The Concise Encyclopedia of
WESTERN PHILOSOPHY AND
PHILOSOPHERS

# The Concise Encyclopedia of
# WESTERN PHILOSOPHY AND PHILOSOPHERS

## New edition, completely revised

*Edited by*

**J. O. Urmson and Jonathan Rée**

London and New York

First published 1960 by
Unwin Hyman Ltd

Second edition 1975
Paperback edition 1976
New edition, completely revised 1989
Paperback edition 1991
Second edition 1991

Reprinted 1991, 1992 (twice), 1993, 1995, 1996 by
Routledge
11 New Fetter Lane, London EC4P 4EE

29 West 35th Street, New York, NY 10001

Printed and bound in Great Britain by
Unwin Brothers Ltd. A member of Martins Printing Group

*British Library Cataloguing in Publication Data*
A catalogue record for this book is available from the British Library

*Library of Congress Cataloguing in Publication Data*
A catalogue record for this book is available from the Library of Congress


ISBN 0–415–07883–0

*Contributors to the original edition (1960)*

J. L. Ackrill
H. B. Acton
A. Hilary Armstrong
A. J. Ayer
Errol Bedford
Karl Britton
Joseph G. Dawson
M. A. E. Dummett
Dorothy M. Emmet
A. C. Ewing
Marvin Farber
J. N. Findlay
Thomas Gilby
Roland Hall
R. M. Hare
R. Harré
H. L. A. Hart
D. J. B. Hawkins
P. L. Heath
Ronald W. Hepburn
Edmund Hill
Walter Kaufmann
I. G. Kidd
G.S. Kirk

Stephen Körner
J.D. Mabbott
Alasdair MacIntyre
D. M. Mackinnon
D. G. C. MacNabb
Philip Merlan
Ernest Nagel
P. H. Nowell-Smith
James O'Connell
D. J. O'Connor
R. S. Peters
Anthony Quinton
Richard Robinson
Erwin I. J. Rosenthal
Gilbert Ryle
Ruth Lydia Saw
P. F. Strawson
F. A. Taylor
Ivo Thomas
J. O. Urmson
James Ward Smith
G. J. Warnock
Alan R. White
Bernard. A. O. Williams

*Additional contributors to the new edition (1989)*

Christopher J. Arthur
Ted Benton
Robert L. Bernasconi
Jay M. Bernstein
Stephen R. L. Clark
Peter Dews
Colin Gordon
Ian Hacking
Alastair Hannay
Ross Harrison
Paulin Hountondji
Richard Kearney
Douglas M. Kellner
David Farrell Krell
Peter Lamarque
Jean-Jacques Lecercle

Genevieve Lloyd
David Macey
Michael Macnamara
Rudolf A. Makkreel
David Papineau
Nicholas Phillipson
Jonathan Powers
Jonathan Rée
David-Hillel Ruben
Peter Singer
Kate Soper
Charles Taylor
Mary Tiles
Jeremy Waldron
Elisabeth Young-Bruehl

# INTRODUCTION

The very idea of an encyclopedia of philosophy is a bit embarrassing. Some people may fancy, from time to time, that they have achieved an encyclopedic grasp of the problems of philosophy. But all you ever get from an actual encyclopedia is a little knowledge about the personalities and problems which make up the **history of philosophy**. And this little knowledge will be enough to convince most people of one thing: that philosophy is such a jumbled and controversial subject that encyclopedic philosophical ambitions are symptoms of megalomania rather than expressions of wisdom.

The first edition of this *Concise Encyclopedia of Western Philosophy and Philosophers* came out in 1960, and it now has the status of a minor classic. Part of its attraction was that none of its large team of contributors disguised their individual voices for the sake of encyclopedic unison. Nevertheless, the majority of these forty nine authors had a common philosophical allegiance: like their editor, J. O. **Urmson**, they were participants in what many would regard as the Golden Age of twentieth-century English philosophy – the "linguistic" movement centered in Oxford in the 1950s, which was inspired by the later **Wittgenstein**, and advocated by **Austin, Hare, Strawson**, and above all **Ryle**. (See also **Analytic Philosophy**.) The main thing that united the Oxford philosophers was their ambivalence about the project of philosophical **analysis**, particularly as interpreted by **logical positivism**. They admired its intellectual unsentimentality and its terse, hard-edged prose; but they rejected its cut-and-dried scientism and its faith in technicalities and formal logic, and they felt uneasy about its condescension towards the classics of philosophy. As one observer of Oxford in the 1950s put it, philosophy was "the subject which now spends its time debating whether it was once correct to describe it as Logical Positivism".

Whatever else one may think of this episode in the history of English philosophy, it was a good moment for compiling an encyclopedia. Urmson's editorial policy, as explained in his Introduction to the first edition, was based on the assumption that "there are no authorities in philosophy", and that "there is no set of agreed results". So he made his Encyclopedia into an incitement to thinking as well as a store of information. Readers could consult the articles on **rationalism** and **empiricism**, for example, to get a straightforward guide to two schools whose disagreement is supposed to structure the whole field of philosophical debate; but if they turned to the magisterial article on **epistemology** they would be told that "their tug-of-war lacks a rope". With the second printing (1967), moreover, readers found initials at the end of each article identifying its author: in the case of Epistemology and several others, it was Ryle himself. Hare wrote on **ethics**; Strawson on **metaphysics**; **Ayer** on **Russell**; **Dummett** on **Frege**; Williams on **Descartes** – to cite only a few examples. And Urmson had extracted perfect miniature samples of their work from his celebrated authors: the result was a remarkable philosophical anthology, as well as an Encyclopedia. Teachers also found that it served well as a textbook for introducing new students to philosophy.

Another of Urmson's objectives was to "range beyond the confines of British and American philosophical fashions". Here too, he had some notable successes: Kaufmann's articles on **Hegel** and **Nietzsche** are classic sources for his famous if tendentious interpretations; in his article on **Husserl**, Findlay was able to air his views about "the strange drop from Phenomenology to Existentialism", and Farber gave a characteristically eccentric interpretation of **phenomenology**.

This new edition reproduces most of Urmson's Encyclopedia, edited and updated where necessary. I have removed about one tenth of the original articles though, either because they are obsolete, or because they are preposterous (like Kaufmann's notorious piece on Heidegger, which concluded, without argument, that "there are probably few philosophers to whose vogue Andersen's fairy tale *The Emperor's Clothes* is more applicable").

This venerable material from the original edition is now supplemented with 80 new articles* from 31 authors. Some of the additions concern things that have happened in philosophy in the past thirty years; others take account of new ideas about old topics; several deal with political or literary aspects of philosophy which might have seemed to the first editor to be of little importance; but most of them have to do with **psychoanalysis**, Marxism and traditions in European continental philosophy which would not have been regarded as intellectually legitimate by English philosophers in the 1950s.

The initials at the end of each article can be decoded by reference to the lists of contributors on p. iv. Initials enclosed in round brackets indicate that the article is a survivor from the first edition; those in square brackets indicate that it is new. So readers can easily tell whose point of view they are being offered, and whether it belongs to the 1950s or the 1980s.

My aim has been to collect the widest range of perspectives on Western Philosophy and Philosophers which could be explained to non-specialist readers, and squeezed into a pocketable book. This Encyclopedia is not meant to resolve questions about the nature of philosophy and its encyclopedias though; in fact it will succeed only if it sharpens them.

Jonathan Rée
*June 1988*

**Note**: Cross references are indicated by **bold type**, for first references only.

* Adorno, "African Philosophy", Alienation, Althusser, Analytic Philosophy, Anderson, Animals, Anscombe, Applied Ethics, Arendt, Atomism, Bachelard, de Beauvoir, Benjamin, Bentham, Bloch, Canguilhem, Chomsky, Davidson, Deleuze, Derrida, Dialectical Materialism, Dilthey, Duhem, Dummett, Feuerbach, Foot, Foucault, Frankfurt School, Gadamer, Gender, Gramsci, Habermas, Heidegger, Hermeneutics, History of Philosophy, Holism, Horkheimer, Humanism, Ideology, Intentionality, Kierkegaard, Kojève, Kripke, Kuhn, Lacan, Lenin, Levinas, Lukács, MacIntyre, Marcuse, Marx, Merleau-Ponty, Metaphor, Modernism, Modernity, Nozick, Philosophy of Mind, Philosophy of Science, Political Economy, Political Philosophy, Post-modernism, Psychoanalysis, Quantum Mechanics, Quine, Rawls, Realism, Relativism, Relativity, Religion, Ricoeur, Rorty, Sartre, Saussure, Schelling, Smith, Structuralism, Transcendental Arguments, Urmson, Weil.

The Concise Encyclopedia of
# WESTERN PHILOSOPHY AND PHILOSOPHERS

# A

**Abelard,** Peter, (c. 1079–1142) born in Brittany, France. The details of his stormy life are to be found in the autobiographical letter known as the *Historia Calamitatum*. Most famous of all the events of Abelard's life is his seduction of Héloise, niece of the Canon Fulbert of Notre Dame; when their child was born they married secretly but Héloise's brothers broke into Abelard's room at night and castrated him. Subsequently Héloise became a nun and Abelard a monk.

Abelard is noted in the history of philosophy for his ability as a **dialectician** and for his contribution to the problem of **Universals**. He studied **logic** under Roscellinus, a nominalist master, and later disputed with the realist theologian William of Champeaux in Paris. The details of this debate, together with an account of the successive positions taken up, are to be found in Abelard's logical treatises *Concerning Genera and Species* and the *Glosses on Porphyry*.

Abelard stands firmly by the principle that only individuals exist and that universal terms, being more than mere names, get their meaning from the abstractive power of the mind. The famous formula that the mind may consider factors separately without considering them as separate from one another gave a convenient dialectical answer to the question as it was raised by **Boethius**.

Abelard also wrote an ethical treatise, *Know Thyself*, which emphasizes the subjective element in human conduct and stresses the importance of intention in the moral qualification of an action.

(J.G.D.)

**Adorno,** Theodor W. (1903–1969), born in Frankfurt; along with Max **Horkheimer** and Herbert **Marcuse**, a major architect of the **Frankfurt School** of Critical Theory. Besides his work in philosophy Adorno was also active as a musicologist (he was student of Alban Berg, and throughout his life a defender of the work of Arnold Schoenberg), sociologist, and literary critic and theorist.

Adorno's most important philosophical works are *Negative Dialectics* (1966) and *Aesthetic Theory* (1970). In *Negative Dialectics* he argues that dialectics must be freed from the totalizing impulse of Hegel's system because the whole of present day society is not a reconciliation of universal and particular, but the domination of particularity by the universality of subjective reason, determined solely by the drive for self-preservation. Subjective reason conceives of knowing as the mastery of things by concepts, where nothing is cognitively significant except what different items share, what makes them the "same". The rule of identity and sameness is realized not only in the philosophical systems of German **idealism**, but also, materially, in capitalism where all use values (particularity) are dominated by exchange value (universality).

Negative dialectics is dialectics without a final moment of unification; its goal is to reveal the non-identity of an item and the concept under which it is usually "identified". Negative dialectics operates for the sake of the object of cognition. For Adorno cognitive utopia would not be a unified science, but a use of concepts to unseal the non-conceptual without making it their equal.

In *Aesthetic Theory* Adorno argues that the kind of non-identity thinking aimed at by negative dialectics is, for the time being at least, adumbrated in modernist works of art. Successful works of art claim us beyond our ability to redeem their claims conceptually. They are particulars demanding acknowledgement while simultaneously resisting being fully understood or explained: in fact it is their unintelligibility which reveals the wounding duality between particularity and universality in modern rationality. Art pre-figures what it would be like to comprehend individuals without dominating them. For Adorno modernist art enacts a critique of subjective reason, and reveals the possibility of another form of reason.

Other noteworthy philosophical works by Adorno are: *Dialectic of Enlightenment* (1947) (written with Max Horkheimer); *Kierkegaard:*

*The Construction of the Aesthetic* (1933); *Against Epistemology: a Metacritique* (1956) (on **Husserl**); *The Jargon of Authenticity* (1964) (on **Heidegger**); *Three Studies on Hegel* (1963); and *Minima Moralia: Reflections from Damaged Life* (1951). See also **Philosophy of Science.**

[J.M.B.]

**Aenesidemus,** *see* Stoics.

**Aesthetics.** Though the division of philosophy into a number of departments has little theoretical value, aesthetics has long been regarded as one of the main departments of philosophy alongside logic, metaphysics, the theory of knowledge and ethics. The word "aesthetics" itself is little over two centuries old and results from a German coinage by the philosopher Baumgarten; thus though the word is ultimately derived from the Greek word *aesthesis* which means "perception", no weight can be put on this etymology. Where we now speak of aesthetics earlier writers would have spoken of the theory of taste or criticism of taste. The *Hippias Major* of **Plato**, in which the sophist Hippias vainly attempts to provide **Socrates** with a satisfactory definition of beauty, is the oldest surviving work in the field of aesthetics and there is a continuing literature from that period.

Aesthetics gains its subject-matter from the fact that people are constantly judging things, whether natural objects, products of the "fine arts" or other man-made articles, to be beautiful, sublime, charming, ugly, ridiculous or uncouth; moreover, they attempt to support or question such judgments and fall into argument about them. The philosophical problems of aesthetics arise from reflection on these data; it will be helpful to list some of them without discussion. What have terms like "beautiful", "sublime", "charming", "ugly", got in common with each other that they do not share with "worthy", "useful", "wicked" and "right"? What is the difference between "beautiful" and "sublime"? How, if at all, can we show judgments of aesthetic merit to be true or justify one

view rather than another? How does aesthetic appraisal differ from ethical and economic appraisal? What is a work of art? Can we have the same aesthetic attitude to works of art as to natural phenomena?

It is natural to find a close parallel between the problems of aesthetics and those of **ethics**. Some would indeed regard it as a mistake, however natural; others would maintain that to speak of a parallel is an understatement and hold that we should start with a general theory of value to be applied with slight modifications to the field of ethics, aesthetics and economics. The most important question of ethics is naturally expressed in some such way as: "Is there any standard of morality beyond the conventions of a group and, if so, what is it?". We can equally naturally ask whether there is any standard of aesthetic judgment and, if so, what it is. This being the case, it is not surprising to find a close parallel between the most common aesthetic and ethical theories. As the ethical **relativist** claims that moral beliefs hold only for an individual or a group so it is claimed that there is no criterion of good taste save that conventionally accepted within a group; as the ethical **hedonist** finds moral worth solely in the production of pleasure, so the aesthetic hedonist claims that the production of pleasure is the sole criterion of aesthetic merit; as some moralists say that goodness is an ultimate moral quality objectively present in things of value, so some have claimed that beauty is an objective quality; similarly we have subjectivist and emotivist theories of meaning in both fields.

The most influential classical discussion of aesthetics was that of **Kant** in his *Critique of Judgment*, especially through his insistence on the preconceptual level of the aesthetic judgment and the formal character of the criteria of aesthetic merit. The precise form of his discussion depends on his view that judgments differ in quantity, quality, relation and modality, so that the problem of aesthetics is mainly to say how aesthetic judgements differ in these four ways from others. In the twentieth century, the best-known theory is that of **Croce** in his *Aesthetics*, to which that of **Collingwood** in his *Principles of Art* is essentially similar; for

Croce the work of art is a sensuous intuition of some emotion of which it is also an adequate expression, the canvas, the written words or the sounds being mere causal aids to others to have the same intuition. The view put forward in Cassirer's *Philosophy of Symbolic Forms*, especially as restated in S. K. Langer's *Feeling and Form*, has also been very influential. It is common to these views to see aesthetic experience as essentially expression, or symbolism, of feeling, and to connect it as such with all use of language and other symbolism; Croce indeed regards general linguistics and aesthetics as one and the same thing. These theories, idealist in tendency, have not gained much support from **analytic philosophers**, but these have notably failed to provide any alternative.

Some philosophers, indeed, deny the possibility of any general aesthetic theory; aestheticians, they say, assume that there is some common feature of experience of all the diverse arts and of natural beauty, and that there is some general criterion of judgment to be found which will be applicable in all these fields; but this assumption they consider to be without any justification. We can say, they hold, what makes us admire this painting, that landscape or that symphony, but we must not expect there to be anything common to all these cases. Whether this extreme scepticism is justified or not, it must be admitted that aesthetics, more than any other branch of philosophy seems doomed either to a pretentious vagueness or to an extreme poverty which make it a poor step-sister to other main fields of philosophical inquiry. See also **Adorno**.

(J.O.U.)

**"African Philosophy"**. The concept of African Philosophy originated as a variant of the general idea of "Primitive" Philosophy, which in its turn is part of the history of European attempts to understand the strange practices of "other peoples". In *Primitive Culture* (1871) the English anthropologist E. B. Tylor (1832–1917) postulated a childish but coherent world-picture called "animism", which he took to be at the basis of "primitive society". Animism, for Tylor,

was a rudimentary scientific theory which attempted to explain natural phenomena by attributing them to the voluntary acts of personal spirits; it was not an arbitrary invention, but a special if naive application of the principle of causality. In this sense Tylor's approach was intellectualist: he went beyond purely emotional factors, such as fear, upon which previous analyses of "primitive culture" had focused, in order to identify its conceptual foundations.

This intellectualist approach did not necessarily involve a rehabilitation of "primitive" culture or an affirmation of cultural equality. "Primitives" were still primitive, "savages" still savage. For Tylor's intellectualism was a form of evolutionist sociology, in which inequalities of development were seen against a background assumption of the ultimate identity of humanity as a whole. Thus it contrasts, on the right hand, with theories of absolute difference, which fragment the idea of "the human race" into several different "races"; and on the left, with the principled egalitarianism which regards actual inequalities of achievement as historical accidents, which do not detract in any way from the equal value of all cultures and peoples.

Tylor drew extensively on **Comte**'s theory that the history both of the individual and of humanity as a whole passes from a theological stage, through a metaphysical one, to a positive or scientific stage. Comte had regarded each of these three stages as based on a specific "philosophy", and held that their historical succession exhibited a progressive acceptance of the limits of human understanding. Thus theology, for Comte, was the earliest and most ambitious form of philosophy. It too had developed in three stages: fetishism, polytheism, and monotheism. Fetishism – the habit of treating inert objects as though they were alive – was thus the absolute beginning of reason. However, according to Comte every member of every society has to go through all the same stages, and moreover no society and no scientific system, however highly developed, could break completely with its origins. So Comte insisted on the functional value of fetishism, as the stage of the initial stirring of conceptual exploration, which left its mark on all subsequent ones.

3

Tylor, in contrast, saw fetishism (or animism, as he re-named it) as an absolutely backward mentality, present in primitive societies but completely overcome in civilized ones. However even Tylor's intellectualism came to be criticized for being excessively generous towards primitive cultures. In *How Natives Think: Mental Functions in Inferior Societies* (1910), the French philosopher Lucien Lévy-Bruhl (1857–1939) complained that the idea of "animism" made the unjustified assumption that "savages" are capable of rudimentary logical thought, so that they are essentially the same as the "civilized adult white man". Lévy-Bruhl suggested that savages are pre-logical and separated from Europeans by a gulf as large as that between vertebrate and invertebrate animals.

The French writer Raoul Allier reached very similar conclusions, on the basis of reports and letters written by Protestant missionaries. In *The Psychology of Conversion amongst Uncivilised Peoples* (1925) and *The Uncivilised Peoples and Ourselves: Irreducible Difference or Basic Identity?* (1927), Allier also challenged the idea of a universal human nature, and described the intellectual methods of "savages" as "para-logical". On this basis he argued that when uncivilized individuals were converted to Christianity they underwent a total crisis, which gave them access not only to a new faith, but to a new humanity.

There was then a reaction against pre-logicism and para-logicism, and a well-meaning revival of intellectualism. Thus in *Primitive Man as Philosopher* (1927) the American anthropologist Paul Radin (1883–1959) described the role of intellectuals in "primitive society" in order to discredit the myth that "primitive man" is totally submerged in society, dominated by the thinking of the group, and lacking individual personality. The French ethnographer Marcel Griaule (1908–1956) pursued a similar task with the Dogon of French Sudan (now Mali). He did his best to efface himself as a theorist, and to act as little more than a secretary, recording, transcribing and translating the statements of some "master of the spoken word". (See for example his *Conversations with Ogotemmêli*, 1948.) With the discovery of

"oral literature", numerous other investigators, including many Africans, have taken the same approach as Griaule.

In this context, "primitive philosophy" means an explicit set of doctrines, rather than the merely implicit animism postulated in Tylor's *Primitive Culture*. But the Dogon cosmogony which was expounded with elaborate beauty by Ogotemmêli is more like a magnificent poem than an exercise in abstract, systematic, critical analysis. It is not clear why it should be categorized as "philosophy" as opposed to, for example, "religion" or "mythology".

Some of the more ardent exponents of this approach therefore attempted to go behind the actual words of their informants in order to reconstruct another, more systematic and philosophical discourse upon which they could be taken to depend. Thus *Bantu Philosophy* (1945), by the Belgian missionary Placide Tempels, depicted a specifically Bantu ontology involving a dynamic conception of the universe based on the idea of complex, stratified plurality of forces. This ontology, he said, contrasted with the static concept of Being; characteristic of scholastic Aristotelianism, which predominated in Europe; and he presented the doctrine in a systematic, deductive form which looks distinctly philosophical. Tempels also argued for the theological conclusion that God has always been present to Bantu thought in the guise of a supreme force. This had important implications for his "missiology" (theory of missionary activity): Allier was mistaken in conceiving of conversion as a total crisis and breakthrough into a new type of humanity; it was a return to the real meaning of authentic Bantu thought, peeling away historical accretions to discover an original revelation of the divine.

But Tempels' generous conception of Bantu philosophy could also be seen as an expression of colonialist condescension. He admitted that the Bantu themselves were not capable of formulating "Bantu philosophy", but claimed that when the ethnologist articulated it for them, they recognized it immediately as representing their own view. But this clearly suggested that their thought was not originally philosophical, but became so only thanks to outside intervention. It is not surprising that in the *Discourse on Colonialism* (1950), Aimé Césaire denounced Tempels for inviting colonists to respect the philosophy of the Africans rather than their rights.

Nevertheless a number of later authors, mostly Africans, have followed Tempels in trying to reconstitute "African Philosophy", or, more cautiously, the philosophy of some particular group of Africans, or "African thought" generally. The theory of negritude developed by Léopold Senghor, from the word coined by Césaire, is closely related to this idea of "African philosophy"; so too are the works of the Rwandan writer Alexis Kagamé (1912–1981) (*The Bantu–Rwandan Philosophy of Being* (1956) and *Comparative Bantu Philosophy* (1976)).

The trouble with all these investigations is that they are based on an antiquarian conception of philosophy, as something which belongs essentially to the past: they are uncritical attempts to restore a philosophy which is supposed to be already given, a collective world-view passively shared by a whole society. They are exercises in what has been called "ethnophilosophy", rather than philosophy itself. Unfortunately, the positive, factual and historical assumptions of ethnophilosophy still dominate African philosophy; but happily they do not have a monopoly.

The alternative is to take the idea of African philosophy more literally, so that it means the contributions which African thinkers make to the sorts of critical and reflexive discussions in which philosophy has traditionally been taken to consist. Then the European history of African philosophy could be replaced by an African history of philosophy, with philosophy defined by its simple if subversive insistence on truth (which of course does not exclude, but on the contrary presupposes being rooted in a historical situation and responding to the extra-philosophical problems of one's society). African philosophy in this sense has a long history – certainly longer than that of ethnophilosophy. More and more Africans are rejecting philosophical antiquarianism as a manipulative impoverishment of the past: they

are refusing to reduce African culture to pure traditions emptied of movement and controversy. Knowledge of old African cultures is no longer the necessary starting point for African philosophy; and it is certainly not the last word. See also **History of Philosophy, Religion**.

[P.J.H.]

**Albert the Great** (1206–1280), also known as Albertus Magnus, Albert of Lauingen and Albert of Cologne; canonized in 1931. Born at Lauingen in Swabia, Albert studied at Padua, where he joined the Dominicans; later he became Bishop of Ratisbon. He taught at Cologne and Paris. Traveller, administrator, theologian, he was an indefatigable experimentalist, especially in botany and zoology. His temper was not unlike that of his contemporary, Roger **Bacon**, who held him in grudging respect. He wrote of **Aristotle** with great sympathy. With his pupil Thomas **Aquinas**, he led the movement which installed in Christian thought an Aristotelianism specifically new to the patristic tradition. But he was the less synthetic and impersonal thinker of the two, though he was more encyclopedic and syncretic. He wrote on Aristotle in the older style of paraphrase and digression, and is closer to **Avicenna** than to **Averroes**. His feeling for the Neoplatonism of Dionysius and Proclus descends through his disciples – Ulrich of Strasbourg, who died in 1277, and Dietrich of Freiburg, who died in 1310 – to Master Eckhart, John Tauler and the Dominican mystics of the Rhineland.

(T.G.)

**Alembert,** Jean le Rond d' (1717–1783), French mathematician, *see* Encyclopedists.

**Alexander,** Samuel (1859–1938), an Australian by birth. As an undergraduate at Oxford he was brought up in the **idealist** tradition of that period. But he became one of the most noted **realist** metaphysicians of his time. He was for many years Professor of Philosophy of Manchester University.

Alexander's great work was *Space, Time and Deity* (1920). The basic stuff of the universe is space-time or pure motion, and everything in it develops out of the primary stuff by a process of emergent evolution. Things or substances are volumes of space-time with a determinate contour; low in the scale of evolution is matter, whence emerges life and finally, so far as we are concerned, mind; but no one can say what will emerge later in the evolutionary process. The next stage to which the universe is striving is at that stage deity; God is in the making but never actual. On this metaphysical foundation, Alexander built a realist theory of knowledge.

(J.O.U.)

**Alienation.** Strictly speaking, to alienate something is to separate it from oneself or disown it. But an extended concept of alienation has gained wide currency in twentieth-century philosophy and social theory. Under converging influences from **existentialism**, the **Frankfurt School, humanism** and **psychoanalysis**, the term "alienation" has been used in numerous diagnoses of the maladies of something called "the modern world". All sorts of alleged symptoms of **"modernity"** – the dichotomies of civilization and barbarism, scientism and irrationalism, town and country, mental and manual labour, atheism and religiosity, individualization and massification, banal popular culture and unintelligible high culture, intellect and feeling, masculine and feminine etc. – have been encompassed within theories of alienation.

Superficially, alienation refers to a subjective feeling of unease, dissociation or exile. At a deeper level, it indicates a kind of structure, in which people find it impossible to "identify" with the social and spiritual conditions of their existence. Ultimately it implies that modernity is the loss or disruption of an original unity, and may also suggest that a day of reconciliation in a "higher unity" is about to dawn.

But alienation is not supposed to be a catastrophe striking humanity from outside; it is essentially a perverted, malign, and self-destructive expression of human creativity itself. Alienation means that people are subject to

an oppression which is – though they may not recognize it – of their own making. In this sense Mary Shelley's story of Frankenstein and his monster provides an exact allegory of alienation.

The concept of alienation achieved popularity as the basis for an alternative to **dialectical materialism** in the philosophical interpretation of Marxism. Humanistic Marxists such as **Marcuse, Sartre**, and the psychoanalyst Erich Fromm (1900–1980) used the term to translate the German words *Entfremdung* and *Entäusserung*, with particular reference to the young **Marx** and his philosophy of labour or *praxis*. In the *1844 Manuscripts* (published in 1932) Marx tried to explain capitalism, or rather "the system of private property", as a form of "alienated labour". As Marx acknowledged, this explanation was indebted to **Feuerbach**, who had argued in *The Essence of Christianity* that "religion is the dream of the human mind" and that the God which people worship is nothing more than their own "alienated self ", inverted and unrecognized. According to the young Marx, the function of labour in modern society is just like that which Feuerbach attributed to worship in **religion**: it creates the power which confronts and overwhelms it. Hence "the *alienation* of the worker in his product means not only that his labour becomes an object, an *outside* existence, but also that it exists *outside* him, independent and alien, and becomes a self-sufficient power over against him – that the life he has lent to the object confronts him, hostile and alien". Moreover, in Marx's theory money itself plays the part of Feuerbach's humanly constructed God: it is "the visible deity, the transformation of all human and natural qualities into their opposites"; thus, "the *divine* power of money resides in its nature as the alienated, externalised and self-estranging *species-being* of humanity: it is the alienated *power* of human beings".

Some Marxist commentators (notably **Althusser**) believe that the theory of alienation is only a regrettable vestige of pre-Marxist ideology. Nevertheless numerous traces of it are to be found in Marx's *Capital*, for example in its doctrine of "commodity fetishism" and in its criticisms of bourgeois theorists like J. S. Mill for "the folly of identifying a specific *social relationship of production* with the thinglike qualities of articles". **Lukács'** *History and Class Consciousness* (1923) was the first work to interpret Marxism in terms of alienation or rather "reification". Later, Lukács followed the theme back to **Hegel**, arguing in *The Young Hegel* that alienation is "the central philosophical concept of the *Phenomenology of Spirit*" (see also **Kojève**). The concept is also at work in **Rousseau**'s social theory, and may indeed be traced much earlier: perhaps it can even be detected in the theology of **neo-Platonism** (see also **Plotinus**) and in **pre-Socratic** doctrines of creation. For the idea that humanity is at odds with itself, and adrift from its spiritual home, is probably co-extensive with religion in general; in which case "modernity" must be considerably older than is commonly supposed.

[J.R.]

**Althusser,** L. (1918– ), born in Algeria, is best known for his writings from 1960 onwards, the main theme of which was a re-working of Marxist orthodoxy and an associated defence of the scientific status of historical materialism. Using ideas derived from French historical **philosophy of science** and from **structuralism**, Althusser argued that **Marx**'s early works, with their "humanist" and "historicist" philosophical basis, should be regarded as "pre-scientific". Later writings such as *Capital* could then be read as containing the elements of a new "scientific" problematic in the theory of social formations and their transformations. Human individuals were to be understood not as the self-conscious sources of their social life, but rather as "bearers" of a system of social relations which exists prior to and independently of their consciousness and activity. In opposition to economic reductionism, Althusser argued for a recognition of the relative autonomy of political, cultural and intellectual practices within a loosely defined "determination in the last instance" by economic structures and practices. This notion of "relative autonomy", together with Althusser's insistence upon the irreducible complexity of social contradictions and struggles, made it possible for a new significance to be given to cultural analysis and to forms of resistance not directly attributable to "class struggle". However, Althusser's "scientism", and his apparent denial of autonomous human agency led to a growing division between Althusser and his younger, more radical followers. Althusser's response was a spate of self-critical writings which appeared to put an end to what was distinctive in the school of Marxist philosophy which he had engendered.

[T.B.]

**Analysis.** "Analysis" is a Greek word, meaning the resolution of a complex whole into its parts. It is opposed to synthesis, which means the construction of a whole out of parts.

Philosophers have always had two main aims, the construction of systems of **metaphysics**, **logic** or **ethics** (synthesis) and the clarification of important ideas (analysis). These cannot always be sharply distinguished, since what is synthesis from one point of view is analysis from another. **Plato**'s *Republic*, for example, may be considered as the construction in thought of a perfectly just society or as the analysis of the idea of a just society. Large parts of **Aristotle**'s *Ethics* are concerned with the analysis of such important ideas as "voluntary action", "virtue and vice", "pleasure", etc.

In recent times continental philosophy has tended to be synthetic and British philosophy to be analytic. For **Descartes** the analysis of concepts was only a preparation for the construction of a system of knowledge based on the "clear and distinct ideas" obtained by analysis; and **Spinoza** sought to construct a view of the world deduced, on the geometrical model, from a small number of definitions and axioms. British philosophers, on the other hand, have tended to be suspicious of constructive metaphysics and to be more concerned with the analysis of thought and experience into their fundamental elements.

Since the beginning of this century the view that analysis is either the whole, or the most important part, or the distinguishing feature of philosophy has been widely accepted in

English-speaking countries. Philosophers who follow this trend often have little in common with each other except the use of the word "analysis" to describe their various activities. All that can be said about their view of the function of philosophy – and even this is not wholly true – is that they take it to be, not the acquisition of new knowledge (which is the function of the special sciences), but the clarification and articulation of what we already know. Three main stands can be detected in the practice of analysis:

(1) G. E. **Moore** questioned an assumption that metaphysicians have been prone to make and which was certainly made by the **idealists** who at that time dominated British philosophy. This was that we do not know all the ordinary humdrum things about the world that we claim to know. Some had said that these things are actually false; others, that even if they were true we could not know them to be true. The world, as it appears to the plain man, is mere appearance; reality is something recondite, wholly unlike what we take it to be, and to be discovered only by profound researches conducted in some new technical language. Against this, Moore held that for the thinker such truisms as that he has a body, that he was born some years ago and that he has existed ever since, are not only true but can be known for certain to be true. Nevertheless he had no wish to assert that metaphysical theories which contradicted these assertions were merely outrageous falsehoods. They were certainly that; but they were also mistaken attempts to answer very genuine and puzzling questions. Briefly, though we cannot seriously doubt the truth of such ordinary statements and though we know, in a sense, what they mean, we may not be able to state clearly and precisely *what* they mean. We do not, in his words, "know their proper analysis" and almost all his philosophical activity was devoted to discovering the proper analysis of propositions whose truth cannot seriously be doubted.

To give the proper analysis of a concept or proposition is to replace the word or sentence which is normally used to express it by some other expression which is exactly equivalent to it and at the same time less puzzling. An analysis, therefore, is a sort of definition, a kind of equation with the puzzling expression, the *analysandum*, on the left-hand side and the new expression, sometimes called the *analysis*, sometimes the *analysans*, on the right. Now most of the ideas that seem to need this sort of clarification are highly complex and the very word "analysis" implies the splitting of a complex form, or replacing an expression that stood for a complex concept by a longer expression that lays bare its hidden complexity. Moore seems to have used this technique with no other aim than that of clarifying our concepts; he had no metaphysical theory and did not suppose that the things mentioned in the analysis were in any sense more real or fundamental than those mentioned in the analysandum. How, indeed, could they be, if the analysandum and the analysis were to refer, as they must, to exactly the same things?

(2) Bertrand **Russell** practised the same sort of definitional analysis as Moore, but for very different reasons and with very different aims. Where Moore sought only clarity and never wished to depart from common sense beliefs, Russell sought metaphysical truth and was quite willing to say with the Idealists that common sense beliefs can be false and ordinary language wholly inadequate as a means of discovering and expressing truth. As a metaphysician, his aim was to give a general account of the universe. His account was the exact opposite of that of the Idealists. They had claimed that only reality as a whole (the absolute) was wholly real; particular things were abstractions from this totality and, as such, only partially real or not real at all. Russell's picture of the world was that of a world composed of "atomic facts", corresponding to each of which there would be a true "atomic statement".

Consider the statement "it is either raining or snowing". This is not made true by correspondence with a complex alternative fact, either-rain-or-snow. It is true if either of the atomic parts of which it is composed ("it is raining" and "it is snowing") is true. Thus compound or "molecular" statements do not correspond or fail to correspond to compound facts; they can be broken down into atomic statements which do, when true, correspond to atomic facts. The aim of analysis was to break down complex facts into their atomic components, the method to analyse complex statements into theirs. Russell's conception of analysis was influenced in two main ways by the fact that he came to metaphysics from the study of mathematics and formal logic. As a mathematician, he regarded all defined terms as theoretically superfluous. Thus if "two" can be defined as "one plus one" and "three" as "two plus one" it is clear that arithmetical operations could be carried on with no numerals other than "one". He had himself claimed to "eliminate" in this way even the notion of "number" by defining it in terms belonging to logic. As a metaphysician, Russell held that if the word "number" could be eliminated by being defined, then numbers are not part of the ultimate constituents of the world which it was his aim to discover. These constituents, whatever they turned out to be, would be only such things as would be named in a language in which all defined terms had been replaced by ultimately indefinable terms.

Secondly, Russell's study of logic had convinced him that the *grammar* of all natural languages is radically misleading. "Horses do not bellow" and "chimaeras do not exist" have the same grammatical form; but while the first denies that certain objects (horses) have a certain property (bellowing), the second does not deny that chimaeras have the property of existing. Rather it says that nothing in the world has the property of being a chimaera. Russell's aim here was that of replacing expressions whose grammatical form was misleading by expressions of "proper logical form", in which the grammatical structure would properly reflect the form of the fact stated. Confronted by the statement, "the average plumber earns ten pounds a week", one might be puzzled by the question "Who is this average plumber?" and perhaps led into wild metaphysical speculation. The remedy was to see that the statement could be translated into "the number of pounds earned each week by plumbers divided by the number of plumbers is ten", a statement from which "the average plumber" has been eliminated. No one is likely to be bemused in such a simple case; but serious consequences, both theoretical and practical, had certainly followed from making the same mistake about more important objects such as "the State" or "Public Opinion". It is clear that in some sense these, like armies, governments, schools and other institutions are abstractions and that to say something about them is to say something, though not the same thing, about the people who make them up. In technical language they were said to be "logical constructions" out of the more concrete objects (people) who compose them. Russell and his followers had high hopes that analysis could be carried to yet deeper metaphysical levels by showing that the things, including people, that we normally treat as being on the "ground-floor level" of experience, were logical constructions out of more fundamental entities.

(3) Russell's views on logic and techniques of analysis were taken up by the **logical positivists**, but used with a very different aim. Where Russell sought a true metaphysical theory, the positivists held *all* metaphysics to be nonsensical and were mainly concerned to establish a sharp line between metaphysics and natural science. Analysis was to be used first for the elimination of metaphysics and secondly for the clarification of the language of science. The word "elimination" here is to be taken in a much more straightforward sense than in connection with Russell. Russell had not claimed that the objects which his analytical method "eliminated" did not, in the ordinary sense, exist; only that they were not metaphysically ultimate. Water exists; but because it is composed of oxygen and hydrogen it is not part of the "ultimate furniture of the Universe"; and this is shown by the fact that the word "water" can be replaced by "$H_2O$". The positivists, on the other hand, used analysis to show that certain words used by metaphysicians and, in consequence, the theories in which those words appear were literally nonsensical.

Since all metaphysics, including Russell's atomism, was to be eliminated, a new aim had to be found for analysis; for metaphysical truth was not merely impossible for us to attain, it was an absurd goal to aim at. It had never been agreed just *what* was to be analysed. Was it to be concepts and propositions, as Moore said? Or facts, as Russell usually said? In practice this had made less difference than might be expected, since the actual technique of analysis had always been the replacement of one *expression* (word, phrase or sentence) by another. The method was linguistic, though both Moore and Russell have always repudiated linguistic aims. With the positivists, aim and method come closer together; for both "concepts" and "facts" come under the ban of being metaphysical, thought is identified with language, and the analysis of linguistic expressions is an end in itself. The clarification and articulation of the language of science can hardly be regarded as an extrinsic aim.

The name "linguistic analysis" is often now used for a general approach to philosophy which has been wide-spread in the English-speaking world. These philosophers differ widely among themselves, for example in their degree of affection towards metaphysics. Their method is certainly linguistic, since it involves paying careful, even minute attention to the actual usage of words, phrases and sentences in a living language; but it cannot, in any clear or strict sense, be called "analysis". What is common to all the linguistic analysts is the belief that the first step towards the solution of a philosophical problem is to examine the key words in the area that generates the problem and to ask how they are in fact used. Thus problems of perception are to be solved, not by condemning ordinary language wholesale and inventing a new vocabulary (impressions, sensations, sense-data), but by asking what precisely we are claiming when we claim to see something. This is the sort of question which Moore asked; but whereas Moore jumped, almost without argument, to the conclusion that the answer must be given in terms of "sense-data", the linguistic analysts try to answer it by exploring the locutions in which the verb "to see" and kindred words actually occur. There is nothing here to which we can point as being "analysis" as we can point to definitional substitution

in Moore and Russell. Perhaps the survival of the name "analysis" is only a just tribute which some philosophers pay to those who have greatly influenced them and from whose work their own work stems. See also **Analytic Philosophy**.

(P.H.N.-S.)

**Analytic.** The terms "analytic" and "synthetic" were introduced by **Kant**, who defined an analytic judgment as one in which the idea of the predicate is already contained in that of the subject and therefore adds nothing to it. Thus "all bodies are extended in space" is analytic, since the idea of extension is contained in that of body. On the other hand "all bodies have some weight" is synthetic since the idea of weight is not so contained. Kant's distinction has been criticized for being too metaphorical – it is not clear what is meant by saying that one idea is "contained in" another – and for being insufficiently general – it applies only to propositions of subject-predicate form.

Various attempts have been made to make the distinction more precise. An analytic proposition is sometimes said to be one the denial of which would be self-contradictory; or it is said to be a covert tautology, on the grounds that, if we define "body", as "extended thing", "all bodies are extended" means "all extended things are extended". It should be noted that on this view the analyticity of a proposition depends on our choice of definitions which is, according to some philosophers, arbitrary. Thus if we defined "body" as "that which has extension and weight", "all bodies have weight" would be analytic. If this is so, we cannot determine from the form of a *sentence* whether or not it expresses an analytic proposition, but must appeal to what the speaker means by it. If these or similar definitions of "analytic" are adopted, it will be seen that analyticity can be extended to propositions not of subject-predicate form.

Analytic propositions, though they may inform us of the meanings of words, can give no knowledge of matters of fact. The philosophy of **logical positivism** was based on a sharp distinction between analytic and synthetic and on the view that all **a priori** propositions must be analytic. Many philosophers now doubt whether this sharp distinction can be maintained. It has been most thoroughly examined by Waismann in *Analysis* (1949–53) and by Quine in *From a Logical Point of View*.

(P.H.N.-S.)

**Analytical Marxism**: a synthesis of **historical materialism** with **analytic philosophy** and **philosophy of science**, pioneered by G. A. Cohen in *KarlMarx's Theory of History: a Defence* (1978).

**Analytic Philosophy.** Analytic philosophy is currently the dominant tradition in academic philosophy in the English-speaking world. It is difficult to define it precisely in terms of characteristic concerns or doctrines. The questions it asks, and even the answers it gives, often have close parallels in the Continental philosophical tradition. It might be argued that it is distinguished by its respect for the findings of the natural sciences, but there are exceptions to this rule. Perhaps the sharpest difference lies at the level of method: analytic philosophy relies heavily on logical and linguistic **analysis** – from which it derives its name.

We will do better to concentrate on tradition rather than definition. Like Continental philosophy, analytic philosophy recognizes **Descartes** as the rationalist father of modern philosophy, followed by the empiricist triumvirate of **Locke, Berkeley** and **Hume**, and then by **Kant**'s attempt to synthesize **rationalism** and **empiricism** at the end of the eighteenth century. After this, however, analytic philosophy's version of history diverges from the Continental one. **Hegel** and **Nietzsche** have no place in the analytic pantheon, and such twentieth-century philosophical movements as **phenomenology, hermeneutics,** and **structuralism** are regarded as unimportant.

For analytic philosophy, the first major philosopher after Kant is Gottlob **Frege**, at the end of the nineteenth century. Frege's researches into the foundations of mathematics led to revolutionary advances in both logic and the philosophy of language. Bertrand **Russell** and Ludwig **Wittgenstein** developed Frege's work on logic and language, and in Russell it was allied to an empiricist epistemology inherited from Hume. This mix of logical analysis and empiricism gave rise to **logical positivism**. The logical positivists aimed to analyse all propositions into their fundamental logical form, and to dismiss as meaningless any propositions whose fundamental constituents did not correspond to elements of sense experience.

The influence of logical positivism waned after the Second World War. Wittgenstein recanted some of his earlier doctrines, and emphasized the social role of language as opposed to its purely representational function. J. L. **Austin** argued that the route to philosophical illumination lay in the sophisticated conceptual distinctions embodied in everyday language. A school of "ordinary language philosophy" emerged, centred on Oxford University, which sought to dissolve philosophical puzzles by attending to the structure of ordinary usage.

Much of the work done under the banner of "ordinary language philosophy" was philosophically shallow, and this particular school had ceased to be of any importance by the 1960s. But in another sense the post-war analytic tradition remained committed to "linguistic philosophy": nearly all analytic philosophers continued to place the analysis of language at the centre of the philosophical stage. Different analytic philosophers, however, drew different philosophical conclusions from it. Thus the American philosophers W. V. O. **Quine** and Wilfrid **Sellars** concurred with the later Wittgenstein in denying that words derive their meanings from sensory ideas in the minds of speakers; but rather than locating the source of linguistic authority in social practices, as Wittgenstein did, they turned to the developing frameworks of scientific theory instead. The influential British philosophers P. F. **Strawson** and Michael **Dummett** drew yet further philosophical morals from the theory of language: Strawson, harking back to Kant, argued that linguistic reference would be impossible if we did not live in a world of reidentifiable spatiotemporal objects; while Dummett argued against metaphysical realism on the grounds that it would be impossible to grasp the meanings of sentences about the world if the world in itself were different from the world as we find it to be.

In Dummett's view, Frege's crucial contribution to philosophy was to show that the theory of meaning is the foundation of all philosophical investigation. However, while it is unquestionably true that the analysis of language has been central to philosophy in the analytic tradition so far in this century, there are signs that since the 1970s it has started being displaced by the **philosophy of mind**.

Treatments of the relationship between mind and language have varied in the analytic tradition. For the founding fathers the function of words was simply to convey ideas from one mind to another, and something of this conception remained even as late as logical positivism. But when Sellars, Quine, and the later Wittgenstein discredited the idea of a self-intimating mental realm which breathed significance into words, most analytic philosophers came to regard linguistic practice as primary, and mental events as little more than dispositions to verbal behaviour. Since then, however, there has been something of a reversion ·to the earlier view that mind is more fundamental than language: a "naturalistic" school of thought has emerged, which rejects the idea of a self-intimating mental realm, but which nevertheless regards the mind as an independent constituent of the natural world.

In *Philosophy and the Mirror of Nature* (1980) Richard **Rorty** argues that, once the traditional conception of mind as a special self-knowing substance is abandoned, any substitute naturalistic conception of mind will be unable to carry the same philosophical weight. Indeed, Rorty argues that the whole analytic tradition is fated to collapse. This is because it is committed, in Rorty's view, to a notion of philosophy as the "queen of the sciences" offering epistemological evaluations of human judgement in general; and the idea of epistemological evaluation, so

Rorty's argument goes, presupposes the traditional distinction between a mirroring non-natural mind and a mirrored natural world.

However, analytic philosophy may be rather more healthy and adaptable than Rorty allows. For a start, while epistemological evaluation clearly requires some contrast between representer and represented, self-intimating mental states as traditionally conceived are not the only possible representers. On the naturalistic conception of the mind mentioned above, for instance, beliefs can be conceived as organizational states of the brain, and yet at the same time can be subjected to epistemological evaluation as better or worse representations of their subject matters. Of course there is a philosophical problem about physical brain states having representational powers; but the task of explaining representation is by no means peculiar to naturalism. It is also true that, on the naturalist conception, mental states are not self-intimating, and so cannot provide the kind of incorrigible foundations for epistemology which were provided by mental states as traditionally conceived: but then there are various non-foundational approaches to **epistemology** open to **naturalism**.

It would be wrong to suggest that analytic philosophy as a whole has taken a naturalistic turn. Many analytic philosophers remain suspicious of the naturalistic conception of mind, and doubt its ability to replace language as the focus of philosophical analysis. This anti-naturalistic tendency has affinities with Rorty's critique of epistemology: the continued emphasis on language tends to go with doubts about the possibility of a perspective from which judgement in general can be evaluated. But those analytic philosophers who have doubts about epistemology continue to articulate them within the analytic tradition, appealing to Wittgenstein and Dummett and Donald **Davidson**, rather than to Martin **Heidegger** and Jacques **Derrida**. Perhaps we are entering a period of increasing convergence between the analytic and Continental approaches; but the sheer power of tradition is likely to keep the two schools distinct for some time to come.

[D.P.]

**Anaxagoras** of Clazomenae flourished *c.* 450 B.C. He was prosecuted for impiety (for describing the sun as a white hot lump of stone) while working in Athens, partly because he was a friend of Pericles. His book *On Nature*, seems to have been written later than **Empedocles'** *On Nature* and tries to overcome the **eleatic** dilemma in another way. In the beginning all the natural substances (not merely a limited number of basic substances like Empedocles' roots) were mixed together; then Mind, "finest of all things and purest", started a rotation which brought the heavier parts to the centre, by vortex-action, to form earth, and the lighter to the circumference. This was a traditional, non-cyclical cosmogony; the production of a plural cosmos did not destroy the initial unity, since still "there is a portion of everything in everything, except Mind". Apparent coming-to-be, as for Empedocles, was caused by mixture. Objects were made up of "seeds", perhaps meaning constituent pieces having the nature of the whole; each seed contained a portion of every natural substance, including the substantial opposites and the main world-masses, but had the appearance of that substance whose portion predominated. Changes, as for example in nutrition, were presumably caused by an interchange of portions so as to alter the predominance in different seeds. Anaxagoras insisted that matter could be theoretically divided *ad infinitum*, and is indeed, what **Zeno** of Elea had denied, "both great and small". He did not attempt to reconcile this with the idea of the predominance of one substance in every seed. In most other details of cosmology and epistemology Anaxagoras was more conservative, often reviving Milesian views. See also **Pre-Socratics**.

(G.S.K.)

**Anaximander** of Miletus flourished *c.* 560 B.C. His scientific activities included making a famous map of the world. Like **Thales** he tried to name a single substance out of which the world originated: for him this was "the indefinite", probably implying a material of indefinite extent to which no precise name could be given because it did not exist within the developed world. From the Indefinite was somehow separated off a nucleus which produced fire and dark mist. The mist solidified at its centre into earth, while the surrounding flame burst to form the heavenly bodies – wheels of fire, each showing through a single aperture in a tegument of mist. The earth is cylindrical, and stays still because of its equidistance from everything else. Physical change within the world occurs through the mutual encroachments and reactions of opposed materials like the hot and the cold, ultimate regularity being assured because these "pay penalty and retribution to each other for their injustice according to the assessment of time". There was a zoogony to parallel the cosmogony: the first living creatures, generated out of primeval slime by the heat of the sun, emerged out of prickly husks on to dry land. Men originally grew up inside a kind of fish, for otherwise they could not have survived their long period of helplessness in childhood. See also **Pre-Socratics**.

(G.S.K.)

**Anaximenes** of Miletus flourished *c.* 545 B.C. He reverted to **Thales'** idea of a definite world-component as originative material, but said that this was *aer*, air or rather mist. For the first time he gave some account of how a single substance could turn into a diversified world: *aer* changed its appearance according to its degree of concentration. Rarefied, it became fire; condensed, water and earth. This was an important new idea; and Anaximenes behaved unusually methodically in citing a specific indication that density can affect, for example, temperature – when the lips are compressed in exhalation. He seems to have chosen air/mist as the basic substance not only because of its apparent meteorological connexion with fire (in the sky) and also with rain, but also because it appeared to fulfil in the world the function of soul, commonly envisaged as breath, in living creatures; soul being motive, directive, and in some way divine. In cosmology Anaximenes was less imaginative than his older contemporary **Anaximander**, often merely elaborating

13

the popular world-picture as exemplified in Homer. The flat earth rode on air; the fiery heavenly bodies went round, not under, the earth, driven by winds; among them were invisible bodies that caused eclipses. See also **Pre-Socratics.**

(G.S.K.)

**Anderson,** John (1893–1962), Scots philosopher who became Professor at the University of Sydney in 1927 and the dominant figure in twentieth-century Australian philosophy. He was noted for his materialistic and deterministic opinions, and also for his outspokenly aggressive attacks on Christianity, patriotism, censorship, and communism, or anything else in which he detected timid intellectual conformism. He never published a book, but his principal articles are collected in *Studies in Empirical Philosophy* (1962).

[J.R.]

**Animals,** biologically speaking, are mobile, sentient organisms, whose cellular structure is less rigid than that of plants, and which do not photosynthesise. The class includes amoebas, tapeworms, sea-urchins, frogs, cats, dogs and people. Any animal, including us, is more like any other animal than either is like a mushroom or a rose; any two animals, if evolutionary theory is correct, are more closely related than either is to anything not an animal. It is this last fact, of evolutionary relatedness, which makes the class of animals something more than a construct. "Animals", unlike "weeds", constitute a real biological taxon, even though (as for other such taxa) there may be or have been organisms at once "animal" and "non-animal".

Although most modern biologists would agree that we are, straightforwardly, members of an animal species, *Homo sapiens*, closely related to other primates (chimpanzees and people, indeed, are more closely related, by biochemical test, than many varieties of fruit fly which are indistinguishable to lay observation), some still believe that people, chiefly in virtue

of their linguistic and forward-looking capacities, are as different from any other animal as animals are from plants. Other animals may mimic what people do in making decisions, formulating theories, painting pictures, engaging in class-conflict and productive labour, but are not "really" doing these things, because not "really" thinking what to do. This distinction between the separate "kingdoms" of plants, animals and people, and their different "souls", goes back at least to **Aristotle** and was mainstream opinion in the West in the next two thousand years. The even more radical claim put forward by **Descartes,** that "animals" (not now including people) did not even have sense-experiences, that they were more like plants than people, had been anticipated – by way of reductio ad absurdum of **Stoic** claims about the irrational nature of all animals except people – by Strato of Lampsacus (mentioned by **Porphyry,** in his work *On Abstinence from Meat-e..ting*): if they only behaved "as if " they were reasoning, then it must be that they only behaved "as if " they were feeling or desiring. Some commentators adopt this merely as a rule of method, not to impute to animals a mental state more complex or anthropomorphic than is strictly necessary; others believe that it is actually true that animals other than people do not have feelings. This doctrine is useful to experimentalists disinclined to take issues of animal welfare seriously.

Cartesians claim that things which cannot speak cannot "think" either, and so cannot ever "be in pain" in anything like the subjective sense in which "we" often are. It is easy, and natural, for us to "project" our own feelings and plans into the animals we live with, and to think that pet dogs are glad to see us, that cats go hunting and veal calves miss their mothers. Sceptics insist that, lacking language, such creatures cannot say even to themselves what they are doing, or what would satisfy them. "Pain" or "pleasure" must be attributed to them in purely behavioural senses, and without any implication that there is "anyone there" who is subjectively in distress or joy, or who reckons her life worth living. On this view there is no real need to anaesthetize (rather than immobilize) animals undergoing surgery. Members of our species who lack language, and should by analogy be thought insensible, are usually given the benefit of the doubt.

The alleged impossibility of our understanding what "animals" do or feel is not usually accepted by people who work with animals and find appropriate rewards and penalties for their charges. The radical incommensurability between "dumb beasts" and "talking people" also raises serious problems for evolutionary theory and for psychology. If we couldn't think until we could talk, how, as a species or as individuals, did we ever learn to talk? It seems more likely that Cartesians, and recent thinkers influenced by **Wittgenstein**'s aphorisms, have exaggerated the importance for experience of the capacity to articulate that experience in the sort of tensed, referential language that people employ. There are, nonetheless, real practical and philosophical problems for those who seek to understand animals "from within", by empathetic identification, not least those posed by our traditional moral categories.

For "animal", as well as its biological or folk-taxonomic meaning, carries moral significance. To treat people "like animals" is to treat them without due regard for their preferences, or their status as free and equal partners in the human community. To behave "like an animal" is to pay no regard to the normal inhibitions and ceremonies of that community. Actually to be an animal (by definition non-human) is to be a creature that cannot really return our friendship, cannot be expected to make or keep bargains, and that is forever excluded from distinctively "human" practices. It follows that those, like the classical **utilitarians** such as **Bentham** or J. S. **Mill**, who thought it proper to take account of "animal pains and pleasures", were thought (e.g. by **Whewell**) to be blind to the higher values of humanity. Taking "animals" seriously meant taking "animal pains and pleasures" seriously in our own lives, and really decent people should not do that.

The doctrine that animals lie outside the realm of justice, that there is no injustice done in dispossessing, enslaving, hurting or killing them, was first articulated by Aristotle (and later Stoics), but was no new thing. All human cultures seem to draw a distinction between their own kind and everything else – though it has been usual, historically speaking, for the class of Non-People to include many whom we would regard as our conspecifics, and the class of People to include at least such honorary members of the community as cattle, horses, pigs or (in the West) dogs. That folk-taxonomic division between the People and the Outsiders has been progressively modified, by philosophers and prophets, until most civilized peoples now accept that all human beings are at least potentially "of our kind", to be treated – if possible – with due respect, as we would ourselves wish to be treated. Humans are, in **Kant**'s phrase, "ends in themselves", whereas animals, as irrational beings, are owed nothing "as of right".

Mainstream Western thought from Aristotle to Kant might qualify the dictum that one could not, whatever one did, treat an animal unjustly (since the animal had no rights to be violated): one might (but should not) treat them wickedly or uncharitably or inhumanely. Deliberate cruelty or callous negligence was a sign of a bad character that might easily result in strictly unjust treatment of one's fellow humans. Pain was a recognizable evil that the decent person did not wantonly multiply. One ought not, in popular morality, to cause animals "unnecessary pain", but one has no obligation not to kill, dispossess, imprison or deprive them. Strict utilitarians, concerned to increase the ratio of pleasure to pain, should add an obligation to increase animal pleasure where one practically can, but are as likely as the rest of us to discount the pleasures animals can experience against those that the exploitative use of animals provides to us.

The political programme of classical liberalism lays it down that the law should be invoked only to protect rights, and not to enforce any particular moral code. It was for that reason that many liberals opposed the first animal welfare legislation. Such laws came between citizens and their lawfully acquired property. One solution was to insist that the law might after all be invoked to decrease suffering, whoever the victim, because no one had any natural right to treat other creatures just as she willed. Another was to claim that animals – by which was usually meant vertebrates more closely related to us ("more evolutionarily advanced") than fishes – had "natural rights" on the same terms as people. Insofar as they were beings with feelings, interests, lives to live, capacities to take (maybe trivial) decisions and to recognize their companions, they lacked no capacity that was shared by all those people who uncontroversially "had rights". If imbeciles had rights (i.e. ought to be protected by law not merely against cruel treatment but against robbery, undue frustration of "natural capacities", enslavement and killing), so also did chimpanzees, horses, dogs and whatever other animals turned out to be at least as mentally developed as the imbecile. Some philosophers concluded that, this being so, imbeciles did not "have rights" after all, and did not need to be protected. If they were it was only to appease public sentiment, which was not (yet) so much engaged on behalf of animals.

The probability is that neither utilitarianism nor a theory of abstract "natural right" is adequate to the task of grounding a reformist view of how "animals" should be treated. A vegetarian way of life would decrease the amount of animal suffering, but at the cost of decreasing gastronomic pleasure amongst repentant carnivores and lessening employment prospects. Utilitarianism does not give an unequivocal answer to the questions "should we eat meat, bait badgers, experiment on apes?" because how much happiness is produced by any particular policy will depend on how we already feel about the policies. If enough people are in fact distressed by badger baiting, the practice might be worth outlawing; if too few, then not – but this does not tell us whether or not to disapprove. A theory of abstract natural right must also grapple with the obvious fact that animals are injured, exploited, and killed by other animals than the human. Their natural rights, if they have them, turn out to be those that **Hobbes** supposed to exist before the State, ones that imposed no duties of care or protection on anyone else.

Those concerned for the welfare of our fellow animals may do better to build on the experience of a shared community life, and on the virtues of loyalty and concern for dependents and friends – accepting that, despite Aristotle, we can be friends with the "non-rational". The actual rights in law of "British beasts" are already more extensive than any "natural rights". Increased understanding of what "animals" are like, how closely related to "us" they are and how poorly they have been served by moralists, may lead to an extension of those protections. The bargains we implicitly make with our domestic animals are at least as real as the **"social contract"** on which political philosophers have laid such stress, and ought not to be so radically rewritten as to leave those animals no better off for their troubles. "Wild" animals, similarly, should be given at least as much respect as the "environment", which is to say the whole living world of which we are a part, and those modes of life adopted, by those who can change their ways, which will enable that living world to continue in good health. "Environmentalism" often stands opposed to the demands of "animal rightists", but the latter are more likely to achieve their goals through environmentalist policies than through the advocacy of abstract rights, or utilitarian calculation.

[S.R.L.C.]

**Anscombe,** G. E. M., Elizabeth (1919– ), one of the most influential English philosophical teachers of her generation, liable to acute dismay about philosophers whose bland fluency prevents thought "about the stuff itself ". She was deeply influenced by **Wittgenstein**, and is his leading translator. Apart from two highly compressed books (*Intention*, 1957; *An Introduction to Wittgenstein's "Tractatus"*, 1959), she has published numerous brief papers, covering topics in the **history of philosophy, metaphysics and epistemology**, and especially **ethics** and the **philosophy of mind**, both of which she sees in terms of the topic of her first book; and in the philosophy of **religion**, where she writes explicitly as a Catholic. Her *Collected Papers* in three volumes appeared in 1981.

[J.R.]

**Anselm** of Canterbury (1033–1109), canonized 1494. He was born at Aosta, Italy. In 1033, Anselm joined the Benedictine Abbey of Bec in Normandy under Lanfranc. He subsequently became Archbishop of Canterbury.

Apart from **Erigena** Anselm was the first systematic thinker of the Middle Ages. Meeting the difficulties occasioned by the **dialecticians** of his day with the celebrated formula "a faith seeking understanding", he was not prepared to substitute dialectic for theology but at the same time he insisted upon a reasoned presentation of traditional Christian belief.

His philosophical writing came in response to a request by some of his monks for a rational meditation on the existence and nature of God which would dispense with reference to scriptural authority. The *Monologion* and *Proslogion* are his reply.

In the former he begins with the experienced occurrence of differences in degrees of value, goodness and being in the objects around us. From this he argues to the necessary existence of an absolute standard, an absolute good, an absolute being in which the relative participates. And this absolute we call God. The argument follows a familiar Platonic method already used by **Augustine** and would later be more fully elaborated by Thomas **Aquinas**.

In the *Proslogion*, Anselm presents his famous **ontological argument**. We may, he says, start with no more than the commonly accepted idea of what we mean when we use the term God, namely a being than which no greater can be thought. This, he says, is a point of departure available even to the fool who, according to scripture, denies the existence of God. Such a being, then, can be said to exist in the mind. But to exist actually is more perfect than to exist in the mind. To deny the actual existence of God, then, is to fall into foolish contradiction. If God is the being than which nothing greater can be thought, he must exist in reality as well as in the mind.

The argument of the *Proslogion* at once aroused controversy and to this day philosophers have not ceased to be sharply divided about it. The monk Gaunilo wrote a *Book on behalf of the Fool* attacking the validity of the conclusion and arguing that by similar argument one might establish the "existence" of anything, for instance of a most perfect island. Anselm in his reply pointed out that only in the unique case of the most excellent of all beings does the argument conclude and that only an infinite being can be conceived necessarily to exist.

In the Middle Ages the Franciscans tended to accept the argument, though **Scotus** required that it be shown that the nature of God is not self-contradictory. Aquinas on the other hand rejected it. **Descartes** accepted the argument; **Leibniz**, like Scotus, required the possibility of God to be accounted for; and **Kant** rejected it.

(J.G.D.)

**Antisthenes** (*c.* 444 B.C.-*c.* 366 B.C.) was the pupil of the rhetorician Gorgias, close friend of **Socrates**, critic of **Plato**, and held to be one of the prototypes of the **Cynics**. From the few fragments that survive of numerous writings, we see the intertwining of three threads: the **Sophistic**, the Socratic, and what was later to become Cynic. He held virtue to be sufficient for happiness. As knowledge necessitating moral action it could be taught, and once gained was unshakeable. Education begins with the study of the meaning of words. Words correspond directly with reality, and a proposition is either true or meaningless, contradiction and false statement being impossible. But practical **ethics** is stressed rather than great learning. Although not an ascetic, Antisthenes especially condemned luxury (wealth and external goods being unimportant), for a man should be rich in his soul. Virtue should be combined with exertion, which yielded the only important pleasure. Hercules was the ideal example of this. Established laws, convention, birth, sex, race, were unimportant in comparison with the law of virtue, by which the state should be governed. Although many of his views are clearly Socratic, the ancients asserted that his importance lay in giving the impulse through **Diogenes** to the way of life later called Cynic, and it is likely that **Stoicism** too was influenced by his practical ethics.

(I.G.K.)

**A posteriori,** *see* A priori.

**Applied Ethics.** There is nothing new about philosophers seeking to apply their ethical ideas to the world in which they live. **Plato** set out his view of the ideal republic, **Aquinas** wrote on the justification for going to war, **Hume** defended suicide, and John Stuart **Mill** attacked the subjection of women. Yet from the early twentieth century until the 1960s, **analytic philosophy** spurned practical questions. **Ethics** was seen as limited to the analysis of moral language, and hence as neutral between different moral views. To enter into practical questions, as Bertrand **Russell** for instance did, was to remove one's philosophical hat and to become a "moralist", on a par with preachers and leader-writers.

The bar against serious study of applied ethics came under pressure in America during the 1960s, when first the struggle for racial equality, and then the resistance to the war in Vietnam, began to raise questions of central importance which were clearly both practical and philosophical. The radicalization of the campuses, with a mounting student demand for courses which were relevant to their present concerns, proved irresistible. Within a few years, an applied ethics course was part of the offering of almost every philosophy department in the English-speaking world. Such courses frequently attracted the largest enrolments of any course in philosophy – an interest soon reflected in new journals such as *Philosophy and Public Affairs*, and in a new, or revived, field of philosophical debate and writing.

Initially the most popular topics in applied ethics were those concerned with equality, the justification of war, and the obligation to obey the state. With the end of the Vietnam war there was a hiatus in discussions of just war doctrine, but these became more prominent again in the 1980s, in the context of concern over nuclear weapons: since traditional just war doctrine condemns the deliberate killing of the innocent, and demands that the gains be worth the costs of fighting the war, can a nuclear war ever be a just war? Discussions of racial and sexual equality have undergone a different change: perhaps because there was such widespread agreement on the issue of equality itself, it is the more controversial positions, such as reverse discrimination, which have had the most attention. Inequality of wealth has been thoroughly scrutinized when it takes the form of distribution within a society – John **Rawls**' A *Theory of Justice* being perhaps the most discussed single work of philosophy since **Wittgenstein**'s *Philosophical Investigations* – but the far greater disparity in wealth between rich and poor nations has received less attention.

Some areas of applied ethics have become virtual sub-specialities of their own, often linking up with other related disciplines. Questions about the environment, and about our relations with the entire non-human world, for example, have opened avenues of inquiry into the nature of intrinsic value, and into the application of principles of equality, rights and justice to those who are incapable of reciprocity, and in some cases are not even sentient. Until recently, most ethical thinking has been, explicitly or implicitly, human-centred. (**Utilitarians** were exceptions, looking to sentience, rather than humanity, as the basis of moral concern.) This tendency has come under strong attack, and an explicitly and exclusively human-centred ethic is now rarely defended. Sentient **animals**, at least, are widely agreed to be of direct moral concern, even if some would still defend the legitimacy of a preference for our own species. On the other hand, attempts to bestow intrinsic value on non-sentient objects like trees, rivers and forests are still highly controversial.

Perhaps the most important sub-speciality in applied ethics at the moment, however, is bioethics. Although this term was originally coined to refer to an ethical approach to the whole biosphere, it has come to be used much more narrowly, as a label for studies in the ethical issues arising from medicine and the biological sciences. Philosophers began by contributing to discussions of abortion and euthanasia, and have gone on to write on the ethics of human experimentation, resource allocation, new developments in reproduction, and future prospects such as sex selection and genetic engineering. They have also played a prominent role in government committees of inquiry which have made recommendations concerning the control of these new developments. Philosophers are now involved in inter disciplinary centres for bioethics in most Western nations. With the creation of the first "bleeper philosophers" – philosophers attached to hospitals who carry a paging device in case they need to be consulted about the ethics of an emergency treatment – philosophy has come a long way from the earlier attitude that it has nothing to contribute to ethical decision-making. See also **Animals, Political Philosophy**.

[P.S.]

**A priori**. *A priori* is a Latin phrase meaning "from what comes before", contrasted with *a posteriori*, "from what comes after". These terms were introduced in the late scholastic period to translate two technical phrases in **Aristotle**'s theory of knowledge. Aristotle distinguished what is prior in the order of nature or more fundamental from what is prior in the order of discovery or known to us first. There are many truths, such as that fire burns or that water will not flow uphill, that we know from experience before we are able to explain why they should be so. Until we discover their causes our knowledge of them must be said to be empirical and not truly scientific. An *a posteriori* argument was an argument from observed effects to unknown causes; for, though the effects are known to us first, the causes are logically prior. An *a priori* argument was an argument from causes to effects or, since the relation of cause and effect was not sharply distinguished by Aristotle from that of logical ground and consequent, from ground to consequent. *A priori* arguments were

held to provide certain scientific knowledge as opposed to probable belief.

From the seventeenth century, for example in **Descartes** and **Leibniz**, *a priori* came to mean "universal, necessary and wholly independent of experience". The term *a posteriori* fell into disuse and *a priori* is now usually contrasted with "empirical" i.e. depending on experience. The term *a priori* is now used of (1) arguments, (2) propositions and (3) ideas.

(1) An *a priori* argument is one in which the conclusion follows deductively from the premises, as for example in a mathematical proof. If the premises are true and the argument valid, no experience is needed to confirm the conclusion and no experience could refute it. By contrast, an argument from experience (empirical, inductive, or probable argument) is one in which the conclusion, however strongly supported by the premises, is not necessitated by them. For example, if we argue that it will rain somewhere in England next January, on the grounds that no January has been known to pass without some rain, this argument, though weighty, is not conclusive. There might be a January without rain even though there never has been one. Since **Hume** it has been generally believed that all natural science contains an empirical element and therefore cannot be *a priori*.

(2) An *a priori* proposition is one which (it is claimed) is independent of experience, except in so far as experience is necessary for understanding its terms. Thus we know *a priori* that a whole is equal to the sum of its parts; for, once we understand the terms involved, we see that this is universally and necessarily true and that no experience could refute it.

(3) Empiricist philosophers – so called because they tend to emphasize the role of experience in knowledge at the expense of *a priori* elements – have sometimes held that all *ideas* are derived from experience. We can (they say) have no idea unless we have either come across an instance of it, as in the case of "red" or "horse", or fabricated it, as in the case of "dragon", out of elements that we have come across. There are, however, some ideas of great importance in philosophy, the origin of which

it is difficult to explain in this way. Among them are the ideas of substance (thing), cause, existence, equality, likeness and difference. Of these it is claimed that, so far from their being derived from experience, we could have no experience without them. This is not to say that we are born equipped with these ideas, but rather that they are presupposed by our being able to have any experience at all. (**Plato**'s *Meno* and **Leibniz**'s *New Essays on the Human Understanding* are classic expositions of this doctrine, sometimes called the doctrine of Innate Ideas. For the empiricist view see **Locke** and **Hume**.)

It is clear that all **analytic** propositions are *a priori*. If "bachelor" means "unmarried man" we need investigate no particular cases to satisfy ourselves of the truth of the proposition "No bachelor is married". But the question whether any **synthetic** proposition can be known *a priori* is one of the most important and difficult in philosophy. The **rationalists** believed that the fundamental principles of science could, like those of logic and pure mathematics, be known *a priori*. Hume argued (in effect) that the principles of logic and pure mathematics were indeed *a priori*, but only because they were analytic. But all knowledge of matters of fact, both common sense and scientific, depended, he argued, on such causal principles as that every event must have a cause and that like causes must have like effects. He claimed to show that these principles are synthetic, cannot be known *a priori* and must be derived from experience.

**Kant** saw the force and the sceptical tendency of Hume's argument and devoted his most important book, the *Critique of Pure Reason*, to establishing the possibility and scope of *a priori* knowledge. He held that such knowledge was possible in mathematics (which he did not regard as analytic) and in physics. With regard to metaphysics he agreed substantially with Hume, but he also undertook to show how it is that men necessarily continue to ask metaphysical questions which it is impossible for them to answer.

In this century the **logical positivists** and many philosophers influenced by them follow Hume in denying the possibility of synthetic *a priori* knowledge. The most difficult problem for them concerns the status of pure mathematics. Mathematical statements are usually regarded as analytic; very few philosophers would now follow J. S. **Mill** in regarding them as synthetic generalizations from experience which have exceptionally good backing but might, nevertheless, not be universally true. Recently, however, the possibility of synthetic *a priori* knowledge has been much discussed, partly owing to doubts about the validity of the distinction between analytic and synthetic, and the issue cannot be regarded as closed. Something akin to synthetic *a priori* knowledge plays an important part in the philosophy of the **Phenomenologists**.

(P.H.N.-S.)

**Aquinas,** Thomas (c. 1225–1274), born at Roccasecca near Aquino on the northern border of the ancient Kingdom of Sicily, canonized 1323. He proceeded from Monte Cassino to the University of Naples where he entered the Dominicans, studied under **Albert the Great** at Cologne and at Paris where he lectured before and after a nine years' appointment as adviser to the Papal Court. A large man, decided and calm, patrician yet modest, he enjoyed the affection even of his adversaries. Ninety-eight items are listed in the catalogue of his works; some run into several folios. Proclaimed Doctor of the Church in 1567, he is the classical systematic theologian of Catholicism.

In 1879, Leo XIII inaugurated the revival of Thomist philosophy, extracted from the earlier *Summa Contra Gentiles* and the *Summa Theologica* (or *Theologiae*) of his maturity. To what extent the result can be appreciated without reference to the witness of Christianity is a matter of some dispute.

According to tradition Aquinas set his colleague, the Flemish Dominican, William of Moerbeke (1215–1286), to provide fresh Latin translations of **Aristotle**. Aristotle's philosophy could otherwise scarcely be separated from the contributions of Arab thinkers, notably **Avicenna** and **Averroes**. It was mingled with Neo-Platonist strains inherited from **Augustine**, Proclus, Dionysius, and **Boethius**. The so-called baptism of Aristotle, however, was no mere surface reconciliation. Aquinas meant to take the philosophical arguments to their deepest level, not to fit them into the existing theological framework. He pressed the distinction between potentiality and actuality to the core of reality itself, and the old problem of the One and the Many turned into the creation by *esse subsistens* of all existents. He showed that a universal and particular Providence followed from knowing and loving at their best. He defended immortality without diminishing the doctrine that the soul is essentially embodied. If he borrowed from Aristotle he certainly made capital gains.

Aquinas' predecessors and most of his contemporaries such as the Franciscan **Bonaventura** and the English Dominican Robert Kilwardby drew no clear distinction between their reflections on a historical and revealed religion and a philosophy which could be its own warrant. He himself calls for careful interpretation of the relations between Reason and Faith. On the one hand he was not a special pleader who treated rational investigation as ancillary to religious belief; on the other he never countenanced a practical separation between them, indeed he fought such a split when it widened into the celebrated Double Truth theory associated with **Siger** of Brabant and the Latin Averroists.

Aquinas' solution was the notion of subordination without subservence. The world is composed of real things which act as true causes, that is, principles and goals of activity, not merely instuments or occasions. To be truly wise about them, and more than narrowly scientific, we must see them in the light of the First Cause. Creatures are real; moreover they interact and are dependent on one another. By a judicious use of analogy, which is treated as a law of being rather than an artifice of logical classification or literary metaphor, the mind can range at large and from its environment discover truth beyond its experience.

But Aquinas does not lose sight of individual and personal substance. This is particularly evident in his psychological and moral philosophy. The philosophical sciences differ from the particular sciences in that they do not stay with the proximate causes but seek reasons more universal, yet not on that account more summary. He does not fall into the philosophism of deducing facts from reasons, or of treating the specialist sciences as applications of metaphysics.

Aquinas' exposition of **Boethius'** *De Trinitate* defines the philosophical disciplines. Logic, which runs through them all, is the study of scientific method and the mental constructions, *entia rationis*, which we place on our experience. Theory isolates what is general and constant in individual and changing facts, and theoretical philosophy may be conveniently according to three degrees of abstraction. First, Natural Philosophy engages objects which not only exist in material processes but cannot be understood without reference to them. Second, Mathematical Philosophy, while considering the implications of quantity, needs no such appeal to the sensible world. Third, Metaphysical Philosophy reaches beyond the material world because its objects are either non-material, for instance, God, or not of necessity material, for instance, substantial unity. As for practice, the chief science is Moral Philosophy, which includes personal ethics, economics (in the Aristotelean sense), and politics.

These headings may serve for a general outline of the parts of his philosophy. A poet and on occasion a writer of distinguished prose, the general run of his expository style is curt and repetitive: sometimes the sparse vocabulary conceals the variety of the ideas and the delicacy of the distinctions. Many of his works were dictated to or written up by secretaries.

I. LOGIC

Aquinas completed a commentary on the *Posterior Analytics* and began one on the *De Interpretatione*. His academic debates on Aristotelian logic fall into two classes, the *Quaestiones*

*Disputatae*, which in the main report his se-
rialised discussion during a teaching-course,
and the *Quaestiones Quodlibetales*, or questions
for special occasions. His general dialectic
begins from induction and proceeds deductively either **a posteriori** for discovery (*via
inventionis*) or **a priori** for assessment (*via
judicii*).

## II. THEORETICAL PHILOSOPHY

Aquinas' welcome for Aristotle's natural and
metaphysical philosophy scandalised some of
his contemporaries. Rejecting **Neoplatonism** he
saw ideas as embodied here and now about us.
Substance and accidents are the first categories
of the material world. Substance is what is able
to exist in itself, accidents are inhering realities,
such as being quantified, qualified, or related. Material processes are shaped by the four
causes – final, efficient, material and formal.
All activity has a purpose or end, *finis*, but
Aquinas' teleological reading of the universe
is not the eighteenth-century Argument from
Design: the finality within the acting thing is
immanent, not imposed. The efficient cause,
*agens*, is the producer. The material cause,
the basic potential subject, and the formal
cause, the actual determinant, are intrinsic and
essential to the effect. All material substances
are composed of matter, *materia prima*, and form,
*forma substantialis*. Bare matter so conceived is
not the ultimate atomic or infra-atomic point
which can be calculated or recorded by scientific apparatus, but the substantial potentiality
common to all material things which are formed
differently in number, degree, and kind under
the action of secondary causes.

The tang of reality infuses his psychology,
which is less a study of consciousness than of
human substance and activity. The Matter-
Form distinction is uncompromisingly applied:
the soul is the substantial form of the body. By
one and the same actuality man is a bodily,
vegetative, sensitive, and intellective being.
This psychophysical unity is defended despite
the difficulties it raises for the immortality of
the soul.

The celebrated five ways, *quinque viae*, sometimes called the proofs for the existence of God,
follow some general themes running through
the universe, namely, change, dependence,
contingency, limited perfection, and utility.
Were they to extend to the whole of reality
we should have no explanation of their presence. Aquinas infers the changeless changer,
the uncaused cause, the necessary being, the
completely perfect, and the ultimate end –
notions all of which combine in the nominal
definition of God.

*He Who Is* transcends our classification of
sorts of being, but we can say what he is
not by a process of elimination, *via negationis*.
Furthermore, Aquinas goes beyond traditional
negative theology by showing that we can think
positively when we are dealing with unmixed
values: to say that God is good means more
than that he is not evil, or that he is the cause
of the goodness we see about us. Goodness is
more properly his than ours, being taken to its
highest strength, *via eminentia*.

## III. MORAL PHILOSOPHY

Moral acts, *actus humani*, are our deliberate
adjustments of means to an end beyond morals.
Morality in the abstract is determined by what
kind of act is performed, good, bad, or indifferent; in the concrete the personal intention
will be either right or wrong. Circumstances
must also be taken into account. Merely as a
moral philosopher he may seem to add little
to the eudemonianism and the typology of
the virtues set forth in Aristotle's *Nicomachean
Ethics* on which he wrote a commentary. Here
he was but on the threshold of his heroic
ideal of theological perfection, which makes
his criticism of the **stoic** standard of passionless
virtue all the more impressive.

Aquinas' synthesis on the nature and divisions of Law dominates his social philosophy.
Law is rational ordinance, not directly a manifestation of might; it is for the common good,
and this means a communion of persons; in
the human community it comes from the ruler
who is the representative, not the owner of
the people; and it must be promulgated. The
Eternal Law in the mind of God is the exemplar
of all law. It is impressed on human minds as
the Natural Law, which is immutable in its

principles though its derivative precepts may be variously developed according to region and period. In contrast, though not in contradiction, stands the Positive Law: its precepts may sometimes reinforce the Natural Law, but as such they are not conclusions from it but rather pragmatic supplements to make the good life easier or to safeguard public order. Aquinas was the first to depart from the traditional view, formed by the Stoics and Augustine, that the civil power, like private property, was *propter peccatum*, a remedy against our anti-social appetites. He revived Aristotle's idea of the State meeting the essential demands of human nature, which, he says, using two terms, is both social and political. "Social" may be taken to mean the moral requirements of living together in community and society, "political" the constitutional forms that are chosen. Human legislation should know its limits, and not seek to cover the whole field of morality.

(T.G.)

**Arcesilaus** of Pitane, *see* Sceptics.

**Arendt,** Hannah (1906–1975), political theorist, was born in Königsberg and educated chiefly at Marburg (with Martin **Heidegger**) and Heidelberg (with Karl **Jaspers**). She fled from Germany in 1933, lived in Paris, and emigrated to America in 1941. Her first major work, *The Origins of Totalitarianism*, published in 1951, remains a classic historical study of Nazism and Stalinism as instances of a novel form a government, totalitarianism. Her next three books, *The Human Condition* (1958), *Between Past and Future* (1961), and *On Revolution* (1963), present basic political concepts and distinctions in challenging interpretations. For example, she analyses work, labor and action, public space/private realm, history, freedom, authority, power/violence, emphasizing their historical evolution as concepts and their present meaning and political relevance. Arendt thought that the precondition for a "new science of politics", neither traditionally liberal

nor conservative, was a radical, critical re-examination of all political thought since the rise of the Greek city-states. In 1963, Arendt published *Eichmann in Jerusalem*, a controversial study of Eichmann in particular and the Nazi genocide in general. This book posed questions about morality and politics that Arendt took up in her last (and unfinished) philosophical study of thinking, willing and judging, called *The Life of the Mind* (1978).

[E.Y.-B.]

**Aristippus** of Cyrene in North Africa (c. 435–356 B.C.) was one of the Socratic circle, a **Sophist**, and the traditional founder of the **Cyrenaic** school of philosophy. While his life and views are in harmony with its tenets, it is possible that these tenets were first systematically formulated by his grandson, also named Aristippus.

He made the goal of his life the enjoyment of present pleasure, eschewing regret for the past and toil for the future. But happiness consisted in the prudent, intelligent control or mastery of such pleasure, not in slavery to it, nor in abstinence. Hence his famous remark on his association with his expensive mistress Lais: "I have Lais, not she me." All acts were indifferent except in so far as they produced pleasure for the doer. Aristippus made his life the art of adapting himself to place, time and person, and playing his part appropriately whatever the circumstances, a virtuosity he displayed especially at the court of Dionysius of Syracuse. It was said of him that he alone could play the dandy or go in rags. He had in fact an extraordinary capacity for enjoyment combined with a great freedom from wants, a combination later to raise a difficult choice of ideals for his successors.

(I.G.K.)

**Aristotle,** (384–322 B.C.) was the son of a doctor of Stagira in northern Greece. For twenty years, from 367, he was a member of **Plato**'s Academy. When Plato died and **Speusippus** became head of the Academy, Aristotle left Athens and went first to Assos (on the coast of Asia Minor) and then to Lesbos. About 342 he was invited by King Philip of Macedonia to go there to supervise the education of the King's son, Alexander. A few years later he returned to Athens to found a new school, which became known as the Lyceum or Peripatos. The school flourished; but in 323 Aristotle left Athens for political reasons and retired to Euboea. There he died in 322.

Aristotle's early writings were mostly intended for a general public. Written in a polished style (some in dialogue form), they were largely Platonic in outlook. These works were well known in antiquity but only fragments survive. The works which we possess are systematic treatises intended for serious students. These works had only a limited circulation in antiquity until texts were edited by Andronicus in the first century B.C.; our text of Aristotle is based ultimately on Andronicus' edition, and so were all translations into Latin and Arabic. Aristotle's treatises have a rather peculiar character, for they are in essence notes of or notes for lectures. A lecturer rehandles his material many times over the years and introduces second thoughts and new ideas, and his notes in their final form may contain parts written at very different dates and not always integrated into a smooth unity. Thus an Aristotelian treatise is not to be thought of as a work written, revised and published in a certain year, but rather as something that has been added to and altered over a period of years without perhaps ever receiving a final rewriting. Moreover what we count as a single treatise may really consist of several originally separate courses strung together by Andronicus or an earlier editor. All this makes the problem of the chronology of Aristotle's writings very complicated and hence makes it difficult to give an account of how his thought changed or developed. These questions have been the subject of much valuable research in recent years but cannot be discussed here.

It is worth saying a word about Aristotle's approach to philosophy. His very name suggests to some people the idea of a dogmatic system of rigid doctrines. But Aristotle's manner is far

from dogmatic: he is always reopening questions and admitting difficulties. Nor is his method dogmatic. He does not argue arrogantly from premises laid down by him as self-evident. He considers carefully what his predecessors have said and what ordinary men say, he assumes that their divergent views will all have some element of truth in them, and he seeks to elicit reasonable solutions to problems by clarifying the issues and qualifying or refining the various inconsistent solutions that have been offered. Finally, it is a mistake to think that the philosophical value of his work must reside in his conclusions (or "doctrines"); it is his skill in analysis and his acuteness in argument quite as much as his positive conclusions which make him a very great philosopher.

The following notes, necessarily superficial, will introduce some of the ideas which recur constantly in Aristotle.

## I. CATEGORIES

Aristotle's categories classify reality: everything that exists falls under one of them – is either a substance or a quality or a quantity or a relation etc. (Aristotle sometimes lists ten categories, usually fewer.) It is because items in different categories have irreducibly different sorts of being that terms like "is" and "one" which are applicable in all categories are in an important way ambiguous (compare the scholastic doctrine of *transcendentalia*). Inattention to this type of ambiguity and to categorial distinctions had led, Aristotle argued, to philosophical paradoxes.

Substance is prior to all the other categories because substances exist "separately" while qualities, etc., exist only as the qualities *of* substance. Individual substances (for example Socrates or this table) are the subjects to which predicates belong and are not themselves predicates of anything else. Aristotle places in the category of substance not only individual substances but also their species and genera (man, animal). For to say that Socrates is a man is not to mention some quality etc. which he has, but to say *what he is*. Moreover science, which studies reality and above all substance, defines and studies species not individuals.

Yet of course species do *not* exist separately as individuals do. There is a deep difficulty in Aristotle's thought here, which may be expressed by saying that his word *ousia* (literally "being") does duty both for our "substance" and for our "essence"; Aristotle assigns to *ousia* incompatible characteristics, some of which really belong to individual substances, others to species or essences.

## II. FORM AND MATTER
A table is wood and glue put together in a certain way. Aristotle distinguishes as separate aspects of the table its matter (the wood and glue) and its form (how it is put together, its structure). Many of his central ideas – and of his puzzles – are connected with this distinction. (*a*) Form is *immanent*: the form of table exists only as the form of this table or that table, that is, as the form of certain matter. There is no separately existing transcendental Platonic Form of Table (or indeed of Man or Justice). (*b*) Form or structure is normally determined by function. It is because of what it has to do that a table has a flat top and four legs. Form may in fact be identified with function: to say what a table *is* is to say what it does or is for. (*c*) Matter is "for the sake of" form, not *vice versa*. If you want an axe – something for cutting down trees – you must of course use iron to make it; but there can be iron without there being an axe. So to state the form or function of something explains it far more than stating what it is made of; the form implies the appropriate matter in a way in which the matter does not imply the form. (*d*) Wood and glue, the matter of a table, are not matter in an absolute sense. In a piece of wood we can again draw a distinction between form and matter, since wood, like everything else, is made of earth, air, fire and water (or of some of these) combined in a certain way. Nor are these four elements pure matter. They can change into one another. This implies a persistent underlying stuff capable of receiving the form of earth, air, etc. but in itself without any form or definite character. This is what Aristotle calls *first* (or "*prime*") *matter*, a characterless substrate which never actually exists on its own but only

in the form of earth, air etc. (*e*) Besides pressing the distinction of matter and form to the extreme concept of prime matter, Aristotle also uses it by analogy in quite different problems. Thus in the definition of a species he treats the genus as the matter and the differentia as the form: the genus is relatively indeterminate, the differentia gives its definite character to the species. This is typical of Aristotle's way of extending the application of key concepts, – which adds a certain unity to his thought at the cost of some obscurity. (*f*) So far form has been the correlative of matter, the form *of* some matter. Aristotle raises the question whether there can be form without matter and says that there can. But his form-without-matter is very different from a Platonic Form. God is form without matter.

## III. ACTUALITY AND POTENTIALITY
A block of wood is potentially a statue, an acorn is potentially an oak; the completed statue and the mature oak are the actualisations of those potentialities. (*a*) There is a close connection between the antithesis form-matter and the antithesis actuality-potentiality. Matter is what has the potentiality of receiving form; form is what actualises the potentiality. So Aristotle sometimes uses the two antitheses interchangeably. (*b*) It is not any and every material that is capable of receiving a given form: an acorn *cannot* become an elm, wood *cannot* be made into an axe. What oaks come from and what axes are made of are particular questions to be answered by separate investigations. Aristotle does not think that they and all similar questions can be adequately answered simply by saying that actual so-and-so's come from potential so-and-so's; *this* is part of a quite general philosophical analysis of the notions of growth and change. (*c*) Aristotle argues that actuality is prior to potentiality in definition, value and time. The actuality has to be mentioned in a definition of the potentiality, but not *vice versa*. The actuality is the end for the sake of which the potentiality exists. And although an acorn exists before the oak it grows into, it is itself the product of some already existing mature oak: "for from the potentially

25

existing the actually existing is always produced by an actually existing thing, for example, man from man, musician by musician; there is always a first mover, and the mover already exists actually". (A table of course is not produced by a table; but it *is* produced by someone who already has the *form* of a table "in his mind".) (d) Since a potentiality implies the possibility of change to the actuality, which is better, there can be no element of potentiality in a perfect changeless being.

## IV. THE FOUR "CAUSES"

Aristotle holds that the full explanation of anything should say what it is made of (material cause), what it essentially is (formal cause), what brought it into being (efficient cause) and what its function or purpose is (final cause). The oddity of describing all these as *causes* is not to be held against Aristotle; "cause" is the traditional translation in this context of a Greek word of wider meaning.

Aristotle holds that in a way the formal, efficient and final causes are identical. It is the essential nature of a table (formal cause) to subserve certain purposes (final cause), and it was the thought of those purposes in the carpenter's mind that brought the table into being (efficient cause). It is the essential nature of a horse to perform certain characteristic functions and exercise characteristic powers, and to do this, to live the life of a mature horse, is just what horses are for; and a horse is produced by horses, that is, creatures already exercising the functions of mature horses.

It should be noticed that the notion of explanation by the four causes applies to things rather than events, is derived from reflection on the process of production (natural and artificial), and implies a kind of universal teleology.

## V. CLASSIFICATION OF SCIENCES

A survey of Aristotle's work in special fields can conveniently be prefaced by an account of how he classifies the various branches of inquiry, a classification of considerable historical importance. His basic division is into theoretical, practical and productive sciences.

Theoretical science studies "what cannot be otherwise" and aims simply at truth. It can be subdivided into three main parts, distinguished by subject-matter: physics deals with things that exist separately but are liable to change, mathematics with things that are changeless but have no separate existence, "first philosophy" (metaphysics) with what both exists separately and is changeless. Practical sciences are to do with "what can be otherwise" and are ultimately aimed at action; the most important practical sciences are ethics and politics. Productive sciences are concerned with making things.

Logic is regarded by Aristotle not as a substantive part of philosophy but as ancillary to all parts. For it studies forms of reasoning and expression common to various subject-matters, and a grasp of it is pre-requisite for the student of any topic. This view of logic is reflected in the traditional name of Aristotle's logical works – the "Organon" (that is, tool or instrument).

## VI. LOGIC

The *Prior Analytics* contains Aristotle's great contribution to formal logic, his theory of the syllogism. This is a purely formal system of remarkable rigour but limited scope. The limitations are that it handles only certain kinds of statement and that the inferences it studies are all inferences from two such statements to a third. The statements in a categorical syllogism all have one or other of the following forms: all A is B, no A is B, some A is B, some A is not B. Modal syllogisms bring in such forms as "all A *may be* B" and "all A *must be* B". Aristotle works out all possible combinations of premises and conclusions, determines which syllogisms are valid, and investigates some of the logical relations between different syllogisms.

The *Posterior Analytics* contains Aristotle's "logic of science". His account of the form a completed science should take is much influenced by the model of geometry and rests on the view that there are in nature "real kinds" whose essence we can know. A given branch of science is about some limited class of objects. It starts from principles and axioms – some common to all sciences, some peculiar to this one – and from definitions of the objects being studied. It then demonstrates by syllogisms that certain properties necessarily belong to the objects in question. This seems remote from what scientists do, and indeed from what Aristotle does in his scientific works; but it must be remembered that it expresses an ideal for the exposition of a completed science rather than a programme for investigators.

Two further points: (*a*) Aristotle is rejecting the notion, which he ascribes to Plato, of one grand comprehensive science; different sciences require different premises. (*b*) Aristotle uses the term translated "induction" to explain how we get indemonstrable starting points from which to make our deduction; but this is not induction in our sense. We are said, for example, to grasp the truth of the principle of contradiction (one of the principles common to all sciences) by "induction"; this means simply that we are led on ("induced") to recognise it as evidently true by noticing one or more instances of it. Aristotle gives a somewhat similar account of how we acquire concepts; having seen a number of men we are able to seize upon the nature common to them all. Grasping the universal, like grasping a universal truth, is a matter of direct apprehension not of inference.

VII. PHYSICS

The study of *physics*, or nature, includes the study of living things, but it will be convenient to treat Aristotle's biology and psychology separately from his more general physical works. The *Physics* and connected works contain discussion and analysis of such concepts as nature, change, chance, time, place, continuity, infinity, growth; proofs that movement is eternal and that there is an eternal Prime Mover; and much doctrine as to the actual constitution and workings of the universe. What Aristotle has to say on this last subject is naturally out-of-date (and would not now be regarded as in a philosopher's province). His analyses of concepts are often subtle and illuminating but cannot be usefully summarised. His treatment of movement and continuity led him to reject as senseless, questions about the velocity (or direction) of a moving body at a given *point* (of space or time); this had unfortunate effects on the study of dynamics.

The argument for a Prime Mover starts from Aristotle's conception of change and causation. There could not be an absolutely first (or last) change. For since change implies pre-existing matter (or potentiality) and a pre-existing efficient cause to impose form on the matter (to actualise the potentiality), there must have existed before a supposed first change something capable of being changed and something capable of causing change. But then to explain why these potentialities (for being changed and for causing change) were actualised at a certain time, and not before, we must assume some actual change just prior to that time, that is, a change before the supposed first change. Change therefore, or movement, must be eternal. But how is eternal change to be explained? Not by the assumption that there is something eternally *self-moving*. The very term "self-mover" is misleading. For the concept of movement or change demands that we distinguish in a "self-mover" one part which causes change and another which undergoes it. We must therefore assume the existence of a being itself *unmoved* which can somehow cause eternal movement. This Prime Mover, eternal, changeless and containing no element of matter or unrealised potentiality, keeps the heavenly bodies moving and maintains the eternal life of the universe. Theology will have something more to say about its nature and mode of operation.

VIII. BIOLOGY

If Aristotle's work on physics suffers from a lack of experiment and observation, the same cannot be said of his biology. He collected a vast amount of information about living creatures and, in spite of some fundamental errors, was better informed on the subject than most of his successors until comparatively recent times. He recognized that theories must wait upon facts; after giving a theory about the generation of bees he says: "the facts have not been sufficiently ascertained". And if at any future time they are ascertained, "then credence must be given to the direct evidence of the senses more than to theories".

Two of Aristotle's important contributions are connected with classification and with teleological explanation. He achieved valuable systematic classifications of animal life, rejecting what he regarded as an inadequate Platonic method – the method of dichotomy – and employing multiple differentiae to distinguish the main classes of creature. He thought of the various species as eternal and not evolved from other species, but as capable of being arranged in a scale leading from the lowest and least developed to the highest and most complex.

Aristotle regards teleological explanation as the essence of the biologist's work: the explanation of material structure in terms of function. Nature, the perfect craftsman, does nothing in vain; and the true explanation of the characteristics of a species must show how they serve some purpose in relation to the life of the members of the species. Aristotle's teleology has nothing to do with one species subserving the interests of another; it is concerned with each species in itself. The job of an embryo is to become a mature animal, live its proper life and reproduce itself; and its parts and characteristics are to be explained as contributing to these ends. "For any living thing that has reached its normal development . . . the most natural act is the production of another like itself, an animal producing an animal, a plant a plant, in order that, as far as its nature allows, it may partake in the eternal and divine. That is the goal towards which all things strive, that for the sake of which they do whatsoever their nature renders possible."

IX. PSYCHOLOGY
The word "*psyche*", commonly translated "soul", really has a wider meaning; plants as well as animals have *psyche*, they are *living*. Living things can be ordered according to the complexity of their powers. Some (plants) have only the power of nutrition and reproduction; others have also the power of perception, desire and movement; men have in addition the power of thought. Aristotle's main discussion of these various psychical functions is in the *De*

*Anima*, which also contains his general account of soul and its relation to body.

A dead man, a body without a soul, is not strictly a man at all, for it lacks just those powers the possession of which defines what it is to be a man. A man (and any animal or plant) is a body-with-soul; and the relation between body and soul is the relation of matter to form. Soul is the form of body, as sight is the form of the eye ("when seeing is removed the eye is no longer an eye, except in name – it is no more a real eye than the eye of a statue"). Soul, the power of life, cannot exist in any and every body (form requires appropriate matter); it is only a body with suitable organs which can possess life. Such a body is *potentially* a living animal or plant; soul is the *actuality* of such a body. This important conclusion (which is closer to **Ryle** than to **Descartes**) enables Aristotle to dismiss the question whether soul and body form a unity: "this is as meaningless as to ask whether the wax and the shape given to it by the stamp are one, or generally the matter of a thing and that of which it is the matter. Unity has many senses . . . but the most proper and fundamental sense . . . is the relation of an actuality to that of which it is the actuality". On this general view to talk of a psychological activity is to talk not of the activity of an immaterial substance inside a body but of the actual functioning of a living body; and Aristotle's accounts of psychological concepts always bring in the relevant physical and physiological facts.

Aristotle allows one exception to the rule that soul is the form or actualisation of body. The activity of *nous* (pure intuitive thought) does not depend on body and may therefore exist separately from it. His doctrine on this point is exceedingly obscure, and it is disputed whether he attributes some sort of immortality to the *nous* in the individual human soul. In general his account of soul dissolves the question of personal immortality as effectively as that of the unity of body and soul.

X. METAPHYSICS
Aristotle expresses two views about "first philosophy" (the name "metaphysics" was given

by an editor to the treatise on first philosophy because it came after – *meta* – the *Physics* in his edition). One view, already mentioned, is that it is the study of changeless, separable substance, that is, theology. The other is that it is not a departmental science dealing with a particular kind of being, but that it studies *being as such*, together with concepts (for example, unity, identity) and principles (for example, the law of contradiction) which are common to all departmental sciences. Aristotle is not very successful in reconciling these two views. Most of the *Metaphysics* is metaphysics in the wider sense – as a brief synopsis of the work will show.

In Book I Aristotle surveys and criticises the views of his predecessors on the ultimate principles of reality in order to confirm his own view that there are four and only four different kinds of "cause". Book III develops a number of problems further discussed later. Book IV discusses the law of contradiction and the law of excluded middle (without trying to *prove* them). Book V is a lexicon of important philosophical terms, various senses of each being discriminated. Books VII and VIII discuss substance and wrestle with the notions of essence, genus, universal, substrate, form, etc. The next books treat of actuality and potentiality, unity, plurality and similar notions. Book XII contains Aristotle's theology. Books XIII and XIV discuss and reject certain views held in the Academy about immaterial substance: there are no such things as Platonic Ideas or Ideal Numbers, and mathematical objects are not substances.

Only Book XII can be further discussed here. In it Aristotle argues again (as in the *Physics*) that there must be an eternal, immaterial Prime Mover – which he now calls "God". God, himself not susceptible of movement, causes movement as an object of desire and love. His life is perpetual activity – activity being perfect and complete in every moment and not, like movement, a process. The only sort of activity which can be ascribed to God is pure thought, uninterrupted intuitive knowledge of the highest object of knowledge, God himself. "It must be of itself that the divine thought

thinks (since it is the most excellent of things), and its thinking is a thinking about thinking".

The outer heavens and the planets are animate beings moved by a desire to imitate the eternal activity of God; the outer heaven comes nearest by its single continuous spatial movement. In nature as a whole there is something similar: the processes of birth, growth and reproduction maintain forever the life of the various species. But of course plants and animals are not *consciously* imitating God (except that man, possessing reason, may do so), nor is God aware of or concerned about them.

## XI. ETHICS

The *Nicomachean Ethics* is certainly one of the best books ever written on the subject. It is rich in analysis of moral and psychological concepts, and in ingenious arguments. The following account will indicate the main lines of the work:

(i) The good life. "Good" is not, Aristotle argues, the name of a single quality. Different kinds of things are called good for different reasons: an axe is a good one if it *cuts* efficiently, eyes are good if they *see* well. To decide what is the best life for man one must ask what are the proper functions of a man (as cutting is the function of an axe); a good man will be one who performs those functions excellently, and his will be the good life. Now the function of something is what it alone can do or what it can do better than anything else. Man is distinguished from other animals by his power of thought. So the functions of a man – the effective performance of which will make him a good man – are those of his activities which involve thought and which therefore he does not share with other animals. Man's possession of reason shows itself not only in his ability to think, but also in his ability to control by thought and principle his desires and conduct; so the virtues of the good man will be not only intellectual but also moral or ethical (that is, virtues of character, *ethos*).

(ii) Moral virtue. Moral virtues, like skills, are acquired by practice. A man becomes generous by being trained or habituated to do the things a generous man would do. He has himself become generous when he has acquired a settled disposition of character so that he now does such things regularly, gladly and without ulterior motive. The "gladly" is important; it helps Aristotle to argue that the virtuous life is pleasant. His ideal is the man who always does what he ought because he wants to; the presence of a moral struggle, the need to conquer desires – these are signs of imperfection.

Moral virtue is concerned with feelings and actions, and in these there can be too much, too little, or the right amount, "the mean". Virtue is a matter of striking the mean between opposite vices: generosity lies between meanness and prodigality. The mean involved is not an arithmetical average, it is the mean "relative to us", that is, it is what is appropriate to a man. There are no simple rules for deciding what *is* appropriate; it is the possession of *phronesis* ("practical wisdom") which enables a man to hit the mean. This doctrine of the mean is more famous than it deserves to be. Aristotle admits to difficulty in bringing *all* virtues and vices into his scheme. More important, that virtue is not just a matter of the right amount is implied by Aristotle's own words: "anger and pity . . . may be felt both too much and too little, and in both cases not well; but to feel them at the right *times*, with reference to the right *people*, with the right *motive*, and in the right *way*, is what is intermediate and best, and this is characteristic of virtue". The doctrine of the mean, in fact, contains little positive moral teaching and is inadequate if considered simply as analysis of vice-virtue concepts.

Supplementary discussions consider responsibility and choice. Aristotle acutely analyses the conditions under which responsibility can be disclaimed, and reduces these to two – duress and ignorance of material facts. Choice he finds to involve deliberation and desire: our desires and character determine our *ends*; we deliberate about the *means* by which we may reach these ends.

(iii) Intellectual virtue: practical wisdom. This intellectual virtue enables a man to get the right answers to practical questions of conduct. It involves skill in deliberation but also presupposes the possession of moral virtue. For to have the right aims is a matter of moral virtue – character determines ends. Moral goodness and practical wisdom are in fact inseparable, each involving the other in its definition.

Three further points about practical wisdom may be noted. Firstly, Aristotle no longer concentrates exclusively on the means-end kind of deliberation. One may see something to be right not as being a means to a future goal but as falling under some moral principle. The means-end terminology common in Aristotle is indeed inadequate to his own account of the good life: the aim of the good man is not to achieve some future goal but to live well all through his life. Secondly, though Aristotle gives simple examples of deliberation, he does not underestimate the complexity of practical questions or suppose they can be settled easily. To appreciate all the factors in a situation and to weigh their various claims one must have an experienced eye for what matters. Age and training are what count here, not mere cleverness. Thirdly, Aristotle does not suppose that deliberation precedes every action (or every right action). But the man of practical wisdom would be able afterwards to justify what he did by reference to ends or principles. Before passing from practical to theoretical wisdom. Aristotle has important discussions of *akrasia* (knowing what one ought to do but not doing it) and of pleasure, its nature and value.

(iv) Intellectual virtue: theoretical wisdom. This intellectual virtue is wisdom about "what cannot be otherwise". It involves intuitive knowledge of unprovable starting-points (concepts and truth) and demonstrative knowledge of what follows from them. This virtue, Aristotle argues, is the highest that man can have: it is to do with the highest objects and it is the virtue of the divine part of man's soul (for no activity but that of pure thought can be attributed to God). The life of theoretical philosophy is the best and happiest a man can lead. Few men are capable of it (and they only intermittently). For the rest there is a second-best way of life, that of moral virtue and practical wisdom.

It is striking how Aristotle, starting from the question what is man's nature and his function *as a man*, ends by finding his highest and most proper activity in the *imitation of God* through the exercise of pure reason, the spark of divinity in him.

### XII. POLITICS

In the *Politics* Aristotle seeks to explain the nature and purpose of a state (a city-state) and so to discover what constitution and laws would be the best. Further, since politics is a branch of *practical* inquiry, Aristotle not only expounds an ideal constitution but also makes sensible suggestions as to how actual cities of various kinds could best be run. The main philosophical interest of the work is in its analysis of political concepts ("state", "citizen", "law" etc.).

### XIII. POETICS

This work must just be mentioned (though it cannot be discussed) because of the enormous – not wholly beneficial – influence it has had in the past both on the writing of drama and on theories of aesthetics. See also **Categories, Metaphor, Philosophy of Mind, Political Philosophy.**

(J.L.A.)

**Atomism.** "Atomism" arose as an explanatory scheme with the ancient Greeks, **Leucippus** and **Democritus**, and **Epicurus**, and the Roman poet, **Lucretius**. At the most fundamental level atomism is the belief that all phenomena are explicable in terms of the properties and behaviour of ultimate, elementary, localized entities (or "fundamental particles"). Thus it prescribes a strategy for the construction of scientific theories in which the behaviour of complex bodies is to be explained in terms of their component parts. That strategy has led to many of the successes of modern physical science, though these do not prove that there actually are "ultimate entities" of the type postulated by atomism.

The atomists accepted the assumption that the things which really exist are permanent and indestructible but this is obviously not true of the everyday objects around us. Their analysis goes "behind" the appearances to minute, unchangeable and indestructible "atoms" separated by the emptiness of "the void". It is the void which is said to make change and movement possible. All apparent change is simply the result of rearrangements of the atoms as a consequence of collisions between them. This seems to lead to mechanical **determinism**, though, in an attempt to leave room for freewill, Epicurus and Lucretius postulated that atoms might "deviate" in their courses.

According to the atomists colour, taste, warmth and so forth are the effects produced in our sense organs by atoms which possess none of these properties: a conclusion which, as they were aware, is difficult to establish on the basis of sense experience itself. The hypothetical properties of the atoms were basically "geometrical" (sharp-cornered, smooth, etc), though "solidity" was needed to distinguish them from empty space (compare **Locke**). The later atomists also regarded "weight" as an intrinsic property of the atoms. Lucretius says that the number of atoms is infinite but the variety of shapes and sizes is finite (arguing fallaciously that otherwise there could be no limit to the size of the atoms).

However if "what exists" is "atoms", what of the "void"? In different ways both **Aristotle** and **Descartes** denied that there could be such a thing as literally "empty space". Physically therefore they saw the world as a *plenum*. Atomism was also associated with atheism, since as Lucretius put it, "Nothing can ever be created out of nothing, even by divine power." Conversely no thing can ever become nothing – so the atomists proposed a strict principle of conservation of matter. The atomists strove to provide a complete picture of the world and included a materialist account of perception and the nature of mind. The mind is simply a fragile and mortal association of certain subtle atoms with those of the body; and they are disordered and dissipated in disease, insanity and death. Visual perception occurs because objects shed physical "images" of themselves in thin atomic films which impinge upon our eyes. These "images" are moving all around us, sometimes in fragments, and are responsible for dreams, phantoms and in their most subtle form for experience of "the gods". This thoroughgoing materialism, and the **hedonist** ethics which Democritus and Epicurus associated with it, were responsible for the disfavour with which atomism was long regarded in European culture.

In the seventeenth century **Gassendi** and Boyle detached the atomic or corpuscular theory from its associations with atheism and **materialism**. Indeed they turned the tables on those, like **Hobbes**, who believed that the material world was a *plenum* and who denied the existence of a real "vacuum" on the grounds that "incorporeal substance" was impossible. In Hobbes' universe not only must the "soul" be material and mortal, but there could be no physical space in which his "corporeal" God could act. Newton, following the example of the Cambridge Platonist Henry More, justified his introduction of "Space" as a real, infinite entity (and by implication, the existence of "hard, massy, impenetrable, moveable particles") by claiming that Absolute Space is constituted by the Omnipresence of God.

Newton sought to make the action of Universal Gravitation across empty space believable by reference to the power of God, but as the investigation of electricity, magnetism and chemical affinity developed in the eighteenth and nineteenth centuries attempts were made to find physical explanations for "action-at-a-distance". In the theories of Boscovich and Faraday the dualism of Atoms and the Void is replaced by an all-pervasive "field of force" in which there are many mathematical centres. (This vision also informs the account of gravitation in Einstein's General Theory of **relativity**.) Paradoxically the attraction of "mathematical atomism" proved an obstacle to the acceptance of Dalton's atomic theory in which "atoms" of many different sizes and weights were proposed, each associated with a different chemical element. That theory provided an explanation of the empirical regularities discovered by experimental chemists, but positivistically inclined scientists regarded atomism as a "metaphysical encumbrance" until the early years of the twentieth century. A critical factor in

convincing the doubters was Einstein's analysis of the "Brownian" motion of microscopic particles, which dimly echoed Lucretius' discussions of the significance of dust dancing in sunbeams. Scepticism over the question of whether "atoms" can be "observed" raises questions about the meaning of "observation" when sophisticated instruments are employed. A thoroughgoing **positivism** will continue to hold that "atomic theories" are simply devices for talking about observable phenomena.

The ancient atomists postulated "atoms" of many different shapes and sizes, but this variety itself stands in need of explanation. Reduction of this variety to one single type of elementary entity would be more "satisfying", though this would not prevent one from asking why this "ultimate entity" had its particular properties. A great simplification in the Daltonian atomic scheme was achieved when it was shown that periodic regularities in the properties of different "atoms" could be explained in terms of inner structures constructed from just three kinds of more elementary particle (electron, proton and neutron). Subsequent collision-experiments generated a profusion of other "elementary" particles, which were eventually largely reduced to order by postulating entities which are yet more fundamental ("quarks"). It might be supposed that this process could continue for ever – without any "ultimate particles" (genuine "atoms") ever being identified. Indeed it is difficult to see how anyone could *demonstrate* that "the end of the road" had been reached. However ordinary concepts of "structure" have come under strain in these explorations, and it is by no means clear that the most elementary entities postulated at present have properties which are explicable in terms of *any* classical atomistic model.

One of the assumptions of the fundamental atomist picture is that the atoms have intrinsic properties of their own and that all "relational properties" can be analysed in terms of these properties and the *spatial* relations of the bodies. (This is another way of saying, "There is nothing but Atoms and the Void".) However **quantum mechanics** indicates that the elementary constituents presently postulated by physical science have properties which cannot conceivably be analysed in this way.

The attempt of the ancient atomists to solve a metaphysical problem about the nature of change resulted in a brilliantly fruitful strategy for the construction of theories in the physical sciences. However there are unanswered philosophical objections to atomism and the very successes it has stimulated suggest that "the stuff of the world" cannot ultimately be understood in terms of atomism.

[J.H.P.]

**Augustine** (354–430), Saint, also known as Aurelius Augustinus and Augustine of Hippo. He was born at Thagaste in Numidia (Souk-Ahras in Algeria on the Tunisian border). His mother was a Christian, his father a pagan. Augustine received a thorough education in rhetoric, a discipline over which the spirit of **Cicero** presided. Before he was twenty he had turned his back on Christianity, intellectually repelled less by the strangeness of its doctrines than by the crudity, in style and content, of its Scriptures. Its canons of behaviour were also uncongenial to him, and as a very young man he was already established in Carthage with a mistress and a professorial chair of rhetoric.

His energetic and curious mind had been fired with a love of philosophy by Cicero's *Hortensius*, now lost, which he read at the age of eighteen. This started him on an intellectual adventure that led him first to Manichaeism, then to the thoroughgoing **scepticism** of the Academics; next, about the time he was appointed to a chair of rhetoric at Milan, to **neoplatonism**; and finally, at the age of thirty-two, to what he himself used to call Catholic Christianity. He was baptized in Milan at Easter 387, about nine months after his conversion.

In 391 he was ordained priest and in 395 bishop of the city of Hippo Regius (Bône, on the Algerian coast). His native genius and his strenuous devotion to his pastoral duties soon made him the intellectual leader of African Catholicism. After an episcopate of over thirty years, during which he won an Empire-wide reputation, he died at Hippo on 28 August,

430, as the Vandals were besieging the city.

It would be a great mistake to suppose that Augustine's philosophy can be scientifically assessed in isolation from his theology. His thought is always concrete, always the expression of his personal experience, and this was an experience of conversion to Christianity followed by a life spent in teaching it. For him Christianity was the true philosophy, and pagan schools of philosophy were so many false or defective theologies.

Truth is one, it is divine (it is indeed what God is), and its possession is happiness, *beatitudo*. Augustine defines beatitude as *gaudium de veritate*, enjoying Truth. Under the pull of Truth his life had a certain splendid simplicity about it; first the quest for Truth, then at his conversion the discovery of it, and after that a life spent in its exploration.

It is wisdom that gives knowledge of Truth, so the quest for Truth is a quest for wisdom. One of the first philosophical problems to engage Augustine was how a man can pass from being unwise to being wise. To do this he must desire the wisdom he lacks. But desire implies knowledge of the thing desired. Desire of wisdom therefore implies lack of wisdom and possession of wisdom, that is knowledge of it, at the same time. This conundrum was posed for Augustine by the Academics, for whom wisdom consisted in knowing that we can know nothing, and he made use of it in his *De Utilitate Credendi* against his Manichee friends, who thought they had all the answers. Dialectically he extricated himself from the *impasse* of scepticism by what has been called the Augustinian *Cogito: Si fallor, sum* (if I am wrong, I am). But his real method was the most un-Cartesian one of what could be described as systematic faith. "Unless you believe, you shall not understand" (Isaiah 7, 9) was one of his favourite texts. (He thought naturally in texts. The older he got, the more biblical his thought and its expression became.) Faith alone can provide the base from which the quest for wisdom must start, because it is both a knowing, which makes love of the thing known possible, and a not knowing, so that love is still desire, not yet enjoyment. Augustine's conversion was his discovery of wisdom by faith, and the beginning of his exploration of it by understanding.

This method is deployed most conspicuously in the *De Trinitate*. In this work too we can assess the extent and the bearing of Augustine's Platonism. His cosmos is constructed on a Platonic dialectic; there is the outer and the inner world, the lower and the higher, the sensible and the intelligible, and the carnal and the spiritual. Progress in wisdom is a movement of the mind inwards and upwards to God at the apex and the centre, an opening of the mind to the illumination of incommutable truth, which is there within and above, always available for its inspection, provided the mental vision has been purified by faith. But this progress is, so to speak, a feeling one's way backwards along the channel of influence which comes downwards and outwards, causing the participating or imaging of the higher order in the lower, Creator in the creature.

The word "Creator" suggests the limits of Augustine's Platonism. His crucial theme of the divine image in the world and in man is more biblical than Platonic, and depends on the wholly biblical doctrine of creation. In virtue too of this doctrine Augustine could regard the material world with a reverence impossible for a thorough Platonist. The goal of his vision was the resurrection of the body, not the soul's release from the prison of the body. His doctrine of evil as no-thing, as a privation, a lack of due order, marks his easy independence of Platonism as much as his emancipation from Manichaeism.

The Incarnation is a doctrine which accords ill with the ultra-spiritualism and intellectualism of the Platonists, but fits smoothly into Augustine's God-imagining world. The divine image in man has been defaced by sin, which upsets the divine order, ruffles the clear surface. It is restored by a transcendent manifestation of divine order, in which the Word, the image *par excellence*, makes up for pride by humility, disobedience by obedience, restores life by enduring death, and innocence by taking the consequences of guilt. The dialectical statement of the Incarnation by St Paul or St John plucks an immediate response from Augustine the trained rhetorician.

The Word incarnate is the Way back for man to the Word who is Truth, and the Way on to the risen Christ who is Life. Restoration must come from above just as creation comes from above. All the initiatives are God's. Hence Augustine's teaching on grace. Human freedom is fully vindicated only when its unconditional derivation from the divine freedom is accepted. Divine grace is shown us in divine charity – "God so loved the world . . . " and the human response is a response of charity, which Augustine would almost say is as natural as falling off a log. *Amor meus pondus meum* ("My love is my weight"), he said. Since, then, his ethics stems from grace before will-power, and from the personal relationship of love before abstract principle, it is quite free from the harsh Puritanism which has often been ascribed to it, and which was far more characteristic of the Pelagianism which he fought so strenuously.

(E.H.)

**Aurelius,** *see* Marcus Aurelius.

**Austin,** John Langshaw (1911–1960), English philosopher. He was White's Professor of Moral Philosophy in the University of Oxford. He had a very considerable influence on the development of **analytic philosophy** since the second world war. His work consists mainly of close examinations of the way words are ordinarily used, without any direct reference to the traditional problems of philosophy. Austin gives an admirable brief account of his reasons for this procedure in his "A Plea for Excuses."

Two of his most important sets of lectures have been published posthumously. In *Sense and Sensibilia* he attempted to show that certain arguments traditional in philosophy that are designed to prove that the direct object of the senses is always a sense-datum and never a physical object derive their plausibility from a systematic distortion of key terms from their normal use. In *How to Do Things With Words* he first restates his doctrine of "performative utterances", but finds it ultimately unsatisfactory and goes on to replace the distinction between performative and statemental utterances by a distinction between locutionary act (saying something with a certain meaning), illocutionary act (what one does, such as promising, in saying something), and perlocutionary act (what one brings about by saying something) as abstractable components of the complete speech-act. This doctrine has influenced later work on the philosophy of language.

(J.O.U.)

**Averroes** (1126–1198); his name is latinized from Ibn Rushd. Philosopher, jurist, judge and physician, he was born at Cordova, Spain, and died at Marrakesh. To the West, Averroes is best known as a commentator on **Aristotle**. On many Aristotelian writings he wrote three different kinds of Commentaries: *Summaries* in his own words, and *Middle* and *Long Commentaries* quoting portions of the text and adding explanatory and critical comments, in the light of classical commentators like Themistius, Alexander of Aphrodisias, and al-Fārābī, **Avicenna** and Avempace (Ibn Bājja). His exposition is lucid and concise, adhering more closely to Aristotle than any of the earlier *Falāsifa* (Muslim religious philosophers). Not having Aristotle's *Politics*, Averroes commented on **Plato**'s *Republic*, which he treated as the second, practical part of the science of politics supplementing Aristotle's *Nicomachean Ethics* which was the first, theoretical part.

The significance of Averroes as a religious philosopher lies in his polemical treatises, his spirited rebuttal of Ghazālī's attack, and his Commentary on Plato's *Republic*. After Ghazālī, philosophy was on the defensive, under constant fire from jurists and theologians. Hence the polemical nature of much of Averroes' writing. He set out to prove the essential agreement between the religious law (*Sharī'a*) and philosophy (*falsafa*) by claiming identity of aim for both in the *Fasl* (*Decisive Chapter on the Agreement between Religious Law and Philosophy*) and in the Commentary on the *Republic*: one is "the companion and foster-sister" of the other. Truth is one and indivisible, only sought and explained in different ways. The theory of Double Truth is wrongly fathered on him; it belongs to the Latin Averroists. Averroes asserts the philosopher's exclusive ability, right and duty to expound the inner meaning of the prophetically revealed Law by demonstrative argument. The theologians use dialectical arguments and confuse the masses. With Plato he distinguishes the few elect philosophers from the masses. With Aristotle he distinguishes three classes of arguments (demonstrative, dialectical and rhetorical or poetical), which he assigns to three classes of believers: philosophers, theologians and the masses. The masses must accept the stories, parables and metaphors of Scripture in their plain meaning. But Scripture contains the whole truth even though its inner meaning is only accessible to the metaphysician. All three classes must accept certain statements in the *Qur'an* (*Koran*) in their literal meaning as religious truth inaccessible to human reason, because they are God's revelation. On these grounds, he maintains and justifies the superiority of the *Sharī'a* over the *Nomos* (secular law). He agrees with Avicenna that this Law teaches true beliefs and convictions in a form accessible to all believers and obligatory on all. The *Nomos* is only concerned with the happiness of the élite, but the *Sharī'a* guarantees every believer his share of happiness.

Averroes' vindication of the *Sharī'a* as the constitution of the ideal Muslim state is combined with a sustained critique of the Muslim state of his time, on the basis of Plato's imperfect constitutions. He adheres to the traditional explanation of prophecy against the theory of the *Falāsifa* and insists, like Avicenna, on the superior and exceptional character of Muhammad as the divinely sent prophetic lawgiver.

(E.I.J.R.)

**Avicenna** (980–1037), Persian philosopher and physician; his name is latinized from Ibn Sīnā.

The most original of the *Falāsifa* (Muslim religious philosophers), he achieved a philosophical monotheism which approaches as closely as possible a synthesis between the tenets of Islam and the teachings of **Plato** and **Aristotle**.

Unlike Fārābī to whom he is greatly indebted, and **Averroes**, whose original contribution is largely contained in his Commentaries, Avicenna succeeded in formulating a *Summa* of philosophy out of a critical study of Aristotle, helped by **neoplatonic** commentators and the **stoics**. His *Shifā* exerted a strong influence on Muslims, Jews and Christians, though, together with his other philosophical writings, it aroused the hostility of the theologians. Ghazālī's *Incoherence of the philosophers* was mainly directed against Avicenna. It forced creative philosophical speculation in Islam on the defensive and even Averroes could not restore it to its former position.

In **logic** Avicenna's strict adherence to Aristotle's concept of cause and effect brought him into conflict with the theologians. His logical determinism clashed with their theological determinism.

In psychology he combined Aristotle with **Plotinus** in his widely accepted idea of the immortality of the rational soul which as form is substance.

More far-reaching is his contribution to **metaphysics**. Like all *Falāsifa* he was helped by Plotinus and Porphyry who tried to harmonize Plato and Aristotle and, by giving Plato's thought a turn towards religious **monism**, enabled Muslims to blend traditional beliefs and convictions with Greek thought. Avicenna's concept of God in whose Being existence and essence are identical, gained wide currency in the West, especially with the Jew **Maimonides** and the Christian Thomas **Aquinas**. So did its corollary that in all created beings essence is separate from existence which is only an accident. Accepting Aristotle's concept of the eternity of matter, Avicenna rejected the theological axiom of "Creation out of Nothing". Moreover, creation is a necessary consequence of God's existence as an absolute, simple unity in whom knowledge, will and power are one with his essence. He is the uncaused First Cause,

hence necessarily the Creator. Maimonides and Aquinas are opposed to the Avicennian concept and maintain the Scriptural position of the creation in time by God's free-will out of nothing.

To close the gap between revelation and reason Avicenna escaped into an intellectual mysticism (in his *Ishārāt, Indications*). The speculative mystic (*ārif*) who attained the highest degree of knowledge, gains intellectual union with God in intuitive perception. Practical philosophy is part of Avicenna's *Metaphysics* because the attainment of human happiness is only possible in society. Prophecy and *Sharīʿa* (prophetically revealed Muslim Law) are indispensable for human survival and happiness. The prophetic lawgiver brings mankind a divine law guaranteeing welfare in this world and bliss in the hereafter. Fārābī identified the prophetic lawgiver with Plato's philosopher-king; Avicenna does not and grants to the prophet spontaneous, intuitive knowledge, thus placing him above the philosopher. The ideal Muslim state with Muhammad's law as constitution is the counterpart to Plato's *Republic* which, together with his *Laws*, illustrated for the *Falāsifa* the political significance of the *Sharīʿa* and the concepts of Justice and Law enabled them to blend Islamic fundamentals with Greek concepts.

(E.I.J.R.)

**Ayer,** Sir Alfred Jules, F.B.A. (1910–1989), born in London. He was educated at Eton and Oxford, where he later held academic posts as Research Student of Christ Church and Fellow of Wadham College. From 1946–1959, he was Grote Professor of the Philosophy of Mind and Logic in the University of London, and in 1959 was appointed to the Wykeham Chair of Logic at Oxford. He is also well known as a broadcaster.

Ayer achieved early fame as the author of *Language, Truth and Logic* (1936), a work which did much to familiarize the English-speaking world with the philosophy of **logical positivism**. Based on first-hand acquaintance with the **Vienna Circle**, it ranks among the clearest and most forthright expositions of the subject in any language. In some respects, also, it represents a synthesis of British and Continental versions of **empiricism**. Ayer agrees with the latter in rejecting **metaphysics** and confining philosophy to **analysis**; but his conception of the analytic method – the translation of problematic expressions into a logically more explicit terminology – is not very different from that of the "Cambridge school"; and he typically makes use of it to resolve traditional cruxes in the theory of knowledge. Material objects, for instance, are not "constructed" out of **sense-data**, but statements mentioning the one can be logically "reduced" to statements mentioning only the other. This linguistic **"phenomenalism"** is put forward as a truth already glimpsed in the writings of **Berkeley** and **Hume**. Apart from its controversial treatment of ethical propositions (as "emotive" rather than factual), the other main feature of Ayer's discussion is his proposal to distinguish a weaker form of the verification principle, designed to exclude metaphysics while preserving the significance of other propositions supposedly more useful to science. Difficulties of formulation have proved greater than expected, and are reviewed, with other matters, in Ayer's introduction to the second edition (1946).

Ayer's later writings (see especially *The Problem of Knowledge*, 1956) have been largely devoted to retrenchment of his position in the light of subsequent criticism. The same epistemological problems are repeatedly attacked, and with substantially the same weapons; but there is less disposition to claim finality for the results. The common sense claims to knowledge of the external world, the past, the self and other people are now scrutinized, not in order to "reduce" or repudiate them, but in order to elucidate the logical grounds for their acceptance. In pursuit of this inquiry, Ayer has been increasingly led to doubt the possibility of analysing claims about material objects into claims about the actual or possible occurrence of sense-data; and he has at length forsaken phenomenalism. His present position seems best described as that of an analytically-minded empiricist, dubious of claims made for "ordinary

language", and without commitments to any really definable school. Ayer is also the author of the article on **Russell** in this Encyclopedia.

(P.L.H.)

# B

**Bachelard,** Gaston (1884–1962), French philosopher and historian of science, more widely known to the English-speaking world for his writings on aesthetics and poetics, but whose approach to the history and **philosophy of science** influenced a whole generation of philosophers passing through French universities, including such figures as **Canguilhem**, **Foucault** and **Althusser**. Bachelard's first degree was in mathematics and he taught physics and chemistry at his local college, in Bar-sur-Aube, whilst working on his doctorate in philosophy. He thus came to the history and philosophy of science from science. This is reflected in his approach to the philosophy of science, which is characterized by an opposition to the imposition of philosophical ideologies (whether **positivist, existentialist, realist** or **phenomenalist**) on science. He insists that any philosophy concerned with **epistemology** must learn from science. It must recognize the distinctive character of twentieth-century science. The overthrow of classical Newtonian physics by the theories of **relativity** and **quantum mechanics** represented a break with past science, which in its turn requires epistemology to break with past philosophies of science. (This view is most succinctly expressed in *The New Scientific Spirit*, 1934.) Bachelard rejects the picture of the development of science as a continuous, gradual accumulation of knowledge in favour of a discontinuous, ruptured development in which what was once taken for knowledge undergoes repeated re-evaluation and re-interpretation. His concern with the development of science and with the objectivity of creative rational thought in science is paralleled by his concern with the subjectivity of non-rational, artistically creative thought, with poetic imagination and reveries. In works such as *The Psychoanalysis of Fire* (1938) and *Water and Dreams*

37

(1942) he draws on Jungian depth psychology for his exploration of the trans-subjective power of poetic images, images which reverberate in the readers' consciousness and lead them to create anew whilst communicating with the poet. Such communication is contrasted sharply with the objectivity required of scientific discourse, which requires that the power of images (which present epistemological obstacles) be broken and that the scientist learn to dream in the austere realm of abstract mathematical structures. This duality of objective and subjective, of concept and image, of the scientific and the poetic, informs not only Bachelard's philosophy, but the whole structure of his written corpus.

[M.T.]

**Bacon,** Francis (1561–1626) was born in the shadow of the English Court which dominated his whole life. He was educated at Cambridge and admitted to the Bar in 1575. In 1584, through the help of his uncle, Lord Burghley, he obtained a seat in the House of Commons. He was befriended by Essex, the favourite of Elizabeth, who tried unsuccessfully to get him made attorney-general in 1593.

Under James I Bacon's fortunes improved. In 1607 he was made solicitor-general and in 1613 attorney-general; in 1617 Lord Keeper and in 1618 Lord Chancellor. He was also created Baron Verulam of Verulam and in 1621 Viscount St Albans. Three days after this final honour Bacon was accused of bribery, found technically guilty, and deprived of office. He had accepted presents from litigants, the usual practice of the time. To quote his own words: "I was the justest judge that was in England these fifty years. But it was the justest censure in Parliament that was these two hundred years." He died in 1626, in retirement, working on his scientific projects.

Bacon had always held that his aim in seeking political advancement was to improve man's estate and to use his wealth and influence to forward the cause of a new science that might contribute to this end. But in spite of repeated attempts he obtained neither a college nor a royal foundation. He lived lavishly, and debts which he accumulated prevented him spending much on the advancement of science during his lifetime; after his death they also prevented the implementation of his will, in which he provided for lectureships in natural philosophy at Oxford and Cambridge.

His actual contributions to learning and science were similarly incomplete – programmatic aspirations rather than concrete pieces of work. In 1603 he laid the foundation for his Great Instauration in his *Valerius Terminus* and in his *De Interpretatione Naturae Proemium*, which were followed by his *Cogitata et Visa*. He announced that he had constructed a new method of scientific discovery. Large natural histories and collections of facts had to be amassed, preferably within a college, and carefully interpreted. The same stress on natural history and a new method of interpretation runs through his *Advancement of Learning* (1605), together with a criticism of previous thinkers and passionate pleas for the use of knowledge to better man's earthly estate.

This was a preliminary to the Great Instauration itself, which was to consist of six parts, the *Advancement of Learning* forming a major section of the first part. The parts were as follows: (1) A classification and review of existing sciences which would make the gaps in them obvious. He fulfilled this portion of his plan in his *De Dignitate et Augmentis Scientiarum* (1623). (2) A new inductive method for putting all human minds on a level in the interpretation of nature. (This he sketched in his *Novum Organum*, 1620.) (3) Natural history or a collection of data and experiments arranged in accordance with the principles laid down in Part 2. (This was extremely fragmentary consisting of his *Parasceve ad historiam naturalem et experimentalem*, 1620; his *Historia Naturalis et experimentalis ad condendam philosophiam: sive phenomena universi*, 1622; and his *Sylva Sylvarum*, 1627, which was a strange collection of facts and fables.) (4) The Ladder of the Intellect, which was meant to consist of fully worked out examples of his method. (There is none of this extant save a preface called *Scala Intellectus sive filum labyrinthi*.) (5) Generalizations reached from natural history without the use of Bacon's special method of interpretation. (Only a preface to this exists called *Prodromi sive Anticipationes Philosophiae Secundae.*) (6) The New Philosophy or Active Science, consisting of the complete science of Nature. This was to be built on the facts of Part 3, established by the methods of Part 2. (None of this is extant.)

Bacon wrote many other works which do not fall into his Great Instauration and which are not easily regarded as anticipations or offshoots of it. Most famous are his *New Atlantis* (his contribution to Utopian literature), *De Sapientia Veterum* (1609), and *De Principiis atque Originibus* (1623–24), an attempt to supplant the Platonic and Aristotelian traditions by a more materialistic theory deriving from **Democritus**. Also in refutation of earlier philosophers he wrote his *Redargutio philosophiarum* (1608) – his treatise on "the idols of the theatre". There are also several other fragments like his *Temporis partus masculus* and his *Delineatio et argumentum*, both of which were anticipatory of his Great Instauration.

Bacon's main contribution to philosophy was in the sphere of scientific method. He was one of the most powerful and articulate rebels against the Aristotelian and Platonic traditions; in many respects he attempted to revive a materialism akin to that of Democritus. He claimed that Aristotelian logic was a useless tool for discovery. It forced assent, but revealed nothing new and dragged experiment along like a captive. Also the final causes which it employed in its explanations had wonderfully corrupted philosophy. They were only appropriate in explaining human affairs. The alternative school of thought, deriving from **Plato**, was equally useless. No trust was to be placed in the abstract axioms of the geometric method. Definitions could not remedy the evil in nature or material objects, because they consisted themselves of words and these words produced others. "Words are but the images of matter; and except they have life of reason and invention, to fall in love with them is to fall in love with a picture". Rationalists are like spiders spinning ideas out of the recesses of their mind. The brute empirics, on the other hand, are no better. For they are like ants, aimlessly collecting data. The bees provide the proper model

for scientific procedure. Order is the secret – the amassing of data or natural history, storing it, and interpreting it judiciously according to definite canons.

In the endeavour to replace rash anticipations of Nature by orderly interpretations the inquirer is brought up against certain deep-seated limitations of the human mind. These bacon called the Idols of the Tribe. Men tend to generalise too readily, to find instances which suit their purposes and to believe more readily that which they prefer. Bacon therefore stressed the importance of looking for the negative instance, of seeking systematically for exceptions to generalizations. Idols of the tribe are also due to other limitations such as the dullness of our perceptual apparatus. But there are also Idols of the Den, which are defects due not so much to human nature generally as to individual differences and idiosyncrasies, both innate and acquired. Then there are Idols of the Market Place, which are due to words and phrases that corrupt and muddle our thinking – especially vague words and words that describe nothing. Finally there are the Idols of the Theatre which arise from systems of philosophy. The remedy for these obstacles was not simply to expose the faulty reasoning of others, but to set out the new method of inquiry clearly for all to use.

This method consisted of accumulating data and dealing with them in a certain manner. Suppose the cause of heat was sought. A table of *presence* had first to be compiled containing all the known instances in which heat was present. A table of *absence* had then to be constructed with instances corresponding to these in the table of presence. A table of *degrees* had also to be compiled containing instances in which heat was present in varying degrees. By examining the tables a generating nature might be found which was co-present, co-absent, and co-variant with the effect or generated nature. An interpretation or "first vintage" could then be made – for example, that motion is the cause or "form" of heat. (These tables are very similar to J. S. **Mill**'s joint methods of agreement and difference and the method of concomitant variations.)

One of the most vexed questions of Baconian scholarship is the status of these "forms" which it was the natural philosopher's business to discover. He distinguished physics which investigates efficient and material causes but "does not stir the limits of things which are much more deeply rooted" from **metaphysics**, which investigates "forms". These are both generic and generating "natures". Heat, for instance, is a limitation of the more generic nature "motion"; and it is also in some way *produced* by motion. Such "forms" do not seem like Aristotelian formal causes because they are generators of other natures and not just correlative with matter. It is often suggested that Bacon had in mind some primitive atomic theory akin to that of Democritus. Yet these "forms" are observables to be discovered by compiling tables whereas Democritan atoms are not observable.

Whatever doubts there may be about the status of these forms, there can be no doubt about Bacon's enthusiasm for projects of a practical sort which a knowledge of the laws of the combination of these forms might permit. He was one of the first to stress that knowledge gives man power over nature and has been heralded as a forerunner of both **utilitarianism** and **Marxism** in this respect. Bacon thought that the aim of his Great Instauration was "knowledge of the causes and of the secret motion of things, and the enlarging of the bounds of human empire, to the effecting of all things possible". He subscribed to the alchemist's ideal of transmuting substances of one kind into substances of another. But he thought that such an undertaking must be based on a thorough understanding of "what is constant, eternal, and universal in nature".

Bacon met with little concrete success either in developing his fundamental science or in inaugurating a college to house it. But he inspired many with his dream of improving man's estate by the employment of scientific method. The Royal Society, which was founded in 1662, was Baconian in spirit. It combined his emphasis on observation and experiment with a concern for inventions of practical use. It was founded by Puritans who believed, like Bacon, that science could reveal the wonders of God's creation and be used to improve man's estate.

Bacon's thought influenced not only the development of science but also the typically British conception of knowledge and scientific method as exemplified by **Locke, Berkeley, Hume,** J. S. Mill, and **Russell**.

Bacon's account of scientific method has been criticized by later thinkers in at least four major respects. First of all he was mistaken in thinking that there is any "inductive" method which could put all men on a level in the matter of arriving at well-founded generalisations. There may be methods for testing generalisations once they have been made, but there are no recipes for arriving at them.

Secondly Bacon failed to distinguish between rash "anticipations" of nature and working hypotheses. Data cannot be collected without some sort of hypothesis, let alone a theory developed. The nineteenth-century logician **Whewell** made much of this defect in Bacon's account.

Thirdly Bacon was profoundly ignorant of mathematics and overlooked its great importance in the development of theories. He rejected the Copernican hypothesis, ridiculed Gilbert's speculations about magnetism, and failed to see the importance of Harvey's work. He understood little of the work of continental thinkers like Kepler and Galileo. This failure to grasp the importance of mathematics led him to overlook the role of deduction in science. For often, when a theory has to be tested, there is a long deductive journey, made possible by mathematics, between postulates and observationally testable consequences.

Finally Bacon ignore problems connected with the *justification* of inductive reasoning, which have troubled philosophers since Hume.

His importance in the history of thought is his stress on the observational basis of science and the search for the negative instance.

(R.S.P.)

**Bacon,** Roger (c. 1214–c. 1292), born in England. Bacon's long career at Oxford and Paris covers the whole of the vital period in the thirteenth century when Greek and Arabic science and philosophy were being assimilated into western thought.

In many respects he appears conservative and traditional like his fellow Franciscan, **Bonaventura**, being no less observant of religion and equally convinced of the supremacy of theological knowledge. Yet he differs profoundly from the latter in his reaction to the new science.

Where Bonaventura saw science as a new, perhaps interesting, field for human investigation, but one which in the long run could only distract men from that contemplative activity to which all men should aspire, Bacon saw a new method, which would radically transform philosophy and theology by applying the new mathematical and experimental techniques to them.

His most characteristic writing is to be found in his *Opus Majus* which, together with the shorter *Opus Minus* and *Opus Tertium* elaborates his views on how to reform the teaching of Christian wisdom. These works were written at the request of Pope Clement IV and urged the political hegemony which would fall to the West as a result of the advance of science. But Clement died and Bacon remained frustrated.

(J.G.D.)

**Barth,** Karl (1886–1968), Swiss theologian, *see* Existentialism, Religion.

**Barthes,** Roland (1915–1980), French critic, *see* Structuralism.

**Beauty,** *see* Aesthetics.

**Beauvoir,** Simone de (1908–1986), born in Paris, was a key figure in French **existentialism** and a founding theorist of modern **feminism**. Though she was profoundly influenced by the philosophy of **Sartre**, with whom she maintained a life-long association, de Beauvoir's alertness to the central weakness of the doctrine of *Being and Nothingness* – its neglect of

the social context of action – was itself an influence on Sartre's shift from a "philosophy of consciousness" to the more Marxist perspective of his later work. An initial focus (see her early novels and *The Ambiguity of Ethics*, 1947) is the moral dilemma posed by the existentialist insistence on our absolute freedom: for whilst freedom from social codes and conventions may be essential to the exercise of responsible moral choice, morality itself would seem to demand that our actions be constrained by a "conventional" concern for their impact on others. Moreover, all choices are in fact made in concrete situations which limit the possibilities of action.

*The Second Sex* (1949) offers a powerful and sustained exemplification of these dilemmas, exploring how the historical oppression of women can be reconciled with their possession of freedom, while at the same time exposing differences in the situation of the sexes which are obscured by philosophy's universalizing pretensions. For while women, in virtue of their humanity, have as much need for autonomy as men have, their cultural relegation to the status of "Otherness" in relation to men has condemned them to forms of dependency and subordination irreconcilable with genuine freedom.

De Beauvoir dismisses any suggestion that women are incapable by nature of transcending their situation. But her positive valuation of transcendence (which implicitly condones the Hegelian and Sartrean association of femininity with immanence) has been unacceptable to some of her readers – as has the political implication that women can only realize themselves by becoming like men.

But in drawing attention to the disparities in the legal and social situation of women, *The Second Sex* helped to inaugurate the practical campaigns (around such issues as abortion and equal rights for women) which led to the growth and diversification of the modern feminist movement.

De Beauvoir is exceptional among philosophers both in the range of her writings (which include novels, journalism and autobiography alongside distinctively philosophical works) and in the extent to which she uses fictional forms to convey philosophical ideas. Of note, too, is her practical adherence to the philosophy she espoused: she lived her life as a project, and not least among her achievements is the record she bequeathed in her memoirs of the existential unfolding of an individual life in its unique and unrepeatable passage from birth to grave.

[K.S.]

**Being,** *see* Metaphysics, Existentialism, Realism, Idealism, Monism, Dualism, Heidegger.

**Benjamin,** Walter (1892–1940), born in Berlin; German literary critic and theorist; he was a close friend of Gershom Scholem, a noted historian of Jewish mysticism, Bertolt Brecht, and Theodor W. **Adorno,** whose philosophy Benjamin's writings significantly influenced. During the 1930s Benjamin was associated with the **Frankfurt School,** in whose journal some of his best-known essays appeared.

Benjamin's philosophical thought circles around his idea of "redemptive criticism". This idea is revealed explicitly in the "Epistemo-Critical Prologue" to his *The Origin of German Tragic Drama* (1928), his "Theses on the Philosophy of History", and in some of his early essays; and implicitly in his historical-critical works, especially the unfinished "Paris – Capital of the 19th Century".

The goal of redemptive criticism was to overcome the modern split between critique, which seeks the truth content of a work of art, and commentary, which seeks to illuminate a work's subject matter. In pursuit of this goal Benjamin developed ideas on the philosophy of history and the philosophy of language, and on critical cognition.

According to Benjamin the idea of history as a progressive continuum, as the slow becoming of truth and human freedom, is a vision from the perspective of the victors – "the continuum of history is that of the oppressor." Redemptive criticism seeks to interrupt this continuum, to reveal the moments of discontinuity in history where its true nature comes to light, and to restore that which continuous, progressive history has dominated and repressed.

While Benjamin's philosophical thought is intensely idiosyncratic and problematic, especially his theologically-inspired philosophy of language, it continues to inspire interest, in large measure because of the way it informs his uniquely powerful critical and historical writings.

[J.M.B.]

**Bentham,** Jeremy (1748–1832), originally expected to follow his father and grandfather as a lawyer working in the city of London. However he revolted against the unnecessary technicality of current legal procedure and devoted himself instead to discovering the fundamental principles of a just, clear, and rational legal system. This led him into a profound examination of the nature of thought, language, law, government, and public morality. Bentham substituted clear expressions for unclear ones, and made the fundamental innovation of substituting at the level of sentences rather than terms (the method of paraphrasis). Unclear sentences are analysed into clear ones and clarity is achieved by closeness to experience, particularly the sensations of pleasure and pain. So, in his account of law, Bentham analysed sentences about rights into sentences about duties, and sentences about duties into sentences about the commands of a person or group backed by the threat of sanctions (that is, the possibility of pain). In this way he established an account of the law as it is. He then took as his leading principle of how the law ought to be the principle of utility (as used in various ways by **Hume,** Helvétius, and Beccaria) declaring at the start of his first main work the "fundamental axiom, it is the greatest happiness of the greatest number that is the measure of right and wrong". This principle also substitutes clear goals, again concerned with pleasure and pain, for unclear. Finally, Bentham added a (relatively standard) self-interest psychology describing how people actually value various states so that the value varies with such factors as certainty, distance, intensity, or duration. With an account of man as he is and an account of society as it ought to be, Bentham spent much time designing institutions, in particular his famous prison, the panopticon, in which these two were united. In these institutions, be they states or prisons, men would naturally (that is, following their own interests) do what they ought to do (that is, promote the greatest happiness of the greatest number). From this follow the utilitarian principles of punishment in which deterrence is its only justification. As Bentham puts it, all punishment is in itself evil (that is, it causes pain); it is only justified therefore if it causes greater good by deterring the wrong acts of others. By taking account of value, this enables the precise quantity of punishment appropriate for every offence to be measured. See also **Utilitarianism**.

[R.H.]

**Berdyaev**, Nicholas (1874–1948) was born in Russia; he remained there until his expulsion in 1922, when he settled first in Germany and then in France. A faithful member of the Russian Orthodox Church, Berdyaev, in most of his work, should be classed as a religious thinker and as a social and political propagandist rather than as a philosopher in the narrower sense of the word; his aim was a practical one – to bring about a Christian social system – rather than theoretical. His fundamental philosophical thesis was a distinction between the material world, subject to natural law and necessity, of which man as an animal is a part, and the higher world of freedom of which man as spirit is a part, a position reminiscent of **Kant**'s distinction of the phenomenal and noumenal worlds.

(J.O.U.)

**Bergson**, Henri Louis (1859–1941), French philosopher, who produced a philosophy of "creative evolution" which made a considerable impression in literature as well as thought during the early years of the twentieth century

(see, for example, the Preface to G. Bernard Shaw's *Back to Methuselah*). This was not only a romantic para-biological theory of a "Life-Force" invoked to counteract materialistic or mechanistic notions of the evolution of life in nature. It was an ingenious speculative theory of the relation of life and matter, correlated throughout with a particular theory of knowledge. Indeed, Bergson's work could either be interpreted idealistically, in which case the theory of knowledge is prior, and we have a certain kind of concept of matter because our minds work in a certain way; or it could be interpreted as an evolutionary realism in which our minds have come to think in a certain way because of the natural history of their evolution. In any case, Bergson's originality lay in the way in which he interpreted a theory of evolution and a theory of knowledge in terms of each other. The theory of knowledge was presented first, in *Essai sur les données immédiates de la conscience* (1889), (the English translation is entitled *Time and Free-will*), and in *Matter and Memory* (1896). Here Bergson draws a sharp distinction between the character of our conceptual knowledge of the external world and consciousness as known from within. The intellect in its scientific study of the external world proceeds by analysis and classification. For analysis, the world must be considered as composed of isolatable objects externally related to each other; for classification these must be regarded as repeatable instances of similar kinds. So the world is interpreted in terms of limited kinds of discrete units, undergoing repeatable arrangements in space. Hence the intellect thinks naturally of static objects in *spatial* juxtaposition; it does not grasp fundamental changes through time, but imagines change as a succession of static states of affairs, spread out in a succession of instantaneous spaces – a limitation which was brought out by **Zeno** of Elea in his paradoxes about motion, and which, Bergson thought, is never transcended by mere concepts, although it may be met practically by devices such as the infinitesimal calculus, where a succession of very small intervals is treated as though they formed a continuous movement. The intellect therefore, Bergson

43

says, "spatializes", and its ideal form of thinking is geometry.

Sharply contrasted is our own self-consciousness. Here change in time is experienced from within; we are aware not of a succession of distinct states, but of our present as arising out of our past and turning into a not clearly envisaged future. The "time" of this inner experience is not external clock time, which is "spatialized time", measured for instance by noting successive positions of the hands of a clock. It is an actual experience of change, in which stages of "before" and "after" interpenetrate each other; this kind of time Bergson calls "duration" (*durée*), and he claims that it is not merely a way of measuring a changing reality, but is the changing reality itself. The state of mind in which we are aware of the quality and flow of inner consciousness is called Intuition. It is a nonconceptual kind of awareness; Bergson even says that it dispenses with symbols; what he here means by "symbol" is not clear, and indeed his own attempts to express and describe Intuition are couched, perhaps inevitably, in metaphors. For a form of consciousness which used neither concepts nor imaginative metaphors would presumably not be explicit thought at all, but *feeling*. Indeed Bergson speaks at times of Intuition as "sympathy", and as "integral experience". In the essay *Introduction to Metaphysics* (1903), he speaks of metaphysics as "the science which claims to dispense with symbols". If this were the whole truth, it is hard to see how it could become articulate knowledge, since any expression must presumably use some form of symbolism. Bergson does not, however, present Intuition as able to work apart from intellect, although he describes these as if they were polar opposites. Intuition is compared with the creative inner excitement which enables a writer to fuse his mass of materials into a unity, which he cannot do unless he has first gathered the materials by intellectual effort. "Any one of us, for instance, who has attempted literary composition, knows that when the subject has been studied at length, the materials all collected, and the notes all made, something more is needed in order to set about the work

of composition itself, and that it is an often very painful effort to place ourselves directly at the heart of the subject, and to seek as deeply as possible an impulse, after which we need only let ourselves go . . . . Metaphysical intuition seems to be something of the same kind. What corresponds here to the documents and notes of literary composition is the sum of observations and experience gathered together by positive science. For we do not obtain an Intuition from reality – that is, an intellectual sympathy with the most intimate part of it – unless we have won its confidence by a long fellowship with its superficial manifestations." In neither case, however, can the "impulse" produce a synthesis out of the materials apart from an integrating idea. Bergson's description of "intuition" seems to be not so much an account of such integrating ideas as of the underlying state of mind out of which they may come. This is a form of feeling intensely concentrated on the present task, but which has behind it the resources of the person's whole past experience. Here Bergson's particular view of *memory* should be taken into account. He holds that consciousness contains implicitly the whole of one's past experience, but the function of the brain of the animal organism is to act as a "filter", letting through selectively into immediate awareness such memories as may be relevant in attending to the situations in which one is placed. But by reversing the practical habits of the intellect (always to Bergson primarily a way of thinking shaped by practical needs), it may be possible through contemplative Intuition to draw on a wider range of the resources of consciousness. Bergson was here impressed by the work of Charcot on amnesia, and by experimental work on hypnotically recovered memories. He was writing before Freud's theory of the unconscious mind had been put forward, and he uses the word "consciousness" broadly and not only for such experiences as are within the focus of attention. Indeed he imagines a rudimentary form of consciousness in all living organisms, and is prepared to interpret them by what he calls an "inverted psychology".

Bergson's theory of knowledge, drawn in terms of the contrast between Intellect and

Intuition, is correlated with a view of the function of these within the process of Evolution. Intelligence, Bergson holds, begins with the making of tools. "Instinct" he describes as an innate power of using natural instruments, either parts of the organism itself, or materials directly found in the environment. Intelligence is first of all a power of making tools as artificial instruments: *homo faber*, the smith, rather than *homo sapiens*, would describe man at the dawn of intelligence. So intelligence starts from the interest in practical construction; it always bears the stamp of this practical interest, and finds its model of intelligibility in artefacts, which are discontinuous, isolatable systems, repeatable as specified types. Instinct on the other hand is continuous with the organizing power of life; but it is unreflective and unadaptive. When it can become disinterested and self-conscious, it is Intuition, and then it can carry forward the original impetus of life into the creation of new forms. Bergson interprets evolution as the outcome of an impulse of life (*élan vital*) manifesting itself in innumerable forms. This is not finalist teleology in the classical sense, which Bergson calls "inverted mechanism", development tied to the realisation of predetermined ends. Nor is it vitalism as ordinarily understood, since no "vitalist principle" is invoked over and above the physico-chemical components of organisms. Rather, the whole of nature is said to be the outcome of a force which thrusts itself forward into new and unforeseen forms of organised structure. These store and utilize energy, maintaining their power of growth and adaptive novelty up to a point, and then relapse into repetitive routine, and ultimately into the degradation of energy. The universe, Bergson says, shows two tendencies: there is "a reality which is making itself in a reality which is unmaking itself". The laws of the tendency to repetition and the dissipation of energy are the laws of "matter"; the counter tendency is the thrust of "life". Here, in *Creative Evolution* (1907), "matter" is represented as a real tendency in nature, inverse to life, and representing the running down of life into uniformity. Bergson also speaks of "matter" as the picture formed by the artificial

fixing of a system of spatialized concepts by the intellect. Possibly the link is to be found in the belief that the more things display the tendency inverse to life, the more they are amenable to this kind of intellectual treatment. But the notion of pure matter, and indeed the notion of a purely free and creative life impulse, would be abstractions. What is routine and mechanical and what is living and creative are never in fact, as Bergson often acknowledges, found in complete separation from each other. But his concern to bring out the difference between them underlies his whole work; and it finds a special application in *The Two Sources of Morality and Religion* (1932). Here Bergson turns from biology to moral and religious sociology. He describes the "closed" morality and religion based on social custom as the conservative force of a limited society making for the solidarity and preservation of a social group. His analysis follows closely that of the French sociological school of Durkheim. The demand for solidarity and stability stops at the cohesion of limited groups. Groups cohering by closed morality are always limited groups, not just by definition, but because their way of life is maintained through real or possible conflict with other groups. Humanity as a whole does not therefore form a group of this kind; and those persons, prophets and saints, who are charged with an outgoing love towards humanity, are drawing on a different source. The analogy of closed morality to the repetitive mechanisms studied by the intellect is apparent; the "open" morality and religion are forms of intuition, and their source is a direct contact with the springs of life in the *élan vital*. In this last book Bergson is prepared to call it "love" which is "either God or from God". Whether he was received into the Roman Catholic Church is not publicly known; he is reported to have held back until just before his death in order to maintain his solidarity with the Jewish people in their time of troubles.

Bergson's works are written in a non-technical, flowing and persuasive style. They show wide knowledge of the biology and psychology of his day, and an enthusiastic, sometimes visionary, power. Other philosophers have, however, remarked on his tendency to write in unexplained metaphors, and on the lack of rigorous exposition of his central concepts, notably those of *durée* and the *élan vital*, and of the case for their supposed identity.

(D.M.E.)

**Berkeley,** George (1685–1753), was born in Ireland, in the neighbourhood of Kilkenny. His ancestors were English and Protestant, but Berkeley passed his early and later years entirely in Ireland, and, though he was always of the Anglican faith, appears to have regarded himself as decidedly an Irishman. He was excellently educated, first at Kilkenny College, and, from 1700, at Trinity College, Dublin, of which he was subsequently a Fellow for many years. He was ordained in 1707, became Dean of Derry in 1724, and Bishop of Cloyne ten years later. He married in 1728. He died in 1753, while supervising the introduction of his son George to Christ Church, in Oxford and his grave is in the Cathedral there.

Berkeley's life is noteworthy, apart from his philosophical writings, chiefly for his attempt in middle life to introduce a university to Bermuda. The aim of this scheme was mainly missionary. Berkeley hoped to attract to his college not only the colonial settlers of America, but also some of the indigenous Indians, there to be trained as ministers of religion and apostles of culture. Berkeley, whose energies, powers of persuasion, and ingenuous charm were remarkable, succeeded in securing much public and official support for his project. He obtained a charter, a large sum of money by private subscription, and the promise from Parliament of a subvention from public funds. But his scheme was impracticable, and was in the end seen to be so. Bermuda – as he was perhaps not clearly aware – is far too distant from the American mainland to have been a suitable site for his purposes; and after he had left for America in 1728, hesitations and doubts began to prevail at home. Berkeley waited abroad almost three years for his grant to be paid over, but in 1731 the Prime Minister, Walpole, let it be known that his hopes were not to be gratified.

The house of Newport, Rhode Island which Berkeley built and inhabited is still preserved.

The works on which Berkeley's fame chiefly rests were written when he was a very young man. By the time he first visited England in 1713, being then twenty-eight, he had already published his *Essay towards a New Theory of Vision* (1709) and his *Principles of Human Knowledge* (1710), and the *Three Dialogues between Hylas and Philonous* were published in that year. In his later philosophical writings he did little more than defend, explain, and at certain minor points amend, the views thus early developed. It is, in fact, clear from his correspondence that for long periods of his later life he did not occupy his thoughts with philosophy at all. In this respect he differs strikingly from **Locke,** whose main work did not appear till he was nearly sixty; and in fact the young Berkeley, who was early acquainted with Locke's writings, is apt to refer to Locke's thoughts as those of a very old man – as admirable, indeed, for one so advanced in years.

Berkeley is a most striking, and indeed a unique, phenomenon in the history of philosophy. There have been many philosophers who have constructed bold and sweeping, and often extraordinary, metaphysical systems. There have been some also, particularly in the English tradition, employed in the clarification and defence of "common sense". There have been thinkers, again, devoted to the defence of religious faith. It is the peculiar achievement of Berkeley that, with astonishing ingenuity and skill, he contrived to present himself in all these roles at once. This achievement exactly suited his temperament, in which a taste for ambitious metaphysical doctrine was combined with strong religious beliefs and with a solid respect for ordinary good sense; but it was of course due only to his insight and intellectual power that he was able so to frame his theories as to yield him rational satisfaction also. His synthesis of these usually incompatible roles is doubtless unstable, and few of his readers have been able to follow him in it. At first, to his great chagrin, he was seen *merely* as a fantastic metaphysician; more recently, he has found occasional defenders, as being *merely* the advocate of "common sense". But if one is to feel the full force of this theories, it is essential to see how in them these diverse aspects are combined.

Berkeley's position is best understood by contrast with Locke's – this course following, in fact, its actual historical development. The picture of the world which, in his student reading, Berkeley found in Locke was roughly as follows: The universe is really a mechanical system of bodies in space. It is *made*, as it were, of Matter; and material bodies really possess just those qualities required for their mechanical mode of operation – "solidity, figure, extension, motion or rest, and number". These bodies operate on, among other things, the sense-organs of human beings, who possess minds – "immaterial substances" – as well as bodies. When this occurs, the mechanical stimulation of the sense-organs and brain causes "ideas" to arise in the mind, and these are the objects of which the observer is really aware. In some respects these ideas faithfully represent the actual character of the "external world", but in others not; ideas of, for instance, sound, colour, and smell have no real counterparts in the world, but are only modes in which an observer so constituted is affected by the appropriate mechanical stimuli.

Now Berkeley soon came to regard this picture of the world as at once ridiculous, dangerous, and detestable. It was ridiculous, he thought, because it clearly entailed a fantastic scepticism, in manifest conflict with good common sense. For how could an observer, who was aware of nothing but his own ideas, know *anything* about Locke's "external world"? Locke himself had asserted, absurdly enough, that colour, for instance, is only an apparent, not a real, feature of that world; but how could he know that, in *any* respect, contemplation of our own ideas apprises us correctly of the world's actual character? A **sceptic** has only to suggest the possibility that our ideas mislead us, not only in some ways, but in every way, as to the character of objects, and it is evident that Locke could in no way counter this suggestion. Locke is thus committed to the ridiculous view that, for all we can *know*, objects in the world may be utterly unlike what we take them to be

– and perhaps that, for all we can *know*, there may be no such objects. This is surely repugnant to any man of good sense.

But Locke's doctrine, Berkeley believed, was also exceedingly dangerous. For, apart from its offering a general pretext for scepticism, its tendency was towards **materialism** and atheism, and therefore, in Berkeley's view, towards the subversion of morals. God was brought in by Locke as the designer, creator, and starter of the great Machine; but how could he show that Matter itself was not eternal? And if it were, would his system not make it possible, and even rational, to deny the existence of God altogether? Again, Locke himself had held that consciousness belonged to "immaterial substances", which doubtless he would have regarded as immortal souls. But he had confessed that he could not disprove the counter-suggestion that consciousness might be just one of the properties of matter, and so, presumably, wholly dependent on the maintenance of certain material, physical conditions. His theory was thus in some danger of permitting – if it did not actually encourage – denial of the existence of God and of the immortality of the soul; and with this denial, in Berkeley's opinion, religion fell, and dragged morality after it.

Finally, it is clear, though it is less explicitly asserted, that Berkeley was utterly oppressed and repelled by the notion that the Universe is really a vast machine. Those metaphors of clocks and engines, wheels and springs, in which Locke delighted, inspired in Berkeley the utmost detestation. The world, he felt, *could not* be really like this – particularly if, in order to maintain that it is, we have to assert that its actual appearance is delusive; that, in fact, the "visible beauty of creation" is to be regarded as nothing but a "false imaginary glare". Why should we deny the evidence of our senses, in order to believe that the Universe is so repulsive?

Now Berkeley perceived – and it struck him as a revelation – what seemed to be a bold but beautifully simple means of eliminating, at one blow, all these horrors and absurdities. It was necessary only to *deny the existence of Matter*. For what would be the consequences of this? First, the actual course of our every-day experience would be quite unaffected. On Locke's own admission, we are never actually aware of anything but our own ideas; to deny the existence, then, of his "external objects", material bodies, is not to take away anything that has ever entered into our experience, and is indeed to leave quite undisturbed the opinions of unphilosophical men. But not only so; it must also put an end to all sceptical questioning. For Locke was obliged to concede to the sceptic that our ideas might mislead us as to the character of things, precisely because he had regarded things as being something *other* than our ideas. But if instead we adopt the view that things – the ordinary objects of experience – are just "collections of ideas", it will then be manifestly impossible to suggest that things may not be as they appear to us, and even more so to suggest that their very existence is doubtful. If an orange is not an "external" material body, but a collection of ideas, then I may be – as of course any man of good sense actually is – entirely certain that it exists, and that it really has the colour, taste, texture, and aroma that I find in it. Doubts on so simple a point could only seem to arise as a result of the needless assertion that things exist, *distinct* from and in addition to the ideas we have.

We may next see how Berkeley counters two serious objections. First, must it not be admitted that our ideas have *causes*? We do not simply produce our ideas ourselves; they plainly come to us from some independent source; and what could this be, if not the "external objects" of Locke's theory? Now Berkeley admits that our ideas are caused; but to take them to be caused in the way supposed by Locke is, he holds, both needless and impossible. It is needless, for we can suppose them to be caused by God; we can suppose that it is directly by the will of God that ideas occur in our minds as they do, with such admirable order and regularity. And it is in fact impossible, he holds, that they should be caused otherwise; for to *cause* is to *act*, and nothing is genuinely active but the *will* of an intelligent being.

But, it may secondly be objected, if Matter is denied, what becomes of physics? It is plainly impossible to dismiss the discoveries of Newton and his fellows as mere moonshine; but Matter, in the form of particles or "corpuscles", is precisely that of which they have discovered and proved so many of the properties. What is there for the laws of physics to hold true of, if there are really no material bodies?

Berkeley's earliest reflections on this objection were rather evasive; but later, notably in the *De Motu* of 1721, he devised a strikingly ingenious reply in which, though running against the main tendency of his age, he anticipated the ideas of many twentieth-century **philosophers of science**. He answered, in effect, that scientific theories are not true of anything at all. Certainly, if correct, they *apply* to the world of our experience, in that they enable us both to predict and in some degree to control its course; but their function is no more than that of predictive devices. The theory of the corpuscular structure of matter, for example, makes possible the exact mathematical expression of formulae, by the use of which we can make invaluable predictions; but there is no need to make the supposition that the corpuscles and particles of that theory actually exist. That there are such corpuscles is a theoretically useful supposition; so long as it proves useful it should continue to be made; but it should never be regarded as a literal truth. Thus, the practice of science need not be disturbed by Berkeley's doctrines; it is necessary only for the scientist to admit that he is not investigating "the nature of things", but rather perfecting the formulation of predictive devices.

It ought to be mentioned here also that, in the belief that the errors of earlier thinkers, notably of Locke, had been due in part to linguistic unclarity, Berkeley devoted the Introduction of his *Principles* to an investigation of language. In that passage he rather unfairly interprets Locke's vague expressions always in their most vulnerable sense. But his own insistence that the essence of language lies in its use, and on the concrete understanding of expressions in definite contexts, makes this one of his most original and stimulating contributions to philosophy.

Two of Berkeley's later works may be mentioned briefly. His *Alciphron* is a long work in dialogue form, in which the tenets of Anglican orthodoxy are defended against various current types of "free-thinking" and **deism**. Though able enough, it suffers from the artificiality of the convention, and has little interest now that the controversies which prompted it are dead. Berkeley's last work was *Siris*, a very extraordinary production, in which a strangely rambling, ponderous, and speculative statement of some part of his earlier opinions leads on to an inquiry into the virtues of tar-water, a medicine which Berkeley made popular, and for the promotion of which he worked in his later years with almost eccentric zeal.

Berkeley's main work was slow to exert any influence on philosophy, though his limited first work on vision became fairly well known. His criticisms of Locke were for the most part powerful and well-taken; and the transition to his own remarkable doctrine of a theocentric, non-material universe, whose *esse* was *percipi* (which existed because it was perceived), and in which human beings were conceived of as conversing directly with the mind of God, was at least a triumph of ingenuity. But this doctrine was too extraordinary to be taken seriously; the fact that, so far as actual experience went, he could represent it as coinciding with the customary views of ordinary people was felt, rightly, to be not enough to make it actually the same; and Berkeley was not welcomed as the defender of common sense. Even his criticism of Locke was deprived of much of its effect, since it appeared to lead straight into a position still less defensible; and his philosophy of science was much less acceptable then than it would be today. It was then generally accepted that physical theory was merely a kind of extension of ordinary observation, revealing truths of just the same kind as those of common experience. Today this has become somewhat difficult to believe; but to deny it then was probably felt, rightly enough in Berkeley's case, to constitute a veiled attempt to undermine the physicist's prestige. There is no doubt that this was Berkeley's intention; he had the bad luck to detest the "scientific worldview", at a time

when that view was in the first flush of its ascendancy.

Today the ordinary student of Berkeley is most likely to regard him as a pioneer of **phenomenalism**. It is certainly true that it was part of his doctrine to maintain that material objects could be reduced to collections of ideas, or of sense-data as his successors would say. This is, moreover, the classic rejoinder to theories of "indirect" perception, such as Locke had classically expounded. It must, however, not be forgotten that Berkeley was not engaged in cool and neutral philosophical analysis. His phenomenalism was primarily an ontological thesis; he genuinely wished to deny that there are any really material things. He was happy, indeed, to believe that ordinary opinions could be so analysed as to conform with his ontology, and he believed that they *ought* to be understood in that way. He was, however, consciously and deliberately, as Locke had been almost inadvertently, a metaphysician, not merely an analyst.

It was remarked above that the result of Berkeley's ingenious attempt to unify metaphysics and common sense is unstable. This instability may be located in his use, adopted from Locke, of the term "idea". Berkeley's use of this term (like Locke's) is not so much ambiguous as insufficiently determinate. When he wishes to bring out the common-sense aspect of his doctrine, he stresses that he means by "ideas" the *things* that we perceive; when he speaks as an ontologist, affirming that *esse* is *percipi* and that matter does not exist, he insists that ideas are "only in the mind". It seems likely that, if his use of this term were more closely scrutinized and made more precise, his theory would become not so much less plausible, as almost impossible to state. In so far as it depends on fluidity at this key point, it does not stand firm.

(G.J.W.)

**Bioethics**, *see* Applied Ethics.

**Black**, Max (1909– ) was born in Russia, but obtained his formal education in England,

and after 1940 taught philosophy in the USA. Black's major interests are in the foundations of logic and mathematics, the theory of knowledge, and the philosophies of language and of science. Although his outlook has been influenced by **Russell**, **Moore** and the **logical positivists**, he has nonetheless been an acute critic of various doctrines advocated by these thinkers. Moreover, while he has been a prominent exponent of the linguistic method of philosophic analysis associated with **Wittgenstein**, he has not been an orthodox follower of this approach. His principal works include *The Nature of Mathematics* (1950) and *The Labyrinth of Language* (1968). See also **Metaphor**.

(E.N.)

**Blanshard,** Brand (1892– ), the most prominent American exponent of a viewpoint developed from the absolute **idealism** which flourished in Oxford in the earlier part of this century. His most important work is *The Nature of Thought* (1939); here he describes, partly in psychological, partly in logical terms the development of human thought. Thought can, and must, be described in psychological terms, but we will not understand its development unless we see it as guided by a logical ideal. The logical ideal is a system, such as is conceived in the coherence theory of **truth**, in which all thoughts are necessarily connected with each other. We must seek necessity everywhere, and attempts to reduce it to the empirical, as in **Hume**'s theory of causation, or to the trivial, as in conventionalist or linguistic theories of the **a priori**, are subjected by Blanshard to sustained attack.

(J.O.U.)

**Bloch,** Ernst (1885–1977), born in Ludwigshafen, was the Marxist philosopher of hope and utopia. Against the reigning positivistic and reductionist philosophies of this century, as well as against Marxism's own scientific variants of the dominant culture, Bloch defended a "process **metaphysics**" oriented toward practice and the future, a philosophy in which "that-which-is-not-yet" surfaces from beneath

social repression to focus and guide revolutionary thought and action.

Bloch's metaphysics of the future, revolving around his concept of the "not-yet", argues that in utopian ideas and ideals we possess anticipations of a radically different future. We are "not-yet-conscious" of what we really desire, but in the unrealized ideals of the past that different future is adumbrated. More significantly, that different future may be really possible even if not all the necessary conditions for its realization are present, for in becoming aware of what is "not-yet-conscious" we give the hoped-for future a practically efficacious place in the present.

There is an indecision in Bloch's thought between its heuristic, practice-oriented side, which seeks to change the present by introducing utopian ideas into it, and its systematic, metaphysical side which labours to underwrite the claims of utopian reason through the development of an expanded conception of "real possibility". Such indecision, however, is systematic and necessary in a theory seeking to make the imagination integral to reason and rationality.

Bloch was a prolific writer. His most important work is the massive *The Principle of Hope* (1954–59). Other significant works include: *Spirit of Utopia* (1918); *Thomas Münzer as Theologian of Revolution* (1921); *Subject-Object, Commentaries on Hegel* (1949); and *Natural Right and Human Dignity* (1961).

(J.M.B.)

**Boethius,** Anicius Manlius Severinus (c. 480–c. 524), born in Rome, into one of the great senatorial families, the *Gens Anicia*. Boethius accepted public service under Theodoric, the Ostrogoth ruler of Italy, and rose to high office. Later, as a result of political intrigue by his enemies he was disgraced and executed. His most celebrated work, the *De Consolatione Philosophiae*, was composed while he was in jail.

Boethius' importance in the history of philosophy, however, rests not only upon the *Consolation*, but perhaps even more upon his effort to translate and transmit to the Latin

West the collected wisdom of the Greeks. His declared intention was to translate and comment on all the works of **Plato** and **Aristotle**, but of this he achieved no more than the translation of the Aristotelian logical writings together with Porphyry's introductory *Isagoge*. For centuries, however, these remained the only sources of Aristotle's philosophy available to western thought.

It is in his commentary on Porphyry's *Isagoge* that Boethius, though he elsewhere gives Aristotle's solution, allows his own platonising sympathies to lead him into the famous formulation of the problem of **universals**, "whether *genera* and *species* actually subsist or are found in the mind and intellect alone". This formulation proved both a starting point and a stumbling block in the controversy which played so large a part in early medieval philosophizing.

Boethius was further instrumental in transmitting a knowledge of Greek scientific methodology by his translations and classification of the four mathematical disciplines, Arithmetic, Music, Geometry and Astronomy. This *quadrivium* of study which follows upon the *trivium* of Grammar, Rhetoric and Dialectic provided a systematic approach by way of the "Seven Liberal Arts" to education. Elaborated later by Cassiodorus and by Isidore of Seville, this arts curriculum survived the Dark Ages in the monastic and court schools of the West, to become fully established in the medieval university system.

The authenticity of his theological writings is now fully accepted. In these Boethius again sets before his heirs a pattern of theological method and of the rigorous application of **logic** to the analysis of Christian doctrine which became a paradigm for subsequent theologians.

Lastly, it would be hard to exaggerate the importance of the *De Consolatione Philosophiae* in the history of European thought. No book was more widely read and it was early translated into the vernacular.

The opening sections give, through the mouth of the lady Philosophy, the conventional answers, **Stoic** and Platonic, of pagan wisdom in reply to Boethius' account of his misfortunes. Thereafter the Christian convictions of

the author give a positive direction to the argument and true goodness is found on analysis to consist only in union with God. There follows a discussion of the problem presented by the existence of evil in a world governed by a benevolent providence and of the difficulty of establishing a relationship between the free human agent and the foreknowledge of God.

The *Consolation* was both a vehicle for the transmission of ancient wisdom and a model for philosophizing for the next thousand years.

(J.G.D.)

**Bonaventura** (1221–1274) was the name given to John of Fidanza, canonized in 1482. Born in Italy, Bonaventura joined the Franciscan order and studied under Alexander of Hales in Paris. Here he later held the Franciscan Chair of Theology contemporaneously with his Dominican counterpart, Thomas **Aquinas**. He died while taking part in the Council of Lyons.

His philosophical doctrines are to be found mainly in his commentary on the *Sentences* of Peter Lombard and in the two short treatises, the *Itinerarium Mentis in Deum* and the *De Reductione Artium ad Theologiam*.

Bonaventura's work in Paris coincided with the debates occasioned by the impact of the full **Aristotelian** corpus of scientific writings upon the West and the rising importance of **Averroism** in the Universities. His philosophical position can best be understood as a relatively conservative reaction on the part of a man who was primarily a theologian and a return to a systematic elaboration of the Platonising philosophical content which is to be found in the writings of **Augustine**. So we find the explicit and formulated presentation in Bonaventura of the typical Augustinian theses concerning man's knowledge of God, the seminal reasons, the soul as a substance, and an illuminationist theory of knowledge.

Bonaventura regards all true speculation as a search for God. This may begin with investigation of the physical world which bears the imprint of its Creator, the *vestigia Dei*. It is only in the study of himself, however, and in acquaintance with his own soul which is

51

an image of God, *imago Dei*, that man can begin to achieve true knowledge. Exercising his memory, his understanding and his will, under the influence of divine illumination, man is led to the contemplation of God, not as a cause through His effects but immediately and ecstatically.

Though Duns Scotus later became the official Doctor of the Franciscans, Bonaventura, the *Doctor Seraphicus*, is perhaps more truly characteristic of the deeply religious outlook of the Order.

(J.G.D.)

**Boole,** George (1815–1864), was born in Lincoln, England. Though entirely self-educated, he became a mathematician of distinction and in 1849 was appointed to the Chair of Mathematics at Queen's College, Cork. Two years earlier, he had published a short book, *The Mathematical Analysis of Logic*, which has come to be regarded as the first substantial step towards modern mathematical **logic**. *An Investigation of the Laws of Thought*, published in 1854, though better known, is important chiefly for its application of Boole's logical algebra to the theory of probability.

Earlier mathematicians, in particular Gregory and Peacock, had shown that algebraic methods can be used to represent relations between entities other than numbers. The basic idea of Boole's logic is the use of methods substantially equivalent to those of ordinary algebra, to operate on variables, $x$, $y$, $z$, . . . , standing for classes and the symbols 1 and o standing respectively for the universal class and the empty class (though the use of these terms was not introduced by Boole himself). In Boole's symbolism, if "$x$" represents a class, say, the class of red things, "$(1 - x)$" or "$\bar{x}$" for short, stands for the complementary class of things that are not red. Operations corresponding to addition, subtraction and multiplication in ordinary algebra are introduced. If "$x$" stands for the class of red things and "$y$" for the class of square things, then "$xy$" stands for the product of the two classes, the things that are both red and square. And "$x + y$" stands for

the class of things that are either red or square but not both. (This exclusive sense of "$+$" distinguishes Boole's algebra from most later versions.)

With this notation we can represent a limited class of statements of logical importance. For example:

All men are mortal

becomes:

$$x(1 - y) = o; \text{ or } x\bar{y} = o$$

(that is, "the class of men who are not mortal is empty".)

Moreover, we can combine these expressions and operate on them in accordance with the rules of the algebra to derive other expressions from them and so solve problems involving logical relations between classes. These include the simple syllogism of classical logic as well as other much more complex problems.

In another application of the algebra to hypothetical propositions, Boole came near to discovering the truth-table technique later developed by C. S. **Peirce** and modern logicians. Boole's ideas were developed by later workers, in particular, by Schröder, and the study of Boolean algebra is a recognized branch of modern mathematics.

(D.J.O'C.)

**Bosanquet,** Bernard (1848–1923), born in Alnwick, England. He gave up his Oxford teaching in 1881 to devote the rest of his life to writing and to social work. He was the last British philosopher to work out a complete system of philosophy covering all types of human experience. His work was influenced mainly by **Hegel** and was based on the conception of individuality understood as the harmony of a variety of differences, the individual as "concrete universal", in contrast with the "abstract universal" found in scientific reasoning operating by general laws and the elimination of differences. This notion of individuality he found expressed in human persons, in works of art, in the State, and supremely in the Absolute as the final ideal transcending and unifying all these subordinate "concrete universals".

Late in his life he fell more under the influence of F. H. **Bradley** and became more doubtful about the power of reason to grasp the unities met with in experience. The individuality of a person or picture required the conception of a type of unity in which the variety could not be so clearly distinguished nor the elements so rationally related as Hegel had supposed.

(J.D.M.)

**Bradley,** Francis Herbert (1846–1924), English philosopher. A research Fellow of Merton College, he lived the whole of his adult life at Oxford. He suffered from poor health and was naturally retiring and reserved, and he devoted himself completely to philosophical thinking and writing. He wrote in a brilliant and trenchant style, with a force and vigour seldom equalled in English philosophy.

He was influenced in his youth by **Hegel** and the German logicians who followed him, but his philosophy was uniquely his own.

In his first book, *Ethical Studies* (1876), he criticizes utilitarian theories from a Hegelian angle and works out a theory of self-realisation which is also Hegelian in its general design. The self is to be realised in self-conscious membership of the state (which is understood as an organic unity of spiritual beings) and not in isolated self-cultivation. The essay in this volume entitled "My Station and its Duties" is indeed the best short statement in English of the Hegelian conception of morality. But in the next essay "Ideal Morality" Bradley passes beyond these Hegelian concepts of rational unity and of moral right as supremely embodied in Law and the State. Many fields such as science and art and philosophy itself provide moral ends and fields of self-realisation independent of national frontiers and civic allegiance; and in the last resort morality itself is unintelligible and internally incomplete and attains its completeness only by moving on into religion.

In *Principles of Logic* (1883) Bradley worked out a complete survey of logical forms showing how each finds its place in the hierarchy of human reason. But he emphasized at every point that all these forms arise from a basic experience of immediate feeling whose unity they all fail to express. They all therefore involve an element of unavoidable subjectivity and error.

*Appearance and Reality* (1893) is Bradley's greatest work. In the first part, he subjects to a relentless dialectical criticism all the general categories of human thought and experience. In arguments reminiscent of **Zeno** of Elea and of **Kant**'s antinomies, he shows that quality and relation, substance and cause, space and time, self and object, are all of them, if taken as real, beset by insoluble contradictions and must therefore be dismissed as "appearance". The absolute reality must have a nature which transcends all these categories. Relations are grounded in the nature of their terms, and no term can be understood apart from its relations. Whether relations are regarded as completely external (in an atomism such as **Russell**'s) or as completely internal (as in the monadology of **Leibniz**), they fail to satisfy the demands of reason. Thus the whole relational mode of thinking – and in the end all modes of thinking – are in one way or another relational – cannot claim to attain knowledge of reality. Reality must have a type of unity unlike anything in our worlds of rational thought, a unity above and beyond relations, a unity to whose nature only the undifferentiated unity of feeling gives any clue. This absolute reality differentiates itself into finite centres of experience which however cannot be identified with human persons because of the element of time which infects all human life. In the second part of *Appearance and Reality* it is argued that each category of human experience, whose final inadequacy had been demonstrated in the first part, must somehow find a place in the real, though taken up and transmuted in it; and each of them has a degree of reality corresponding to the extent to which it is comprehensive and self-consistent.

In his later work Bradley did not go back on his fundamental metaphysical position and the suprarational and even mystical or religious view of the real to which it leads. At the time of his death he was working on a long essay on relations, and the incomplete draft published in the posthumous volume of his *Collected Essays* gives the best exposition available of this central part of his philosophy. But he developed steadily the positive argument of the second part of *Appearance and Reality* by emphasizing more strongly the partial truth to be found in the various logical and epistemological categories which many of his readers thought he had intended totally to destroy, and by elaborating his theory of degrees of truth. Each of these categories is now justified in its own sphere and degree; what is resisted is the claim of any one of them to be (or to be the model for) the whole truth. At the same time, and no doubt for similar reasons, his work became less polemical and his style more mellow and tolerant.

Bradley's position in the history of philosophy is thus a curious one. He was probably the only first-rank philosopher England produced in the nineteenth century; and in brilliance and acuteness his only previous rival was **Hume**. Yet his influence was slight and his followers few. This was partly because he came at the end of the idealist movement, and partly because he was a very unorthodox representative of it, so that the few later idealists looked back not to him but to Hegel for their inspiration. There are indeed strands in theology which recall his metaphysical position, but they do not seem to have had any links with his work. Though his main tenets have won little acceptance he can still be read with profit for three reasons: first for the vigour and effectiveness of his style; secondly, because his devastating criticisms of utilitarian, associationist, individualist, and pragmatist theories remain of use against such tendencies, which are liable to tempt each new generation of philosophical students; thirdly because his work in philosophical psychology on such subjects as memory, imagination, and introspection has permanent importance.

(J.D.M.)

**Braithwaite,** Richard Bevan (1900–88), English philosopher, based in Cambridge. Though mainly a philosopher of science, he was also interested in giving an account of religious belief which would make it tenable for the thoroughgoing empiricist, and in putting moral choice on a rational basis by applying the mathematical theory of games to conflict-situations. This use of the theory of games developed by statisticians is the chief innovation in his main work *Scientific Explanation* (1953), where he draws on it for "the prudential policy" for making choices between statistical hypotheses; this provides a rejection procedure, and so guarantees that probability statements have an empirical meaning, by allowing them to be *provisionally* refutable by experience, the rejection being subject to revision after each new series of tests. This procedure is unnecessary for the limiting case, that of universal statements, which are of course open to *conclusive* refutation (by a single counterinstance). In the same book he explains the use of "models", theoretical concepts, and mathematical reasoning in scientific theories, and also discusses the status of laws of nature.

(R.HALL)

**Brentano,** Franz, (1838–1916), German-Austrian philosopher, who made important contributions to philosophical psychology. Born in the Rhineland, Brentano became a Professor of Philosophy at the Catholic University of Würzburg, but resigned his chair and his priesthood after the declaration of Papal Infallibility in 1871. He accepted a philosophical chair at Vienna, but resigned it in 1880, returning later as an instructor. His last years were spent in Florence. His two most important works are *Psychology from the Empirical Standpoint* (published 1874, second edition 1911), and *The Origin of Ethical Knowledge* (published 1889), which influenced **Moore** in writing *Principia Ethica*. His posthumously published work is considerable and valuable.

In his *Psychology* Brentano is out to provide a "psychognosy", that is a logical geography of mental concepts, which will serve as an indispensable preliminary to an empirical psychology. He assumes without question that the world contains *two* sorts of "phenomena", the physical and the "psychical", and seeks to find (*a*) some feature or features which will be *distinctive* of "psychic phenomena"; (*b*) certain "basic classes" into which psychic phenomena may be divided.

As regards the differentiae of the psychical, Brentano holds these to be (*a*) **"intentionality"** or directedness to objects; (*b*) direct and inerrant revelation to an "inner perception", which is one with the act perceived. By the term "intentionality" (derived from the Scholastic *esse intentionale*) Brentano means what is revealed by the fact that most mental verbs are senseless (or only elliptically significant) in the absence of appropriate *object*-expressions, which state *what* the mental activity expressed by the verb is concerned with. Thus if I am said to observe, my observation is for example *of* a house or a tree; if I am said to doubt, my doubt is, for example *about* the equality of 2 + 2 to 4; if I am said to be pleased, there must be something I am pleased *with*, etc. etc. In his second edition Brentano makes the all-important point that intentionality is not a relation between the mind and an object: it is merely *relational* or *relationlike (relativlich)*. A relation to an X would entail that an X *existed*, whereas a mental directedness to an X usually does not. What is distinctive of Brentano's position is that he thinks this "relationlikeness" is ultimate and needs no further analysis.

In his classification of Mental Phenomena Brentano admits only three Ground-Classes: (*a*) Presentations (*Vorstellungen*) in which some object is simply present to mind; (*b*) Judgments, in which something is *accepted* as real or factual, or *rejected* as the reverse; (*c*) Phenomena of Love and Hate, that is cases of affective-conative acceptance or rejection. In the case of (*a*) there is no distinction of correctness or incorrectness, but in the case of (*b*) there is such a distinction, the criterion of which is an inward self-evidence (*Evidenz*). In regard to (*c*) Brentano holds that certain acts of liking, disliking or preferring have an inwardly self-justifying character which mediates the knowledge of what is absolutely good, evil or better. Pleasure, for example, is absolutely good.

(J.N.F.)

**Broad,** Charlie Dunbar (1887–1971), English philosopher, based at Cambridge. Strongly influenced by many previous Cambridge philosophers, including **Russell** and **Moore** as well as W. E. Johnson and **McTaggart**, he owed little to foreign influences, and nothing at all to **Wittgenstein**. Broad claimed for himself neither the task of construction nor of demolition, but "at most the humbler (yet useful) power of stating difficult things clearly and not too superficially". While admitting that speculative philosophy has value he doubted that any attempt to construct one could be profitable without there first being a considerable advance in critical philosophy. This type of philosophy makes progress, according to Broad, in so far as it replaces vague and instinctive beliefs by clear and analysed beliefs which have stood up to criticism. In carrying out parts of critical philosophy in this sense in a series of large books, he dissected existing theories and possible alternatives and the arguments for and against them, as for example in *The Mind and its Place in Nature* (1925), where seventeen different theories of the relation between mind and matter are considered, the one most favoured being one type of "emergent materialism". Broad took an interest in psychical research: though not prepared to accept the possibility of survival, he regarded alleged paranormal phenomena as due to the persistence after death of a "psychic factor", which had previously formed with the brain and nervous system a compound of which mentality was an emergent quality. Broad also wrote on ethics, though here his interpretations of some great philosophers are highly questionable. His greatest achievement, and the most difficult to follow, was his monumental *Examination of McTaggart's Philosophy* (1933–38).

(R.HALL)

**Butler,** Joseph (1692–1752), Bishop, holds a lastingly important place in English moral philosophy and philosophy of religion. His ethical thought is contained primarily in his *Fifteen Sermons* (1726) and his *Dissertation upon the Nature of Virtue*: his philosophy of religion in *The Analogy of Religion* (1736), to which the *Dissertation* was an appendix. These two sides of Butler's thought are most closely interconnected; for conscience is not only the crucial concept of his ethics, but it also provides an impressive disclosure of the being and nature of God. Virtue, to Butler, is natural to man, vice a violation of our nature, a kind of self-mutilation. Human nature is a complex structure that Butler likens to a watch with intricately cooperating parts, to a political constitution, and to a body with its component members. The full realising of this nature (and the attainment of virtue) involve the hierarchical subordination of its various elements under conscience. The promptings of hunger and thirst, appetition of all kinds, form the base of the hierarchy, as Butler conceives it. This group of "particular passions" is disciplined and regulated by benevolence and by self-love – thought of not as the indulging of the passions, but as the control and management of them with a view to one's long-term, total well-being. Butler denied that self-love and benevolence were mutually antagonistic principles; indeed, the policies they initiate tend to coincide – for the most part in this world, and perfectly hereafter. Conscience is an essentially reflective and rational principle. It refuses to reduce all duties to one alleged supreme duty such as the production of the general happiness; our duties are multiple; and only God, with his synoptic and omniscient view, could afford to play the utilitarian. A measure of agnosticism pervades Butler's thought on account of his strong sense of human ignorance (the *Fifteenth Sermon* is devoted to this theme). Perhaps the most memorable feature of his ethical thought, however, are the many shrewd analyses that make up his moral psychology; analyses of such concepts as forgiveness, resentment, self-deceit, compassion. Particularly effective among these are his arguments against **Hobbes'** egoistic interpretation of pity.

*The Analogy of Religion* was conceived as an answer to **deism**. The deists held that a natural and rational religion escaped a great many intractable difficulties that beset a religion based on alleged revelation. But Butler maintained that analogous difficulties belong to *both* spheres, although they are decisive against

neither. "The design", he wrote, "of the following treatise will be to show, that the several parts principally objected against in this moral and Christian dispensation . . . are analogous to what is experienced in the constitution and course of Nature, or Providence; that the objections themselves which are alleged against the former, are no other than what may be alleged with like justice against the latter, where they are found in fact to be inconclusive." As this suggests, Butler does not claim *a priori* certainty for his apologetic, but only a probability high enough to satisfy faith.

(R.W.H.)

# C

**Cajetan,** Thomas de Vio (1468–1534), born at Gaeta, Italy, died in Rome. He was Dominican Master-General, later Cardinal, and the classical commentator on the *Summa Theologica* of Thomas **Aquinas**. His criticism of **Scotism** brought him to the problem of analogy, the use of the same name for different objects in more than a purely equivocal or **metaphorical** sense. He distinguished two proper types: analogy of attribution, based on a causal connection; and analogy of proportionality. Only this, he held, meets the requirements of metaphysical thinking. Most Thomists have agreed with him, including John of St Thomas (1589–1644). But not Francis Sylvester of Ferrara (1474–1528), his successor as Master-General and the author of the classical commentary on the *Summa Contra Gentiles*, who tried to vindicate attributional analogy.

(T.G.)

**Cambridge Platonists.** A group of English philosophical theologians, centred on Cambridge and predominantly Puritan, who wrote and preached in the later seventeenth century. Best known among them are Ralph **Cudworth**, Richard Cumberland, Henry More, Benjamin Whichcote, John Smith and Joseph Glanvill.

Their writings contain a mass of erudition, philosophical, mystical, ancient and "modern", often uncritically employed and on the whole lacking logical coherence. The thought of **Plato**, in particular, is seldom accurately differentiated from the speculations of **neoplatonists**. Nonetheless, the Cambridge Platonists made a considerable impact on the history of ideas, in **epistemology** and **ethics** as well as in theology. They attempted to disengage theological thinking from the polemics of the reformation and the earlier seventeenth century, to restore the emphasis upon religion as above all a way of living and to give primacy to religious – often mystical – experience. To Henry More, who was most in sympathy with mysticism, the path to knowledge of God was not learning but moral purification, a view that carries echoes of **Plotinus**. Joseph Glanvill's *The Vanity of Dogmatizing* is in the main a repudiation of intellectual pretention and arrogance, whether among the over-revered Ancients, in the scholastics or in moderns infected with the same vice. Real understanding, to Glanvill, starts only from a wholesome scepticism. The Platonists had themselves, however, a humble confidence in reason. Whichcote repeatedly reminded his reader that reason is "the candle of the Lord". Irrationalisms were indeed as much part of their target as scholasticism; and the reconciliation of reason and revelation was the dominant aim of their work. The controversial issue to which they were most single-mindedly devoted was undoubtedly the refutation of the philosophy of **Hobbes**. Against his claim that matter and motion were adequate concepts for a philosophy of nature, Cudworth protested: "as if there were not as much reality in fancy and consciousness as there is in local motion". The *activity* of mind, the reality of noncorporeal spirit, were thus strenuously argued for by the Platonists against all brands of materialism. More insisted that spirit must be thought of as extended for otherwise it would lack full reality, so he regarded infinite extension as an attribute of God. Also against Hobbes, the Platonists affirmed that moral right and wrong, good and bad are "eternal and immutable", the products of no decrees, orders or agreements, whether human or divine.

(R.W.H.)

**Canguilhem,** Georges (1904– ), French philosopher based at the Sorbonne, who specialized in the history and epistemology of the life sciences. Canguilhem trained as a medical doctor, and his thesis on *The Normal and the Pathological* (1943; republished with supplementary essays, 1966) honed his interest in the origin and transformation of concepts. His ability to combine detailed historical analyses with major speculations on **ideology** and rationality was an inspiration for a whole generation of students, including **Foucault**, whose *Birth of the Clinic* (1963) is a notable development of Canguilhem's approach.

Canguilhem shared with **Bachelard** (whom he succeeded as director of the Institute for the History of Science and Technology in Paris) a belief that there are radical breaks in the development of knowledge. Science, for Canguilhem, was a matter of constituting the world and determining possible ways of interacting with it, rather than of uncovering the hidden structure of nature. The distinction between normal and pathological states, for example, was not a fact about the body and its organs but a way of structuring medical thought, and could be understood only by analysing its specific historical origins.

Canguilhem combined detailed studies of scientific research and its controversies with wide-ranging analyses of the situations in which they occurred. Thus his most characteristic work, *The Formation of the Concept of Reflex in the 17th and 18th Centuries* (1955), is both an essay about a single organizing idea and a study of the very concept of "life", which turns out not to have been a transparent constant of human thought but, on the contrary, to have undergone sharp alterations which have redirected the entire course of medical inquiry. Further reflections on this theme are to be found in his *The Understanding of Life* (1965). See also **History of Philosophy, Philosophy of Science**.

[I.H.]

**Carnap,** Rudolf (1891–1970), born in Germany. He taught philosophy at the University of

Vienna and later at the German University in Prague, but left Europe in 1936 for the USA, where he was Professor of Philosophy at the University of Chicago and from 1954 at the University of California in Los Angeles. He is generally acknowledged to be the leading exponent of **logical positivism**, the internationally influential philosophical movement that originated with the **Vienna Circle**. This was an informal discussion group of scientifically oriented thinkers, who combined a sympathy for the anti-metaphysical positivism of the Viennese physicist-philosopher **Mach** with the cultivation of logical analysis as practised by **Russell** and the early **Wittgenstein**. Carnap was a member of this group for some years; and eventually he served as co-editor of *Erkenntnis*, the semi-official organ of logical positivism, until it became a casualty of the Second World War. He still continued to be an editor of the *International Encyclopedia of Unified Science*, an uncompleted series of monographs designed by the late Otto Neurath, another member of the Vienna Circle, to exhibit the essential methodological unity of the major scientific disciplines.

Carnap was a prolific contributor to the theory of knowledge, mathematical **logic**, the **philosophy of science**, and the foundations of probability and induction. His writings are a large storehouse of ingenious technical analyses and innovations, and models of formal precision and clarity. They also exhibit Carnap's readiness to revise his ideas repeatedly.

One of Carnap's long-standing concerns was the construction of an adequate criterion of cognitively meaningful discourse. He first adopted and developed a stringent form of what is commonly called "the verifiability theory of meaning". He maintained, in effect, that the meaning of a statement consists in the sensory or introspective data which establish the statement directly and conclusively. However, although it can readily be shown that on this criterion metaphysical utterances whose alleged content transcends the domain of possible experience are nonsensical (and not even false), Carnap soon recognized that the criterion also rules out as meaningless most if not

all scientific statements. For various technical reasons he also came to view as unpromising the task he had set for himself (in his first major book, *The Logical Structure of the World*, 1928) of indicating in detail how every purportedly factual statement may be translated into statements about sense-data; and he eventually came to doubt the feasibility of such translations even into the language of everyday affairs and experimental physics. He subsequently sought to develop a more liberal version of the verifiability criterion of cognitive significance, one which could be a guide in constructing symbolic systems for theoretical science but which would also help to demarcate metaphysical vagary from genuine scientific hypothesis. The general import of Carnap's proposed criterion was that a statement is meaningful if, and only if, the statement itself or some of its logical consequences can be tested by sensory observation.

Carnap's ideas on the province of philosophy underwent an analogous liberalization. In *The Logical Syntax of Language* (1934), in which he formulated some of his characteristic views on logic, mathematics and the philosophy of science in rich detail, he defined logical syntax as the study of how the signs in a language are related to one another in virtue of their purely structural properties. He maintained that the laws of logic and mathematics make no assertions about any subject matter, but are simply linguistic structures whose *a priori* necessity within the language in which they occur is derived entirely from conventionally instituted syntactical rules. Moreover, he declared that philosophical controversies are usually generated by the confusion of "pseudo-object" statements (such as the claim that time extends infinitely in both directions, which he held to be equivalent to the syntactical statement that any positive or negative real-number expression can be used as a time-coordinate) with genuine statements about some non-linguistic subject matter. He concluded that philosophy should be identified with the logical syntax of the language of science. This recommendation apparently made illegitimate any consideration of the relations of signs to what they represented,

58

and in particular outlawed any analysis of what is meant by factual truth. However, as was made evident by the work of Alfred **Tarski**, it is possible to develop a precise theory of semantics, which is concerned with the relations of signs to what they signify; and indeed, Carnap eventually made important contributions to this branch of logical analysis. In any event, he now enlarged his earlier conception of the scope of philosophy, and identified the latter (using the terminology of Charles **Morris**) with the semiotical analysis of the structure of cognitive discourse.

Carnap's main preoccupation during later years was with the technical development of the logic of inductive inference. On his view, statements such as "It is highly probable on the available evidence that Smith is guilty as charged" cannot be explicated in terms of empirically ascertainable relative frequencies in some class of repeatable events, as can be done for a statement like "The probability of obtaining heads with a fair coin is one-half" (which in effect asserts that in a long series of tosses a coin falls uppermost about half the time). In statements of the first type, Carnap believed, the word "probable" refers to a logical relation between the evidence and the hypothesis based upon it. Since it is this logical sense of probability that Carnap thought is the relevant one in evaluating the weight of the evidence for some conclusion in inductive inquiries, he attempted to construct an explicit symbolism for this logical relation, and also devised a variety of numerical measures for degrees of logical probability. However, although Carnap had already erected an imposing structure of ideas and theorems on this subject, the structure was not completed, and its eventual value for scientific practice remains an open question.

(E.N.)


**Carneades,** *see* Scepticism, Sceptics.


**Cartesianism,** *see* Descartes.

**Cassirer,** Ernst (1874–1945) built up his original reputation as an historian of philosophy, especially of that of the seventeenth century, and as a philosopher of science; but in his last years, which he spent in the United States, his original philosophical work came to be highly valued there and his influence can be traced in the writings of American philosophers such as S. K. Langer and C. W. Hendel. He was a product of the famous neo-Kantian school of Marburg and spent most of his teaching life at Berlin and Hamburg; but on the advent to power of the Nazis he moved first to England, then to Sweden and finally to the United States. He never rejected the Kantian philosophy which he learnt at Marburg, though he developed it. **Kant** had taught that human experience was conditioned by the categories, the forms of thought under which all phenomena were subsumed; in his *Philosophy of Symbolic Forms* (1923–29) Cassirer maintained that in addition to the Kantian categories informing scientific thought there are also forms of mythical thinking, historical thinking and everyday practical thinking, which could be brought to light by the study of the forms of expression in language. Each of these kinds of thinking is valid in its own right, and though scientific thought is a later development than mythical thought the latter is not merely primitive science. Cassirer's thought is difficult and expressed at very great length; his works all contain long and learned discussions of the linguistic, anthropological and philosophical work of his predecessors.

(J.O.U.)


**Categories. Aristotle** borrowed "categoria" from legal parlance, where it meant "accusation", and stretched it to mean anything that could be asserted truly or falsely of anything. If we complete "Socrates is . . . " with any noun or adjective, or "Socrates . . . " with a verb, we ascribe a predicate to Socrates. Aristotle saw that predicates are of different types. To say of what kind Socrates is, for example a man or an animal, is very different from saying merely where or how heavy he is. Aristotle distinguished several ultimate predicate-types or categories.

(1) Kind, for example " . . . a man".

(2) Quality, for example " . . . pale".

(3) Quantity or size, for example " . . . six-foot".

(4) Relation, for example " . . . older than Plato".

(5) Location, for example " . . . in Athens".

(6) Time or date, for example " . . . in the fifth century B.C.".

(7) Action, for example " . . . argues".

(8) Undergoing, for example " . . . being prosecuted".

Aristotle called several of his predicate-types after ordinary interrogatives, like What? Where? How big? and When? Any answer to "What is Socrates?" specifies a Kind, any answer to "Where" a Location, and so on. All predicates of one type will answer, truly or falsely, one interrogative and will not answer any other interrogative.

To most predicates, for example " . . . laughs" or " . . . shrewd", there correspond abstract nouns, like "Laughter" or "Shrewdness". If we ask What, ultimately, is Laughter? or Shrewdness? or Slavery? the answer names the appropriate category. "Laughter is an Action"; "Shrewdness is a Quality"; "Slavery is a Relation". But not all abstract nouns correspond to predicates. "Possible" is not a predicate, for example, of Socrates, so we cannot ask to what category possibility belongs. Predicates of Kind, like " . . . a man" and " . . . gold" do not naturally yield abstract nouns. We speak of the brightness or remoteness of Venus, but not of her "heavenly bodihood". Her brightness or remoteness might alter or cease, but Venus could not become less or more of a body. If she ceased to be a body she would cease to be at all.

Moreover, to find a particular instance of brightness we have to find a particular *bright star* or *bright torch*, etc. An instance of brightness can be found only in a member of a Kind. But we find a specimen of *star* or *torch*, just in finding a star or torch. Brightness is something that, for example, *this star* possesses. But being a star is not something extra that *this star* also possesses

– else the question "Of what Kind is it?" would arise again about the possessor of this postulated property of being a star.

What made Aristotle want to discriminate predicate-types was perhaps partly this. When a thing alters, it ceases to be what it was. So, apparently, Socrates, who is getting warm, being no longer what he was, cannot still be a man or Xanthippe's husband; which is absurd. To resolve this paradox it is helpful to be able to say that Socrates has changed from having one quality to having another, but this is not a change from one to another Kind, or from one to another Relation. We specify the general field of a change by specifying the category of the predicates between which the transition is. Though Socrates is never continuously the same age, he is continuously a human being. Not everything is in flux.

**Kant** gave to the word "category" a different philosophical use. For him a category is a structural principle exemplifiable in scientifically ascertainable facts. Thus all facts of the form "X's happening was due to Y's happening" come under the category of Cause and Effect. We know, before we find out the actual explanation of X, that there has to be an explanation with this structure.

Today the word "category" is used by philosophers, if at all, for any supposedly ultimate type, without any settled convention about what it is a type of. Without *ad hoc* elucidations the word is therefore nowadays a vague one.

(G.R.)

**Chomsky,** Noam (1928– ), American linguist, whose *Syntactic Structures* (1957) revolutionized linguistics by centring it on grammar, and turned grammar itself into a powerful formal theory. A grammar, according to Chomsky, is a device which produces all and only the grammatical sentences of a language. Although this set is infinite, the grammar must be finite. The only kind of grammar which matches actual human competences is, according to Chomsky, one which postulates a "deep structure" together with a set of "transformational rules" which generate "surface structures". Such a "transformational grammar" can be seen as revising Saussure's distinction between *langue* and *parole*, which is fundamental to **structuralism**.

According to Chomsky, transformational grammars are not just scientists' theories; they are actually encoded in language-users: thus to know a language is to know, implicitly, its grammar. In *Language and Mind* (1968) Chomsky argued that his analyses of linguistic competences in terms of abstract mental structures could be generalized into "a remarkably favourable perspective for the study of human mental processes"; and this vision inspired the subsequent development of "Artificial Intelligence" at the border between computing science and psychology.

Chomsky holds that it is impossible that children should learn a language from scratch: they must, he believes, be already equipped with "innate knowledge" of "linguistic universals". According to Chomsky, this theory places him in the Cartesian, "rationalist" tradition in philosophy, as opposed to the Lockean "empiricist" one; and moreover supports the belief in the worth of all human beings which underlies his outspoken anarchistic socialism.

[J.R.]

**Chrysippus,** (*c.* 280–207 B.C.) of Soli, Cilicia, succeeded Cleanthes in 232 as third head of the Stoa. On coming to Athens about 260, he became a pupil in the Academy of Arcesilaus, from whom he acquired an extreme virtuosity in logic and dialectic. When converted to the Stoa, the School was suffering from divergent theories in the unorthodox systems of Ariston and Herillus, and from a severe attack from Academic **scepticism**. Chrysippus, in an enormous literary output which displayed his dialectical power, repelled attacks and formulated in great detail what became the definitive system of **stoicism**, justly winning the title of Second Founder. He was not an original thinker; he exercised his skill in refurbishing the fundamental doctrines of **Zeno** of Citium. "Give me

the doctrines", he said with characteristic dry humour, "and I shall supply the proofs." But his relentless logic led to differences of detail most noticeable in his psychology and theory of knowledge. And as his logic drove him towards extreme positions, so the paradoxes inherent in Stoicism were spotlighted. To his boast "Without Chrysippus, there would have been no Stoa", Carneades, the most formidable opponent of Stoicism, could answer, "Without Chrysippus, there would have been no Carneades".

(I.G.K.)

**Cicero,** Marcus Tullius (106–43 B.C.), Roman lawyer, politician and writer. Trained in philosophy from youth up, auditor and friend of the leading professors of the Academy, Stoa and Epicurean School, he maintained his interest and reading during his busiest years in public life. In 45, personal distress and political helplessness unleashed his full energies on making Greek philosophy accessible in Latin literary form. Within the next two years appeared a long series of works in dialogue form which covered the various departments of contemporary philosophy by expounding and criticising the doctrines of the three leading Schools. By temperament and training an Academic **sceptic**, in **ethics** he followed and widened the electicism introduced to the Academy by Antiochus. He admired the noble ideals of **stoicism**; to **Epicurus** he was unsympathetic. He thought of himself as a translator (in some cases his source books can be traced, for example, to Clitomachus, Philo, Antiochus, Panaetius, Posidonius), but he claimed the right of independent presentation and criticism. His aim was perhaps to naturalize Greek philosophy, as his predecessors, beginning with translations, had naturalized Greek literature; he thought with reason that the impact of his mastery of language and style could initiate the process. The creator of a Latin philosophical vocabulary which was to become current, his influence was immense, and he remains invaluable as a source for the three dominant Schools of his time.

(I.G.K.)

**Clarke,** Samuel (1675–1729), English philosopher who championed a Newtonian philosophy in opposition to the prevailing Cartesian climate of thought in the Cambridge of his day. In a famous correspondence with **Leibniz**, he maintained that space and time were infinite homogeneous entities, as against Leibniz's claim that they were ultimately relational. In *A Discourse Concerning the Being and Attributes of God* (the Boyle lectures, 1704–05), he contended against "deniers of natural and revealed religion", **Hobbes** and **Spinoza** being notable targets. Morality is based, according to Clarke, not on the sheer power or the command of God, nor upon "contracts" brought into being by human communities, but on independent and self-evident relations between situations and the kind of actions they demand. A mistaken moral judgement is of the same logical order as a contradiction in mathematical reasoning. Joseph **Butler** found this rather too abstract a presentation of moral philosophy. But the most powerful criticism came from **Hutcheson** and **Hume**, who denied that moral judgment lay in the perceiving of relations, or in the activity of reason alone.

(R.W.H.)

**"Cogito ergo sum",** *see* Descartes.

**Cohen,** Morris R. (1880–1947), born in Russia. He emigrated to the United States as a boy, and taught philosophy in New York. Cohen was an outspoken **naturalist** in his general outlook, and a vigorous exponent of liberalism conceived as a faith in rational analysis. He subscribed in essentials to a philosophical **realism** that had been advocated by the early **Russell**, maintaining that philosophy, like the sciences, succeeds in making significant intellectual advances only when it grapples in piecemeal fashion with limited and clearly formulated problems.

Cohen believed that the truths of **logic** formulate the absolute invariants exhibited by all possible objects. On the other hand, he construed the laws of the positive sciences to be expressions of relations which are invariant only in certain specialized domains. He therefore maintained that factual statements are inherently incapable of a purely rational demonstration. Accordingly, he recognized a fundamental polarity between what he called the rational and the empirical elements in existence; and his writings contain spirited criticisms of philosophies that ignore these as well as other polar aspects of nature. He expounded this principle of polarity in his major book, *Reason and Nature* (1931), which contains, in addition to an uncompromising critique of anti-rational currents in contemporary philosophy, a generalized account of scientific method, and numerous analyses of philosophic issues that are raised by the substantive materials of **mathematics**, physics, biology, the social sciences, and ethical theory.

(E.N.)

**Collingwood,** Robin George (1889–1943), English philosopher. He spent all his working life at Oxford, first as an undergraduate, then as a Fellow of Pembroke College and finally as Professor of **Metaphysics**. In addition to his main life's work in philosophy he was a very eminent authority on the archaeology and history of Roman Britain.

He was a very original philosopher, and the bold, fresh style in which he argues out his position makes him an unusually stimulating and exciting author even for readers who are not in agreement with him. Contrary to his own statement in his *Autobiography*, his views appear to have undergone considerable change (on this point see the excellent Editor's Preface to the *Idea of Nature*); this fact, together with his originality, makes it difficult to give a summary account of his views. Brought up in the Oxford realist school, led by Cook **Wilson** and **Prichard**, he early reacted to a position more nearly in sympathy with **idealism**; in his *Essay on Philosophical Method* (1933), perhaps the best of his earlier writings, he took the view that philosophy was essentially an attempt to set forth human knowledge in systematic form. But he insisted that this system was but a transmutation of knowledge already possessed in a less developed form – thus moral philosophy should present in systematic rational form our existing moral beliefs, transmuting but not challenging or adding to them. The other main contention of this work was that philosophy works with concepts which overlap in a way not found in science and that this gives philosophy its special character and methods of argument. In later life, however, Collingwood became more sceptical; in *An Essay on Metaphysics* (1940), ostensibly a continuation of the *Essay on Philosophical Method*, he abandons the view that philosophy has a distinctive character and sees it rather as a part of history. Metaphysics now has the purely historical task of bringing to light the absolute presuppositions of human thought at some date in history; to any metaphysical statement in traditional form should be supplied at the beginning the "metaphysical rubric" that "it was an absolute presupposition of thought at such and such a time that . . . ". No assessment of the merits of these presuppositions is apparently possible. In identifying philosophy and history he adopted a position, similar to that of **Dilthey** and **Croce**, which gave an appearance of unity to his historical and philosophical interests. The specimens of the tracing of absolute presuppositions at the end of the *Essay on Metaphysics* and in his *Idea of Nature* are of great independent interest.

Collingwood's views on the nature of history are of great interest though expressed in essays of uneven merit (see his *Autobiography* and the posthumous *Idea of History*). He expresses great contempt for "scissors and paste" history, and takes very seriously the view that history is the history of human thought and that the task of the historian is to relive the thoughts of the people of whom he is treating. He was also a major contributor to aesthetics, especially in his *Speculum Mentis* (*The Map of Knowledge*), (1924) and *The Principles of Art* (1938).

(J.O.U.)

**Comte,** Isidore-Auguste-Marie-François-Xavier (1798–1857), French philosopher, born in Montpellier in January 1798 of Catholic parents. He went to the *École Polytechnique* at Paris in 1814. In 1816 he was a leader of a student revolt which resulted in his expulsion together with the rest of the students of his year. In 1817 he became secretary to Saint-Simon, the socialist writer. Saint-Simon influenced him greatly, but because of Comte's greater scientific knowledge and superior powers of exposition it has been held that he was the principal author of much that was published in Saint-Simon's name at that period. In 1822 there appeared under Saint-Simon's auspices Comte's *Plan of the Scientific Works necessary for the Reorganization of Society*, in which most of the ideas of his completed philosophy are contained. In 1824 Comte quarrelled with Saint-Simon and left his service.

In 1826 Comte began a course of public lectures on his "Positive Philosophy", but had to abandon them owing to mental illness. The next year he tried to drown himself in the Seine. In 1829 he restarted his public lectures, which were published in six volumes from 1830 to 1842 with the title of *Course on Positive Philosophy*. This is his major work. In it he sets out his theory of knowledge and the sciences and lays the foundations for the new science, which he first called "social physics" and then "sociology". The central thesis is that the attempt to discover extra-mundane causes of the natural world, whether in theological or in metaphysical terms, should be abandoned in favour of the positive method of correlating the facts of observation with one another. The positive sciences, he argued, have been developed progressively, with the earlier ones forming the necessary basis for those that came afterwards. The sequence he sets out, in ascending order of complexity is: mathematics, astronomy, physics and chemistry, and biology (in which he includes psychology). There remains sociology, of which Comte claims to be the founder. As conceived by him, this science consists of the statics and the dynamics of society. As to the former, he held that the various elements are so closely bound together in a "social consensus" that no part can be radically changed without serious effects upon the whole. As to the latter, he held that intellectual development was the prime cause of social change, and that therefore human society passes through the same theological, metaphysical and positive stages as the sciences. There was thus to begin with a theocratic and traditional stage which later was organized between the secular power of kings and the spiritual power of priests. At the metaphysical stage there is a sort of anarchy during which both temporal and spiritual authority are attacked. This transitional stage would be succeeded by the positive era when men of science would form a new and durable spiritual power. An ordered society would then be based on the co-operation that positive knowledge of social facts would bring with it.

Comte had hoped for a professorship at the École Polytechnique, but obtained only minor teaching and examining posts there. J.S. **Mill** and Littré organized financial support so that Comte could continue with his researches. In 1844 Comte made the acquaintance of Clotilde de Vaux. Comte claimed to have been taught by her the importance of subordinating the intellect to the heart, and after her death in 1846 his writings take on a new emphasis. It is not merely by means of the natural and social sciences and by the spiritual power of scientists that society is to be regenerated, but by means of a secular religion, the Religion of Humanity, of which Comte was to be the High Priest. The details of this new religion are set out in *The General View of Positivism* (1848), *The Catechism of Positive Religion* (1852), and the four volumes of *The System of Positive Polity* which appeared between 1851 and 1854. Having made arrangements for the perpetuation of the cult, Comte died in 1857.

Comte's later writings are a strange mixture of absurdity and insight. On the one hand, there is the Religion of Humanity, with details for the worship of the Great Being (symbolized by the female form) in chapels containing the busts of the benefactors of mankind. There is the Positivist Calendar with months named after Moses, Archimedes and Frederick II, and with days for the celebration of great men (among whom Comte gratefully included

friends who had vainly worked on his behalf in the matter of the professorship at the École Polytechnique). On the other hand, Comte had pondered seriously about the ritual and ideology of a society from which religious beliefs and institutions had been eliminated. He saw that in the absence of unifying sentiments a scientific society might degenerate. One of his ideas was that there were moral implications in the scientific activity itself. Thus he held that submission to the facts of nature curbed the exorbitance of egoism, that the acceptance of a scientific argument had a certain kinship with justice, and that understanding was very close to sympathy. Yet his principle of the subordination of the intellect to the heart is an admission that there is more in morality than can be got from science. The intellect, he held, in a phrase that echoes and yet corrects **Hume**, should be not the slave but the servant of the heart. See also **Philosophy of Science**.

(H.B.A.)

**Conceptualism.** Conceptualism is the view that the objects of thought and the meanings of general terms are concepts, these being mental entities which exist only in minds and are formed or constructed by them. On this view when I think about redness, when, for example, I infer from the fact that something is red the fact that it is coloured, I am scrutinising the concept of red that I possess and discovering that it contains as a part the concept of colour. Again, when I recognize something as red, what I do is see that it falls under or satisfies the concept. Stated in this way the theory has a somewhat uninformative appearance. It seems to repeat, in less familiar words, the state of affairs to be explained. It is more compelling in the form of imagism where the concept is identified with mental imagery of some kind. Imagery is used as a standard of classification. To tell if a thing is red I must compare it with my standard imagery of red. For **Locke** this imagery was abstract. **Berkeley** found abstract and indeterminate images unintelligible and proposed instead a theory of representative images. But a specific representative image will have a multitude of features and so will be ambiguous. **Hume's** theory of a series of similar images overcomes this difficulty. Conceptualism, like other theories of **universals**, is implicitly regressive. To use a mental standard of classification I must compare the things to be classified with the standard and this comparison is itself a classificatory undertaking, requiring the use of a further mental standard and so on. A difficulty peculiar to imagism, the price, perhaps, of its ready intelligibility, is that it seems psychologically false. The use of images in recognition is the exceptional case. It is often said that images are themselves symbolic in character and thus raise the same problems about meaning as words.

(A.Q.)

**Condillac,** Etienne Bonnot de (1715–1780), born in Grenoble, France. He took holy orders early in life. In Paris he came into contact with **Diderot** and others of the **encyclopedists**, by whom he was greatly influenced; he was also for long a friend of **Rousseau**. He began as a disciple of **Locke**, whose philosophy was very popular among advanced thinkers in France at that time and in his first book, the *Essay on the Origin of Human Knowledge*, he is mainly content to follow Locke's views. But in his main work, on which his fame rests, the *Treatise on Sensations* of 1754, he goes further in an empiricist direction than Locke had ever gone. Not only are all our ideas derived from sensation but all the activities of the mind are mere transformations of sensations; a memory, for example is a mere after-effect of sensation and attention is the occupation of consciousness by one sensation to the exclusion of others. Condillac expounds this doctrine by the device of imagining a statue being gradually endowed with senses, first smell, then touch, and so on; he can thus consider the contribution of each separately. It is important to his doctrine that he conceives of sensations as arousing pleasure and pain at the promptings of which our wants, instincts and habits are formed.

This doctrine, which Condillac expounds with grace, simplicity and clarity had a great success in France for a time, where it supplanted Cartesianism in popularity; but his views have had a more abiding influence in Britain, largely because of their influence of James **Mill**, Bain and Herbert **Spencer**.

(J.O.U.)

**Condorcet,** Marie-Jean-Antoine-Nicolas Caritat, Marquis de (1743–1794) was one of the **encyclopedists** in eighteenth-century France. He was early a supporter of the Revolution but was soon proscribed and went into hiding where he wrote his most famous work, the *Sketch for a Historical Picture of the Progress of the Human Mind;* he was captured and imprisoned and immediately died, possibly from poison. Condorcet was many-sided; he wrote biographies of Voltaire and Turgot and his *Essay on Methods of Analysing Probability in its Relation to Majority Decisions* (1785) is an important document in the history of the theory of probability. But it is as a philosophical theorist of progress that he is best known. He believed in a permanent human nature and invariant moral principles derived from this nature and independent of custom and religion (of which he was a fierce opponent); progress was therefore a matter of improving institutions and education. He distinguished ten epochs of human society, beginning with the hunter, then the pastoralist, then the agriculturalist; the eighth stage was that of scientific culture inaugurated in the sixteenth century, and the triumph of this culture ensured indefinite further progress. The ninth period began with the French Revolution and the tenth was yet in the future. For his idea of indefinite progress he relied on an analogy with the sciences. Though the human intelligence is essentially limited, there can always be progress in mathematics and the other sciences; similarly an indefinite progress in human affairs does not presuppose perfection in human nature. These views, very influential in their time, were severely attacked by Malthus and others of his school in the nineteenth century.

(J.O.U.)

65

**Contract, Social,** *see* Social Contract, Hobbes, Locke, Rousseau, Hume, Political Philosophy.

**Cook Wilson,** *see* Wilson, Cook.

**Cosmological Argument,** *see* Theism.

**Cratylus** of Athens was a sophist who lived around 410 B.C. He developed an extreme form of Heracliteanism and according to **Aristotle** influenced the young **Plato** to think that there could be no knowledge of the unstable physical world. In Plato's *Cratylus* he was shown as defending the natural correctness of names – a development of **Heraclitus'** view that a thing's essence is often revealed in its name. Aristotle asserted that he also went beyond Heraclitus in saying that you could not step even once into the same river, and that he ultimately avoided speech and merely pointed. Cratylus seems to have been an extravagant and somewhat uncritical person, who must have found difficulty in reconciling his exaggerations of Heraclitus' beliefs in the ultimate impermanence of objects and the significance of some names. There are points which suggest that Plato's interpretation of Heraclitus as having posited constant and universal physical change was derived rather from Cratylus' exaggerated version. See also **Pre-Socratics.**

(G.S.K.)

**Critical Philosophy,** *see* Kant.

**Critical Theory:** the interpretation of Marxism associated with the **Frankfurt School.**

**Croce,** Benedetto (1866–1952), born in Naples. His first scholarly work was on the history and antiquities of that area. He turned to pure philosophy after a considerable period as an historian and art critic, and to the end of his life he continued to work in those fields.

He held no academic post, but was Minister of Education in the Italian government from 1920–21, and again after the Second World War. He retired from active politics on the advent of Fascism, with which he never compromised.

Croce's main fame is in the field of **aesthetics,** but his aesthetic theory is essentially part of his general philosophical system which is a form of idealism indebted to **Hegel.** His general system he called the philosophy of the spirit. Spirit is for him the sole reality, and the physical world is a construction of the mind; but spirit is not a transcendent something beyond experience: it is the world. Though spirit is one it contains four varieties of experience: cognitive experience of the particular, where the spirit expresses itself in particular embodiments, the sphere of aesthetics; second, cognitive experience of the universal, the sphere of logic; third, practical experience in particular matters, the sphere of economic interests; fourth, practical experience concerned with the universal, the sphere of ethics. History is the description of the activity of spirit in these four grades; philosophy can be regarded as a systematic account of the task and methodology of history and Croce often says that philosophy and history are one; hence the systematic treatise on the spirit contains a final part on the theory and history of historiography.

Croce stated his aesthetic views not only in the first volume of the *Philosophy of the Spirit* but also in a shorter *Breviary of Aesthetics* and an Encyclopedia Britannica article, *Aesthetics.* Art, Croce holds, is vision or intuition; a work of art is an image produced by the artist and reproduced by his audience. The physical artefact is produced by the artist to perpetuate and aid reproduction of his image, which is the true work of art. But we cannot separate the artist's intuition from its expression: a poetic thought is nothing outside its metre, rhythm and words, and intuition and expression are one; technique is involved in mixing paints, writing down notes, or cutting stone, but the poem, the sonata and the novel are complete before the mechanical work of writing down is undertaken. Artistic imagination must be distinguished from mere fancy: it is productive imagination expressing some feeling or emotion, though we must not separate the feeling as content from the image as its form; art is the *a priori* aesthetic synthesis of feeling and image.

Art then is simply the representation of feeling in an image. Though this will normally give pleasure we must not be misled into thinking that art is the utilitarian act of producing images as a means to pleasure; nor is art a moral activity; nor again must we confuse art with conceptual knowledge.

Since art is an activity of spirit it is a mistake to claim that there can be beauty in nature; but nature, as much as a block of carved marble, can prompt and fix in our memories an aesthetic image: "nature is mute if man does not make her speak". Expression and beauty are a single concept in different words.

Such is Croce's theory of aesthetics in a narrow sense. But for Croce aesthetics is the field of the whole of the manifestation of spirit in which it expresses itself in particular embodiments; thus it includes all expression except pure logical thinking. This accounts for Croce's claims that his aesthetics is also a general theory of linguistics: language is in general the medium of self-expression; hence, Croce says, any use of language is identical with poetry. Croce's closest follower in the English-speaking world was **Collingwood**.

(J.O.U.)

**Cudworth**, Ralph (1617–1688), English philosopher, the most distinguished among the **Cambridge Platonists**. He published his chief work, *The True Intellectual System of the Universe* in 1678; his *Treatise Concerning Eternal and Immutable Morality* appeared posthumously in 1731. Cudworth took as his task the welding together of the new science of his day and a broadly Platonic tradition of metaphysics and theology. The universe, to him, is not a mechanism, once fashioned and set in motion by God and thereafter self-regulating: nor is it the theatre of God's constant miraculous intervention. Rather, God works by way of a semi-autonomous "Plastic Nature", reminiscent

of the Platonic "World-Soul". Cudworth vigorously combated atomistic and materialistic metaphysics, stressing in particular the active, spontaneous and creative powers of the mind.

Right and wrong, to Cudworth, cannot be established by the arbitrary fiat of ruler or deity. Both the Calvinist and Hobbesian concern with will and power as ultimates are criticized in terms of a morality "eternal and immutable". Happiness and freedom are seen as release from self-concern, religion consisting crucially in the choice and pursuit of a way of life. Of philosophers influenced by Cudworth the most significant is Richard **Price**, whose theory of knowledge, though not his moral philosophy, might almost be called a restatement of Cudworth's.

(R.W.H.)

**Cynicism** is the name applied to the philosophical movement or way of life inaugurated in the second half of the fourth century B.C. by **Diogenes** of Sinope, from whose nickname, *Kuōn*, the Dog, it was so called. It continued in phases of varying popularity and purity until the end of the Graeco-Roman world in the sixth century A.D. Since it was never an organized School with official dogmas, but a succession of individuals emulating the life and practices of Diogenes, considerable variation is found, but a traditional core of precept and behaviour can be extracted.

The end of life is happiness, achieved only by living in accordance with nature, to do which is self-sufficient and constitutes virtue. But this statement is common to both Cynicism and **Stoicism**: they differ in the interpretation placed on it. To the Cynic happiness depends on being self-sufficient, which is a matter of mental attitude. His method of becoming self-sufficient was actively to dissociate himself from any influence, external or internal, whose ties, responsibilities or distractions might fetter his individual freedom. For example, his attitude to prosperity was not one of untroubled indifference whether he gained it or lost it, but of uncompromising hostility. Money is the metropolis of all evil, the whip of desire.

So the solution does not lie in moderation or temperance, but in the eradication of money and of the lower desires. Property may involve ties; the true Cynic has no property at all. In the same way he will attack all ties of family and community, all conventional external values of birth, class, rank, honours, reputation. As the opposite of nature is convention, life according to nature is life stripped of all the accretions of convention, or positively, a life in accordance with the bare minimum necessary for existence. The driving force is the search for the inviolability of the individual under any circumstances. The more one has, the more one wants; the further one is involved, the wider one's needs; the greater one's needs, the more vulnerable one is. But if all needs apart from the absolutely basic are the result of convention and not natural, a man can be free by unshackling himself from them. This is apparent from the conduct of animals who are not bound by convention, and from the ideal of the gods who have no needs at all.

But this asceticism did not involve leading the life of a hermit. The Cynic lived in the full glare of the civilization he condemned, for two reasons. The way of life he led demanded continual practice against his enemies – convention, pleasure, luxury – to keep his body and mind in fighting trim. For example, to form and test *apatheia*, or lack of emotion, he had to face insults. Secondly, Cynicism was a militant evangelism; as the Scout of Mankind, the Cynic had to explore human conditions; as the Doctor, to cure men's minds. Conventional education and the learning of the Philosophical Schools were alike reviled. Cynicism as a purely practical ethic could be taught only by the personal example of the Cynic's life, (hence his extreme behaviour and deliberate public contravention of conventional decencies for illustration), and by the precepts distilled from his experience. These precepts often contained illustrations from the uninhibited behaviour of animals and the example of Heracles of virtue in endurance. But Cynics were principally characterized by a fearless, shameless freedom of speech in criticism, a mordant wit and repartee which gave birth to numerous apophthegms,

and to a new philosophical *genre*, the satirical diatribe. This was misused by the less reputable members of the sect, but in the hands of the true Cynic, it was a surgeon's knife, sharpened by his labours, impartially wielded to cut the cancer of false values, illusory conventions, pretensions and sham from men's minds.

Cynicism was another, and the most drastic, of the philosophies of security which were a common feature of the Hellenistic Age (see Stoicism, Epicureanism). Arising at a time of great social and economic insecurity, when the old values of the Greek city state, already weakened, were tottering under the impact of Alexander, it offered the individual, whatever his status, freedom from fear of misfortune, by schooling him to hold valuable only that which could never be taken from him. The embodiment of this self-sufficiency was Diogenes himself. Subsequent Cynics tended to stress one aspect or another of his doctrines. His pupil Crates of Thebes, who gave away his fortune to become a mendicant healer of men's souls, was well-loved as a kind of poor man's consultant. In the third century B.C., when Cynicism flourished, Bion of Borysthenes and Menippus developed Cynic literary satire; Cercidas of Megalopolis, prominent in politics, applied his beliefs to a doctrine of social reform; Teles was a third-rate mendicant preacher of a type later to become common. After lying dormant in the second and first centuries B.C., Cynicism blazed in the Roman Empire. Apart from prominent adherents like Demetrius, Dio, Demonax, Oenomaus of Gadara, Peregrinus Proteus, Sallustius, we hear of a swarm of riff-raff charlatans imposing on the populace under the Cynic beggar uniform of cloak, knapsack and stick; they particularly disgusted men like Lucian and Julian who yet admired Cynic ideals. Indeed it was a philosophy peculiarly open to abuse, and when falling short of the highest principles especially repugnant. For the Cynic was something akin to a god, and something akin to a beast.

Perhaps the greatest philosophical importance of Cynicism lay in its influence on Stoicism, strong at the beginning in Zeno of Citium and Ariston, and later revived in the first century A.D. by Musonius and **Epictetus**, in one of whose *Discourses* (iii. 22) the noblest expression of its ideals is found.

(I.G.K.)

**Cyrenaics.** A School of **hedonistic** philosophy, founded by **Aristippus** of Cyrene, the friend of **Socrates**, or by his grandson of the same name; flourished at the end of the fourth and first quarter of the third century B.C. when Theodorus, Hegesias and Anniceris led branching sects; thereafter the School disappears before the advance of **Epicureanism**.

**Ethics** was regarded as the only useful branch of philosophy; the end was the enjoyment of the particular pleasure of the moment, which was the sole good to be desired for its own sake. This view is based partly on the observation that the prime natural instinct in all living beings is pursuit of pleasure and avoidance of pain, partly on an epistemology which denied knowledge of external objects and restricted it to the field of sensations. Pleasure and pain are motions and as such positive sensations, mere absence of pain is neither. Neither the past nor the future provokes immediate movement; the philosopher will feel no regret for the past nor toil for the future; nor, since only his immediate sensations are knowledge, will he countenance vain opinion, envy, or superstition. Present gratification, accordingly, is the only goal, and all actions, states, social and moral virtues are indifferent in themselves and good only in so far as they produce this end. But the Cyrenaics also maintained that happiness lies not in slavery to pleasure, but in mastery over it. Pleasures differed in degree, and a present pleasure might be followed by a more violent pain, and hence the consequences of an act could not be ignored. Faced with choice, the philosopher's weapon is rational practical intelligence which can be taught and trained; the art of life lay in the intelligent manipulation of circumstances and the prudent adaptation of oneself to them for one's present gratification. Thus the Cyrenaic answer to the problems of a troubled age was not renunciation and dissociation like the **Cynics**, but to accept the vicissitudes of fortune and attempt

the intelligent control of them for a personal hedonistic end. The master of a horse or ship, they said, is not one who declines its use, but one who knows how to guide it in the right direction.

But the difficulty of reconciling sensuous end and rational means and external stimulus and the control of reason, troubled the School. Theodorus attempted to free himself from external dependence by redefining the end, although still sensual, as a state of mind, joy, brought about by wisdom. In Cynic fashion he advocated self-sufficiency. Gratification could be gained by any act on the basis of utility to the doer. Hegesias stressed that pleasure and pain depended to a large extent on our attitude to external circumstances; poverty, riches, birth etc., being not in themselves pleasant or painful; but he showed clearly the pessimism likely to result from the original position, by admitting that happiness was not realizable and that the philosopher could only alleviate the preponderance of pain. Anniceris softened the position in another direction, by making some allowance for the pleasures of friendship and patriotism, thus raising the problem of altruistic feelings previously denied by the egoistic hedonism of the School. The School is mainly interesting as a curtain-raiser to the more elaborate and successful philosophy of **Epicurus**.

(I.G.K.)

# D

**Damascius,** *see* Neo-Platonism.

**Davidson,** Donald (1917– ), American philosopher born in Springfield, Massachusetts. Although he has never written a full-length book, Donald Davidson is one of the most influential post-war analytic philosophers. In the series of articles collected in *Essays on Action and Events* (1980) and *Inquiries into Truth and Interpretation* (1984) he has developed a philosophical system involving a number of interlocking themes from the **philosophy of mind** and the philosophy of language.

In the philosophy of mind, Davidson aims to reconcile the physical basis of mental life with the fact that explanations in terms of mental events do not involve the kind of general laws that govern physical phenomena. His solution is "anomalous monism": although each mental event is identical with a physical event, in considering events as mental we adopt a different perspective, with different principles of organization, from the perspective of the physical sciences.

The link between mind and language, according to Davidson, is that we can only know what people think if we know what their sentences mean. To know the meaning of a sentence is a matter of knowing its truth condition, but the identification of truth conditions hinges in turn on what thoughts can intelligibly be attributed to a speaker. Davidson draws general philosophical conclusions from these constraints on interpretation; in particular, he concludes that there is no possibility of radical divergence in human conceptual systems. See also **Metaphor**.

[D.P.]

**de Beauvoir,** Simone, *see* Beauvoir, Simone de.

**Deconstruction,** *see* Derrida, Structuralism, Postmodernism.

**Deduction** is one of the technical terms of **logic**. There it is used to denote arguments which are such that if their premises are true the conclusion must also, as a matter of logic, be true. A deductive argument is thus distinguished from an **inductive** argument in which, however convincing it may be, the premises could conceivably be true and the conclusion false. In this use of words the "deductions" of Sherlock Holmes and of all non-technical language are counted as inductions. In the use of logicians the arguments of mathematics are the most notable examples of extended deductive arguments.

(J.O.U.)

**Deism** is the belief that there is a good and wise Supreme Being who created the world but no longer intervenes in it; the God of the deists is an eighteenth-century deity in every respect, to be known only by the methods of rational argument and more particularly by those arguments which lead to a First Great Cause and to an Intelligent and Benevolent Designer. The importance of deism in the history of ideas is largely due to its use by Voltaire and others as a weapon against Catholic orthodoxy. Its main importance in the history of philosophy is that it provoked Bishop **Butler** to write *The Analogy of Religion Natural and Revealed.* Butler tries to show that the doctrines of revealed religion and the course of nature are sufficiently alike that they probably both have the same author. In particular there are no intellectual difficulties in accepting a theology of revelation which do not arise for the believer in a purely natural and rational theology. But the interest of Butler's arguments on, for instance, immortality, is happily independent of their connection with deism. What Butler's arguments do point to in deism is the fact that in its most vulnerable points it is no stronger than revealed religion. While the deist aims his polemics at the Trinity and the Incarnation, he is himself undermined by sceptical attack on the very existence of God. Moreover deism is entirely a religion of the intellect. Whether God exists is for the deist a question of the same order as whether atoms exist. Deism, therefore, even if true, would have little of the type of interest which most religious doctrines possess. The classic deistic statements are John Toland's *Christianity Not Mysterious* (1696), the author of which acknowledged a debt to **Locke**, and Matthew Tindal's *Christianity as Old as the Creation, or the Gospel a Republication of the Religion of Nature* (1730). See also **Religion, Theism**.

(A.MACI)

**Deleuze,** Gilles (1925– ), French philosopher, started his career as a gifted but conventional historian of philosophy, with studies of **Hume**, **Kant**, **Bergson** and **Spinoza**. With *Nietzsche and Philosophy* (1962) and especially *Difference and*

*Repetition* (1962) and *Logic of Sense* (1969) he emerged as a major philosopher of desire and difference. After 1968, he collaborated with the psychoanalyst Felix Guattari (*Anti-Oedipus*, 1972; *A Thousand Plateaus*, 1980). His position is fundamentally anti-Hegelian: against the concepts of Totality, origin and hierarchy, he develops a philosophy of difference and multiplicity which is etymologically an-archic. His work contains a powerful critique of the reductionisms which dominate contemporary French culture: against the Oedipal reductions of **psychoanalysis**, with its interpretation of desire in terms of Law and lack, he celebrates desire as positive, productive, excessive and proliferating; against the economistic reductions of **Marxism**, he gives a picture of society in terms of flows and cuts, semiotic machines rather than structures, lines of flight and bodies without organs; against **structuralist** reconstructions of language, he stresses the multiplicity of semiotic levels, the struggle of minor against major dialects, the importance of pragmatic strategies and collective arrangements of utterance. This central opposition is best embodied in the metaphors of the hierarchized tree and the proliferating rhizome. The material of Deleuze's analyses often comes from literature or art: he has written extensively on Proust, Lewis Carroll, Kafka, Francis Bacon and the cinema.

[J.-J.L.]

**Democritus** lived in the fifth century B.C. He was a native of Abdera, Greece, which was probably also the birth-place of **Leucippus** with whom he is associated as a founder of the **atomic** theory. It is probable that Leucippus first propounded the theory and Democritus elaborated it. We have much information about his life, of which a great deal is improbable – he is said to have been educated by the magi and to have blinded himself to free himself from the distractions of sense. It seems, however, that he was the son of wealthy parents, and that as a young man he travelled much, including a tour of Egypt and the nearer East, thus reducing himself to poverty. On returning home he won renown by his learned work; he wrote not only on general atomic theory and cosmology but on sense-perception, biology, music and many other subjects; some of his work, such as his attempts to explain colour in terms of the atomic theory, seems to have been based on experiment. He also developed an ethical system which is essentially that held later by **Epicurus**. The goal is happiness, which consists largely in tranquil freedom from fear and anxiety. Mental well-being is more important than the pleasures of sense because the latter are fleeting and frequently lead to pain; though well-being is alone of value wisdom is of great importance since through it alone can we know what pleasures are worthy of pursuit and how to attain them. Considerable fragments, but no complete works, by Democritus survive, and many of these fragments show plainly a mind of great power and subtlety.

(J.O.U.)

**Deontology**: the position which regards the fact of duty as fundamental for the understanding of moral thought. In particular deontologists have been contrasted with **utilitarians**, who regard the obligatoriness of actions as derivative from the goodness of the results that the action will achieve. In recent controversy the most obvious examples of deontologists have been **Prichard, Ross** and the Intuitionist school. The word "deontology" is derived from a Greek word "deon" which means approximately "obligatory".

(J.O.U)

**Derrida,** Jacques (1930– ), French philosopher, born in Algeria, educated at the Ecole Normale Supérieure in Paris, where he also taught. His thought – often discussed under the rubric *deconstruction*, a term derived from **Heidegger** – first had a revolutionary impact on literary criticism and "philosophy of literature"; only recently has Derrida been recognized as a remarkably original voice in philosophy and the history of philosophy.

His early work on **Husserl**, *Voice and Phenomenon* (1967), introduces most of his ideas concerning "deconstruction". These ideas centre on theories of signification, indication, ideality, and sense or meaning generally; on the transcendental/empirical parallelism in metaphysics and epistemology since **Kant**; on theories of time and the "spacing" of time; on the metaphysics of presence as analysed by Heidegger; on theories of intersubjectivity, alterity, and *Lebensphilosophie* or "philosophy of life"; and on the privileging of the voice and living speech in traditional philosophy, with the concomitant suppression of writing. The deconstructive strategy, in brief, is as follows. Derrida shows that prior metaphysical, epistemological, ethical and logical systems have been constructed on the basis of conceptual oppositions such as transcendental/empirical, internal/external, original/derivative, good/evil, universal/particular. One of the terms in each binary set is privileged, the other suppressed or excluded. By analysing the denigrated or marginalized terms and the nature of their exclusion, Derrida demonstrates that the preference for one term over its opposite is ultimately untenable: the privileged term has meaning only in so far as it is contrasted with its ostensibly excluded opposite. In other words, the privileged term is constituted by what it suppresses, and the latter returns to haunt it. Thus the privileged term never achieves perfect identity or conceptual purity; it is always already parasitic on or contaminated by the "marginalized" term. In *Of Grammatology* (1967) Derrida develops his understanding of the *trace* or *arché-writing* by deconstructing the dream of plenitude, proximity and perfect presence that dominates Western metaphysics. Important strands of his notion of **trace** arise from Freudian **psychoanalysis**, **Levinas'** "trace of the Other", Heidegger's history of being, **Rousseau's**, **Saussure's** and Lévi-Strauss' condemnations of (but ultimate appeals to) writing, and **Nietzsche's** genealogy of *differential* force.

Derrida's deconstructionist readings of a number of important philosophers have already become classics, and no doubt many of his more recent books and articles will attain that status. See especially his work on **Plato** ("Plato's Pharmacy", in *Dissemination*, 1972); on **Kant**

("Parergon", in *Truth in Painting*, 1978; "Mochlos – or The Conflict of the Faculties", 1980); on **Hegel** ("The Pit and the Pyramid", in *Margins of Philosophy*, 1972; and *Glas*, 1974); on **Freud** ("Freud and the Scene of Writing", in *Writing and Difference*, 1967; and *The Post Card*, 1980); on Nietzsche (*Spurs*, 1978; and *Otobiographies*, 1984); and on Heidegger ("The Ends of Man" and "Ousia and Grammè", in *Margins*; "The *Retrait* of Metaphor", "Geschlecht I" and "Geschlecht II", in *Psychè*, 1987; and *Of Spirit: Heidegger and the Question*, 1987). Interspersed with his readings of philosophers are essays and books on literary figures (e.g. Mallarmé, Joyce, Artaud, Bataille, Blanchot, Barthes, Celan, Jabès, Ponge), on political topics such as philosophical nationality and nationalism, apartheid, feminism, the Holocaust and nuclear disarmament, as well as works on law, education, art and architecture.

While it is impossible to summarize a thought that is still in the making, one can nevertheless discern how the notion of the *trace* – which, Derrida insists, always was an affirmative idea, never a negative one – has been transformed in recent work on the promise of memory and on an affirmation prior to questioning.

[D.F.K.]

**Descartes**, René (1596–1650). Descartes was born at La Haye, a small town in Touraine, France, and educated at the Jesuit college of La Flèche; for his teachers he retained a lively admiration, but was dissatisfied with the course of instruction, finding that for the most part it consisted of the transmission of the received opinions of the ancients, and that mathematics alone gave any certain knowledge. In 1618 he departed for Holland to serve as a soldier under Maurice of Nassau. The following year he was in Germany where he had dreams or visions which apparently revealed to him some fundamental part of his philosophy – most probably, the unity of mathematics and science. He did not at once set himself to write works of philosophy or science, but travelled widely. In 1628 he wrote the *Rules for the Direction of the Understanding*, an unfinished work, not published in his lifetime, which sets out for the first time the rules of his "method", which was to be a method of both science and philosophy.

In the same year he went again to Holland, where with brief interruptions he remained until 1649. In 1634 he had completed and was about to publish his treatise called *Le Monde*, when he heard of the condemnation of Galileo by the Inquisition for teaching, as did the treatise, the Copernican system, and he withdrew it from publication. In 1637, however, he published three short *Discourses* on physical and mathematical subjects, prefaced by the celebrated Discourse on Method. Besides being in other respects revolutionary, this was the first great philosophical work to be written in French, and created a style which became a model for the expression of abstract thought in that language. In 1640 he suffered a grievous blow from the death, at the age of five, of his illegitimate daughter Francine, for whom he cared deeply.

In 1641 he published his *Meditations on the First Philosophy*, together with six sets of *Objections* from various distinguished persons (including **Hobbes** and **Gassendi**) to whom Descartes had submitted the work, and Descartes' *Replies to the Objections*; altogether these form one of the most important texts of Descartes' philosophy. He followed this in 1644 with the *Principles of Philosophy*, which contains besides other things his views on cosmology, cautiously set forth. This work was dedicated to Princess Elizabeth of Bohemia, a woman of intelligence and sensibility with whom Descartes was in correspondence.

In 1649 Descartes yielded, after much hesitation, to the requests of Queen Christina of Sweden that he should join the distinguished circle she had assembled in Stockholm, and should instruct her in philosophy; in this year he also published the work called *The Passions of the Soul*. The next year, however, as a result of the Swedish climate and the severe régime demanded by the Queen, he caught pneumonia, and died on February 11th, 1650.

Descartes' character has been the subject of much discussion and analysis: his exaggerated secrecy, which led him increasingly to disguise both his interests and his whereabouts, together with his ambiguous relations to the Church, have given rise to many hypotheses, of which perhaps the most fanciful is that he was a Rosicrucian. However, there is no real doubt that his Catholicism was sincere; he believed that his philosophy was in accordance with the faith and constituted the only way of reconciling it with the contemporary advances in natural knowledge. His principal aim was to avoid any prejudiced and hasty judgment of his views that would result in their being misguidedly suppressed. In his attitude to his philosophy, he was self-confident, proud, almost visionary, and did not underestimate his own vocation as a solitary and privileged discoverer of the truth. However, he also enjoyed social life; and had a number of distinguished and devoted friends, with whom he conducted an ample correspondence, which is happily preserved and is of the greatest interest.

## I. THE QUEST FOR CERTAINTY

Descartes was not only a metaphysician, or a philosopher in the modern sense; like many other "philosophers" of the seventeenth century, he was also a natural scientist, with interests in such subjects as physics and physiology. Above all, he was also a mathematician; the use of the term "Cartesian co-ordinates" in analytical geometry commemorates his invention of such a system (even though in its present form this branch of mathematics owes more to the work, unpublished for many years, of Descartes' contemporary Fermat). Descartes' concern with mathematics, and his own contributions to its powers, above all as an instrument of science, profoundly influenced his philosophical system. In the first place, he believed that the essence of a natural science was the discovery of relationships which could be mathematically expressed; that all natural science must be capable of being unified under mathematics; and that the world, in so far as it can be scientifically explained, must be of such a nature as to admit of mathematical treatment. Second, he thought that mathematics gave in general a paradigm of certain knowledge, and of the methods of acquiring it; hence he set himself to discover in what this certainty consisted, and to test all beliefs by the criterion of such certainty, by methods as clear and effective as those of mathematics.

The criterion of certainty which he was to apply to all received beliefs was expressed by Descartes in the rule – one of the celebrated rules of his "method" – that he would accept only those beliefs that appeared to him "clearly and distinctly" to be true. By "clarity and distinctness" he meant that kind of intrinsic self-evidence which he found to characterise the simplest propositions of mathematics and **logic** – propositions which anyone could see to be true by the "natural light" of reason. Such propositions Descartes also characterised as *indubitable*, in the sense of being not just very hard to doubt, but intrinsically incapable of being doubted; and it is in the form of a search for the indubitable that Descartes' attempt to find certain knowledge takes its most characteristic form. He set himself to doubt anything that admitted of doubt, and to see whether anything was left over that was immune to this process. His application of this procedure of "methodical doubt" is explained principally in the *Discourse on Method* and (in a strikingly dramatic form) in the *Meditations*.

He found that he could doubt many things generally considered very certain: for instance, the existence of physical objects around him. He reasoned that, although he felt very certain at a particular moment that he was seeing and feeling various physical objects, he had on many occasions felt just as certain of such things when later it had turned out that he had been dreaming, and all the things he had supposed to be around him had been illusions. How then could he be certain that the things apparently around him at this moment were not also illusions? He could even doubt that he himself had a body: his body was one physical object among others, and it might be that this, too, was an illusion. What then could be immune to doubt? At least one thing – that he was doubting; for if he doubted this, it would still certainly be true that he was doubting. From this it followed that he could not doubt that he was thinking, for doubting was only a kind of thinking. Hence he had found at least one indubitable proposition: "I am thinking".

From this, however, there followed another, "I exist", for it was self-evident that nothing could think without existing. Thus Descartes could be certain of his own existence because he was thinking – a truth expressed in the famous Cartesian formula "*cogito, ergo sum*", "I am thinking, therefore I exist".

The expression "I am thinking" in this formula is not, however, to be taken only in the narrow sense of "I am doubting". Although, principally in the *Discourse*, Descartes does approach the *cogito*, (as the formula is often called) by way of the impossibility of his doubting that he is doubting, it is quite clear that more is established in the *cogito* than the one proposition "I am doubting". Under the term *cogitationes* (thoughts) Descartes includes a much wider range of what might be called "private experiences", all of which he regards as immediately evident to consciousness and indubitable. For instance, although Descartes can doubt that there are objects around him and that he has a body, he cannot doubt, he holds, that at least he is having experiences as if such objects were there. The certain existence of such *cogitationes*, regarded merely as subjective experiences, is recognized in the *cogito*; all the experiences of which he is in this way immediately aware are, Descartes reflects, in some sense *his*; and he must exist to have them.

But what is the manner of this existence? He has seen that he can doubt that he has a body, but not that he exists so long as he is thinking; hence, he concludes, the "I" that he has proved to exist is something whose essence is to think. Thus he has proved his existence as a "*res cogitans*" or "thinking being"; or, as he also puts it with dubious justification, as a *substance* whose essential attribute is that of thought.

At this point Descartes turns naturally to the *content* of his thoughts. He finds that he has, among other ideas, the idea of a Perfect Being or God, and reflection on this idea leads him to the conclusion that there must be something outside himself corresponding to this idea – that God must exist in reality, not merely in Descartes' thoughts. Two lines of reflection lead him to this conclusion, both of them derived from scholastic or patristic sources. One is substantially the same as **Anselm**'s ontological proof of the existence of God. The other relies on an application to the realm of ideas of the principle that the less cannot give rise to the greater. An idea of a perfect thing, Descartes argues, could not be brought into being by an imperfect agency. But he himself is imperfect, as is shown by his state of doubt, which is inferior to knowledge. Hence there must really be a Perfect Being, who is the origin of this idea. This argument is derived from **Augustine**; as indeed is the principle behind the *cogito*, that to doubt one's own existence is self-defeating or impossible.

Since he has established that a Perfect Being exists, Descartes has a warrant to reintroduce at least some of the beliefs which he had eliminated in the doubt. For, he reasons, a Perfect Being would not allow him to be deceived to such an extent that he would naturally and systematically believe in such things as external objects if they really did not exist. Hence Descartes feels justified in accepting, though with reserve, some of the most basic beliefs of common sense. In particular, the proof of the existence of God introduces an idea of *permanence* hitherto lacking. The proof of Descartes' own existence in the *cogito* was, strictly speaking, only a proof that he existed so long as he was thinking; even though Descartes seems to have tried, illegitimately, to transcend this limitation already by speaking of himself as a thinking *substance*, that is, an enduring thing. The idea of God as a conserving principle may help to overcome this limitation. Again, Descartes sometimes says that it is only the existence of God that validates memory, and so *deduction*: a process which, unlike the instantaneous steps of *intuition*, presupposes the reliability of memory. Since, however, Descartes has already relied on deduction in his somewhat complex proofs of the existence of God, if not in the *cogito* itself (a much disputed point), there is a strong suspicion of a circular argument here.

Descartes is in further difficulties at this point. He must admit that we are sometimes deceived – this was the starting point of his whole inquiry. How is this fact to be reconciled with the existence, now proved, of a Perfect Being who would not deceive us? Descartes'

answer is that the origin of our being deceived is our misuse of our will, of that freedom which also allows men to do moral evil in despite of God. This misuse of the will consists in an overhasty assent to propositions that are not really self-evident, and it can affect even deductive reasonings – thus we make mistakes in mathematics. But if this is so, it may be objected, can we ever be sure that we have taken enough care, that our imperfect nature may not have led us into error? In particular, may not Descartes be mistaken about even the foundations of his philosophical system? Here Descartes merely asserts that God would not allow us to misuse our will to that extent; but this is hardly satisfactory, since the existence of God is itself one of the things proved in the system by reasonings to which these doubts apply. Here again, the argument seems circular. Accusations of circularity were frequently made against Descartes' system in his lifetime, and have been constantly discussed since.

## II. MIND AND BODY

Among the physical objects which he now believes with some firmness to exist, Descartes finds one – what would normally be called his own body – which is in a peculiar relation to the mind, thinking substance, or, as he also calls it, soul, whose existence has been proved in the *cogito*. For one thing, his will can move this body immediately, unlike any other; for another, things that happen to this body affect the mind in peculiar ways; for instance, when this body is struck, pain is experienced, and when some sorts of desire are experienced, we know (as Descartes puts it, "Nature teaches us") that the body has some need. These latter facts, in particular, mean that the soul is united to the body in a peculiarly intimate way. "My soul is not in my body like a pilot in a ship" said Descartes, echoing Thomas **Aquinas**; if it were so, the soul would be able only to move the body, not also to feel "through" it.

Ultimately, Descartes holds, the peculiar nature of this union cannot be explained. In this connection, he wrote to the Princess Elizabeth, there are three basic and unanalysable notions – the body, the soul, and the union between them. Nevertheless, elsewhere Descartes attempts to explain at least some features of the union. In particular, he holds against much ancient and traditional opinion that the soul is not the principle of life of the body. The body, as a body, is just a machine with its own internal economy and sources of energy, and "it is not that the body dies because the soul leaves it, but that the soul leaves it because the body has died". While the body is alive, however, a soul is joined to it in such a way that some of the movements of the body are produced by the soul, and some experiences of the soul are produced by changes in the body. In the *Passions of the Soul* Descartes suggests that there is in the body a physical place of this interaction, and that this is the pineal gland at the base of the brain. This gland, he supposed, could be moved directly by the soul, and thus agitate the "animal spirits" which, in common with many seventeenth-century theorists, he believed to flow and to transmit movement to all parts of the body; in the opposite direction, changes in the animal spirits induced by stimuli to the body could move the gland and thus affect the soul.

This naive causal account of the relations of soul and body was thought unsatisfactory even by many Cartesians. The **occasionalism** of **Malebranche**, and, in one of its many applications, the "pre-established harmony" of **Leibniz** were other seventeenth-century attempts to solve the problem.

Descartes held that this problem arose only in the case of human beings. In the case of **animals**, he seems to have thought that all their movements were produced by purely mechanical causes in a system of stimulus and response, and that they were accordingly merely machines, having in the proper sense no souls. However, Descartes is not always consistent on this issue, which raises important problems about his concept of consciousness.

The problem of the union of soul and body is, in a very real sense, central to Descartes' metaphysics. In his view, which is the classical expression of **dualism**, there are in the realm of created beings two and only two fundamentally different sorts of substances or existing things: "thinking" and "extended" substances, souls and

matter. This dualistic view was the heart of Descartes' attempt to reconcile the Catholic faith and the advances of seventeenth-century science. Although there was some causal interaction between souls and bodies, he thought that he had sufficiently isolated souls from the realm of extension, which alone was subject to the mechanical laws which science was developing. Natural science, he believed, could ultimately complete a deductive theory of all mechanical changes in extended nature, and so of all physical events, since every physical event must be only a change of motion in extension: these would include all movements of human bodies which were not the product of **free-will**, but free-will and the soul itself would remain essentially outside the reach of the scientific laws.

Apart from the difficulties already mentioned concerning the relations of soul and body, one notable problem about Descartes' dualism is the question of the number of each type of substance. It is clear that on Descartes' view there can be an infinite number of thinking substances or souls. The case is different, however, with extended substance: Descartes seems to have held, in effect, that there could be only *one* extended substance, which constituted all of mechanical nature. This substance could be more or less dense, but not discontinuous: Descartes holds that the notion of absolutely empty space is unintelligible, and that a vacuum cannot exist. Influenced by a purely geometrical concept of extension, he in fact equates extended matter and space and is faced in consequence with many difficulties, particularly in his theory of motion. These views were effectively attacked by Leibniz as was Descartes' related belief that the quantity of motion in the universe remains always constant.

III.  NATURAL SCIENCE

The only essential property of matter, on the Cartesian view, is extension. The idea of extension is, like the idea of God and the fundamental ideas of mathematics, innate; by "innate" ideas Descartes means **a priori** notions which the mind can find in itself alone and which it does not derive from experience. Moreover, we can form clear and distinct ideas of other qualities which can belong to physical objects, viz. size, shape, motion, position, duration and number: all these are "modes" of extension. Since we can clearly and distinctly conceive these qualities, we know *a priori* that it is possible that there should be in reality physical objects possessing them. However, we in fact have more than the mere innate idea of these qualities as possible attributes of physical objects; we also have what Descartes calls "adventitious ideas" – that is, ideas formed in our minds without our willing them, and apparently caused by some outside source – of objects around us actually possessing these qualities. Since God is no deceiver, we have good reason to think that such objects actually exist.

The objects around us appear to have other qualities besides these, as we also have sensations of such things as colours, sounds, odours, tastes, degrees of hardness etc. About these qualities (often called in the seventeenth-century "secondary" qualities, as opposed to the former group of "primary" qualities) Descartes holds that we can have little certainty. The ideas of them are confused and unclear, and while he thinks that the goodness of God makes it probable that there are in the physical objects real differences corresponding to the differences of these various sensations, he finds unintelligible the notion that these various qualities as given to sensation actually exist in the objects. Thus Descartes, although he does not commit himself firmly on the point, leans towards the view found in Locke and others, that primary qualities exist in objects, but secondary qualities, as we perceive them, do not. He shares with Locke the representative theory of perception that goes with such a view. He differs from Locke, however, both in the exact list he gives of primary qualities, and in holding that, although we have ideas of sensation, none of our knowledge of physical objects really comes from sensation. Sensation can give us only unclear and confused ideas, and we understand physical reality only by an act of the intellect, through the ideas of extension and its modes, which can be made clear and distinct.

Descartes' conception of a complete natural science, consonant with his other views, is of an entirely deductive system derived from self-evident *a priori* premises. These premises were ultimately of a philosophical or metaphysical character. Metaphysics and science are for him fundamentally one, and in his *Principles* he indeed attempts to derive the first principles of his science from reflection on the nature of God. Every physical event, including changes in the human body, was governed by the same physical laws – thus medicine, ultimately, must be part of the one physical science. All the sciences were one with physics, and physics one with philosophy, a state of affairs which Descartes pictured in his description of the Tree of Knowledge, of which the roots were metaphysics, the trunk physics, and the branches the other sciences.

This science Descartes expected to be of not merely theoretical interest. In common with his older contemporary, Francis **Bacon**, he frequently emphasises the practical benefits to be expected from the scientific study of nature; in particular he hoped that the study of physiology might enable man to discover the causes of senescence and thus to prolong life.

Despite the entirely *a priori* character of the science which he imagined, Descartes admitted, from the beginning, and increasingly after discouraging experience, that experiments were necessary to the discovery of physical truths, and he himself engaged in many experiments, for example in physiology and optics. The need for these experiments and their function are not entirely clear granted the nature of his system and its *a priori* claims, and his interpreters have found many problems in his various and not entirely consistent accounts of this matter.

IV. HISTORICAL INFLUENCE

The influence of Descartes on the history of philosophy has probably been greater than that of any other thinker, with the exception of **Aristotle**. It extended far beyond the Cartesians, such as Malebranche who adopted many of his views, or even the other **rationalists**, who agreed with much of his general account of the nature of philosophy and science. In particular, the British **empiricists**, who rejected almost all his conclusions, were so profoundly affected by his approach that the eighteenth-century Scots philosopher **Reid** stated not so much a paradox as the truth in writing that Malebranche, Locke, **Berkeley** and **Hume** shared a common "system of the human understanding" which "may still be called the Cartesian system". The same influence, in very various forms, has continued to the present day.

What influenced all these philosophers was the most revolutionary element in Descartes' thought, his placing at the centre of philosophy the **epistemological** question "how do I know . . . ?" Descartes was effectively the first to try to abandon the impersonal "God's eye view" of the world common to earlier philosophers, and to ask, not just what the world was like, but how one could know what the world was like. Descartes also transmitted to his successors the view that there could be only one valid method of answering these questions, the method of starting from the immediate data of consciousness, which alone were indubitable, and attempting to "work out" from them to an external world. Descartes himself attempted to do this by appealing to the existence and nature of God. His arguments here represent some of the most traditional elements in his thought; when these were called in question, not just in detail but in principle, other philosophers were left with the task of constructing an external world from the immediate data of consciousness without such transcendental aids.

Thus the philosophy of Descartes, which is itself a transcendental religious metaphysics as well as a philosophy of the New Science, contained the seeds of the empiricism and subjective idealism that came later. It is perhaps only in very recent years that philosophers have determinedly called in question the fundamental Cartesian principle which underlies these systems, that there are immediate data of consciousness, more certain than anything else, from which philosophy must start in its search for knowledge. See also **Philosophy of Mind**.

(B.A.O.W.)

**Determinism.** The thesis of determinism is, roughly, that any event whatsoever is an instance of some law of nature. It is not easy to state this thesis in a precise manner; it is most usually stated in the form: every event has a cause, or nature is uniform; a famous and very graphic formulation by Laplace is that given a knowledge of the state of the universe at some date it is in principle possible to predict all the subsequent history of the universe. The thesis cannot be proved or disproved; we cannot prove it since to do so would require the provision of a deterministic explanation of the totality of events; we cannot disprove it since any failure to find a deterministic explanation of an event can always be regarded, and usually is regarded, as a temporary lacuna in scientific knowledge. The famous problem of the justification of **induction** can be stated in the form: science presupposes the principle of determinism, and if this principle is unprovable then science rests on unprovable presuppositions. **Hume** was responsible for the classical statement of this problem, to which philosophers have never found an agreed solution. It appears, however, that the deterministic hypothesis has been abandoned in some fundamental physical inquiries in which statistical laws are sought regarding events for which, taken singly, no deterministic explanation is sought. For this, and other reasons it is commonly suggested that the principle of determinism should not be regarded as a true or false statement but as a methodological principle which may or may not be used in a scientific investigation (see **quantum mechanics**).

Frequently, however, the thesis of determinism is understood to involve the thesis that the will is not free, that choice is illusory and that how we act is determined. There are philosophers who accept the principle of determinism but regard it as compatible with the **freedom of the will**, but it would be misleading to speak of these philosophers as determinists. The principle of indeterminacy in physics can be thought to provide a solution to the problem of the freedom of the will only at the expense of confused thinking, for there is no way of basing human responsibility on the impossibility of simultaneously determining the position and momentum of elementary particles.

(J.O.U.)

**Dewey,** John (1859–1952), American philosopher, who was guided by the idea that philosophy is a thoroughly human undertaking which must be judged in terms of its social or cultural impact. Dewey was an uncompromising naturalist with a vigorous distrust of anything that smacked of the esoteric. Philosophizing is a mode of human behaviour; it arises in certain contexts rather than others; and it should be judged in terms of its capacity to meet the challenge of the very conditions which give rise to it.

One can say that Dewey replaced the problem of truth with the problem of value. His tendency is to replace the question "what conclusion is true?" with the question "what conclusion, considering the conditions of the problem which gives rise to our thinking at all, is the one which we *ought* to come out with?"

Dewey was strongly influenced by C. S. **Peirce**'s contention that all thought is a movement from a doubtful to a settled situation of belief. Thinking (or intellection) is a form of activity engaged in by a human biological organism whenever habitual patterns of action are disrupted. · Its function is described by Dewey in five stages. (1) Given the breakdown of habit, the organism nonetheless presses on to further action. Overt action being thwarted, it resorts to "suggestions". (2) "Intellectualization" takes place as the problem is formulated as one to be solved. (3) The next step is the imaginative construction of "hypotheses" which might serve as guides in the actual search for an answer. (4) "Reasoning" consists in deducing from a hypothesis the actual differences it would make in the course of experience. (5) Experiment itself, or "testing", is the action (overt or imaginative) of checking the hypothesis against those differences of fact entailed.

In his earlier writings Dewey tended, following **James**, to state his position as a view concerning the meaning of truth. Thus, he tended at first to say that what we *mean* by "true" is contained in a description of the criteria to be satisfied by any "proper" end result of the process just described. Such a description would provide the full import of Dewey's notorious remark that "the true is that which works". Nonetheless, under vigorous attack, especially by **Russell**, Dewey's way of talking significantly changed. Russell argued that one must carefully distinguish the *meaning* of truth from the *criteria* we apply in establishing its presence. Thus, in order to establish that "Caesar crossed the Rubicon" is true, I must no doubt engage in future research and establish that, when adopted as an hypothesis, it "works". But what I *mean* in calling the proposition true is that it "corresponds" in some sense with what actually took place a good many years ago. But Dewey's concern was with the conditions under which the hypotheses we adopt are or are not *warrantedly assertible*. It was those conditions which must be our guide in judging discourse, not esoteric notions about truth by correspondence. Russell's response was that, difficult as it is, the notion of truth by correspondence cannot be avoided, and that Dewey, while ostentatiously ushering it out of the front door, surreptitiously introduces it through all the back windows.

For Dewey the first task of **ethics** is to understand the nature of the biological organisms whose conjoint behaviour constitutes the social context. The second task is to understand the kinds of problem-situation which give rise to our effort to distinguish good conduct from bad. Dewey states the main outlines of his moral theory in a book significantly entitled *Human Nature and Conduct* (1922). Human nature is analysed in terms of three key concepts: impulse, habit and intelligence. The dynamic character of the human organism is expressed in the concept of impulse. Habits in turn are conceived as those relatively stable patterns of activity which result from the constant interplay of impulse from within and social pressures from without. Intelligence is described in functional terms as the form of activity whereby, when habits are frustrated or upset, the organism seeks to reinstate action. Thus, degree of intelligence will be judged in terms of the degree of permanence with which action is reinstated relative to the problem which thwarted action in the first place.

This is now introduced as a clue to the moral philosopher's search for the good for man. Dewey proposes the following definition: "Good consists in the meaning that is experienced to belong to an activity when conflict and entanglement of various incompatible impulses and habits terminate in a unified orderly release in action." In short, we *ask* the question "what is good?" only relative to a general type of problem-situation.

Societies, like individuals, are dynamic and active. Like individuals they develop habits which break down under pressures and strains. Thus the role of intelligence at the social level is comparable to the role of intelligence at the level of individual action. Societies must seek to establish patterns of activity stable enough to resist shock; a course of action must always be judged according to its degree of success in removing the conditions of breakdown.

Dewey had no respect for those who approach problems "from the top down". It seemed to him that political philosophy had for too long sought the justification of courses of action in elaborate metaphysical doctrines. Social science should tackle concrete problems by running through the five stages of intelligent activity. It should run the risk of bold hypothesis and tackle the task of checking every hypothesis against the evidence.

Dewey's philosophy of education is an integral part of his general social philosophy. Education should be based upon the premise that all genuine thought grows out of real problem-situations. If education is to proceed "from the bottom up" it will adjust itself to real problems felt by the child, and will educate it by training him to invent hypotheses, think out their consequences, and test them in actual practice. The emphasis is on what the child feels as a real problem in contrast to what the teacher preconceives as gospel.

Dewey attacked **Metaphysics** on two rather different grounds. The first is that metaphysical thinking really makes no difference at all so far as the progress of man's intelligent control of nature is concerned. The second is that

metaphysical thinking makes a very great deal of difference – for the worse. It is said to block inquiry, to make philosophy dogmatic and stagnant, to close men's minds to possibilities inherent in natural science.

Dewey attacked **religion** on both these grounds, and they may very well be compatible. But Dewey was not an iconoclast, and he coupled his attacks upon religion with a positive claim that his way alone would lead to a release of the religious energies of mankind. "If I have said anything about religions and religion that seems harsh," he wrote, "I have said those things because of a firm belief that the claim on the part of religions to possess a monopoly of ideals and of the supernatural means by which alone, it is alleged, they can be furthered, stands in the way of the realisation of distinctively religious values inherent in natural experience. For that reason if for no other, I should be sorry if any were misled by the frequency with which I have employed the adjective 'religious' to conceive of what I have said as a disguised apology for what have passed as religions. The opposition between religious values as I conceive them and religions is not to be bridged."

(J.W.S.)

**Dialectic**. The word "dialectic" comes from the Greek verb meaning "to converse", and originally meant "the art of conversation, discussion or debate". **Aristotle**, in saying dialectic was invented by **Zeno** of Elea, was presumably referring to Zeno's paradoxes, which refuted some hypotheses of opponents by drawing unacceptable consequences from them. But it was first applied generally by **Socrates**, who, as presented in the earlier dialogues of Plato, constantly practised two techniques, both hypothetical in form: refuting his opponents' statement by getting them to accept as an ultimate consequence of it a statement contradicting it (*elenchus*), and leading them on to a generalisation by getting them to accept its truth in a series of instances (*epagoge*, translated "induction").

**Plato** himself regarded dialectic as the supreme philosophical method, "the coping-stone of the sciences", and it was to be the final stage in the formal education of his philosopher-kings. But his references to dialectic, though always laudatory, are often vague, and he may have had various conceptions at different times. It seems always to have involved the search for unchanging essences, for example, above all for the idea of the Good, but almost any form of non-specialised abstract reasoning could fall under it. Sometimes it was certainly the method of refuting hypotheses, and at a later stage it included the method of "division" of a genus into species, one of which was then divided, and so on as long as repetition was possible.

Aristotle put dialectic on a sound footing for the first time in his *Topics*, which is a manual for finding arguments for or against given positions, or *theses*, such as "Every pleasure is good". Such theses were probably debated in Plato's Academy, and he wanted to provide general methods for dealing with them. He says that his book is useful for three purposes: training, discussions, and the philosophical sciences. In the process he discovered many basic principles of formal **logic**, a subject which he developed in his *Analytics* as a theory of demonstration by contrast with dialectic, which is restricted to reasoning from mere opinions. But formal logic came to be called dialectic, by the **stoic** logicians and in **medieval philosophy**.

A descendant of the debates in the Academy was the medieval disputation, in which the contestants continued, mainly by syllogistic reasoning, to maintain theses and *antitheses* (their opposites). By this means candidates in medieval universities were examined for degrees.

**Hegel** gave a new turn to dialectic, which he regarded as a process not merely of reasoning, but found in history, and in the universe as a whole, consisting of a necessary movement from thesis to antithesis, and then to a *synthesis* of the two. It is the Hegelian dialectic which was taken over by **Engels** and made part of his philosophy of **Dialectical Materialism**.

(R.HALL)

**Dialectical Materialism** is, according to some authorities, the "philosophical basis" of Marxism. Its origins can be traced back to 1845, when **Marx** and **Engels** wrote a bulky manuscript intended to reveal that the "Young Hegelians" (especially **Feuerbach**, Bauer and Stirner) were merely second-rate copies of the French **ideologists**. They were sheep in wolves' clothing: they pretended to be "revolutionary philosophers" but "their bleating merely imitates in a philosophic form the conceptions of the German middle class." Marx and Engels declared that real revolutionaries must replace this "idealist outlook" with "materialism"; they should "set out from real active human beings" instead of pretending to "descend from heaven to earth". This manuscript, entitled *The German Ideology*, was left, as Marx put it, "to the gnawing criticism of mice": Part One was eventually published in 1926; the rest in 1932.

In the 1870s, the German reformist socialist Eugen Dühring brought out several books purporting to derive a policy of class cooperation within the nation-state from a materialistic philosophy of nature and history. Dühring denounced Marx for "performing dialectical miracles for his faithful followers" and attacked "dialectics" in general, by which he meant the supposedly Hegelian claim that "contradiction is objectively present not in thought . . . but in things and processes themselves and can be met with in so to speak corporeal form".

Engels responded to this attack in *Anti-Dühring* (1878), arguing that the idea that reality is "contradiction-free" is valid only "so long as we consider things as at rest and lifeless, each one by itself, alongside and after each other". Drawing on a wide acquaintance with the natural sciences, Engels argued that motion and life could not be understood from this "mechanistic" and "metaphysical" point of view, and that dialectical contradictions really do exist in the objective natural world.

Engels gave a lucid restatement of this position in *Ludwig Feuerbach and the End of Classical German Philosophy* (1886), where he argued that in reacting against **Hegel's** idealism, Feuerbach had simply reverted to pre-Hegelian, mechanical materialism. He had continued to regard

81

philosophy as "an impassable barrier, an unassailable holy thing"; hence, "as a philosopher, he stopped half way: the lower half of him was materialist, the upper half idealist". It was Marx alone (Engels self-effacingly said) who had, forty years earlier, seen the way forward: whilst opting for materialism, he had retained Hegel's "dialectical method". In this way "the revolutionary side of Hegel's philosophy was taken up again but freed from the idealist trammels which, in Hegel's hands, had prevented its consistent execution." Unlike the Hegelians, Marx had put matter first; but unlike the "mechanical materialists" he did not think of matter in terms of "*things*, as given, as fixed, as stable" but in terms of "dialectical processes", driven by "real contradictions". This provided Marx with a philosophical outlook on nature as a whole, and also on society as a part of nature.

Engels' vivid account of the place of Marxism in the history of philosophy had a wide appeal in the international socialist movement. It corresponded to some of the ideas already being propagated by the German worker-philosopher Joseph Dietzgen (1828–1888); and in 1892 the Russian revolutionary Georg Plekhanov (1856–1918) invented the name under which it was to become famous: "dialectical materialism". In 1909 **Lenin** asserted boldly, though quite falsely, that "Marx and Engels scores of times termed their philosophical views dialectical materialism".

The textual basis for "dialectical materialism" was extended in 1925 with the publication of some fragments and drafts of a work on *The Dialectics of Nature* which Engels had left unfinished at his death. This codified dialectics into three "laws" which were said to have been "abstracted" from the "history of nature and human society". These were "1) the law of the transformation of quantity into quality and vice-versa; 2) the law of the interpenetration of opposites; and 3) the law of the negation of the negation." With the help of this formula, dialectical materialism was taken up as part of the propaganda of the Third International, achieving its most forceful statement in Stalin's chapter on "Dialectical and Historical Materialism" in the *History of the CPSU(B)* (1938). This made a sharp and influential distinction between "dialectical materialism", which was the Marxist philosophy of nature, and "historical materialism", which was "the application of dialectical materialism to society and history". In this form, and as elaborated by Mao, dialectical materialism became the best-known philosophical doctrine ever.

Dialectical materialism has offered a tempting target for philosophical critics of Marxism (such as **Popper**) who have questioned, in particular, whether "dialectical contradictions" (as distinct from clashes of forces) can coherently be attributed to inanimate natural processes, particularly if these are interpreted materialistically. However, its credentials as the authentic "philosophical basis" of Marxism are themselves very questionable, and it is doubtful whether Marx's own theoretical achievements presuppose dialectical materialism in any way. Throughout the twentieth century, many of the most vital Marxist philosophers (**Lukács,** the members of the **Frankfurt School, Gramsci,** and **Sartre,** for instance) have been more or less explicitly hostile to dialectical materialism. For them, the live philosophical issues in Marxist theory are **alienation, ideology** and art; the nature of freedom, practice, and labour; and the changing relations between society and nature, none of which has any place on the philosophical agenda of orthodox dialectical materialism. Their interpretation of Marxist philosophy often implies, moreover, that the very idea that knowledge stands in need of a "philosophical basis" is "idealistic"; which suggests that "dialectical materialism" is itself a form of "German Ideology".

[J.R.]

**Diderot,** Denis (1713–1784), a cutler's son, born at Langres, France. He received his final schooling at the Jesuit College of Louis-le-Grand in Paris. A man of encyclopaedic learning, he was a natural choice as editor of the *Encyclopédie* (see **Encyclopedists**). At first associated with d'Alembert as co-editor, he became sole editor following the latter's withdrawal in 1757. From 1747 till the appearance of the seventeenth and final volume in 1765, he wrote numerous articles himself on philosophy, religion, political theory and literature, took particular interest in the sections on trade and applied science, and edited the articles of the other contributors. This achievement alone would have established his reputation.

The philosophy of Diderot is found in *Philosophical Thoughts* (1746); *Letter on the Blind* (1749); *Thoughts on the Interpretation of Nature* (1754); and in works of fiction such as *D'Alembert's Dream* (1769).

Following **Locke**, Diderot was a convinced empiricist, accepted scientific "facts" and rejected all metaphysical systems, especially Christian revelation, and the Church's claim to dominate the mind.

(F.A.T.)

**Dilthey,** Wilhelm (1833–1911), German philosopher and historian. Best known for his writings on the theories of history and the human sciences, Dilthey also had a significant influence on the development of **hermeneutics** and **phenomenology**, literary criticism and the methodology of the social sciences. Viewing his overall philosophical task as a Critique of Historical Reason, Dilthey sought an epistemological grounding for the human sciences (*Geisteswissenschaften*), which include the humanities as well as the social sciences.

Dilthey's delimitation of the natural and human sciences is set forth in his landmark work, *Introduction to the Human Sciences* (1883), and subsequently elaborated in the "Ideas Concerning a Descriptive and Analytic Psychology" (1894). The natural and the human sciences are both empirical, but the former deal with the outer experience of nature, while the latter are based on inner, "lived" experience which provides a direct awareness of the human historical world. The distinction is ultimately epistemological; the difference between their tasks is characterized as that between explanation and understanding. The natural sciences seek causal explanations of nature – connecting the discrete representations of outer experience through hypothetical generalizations and abstract laws. The human sciences aim at an understanding (*Verstehen*) that articulates the fundamental structures of life given in lived experience. Finding lived experience to be inherently connected and meaningful, Dilthey opposed traditional atomistic and associationist psychologies and developed a descriptive psychology that **Husserl** recognized as anticipating phenomenological psychology.

Although Dilthey first thought that descriptive psychology could provide a neutral foundation for the other human sciences, in his later hermeneutical writings he rejected the idea of a foundational discipline or method. In the *Formation of the Historical World in the Human Sciences* (1910), he claims that all the human sciences are interpretive and mutually dependent. Hermeneutically conceived, understanding is a process of interpreting the "objectifications of life," the external expressions or manifestations of human activity and spirit. The understanding of others is attained through these common objectifications and not, as is widely thought, through empathy. Moreover, to fully understand myself I must observe the expressions of my life in the same way that I observe the expressions of others.

Whereas the natural sciences aim at ever more comprehensive generalizations, the human sciences place an equal value on the understanding of individuality and universality. Dilthey regards individuals as points of intersection of the general social and cultural systems in which they participate. Any psychological contribution to the understanding of human life and its expressions must be integrated into this more public framework. Although universal laws of history are rejected, the more systematic human sciences (e.g., economics, sociology) can establish uniformities limited to specific systems.

In his philosophy of life, Dilthey conceived of life as the nexus of all that is real. He focused on value, meaning and purpose as three of the principal categories of life, but maintained that there is an indeterminate number of categories available for reflection of life in general.

Such reflection receives its fullest expression in a *Weltanschauung* (world-view), an overall perspective on life encompassing the way we perceive the world, evaluate and respond to it. Dilthey distinguished three recurrent types of world-view in Western philosophy, religion and art: naturalism (e.g., **Hume**), the idealism of freedom (e.g., **Kant**), and objective idealism (e.g., **Hegel**).

[R.A.M.]

**Diogenes of Apollonia,** *see* Pre-Socratics.

**Diogenes,** son of Hicesias, lived in Greece in the fourth century B.C. A prominent citizen of Sinope, he was exiled about the middle of the fourth century, allegedly for defacing the debased currency then appearing in Sinope; thereafter he lived at Athens and Corinth, becoming the prototype of **Cynicism**. It is likely that he was influenced by some aspects of **Antisthenes'** teaching, although Antisthenes was probably dead before Diogenes reached Athens. There is thus a tenuous thread leading back to **Socrates**, and there is some point in the alleged remark of Plato, that Diogenes was a Socrates gone mad.

Virtue, which alone produced happiness, was achieved through the attainment of self-sufficiency, the means to which was freedom from any external family or public restriction or internal disturbance of desires, emotions or fears. By rejecting all property, external goods, conventional values, he reduced his needs and vulnerability to the barest natural minimum, retaining mastery of the kingdom which could not be taken from him – his own soul. His aim was to live in accordance with nature; everything else was convention of illusory value, against which he carried on uncompromising warfare, and he sought in his life and teaching to deface its currency in the eyes of others, as he and his father had defaced the debased currency at Sinope. As a practical ethic this required continual practice and training, both physical and mental. For example, he would embrace a bronze statue in winter to train the body in hardship and eradicate physical desire; he would court insult to test the subjugation of emotion in his mind. Indeed continual endurance of hardship, of which Heracles was the often quoted ideal, was a necessary concomitant of the stark poverty of the Cynic way of life. Diogenes' own life as a stateless beggar sleeping where he could in Athens, was a practical demonstration of this. Theoretical education and learning were despised. Possessed of a cutting wit and repartee, his attack on convention knew no restraint of fear, authority or decency, either in word or deed, as he deliberately went to extremes to underline his points; hence his nickname, the Dog, from which, in Greek, came the word Cynicism. He is unreliably credited with some written works, notably a *Republic* and some tragedies illustrating his philosophy.

(I.G.K.)

**Diogenes Laertius,** *see* History of Philosophy.

**Dogmatism,** the opposite of **scepticism**.

**Dualism.** "Dualism" is the name for any system of thought which divides everything in some way into two categories or elements, or else derives everything from two principles, or else refuses to admit more or less than two substances or two kinds of substance. Although of course dualistic systems have to be justified by arguments, what leads some philosophers to dualism is the urge to tidy up and simplify our picture of the world, an urge which would drive them on to **monism** if they were not prevented by respect for some radical and irreducible difference which their dualism expresses. The **Pythagoreans** afford an early example of this blockage of the unifying tendency, in their case by a whole series of opposites, which they reduced in turn to two basic principles, the Limit and the Unlimited.

The term, which was introduced by Heyde about 1700 to cover such theological views as Manichaeism has the same ambiguities as monism, and can likewise be applied to at least three distinguishable and logically independent ontological views. The most outstanding and influential example of dualism, giving precise formulation to what is probably the common-sense view, and going back at least to **Anaxagoras**, is **Descartes'** division of the world into "extended substance" (matter) and "thinking substances" (minds); this kind of dualism might be called *attributive*, as claiming that there are two kinds of attributes and thus that all substances are of just two ultimate kinds. This distinguishes it from *substantial* dualism, the view that there are precisely two substances, which does not *by itself* have the same psychological attractiveness: for once admit that there is more than one substance, and it seems arbitrary not to admit several, unless the two admitted are of fundamentally different kinds. For the same reason, a third possibility, a *partial* dualism, claiming that regardless of the number of ultimate kinds of substance some one kind has just two substances belonging to it, is unattractive. It was in fact rejected by Descartes, who allowed only one substance in the material realm, but in the mental realm a plurality of them.

The term "dualism" can also be applied rather more loosely to philosophical systems which have as their core some important opposition, as in **Plato** between the world perceived by the senses and the world of Forms known by the mind, or in **Kant** the distinction between the phenomenal and the noumenal world. See also **Philosophy of Mind**.

(R.HALL)

**Ducasse,** Curt John (1881–1969), American philosopher, born in France, and educated in France, England and USA. His most important book was *Nature, Mind and Death* (1951). In Part I he discussed the subject matter and method of philosophy, holding that philosophical questions are essentially semantical and about the analysis of value-terms. Part II analysed such fundamental categories as those of substance and causation. Part III defended a view of perception according to which what is sensed is an "internal accusative" of the sensations

and that perception proper always involves interpretation, conscious or unconscious. Part IV contained Ducasse's discussion of the relation of mind to body and of the possibility of survival; after a general discussion of traditional views and their difficulties and of the empirical evidence for survival he tentatively suggested a modified version of metempsychosis as the most plausible hypothesis.

(J.O.U.)

**Duhem,** Pierre (1861–1916), French philosopher of science, was one of the outstanding French theoretical physicists of his generation on account of his austere and rigorous analysis of thermodynamics. He also established himself as a leading historian of science in a series of monumental investigations of the mechanics, astronomy and physics of medieval and renaissance precursors of "the scientific revolution". However it is chiefly because of his book *The Aim and Structure of Physical Theory* (1906) that he is still discussed by philosophers of science. As a young student he was at first attracted by the idea of science discovering real mechanism hidden behind phenomena, but this ambition was severely battered by his later teachers and he began instead to pursue the Newtonian ideal of inferring laws by induction from experiment. However when Duhem himself came to teach he found it impossible to sustain this approach and was driven to adopt the positivist and conventionalist stance which characterizes his mature thought. This implied that no metaphysical conclusions can be derived from physics; but, as an orthodox Catholic, Duhem maintained a philosophically **realist** view of theology. He gives his name to the "Duhem-Quine argument" according to which no scientific hypothesis can ever be conclusively refuted, since one can always adjust other hypotheses to protect it.

[J.H.P.]

**Dummett,** Michael (1925– ), English philosopher of mathematics, based at Oxford. He regards the construction of a systematic theory of meaning as the main task of philosophy, if not the sole legitimate one, and takes his inspiration from **Frege**. (Dummett's works include *Frege: Philosophy of Language*, 1973; second edition 1981, and *The Interpretation of Frege's Philosophy*, 1981, as well as the article on Frege in this Encyclopedia.) However, he rejects Frege's central belief that mathematical and logical rationality presuppose a "platonic" **realism**; see **Analytic Philosophy**.

[J.R.]

# E

**Edwards,** Jonathan (1703–1758), born in South Windsor, Connecticut, is now widely recognized as one of the most brilliant and original philosophical minds produced by America. He stood midway between the Calvinist theological mind of the seventeenth century and the Lockean **empiricist** temper of the eighteenth century. In his own time the significance of his major writings was missed on both sides. For close to two centuries his reputation was confined to the field of specialized theology and distorted by failure to grasp his central philosophical intent. Not until the twentieth century was his role in the drama of eighteenth-century thought reconsidered and gradually understood.

The traditional conception of Edwards was that of a man who in early life showed great promise as a philosopher steeped in the writings and the spirit of Newton and **Locke**; who later as a Calvinist minister sought to revive the fundamental axioms of Calvinism at a time when they were losing their hold on English-speaking minds; who therefore must be considered as an "anachronism" smothering his latent philosophical promise with Hell-fire sermons and esoteric treatises which sought to justify them.

A proper understanding of Edwards will recognize that all of his mature writings are careful and brilliant attempts to defend and reinterpret the fundamental axioms of Calvinism in terms precisely of that deep understanding and profound grasp of the spirit of Newton and Locke

which he never for a moment abandoned. He did straddle, as it were, an impossible fence. His subtle revision of the import of Calvinism made him unpopular among the defenders of the orthodoxy he was trying to save; his use of the new philosophical spirit to revive religious orthodoxy at all made him anathema to the run-of-the-mill proponents of the secularized spirit of the "Enlightenment". The fact remains that Edwards' major writings show a deeper understanding of the new philosophical insights of the eighteenth century than do the commonly adulated works of later Americans such as Franklin and Paine.

His major works were three; and each was designed to reinterpret a fundamental Calvinist axiom in the light of Newton and Locke. The axiom of Determinism is defended in the treatise on *Freedom of the Will* (1754). This treatise remains one of the classic defences of determinism. The axiom of depravity is defended in the treatise on the *Nature of True Virtue* (1765). The brilliance of Edwards' revision of the concept of depravity is difficult to overestimate. The argument rests throughout upon a thoroughgoing Lockean psychological analysis; its logic is impeccable, and one is struck by the independence of the argument from any appeal to theological matters such as the story of the Fall of Man. The central theological axiom of Calvinism – the axiom of God's omnipotence and inscrutability – recurs in all of Edwards' writings; but the pivotal document in which he takes his stand on the source of man's knowledge of God is the treatise on the *Religious Affections* (1746). Here too Edwards' argument is based upon a thoroughgoing Lockean empiricist psychology. His defence of the emotive basis of religious experience (designed as a defence of the Great Awakening) is one of the most forward-looking documents of the time. The late eighteenth century committed the great mistake of proclaiming an utterly unempirical "argument from design" as the touchstone of empiricism in religion. Edwards on the contrary saw clearly that the only consistent way to endorse empiricism in religion is to endorse mysticism. The empirical demand is the demand that you have experience of that whereof you speak; and if you speak of God this is a demand for the mystical strain. .Edwards' defence of the thesis that such experiences are always essentially emotive in character is an astonishing foreshadowing of claims usually associated with William James' monumental *Varieties of Religious Experience* published nearly two centuries later.

(J.W.S.)

**Eleatics**: the name given to the philosopher **Parmenides** and his follower **Zeno**, who lived in Elea (a Greek colony in southern Italy) and argued that reality must be single and unchanging, and by implication that the plural sense-world is illusory. Also counted as an Eleatic, because he accepted these views, was Melissus of Samos, who flourished c. 440 B.C.; he amended Parmenides by arguing that Being was infinite, not finite, and incorporeal. He also produced an explicit argument against sensation: we perceive plurality, yet we also perceive that things change, which on Eleatic premises is logically impossible; therefore perception is false, and if there are many they must be of the same kind as the Eleatic One. This conclusion may have aided **Leucippus** in his conception of **atomism**. **Xenophanes**, too, was often regarded in antiquity as an Eleatic, because of the superficial resemblance of his one god with Parmenides' one Being; but Parmenides' logical process of inference is so radically different from Xenophanes' reversal of Homeric anthropomorphism that there were probably no close links between the two thinkers. The Eleatics – their leader, Parmenides, in particular – had a profound effect on the development of Pre-Socratic thought. The material **monism** of the Milesians and the structural monism of **Heraclitus** were replaced by systems that envisaged a plurality of essentially immutable elements, and which had now to face the question of the validity of sensation. See also **Pre-Socratics**.

(G.S.K.)

**Emotivism**: the doctrine, associated chiefly with **logical positivism**, that value judgments in general, and ethical judgments in particular, express emotions rather than representing facts; see **Empiricism**, **Ethics**.

**Empedocles** of Acragas in Sicily, flourished c. 450 B.C. He was a doctor, also a keen democrat; his mystical claims (e.g. that he was a god, having previously been "a boy, a girl, a bush and a bird and a dumb fish in the sea") gave rise to extravagant biographical inventions. To meet **Parmenides'** dilemma he claimed in his physical poem "On Nature" that apparent coming-to-be and perishing were caused by the mixture and separation of eternally-existing "roots" or elements – fire, water, earth, and air (the corporeality of which Empedocles verified by observation). Attraction and repulsion of the roots were caused by specific motive agents, Love and Strife, which also possessed size and bulk. An equivalent to Parmenides' "sphere" of Beings was reproduced when Love permeated the roots and mixed them together; then Strife gradually entered the sphere which was described as a god and caused plurality to assert itself. Thus the senses, if properly used, were *not* necessarily deceptive; in fact sensation was caused by physical effluences from objects entering pores in the sense-organs and meeting with corresponding roots there; thus fire activates fire in the eye, in vision. Empedocles avoided the apparent coming-to-be of traditional cosmogonies by making the entry of Strife into the sphere merely one stage out of four in a never-ending cosmic cycle: domination of Love, entry and gradual increase of Strife, domination of Strife, entry of Love. Our world belongs to the second of these. Corresponding with the transitional stages were two evolutionary stages: when Love is in the ascendant, first disunited limbs, then monsters; when Strife increases, first "whole-natured forms", then our world. In a second poem, "Purifications", Empedocles described a personal cycle of innocence, pollution, fall, purification, and deification. Verbal resemblances with the physical poem suggest that this cycle had some correspondence with the cosmic one. Pollution is caused by bloodshed and strife, and leads to successive incarnations of the type also envisaged by **Pythagoreans** and Orphics. See also **Pre-Socratics**.

(G.S.K.)

**Empiricism.** In its ordinary use, the term "empiricism" (from the Greek "empeiria" = "experience") means the employment of methods based on practical experience, rather than on an accepted body of theory. But in philosophy the word is used only in a quite different, and technical, sense to refer to the philosophical theory that all knowledge is derived from experience. "Radical empiricism" was the name given by William **James** to his own version of this theory.

Empiricism has been developed mainly by a succession of British philosophers, of whom the most important are **Locke, Berkeley, Hume** and John Stuart **Mill**. Although such movements as **Encyclopedism** in France have been inspired by empiricist ideas, empiricism has never taken hold on the Continent, whereas in Britain it has been the dominant tradition in philosophy since the seventeenth century. Moreover, Continental empiricists, like the Frenchman **Condillac**, have always been directly or indirectly influenced by British philosophy.

The general principles of empiricism are opposed primarily to those of **rationalism**, and it was as a reaction against the systems of **Descartes, Spinoza** and **Leibniz** that modern empiricism originated. There are two central questions at issue between rationalists and empiricists. The first concerns **a priori** concepts (or "innate ideas" as they were misleadingly called in the seventeenth century), that is, ideas which, it is claimed, are not derived from sense-experience but independently produced by reason or intellect. Rationalists allow that some concepts are empirical (for example, that we derive our idea of redness from our experience of seeing red objects), but they maintain that our knowledge of the world also involves *a priori* concepts like those of cause and substance. It is fundamental to empiricism to deny the existence of such ideas. Empiricists

therefore argue either that allegedly *a priori* concepts can be analysed or broken down into a combination of simpler concepts derived from experience, or sometimes, and more radically, that they are not genuine concepts at all (for example, that "substance", as a metaphysical term, is simply a word to which no meaning can be assigned). The second dispute between rationalists and empiricists concerns *a priori* propositions or statements. It is generally agreed that all necessary truths are *a priori*, since we can learn from experience only what has been and is likely to be the case, not what *must* be so. Empiricists, who believe that we have no means of acquiring knowledge except through observation of what actually happens, contend that necessary truths are true by definition, or **analytic**. Rationalists, on the other hand, hold that some *a priori* statements are synthetic; that is, that they tell us something about the nature of the world. The assertion "every event must have a cause", for example, has been said to be a self-evident principle of this kind: *a priori* because it states a necessary connection, and synthetic because it is not simply true by definition (as "every *effect* has a cause" is). It is characteristic of empiricism to deny that reason can assure us of the truth of a genuinely synthetic statement and therefore that any proposition can be both *a priori* and synthetic.

As a result of their disagreement over these matters of principle, rationalists and empiricists have very different attitudes towards natural science and towards metaphysics. Rationalists have been inclined, broadly speaking, to think of beliefs based on experience as infected with error. For them, an understanding of the world is not to be gained through sense-perception, which is confused, but through metaphysical speculation. But precisely because metaphysics claims to give knowledge of a reality transcending experience, metaphysical inquiry depends upon our having *a priori* concepts. The empiricist tradition has therefore been antagonistic to metaphysics, and has set a high value on science as a means of acquiring knowledge. Hume described Newton as "the greatest and rarest genius that ever arose for the ornament and instruction of the species".

The solutions that empiricists offer to particular philosophical problems are essentially applications of the general principles that have been described. Hume's account of causation is a classical example of this. Hume is well aware that the relation of cause and effect presents crucial difficulties for empiricism and that he has to show that the idea of a cause originates in experience. He maintains, and in this he has been generally followed by later empiricists, that the causal connection between two events is, in effect, their regular succession, which is a matter of observation. He allows that the idea of a cause involves the idea of necessity, but this he also traces to its origin in experience. The repeated observation of B following upon A produces in us the habit of thinking of B when we perceive A. It is the experience of this habit of thought which is the source of our idea of necessity. "Necessity", Hume writes, "is something that exists in the mind, not in objects". He claims therefore to have refuted the rationalist account of causation as a necessary connection between objects, and to have shown that the idea of causation is a complex one that can be analysed into simpler elements (for example, the idea of regular sequence) each of which is derived from experience.

Another typical application of empiricist principles is to the theory of mathematics. Mathematics has always been regarded as a stronghold of rationalism, since on the face of it, mathematical propositions are *a priori* and synthetic. $7 + 5 = 12$: it seems both that this *must* be so and that it is a truth about objects that we can know in advance of any experience of them. This challenge has been met by empiricists in two ways, by denying either the *a priori* or the synthetic character of mathematics. The first course is that taken by J. S. Mill, who treats mathematics as a generalisation from experience. $7 + 5 = 12$ is, according to him, a law of nature based on observation. If, however, arithmetic is not necessarily true and is only established by experience, it remains possible that it might also be falsified by experience, difficult though it may be to imagine what that experience would be like. Few empiricists have been prepared to swallow

this paradox. They have usually taken the other alternative, of asserting that mathematics is analytic, not synthetic. According to this view, mathematical propositions are true by definition. $7 + 5 = 12$ is a necessary truth, only because we define "7", "+", "5", "=", and "12" in such a way as to make it so. Mathematics therefore does not, as rationalists have thought, give us any information about the nature of the world. Though there are considerable technical disagreements about the nature of mathematics between present day empiricists they all agree on the essential point that its truths are necessary only because they are in this way uninformative.

Empiricism is primarily a theory of knowledge, but its influence has also been considerable in the field of **ethics**. The reason for this is that empiricists have had to work out an ethical theory that is consistent with their general account of knowledge, rather than that they have always been especially interested in ethics. Moral concepts (like rightness, obligation, duty and so on) must, if they are genuine concepts and if empiricism is correct, be derivable from experience like any others. But according to rationalists this derivation is not possible. We can see that a man is behaving ungratefully, but we cannot similarly see that his ingratitude is wrong. Our idea of wrongdoing, it is said, is not based on experience, and we know that ingratitude is wrong only because reason intuitively grasps the *a priori* connection between these two ideas. The basic principles of morality are self-evident, in the sense that they neither can be, nor need to be, justified by argument or observation. The reply of empiricists in the eighteenth century to this intuitionist theory was, in Hume's words, that "morality is more properly felt than judged of". Moral ideas are derived from *inner* experience. We do not, admittedly, observe the wrongness of an action, but we *feel* it, and it is this feeling that we put into words when we say that the action is wrong. (See Hume's *Treatise of Human Nature*, Book 3, Part I). This point of view (often called the moral sense theory) was characteristically combined in eighteenth-century empiricism with the theory that our only duty is to produce as much happiness as possible (utilitarianism). Although utilitarianism is not an essential part of empiricist ethics, this combination is an understandable one. For, since they do not believe that moral principles are self-evident, it is natural for empiricists to hold that morality is justified by its tendency to bring about human happiness, which makes an appeal to each person's instinctive feelings of sympathy. Contemporary empiricists have come to realize that it is unsatisfactory to treat moral judgments as statements about feelings, and to regard ethics as a branch of the science of human nature, in the manner of Hume. They have therefore tended to argue that moral principles do not assert *a priori* truths, because they assert nothing, their function being solely the practical one of influencing behavior. It has been suggested that moral judgments are really commands (for example, "stealing is wrong" = "do not steal") or that they are expressions of feeling (not *statements about* feelings) having no objective validity. This "emotive theory of ethics" rests on a naive view of language, and it has been widely criticized.

If the empiricism of recent times is compared with that of the eighteenth and nineteenth centuries the most significant advance that can be seen to have been made is the clear separation of logical from psychological issues. The older empiricists were primarily interested in problems, of the kind that have been mentioned, about the analysis of concepts and the logical status of propositions, rather than in psychological problems about the origin of ideas. Nevertheless they were often confused about the questions they were debating and wrote as if their intention was to give a natural history of the mind. Hume and J. S. Mill, for example, felt themselves to be committed to an atomistic psychology, which explained all mental activity in terms of the association of ideas. Modern empiricists, on the other hand, recognise that their philosophy is compatible with any psychological theory that is based on observation, and leave psychology to the psychologists.

The establishment of empiricism purely as a thesis about the logical structure of knowledge

has been an important stimulus to the development of mathematical logic. It has also led to the conception of philosophy as the **analysis** of concepts and propositions, and therefore to an increased hostility to speculative philosophy and to metaphysics in particular. This hostility found its most extreme expression in **logical positivism**, advocated in the twenties and thirties principally by the group of philosophers known as the **Vienna Circle**. The positivists held that apart from the formal or analytic statements of mathematics and logic, no statements were significant except those which could be verified by observation. Metaphysical and theological assertions were consequently rejected, not as unproved, but "nonsensical" or "meaningless".

(E.B.)

**Encyclopedists.** The first intention of the Paris printer and publisher, Le Breton, was to translate the English *Cyclopaedia* of Ephraim Chambers (1727), but when **Diderot** and d'Alembert became co-editors the scope was enlarged until it became the *Encyclopédie ou Dictionnaire Raisonné des Sciences, des Arts et des Métiers* (1751–65). This great work in seventeen folio volumes was a monument to the erudition of the French intellectuals or *philosophes*, intended to provide information on every branch of knowledge, and giving special attention to the application of science to industry, trade and the arts.

Chief among the contributors was Diderot, who, besides having the general direction of the work, wrote an immense number of articles – on religion, ancient history, political theory (his article "Political Authority" is the most outspoken pronouncement in the whole work), philosophy, beer; and he also wrote copiously on the applied arts. D'Alembert, who was a member of the *Académie des Sciences* before he was thirty, wrote his celebrated "Preliminary Discourse", in which he traced the growth of knowledge from the beginning. Although chiefly concerned with geometry, mathematics and the sciences, he wrote the notorious article "Geneva" in 1757 which provoked the ire of the local clergy (identified therein with

Socinianism) and also the wrath of **Rousseau**, because d'Alembert had deplored the absence of a theatre in Geneva. This called forth Rousseau's indignant "Letter to d'Alembert". Disgusted with the outcry over this article and for other reasons of prudence and ambition, d'Alembert withdrew his collaboration at the end of 1757, leaving Diderot to carry on alone. Luckily Diderot's devoted friend, the Chevalier de Jaucourt, who had studied medicine in Geneva, Leyden and Cambridge, then became the general factotum of the work, and wrote articles on the widest variety of topics – philosophy (he had previously published a study of **Leibniz**), politics and literature, war, despotism, government and monarchy etc. Some critics claim that he was as important and as devoted to the enterprise as Diderot himself.

Rousseau wrote on music, but a more important contribution on "Political Economy" foreshadowed some of the theories of *The Social Contract*. Later, Rousseau came to regard the *Encyclopédie* as the work of the devil; he quarrelled not only with d'Alembert but with Diderot as well, and he fiercely abused all the philosophers and their works. The fifth volume opened with a notable tribute to Montesquieu, author of *The Spirit of the Laws* (1748), whose influence on the *Encyclopédie* was all-pervading. None the less, Montesquieu stood aloof; refusing to write on "Despotism" and "Democracy", he sent an incomplete article on "Taste", which was finished by Voltaire. Nor did the latter, despite interest and encouragement, contribute much. His articles are more important for their style than for their content, the article "History" excepted. Voltaire's friend, Marmontel, an indifferent novelist and playwright, contributed articles on literature.

Although the editors claimed that the *Encyclopédie* had attracted the most eminent contributors, two outstanding personalities found its atmosphere too bellicose: Buffon, author of the great *Natural History* in forty-four volumes, who may have contributed one article on "Nature"; and Duclos, a court historian, who wrote only on "Declamation" and "Etiquette". The King's physician, Quesnay, contributed two outstanding articles, "Farmers" and

"Seeds", products of physiocratic principles. From the same physiocratic school of thought came Turgot, famous later as Intendant and Minister. He wrote on "Fairs and Markets" condemning barriers to free enterprise; on "Foundations", showing the disadvantage of unchangeable bequests; a learned article on "Etymology" and another on "Existence". The German Baron d'Holbach wrote on mineralogy and chemistry, and there are grounds for attributing to him the entry on "Representatives" which maintains that a state cannot be prosperous and happy unless the king invites the cooperation of all elements of the population. For the rest, his general philosophy is contained in his notorious *System of Nature* (1770) where he insisted that kings are the defenders of the liberty of their subjects. Holbach was an atheist and as such was attacked by Voltaire.

The great majority of the articles are factual and objective, written by specialists without an axe to grind. Other articles, however, were more barbed. Whereas opinions on politics were moderate, for republicanism had no adherents, contributions connected with philosophy (deeply permeated with Lockean empiricism) and religion were double-edged, despite orthodox professions. For instance, under "cowl", the absence from monasteries of "sound philosophy" is deplored, and under "Encyclopedia" occurs the bland statement that the contribution of the Sorbonne to knowledge will be theology, sacred history, and the history of superstitions. One needs to read between the lines and to follow the cross-references to see how sceptical these articles are about religion. Because of this attitude the *Encyclopédie* was suspect from the beginning, and in the course of its chequered career it came into conflict with the Jesuits, the Jansenists, the Sorbonne, the Pope, the Parlement, the devout party at Court, and private enemies. The first suppression in 1752, thanks to Jesuit intrigue, was repeated in 1759, owing largely to the outcry against the materialsim of *On the Mind*, a work of Helvétius, a friend but not a contributor. The public prosecutor assumed that this work was the very quintessence of *philosophe* doctrine and it was condemned to be burned. Its fate brought about the second suppression of the *Encyclopédie* but in neither case was the ban enforced for long, and the work went on despite hostility. In 1757 a lawyer called Moreau published a pamphlet in which the *philosophes* were called *Cacouacs*, a pejorative definition which caused them intense annoyance. In 1760 Pallissot pilloried the *philosophes*, chiefly Diderot and Rousseau, in a comedy of that name. Other enemies were Boyer, a former bishop, and the poet Le Franc de Pompignan, both of whom were devastatingly ridiculed by Voltaire. But the man who gave most annoyance was Freron a gadfly or rather hornet journalist (Frelon) whom Voltaire subjected to petulant but ineffective criticism.

Throughout these vicissitudes, Diderot stood firm. Thanks to his efforts the seventeenth and final volume of text appeared in 1765, and the indispensable eleven volumes of plates were complete by 1772. Diderot's avowed aim, which was "to change accepted habits of thought" was in large measure realized.

(F.A.T.)

**Engels,** Friedrich (1820–1895), German socialist, was the friend, collaborator and financial supporter of **Marx** during his residence in Britain. To Engels rather than to Marx we owe the exposition of the fundamental tenets of **dialectical materialism**. His most important philosophical works are *Anti-Dühring* (1878) and *Ludwig Feuerbach* (1886), in which he treats of materialism and **idealism**, dialectical and mechanistic **materialism** and the materialist reorientation of Hegelian **dialectics**; and *The Dialectics of Nature* which contains his fullest statement of the laws of development, but which is incomplete and was not published till 1925. Engels was also co-author with Marx of the *Manifesto of the Communist Party*.

(J.O.U.)

**Epictetus** (*c.* 55–*c.* 135 A.D.), a **stoic** of Hierapolis, Phrygia. A freed slave of Nero's secretary, and pupil of the stoic Musonius, he set up a school in Nicopolis when Domitian banished the philosophers from Rome in 89. His stoicism underlines freedom, providence, practicality, humanity. A man must choose between slavery to externals and freedom in the inviolability of his moral purpose, which alone is completely in his power, unassailable by all external ills. No man can be injured by another, he can only injure himself. For the governing, indeed divine, principle in man is his moral will; hence his sole active duty is to exercise it rightly, and by recognizing the rule of divine providence in the universe of which he is an integral part, to accept God's will. Impatient of academic theorising, he concentrated on a practical ethic illustrated by everyday examples; **Socrates** and **Diogenes** were his heroes. His message was not, like that of many stoics, to an intellectual, social or governing élite, but to the common brotherhood of ordinary men. The humanity and nobility of his teaching shine in the *Manual* and four surviving books of lectures we have from the notes of his pupil Arrian. Failure is human and should not deter one from remaining intent on the ideal; only sham and pretence are denounced. His later influence on both pagan and Christian thought was widespread.

(I.G.K.)

**Epicurus** (342–270 B.C.), an Athenian citizen. He was brought up in Samos, returned to Athens for a short period of study as a young man, and then spent some years in Asia Minor. He finally returned to Athens in about 306 B.C. where he set up his school in the garden where he taught until his death.

The modern notion of an Epicurean as a man given up to voluptuous high living is based on the slanders of later Greek writers and not on the life or teaching of Epicurus.

Epicurus is best know for his **hedonism** and **atomism**; yet in neither field was he original. The only contribution that he made to the theory of atomism, the view that atoms originally fell in a kind of rain in parallel courses but that some few atoms swerved by a free choice, thus setting up collisions is a regression rather than an improvement. And the essentials of the ethics of Epicurus can be found in the ethical fragments of **Democritus**.

Epicurus was unoriginal in theoretical matters because his interest was essentially practical; he was a secular evangelist who had to preach the secret of true happiness. Thus Epicurus taught the atomic theory because men were haunted with fear of gods and demons, terrified of death and the torments of the underworld, and thus unhappy. The mechanistic doctrines of atomism, which denied to the gods any control of nature and treated the soul as a concourse of atoms which was dissolved at death, were an antidote to these terrors. But a purely mechanistic atomism might suggest that man was a mere machine; the doctrine of the voluntary atomic swerve was an antidote to this danger; "it were better to follow the myths about the gods than to become a slave to the destiny of the natural philosophers".

Epicurus' moral views have been much misunderstood and misrepresented. The theoretical basis is that pleasure alone is good and always good. It consists in the driving out of pain, and when pain is ended pleasure can only be varied but not increased. Pleasure is either bodily, perfect health being its highest form, or mental, when it is freedom from fear and anxiety. But though all pleasure is good in itself some pleasure brings pain with it as an inevitable consequence; therefore not all pleasure is desirable. Therefore wisdom is of the greatest importance since it is by wisdom that we are able to make the best choice of pleasures.

But Epicurus was much more concerned with the wise choice of pleasures than with theory. In the letter to Menoecus he says: "When we maintain that pleasure is an end, we do not mean the pleasures of profligates and those that consists in sensuality . . . but freedom from pain in the body and from trouble in the mind. For it is not continuous drinkings, nor the satisfaction of lusts, . . . but sober reasoning, searching out the motives for all choice and avoidance." Pains of the mind are much more important than those of the body, which are either bearable or produce death, which is no evil. Death "is nothing to us, since so long as

we exist death is not with us, but when death comes then we no longer exist." Moreover, though virtue is not in itself a good, no man can live the happy life unless he lives virtuously and the virtuous life is pleasant as such.

Epicurus believed in gods who did not control nature; they lived a life of infinite bliss which would be spoilt if they worried about human affairs. Epicurus practised a disinterested worship of the gods conceived as exhibiting the ultimate beatitude.

Epicurus' practical teaching is thus paradoxical. He is a theist who regards ordinary religion as evil; a hedonist who advocates a simple virtuous life of study; a supporter of virtue and the pursuit of truth who holds them to have no value in themselves. Epicurus seems to have endeavoured to live the life he preached; he gathered a simple community of disciples round him in his garden; we are told that "he exceeded all others in the bulk of his works", of which some seventy or eighty pages survive; and on his deathbed he spoke contemptuously of his severe pains as weighing nothing against his joy of mind.

Among the surviving writings of Epicurus may be singled out the letter to Herodotus containing the earliest extant complete account of the general atomic theory and the letter to Menoecus containing a short account of ethics. The philosophical poem by **Lucretius**, *De Rerum Natura*, also well brings out both the doctrines and the practical attitude of Epicurus.

(J.O.U.)

**Epistemology.** There is a wide-ranging, loosely knit set of philosophical problems concerning such notions as those of knowing, perceiving, feeling sure, guessing, being mistaken, remembering, finding out, proving, inferring, establishing, corroborating, wondering, reflecting, imagining, dreaming and so on. This part of philosophy is often called the Theory of Knowledge, or Epistemology – the latter word deriving from the Greek *Episteme* = knowledge or science.

Some of the problems revolve around the notion of a science, in the sense in which we take astronomy to be a science, but astrology not. A fairly typical problem of this kind is the problem why in pure **mathematics** there are conclusive proofs of theorems, when no such demonstrable certainties can be found or even looked for in, for example, history or medicine. It would be absurd for a mathematician to rest content with mere plausible conjectures or even with highly probable hypotheses. Scientists of other sorts seem not be in a position to aspire higher than high probabilities. We incline to say that a body of truths ranks as a real science only when these are conclusively established; and then we find ourselves forced to say that, judged by this rigorous standard, even physics and chemistry are not really sciences; and this conclusion conflicts badly with our ordinary ideas.

Other problems in the Theory of Knowledge centre not upon the notion of a science, but upon the notions of our personal investigatings, inferrings, perceivings, rememberings, imaginings, and so on. How can I tell for certain whether the stick half immersed in water is bent or not? How can I tell for certain whether I really recollect a past event or am merely imagining it, and whether I am now awake or dreaming? Might I not be the victim of one continuous illusion?

Whatever sorts of things we may want to find out, our attempt may fail in one of two ways. We may be simply baffled, or we may get something positively wrong. We can be stumped or we can make mistakes in calculating, in counting, in reasoning, in visual estimates of speeds and distances, in recognizing people or places, in recollecting, as well as in more executive things like spelling, aiming and treating the sick. What safeguards have we against mistakes? How, if at all, can we ever know anything? For in knowing, unlike believing, surmising and feeling confident, we cannot be wrong.

When we consider conflicting opinions about what exists and happens in the world around us, e.g. about the relative heights of two church-steeples or about the migration-dates of cuckoos, we think we could decide between the true and the mistaken opinion by, in the one

case, simply measuring the heights of the two steeples, and in the other case by observing the arrivals and departures of cuckoos for a number of years in succession. But then we have to face the fact that there are mistakes of measurement and even mishearings of the first cuckoo. How could we decide between conflicting measurements or between conflicting reports of birdwatchers? At this point we are inclined to say that the ultimate decision, if only we could attain it, would be given by sense impressions unadulterated by any assumptions, guesses or expectations – by pure hearings, seeings or tastings in which there is not yet any place for slips or misjudgments. Here perhaps we have the absolutely firm foundation on which we might build knowledge of the world around us. The difference between having knowledge of something in the world around us and merely having a fallible opinion about it would be that the former would be at all points supported by sense-impressions, where the latter, though suggested by them, would be at best only partly supported by them. Where I am or may be mistaken, I have let my imagination jump ahead of the required impressions.

This sort of account of the difference between knowledge and fallible opinion will not be applicable inside the fields of purely abstract truths and falsehoods, like those of pure mathematics; nor yet inside some other fields, like those of ethics. Nor can my knowledge about my present wishes, fears, imaginings and broodings rest on the support of what I see with my eyes or taste with my tongue. It is for our knowledge only of what exists and happens in the world surrounding us, as well as in our own bodies, that sense-impressions, it seems, furnish the granite foundations.

In every case in this field where we would normally claim to be not merely guessing or believing something, but to have discovered or made certain of it, the fact which we claim to know goes beyond any particular momentary visual or auditory impression. If I assert that the cuckoo has arrived, I am asserting more than that at a certain moment I heard a noise of a certain sort. How then can we go beyond our present impressions and still sometimes claim to know? The natural answer to give is that we *infer* from e.g. the sound that we have heard to the ulterior conclusion that the cuckoo has arrived. Our knowledge of the world around us, together with our mere beliefs and conjectures about this world, are all conglomerations of interlocking conclusions inferred, sometimes legitimately, sometimes riskily and sometimes illegitimately from our impressions. Knowledge, unlike belief and conjecture, would be the product solely of legitimate and riskless inferences. But then what, if anything, can guarantee our inferences themselves against being mistaken? Even if the impressions from which we infer are exempt from slips, still the inferences that we draw from them are not so exempt.

If we knew, somehow, from the start some completely exceptionless causal laws, to the effect that whenever such and such a sequence of sense-impressions is had, then such and such other sense-impressions will always follow, then in any particular case we could, without risk of error, infer from the sense-impressions of the present moment to their successors in the next few moments. But we do not start off with any such knowledge. If we get bits of such knowledge, we get them late in the day, after a great deal of observation and experimentation. We discover the ways in which things always or sometimes happen only by finding them happening and collating our findings; and even then the laws and regularities that at any particular time we claim to have ascertained are always subject to subsequent correction. Nature is never without her surprises. The unpredicted sometimes happens and the predicted sometimes fails to happen. So it begins to look as if knowledge about the world around us, going beyond our impressions of the moment, cannot be got at all. For it would have to be knowledge by inference; but we possess, to start with, no warrant to make any such inferences. If we make jumps beyond our present impressions, we can have, to start with, no warrants for making them; and even if they happen to turn out right, this, by itself, cannot justify us in making the same jump on the next similar occasion. One lucky guess may be succeeded by another lucky guess. But we have no reason

to expect it, however much we, like gamblers, are irrational enough to trust that our successes will continue.

So far we have been not expounding but rather reconstructing a line of thought that was operative in especially **Locke, Berkeley** and **Hume**. We have contrasted our fallible perceptions and inferences with knowledge of what exists and happens in the world around us, with the disappointing upshot that this knowledge seems to be forever out of reach. Those very matters of everyday fact which we are inclined to adduce as obvious instances of things known and not merely guessed or opined – such as that the cuckoo has reached England, or that this church-steeple is taller than that one – seem unable to live up to their promise. The granite foundation of mistake-proof sense-impressions seems unable to carry any mistake-proof superstructure. Perhaps all that I can know from perception is that I am at this moment seeing such and such colours, smelling such and such smells, and hearing such and such noises, and these seen colours and heard noises are untrustworthy clues, if they are clues at all, to what exists or happens in the world around us – if there is such a world.

Considerations like these have led many thinkers to reverse the whole direction of the inquiry. Knowledge, as opposed to guesswork and opinion, is to be found where the sciences at their peak are to be found. What is known to some and is in principle knowable to all is any body of truths conclusively established by the rigorous methods of true science. We can get beyond guesswork and fallible opinion to knowledge by operating as geometricians and arithmeticians operate, namely by pure thought, not vitiated by the deliverance of our senses. Where we can calculate and demonstrate we can know. Where we can only observe and experiment we cannot know. No set of sense-impressions can yield knowledge. Only by exercises of pure thought can we ascertain truths. In the most exacting sense of the word "science" there cannot be empirical sciences, but only purely ratiocinative sciences. Holders of this kind of view are called "**rationalists**". This programme leaves us discontented. We object that even granting that in pure mathematics we can discover uncontradictable truths, still these truths are bound to be completely abstract truths. Pure geometry cannot tell us the positions or dimensions of actual things in the world, but only, for example, that *if* there is something in the world possessing certain dimensions, *then* it has certain other dimensions. Geography could get nowhere without geometry, but geometry by itself cannot establish the position or even the existence of a single hill or island. Truths of reason win the prize of certainty only at the cost of being silent about what, if anything, actually exists or happens. Pure reason can arrive at uncontradictable truths, but none of these truths of reason can ever also be or yield truths of fact. We cannot learn merely from the theorems of Euclidean geometry or from the formulae of algebra whether Ptolemaic or Copernican astronomy is true, or even whether there exist any stars at all.

If these attainable certainties are, by themselves, too factually empty to yield knowledge of the actual world, and if sense-impressions, by themselves, are too anarchic to yield reliable inferences to what exists and happens in the actual world, there seems to remain just one escape-route from the depressing conclusion that we cannot possibly know a single bit of what we most want to know. This escape-route was the one first suggested by **Kant**. Knowledge of what exists and happens must have for its foundation not just the formal and therefore uncontradictable truths of pure reason, nor just the uninterpreted and therefore mistake-proof impressions of the senses, but the truths of reason as the principles organizing the sense-impressions, and the sense-impressions as the concrete material to be organized by the truths of reason. It is the application of the formal certainties of the abstract sciences to what we get by sheer seeing, hearing, etc., that enables us first to make anything at all out of our impressions, and then to sift out what really does exist and happen from what we precariously and often mistakenly suppose to exist and happen. We continue, of course, to be the frequent dupes of illusions and precipitate

assumptions. But we know in principle how to check and correct them. We know the methods of making certain; and the principles of our procedures of making certain are the abstract truths of pure reason being put to work as our canons of objectivity in our experimental investigation of the world around us. Pure reason tells us no matters of fact. But it does provide, so to speak, the acid for our acid tests. When we progress beyond the infantile stage of mere sentience to the stage when we try to ascertain things, our investigations begin to be controlled not just by an Utopian ideal of mistake-proof knowledge, but by operative, though initially inarticulate procedures of testing. We begin to look, feel and listen experimentally, methodically and suspiciously. Though we make plenty of mistakes, we begin to take cautionary steps to prevent them and remedial steps to rectify them. We become alive to the contrast between "real" and "apparent" as we master the manifold techniques of deciding between them. We now begin to use our eyes, fingers and ears with some degree of judiciousness, and our seeings and hearings are now exercises not only of our senses but also of our wits. For our still frequent perceptual mistakes, e.g. for our misestimates, misrecognitions and non-discriminations, we properly confess to having been, not deaf or blind, but silly. Perception calls not only for sentience but also for rationality, though not, save in unusual circumstances, for explicit ratiocinations.

The possibility of mistakes always exists; but the possibility of detecting, correcting and forestalling mistakes also always exists. To be judicious is not indeed to be immunized against mistakes, but it is to know how to forestall and correct them. What exists and happens in the world around us is, in principle, ascertainable to creatures who possess both Sentience and Reason, i.e. to creatures who can examine judiciously.

It is important to be on one's guard against a tendency, deep-seated in all of us, to think of people as if they were, like large stores, divided up into departments. We tend to speak as if a person consisted, somehow, of one internal employee or agent called his "Reason", of another called his "Memory", of a third called his "Imagination", of a fourth called, in the plural, his "Senses", or in the singular, his "Sight", his "Hearing", and so on. Now we can indeed properly *distinguish* these and many other human capacities. My memory may be deteriorating with advancing age, while my sight and hearing remain as good as before, and my ability to calculate or argue may even be improving. The lessons, stimulations and exercises which develop the powers of the young musician are not at all like those which develop the powers of the young engineer or geometrician – or, of course, of the young swimmer or skater. The danger is that we may pass from correctly distinguishing, say, the violinist's musical taste from his manual dexterity to personifying his Taste and his Manual Dexterity as separate, internal functionaries; and so puzzle ourselves by questions like, Are his Taste and his Dexterity related as Master to Servant, as Partner to Partner, or even as Rival to Rival?

Questions akin to these have often been raised in epistemology. People have asked whether our knowledge is given to us by our Intellect or by our Senses, and whether our mistakes are the faults of our Senses or of our Imaginations – as if these distinguishable capacities were themselves separate and semi-personal investigators quarrelling with one another inside our minds, and giving to us, their employers, conflicting reports about the world. But it is we ordinary people who try to ascertain things, and while we can certainly differ in eyesight, hearing, memory, judiciousness, inventiveness, and in our capacity to calculate, systematize, experiment, and so on, still these distinguishable abilities are not themselves observers, experimenters, calculators, theorists – or reporters. For the sake of picturesqueness we may say that our Eyes notify us of things; that our Ears or Memories have given us false reports; that our Reason has convinced us; that our Imagination has invented things; and even that our Consciences reproach us. But in serious, theoretical discussions we need to avoid such tempting personifications.

There is another model to which we are tempted to shape our theories of knowledge, what may be called the "Container-model". We are tempted to suppose that because, what is true, a person who at one date had not yet learned what pineapples taste like, or what "isosceles" means, may at a later date have learned these things, therefore there must by the later date have come to exist inside him something that can be called "the idea of the taste of a pineapple" and "the abstract idea, notion or concept of 'isosceles'"; somewhat as a bird-cage, formerly empty, may now house a canary, or as a picture-gallery may now have hanging on the wall a newly acquired picture. Using this Container-model, we are inclined to assume that in order to find out whether we have yet learned what pineapples taste like, or what "isosceles" means, we can and must, so to speak, peer inside our own minds in order to see whether the required idea or notion is there or not. Yet when we try so to peer inside our own minds, we find the task oddly baffling. What sort of an internal thing can I be looking for when I try to peer into my own mind for the abstract idea of "isosceles"? Certainly most people, though not all, can see in their minds' eyes things like familiar faces, houses and coloured or colourless patterns. But the taste of pineapple can naturally not be visualized at all, nor, by most people, even tasted "on the mind's tongue"; and what we visualize, if anything, when thinking of isosceles triangles, we visualize far too nebulously to meet the very precise requirements of Euclid's definition of an isosceles triangle. Yet very likely we can, without hesitation or error, discriminate the taste of pineapples from that of oranges, bananas, raspberries, etc., and we can decide, without hesitation or error, whether a triangular figure of certain dimensions is or is not isosceles. We have learned and we now know the taste of pineapples and what "isosceles" means, without there existing anything "inside our minds" to be found by inward peering.

To learn is indeed to acquire something or to come into possession of something. But what is acquired is not a thing but an ability, such as the ability to discriminate one taste from others, or the ability to classify geometrical figures, given their dimensions. When the schoolmaster wishes to find out whether a pupil has yet got the ideas of "square number" and "square root", he tests him on some arithmetical problems. The pupil has the ideas if he can tackle the problems; he has not got the ideas if he cannot yet tackle them. This is what it is to have the ideas.

It follows that the question How do we acquire our ideas? has as many different answers as there are different kinds of acquired mental abilities. We become familiar with the taste of pineapples by tasting not only pineapples but also many other kinds of fruit, by comparing these tastes and perhaps also, what is very difficult, by trying to describe in words these different tastes. We get the ideas of "square number" and "square root" only when, having learned to count, add, subtract, multiply and divide, we learn to multiply numbers by themselves and to work out what number, if any, multiplied by itself produces a given number. Correspondingly different kinds of accounts would have to be given of our acquisition of the ideas of "check-mate", "vacuum", "volt", "equator", "joke", "weed", "magneto", "risk", "virus", "dragon", "impossibility", "to-morrow", "debt", and so on. The doctrine that all our ideas come from sense-impressions, though unhelpful, is true enough if it means only that an infant born blind, deaf and without the senses of smell, taste and touch would never learn anything at all. It is false if it means that we get the idea of "square root", say, or "tomorrow" in just the same way as we get the idea of the "taste of pineapples", – and even this latter idea is got not just by having a certain taste-impression two or three times, but by having this impression, noticing it, comparing it with other tastes, and perhaps trying to describe in words the differences and similarities between these tastes. To have learned something, however primitive, from one's sense-impressions, is always more than just to have had those impressions. It is to have become able to cope, in some degree, with some kinds of task or problem, however elementary.

Epistemologists are commonly divided into **empiricists**, like **Locke**, **Berkeley** and **Hume**, and **rationalists**, like **Plato**, **Descartes**, **Spinoza** and **Leibniz**. The Empiricists are said to maintain that all our ideas come from experience; the rationalists that some of our ideas come not from experience but from reason or thought. But what does this apparent tug-of-war amount to? What does "come from" mean? What does "experience" mean? The technical phrase "sense-experience" is used to denote the mere having of sense-impressions. In this use, philosophers sometimes speak of a particular momentary sense-experience. In contrast with this technical idiom, we commonly use "experience" in another way, to cover continuous or repeated practice in something or accumulating familiarisation with it. Thus a chessplayer may have had much or little experience of match-playing in chess; but he would not describe himself as having had, on a particular afternoon, an experience of match-play. Experience, in this use, is what makes a person more expert than he had been. He has learned by having a certain amount of practice. He has tested and developed his abilities by exercising them. An experienced chairman is a man who has been in the chair a lot of times and in a lot of more or less difficult situations.

That all knowledge, e.g. all expertness and all competence, comes from experience, in the second sense, i.e. from training and practice, is an uncontentious truth – at least if safeguarded by the proviso that much of what we learn comes from instruction by others. But this is not at all the same thing as to say that whatever is known is inferred from premises provided, ultimately, by particular sense-experiences, though this is a theory maintained, with reservations, by some empiricist philosophers. The truth that we are not born already knowing anything, i.e. that no ideas are innate, is sometimes erroneously identified with the proposition that whatever we ascertain, when we do come to ascertain things for ourselves, we get by inference from our sense-impressions. But it is obvious that even if, what is questionable, we ascertain some facts by inference from our sense-impressions, when we have learned from training and practice to do this, still this account will not by itself cater for the enormous differences between, for example, ascertaining that the cuckoo has arrived, ascertaining that the king is check-mated, that the ship is now crossing the Equator, that there is a risk of thunder tomorrow, that a certain sentence is ungrammatical or that a certain metal object is a magneto. To ascertain things of these different kinds, we have to have acquired special abilities from special kinds of training and practice. The mere combination of good eyesight with good wits would not enable anyone to tell that the king is checkmated. He must also have studied and practised the game of chess.

Conversely, however, if an ultra-rationalist were to argue that since we cannot ascertain anything merely from having sense-impressions, therefore our only way of finding out what exists and happens is to do what Euclid did, namely to deduce theorems from axioms, without any recourse to observation or experiment, his position would also be untenable. If, which is rare, he holds that we are born knowing both these axioms and these techniques of deducing consequences, he is saying that we have masteries of things without ever having mastered them, i.e., that we know without having learned, and hence are experts, though totally inexperienced. But even if, as is more common, he allows that knowledge of abstract truths and of the techniques of deriving consequences from them itself requires experience, in the sense of training and practice, he still cannot show that this special kind of training and practice can replace the other special kinds of training and practice which make us more or less experienced observers and experimenters – or, for that matter, the other special kinds of training and practice which make us more or less experienced draughtsmen, speakers or dancers. The experience which is omitted from the theories of the empiricists is the experience which is omitted from the theories of the rationalists. Craving for something to avert the possibility of mistakes, the one finds its haven of safety in uncorrupted sense-impressions, the other in uncorrupted ratiocination. But the successful investigator is he who has made sure, not he who has remained in safety.

Where mistakes are possible, the avoidance, detection and correction of them is possible. Knowledge comes not by some immunization against the chance of error, but by precautions against possible errors – and we learn what precautions to take by experience i.e. training and patience. It is the expert, not the innocent, who knows.

To take a concrete example. If we ask how anyone can tell for certain whether the king is checkmated, the right answer would be that this can be ascertained by a spectator who has adequate eyesight and uses his eyes; has adequate wits and uses them, i.e. is not absent-minded or distracted, but is attending to the game; and lastly who has become, through training and practice in the game, expert enough to consider possibilities and to eliminate them. But if, instead, we asked whether the checkmate is ascertained by the spectator's Reason or by his Senses, and whether he was saved from being mistaken by the infallibility of his sense-impressions or by the uncontradictability of his formal principles, we should have debarred ourselves from getting a sensible answer, since these questions, unless taken as merely picturesque, are themselves not sensible questions. The spectator was not saved from making mistakes; he took good care not to make them. He was not notified by reports from his Intellect or by reports form his Senses that the king was checkmated; he found it out by visually studying the chessboard with his wits about him. He knew what to look for, since he had previously learned by training and practice how to play chess and how to follow games played by others.

Similarly, if asked whether the spectator has the abstract idea of "checkmate", we need to construe the question as asking whether he has learned and still remembers what it is for a king to be checkmated, and whether, therefore, he can tell by suitably careful inspection whether at any particular point in any particular game the king is or is not checkmated. To this question the answer is obviously "yes". But if we construe the question as asking whether the spectator has something special in his mind's eye, like a clear or blurred picture of a checkmate, we should answer first that there could be no picture of what is common to all checkmates; and second that it does not matter what, if anything, he visualizes when he hears or uses the word "checkmate". What matters is whether he has learned what it is to checkmate, to be checkmated and decide on inspection that the king is, or is not, checkmated. If he has learned and remembers these things, then he has the idea of checkmate, whether he happens to visualize things or not. If he has not learned them or has forgotten them, then he has not got the idea, whatever he may happen to see in his mind's eye on hearing the word "checkmate". If we forswear the personification of capacities and forswear the Container-model, we shall not suffer much from dividedness of mind between Rationalism and Empiricism. Their tug-of-war lacks a rope.

(G.R.)

**Erigena,** John Scotus (*c.* 810–*c.* 877), also known as Eringena ("Irish born"). He left Ireland to live and work at the court of Charles the Bald, King of the West Franks.

In common with other Irish monks of the time Erigena knew some Greek and much of his work consisted in translating and commenting on Greek patristic writings. His chief philosophical work is, however, *Of the Division of Nature,* a sustained speculative treatise on the evolution of the universe in the **neoplatonic** style of Proclus. For its comprehensiveness and speculative power it stands unique in western thought, from the time of **Boethius** to that of **Anselm**.

Erigena begins from the principle that all that exists is a divine manifestation which is to be understood by a dialectical penetration of revelation. The dialectic consists in the application of the well-known neoplatonic method of division and analysis to the study of Nature.

So elaborated, Nature is subject to four main divisions: nature which creates but is not created, nature which creates and is created, nature which does not create but is created,

nature which neither creates nor is created. So all reality consists either of God (the uncreated) or of creatures which go forth from and return to God.

Being a Christian, Erigena tried to avoid the pantheistic conclusions of such a system by distinguishing the divine from the human as that which is not from that which is. Erigena had no immediate followers and his work exerted little historical influence. There is however, considerable systematic affinity between his speculations and later mysticism.

(J.G.D.)

**Ethics**. Out of the many sorts of inquiry for which the term "ethics" has at one time or another been used, three groups of questions may be selected as the most important to distinguish from one another: (1) *Moral questions*: for example, "Ought I to do that?"; "Is polygamy wrong?"; "Is Jones a good man?". In this sense "ethical" and "moral" mean much the same. (2) *Questions of fact about people's moral opinions*: for example, "What did Mohammed (*or* what does the British Middle Class, or what do I myself) in fact think (or say) about the rightness or wrongness of polygamy?" (3) *Questions about the meanings of moral words (for example, "ought", "right", "good", "duty"); or about the nature of the concepts or the "things" to which these words "refer"*: for example, "When Mohammed said that polygamy is not wrong, what was he saying?" These three sorts of questions being quite distinct, the use of the word "ethics" to embrace attempts to answer all three is confusing, and is avoided by the more careful modern writers. No generally accepted terminology for making the necessary distinctions has yet emerged; but in this article we shall distinguish between (1) morals, (2) descriptive ethics and (3) ethics, corresponding to the three sorts of questions listed above. The case for confining the word "ethics" (used without qualification) to the third sort of question is that ethics has usually been held to be a part of philosophy, and the third group of questions, which are analytical or logical inquiries, or, as older writers might say, metaphysical ones, is much more akin than the first two groups to other inquiries generally included in philosophy. Thus ethics (in the narrow sense) stands to morals in much the same relation as does the **philosophy of science** to science. The student of ethics will nevertheless have to get used to a variety of terminologies; he will find plain "ethics" used for what we have just called "morals" ("normative ethics" is another term used for this); and he will find, for what we have just called "ethics", the more guarded terms "the logic of ethics", "metaethics", "theoretical ethics", "philosophical ethics" and so on. Works called "ethics" usually contain questions and answers of all three kinds, and the student of ethics must be prepared to find in them ambiguous remarks in which it is' not clear *what* sort of question the writer is trying to answer. It is, for example, only too easy to confuse a moral statement with a descriptive ethical one, especially when one is talking about one's own moral views; but it is nevertheless vital to distinguish the moral judgment "It would be wrong to do that" from the descriptive ethical statement "I, as a matter of psychological fact, think that it would be wrong to do that". The first task, therefore, for anybody who takes up the subject, is to learn to distinguish these three types of questions from one another; and for this purpose the following rules may be found helpful. A writer is making a *moral* statement if he is thereby *committing* himself to a moral view or standpoint; if not (that is, if he is merely writing in a detached way about moral views which are or may be held by himself or other people), it is either a *descriptive ethical* or an *ethical* statement; and this is normally indicated by the form of the statement, the moral words being "insulated" by occurring inside a "that"-clause or quotation-marks. Which of the two it is can be decided in the following way: if the truth of the statement depends on what moral opinions are *actually held* by people, it is a *descriptive ethical* statement; but if its truth depends only on what is *meant* by certain words, or on *what people would be saying if* they voiced certain moral opinions, it is an *ethical* statement. Thus, for example, ethics in the narrow sense is concerned directly neither with

whether polygamy *is* wrong (a moral question) nor with whether anybody in fact thinks it is wrong (a descriptive ethical question) – though ethics may have a bearing on these two questions, as mathematics has on physics; it is concerned with the question "Precisely what is one saying if one says that polygamy is wrong?"

## 1. RELATIONS BETWEEN THESE INQUIRIES

Throughout the history of the subject, the chief incentive to the undertaking of all three sorts of inquiry has been the hope of establishing conclusions of the first kind (that is, moral conclusions) by means of a philosophical inquiry. It is from this motive that inquiries of the second and especially the third kinds have mostly been undertaken. Clearly the study of the meaning of the moral words is closely related to the study of what makes arguments containing them cogent or otherwise. One of the best ways of obtaining a clear view of the subject is to consider the mutual relations between these three kinds of inquiry, and the bearing that they can have on one another.

(1) *Descriptive ethics and morals.* Some writers have proceeded directly from descriptive ethical premises to moral (normative ethical) conclusions. For example, the Greek **hedonist** Eudoxus argued that since everyone thought pleasure to be the good, it must *be* the good. In a similar way some modern writers have held that the task of the moral philosopher – the utmost he can do by way of establishing moral conclusions – is to examine carefully the opinions that are accepted by his society or by himself and reduce them to some sort of system. This is to take received opinions as data, and to regard as established a moral system that can be shown to be consistent with them. This type of argumentation will not, however, appear convincing to anyone who considers the fact that a person (for example, in the ancient world) might have said "Everyone thinks that it is legitimate to keep slaves, but may it not be wrong?" Universal assent to a moral principle does not prove the principle; otherwise the moral reformer, who propounds for the first time a new moral principle, could

be put out of court all too easily. Still less does it follow, from the fact that some limited set of people hold some moral opinion, that that opinion is right.

(2) *Descriptive ethics and ethics proper.* The commonest way, however, in which it has been sought to bring descriptive ethics to bear on moral questions is not directly but indirectly. It has been thought that a descriptive ethical inquiry might lead to conclusions about the *meanings* of moral terms (conclusions, that is to say, in ethics proper); and that in turn these might be used to prove moral conclusions. Those who have argued in this way have been attracted by a seductive analogy between moral terms and other predicates and adjectives. For example, it might be held possible to prove in the following way, to anyone who disputed it, that post-boxes in England are red: we should first establish by observation that everybody says that things are red when they have a certain recognizable quality, and that they are not red when they do not have this quality; we should conclude from this, that "red" *means* "having this quality". This is the first step. We should then ask our disputant to observe that post-boxes in England have this same quality; and since we have already established that "having this quality" is just what "red" *means*, he can no longer deny that the post-boxes are red. It might be thought possible to use the same argument in ethics to prove, for example, that certain kinds of action are right. But unfortunately the analogy breaks down at both steps – at the step from descriptive ethics to ethics proper, and at the step from ethics to morals. That conclusions about what people *mean by* "right", for example, cannot be proved by finding out what they *call* right, is evident from the case of the moral reformer just mentioned. If he said that slavery was not right, when slavery was one of things universally agreed to be right, he would, if the proposed argument were valid, be like a man who said that post-boxes were not red when everybody agreed that they were red; we should be able to accuse such a man of misusing the word "red" – for "red" *means* the colour which post-boxes are, so how can he deny that they

are red? But the moral reformer can deny that slavery is right while still using the word "right" in the same sense as that in which his contemporaries, who think that slavery is right, are using it. This example shows that there is an important difference between moral words and words like "red" – a difference which invalidates the superficially plausible argument from descriptive-ethical premises to conclusions about the meanings of moral words.

(3) *Ethics and morals.* But the second step in the proposed argument is also invalid, for a very similar reason. We cannot, even if we can establish the meaning of the moral words, pass from this to conclusions of substance about moral questions. This may be shown by the following example: suppose that there are two people who know everything about a certain action (including its circumstances and consequences), and still dispute, as they may, about whether it was wrong. Since they are in dispute, they must be using the word "wrong" with the same meaning; for if this were not so, there would be no real dispute, only a verbal confusion. But since they can continue to dispute, even though they are in agreement about the meaning of the word, it follows that knowledge of the meaning of the word cannot by itself, or even in conjunction with what they both know about the action, determine whether the action is wrong. Some *other* difference must remain between them (a moral difference) which is neither a difference about what the action is (for this they know in the fullest detail) nor about the meaning of "wrong" (for about this they are agreed). The plausible argument which we have just rejected is a particular application of a type of argument often used in philosophy, and known as "the argument from the paradigm case". Without discussing here whether the argument is cogent in other fields, we can see that it is not in ethics. The assumption that this argument has unrestricted force is linked with the assumption that to discover the use of a word is always to discover to what things it is correctly applied. This is not true of words like "is" and "not"; and it seems not to be true of moral words either. This assumption (to take

another example) leaves us with no way of distinguishing between the uses of the two sets of words "Shut the door" and "You are going to shut the door"; for all the words in both sets, in so far as they "apply" to anything, apply to the *same* things.

## II. NATURALISM

The arguments so far considered and rejected all exhibit a common feature. In them, moral conclusions are allegedly derived from premises which are not themselves moral judgments: in the one case the premise was a statement of sociological fact about what people think on a moral question; in the other it was a statement of linguistic fact about how (with what meaning) people use a certain word, together with another premise giving the description of an action whose wrongness is in dispute. This feature is common to a great many arguments which have been used by ethical thinkers; and it has been frequently stated that any argument which derives moral conclusions from non-moral premises must be invalid. A famous statement to this effect was made by **Hume** in *Treatise of Human Nature* (1739–40), III, 1, i. Hume based his rejection of such arguments on the general logical principle that a valid argument cannot proceed from premises to some "new affirmation" not contained, at any rate implicitly, in the premises. The correctness of Hume's view ("no *ought* from an *is*") depends, therefore, on the assumption that moral judgments contain an element in their meaning (the essentially moral element) which is not equivalent, even implicitly, to anything in the conjunction of the premises. It is this assumption which is challenged by those ethical theories known as **naturalist**. The term "naturalist" has been used in a variety of ways, but will be used here as follows: an ethical theory is naturalistic if, and only if, it holds that moral judgments are equivalent in meaning to statements of non-moral fact.

It must be noted that, on this definition, a statement of moral opinion (that is to say a statement in the first of the three classes listed at the beginning of this article) cannot be called naturalistic; for naturalism is a view about the meanings of moral terms, and nobody is committed to any form of it who confines himself to merely *using* moral terms without taking up a view about their meaning, definition or analysis. In general, no view can be naturalistic unless, in the statement of the view, the moral words occur inside quotation marks or a "that"-clause or are *mentioned* (not used) in some other way, and remarks are made about their meaning or their equivalence to other expressions. That is to say, only statements in ethics proper, as contrasted with descriptive ethics and with morals, can be naturalistic. Thus the view that the right action (the action which ought to be done) in a given situation, is that which would produce the greatest balance of pleasure over pain, is not naturalistic, since it does not seek to *define* "right", but only to say what actions *are* right. To be a naturalist, a utilitarian of this sort would have to hold, in addition, that his view was true in virtue of the meaning of "right" – that is to say, that "right" *meant* "producing the greatest balance of pleasure over pain". If he refrains from trying to prove his theory in this way, "refutations of naturalism" pass over his head.

It must also be noticed that, on this definition of naturalism, to call a definition of a moral word "naturalistic" does not imply that the properties in terms of which it is being defined are empirical, that is, perceived by the five senses. As **Moore**, who coined the expression "the naturalistic fallacy", observed, the same "fallacy", as he thought it was, is committed if the properties are "properties of supersensible reality", given only that they are not moral properties. Thus a philosopher who *defines* "right" as meaning "in accordance with the will of God" is, in this sense, a naturalist, unless the word "God" itself is held to be implicitly a moral term. The most important argument by which Moore sought to "refute naturalism" may be restated as follows, using the example just quoted: if "right" meant the same as "in accordance with the will of God", then, "whatever is in accordance with the will of God is right" would mean the same as "whatever is in accordance with the will of God

103

is in accordance with the will of God"; but according to our actual use of the words it seems to mean more than this mere tautology. (Note that, as before, there is nothing in this argument which forces anybody to abandon the *moral* view that whatever is in accordance with the will of God and only what is in accordance with it is right. It is only the attempt to make this view true by definition which is naturalistic.) It has been held, though not by Moore, that what is wrong with naturalistic definitions is that they leave out the commendatory or prescriptive element in the meaning of words such as "right" and "good" (*see below*).

## III. INTUITIONISM

The work of Moore convinced certain philosophers, that naturalistic definitions of moral terms had to be ruled out. But Moore and his immediate followers showed a great reluctance to abandon what had been the traditional view of the way in which words have meaning. It was taken for granted that the way to explain the meaning of an adjective, for example, was to identify the property which it "stands for" or "is the name of"; all adjectives have the same logical function, that of "standing for" a property, and the differences between them are not differences in logical character, but simply differences between the properties for which they "stand". When, therefore, it became accepted that moral adjectives did not stand for "natural" (that is, non-moral) properties, it was concluded that they must stand for peculiar moral properties, thought to be discerned by "intuition".

There are two main forms of ethical intuitionism. According to the first, we are supposed to intuit the rightness, goodness, etc. of concrete individual acts, people, etc.; general moral principles are arrived at by a process of induction, that is, by generalization from a large number of these instances. According to the second, what we intuit are the general principles themselves (for example, "promise-breaking is wrong"); by applying these, we ascertain the moral properties of individual acts and people. The second view has the merit of

emphasising a very important fact about the logical character of moral words, namely that the moral adjectives, etc. differ from most other adjectives in the following way: we call a thing "red", for example, because of its redness and nothing else; it could be similar in every other way and yet not be red. But when we call a person "good" or an act "right", we call them good or right *because* they have certain other characteristics – for example, an act is called wrong because it is an act of promise-breaking, or good because it is the act of helping a blind man across a road. The intuitionists sometimes express this feature of moral adjectives by saying that they are the "names" of "consequential" or "supervenient" properties. Even if we reject the idea that all adjectives have meaning by being the names of properties, this remains an important discovery. It has sometimes been thought that Hume's "no *ought* from an *is*" was a denial that we can, for example, call an act good *because* it is an act of a certain kind. This is a misunderstanding; what Hume was denying was that it *logically followed*, from an act's being of a certain kind, that it is good. The difference is crucial, but obscure. It has been one of the main problems of recent ethics to give a satisfactory account of the connexion between, for example, goodness and what were called "good-making characteristics". The intuitionists reject the naturalist explanation that this connexion is due to an equivalence in meaning between moral words and words describing the characteristics of things in virtue of which we apply moral words to them. But they give no adequate positive account of the connexion, contenting themselves, for the most part, with saying that it is a "synthetic necessary" connexion discerned by "intuition". The explanatory force of this account is impaired by the failure to say clearly what "intuition" is or what is meant by "synthetic necessary connexion".

But the chief argument brought against ethical intuitionism of all sorts is the following, which is to be compared with that in section II (3). Intuition is supposed to be a way of knowing, or determining definitively and objectively, the truth or falsity of a given moral judgment. But suppose that two people differ on a moral question, and that both, as may well happen, claim to intuit the correctness of their own views. There is then no way left of settling the question, since each can accuse the other of being defective in intuition, and there is nothing about the intuitions themselves to settle which it is. It is often objected further, that what "moral intuitions" people have will depend on their various moral upbringings and other contingent causes. In fact, the intuitionists, who often claim to be "objectivists", belie this claim by appealing to a faculty of intuition which is unavoidably subjective. This illustrates the extreme difficulty, to be referred to below, of stating any clear distinction between "objective" and "subjective" in this field. Intuitionism has waned since the early years of this century. Writers on ethics have tended, either to revert to some form of naturalism, open or disguised, or to pass on to one of the kinds of view, to be described below, which recognise that "good", "right", etc. have, logically, a quite different role from that of other adjectives, and that it may be misleading to call them "the names of properties".

## IV. RELATIVISM AND SUBJECTIVISM

Great confusion has been caused in ethics by lumping together, under the title "subjectivism", theories which are quite different from one another. Before considering subjectivism proper, we must first distinguish from it the *moral* view which is best called **relativism**. A typical relativist holds that we ought to do that, and that only, which we *think* we ought to do; on this theory, the mere having of a certain moral opinion by a person or a society makes that moral opinion correct for that person or society. Since this is a *moral* doctrine and not an *ethical* one (that is, since it says what we ought to do, not what "ought" means) it is not naturalistic (see above); but it is open to the objection that it makes it impossible to say that another person's moral judgment is wrong – indeed, it has the paradoxical consequence that two people who differ about a moral question must both be right. This seems to be

at variance with the common use of the moral words; we have here an illustration of a way in which ethics (the study of the uses of the moral words) can have a negative bearing on a moral question – it enables us to *rule out* a moral view as involving logical paradox, but not to *prove* one. It may also be objected to relativism that it does not do what a moral principle is expected to do, viz. guide us in making our decisions on particular moral questions. For if I am wondering what to do, it is no use being told that I ought to do what I think I ought to do; for the trouble is that I do not know what to think. Relativism is mentioned, not for its own value, but because confusion of other views with it has bedevilled nearly all discussion of the views which we are about to consider. These are by contrast all ethical views (that is, views about the meanings of the moral words). They do not commit the holder of them to the acceptance or rejection of any substantive moral opinions.

The first is a form of naturalism, which is not now often avowedly held, but dates from a time when it was thought that a moral sentence must have meaning in the same way as other indicative sentences, viz. by being used to state that a certain object possesses a certain property (see above section IV). It being unplausible, for many reasons (some of which have been given in section III) to hold that the properties in question are "objective" properties of objects, it was suggested that they are "subjective" properties – that is, properties of being related in certain ways to states of mind of the maker of the statement in question. Thus "He is a good man" was held to mean "He, as a matter of psychological fact, arouses in me a certain mental state (for example, a feeling of approval)". This theory makes a moral judgment equivalent to a descriptive ethical statement (see above, section I). If it is taken literally, it is open to the objection that it makes moral disagreement impossible. For if two people say, one that a man is a good man, and the other that he is not, they are, on this view, not disagreeing with each other; for one of them means that he (the speaker) is in a certain mental state, and the other means that *he* (the second speaker) is not in that state; and between these statements there is no contradiction.

Because of this objection, the view has been generally abandoned in favour of others which hold that in a moral judgment we are, not giving information about our mental state, but engaging in a use of language different from the giving of information. This development has been part of the recent realisation by philosophers that it is a mistake to regard all kinds of sentences as having the same logical character and role. For at least two reasons it is best to confine the name "subjectivism" to the view just considered, and not to extend it to those described below. First of all, the terms "objective" and "subjective" have a tolerably clear meaning, and draw a graspable distinction, when they are used to mark the difference between statements of "objective" fact about objects, and statements of "subjective" fact about the speaker (though even here there might be confusion; for in a sense it is an objective fact that the mind of the speaker is in a certain state). But the distinction gets lost when moral judgments are held not to be statements of fact, in the narrow sense, at all. This may be seen by comparing the case of imperatives (though it is not suggested that moral judgments resemble these in all respects). An imperative expresses neither an objective statement nor a subjective statement, since it does not express a statement at all; nor does it express a "subjective command"; for it is hard to understand what this would be. So, if it be asked "Is the command 'Shut the door' *about* the door or *about* the mind of the speaker?", the answer, in so far as the question is meaningful, must be "About the door". And in the same way the moral judgment "He is a good man" may be held to be, in the strongest possible sense, "about" the man in question, and not about the mind of the speaker, even by someone who holds that it is not (in the narrow sense) a *statement of fact* about the man. Thus criticisms of the theories to be described in the next section, on the ground that they turn moral judgments into remarks about the mind of the speaker, are misdirected, and should

be reserved for subjectivism as described in the present section. The same applies to the criticism that these theories "make what is right depend on what the speaker thinks is right".

Secondly, the division between those views which hold that moral judgments are used to give some sort of information, and those which hold that they have a quite different function, is the most fundamental in ethics, and should not be concealed by using a term which straddles it. Views of the first sort (for example all the ethical views so far considered) are called "descriptivist"; views of other kinds, including those considered in the rest of this article, are called "non-descriptivist".

## V. EMOTIVISM

Though emotivism was, historically, the first kind of non-descriptivism to be canvassed, it is a mistake to think of it as the only kind, or even as commanding general support among non-descriptivists at the present time. It is common even now for non-descriptivists of all kinds to be misleadingly called "emotivists", even though their theories do not depend on any reference to the emotions. Emotivism proper embraces a variety of views, which may be held concurrently. According to the best-known, moral judgments have it as their function to "express" or "evince" the moral emotions (for example, approval) of the speaker. According to another version, their use is to arouse or evoke similar emotions in the person to whom they are addressed, and so stimulate him to actions of the kind approved. A. J. **Ayer** when he wrote *Language, Truth and Logic* (1936), which contains the most famous exposition of emotivism, attributed both these functions to moral judgments; but he has since abandoned emotivism, though remaining a non-descriptivist. C. L. **Stevenson** put forward a kindred view, with the difference that, instead of the word "emotion", he most commonly used the word "attitude". An attitude was usually thought of by him as a disposition to be in certain mental states or to do certain kinds of actions. Stevenson's "attitudes" are much closer to the "moral principles" of the older philosophers (especially **Aristotle**) than is usually noticed by those who use the misleading "objectivist-subjectivist" classification. Stevenson made the important qualification to his view that, besides their "emotive meaning", moral judgments may also have a "descriptive meaning". In one of his several "patterns of analysis" the meaning of a moral judgment is analysed into two components: (1) a non-moral assertion about, for example, an act (explicable naturalistically in terms of empirical properties of the act); and (2) a specifically moral component (the emotive meaning) whose presence prevents a naturalistic account being given of the meaning of the whole judgment. This specifically moral element in the meaning is the function which these judgments have of *expressing* attitudes and *persuading* or *influencing* people to adopt them, towards the act described. Stevenson's views did not, of course, find favour with descriptivists; and even non-descriptivists who have written after him, while recognizing the seminal importance of his work, have for the most part rejected the implied irrationalism of the view that the only specifically moral element in the meaning of moral terms is their emotive force. This, it has been felt, makes moral judgments too like rhetoric or propaganda, and does insufficient justice to the possibility of reasoned argument about moral questions. If moral argument is possible, there must be *some* logical relations between a moral judgment and other moral judgments, even if Hume was right to hold that a moral judgment is not derivable from statements of non-moral fact. Stevenson has some important things to say about moral arguments, but his account of them has been generally held to be inadequate.

VI. OUTSTANDING PROBLEMS

Most of the main problems which occupy ethical thinkers at the present time arise from the complexity of the meaning of moral terms, which combines two very different elements.

(1) *The evaluative or prescriptive meaning* (these more non-committal terms are now often preferred to Stevenson's "emotive meaning"). It is not necessary, and probably false, to attribute to moral judgments, as such, any impulsive or

causative force or power to *make* or *induce us to* do what they enjoin; but even descriptivists sometimes admit that moral judgments have the function of *guiding* conduct. It is indeed fairly evident that in many typical cases we ask, for example, "What ought I to do?" because we have to decide what to do, and think that the answer to the "ought" question has a bearing on our decision greater and more intimate than that possessed by answers to questions of non-moral fact. To take another example, it is fairly evident that there is an intimate connexion between thinking A better than B, and preferring A to B, and between the latter and being disposed to choose A rather than B. This intimate connexion is emphasized in the old tag (whose substance goes back to **Socrates**): "Whatever is sought, is sought under the appearance of its being good". It would follow from this that to call a thing good is thereby to offer guidance about choices; and the same might be said of the other moral terms. Descriptivists, however, refuse to admit that this feature is part of the *meaning* of moral terms.

Their principal opponents, who may be called "prescriptivists", hold that it *is* part of the meaning. Moral judgments, on this view, share with imperatives the characteristic that to utter one is to commit oneself, directly or indirectly, to some sort of precept or prescription about actual or conceivable decisions or choices. In typical cases, disagreement with a moral judgment is displayed by failure to act on it − as when someone has told me that the right thing to do is such and such, and I immediately do the opposite. Such a view does not, like the emotive theory, make moral argument impossible; for according to some prescriptivists logical relations may hold between prescriptions as well as between ordinary statements.

Prescriptivists have to face, like Socrates, the difficulty that in cases of so-called "weakness of will" we may choose to do something which we think bad or wrong. The most promising line for prescriptivists to take in answer to this objection is to point out that in such cases either the chooser is *unable* to resist the temptation (as is indicated by the expression "*weakness* of will"; cf. also St Paul, Romans 7, 23); or else he thinks the thing bad or wrong only in some weaker, conventional sense, having the descriptive meaning of "bad" or "wrong" but lacking their prescriptive force.

(2) *The descriptive meaning.* The second main feature of moral judgments is that which distinguishes them from imperatives: whenever we make a moral judgment about, for example, an act, we must make it because of *something about* the act, and it always makes sense to ask what this something is (though it may be hard to put a reply into words). This (although it has been denied by some recent thinkers) follows from the "consequential" character of moral "properties" (see above, section IV). To every particular moral judgment then, there corresponds a universal judgment to the effect that a certain feature of the thing judged is, so far as it goes, a reason for making a certain moral judgment about it. For instance, if I say that a particular act is good because it is the act of helping a blind man across a road, I seem to be adhering thereby to the universal judgment that it is good to help blind people across roads (and not merely this particular blind man across this particular road). Those who accept this argument may be called "universalists"; and their opponents, who do not, may be called "particularists". A universalist is not committed to the view that, if it is a good act to help a blind man across a road on this occasion, it would be a good act on all occasions (for example, it would not be a good act if the blind man was known to be hopelessly lost and his destination lay on this side of the road); he is committed only to the view that it would be a good act in the absence of something to make a difference between the two acts – something more than the mere numerical difference between the acts.

The universalist thesis is closely connected with the thesis that moral judgments, besides their function as prescriptions, have also a descriptive meaning (see above, section VI). On this view, in calling an act, for example, good, we are commending it (the prescriptive element in the meaning), but commending it because of something about it. These two elements are well summarized by the *Oxford English Dictionary*'s first definition of "good": "The most general adjective of commendation, implying the existence in a high, or at least satisfactory, degree of characteristic qualities which are either admirable in themselves or useful for some purpose". The word "characteristic" is important; it draws attention to the fact that the word which follows "good" makes a difference to the qualities which a thing has to have in order to be called good (for example, a good strawberry does not have to have the same qualities as a good man). In the case of some words (for example, "knife"), if we know what they mean, we know some of the conditions that have to be fulfilled before we can call a thing of that kind good. Some philosophers (for example **Plato** and Aristotle) have held that the same is true of all words – that, for example, if we could determine "the nature of man" we should therefore be able to say what makes a man a good man. But this type of argument may be based on a false analogy between words like "man" and words like "knife".

A more promising way of bringing the universalist thesis to bear on moral arguments (and thus to some extent satisfying those who insist that ethical studies should be relevant to moral questions) is that exemplified by the "Golden Rule" and worked out in some detail (though obscurely) by **Kant** and his followers. In certain cases it may be a powerful argument, if a man is contemplating some act, to ask what it is about the act which makes him call it right, and whether, if some other act possessed the same features, but his own role in it were different, he would judge it in the same way. This type of argument occurs in two famous passages of Scripture (2 Samuel 12, 7 and Matthew 18, 32). It has been held that a judgment is not a *moral* judgment unless the speaker is prepared to "universalize his maxim". But this raises the vexed question of the criteria for calling judgments "moral judgments" – a question which is beyond the scope of this article. This question, and the whole problem of the relation between the prescriptive and the descriptive elements in the meaning of moral judgments, continues to tax ethical thinkers.

(R.M.H.)

**Existentialism.** The name of a philosophical trend or tendency whose central figure is **Heidegger**, and of which the following marks may be noted:

(1) Hostility to abstract theory for obscuring the roughnesses and untidinesses of actual life. This may take the shape, as in **Augustine's** *Confessions*, of a profound self-analysis, or as in **Pascal's** *Pensées*, of an insistence that the mathematical methods of the exact sciences must be contested in the name of a flexible and less restricted concept of the varied and different styles of commerce with the natural and human environment. Etienne **Gilson** claims that **Aquinas** should be classed as existentialist, whereas the Platonic essentialist tradition should be viewed as asserting the priority of essence over existence.

(2) The task of the moral philosopher is seen as continuous with that of the novelist or dramatist. (**Sartre** and **Marcel** achieved distinction as writers and dramatists as well as philosophers.) In this one may discern a continuity between existentialist philosophizing and **phenomenological** criticism of **Kant's** formalistic ethics. The existentialist bias in favour of the particular and the concrete conflicts with Kant's attempt to lay bare the universal principle of all moral action, though it harmonises with his doctrine of the primacy of practical over theoretical reason.

(3) Existentialist thought is sometimes profoundly religious (as in **Kierkegaard**), and sometimes overtly atheistic (as in Jean-Paul Sartre). But in existentialist atheism there is discernible an almost obsessionally religious note. Thus Albert Camus' novel *The Plague* (1947) displays a preoccupation with the problem of an atheistic sanctity which is unmistakably religious in its undertones.

(4) Kierkegaard saw himself as offering a corrective to the dialectical rationalism of **Hegel**, and its philosophical interpretation of the Christian religion. One might say that professional philosophers will always find in the writings of existentialist thinkers, resources to correct restricted and confined paradigms. One might mention in this connexion **Wittgenstein's** regard for Augustine's *Confessions*, and for the stories of Tolstoy. The enlargement of the academic imagination by recollection of the actual poignancy of human life and experience is often achieved through insights to be found in the diffuse, and sometimes unbalanced, writings of the existentialists.

The influence of existentialism in contemporary theology is better sought in the work of Paul Tillich, and of Rudolf Bultmann than of Karl Barth. The latter's early work owes much to Plato as well as to Kierkegaard and Dostoevsky; and his later work is more in debt to **Anselm** than to existentialist thinkers. Indeed members of his school have been known to accuse those who pursue the method of existentialism in theology, of continuing the disastrous inheritance of Augustine's self-absorption!

(D.M.M.)

# F

**Fallacy.** The term "fallacy" is used in logic to refer to an invalid argument or form of argument. Strictly, therefore, only arguments, not statements, can be said to be fallacious; an argument with true premises and conclusion may be a fallacy, while an argument with false premises and conclusion may be exempt from fallacy. If the premises of an argument are true and the conclusion false there must be a fallacy in it; in no other case can we determine whether an argument involves a fallacy simply by considering the truth or falsity of the statements it comprises.

It should be noted that the term "fallacy" applies properly only to a deductive step in an argument (see **deduction**); what would be a fallacy regarded as a deduction might well be perfectly sound in a merely probable argument. Thus there is a fallacy known as the fallacy of affirming the consequent which is of the form "If p then q; but q; therefore p". An example would be "If it has been raining the roads will be wet; but the roads are wet; therefore it has been raining". Here the conclusion does not follow, for there may in fact have been no rain but only a burst main; but clearly wet roads are a good ground for suspecting that it has been raining.

The ways in which arguments can be bad are numberless; many of the traditionally named fallacies are of little interest and may be found in any traditional logic book. But some of the more interesting named fallacies will be briefly explained.

(1) *Denying the antecedent.* Of the form "If p then q; but not p; therefore not q"; e.g. "If it has been raining the roads will be wet; but it has not been raining; therefore the roads will not be wet".

(2) *Petitio principii* (begging the question). This is the assumption of a premise which cannot be known to be true unless the conclusion is known to be true. Sometimes it is said that to take as a premise a proposition which cannot be true unless the conclusion is true involves begging the question; in which case, as some have not shirked saying, every valid argument would be a case of begging the question.

(3) *Simple conversion.* This is to conclude from "All A is B" to "All B is A"; it is of course valid to conclude from "No A is B" to "No B is A".

(4) *Undistributed middle.* This fallacy consists in arguing syllogistically with premises in which the term occurring in both (the middle term) is in neither premise used to refer to everything to which it can refer (to its whole extension). Thus in "All liars are rogues and all thieves are rogues, therefore some thieves are liars", the middle term "rogues" is undistributed in both premises; in neither is anything said about the whole class of rogues.

(5) *Ignoratio elenchi.* This is to produce a proof which does validly prove something, but not what it was required to prove.

(6) *Equivocation.* An argument in which a term is used in different senses at different stages of the argument.

(7) *Post hoc ergo propter hoc.* An argument from the fact that something followed on something else to the conclusion that it must have been caused by it. Many superstitions are supported by this argument; bad luck after walking under a ladder or breaking a mirror or spilling salt is held to be due to doing so. But regular sequence is clearly a valid ground for an inductive argument to a causal relationship.

(J.O.U.)

**Fatalism,** *see* Freedom of the Will, Determinism.

**Feminism,** *see* Gender.

**Feuerbach,** Ludwig Andreas (1804–1872), German philosopher born in Bavaria. At the University of Berlin he was influenced by **Hegel**'s lectures. He is best known for his *Essence of Christianity* (1841). His philosophical manifestos, e.g. *Principles of the Philosophy of the Future* (1843), were welcomed by the young **Marx**.

Feuerbach's philosophy (or anti-philosophy as he conceived it) was a **humanism** and a naturalism: "man on the basis of nature" is the touchstone. His position is distinguished from crude empiricism by a phenomenological approach derived from his Hegelian training.

Thus his critique of **religion** is a reinterpretation of it as an unconscious projection of truths about human nature, especially its "species being" (*Gattungswesen*): while individuals are limited, humanity as a whole actualizes *Gattungswesen* in its totality, and this is expressed in religious imagery as God's plenitude. It is experienced most immediately when individuals recognize each other in an I–Thou relationship. This humanist reading of religion influenced modern theology.

Feuerbach's critique of philosophy follows the same course: speculation hypostatizes the abstractions generated in human thought, as if they had a real existence apart from it. But truth exists there in inverted form: hence Feuerbach advised readers of Hegel to "reverse subject and predicate".

Reading Feuerbach encouraged Marx and **Engels** in their turn to **materialism** and the theory of **alienation**.

[C.J.A.]

**Feyerabend,** Paul (1924– ), philosopher of science born in Vienna who has worked mostly in Britain and California, whose inquiries brought him to the conclusion (similar to that of **Kuhn**) that orthodox views of scientific progress are a myth; and that there is no such thing as "the scientific method". His works include *Against Method* (1975) and *Science in a Free Society* (1978); his collected *Philosophical Papers* appeared in two volumes in 1981. See also **Philosophy of Science, Relativism.**

**Fichte,** Johann Gottlieb (1762–1814), German philosopher, was of Saxon peasant stock. Aided by a local landed proprietor he studied theology, philology and philosophy at Jena and Leipzig. He met **Kant** in 1791 and became his close student and disciple. In 1794 he became professor at Jena but was dismissed in 1799 on a charge of teaching atheism. An ardent patriot, he delivered his *Addresses to the German Nation* in Berlin in 1807–08 and was largely instrumental in the rebirth of Prussia after her defeats at the hands of Napoleon. He became professor at the new University of Berlin in 1810.

Fichte held that there were two possible methods in philosophy, dogmatism which deduces the idea from the thing and **idealism** which deduces the thing from the idea. Which method one follows depends on one's mental make-up, but idealism is preferable since we cannot explain consciousness satisfactorily in terms of being, as dogmatism would do, but can construct experience, though not the thing-in-itself, from consciousness as a datum. Thus Fichte discarded the thing-in-itself and instead of deriving the nature of the thinking self from the manifold of experience, like Kant, he set out to deduce the manifold from the activity of the ego. The clearest statement of this not very easy doctrine is perhaps to be found in his *Introduction to the Theory of Knowledge* (1797).

Fichte's ethical views were developed in his *Theory of Morals* (1798). We may act so as to cause ourselves self-contempt or esteem, the latter being conscience. Moral action must spring from conscience not from obedience to authority. The basic ethical demand is that we should act according to our conception of duty, our conception of the action which we would acknowledge as ours without reservation through all time. Thus the moral life is a series of actions leading to the complete spiritual freedom of the ego. Moral evil arises from our lazy incapacity to think out our actions to the full. Certain individuals have the power to act morally in a pre-eminent way and these people through their example are an inspiration to others; in this fact lies the basis of religion and a church is a union of individuals associated for the purpose of stimulating and strengthening moral conviction.

The State, according to Fichte, has the task of ensuring that all men limit their freedom by regard for the freedom of others; but it can only do this if it also attempts to secure the same rights for all, which it can do only if it ensures that all men have property and economic self-dependence. In the light of this view Fichte was led to some socialistic doctrines about economic matters, including the transference of all foreign trade to the state. But, contrary to received legend, he did not share the organic view of the state typical of many German idealists.

(J.O.U)

**Foot,** Philippa (1920– ), English moral philosopher. In a series of concentrated articles starting in the 1950s, she has attacked **emotivism** and **prescriptivism** by arguing that moral considerations are "necessarily related in some way to good and harm", and that there is no separate "evaluative element" in the meaning of moral terms (see **ethics**). Like **Nietzsche**, she sees no logical reason why people ought to care about morality; but she holds that "morality may be stronger rather than weaker if we look this fact in the face". Her principal papers are collected in *Virtues and Vices* (1978).

[J.R.]

**Foucault,** Michel (1926–1984), French philosopher and historian, born in Poitiers, who worked most of his life in Paris. Foucault's work is a distinctive fusion of philosophical and historical investigations. From the **Hegelian** tradition which dominated the post-war French intellectual climate of his youth, it retains two major traits: a concern to theorize relations between general history and the history of thought, and a preoccupation with the human subject, or with how individuals are constituted as knowing, knowable and self-knowing beings. It discards, from the same tradition, the idea of history as a total process with an intelligible overall meaning and direction. It also rejects the goal of a definitive science (or sciences) of the human subject.

Each of Foucault's historical studies deals with concepts which have been used in particular periods (usually, Europe from the seventeenth century to the present; in his last books, Greek and Roman Antiquity) and thematic fields (psychiatry, medicine, linguistics, penal practice, sexual conduct) to articulate systems of thought about human beings. Foucault examines the intimate and sometimes morally disconcerting relationships between such knowledges and the social practices, techniques and power-relations through which they are developed and applied. One of his recurring lessons is that the nature and limits of the thinkable, both in theory and in practice, have changed more often, more radically, and more recently than we tend to suppose. Concepts such as those of normality or sexuality, through which we now think our selves and our identity, are contingent and potentially dispensable historical constructs. Foucault acknowledges **Nietzsche's** inspiration. His later work, notably *Discipline and Punish* (1975), contains a "genealogy of morals" which demonstrates, for example, that punishment is a practice whose meaning can change fundamentally over time, and that familiar values may have forgotten, accidental, and possibly ignoble antecedents.

Like their historical content, the ethical implications of Foucault's analyses are complex and challenging. Power and freedom are not seens as incompatible. Power, or our capacity to act on others, is not an intrinsic evil, but an ineluctable social fact. Freedom is a practice which can never be made safe by institutional guarantees. Our task is to invent modes of living which avert the risk of domination, the one-sided rigidification of power-relations. Enlightenment, the modern commitment to the pursuit of rationality, is a fortunate fact but also a source of intrinsic dangers. The search for truth, especially perhaps for the truth about ourselves, is not a sure path to freedom. In showing the historically various forms taken by the concern for truth, Foucault's intention is not to repudiate that concern as vain or culpable, but rather to assemble analytical resources enabling us to exercise it more critically and freely. His work ends in a reassertion of the practical and moral value of philosophy, which, as an effort to think the unthought, is always a thought against one's self and a readiness to "refuse what we are".

[C.G.]

**Frankfurt School:** the Institute for Social Research founded as an autonomous section of the University of Frankfurt in 1923. Its first director, Carl Grünberg, saw it as a centre for historical and sociological inquiry inspired by Marxist theory. Within a few years, however, leading members of the Institute, including **Horkheimer, Adorno, Benjamin,** and **Marcuse** were giving equal emphasis to purely theoretical work, incorporating elements of **psychoanalysis** and **existentialism** into a new form of Marxism known as "critical theory". Critical theory is centrally concerned with problems of aesthetics, culture and **modernism**; it is Hegelian in inspiration and strongly opposed to Soviet Marxism and **dialectical materialism.** During the Nazi period the School dispersed and eventually regrouped in New York; it moved back to Frankfurt in 1949, where **Habermas** emerged as its leading figure.

[J.R.]

**Freedom of the Will.** The cluster of problems about the freedom of the will arises from an incompatibility, real or apparent, between sets of beliefs none of which we are ready to abandon. On the one hand we believe that we can sometimes choose whether to act in a certain way or not; we believe that we are responsible for so acting or refraining from action; we believe that for those parts of our history which do not lie within our choice we cannot be held responsible. On the other hand we believe that nature is uniform, that whatever happens results from and can be explained by a set of causes and conditions, and in particular that our actions result from our inherited character as modified by environment. But if all that happens is determined by its context then it would seem that our actions are determined by their context and our choices are determined by their context; in particular, if our actions arise from an inherited character as modified by our environment, then it would seem that we are no more responsible for our actions than we are for our inherited character and environment.

Moreover a mere denial of the principle of **determinism**, unplausible in itself, does not obviously eliminate the problem; for if our actions do not arise out of our character as modified by environment it is hard to find any other account of their genesis which will make us responsible for them; certainly we are hardly to be held responsible for what occurs purely fortuitously.

No solution to these problems has been found which commands anything approaching general consent. Those philosophers who regard determinism as incompatible with freedom and therefore deny or weaken the deterministic thesis are usually called **libertarians**; they have had no conspicuous success in finding an account of human action which makes responsible choice intelligible. Those philosophers who retain the doctrine of determinism and accept that we have not in a full sense freedom to choose are known as determinists. Many philosophers are, however, unwilling to accept either of these paradoxical positions and try instead to show that the opposition between determinism and

freedom is only apparent. Thus it is frequently said that the true antithesis to acting freely is acting under compulsion; but, it is said, laws of nature are descriptive, not prescriptive and do not constrain; even the laws of motion describe how things do in fact move and do not compel them so to move. Consequently they maintain that we do in fact often act freely (not under constraint) even though our actions can always in theory be subsumed under (descriptive) natural laws. It is not however clear that in these contexts compulsion is the antithesis of freedom; and though I do not digest my food under compulsion it would be odd to say that I do it of my own free will.

It is, however, true that the determinist at least need not think of laws as prescriptive. Those who think that human actions are in some way prescribed are called fatalists or predestinationists. According to the doctrines of fatalism and predestination some powerful entity (Fate or God) has a plan according to which things happen in a prearranged fashion; the laws of nature can, but need not, be thought of as prescribed by fate or God as a method of executing the plan. Thus the fatalist and predestinationist accept, as the philosophical determinist does not, that human action is purposively determined or compelled; notoriously doctrines of creation and divine foreknowledge raise problems about human responsibility for the theologian.

(J.O.U.)

**Frege,** Gottlob (1848–1925), German philosopher. Frege's historical importance is twofold: as the founder of modern mathematical logic, and as a philosopher of **logic** and of **mathematics**. He invented the notion of a *formal system* with the intention of attaining the ideal of mathematical rigour, and in *Concept-Script* (*Begriffsschrift*, 1879) gave what was at once the first example of a formal system and the first formulation of the sentential and predicate calculi. He drew for the first time the distinction between axioms and rules of inference and introduced the device which distinguishes modern logic from its predecessors and makes it superior to them, the use of variables and (nested) quantifiers.

Frege then turned to the application of his formal system to arithmetic. In doing so, he discovered the possibility of formalizing arithmetic without introducing any non-logical concepts or axioms, at least if the notion of a class or set is admitted as a logical one. This possibility rested on the famous definition of a cardinal number, later rediscovered by **Russell**, as the class of all classes which can be mapped one-to-one on to a given class, together with the definition of the ancestral of a relation (that is, the transformation of a recursive into an explicit definition) which had already been given in *Begriffsschrift*. The definition of cardinal number follows naturally from the discovery that the fundamental numerical notion is that of "just as many as". An unreflective person, asked what it meant to say that there were just as many things of one kind as of another, might reply that it meant that if one counted up the first set and then counted up the second, one would arrive at the same number. But Frege observes that it is possible to say that a set has just as many members as another set without being able to say how many each has; thus if a waiter checks that there is just one knife to the right of each plate, then he knows that there are just as many knives as plates on the table. He has mapped the set of plates one-to-one on to the set of knives by means of the function "object to the immediate right of". Moreover, counting itself is a particular case of setting up a one-to-one mapping; for what I in effect do when I count a set of objects and find that there are *n* of them is to define a function on the set whose values are the numbers from 1 to *n*. Finally to explain "just as many as" in terms of one-to-one mapping gives a sense to saying of some infinite set that it has just as many members as another set, whereas of course an infinite set cannot in the ordinary sense be counted.

In order to prepare the way for the symbolic work Frege wrote *The Foundations of Arithmetic* (1884), expounding his theory without symbolism. This is a classic of philosophical exposition, and contains an entirely effective annihilation of then prevalent philosophical accounts of numbers and of arithmetic. It also contains some profound philosophical insights. In order to answer such a question as "What is the number 1?", Frege says, we have to give an account of the sense of sentences in which the symbol "1" occurs. We must not make the mistake of asking for the meaning of a word in isolation: only in the context of a sentence does a word have meaning. If we ask for the meaning of a word in isolation, we shall be inclined to answer by describing the mental images which are called up in us by hearing the word. But these mental images are entirely irrelevant to the sense of the word. The same word may call up different images in the minds of different people; different words may call up the same image in the mind of one individual. In any case the image cannot determine the sense of sentences containing the word. Elsewhere, Frege distinguishes two features of the meaning of a word: the images and associations which the word calls up, which Frege calls the "colouring" of the word; and the sense properly so called. Colouring is subjective, and can vary from person to person. The sense of the word is objective; it is that feature of the meaning which alone is relevant to the determination of the truth-value of a sentence containing the word. When we know how to determine the truth-value of sentences containing the word, then we know all there is to know about the sense of the word; nothing further can be demanded. Among the most important sentences in which a singular term can occur are those expressing judgments of identity: Frege points out that stipulating the criterion of identity for Xs is a necessary part of determining the sense of the word "X". It is evident that the first part of **Wittgenstein**'s *Investigations* is deeply indebted to these ideas of Frege.

In a famous article published in 1892, Frege introduced a distinction which had not occurred in *The Foundations of Arithmetic*, that between the sense and the reference of a word. The reference of a singular term is the object about which we are speaking when we use a sentence containing it. But we must not think with J. S. **Mill** that the meaning even of a proper name consists just in its having the reference that it has; its sense is not uniquely determined by its reference. Thus, to use an example given by Frege elsewhere, one explorer might discover a mountain to the south and give it a name, while another explorer gave a different name to the same mountain seen to the north, and it might be many years before it was realized that it was the same mountain they had seen; the two names would then have different senses but the same reference. The sense of the whole sentence is a *thought* (somewhat analogous to the "proposition" of Russell); the thought is what is primarily said to be true or false, and is something immaterial though objective. Hence the reference cannot be a constituent of the thought; if I am talking about Everest, the mountain itself cannot be part of the thought I express. All the same, I do succeed in talking about the mountain itself, and not some shadowy correlate of it; the reference is in general something non-linguistic, something "in the world".

Whether an expression is a proper name or not is for Frege a question only of its logical behaviour. Thus "red" and "5" (used as nouns) can count as proper names since "red is a primary colour" and "5 is a prime number" are logically of exactly the same form as "Krushchev is a clever man". If an expression functions like a proper name, and possesses a definite sense, then it *is* a proper name; and it has a definite sense if we have assigned a sense to all the sentences in which it can occur. Whether an expression has a reference or not depends upon whether we should ordinarily say that there was something answering to that designation; for example, "the perfect number between 10 and 30" has a reference in virtue of the fact that, as we should ordinarily say, there is a number which is perfect and between 10 and 30. The idea that there is a further philosophical question as to whether there *really* exists an object for which the expression stands arises from the fallacy of "asking after the reference of a term in isolation". Frege calls an "object" anything which is the reference of a singular term; for him it is as legitimate to speak of numbers

(and other "abstract entities") as objects as of men or cities as objects. Hence arithmetic is a collection of truths about objects just as much as any other science, and it is the task of the mathematician to *discover* these truths, which hold good independently of whether we discover them or not.

Frege distinguishes two fundamentally different types of expression, which he calls "saturated" and "unsaturated". Singular terms are saturated, as are complete sentences. Unsaturated expressions are predicates like " . . . is tall", relational expressions like " . . . bores . . . " and functional expressions like "the capital of . . . ", in short expressions containing gaps which become saturated when the gaps are filled by saturated expressions. Unsaturated expressions are not merely sequences of words which could be written down on their own, for it is required that we can indicate where the gaps occur and which gaps must be filled with the same term and which may be filled by distinct terms (variables are a device for indicating this). Thus an unsaturated expression is rather a *feature* in common to several sentences than an isolable *part* of those sentences. An unsaturated expression has a reference as well as a saturated one; but its reference is an unsaturated kind of thing, something which can no more be thought of as standing on its own than can the expression which denotes it, and which is therefore totally unlike an object. The reference of a predicate Frege calls a "concept" ("property" would be a happier term in English), that of relational and functional expressions "relations" and "functions". The reference of an unsaturated expression is to be distinguished from its sense just as sharply as the reference of a proper name from *its* sense; concepts, relations and functions are just as much "in the world" as are objects. If we say that Jupiter is larger than Mars, the relation holds between the *references* of the words "Jupiter" and "Mars", and not between their senses, and hence must be a feature of the world (the "realm of reference") as are the planets themselves. It is nevertheless an entity of a quite different kind; if an expression stands for a concept or a relation, it cannot stand for

115

an object, and indeed it cannot even be sense to try to say about a concept what it makes sense to say about an object, or conversely. We do talk about concepts, however: if I say, "God exists", I am not ascribing a property to a particular object, I am talking about a certain *kind* of thing, about a property or concept, and saying about it something that it makes sense to say only about a property, viz. that there is something which has it, that there is something of that kind. Number-statements are to be understood in the same way; "There are three trees in the garden" says something about the concept *trees in the garden*, and cannot be understood as an assertion about an object.

If we want to understand the nature of concepts and relations, we must consider functions in mathematics. The number 4 is a certain function of the number 2, namely its square, but it is not itself that function. In fact we cannot as it were isolate the function, but only particular numbers which are that function *of* certain other numbers. Indeed, Frege is able to regard concepts and relations as special cases of functions, since he holds that a sentence as a whole has a reference, namely its truth-value; concepts and relations are thus functions whose value is always truth or falsity. This doctrine cuts clean through the old controversy between nominalists and realists. For Frege the colour red, for example, is a genuine object, and the reference of the *noun* "red"; but it cannot be the reference of the *adjective* "red" and is not alluded to in the sentence "Tulips are red".

The doctrine leads in Frege's formal system to a rigorous distinction of type between predicates; classes are, however, treated as *objects* (entities of lowest type). This is an illustration of the interdependence between Frege's philosophy of logic and his formal system. A formal system is to be constructed not merely with an eye to convenience, but ought to mirror the essential features of language (this was in essence Frege's retort to Peano's objection that his assertion sign was formally redundant). This does not mean that a formal system has to copy natural language: the use of variables and quantifiers, for instance, solves the problem of

generality not by giving a coherent account of the devices used to indicate generality in natural languages, but by inventing a totally new device (the theory of quantification seems a better claimant for the title "paradigm of philosophy" than Russell's theory of descriptions). Natural language may actually be incoherent and can be criticised as such; thus Frege regards it as a defect of natural language that in it singular terms may be formed which have a sense but no reference. The modern quest for an ideal language was initiated by Frege.

In 1893 and 1903 Frege published two volumes of his masterpiece, *The Basic Laws of Arithmetic*, which sets out his construction of arithmetic out of logic in his logical symbolism. The theory contains "naive set theory", that is, the assumption that for every property there exists a class having as members precisely those objects which have that property. Shortly before the publication of volume II Russell wrote to Frege explaining the contradiction he had found in naive set theory. Frege hastily added an appendix stating how the contradiction could, as he thought, have been avoided by weakening one of his axioms. Lesniewski later proved that a further contradiction would arise, but it is doubtful if Frege discovered this; but in any case many of the proofs would have broken down under the revised axiom, and Frege lost heart for rewriting and completing the book. At the end of his life he came to consider the whole theory of classes, and the project of deriving arithmetic from logic, an error. Frege produced little work of interest after 1903; and probably did not follow the work that was being done in the subject he had founded. Nor did he receive much credit in his lifetime. The work he had done was transmitted to other logicians through the writings of Peano, Russell and **Whitehead**; only Dedekind, Zermelo and Russell gave him the credit that was his due. He was little known among philosophers, although three of great importance were profoundly influenced by him – **Husserl**, Russell and Wittgenstein. In recent times there has been a great awakening of interest in him; logicians are fully aware of his work, and some such as Church, **Carnap** and **Quine**, have been directly influenced by him. Perhaps

Frege's greatest achievement in philosophy, in which he was followed by Wittgenstein though not by Russell, was to reject the Cartesian tradition that **epistemology** is the starting-point of philosophy, and reinstate philosophical logic as the foundation of the subject.

(M.A.E.D.)

**Freud**, Sigmund (1856–1939), *see* Psychoanalysis.

# G

**Gadamer,** Hans-Georg (1900– ), German philosopher, the main exponent and developer of the idea that **hermeneutics** is the most fundamental of all disciplines. Much of his work takes the form of lucid and self-effacing essays on the figures he sees as dominating the **history of philosophy**: not only his friend and teacher **Heidegger**, but also **Plato**, **Aristotle**, **Hegel**, and **Husserl**. Collectively, these essays plead for a recognition that philosophy consists essentially in the interpretation of philosophical tradition. With the publication of his *Truth and Method* (1960), it became clear that this historical approach to philosophy was based on a general theory about the universal ontological significance of "the phenomenon of understanding".

Following Heidegger, Gadamer rejects the idea that understanding or interpretation is the activity of a "subject" confronting an independent "object". This dichotomy of subject and object is itself, he argues, a hasty interpretation with limited validity, and so are all the other dualisms characteristic of **modernity**, especially that between art and science. For, in spite of **Kant's** "subjectivisation of aesthetics", art makes no less a "claim to truth" than science. Once we have discovered how truth can happen in art, according to Gadamer, we can begin to see how understanding in general – including scientific understanding – works. We will realise that it consists not in the pure and timeless relation between subjective representations on the one

hand and objective phenomena on the other, but in historically situated "events" where interpretative "horizons" are enlarged, and eventually "fused" with others gathered from the past. "Understanding," he says, "must be conceived as part of the process of the coming into being of meaning, in which the significance of all statements – those of art and those of everything else that has been transmitted – is formed and made complete."

Gadamer's conception of understanding as part of "the historicity of our existence" also leads him to reject the "prejudice against prejudice" which he regards as another commonplace of modernity. Recognition of authority, he argues, is really a condition of knowledge, rather than its enemy. Our prejudices "constitute our being": they are the "biases of our openness to the world" and "the initial directedness of our whole ability to experience." Some left-wing critics such as **Habermas** have seen this as involving a universal endorsement of supine conservatism since, they argue, it implies that any demand for radical change must be irrational and a misinterpretation of tradition. Gadamer however sees these criticisms as mistakenly presupposing an "unconditional antithesis between tradition and reason", and an "objectivist" view of the past. Tradition, for Gadamer, does not "persist by nature because of the inertia of what once existed"; on the contrary, it is "an element of freedom" which perpetually "needs to be affirmed, embraced, cultivated". Hence even in the most fundamental revolutions, according to Gadamer, "far more of the old is preserved. . .than anyone knows."

[J.R.]

**Gassendi,** Pierre (1592–1655), French scientist. Gassendi was not a man of great originality, yet his indirect influence on the course of philosophic and scientific speculation was important and profound. Both **Hobbes** and **Descartes** knew him well and derived from him, not so much specific doctrines or solutions of philosophic problems but rather certain habits of thought. Gassendi set himself the task of providing an explanation for the doctrines of the current orthodoxy that would be based upon the scientific theories of the ancient **atomists** and the moral views of **Epicurus**. For example, he regarded mental activities as fully explicable in terms of physical distortions of the material of the brain and he elaborated a most complex theory of "traces" to account for the intelligent behaviour of men and animals. Typically, his solution of the problem of the interaction of imperishable soul and perishable brain was a para-mechanical one. If both Brain and Soul pursued the same goals, they would for that reason act together, a doctrine similar to, but much simpler than **Leibniz's** pre-established harmony. Gassendi also exerted a marked influence on moral and political theory, for he reintroduced to Europe the Epicurean doctrine that the highest moral good was to be sought in "tranquility of soul", a notion which is a likely progenitor of Hobbes' "peace". We act for the preservation of our soul's tranquility, which is not always the pursuit of pleasure.

(R.HAR.)

**Gender.** "Gender", as distinct from "sex", is whatever there. is to being male or female that cannot be attributed to innate bodily differences. Sex, we are told, is biologically given; gender is socially constructed. But opinion differs as to where sex stops and gender starts. For many feminists, gender is malleable without limit; but others question this conception of free-floating gender, and also challenge aspects of the western philosophical tradition on which it rests.

The idea of gender as transcending bodily sex differences is of course a modern one. But it has its roots in traditional philosophy, with its aspirations to the transcendence of body by mind and consciousness; or of animality by human nature; or of the passivities of nature by autonomous will. And the concept of gender also has links with the traditional philosophical concept of the person. Gender transcends sex. But for those feminists who rest claims to sexual equality on the supposed fundamental sameness of men and women, it is itself transcended by personhood. As persons, what sex we are is not

essential to us. The rational mind is neither sexed nor gendered.

The idea of the sexless soul, which reinforces the idea of gender as changeable, goes back to **Plato's** discussion of the female guardians in Book Five of the *Republic*. The sexual equality of the guardians rests on their sameness of soul, which co-exists with bodily difference. Women should be given the same education as men, to fit them for the same social roles. But in *Emile* (1762) **Rousseau** claimed that Plato had really excluded femaleness from the Republic: the female guardians did not really have female gender.

Modern feminists have often seen this pattern repeated in women's access to institutions and professions structured around men. In reaction to the disappearance of female gender into a supposedly gender neutral norm, there has been a trend in more recent feminism towards an affirmation of female difference. This has been accompanied by a move to bring gender closer to sex, repudiating the philosophical assumptions implicit in the picture of gender as "free-floating", especially **Descartes'** model of the mind-body distinction.

Some feminists also argue that social arrangements should reflect the different relations of the sexes to the biological facts of reproduction. Such versions of feminism echo Rousseau's insistence that male and female are different ways of being human, and that female reproductive capacities are central to the difference. They believe in "taking biology seriously", highlighting the connections between femaleness and nurturance, and then arguing that the philosophical dichotomy between mind and body deludes us into advocating the fundamental sameness of men and women.

Although such feminists are at pains to distance themselves from biological determinism, they continue to construe the relations between gender and sex in causal terms. The problem, however, is to see what there is to "sex" that can provide the cause or ground of the approved forms of social arrangement. How do we know where the biological facts end and the social construction of nurturance as female begins? A merging of cultural and biological facts of reproduction is of course exactly what we should expect, if we do repudiate the sharp dichotomies inherited from the philosophical tradition. But to the extent that they do merge, the idea of sex as grounding gender becomes confused.

An alternative approach has been to see gender as the human response to the fact of sex differences, rather than their causal product – as our enactment of sex differences, our response to their significance. This view seeks to expose as illusory the Kantian ideal of a personhood that transcends sex difference, in favour of seeing gender as integral to personhood. But this view also has difficulty in identifying the natural facts to which gender is supposedly the truthful response.

We seem to have here a conceptual impasse. We can think of gender as floating free of sex. But then femaleness either disappears into a human norm, which coincides with socially constructed maleness; or it survives only as a complement to the essentially human. Alternatively, we can try to affirm femaleness by bringing gender closer to sex; but this may only perpetuate and rationalise existing sexual stereotypes, by naturalising them.

A possible way out of this impasse is to see gender as neither a causal product nor a response to pre-existing difference, but an expression of power, with no existence independent of the dominance of men over women. According to this view, what is fundamental is the political fact that maleness is the standard with reference to which both sameness and difference are judged: sameness means being the same as men; difference is being different from men. Hence a feminist affirmation of what differentiates women from men is fraught with problems. For women to affirm difference is to confirm their powerlessness.

Some feminist philosophers have argued that the philosophical tradition has helped form this identification between maleness and the human norm: that philosophical ideals of reason, autonomy and personhood have privileged maleness as transcending and excluding the feminine; and that female gender has been constructed by those exclusions. But if the philosophical tradition has contributed to our present quandaries about sex and gender, it also offers resources for rethinking sexual difference; and from this perspective many of the old philosophical debates take on new dimensions.

For example, much of the contemporary dissatisfaction with our ways of thinking of sex and gender focuses, as we have seen, on Descartes' view of the mind. But on a Spinozistic view of the mind–body distinction, sex differences would reach right into the mind. The mind, for **Spinoza**, is the "idea of the body". As ideas of differently sexed bodies, minds would have to be sexually differentiated. But does that commit us to a distinction between male and female minds? Why should the idea of a male body be male, any more than the idea of a large body is large? But the claim is not ludicrous. The idea of a large body reflects the "powers and pleasures", in Spinoza's phrase, of such a body. And to the extent that the powers and pleasures of bodies are sexually differentiated, it will be appropriate to speak of male and female minds. A female mind will be one whose nature, and whose joys, reflect those of a female body.

Moreover, there is for Spinoza a continuity between the individual body and the socialized body. The powers of bodies are enriched by good forms of social organization, which foster the collective pursuit of reason. They are also diminished by bad forms of social organization, and by exclusion from good ones. If we take seriously the implications of Spinoza's theory of the mind, female minds will be formed by socially imposed limitations of the powers and pleasures of female bodies.

On this way of looking at sex difference, there is no sexless soul, waiting to be extricated from socially imposed sex roles. But nor is there any authentic male or female identity, existing independently of social power. With gender there are no brute facts, other than those produced through the shifting play of the powers and pleasures of socialized, embodied, sexed human beings.

[G.L.]

**Geulincz,** Arnold (1624–1669), *see* Occasionalism.

119

**Gilson,** Etienne Henri (1884-1978), French philosopher. The vastly increased knowledge of **medieval philosophy** we now have is largely due to his work. He started from an interest in **Descartes** and was first led to medieval philosophy in an attempt to understand better the philosophical antecedents of the Cartesian philosophy; medieval philosophy then began to absorb his attention and he came to accept the position of Thomas **Aquinas** on essential points. His most important historical work, *The Spirit of Medieval Philosophy*, was first published in French in 1932. He has also written independent philosophical works in the Thomistic tradition, including *God and Philosophy* (1941).

(J.O.U.)

**Glanvill,** Joseph (1636–1680), *see* Cambridge Platonists.

**Goodman,** Nelson (1906- ), American philosopher of language. In his view, philosophy aims at giving precise structural descriptions of the world, by formulating definitions which exhibit things as patterns of various elementary components of experience. In his first book, *The Structure of Appearance* (1951), he offered such definitions for a number of individual items in phenomenal experience (such as colour spots), using for his primitive building blocks directly presented qualitative characteristics, such as specific shades of colour and places in the visual field. He has been a vigorous proponent of **nominalism**, refusing to postulate such abstract "Platonic" entities as classes. Although Goodman has made extensive use of modern logical techniques, he has not hesitated to reject portions of logic, mathematics and scientific theory that do not satisfy his nominalistic requirements. He has, like **Quine,** been highly critical of the widely employed distinction between synthetic and **analytic** statements.

A problem that has occupied much of Goodman's thought is the clarification of what is to be understood by contrary-to-fact conditionals, such as "If this match had been scratched it would have ignited." He has canvassed various difficulties that he thinks face attempts at explicating precisely the sense of the connective "if-then" in such statements; and he has shown that this problem is intimately related to the problem of formulating the difference between statements expressing laws of nature (e.g., "Water expands on freezing") and those expressing merely accidental universality (e.g., "All the coins in my pocket to-day are made of silver"). In *Fact, Fiction and Forecast* (1955), Goodman advanced some ideas toward resolving these questions, and has also suggested in what way he thinks those ideas are relevant to the analysis of inductive inference. Later works include *Languages of Art* (1968) and *Ways of Worldmaking* (1978). See also **Relativism.**

(E.N.)

**Gramsci,** Antonio (1891–1937), Italian marxist, born in Sardinia, whose activities in opposing the Fascists led to his arrest in November 1926. Gramsci spent the final ten years of his life in Fascist prisons and clinics. His major theoretical work, the *Prison Notebooks*, first published 1948–51, was written during his incarceration.

Gramsci's philosophical aim was to reconstruct Marxism as a political philosophy, a philosophy of praxis; and thus to move away from the historical materialist conception of Marxism as a scientific theory of economy and society. To this end he attempted to incorporate into Marxist thought, in radically altered form, the brand of Hegelianism and historicism he has learned from the writings of the Italian philosopher Benedetto **Croce.**

For Gramsci "philosophy" is a social activity; it is the universe of cultural norms and values, the world-view, shared by all as common sense. All philosophy, then, is historically concrete, belonging to a people, a time and place, even if "philosophers", those who produce specifically philosophical writings, are unaware of it as such.

In conceiving of philosophy in this way Gramsci was attempting to refute the standard Marxist conception of the economy as the base or infrastructure which determines society's political and cultural superstructure. For Gramsci, politics, as the transformation of common sense, and the introduction of new philosophical perspectives, represents an independent element in historical change; and as such it was essential to the possibility of revolutionary change in the West.

Central to Gramsci's conception of historical change and political education is his concept of "hegemony". This refers either to the consensual basis of an existing political system, achieved when a ruling class imposes its worldview as common sense; or to the attainment of a new common sense by a dominated class. For Gramsci, ideological struggles are, properly speaking, struggles for hegemony, struggles for the hearts and minds of the people.

In identifying philosophy, history and politics Gramsci transformed the Marxian problematic of **ideology** into the question of the "fate" of "the political" in modernity.

[J.M.B.]

**Green,** Thomas Hill (1836-1882), English philosopher, educated at Oxford. Green helped to spread into England the influence of **Kant** and **Hegel** against the prevalent trends of empiricism and utilitarianism. The only book of his which appeared in his lifetime was his edition of **Hume**, and his influence was exercised mainly through his lectures at Oxford which were posthumously published.

He maintained that the world was to be thought of as a network of relations, and that mind was required not only to apprehend but also to constitute and sustain these relations. What are the terms related in this network? Any term we may seek to isolate turns out to be itself a network of relations too; and any attempt to find in feeling or sensation the ultimate data of experience must fail. Here Green comes very close to Hegel. The distinction between appearance and reality is not a distinction between a mental world and a world independent of mind, but one between mind as limited and human and mind as universal and absolute – the mind which sustains the universe.

In **ethics** too Green goes a long way with Hegel. Desires are not, as in an animal, isolated forces. In each desire the human self seeks its own satisfaction as a whole. Only thus can a man hold himself responsible and a free agent. Here, however, Green began to diverge from Hegel. The good is personal to the individual whose good it is, even though, being naturally social, he can achieve full satisfaction only if he confers good on others. Green firmly rejected any notion of a corporate self. The divergence dominates his political theory. He noted how **Rousseau's** conception of a common good led him to that of a general will. But beyond this lay Hegel's view of the State as a unity higher than that of the individual and beyond this again lay extremes of totalitarian authority and nationalistic state-worship. Green's solid English liberalism rejected all such conclusions. He maintained the importance of individual responsibility and of individual rights. But his final position involved serious difficulties. A "common good" means that a man benefits others only "so far as he finds the thought of their being perfect necessary to his own satisfaction". On the other hand, individual rights are not allowed, as in **Locke** or J. S. **Mill**, to serve as a bulwark against social authority; indeed they depend for their existence on social recognition. See also **Political Philosophy**.

(J.D.M)

**Grotius,** Hugo (1583-1645) a Dutch thinker whose ideas exerted an influence out of proportion to their philosophical acuteness. Their context was political upheaval and assassination, lawlessness at sea, and the Thirty Years War. His belief in toleration and rational ways of settling disputes was based on a profound respect for truth which was in the humanistic tradition of Erasmus. He believed that piety based on what was common to different interpretations of the Christian religion, together with reticence about doctrinal disagreements, was a sufficient basis for reconciliation between Catholics and Protestants.

His rational outlook was, no doubt, partly the product of his early training by the great scholar Scaliger, who was one of the first to stress grammatical cogency rather than doctrinal convenience in interpreting Scriptural texts. Grotius was an infant prodigy – mastering Latin and Greek by the age of twelve and a Doctor of Law at the University of Leyden at sixteen. As advocate for the Dutch East India Company he became involved in a controversy arising from the seizure of a Portuguese galleon in the Straits of Malacca. Grotius was led to investigate the general grounds of the lawfulness of war. His *On the Law of Booty*, written in 1604 and re-discovered and published in 1868, was the result; it led to his abiding interest in International Law and formed the basis of his later masterpiece *On the Law of War and Peace*, 1625. Grotius upheld the general principle that the ocean is free to all nations.

Grotius' contribution to philosophy consisted mainly in his unequivocal defence of natural law as a rationally discernible set of principles binding on citizens, rulers, and God alike. The validity of such a law upholding the security of property, good faith, and fair dealing was a commonplace of Christian thought. But the disunity of Christendom after the Reformation and the secular challenge to the authority of the church, which was one of the legacies of the Renaissance, had made its validity difficult to defend on religious grounds. Furthermore the policy of Realpolitik pursued by the rulers of the new nation states, as popularized by Machiavelli, made the content of the old law of nature look somewhat artificial. Grotius therefore sketched a foundation for the law of nature which would make it independent of religion and based on a proper understanding of human nature.

Natural law, claimed Grotius, is "a dictate of right reason, which points out that an act, according as it is or is not in conformity with rational nature, has in it a quality of moral baseness or moral necessity; and that, in consequence, such an act is either forbidden or enjoined by the author of nature, God." It was not obligatory because God commanded it; rather God commanded it because it was obligatory. "Just as even God, then, cannot cause that two times two should not make

four, so he cannot cause that which is intrinsically evil be not evil." In other words Grotius assimilated moral knowledge to mathematical knowledge.

Grotius held, furthermore, that as men were, as **Aristotle** and the **Stoics** had taught, social by nature, they had a natural interest in the maintenance of a social order. The rules of natural law, therefore, were self-evident to man as a social animal endowed with reason, "for the very nature of man, which even if we had no lack of anything would lead us into the mutual relations of society, is the mother of the law of nature."

Grotius maintained that all other laws were subordinate to natural law. The civil law, for instance, depended for its validity ultimately on the natural obligation of good faith in keeping covenants. Grotius' treatment of the Law of Nations was particularly interesting and important; for he transformed what had been a system of private law establishing relations between subject and subject belonging to different nations into system of public law establishing relations between state and state.

(R.S.P.)

# H

**Habermas,** Jürgen (1929– ), is the most influential contemporary representative of Critical Theory, a tradition of Marxist social philosophy which originated in Germany in the 1930s, amongst members of what has come to be known as the **Frankfurt School**. Like earlier members of the School, including Theodor **Adorno** and Herbert **Marcuse**, Habermas is concerned with the predominance of "instrumental reason" in modern industrial societies. Instrumental reason deals with the relation between means and ends, but leaves the determination of ends outside its scope. For many modern philosophers, this is the only kind of reason. Such views, Habermas argues in his early work, encourage the "scientization" of politics: political questions are reduced to problems of technical control, and the "public sphere" of debate and discussion concerning social goals is eroded. Habermas also believes that earlier Critical Theory failed to clarify the broader conception of reason to which it implicitly appealed.

Habermas' solution to this difficulty is to shift the philosophical emphasis from the subject–object relation to the process of inter-subjective communication. Thus, in his main contribution to **epistemology**, *Knowledge and Human Interests* (1968), he argues that the existence of society depends on two forms of action, labour (instrumental action) and social interaction (communicative action). These form the basis of distinct human interests, which in turn guide the formation of categorically different kinds of knowledge, Hermeneutic and critical modes of enquiry, directed towards understanding others and uncovering unconscious compulsions, arise from communicative action, and cannot be reduced to "empirical-analytic" enquiry, which arises from instrumental action and aims at the prediction and control of objective processes.

Subsequently, Habermas has worked on a "universal pragmatics", an account of the normative commitments which are constitutive of linguistic communication. In particular, he wishes to show that, when we attempt to reach agreement through discussion, we cannot help but assume that the conditions under which an unconstrained consensus could be reached have already been realized. Thus an "ideal speech situation", characterized by equality and reciprocity of participation, is an immanent goal of communication, and makes possible a critique of inequalities of social power which is not simply based on personal value-commitments.

This account of communication is a central component of Habermas' comprehensive reformulation of social theory in *The Theory of Communicative Action* (1981). Here Habermas argues that the pathologies of contemporary society can be diagnosed in terms of the invasion of the 'life-world' (the domain of social existence which is communicatively organized) by quasi-autonomous "systems" of bureaucracy and the economy. Opposition to this invasion is no longer located only in the working class,

but rather amongst all those social movements which attempt to expand solidaristic forms of social life, and to bring the dynamics of money and power under democratic control. See also **Philosophy of Science**.

[P.D.]

**Hamilton,** Sir William (1788–1856), Scottish philosopher. He spent some time at the Bar and was Professor of history and then philosophy in Edinburgh. In philosophy his starting point was the common-sense position of **Reid** and the Scottish school; his lectures, later published as *Lectures on Logic* and *Lectures on Metaphysics* were of great weight in the development of the Scottish philosophical tradition.

Hamilton's main work was the *Philosophy of the Unconditioned* (1829). In this work he proceeds, by means of a critical examination of the views of **Kant, Schelling** and **Comte** to a theory of knowledge whose main thesis is that to think is to condition. This means that when we think of anything we inevitably determine it by its relation to something else by which it is conditioned; thus every part is a whole of parts and every whole is itself part of some greater whole and the idea of the absolute whole or part is an absurdity. Similarly we cannot think of an unconditioned beginning and can only understand a beginning as conditioned by another phenomenon; the conditioning phenomenon is thus the cause and the concept of cause is made by Hamilton merely a special case of the general principle of conditioning. Hamilton took it that this philosophical view made it impossible to attain absolute truth by philosophy and that we must be satisfied with an enlightened ignorance. But though we cannot know the unconditioned we cannot but have some faith about it; the unconditioned is God who, as unconditioned, is completely incomprehensible.

Hamilton is now best remembered as the subject of J. S. **Mill's** *An Examination of Sir William Hamilton's Philosophy* and as the inventor of a variant of the **logic** of the syllogism in which the predicate as well as the subject is quantified (that is, in which we have not simply the proposition, all S is P and some S is P, but rather all S is all P, all S is some P, Some S is all P and some S is some P).

(J.O.U.)

**Hampshire,** Stuart (1914– ), English philosopher based at Oxford. His *Thought and Action* (1959) is an important exploration of the way in which people's knowledge of their own actions differs from the objective empirical knowledge which then preoccupied **analytic philosophy**.

**Hare,** Richard Mervyn (1919– ), English moral philosopher who taught at Oxford. His main position is set out in *The Language of Morals* (1952), *Freedom and Reason* (1963) and a number of papers which have been published in collected form. This position is commonly called **prescriptivism**. Hare holds that the primary task of the moral philosopher is to clarify the nature of moral terms and judgments, and that such clarification can have considerable influence on practical questions. Moral judgments, he holds, differ from descriptions of the world, not in subject matter, but by being imperatives whose primary function is to guide choice. But moral judgments are not mere commands, for they are essentially universalizable. Also notable are Hare's critical reformulation of **Moore's** arguments against naturalism, or descriptivism, and his attempt to show that there can be a logic of imperatives as well as of indicatives. Hare is the author of the entry on **ethics** in this Encyclopedia.

(J.O.U.)

**Hartmann,** Karl-Robert-Eduard von (1842–1906), known chiefly for his *Philosophy of the Unconscious* (1869), the most widely-read of all German philosophical books of its time. Hartmann claimed to produce a synthesis of **Hegel** and **Schopenhauer**; taking from Hegel the notion of the rational Idea and from Schopenhauer that of the Will, Hartmann saw these as elements in a new ultimate – the

Unconscious. The rational Idea is properly the guide of the blind Will, but the pessimistic Hartmann regarded them as at variance in sinful man. His reputation has now much declined.

(J.O.U.)

**Hartmann,** Nicolai (1882–1950), German philosopher, one of the few speculative metaphysicians in the grand style of the twentieth century. Hartmann considered that the European tradition in philosophy since **Descartes** had been to start with the subject, the thinker; this, he held, was a fundamental mistake. Knowledge, he said, was the apprehension of an independent reality, an apprehension as immediate as is, according to Descartes, our apprehension of the self. Properly understood, all philosophical problems are ontological; they are attempts to understand the kind of being presented to us. Metaphysical problems such as that of **free will** and of the relation of life to the mechanical are, according to Hartmann, essentially insoluble.

Hartmann's ethical work is indebted to **Husserl** and the **phenomenologists** in its method. There are two kinds of value, that which is possessed by the things and situations with which agents deal and that which is possessed by agents and their actions. Specifically moral value is to be found in the disposition of the agent, and it is in this connection that Hartmann gives his famous analysis of the virtues. For an agent and his actions to have value they must be free; they must therefore be to some extent exempt from determination by natural law and not determined even by values. In accordance with his general position on the insolubility of metaphysical problems Hartmann admits that he cannot understand how man can be free in this way; but he is sure that such freedom is presupposed in morality.

(J.O.U.)

**Hedonism,** from the Greek "hedone" which means pleasure. Three quite different views have been called "hedonism". First, ethical hedonism, the moral view that the only thing which is good is pleasure. **Epicurus** and **Bentham** are famous examples of moralists who have held this view. Secondly, psychological hedonism, which is the psychological theory that we can desire nothing but pleasure; though this view has often been confused with ethical hedonism it is strictly incompatible with it, for if we can desire nothing else it is as pointless to recommend desires for pleasure as it is pointless to recommend falling when one is released in mid-air. This theory, frequently held by earlier British empiricists, was heavily attacked by **Butler**; but it nonetheless appears as a support for ethical hedonism in J. S. **Mill**'s *Utilitarianism*. Thirdly, the view that the notion of "good" is to be defined in terms of "pleasure". Thus **Locke** in his *Essay* (II.xx.2) says "That we call *good* which is apt to cause or increase pleasure, or diminish pain in us." This view also has been confused with ethical hedonism in spite of the fact that "pleasure alone is good" can have no moral content if it is a mere definition.

(J.O.U.)

**Hegel,** Georg Wilhelm Friedrich (1770–1831), born in Stuttgart, Germany, was one of the most influential philosophers of all time: indeed, the history of philosophy since his death could be represented as a series of revolts against him and his followers. A little more than a century after his death, few followers were left, but much of his thought had been absorbed by his opponents, and to gain some historical perspective on **Kierkegaard** and **Marx**, on Marxism and **existentialism**, on **pragmatism** and **analytic philosophy**, Hegel's influence must be taken into account as one of the key factors.

Hegel himself published only four books: *Phenomenology of Spirit* (1807); *Science of Logic* (1812–16); *Encyclopedia* (1817; thoroughly rewritten edition 1827; revised edition 1830), and *Philosophy of Right* (1821). All of these works, as well as his posthumously published lectures on the philosophy of history, the philosophy of art, the philosophy of religion, and the history of philosophy, have been translated into English.

Hegel's philosophy may be conveniently divided into three phases. The first antedates the publication of the Phenomenology. The second is represented by that book. The third is represented by his later works, beginning with his *Logic*. In the first phase we encounter an as yet non-professorial Hegel, who could hardly be more different from the popular image of the man.

Hegel's earliest writings – drafts and essays he wrote in his twenties – were first published in 1907 under the misleading title *Hegel's Early Theological Writings*. In some of these essays, notably in "The Positivity of the Christian Religion", Hegel's style is brilliant, eloquent, and picturesque, his criticism of the Christian churches, both Catholic and Protestant, and even of Jesus himself, is frequently vitriolic, and his opposition to all dogma and authoritarianism uncompromising. He does not oppose all religion but finds Christianity incompatible with reason and human dignity. In the oldest fragments, he considers the possibility of a wholly rational religion which would help us to attain a harmonious personality and a high level of morality.

By 1800, Hegel felt that the sort of criticism in which he had earlier engaged was all too easy, obvious, and pointless. It would be a more challenging task to show how Christianity and other beliefs held by eminent men of the past had not been "bare nonsense". Perhaps one could even "deduce this now repudiated dogmatics out of what we now consider the needs of human nature and thus show its naturalness and its necessity". This programme, sketched in 1800 in a preface to a never written work, marks the transition to Hegel's second phase and to his *Phenomenology of Spirit*.

The use of "necessity" in the last quotation foreshadows one of the central confusions of Hegel's subsequent philosophy. He uses "necessary" as a synonym of "natural" and an antonym of "arbitrary" and "utterly capricious" and he does not distinguish between giving some reasons for a development and demonstrating its "necessity". In this sense he finds reason in history, but he does not claim – as many interpreters suppose – that historical events or particular entities can be "deduced" in any ordinary sense.

Although Hegel declares in the important preface to his *Phenomenology* that he aims to elevate philosophy to the status of a science, the book – and much of his later philosophy, too – is best understood in the perspective supplied by his early writings: what he wants is still a substitute for traditional Christianity – a world view that eliminates whatever is incompatible with reason and human dignity while preserving whatever was sound in Christianity and in the thought of all the great philosophers of the past. His prose, though still occasionally picturesque, has on the whole become involved and heavy, and his criticism no longer takes the form of sarcastic denunciation or outright ridicule: rather it consists in relegating all past positions, including various forms of Christianity, to the role of more or less remarkable, though plainly unsatisfactory, anticipations of the philosophic system that Hegel distils out of the cauldron of history.

In spite of the scorn which Hegel's critics have lavished on his allegedly arrogant claims for his own system, the view of the **history of philosophy** on which these claims are based has been almost universally accepted; and when his claims are understood in terms of this view they prove to be much less presumptuous. Hegel does not pit his own philosophy against rival philosophies, past and present, by way of saying: they are wrong and I am right. He repudiates the common conception of philosophic disagreement which one might call the battlefield view of the history of philosophy. The history of philosophy must be understood, he insists, in terms of development. It was Hegel more than anybody else who established the history of philosophy as a subject of central importance, and almost all texts on the subject show, albeit in varying degrees, his influence.

Hegel, then, does not look at his system as in any sense peculiarly his own philosophy. He is not contemporaneous with his predecessors but able to draw on their cumulative efforts. He can see how the excesses of one are in time pointed out by his successor who, in turn, may well go to the opposite extreme. All along,

there is a continual refinement, an increased articulateness, and, as it were, a progressive revelation of the truth.

This raises the question what Hegel expected from the future. Did he admit that his own system was not final? Hegel never supposed that history would stop with him. In his lectures on the philosophy of history he referred to the United States as "the land of the future", while insisting that it must be left out of account at present, since it is the task of philosophy to comprehend "that which is" and not to speculate about the future. The same course of lectures culminates in the pronouncement: "To this point consciousness has come." If he had foreseen the insights of future philosophers, he would have embodied them in his own system. Since he could not foresee them, he did not talk about them.

For all that, he might have stressed, at least occasionally, that his own system was not final, instead of stressing, as he often did, that it was, if only at the time of speaking, the last word. This is surely a fault, but there are at least two extenuating circumstances. The first is that few great philosophers have not been guilty on the same score: from **Plato** to **Wittgenstein**'s preface to his *Tractatus* it is encountered in classic upon classic. Secondly, there was a peculiarly apocalyptic atmosphere in German philosophy in Hegel's day. We can trace it back at least to **Kant**'s announcement, in the preface to his *Critique of Pure Reason* (1781), that he hoped philosophy would at long last attain the truth by the end of the century. **Fichte** tried to keep Kant's promise in 1794; **Schelling**, at first enthusiastic about Fichte's effort, soon struck out on his own in an attempt to build on the foundations laid by Kant and Fichte, and published his own *System of Transcendental Idealism* in 1800. Hegel felt that he was completing what Kant, Fichte, and Schelling had begun. In addition, there was a widespread feeling that an era was coming to an end, and Hegel, like the old Goethe, felt that the civilisation he had known was drawing to a close, that he was looking back upon European history and in some sense summing it up. To cite his preface to the *Philosophy of*

*Right*: "When philosophy paints its grey on grey, a form of life has grown old, and with grey on grey it cannot be rejuvenated, but only comprehended. The owl of Minerva begins its flight only at dusk."

In the *Phenomenology* these tendencies are less prominent than in Hegel's later work. It is a work of youthful exuberance, although the preface makes clear that the author's desire is to put an end to romanticism in philosophy. What is wanted is not inspiration and edification, sentiment and intuition, but the exertion of careful and rigorous conceptual thinking – not the enthusiasm of a coterie but the discipline of a science.

Even if one sympathizes with these programmatic declarations and with Hegel's sharp and perceptive criticism of romanticism, one may yet conclude that his own brand of rigour was misconceived from the start. The great central idea of the *Phenomenology* is that different outlooks correspond to different states of mind, different stages in the development of the spirit, and are not, taken as a whole, true or false, but rather more or less mature. The book is the story of the education of the spirit, and this framework allows for many penetrating observations. But it is marred by two pervasive faults: first, the above-mentioned confusion about necessity affects Hegel's attempts to show how one stage necessarily issues in the next; secondly, he assumes not only that *some* outlooks and positions are best understood in terms of a developmental sequence, but – and this assumption is surely untenable – that *all* outlooks and positions can be reasonably arranged in a single development, or even on a scale of rising maturity.

One further flaw in the *Phenomenology* is that it is never altogether clear whose "spirit" Hegel is discussing. Often it is clearly the human spirit, and Hegel seems to be writing about the education of humanity. But at other times, "spirit" seems just as plainly an *alias* of God. Hegel clearly did not believe in a transcendent God, omniscient and omnipotent from all eternity; but he did believe that the force which is at work in the development of the material universe and eventually fashions man and finds expression in man's spirit, may legitimately be named after its final and highest manifestation – even as we call an embryo an undeveloped human being. According to Hegel, it is only in man that the spirit achieves self-consciousness, and it knows only what man knows.

Instead of repudiating traditional conceptions of the Trinity, the Incarnation, or of God, Hegel often uses Christian terms and praises Christianity for realising that God is spirit, that God becomes man, etc. This gives rise to the paradox that "God" finds out about himself only in Hegel's system. The paradox disappears when we say that Hegel did not believe in "God" but, like many philosophers and theologians, did not make a point of this fact, preferring to pour new wine into old skins.

Hegel's *Logic*, the work which inaugurates his third and final phase, is marred to an even greater degree by pseudo-demonstrations and a confused notion of necessity. Again, much remains after allowance has been made for these great faults: above all, perhaps the most sustained attempt since **Aristotle** to articulate the meaning of philosophically interesting and important terms and their relation to each other.

Unfortunately, many readers have never got beyond the first three terms: Being, Nothing and Becoming. Partly as a result of this, partly because it is a commonplace in the literature, they suppose, mistakenly, that all of Hegel is reducible to the three-step of Thesis, Antithesis, and Synthesis. As a matter of fact, he does not speak of theses, antitheses, and syntheses at all, although his immediate predecessors, Fichte and Schelling, did; and neither his analyses in the *Logic* nor his dialectic in general can be reduced to any such three-step.

The point is even more obvious in Hegel's philosophy of history. He divides world history into three stages: in the first, in the ancient orient, only one is considered free (the ruler); in the second period, in Greece and Rome some are free; in the modern world all are considered free, at least in principle. Some English translations, however, introduce the word "antithesis" in all kinds of places to render words that literally mean "other" or "opposite"; and secondary sources perpetuate the legend that Hegel construed everything mechanically in terms of three concepts which he actually spurned.

His *Encyclopedia* contains his entire system in outline form. A shorter version of his *Logic*, slightly rearranged, (sometimes cited as his "Lesser Logic") comprises Part One; his philosophy of nature, subdivided into mechanics, physics, and organics, constitutes Part Two; and his philosophy of spirit forms the third and last part. The philosophy of spirit is also divided into three parts, and each of these in turn into three sub-parts; but these tripartite divisions cannot be reduced to theses, antitheses, and syntheses. Subjective spirit comprises sections on anthropology, the phenomenology of the spirit, and psychology. Then comes objective spirit which contains sections on right, morality, and ethical life. Finally, the whole system culminates in a chapter on absolute spirit which is divided into sections on art, revealed religion, and – the pinnacle – philosophy.

The state is discussed in the section on ethical life (*Sittlichkeit*) after family and civil society. It belongs in the sphere of objective spirit – that is, of spirit embodied in institutions. This whole realm is the basis on which art, religion, and philosophy develop. "Although it is true that all great men have formed themselves in solitude, they have done so only by assimilating what had been created by the state."

Hegel's philosophy of objective spirit is developed in more detail in his *Philosophy of Right* and in his lectures on the philosophy of history, from which the last quotation is taken. His philosophy of absolute spirit is elaborated in the eight volumes of his lectures on art, religion, and the history of philosophy.

After Hegel's death, his followers quickly divided into two camps: a right wing that made the most of Hegel's theology and tried to infuse new life into Protestantism, and a left wing of so-called Young Hegelians who included brilliant atheists and revolutionaries – most notably Ludwig **Feuerbach** and Karl

Marx. Marx accepted Hegel's preoccupation with history and development but claimed that Hegel had stood man on his head, as if spirit and ideas were fundamental, while he, Marx, had turned Hegel right side up again by pointing out that material factors are basic.

Kierkegaard also protested against the Hegelian theologians. He repudiated any attempt to transcend faith or even to comprehend Christianity, which, he insisted, is absurd but must be believed, or any attempt to hide from the problems of one's own concrete existence in a system.

During the latter half of the nineteenth-century, Hegelianism came to England and profoundly influenced T. H. **Green**, B. **Bosanquet**, F. H. **Bradley** and J. M. E. **McTaggart** against whom, in turn, G. E. **Moore** and Betrand **Russell** revolted at the beginning of the twentieth century. In the United States, William **James** rebelled against the Hegelian idealism of Josiah **Royce** and of dozens of less gifted philosophers. John **Dewey** was a Hegelian when young. In Italy, **Croce** developed the Hegelian tradition. In France Jean-Paul **Sartre**'s *Being and Nothingness* leans heavily on Hegel. Beyond that, the historical approach to art, religion and literature, no less than philosophy, owes a great deal to Hegel. Perhaps no other thinker since Kant has had a comparable influence. See also **Political Philosophy**.

(W. K.)

**Heidegger**, Martin (1889–1976), taught at Marburg University from 1923 to 1928 and at the University of Freiburg-im-Breisgau from 1928 to 1958. His life-long preoccupation with the "question of being" was first formulated in his unfinished magnum opus, *Being and Time* (1927), and then revised in lectures, books and essays until his death. Heidegger's *Seinsfrage* arose from a number of sources, among them: **Aristotle**'s physics, metaphysics and ethics, interpreted in the light of his mentor **Husserl**'s phenomenological method, **Kant**'s *Critique of Pure Reason*, and the historical and **hermeneutical** investigations of Wilhelm **Dilthey**. Aristotle inspired Heidegger to challenge

Husserl's neo-Kantian thesis concerning "acts of consciousness" as the sole resource of philosophy by asking: How does the being of *acts* relate to the being of the *objects* of those acts? Thus the question of being was from the outset a question concerning **truth**, understood not as the correspondence of propositions to states of affairs but as disclosure, unconcealment, and what Heidegger later called the "clearing of being", *die Lichtung des Seins*. Dilthey encouraged Heidegger to challenge Husserl's emphasis on "evidence" as the sole philosophical recourse by asking: What sort of *historical* self-understanding lies behind philosophy's search for apodictic and adequate evidence; indeed, behind its fascination with *cognition* and theory of *knowledge* in general?

Heidegger first elaborated the question of being as *fundamental ontology*, the "science" of being. He set out in *Being and Time* to revise all the categories which prior philosophers had applied to the relations between human beings and their world. Fundamental ontology, as enquiry into being, was itself a possibility of human being (which Heideger called *Dasein*, "being-there" or "existence"). Dasein always operates within a prevailing understanding of being, or *Seinsverständnis*, even when it is not philosophizing. Traditional epistemologies and metaphysical systems appeared to have forgotten the salient features of human being as being-in-the-world: our manipulation of tools in the workaday world, a manipulation that does not depend on concepts such as "extended substance" or "primary and secondary qualities", our absorption in a kind of "public self" that defines most of the possibilities that shape our lives; and the occasional upsurge of an anxiety that exposes human being as eminently finite and mortal. None of these things pertains to our "knowledge": *knowing* the world is not the primary way of *being* in the world. Heidegger's reading of **Augustine**, Luther, **Kierkegaard** and **Nietzsche** had convinced him of the "falling" character of the world and the need for human existence, as "concern" (*Sorge*), to resist the everyday, public world. Such resistance does not take the form of an epistemological solipsism; rather, it is a matter of confronting without subterfuge one's own impending death. In this way one achieves an *appropriate* relation to one's own death. This proper relation to the finitude of Dasein Heidegger called *Eigentlichkeit*, a word that came to be translated by French (and English) existentialists as "authenticity". Such an appropriate or "ownmost" relation to the possibility of one's own death reveals *temporality* and ultimately *time* itself as the horizon upon which the meaning of being is projected.

In essays and lecture courses of the 1930s and 40s Heidegger expanded the scope of his question beyond human being to being as a whole, *das Seiende-im-Ganzen*. Actually, the tendency of human dispositions and moods to reveal being *as* a whole had long been noted by Heidegger. The expansion thus did not so much abandon the ontology of Dasein as exceed its terms of reference in the direction of "metaontology". Yet Heidegger soon let the vocabulary of ontology recede altogether: the guiding and the grounding questions of **metaphysics** now became his principal concern. What is being? Why *is there* being, why not far rather *nothing*? How and why are beings understood as grounded in another being – e.g., a Creator-God? Heidegger's pursuit of the grounding question of metaphysics uncovered what he called the history or destiny of the truth of being: *Seinsgeschichte/Seinsgeschick*. That history or destiny, viewed as a whole, unfolded essentially as oblivion of being, *Seinsvergessenheit*, the self-occultation of being. Nevertheless, the history of being consisted of more or less well-defined epochs: (1) early Greek thinking, which experienced the clearing of being without preserving that experience in texts, leaving only mere traces of being; (2) **Plato** and Aristotle, who founded metaphysics – in which "being" is accepted uncritically as "permanence of presence" – and who thus in some sense initiated the forgetting of the question of being, yet in whose works reminiscences of the great Greek tradition can still be found; (3) Latin and **medieval** thought, which at least in its orthodox representatives obscured the Greek tradition and perpetuated an inferior version of Greek ontology; (4) modernity, which from

129

Descartes and Leibniz onward sought security no longer in sanctity but in certitude of cognition. The epochs of being thus culminate in the age of *technology*, and because technology closes off all other ways in which beings are disclosed, the age of technology completes the history in which being is forgotten. Ours is the epoch of *nihilism*. Modern science itself is part of the technological framework of beings, it is by no means the master of technology. Contemporary philosophy, with its compulsion to epistemological rigour, formal precision, calculability of truth, clarity and "cashable" value of argument, exhibits both a Cartesian heritage and a technological destiny. Contemporary thinking is bound to be one-track thinking. "The most thought-provoking thing in our thought-provoking time", wrote Heidegger in 1951, "is that we are still not thinking".

In writings after World War Two, such as the famous "Letter on 'Humanism'", Heidegger turned increasingly to the theme of *language*, especially the language of *poetry*. Language is not in Heidegger's view the vehicle of thought. Nor is it subject to manipulation – except as flattening out and vulgarizing. Nor, finally, does its "normal" use, even in "speech acts", allow it to serve as the arbiter of philosophical disputes. Heidegger's every effort is to *hear* in language what he calls *Ereignis*, the event by which human beings, as mortals, are claimed and called upon to think. *What* they are called upon to think will vary from epoch to epoch, but it will invariably have to do with what he calls the "granting" – the bestowing and preserving of time and being, and thereby of the particular ways in which being as a whole is revealed: in our time, for example, as a stockpile of resources awaiting exploitation.

Heidegger is without doubt the most powerfully original and influential philosopher of the century in the Continental tradition. **Phenomenology, existentialism** and deconstruction are unthinkable without him, but so are philosophy of literature and many social-critical or neo-Marxian strands of thought. His importance in the English-speaking world is also growing steadily, because no other contemporary thinker so unsettles the analytic enterprise.

While convinced analytical philosophers fulminate against him, or try to ignore him, their students have long been reading him. Yet the greatest single obstacle to the reception of Heidegger's work both in the Anglo–American world and on the Continent is his commitment during the 1930s to National–Socialism. While his active engagement (as rector of Freiburg University in 1933–34) was brief, his anti-liberal, anti-democratic sentiments perdured. For reasons that resist all explanation, he failed to speak out after the War in condemnation of Nazi atrocities. Even if his reasons for refusing had more to do with a Kierkegaardian contempt for publicity and our media-dominated lives than with crass indifference, that silence more than anything else inhibits the reception of his thought. However, much research and writing are being done today on Heidegger's politics, and a more insightful and differentiated evaluation is becoming possible. Such nuanced responses are important if one of the most significant voices in contemporary European thought – its metaphysics, its philosophy of language and poetics, science and technology, religion and art, its political theory and praxis – is not itself to be silenced.

Major works by Heidegger include: *Being and Time*, 1927; *Kant and the Problem of Metaphysics*, 1929; "On the Essence of Truth", 1943 [1931]; "The Origin of the Work of Art", 1950 [1935]; *Introduction to Metaphysics*, 1953 [1935]; *Nietzsche*, 1961 [1936-1941]; "Letter on 'Humanism'", 1947; *What is Called Thinking?*, 1954; "The Question Concerning Technology", 1954; *Identity and Difference*, 1957; *On the Way to Language*, 1959; *On Time and Being*, 1969 [1961].

[D. F. K.]

**Heraclitus** of Ephesus, Greek city of Asia Minor, flourished c. 500 B.C. Of aristocratic family, he withdrew from society and in notoriously obscure terms attacked the Ephesians, and men in general, for their stupidity. Men failed to apprehend the *Logos*, a kind of common structural characteristic of all natural objects, in part identifiable with fire. He believed that things in the world were divided into opposites – an analysis shared by **Anaximander** – and that change could be expressed as between opposites. These, apparently plural and discrete, were actually "one and the same", being connected in a "joining that stretches in both directions" by the Logos, which ensured the ultimate balance and continuity of changes between opposites. Thus Heraclitus saw the unity of the world in its structure and behaviour rather than in its material. Fire, nevertheless, is the primary material, and controls the "turnings" into each other of the three great cosmic components, fire, sea and earth. Change, or "strife" as Heraclitus called it, was necessary for the continued unification of opposites: not perhaps continuous change in everything (as **Plato**, thinking rather of the exaggerated Heracliteanism of **Cratylus**, maintained) but the certainty of ultimate change between opposites. Wisdom consists in understanding the Logos, how the world works; for man is a part of the world, himself governed by the Logos, which exists in his soul as its active and fiery part. This fiery part, which must be preserved from the moisture produced by sleep, stupidity, and vice, makes contact with the Logos-element in outside objects, and in some form can survive even death. Thus Heraclitus produced a surprisingly coherent system, which gave a real motive for philosophy, and which for the first time gave some account of epistemology. Its obscure presentation, and **Parmenides'** re-alignment of thought, prevented it from being as influential (until the **Stoics**) as it deserved to be. See also **Pre-Socrates**.

(G. S. K.)

**Hermeneutics** is the theory and practice of interpretation (Greek: *hermeneia*). Originally applied to biblical criticism, the concept of hermeneutics was extended by Schleiermacher (1768-1834) and especially **Dilthey** to cover the whole of human existence, and made the basis for a projected science of the human as distinct from the natural world. The concept has been further developed within **phenomenology**, particularly by **Gadamer** and **Ricoeur**, and

usually carries the implication that whilst some interpretations are better than others, none can ever be final. See also **Psychoanalysis**.

[J.R.]

**Hesiod,** *see* Pre-Socrates.

**Historical Materialism,** *see* Dialectical Materialism, Marx, Ideology.

**History of Philosophy.** It has commonly been agreed (too readily, perhaps) that the task of a scientist is to produce theories, and that theories are good or bad depending how adequately they describe or explain established facts. On this view, the study of the history of science, though it can be entertaining or chastening or inspiring, is a distraction from science proper. "A science which hesitates to forget its founders," as **Whitehead** said, "is lost."

Philosophers who have aspired to model their discipline on the progress of the sciences have therefore disdained the study of the history of philosophy. **Kant**, for example, made a division between the authentic philosophers, "who endeavour to draw from the fountain of reason itself," and their boring colleagues, the "scholarly men to whom the history of philosophy is itself philosophy." **Analytic philosophers** have typically taken the same view; as **Quine** put it, "there are two kinds of people interested in philosophy, those interested in philosophy and those interested in the history of philosophy."

In practice, however, would-be scientific philosophers have seldom succeeded in confining their attention to a supposedly ahistorical "fountain of reason". Whereas scientists have often discussed theories without caring about their original formulation or context, philosophers have repeatedly succumbed to historical curiosity. Many of them (**Russell** for example) have produced both detailed studies of particular events in philosophy's past, and synoptic surveys of periods, movements, or even the "history of philosophy" taken as a whole.

131

They have attempted to square this with their philosophical conscience by appealing to a distinction between their own approach to philosophy's past, which they take to be "purely philosophical," and that of Kant's "scholarly men", which they dismiss as "merely historical". The practical utility of this distinction is evident: it permits philosophers to insulate their histories of philosophy from historical criticism. Its theoretical justification is obscure however; and it is hard to see why philosophers should bother with the past at all, if they are as uninterested in history as they claim. May it be that the entanglement of philosophy with its past is inevitable, even though unwelcome to some philosophers?

There are three main ways in which philosophy gets involved with its past. The first can be described as *connoisseurship*: just as poets or painters learn to be discriminating about their art, and hence capable of meaningful innovation, by acquainting themselves with existing masterpieces, so it is, presumably, with philosophers as well. Indeed the significance of a work of art, or poetry, or philosophy, may be wholly mysterious unless it is seen in relation to the past works to which – implicitly or explicitly, negatively or positively – it refers. This is especially true of philosophy, which is as often engaged in the exposure and diagnosis of plausible errors in the works of the illustrious dead, as with positive expositions of evident truths.

An even closer connection between philosophy and its past can be identified under the rubric of *canonicity*. The canon is, strictly speaking, the list of the books of the Bible which are accepted as genuine or inspired; by extension, it is the set of acknowledged masterpieces in which a practice acknowledges, or claims, its legitimate ancestry, and thereby forges a sense of its identity. If a discipline is uncertain or divided about its aims, objects and methods (as seems to be chronically the case with philosophy) then its canon becomes especially vital to it. The unity of the field of philosophical issues, and the cohesion of communities of philosophers, will depend on agreement about the contents of the philosophical

canon. And specific theoretical projects, such as **analytic philosophy**, **empiricism**, or **phenomenology**, or indeed 'Western philosophy' or 'philosophy' itself, will define themselves very largely in terms of their rival canons. Controversies as to the canonical status of works by, for example, **Heraclitus**, **Spinoza**, **Hegel**, **Nietzsche**, **Green**, **Heidegger**, or **Kripke** turn out to be debates about philosophy's nature and future, disguised as discussions of its past.

The third and most intimate link between philosophy and its past is provided by *plot*. By means of plot, the history of philosophy is divided into periods, and partitioned between various schools of thought, in such a way that it exhibits a philosophically meaningful development over time, probably leading to some present or imminent crisis. (If the addition of an idea of completeness to the objects of philosophical connoisseurship turns philosophy's past into a canon, then the addition of significant organization in time to the canon, produces philosophy's past as plot.)

These three kinds of connection between philosophy and its past can be traced back to **Socrates**, a connoisseur who defined himself against the historical background of the sophists; to **Plato**, who canonized past philosophers as participants in his dialogues; and to **Aristotle**, who conceived philosophy as a continuing cooperative enterprise whose plot should display rational progress. **Cicero** systematized the Aristotelian story by dividing philosophy into four Schools – **Epicurean**, Stoic, Academic (Platonic) and Peripatetic (Aristotelian); and **Seneca** drew the obvious eclectic moral; "we must imitate the bees," he said, "who raid whichever flowers they need for making their honey."

The classical view of the canon and plot of philosophy's past was crystallised in Diogenes Laertius' gossipy *Lives of the Philosophers*, written in the third century AD, which defined philosophy in Europe throughout the middle ages and the renaissance. Georg Horn was the first to mount a systematic challenge to Diogenes. His *Philosophical Histories* (1655) added postclassical authors to the philosophical canon, and organized ancient (pagan) and modern

(Christian) philosophy into a single "Judaeo-Christian" plot, in which Jesus Christ played a pivotal role. But Diogenes was not definitively displaced until the appearance of Johann Jakob Brucker's *Critical History of Philosophy* (1742–4) – a monumental work which firmly established a three-part plot for the history of philosophy, with ancient philosophical wisdom at the beginning, medieval scholastic darkness in the middle, and modern eclectic enlightenment at the end. This tightly articulated history had the fateful effect of presenting the whole history of philosophy as culminating exclusively in Western Europe. (See **African Philosophy**.)

For Hegel the historicity of philosophy was a cardinal philosophical problem: true philosophy would have to go behind the apparently self-defeating quarrels of the past, and the complacent eclecticism of modern enlightenment as celebrated by Brucker, in order to reveal an underlying intellectual unity in the history of philosophy as a whole. According to Hegel, all true philosophers incorporated the principles of their predecessors, even if they thought they rejected or ignored them; despite appearances, therefore, the plot of philosophy's past expressed a single unified argument, and "the same Architect has been directing the work for thousands of years". Whether they knew it or not, philosophers could only articulate this inherited argument for the benefit of their own age, and clarify its implications for the future. Philosophy might attempt to escape its past, but it was impossible that it should succeed.

Of course philosophers may still try to avoid a Hegelian submission to history by imitating the progress of the sciences. But unfortunately for them, this unhistorical concept of scientific progress has been discredited by the progress (if such it is) of the **philosophy of science**. **Popper**'s theory of science as a cycle of arbitrary conjectures and systematic refutations, followed by **Kuhn**'s idea of scientific revolutions as instituting new paradigms incommensurable with the old, and **Bachelard**'s idea of the "breaks" which inaugurate the different sciences, have all suggested that criteria of scientific truth may themselves be contingent and perspectival. **Rorty** has drawn negative conclusions about the whole of "traditional philosophy". **MacIntyre** however has attempted to get round the difficulty by arguing that whilst both science and philosophy are "essentially historical", they are still rational, and indeed that they could not be rational unless they were embedded in particular traditions. On this view, the distinction between historical and philosophical approaches to philosophy crumbles, and many elements of Hegelian historicism are reinstated.

However, Hegel's view of the history of philosophy tends to conceal the arbitrary artifice in the smooth idea of a self-contained tradition called "(Western) philosophy" which fuses Jewish, Christian and ancient Greek elements. **Marx** tried to escape Hegel's emollient philosophical historicism (if not his Eurocentrism) by replacing a history of modes of philosophising by a history of modes of production. Both **Kierkegaard** and Nietzsche revolted against Hegel's homogenized conception of history by affirming the awkward and absurd irreducibility of the "actually existing individual". Heidegger and **Derrida** have argued that the development of philosophy as recounted by Hegel is really an increasingly disastrous forgetting of philosophical questions, rather than a triumphantly progressive solution of them. And **Foucault** has suggested that the whole conception of a Western philosophical tradition benignly seeking the truth is a systematic concealment of the processes in which political powers establish and legitimate themselves through a violent exclusion of those whom they define as mad or otherwise beyond the bounds of reason. Such attempts to "invert" Hegel – whether Popperian, Marxist, Nietzschean, or Foucaldian – all agree with Hegel on one point, though: detached objectivity is impossible in any history of philosophy, or for that matter in an encyclopedia.

[J. R.]

**Hobbes,** Thomas (1588–1679), English philosopher educated at Oxford. In 1608 he became tutor to the young son of William Cavendish,

Earl of Devonshire. He spent the rest of his long life in similar employment, mainly with the Cavendish family. He was tutor to Charles II during his exile in Paris in 1646.

Hobbes' intellectual history can be conveniently related to his three visits to the continent. His first, in 1610, inspired him with a desire to master the thought of the ancient world. His dissatisfaction with Aristotelianism was probably encouraged by his talks with Francis **Bacon**. In 1628 he published a translation of Thucydides, partly to warn his fellow-countrymen of the dangers of democracy.

In 1628, during his second journey to the continent, he developed both a passionate interest in geometry whose method he thought he might use to present his conclusions about democracy as irrefragable demonstrations. He thought, like Bacon, that knowledge meant power, and hoped to cure the ills of a society on the verge of civil war by sketching a rational reconstruction of society like a geometer's figure.

Hobbes' third journey to the continent provided the final ingredient for his natural and civil philosophy; for he visited Galileo in 1636 and conceived the imaginative idea which permeated his whole philosophy – the generalization of the science of mechanics and the geometrical deduction of the behaviour of men from the abstract principles of the new science of motion.

Hobbes claimed originality for two main parts of his philosophy, his optics and his civil philosophy. His *Little Treatise* (1630–37) was an attack on the Aristotelian theory of sense and a sketch for a new mechanical theory. On returning to England his thoughts turned again to politics, owing to the turbulent state of the country. In 1640 he published his *Elements of Law*, while Parliament was sitting. This demonstrated the need for undivided sovereignty. When Parliament impeached Strafford, Hobbes fled to the continent, priding himself in later times on being "the first of all that fled". In *De Cive* (1642, published in English in 1651 under the title *Philosophical Rudiments Concerning Government and Society*), he tried to demonstrate conclusively the proper purpose and extent of the civil power, and the relationship between church and state.

Hobbes' originality consisted not simply in his views about optics and politics but also in the links which he forged between them. He thought that an all-inclusive theory could be constructed starting with simple movements studied in geometry and culminating in the movements of men in political life. He envisaged a deductive trilogy comprising works on Body, Man, and Citizen, but events constantly interrupted his project. He started on his *De Corpore* soon after the publication of *De Cive*, but after the arrival of Charles II in Paris Hobbes started work on his masterpiece, *Leviathan*, which stated in a pungent form his views on Man and Citizen. It was published in 1651 and soon afterwards Hobbes was permitted by Cromwell to return to England. For Hobbes used the **social contract** theory to demonstrate the necessity of an absolute sovereign – by consent, not by Divine Right. So his doctrine could be used to justify any government, provided that it governed – first of all that of Cromwell and later that of Charles II.

After his return to England Hobbes soon became involved in a dispute with Bishop Bramhall on the subject of **free will**. His *Questions Concerning Liberty, Necessity, and Chance* was the result (1656). Hobbes was then led into a most humiliating controversy; for in chapter 20 of *De Corpore* (1655) he had inserted an attempt to square the circle. This was seized on by John Wallis and Seth Ward, both of them Puritans and foundation members of the Royal Society, who were irritated by Hobbes' criticisms of the universities and ruthlessly exposed his mathematical ineptitude. The wrangle lasted for about twenty years.

Hobbes' energy was remarkable (he played tennis up till the age of seventy). In 1657 he published the second part of his trilogy, the *De Homine*. After the Restoration Hobbes was received at Court, where his wit was appreciated. But at the time of the Plague and Great Fire some reason was sought for God's displeasure, and a bill being brought before Parliament for the suppression of atheism, a committee was set up to look into *Leviathan*.

The matter was however dropped, probably through the intervention of the King; but Hobbes was forbidden to publish his opinions. He turned to history and in 1668 completed his *Behemoth* – a history of the Civil War, interpreted in the light of his opinions about man and society. It was published posthumously in 1682. He was also sent Bacon's *Elements of Common Law* by his friend John Aubrey and, at the age of seventy-six produced his *Dialogues between a Philosopher and a Student of the Common Laws of England*. (Published posthumously in 1681.) At eighty-four he wrote his own autobiography in Latin verse and at eighty-six published a translation of the *Iliad* and *Odyssey*. He died at the age of ninety-one.

CONTRIBUTION TO PHILOSOPHY

(1) *Philosophical method.* Hobbes, like his contemporaries **Bacon** and **Descartes**, believed that natural reason was in decay for want of a proper method and clouded over and corrupted by the vaporous doctrines of the Schools.

Hobbes saw philosophy as a necessary preliminary to rational government and the avoidance of civil war – the worst of all evils, from which come "slaughter, solitude, and the want of all things." But he understood philosophy in a very wide sense: "such knowledge of effects or appearances as we acquire by true ratiocination from the knowledge we have first of their causes or generation. And again, of such causes or generations as may be from knowing first their effects." Like all his rationalist contemporaries, he believed that the reality beneath the deceptive appearances of sense was geometrical in character. Hobbes regarded the use of reason as a kind of adding and subtracting "of the consequences of general names agreed upon for the marking and signifying of our thoughts".

(2) *The metaphysics of motion.* Hobbes' analysis was, as a matter of fact, usually subservient to his wider speculations. For his dream of a trilogy covering Body, Man, and Citizen coloured all his work. He conceived of the actions of men as particular cases of bodies in motion, explicable in terms of all-pervasive mechanical laws. This was made plausible by the introduction of the concept of "endeavour" to postulate infinitely small motions of various sorts – especially those in the medium between man and external objects, in the sense-organs, and within the body. The phenomena of sense, imagination and dreams were regarded as appearances of minute bodies conforming to the law of inertia, and the phenomena of motivation were explained as reactions prompted by external and internal stimulation. Hobbes became famous, however, (and notorious), for his suggestion that all human motivation is a particular case of one of two basic bodily movements – appetite, or movements towards objects, and aversion, or movements away from them.

(3) *Politics.* In his political writings these basic responses appeared as the desire for power and the fear of death, which were the reality beneath all the appearances of political behaviour. Hobbes thought that a multitude of men became a commonwealth by the device of authority in which men gave up unlimited self-assertion against each other – their "rights of nature" – and authorised a man or a body of men to act on their behalf. This "social contract", which was presupposed by sovereignty was a consequence of the overwhelming fear of death which haunted men in a state of nature. Hobbes also deduced from this "ideal experiment" that such a sovereign *must* be absolute, the sole reason for the institution of government being the safety of the people.

(4) *Ethics.* This deductive scheme determined the general pattern of Hobbes' thinking about morals, law, and religion. In moral philosophy he held that the rules of civilized behaviour (then called "natural law" or "the laws of nature") were deducible from rules of prudence which any reasonable man must accept who is afraid of death. Civilization, he contended, is based on fear, not on natural sociability. By "good" we mean what is an object of desire, by "evil" what is an object of aversion. He believed, too, in **determinism** and made important contributions to the **free will** controversy by maintaining that "free" is a term properly applied to man and to his actions,

not to his will, which is but "the last appetite in deliberating". A man is free if there is no constraint on his actions; but his actions are necessitated, as they have causes, even though they may be free. For "contingent", not "free" is the opposite of "necessitated". Hobbes was also singularly clear-sighted on the subject of punishment. He held that punishment is by its nature retributive; but its *justification* must be sought along **utilitarian** lines.

(5) *Law*. Hobbes is famous for his view that law is the command of the sovereign. This was, historically speaking, a very important thesis in that it attempted to make clear the procedural difference between statute law (which was then in its infancy) and the Common Law. It also insisted on distinguishing the questions: "What is the law?" and "Is the law just?"

(6) *Religion*. Hobbes' views on religion were, to a large extent, directed to showing that there were general grounds as well as scriptural authority for the belief that the sovereign was the best interpreter of God's will. Religion was a system of law, not a system of truth. To establish this Hobbes distinguished between knowledge and faith. He suggested that we could *know* nothing of the attributes of God. The adjectives which we used to describe him were expressions of our adoration, not products of reason. He was particularly vehement in defending what he called the "true religion" against the twin threats of Catholicism, with its extra-mundane authority, and the Puritans who took seriously the priesthood of all believers. In the course of this onslaught he dealt mercilessly, from the point of view of mechanical metaphysics, with the concepts of Scripture, such as "spirit", "inspiration", "miracles" and "the kingdom of God". On the problem of evil he pointed out very acutely that the only solution was to stress God's power. Did not God reply to Job "Where wast thou when I laid the foundations of the earth?"

(7) *Philosophy of language*. Many modern philosophers hold that Hobbes' outstanding contribution to philosophy was his theory of speech. He tried to combine a mechanical view about the causes of speech with a nominalist account of the meaning of general terms. He

was particularly vitriolic about the scholastic doctrine of essences. Names could be either names of bodies, of properties, or of names. If one of these classes of names was used as if it belonged to another class, an absurdity would be generated. "**Universal**", for instance, was a name for a class of names, not for essences designated by names; such names are "universal" because of their use, not because they refer to a special type of entity. Similarly redness (which is a property) is not in blood in the same way as blood (which is a body) is in a bloody cloth (which is another body). In this sphere Hobbes used crude distinctions; but he anticipated modern techniques of logical analysis by supplementing the demand for concreteness and clarity of speech by a theory of how absurdities are generated by insensitivity to the logical behaviour of different classes of terms. But of much more general importance was his insistence that speech was essential to reasoning and that it was reasoning, in the sense of laying down definitions and drawing out the implications of general names, that distinguished men from animals.

(8) *Assessments of Hobbes*. Hobbes' contemporaries were alarmed at his denial of any sort of extra-human authority, at his thoroughgoing doctrine of human selfishness, and at his suggestion that we can know none of God's attributes. **Spinoza**, who owed a lot to Hobbes, purged his political doctrines of their inconsistencies and converted political philosophy into a theory of power. **Locke** criticized Hobbes mainly for his doctrine of human selfishness and for his willingness to substitute the terror of an arbitrary sovereign for that of a state of nature. **Leibniz** was full of admiration for Hobbes – especially for his nominalism – but aghast at his determinism and agnosticism about God's attributes. During the eighteenth century criticism was focused on Hobbes' account of the passions – especially his attempt to show that benevolence is a special case of self-love. The **utilitarians** regarded Hobbes as their intellectual ancestor and were impressed by his individualism, his mechanical psychology, his nominalism, and his theory of law and punishment. And **Marx** viewed Hobbes as a pioneer of materialism and

approved of his determination to use knowledge for practical purposes rather than merely to understand. Modern philosophers have tended to criticize Hobbes for his naturalism in ethics and for his mechanical account of man. They have, however, dwelt on the startling similarity between Hobbes' account of a state of nature and international affairs. They have praised Hobbes for his interest in language, for his analytic techniques, and for his clarity in handling political concepts. And even if they disagree with most of the details of his scheme, they accord Hobbes the doubtful honour of being the father of modern psychology and one of the first systematic social scientists. See also **Cambridge Platonists**.

(R.S.P)

**Hocking,** William Ernest (1873–1966), born at Cleveland, Ohio. He was a disciple of Josiah **Royce**; and, in a period during which most professional philosophers in America abandoned the kind of philosophical **idealism** advocated by Royce, Hocking defended it with an eloquence which made him a significant factor in American intellectual history. His influence was especially strong in religious and theological circles. His most important books were *The Meaning of God in Human Experience* (1912), and *Human Nature and Its Remaking* (1923).

(J.W.S)

**Holbach,** Baron d' (1723–1789), Franco-German exponent of materialistic atheism, see Encyclopedists, Materialism.

**Holism** (from the Greek *holos*–whole) is the general thesis that wholes are more than the sum of their parts. It is a rational, rather than mystical, alternative to atomism and scientific mechanism. The doctrine inhabits many disciplines: in political philosophy, for example, holism opposes individualism by collectivism; in historiography and social science, it maintains that the objects of social inquiry are wholes rather than individual actions; in psychology, it sets the focus on Gestalts, not elements; and in the philosophy of biology, it opposes both mechanism and vitalism, asserting that life consists in the dynamic system of the organism.

While predecessors like **Spinoza** and **Hegel** thought in a holistic way, the term "holism" was coined by the South African statesman-scholar J.C. Smuts (1870–1950), who argued that wholes – both animate and inanimate – are real, while parts are abstract analytical distinctions, and wholes are flexible patterns that are not simply mechanical assemblages of self-sufficient elements. Like **Bergson**, he rejected Darwin's theory of natural selection and argued for "internal holistic selection", though as a natural rather than immaterial principle.

Among analytic philosophers, **Quine**, for example, has opposed the atomistically formulated verifiability theory of meaning in claiming that it is not an isolated statement, but the whole ensemble of assumptions involving it, which is amenable to empirical testing.

**Popper**, though maintaining that scientific method is applicable to the study of individual aspects of social systems, has rejected holistic attempts to formulate laws holding for social wholes, regarding the latter as theoretical constructs.

[M.M.]

**Hook,** Sidney (1902– ), American philosopher born in New York, has written extensively on the philosophy of Karl **Marx** (*Towards the Understanding of Karl Marx*, 1933; *From Hegel to Marx*, 1936). He defended Marxism as a version of American **pragmatism**, rather than as **dialectical materialism**. But with the passage of time he decided that what he approved therein was certainly not what the usual "Marxists" advocated (*Marx and the Marxists, the Ambiguous Legacy*, 1955). His later work expressed rancorous disillusion with Marxism.

(J.W.S)

**Horkheimer,** Max (1895–1973), German social theorist born in Stuttgart; along with Theodor **Adorno** and Herbert **Marcuse** he was one of the central architects of the **Frankfurt School** conception of "Critical Theory".

Horkheimer assumed the directorship of the Institute for Social Research in 1930, guiding it throughout the period of its greatest productivity; he edited the Institute's journal, *Zeitschrift für Sozialforschung* (1932–39), and oversaw the Institute's move from Frankfurt to New York in 1935 and its return to Frankfurt in 1949.

Horkheimer is best known for the numerous essays he wrote for the *Zeitschrift*, now collected in the two-volume *Kritische Theorie*; and for *Dialectic of Enlightenment*, which he wrote in 1944 with Adorno.

In his writings of the 1930s, most notably in "Traditional and Critical Theory" (1937), Horkheimer developed an original version of the sort of philosophy of praxis inaugurated by Georg **Lukács**. Increasingly, however, Horkheimer saw the impossibility of an integration of philosophy and social science, and of critical theory and revolutionary practice.

After the War, Horkheimer's critical theory became a critique of "enlightened" reason and rationality. Reason, it was argued, has been reduced to instrumental, means-end, reason, suppressing difference and particularity through the establishment of regimes of identity. The model for such regimes was the domination of (concrete) use values by (abstract) exchange value. Reason's critical and paradoxical autocritique is made in acknowledgment of suffering, and in the name of the entirely other, what is dominated and suppressed by the regimes of identity thinking and practice.

[J.M.B]

**Humanism.** Entering philosophical vocabulary by way of the *studia humanitatis* associated with the focus of Renaissance education on Classical culture, "humanism" established itself in the late nineteenth century as an umbrella term for any disposition of thought stressing the centrality of "Man" or the human species in the order of nature.

Today, in the Anglophone world, humanism is more or less synonymous with atheism or secular rationalism. In the Continental tradition, however, it has come to designate (often pejoratively) any philosophy (**Feuerbach**, the young **Marx, phenomenology, existentialism,** for example) premised on ontological differences between humanity and the rest of nature, and according priority to it in the explanation of society, history and culture. According to humanists, there are qualities and capacities peculiar to human beings which make their products – whether historical events, economic systems or literary works – unamenable to the objective and reductive analyses associated with standard scientific explanation.

While the epistemological reference of humanism is to the human subject as the locus of experience and source of knowledge, the political stress falls on human agency and hence control over historical process. Marxist and socialist humanists have wanted to respect the "dialectic" between human agency and the circumstances in which it is exercised, but there has been a certain polarization in their argument: the existentialist approach has placed an emphasis on consciousness which is difficult to reconcile with the idea of "unwilled" social forces whilst the Hegelian-Lukácsian school has emphasized the loss of humanity inflicted by generalized processes of reification and **alienation**, though perhaps at the cost of making them appear inescapable.

In contrast to both these positions, **structuralist** and "post-structuralist" anti-humanists either insist on the subordination of individuals to economic structures, codes and regulating forces (modes of production, kinship systems, the Unconscious, etc.) or attempt to "deconstruct" the very idea of a "human meaning" prior to the discourse and cultural systems whose qualities it is supposed to explain. Thus, Jacques **Derrida** had detected a "humanist" residue even in **Saussure's** structural linguistics in so far as it allows the sign to retain a reference to a "signified". More generally, humanist argument has been rejected by these schools of thought for its "mythological anthropology", teleology and ethnocentricity.

[K.S.]

**Hume,** David (1711–1776), Scottish philosopher. He never held any academic post, though he once (1745) stood unsuccessfully for the Chair of "Ethics and Pneumatic Philosophy" at the University of Edinburgh. His ruling passion, he tells us, was a love of literary fame, and this he achieved in his lifetime mainly by his essays on moral, political, and economic subjects, and by his historical works. The only post of any importance which he held was that of secretary to the British Embassy in Paris (1763–69), where he cut a considerable figure in French society. Though not without friends among moderate churchmen, he was certainly a sceptic and an opponent of all established religions, and enjoyed notoriety as an "Infidel".

Hume's first philosophical work, *A Treatise of Human Nature* was completed by 1737, when he was twenty-six years of age. It was the product of ten years of unremitting and exhausting intellectual effort.

The aim of the *Treatise* was ambitious; to remedy the defects of all previous philosophies, which seemed to Hume to "depend more upon invention than experience", by establishing the foundations of a genuinely empirical science of human nature. The first step was to investigate the understanding and the passions, on which all human judgments and actions depend. The *Treatise* was divided into three books, "Of the Understanding", "Of the Passions" and "Of Morals", and was intended to lay the foundations of the science of man, for "There is no question of importance, whose decision is not comprised in the science of man".

I.  IMPRESSIONS AND IDEAS

The mind, Hume said, consists of nothing but perceptions, and these are of two kinds, impressions and ideas. Roughly speaking, impressions are what we call sensations, feelings, emotions. Ideas are what we call thoughts. Impressions are forceful and vivacious and ideas are but faint copies of them.

Impressions are of two kinds, primary impressions of sense, which arise in the soul "from unknown causes", and secondary impressions of reflection which arise as the result of our ideas. Aversion, for instance, is caused by the idea of pain, itself a copy of the primary impression of pain.

Ideas are of two kinds, simple and complex. The simple ideas are copies of simple impressions and always resemble and are derived from impressions we have actually had. Complex ideas are combinations of simple ideas and need not mirror any actual combination of impressions (if they do, and do so vividly, they are memories). Thus we are able to think of dragons and other things which we have never perceived. We never have a simple idea which is not derived from a corresponding impression; and all our complex ideas are constructed out of simpler ideas derived from impressions. This, Hume says, is the same as to say that we have no "Innate Ideas"; all our ideas are derived from experience. The objects of our thoughts are confined to such as we have experienced, or conceivably might experience, by the senses or inner feeling.

All these propositions, Hume thinks, are evident from experience, known from observation of our own minds. Empiricism is an empirical truth.

Though the fancy may join ideas as it pleases, it tends usually to join those whose corresponding impressions have been either alike, contiguous in time or place, or related as cause and effect. Hume attached the very greatest importance to these principles of association. "Here is a kind of *attraction*, which in the mental world will be found to have as extraordinary effects as in the natural, and show itself in as many and as various forms." "These are the only ties of our thoughts, they are really *to us* the cement of the universe."

The meaning of a word, according to Hume, is the range of ideas associated with one another by resemblance, with which the word is associated by contiguity; in plain English, all objects sufficiently like those in whose presence we have heard the word used. Understanding a word is the activation of these associations.

Space and Time present difficulties. They are neither impressions nor associated groups of impressions. Each is a "manner" in which impressions appear to us, and which is mirrored in the manner of appearance of the resulting ideas. Time is the "manner" in which all perceptions occur, i.e. sucessively or simultaneously. Space is the manner in which coloured and tangible points are disposed, i.e. alongside one another. Since size and duration are defined in terms of the manner in which unitary perceptions are disposed, these latter cannot themselves have size or duration, and are consequently simple and indivisible. Since no ideas are infinitely divisible, we have no idea of infinite divisibility, and it is therefore inconceivable, whatever the mathematicians may say.

## II. CAUSAL REASONING

Reasoning, according to Hume, consists in the discovery of relations. These may be either "relations of ideas", which yield demonstrative reasoning, showing what is conceivable and what is inconceivable (i.e. absurd or self-contradictory), or relations in which objects happen as a matter of fact to stand one to another. That three is half six, and the internal angles of a triangle equal to two right angles, are relations of ideas, depending on the nature of the ideas related. That mercury is heavier than lead, that Caesar was murdered in the Forum, that the number of the planets is nine, are matters of fact, which could conceivably have been otherwise. A matter of fact, since the opposite of it is conceivable without absurdity or contradiction, cannot be demonstrated. Its truth or falsehood can only be learned from experience. The only important field of demonstrative reasoning, Hume said, was mathematics. Consequently any books, such as most works on Metaphysics and Theology, that contain neither mathematical demonstrations nor empirical reasoning concerning matters of fact, can contain "nothing but sophistry and illusion", and should be "committed to the flames".

Though matters of fact cannot be demonstrated, they can be inferred with probability. The relation on which such inferences depend is cause and effect. There is no other relation,

according to Hume, which enables us to infer the existence of an object which we have not observed from the existence of one which we have. This relationship is therefore of "prodigious consequence", and the account Hume gives of it is the most fundamental feature of his philosophy.

Hume insists that neither the proposition that everything has a cause, nor any proposition assigning a particular cause to a particular occurrence is demonstrable. A *priori*, it is perfectly conceivable that some events should be fortuitous, and that anything should cause anything. Nothing but experience teaches us of the orderliness of nature, and what in particular causes what.

But how does experience teach us that one thing is the cause of another? The cause, we all suppose, immediately precedes the effect and is contiguous to it in space. These features we can verify by our impressions of sense. But there is a third feature which we cannot so verify. The effect *necessarily* follows the cause. It is this *necessary connexion* that enables us to infer the one from the other. And it is not a *logical* connexion, demonstrable or self-evident like the proportions of numbers. What is it then?

Hume's answer is as follows. The necessary connexion we seek is the foundation of the inference from cause to effect. Let us then see what is the foundation of the inference in common life; if we can find it, *that* must be the necessary connexion. It is not far to seek. If, for instance, flame has always been attended by heat, and has never occurred without it, then when we see a flame we infer the presence of heat, and "without further ceremony we call the one cause and the other effect." The necessary connexion we refer to when we say flame causes heat, consists in nothing but the fact that heat has regularly followed flame in the past, and that we cannot help expecting it to do so again. The "must" of causal necessity expresses only our readiness to infer, and this is due to experienced regularity.

Hume subsumed this account of causal inference under the general principle of association of ideas. Seeing the flame is an impression, associated by resemblance with the ideas of flames seen in the past, each of which is associated by contiguity with the idea of heat. So the impression of flame readily evokes the idea of heat. The vivacity of the impression transfers itself in part to the associated idea, and the frequent repetition of the transition from impression to associated idea gives it a customary facility, a kind of felt unavoidability. These two features, the vivacity of the idea, and the steadying click of custom, make it what we call a *belief*. Where the regularity in past cases is unbroken, and the custom consequently full and perfect, we have *certainty* and *empirical proof*. Where either the regularity or the resemblance of the present case to the past cases is imperfect, the inference is uncertain, and we speak of *probability*.

## III. SCEPTICISM

So far Hume has attempted to present a constructive theory of knowledge, sceptical only in so far as it undermines the pretensions of Metaphysicians and Theologians to demonstrate matters of fact *a priori* (e.g. the existence of God, or how the world began), and the pretensions of natural scientists to prove exact and final truths, or provide rational explanations *a posteriori*. It opens the way for a tentative and descriptive science of man, in every way as respectable as the physical sciences. But when Hume discusses the fallibility of both reason and the senses, and the nature of the mind, he reaches conclusions so sceptical, that no science could possibly be founded on them.

Hume's argument against the efficacy of reason is designed to support his preceding contention that belief is a psychological state due to instinct and habituation, not the completion of a logical exercise. If the exercise of reasoning were ever carried to its logical conclusion it would destroy all assurance of anything. Belief therefore, since it undoubtedly occurs, is due to something else; it is natural, not logical. The sceptic's arguments fail to carry conviction because they are "remote and strained", carrying us far beyond the experiences of common life, not because they are invalid.

But now the baby of science has been thrown out with the bath water of metaphysics, as Hume realizes: "Shall we then establish it for a general maxim that no refined or elaborate reasoning is ever to be received? By this means you cut off all science and philosophy."

Hume need not have despaired. His arguments for the self-destructiveness of reason are fallacious. We make, say, a calculation according to sure mathematical principles. But we may have made a mistake. Our conclusion has then only that degree of probability which is the probability of our not having made a mistake. But in estimating this probability we may again have made a mistake and the probability of our original conclusion sinks to the probability of our not having made this second mistake. And so on *ad infinitum*. This process would, according to Hume, ultimately reduce the probability to zero. But there is no reason why these probabilities should decrease. The probability of a firm's profits for the year being what the accounts show is equal to the probability of there being no error in the books. But the probability of the auditors being right in thinking that there is no error may well be greater than the original probability of the accounts being correct.

Hume's account of sense-perception is equally unsatisfactory. All the perceptions of the mind are impressions or ideas. How do these give rise to knowledge of physical objects? The impressions of sense are interrupted, and part of, and dependent on us. Physical objects are relatively permanent, distinct from, and independent of us. They are not therefore known by sense alone. Nor can they be inferred by an argument from effect to cause. For to know that a given sensation is due to a certain material thing, we must have been able to observe the two separately and notice the constant conjunction between them. And how we can observe the material thing as something distinct from the sensation is precisely the question at issue.

Neither sense nor reason then produces our belief in material things. Hume concludes that it must arise from the imagination. By certain weird "propensities", quite different from the orthodox principles of association of ideas, we are impelled to construct a picture of a relatively permanent and regular world in which the gaps in those interrupted series of impressions we call mountains and fires are filled with fictitious unperceived impressions. This "world" provides the material for the casual investigations of natural science, which soon convince us that impressions and their sensible qualities, such as colour and warmth, are wholly dependent on our perception of them and cannot have an independent existence. Science consequently bids us accept an unimaginable world of atoms with no qualities at all, and sense and imagination bid us accept a world which is scientifically impossible. "Carelessness and inattention" are the only remedies for this, as for all other sceptical quandaries.

## IV. THE HUMAN MIND

Hume's account of the mind is similar. There is nothing discoverable but impressions and ideas. These are just so many distinct occurrences, like the successive pictures in a cinema display. But there is no screen and no audience. The perceptions stand in relations of succession, similarity and causation. There is no other real bond between them. The self is a mere figment, an imaginary string on which the beads are strung. "I am nothing but a bundle of perceptions." But who or what imagines the string? How is the series conscious of its own serial existence? Hume cannot answer, "pleads the privilege of a sceptic" and says the question is too hard for him.

The absurdities of Hume's accounts of sensory perception and of the mind arise from the starting point of his philosophy – the doctrine of impressions and **ideas**. These, supposed by Hume to be the undeniable elements of which experience is composed, are in fact but the fragments of a metaphysical ghost exploded by Hume himself. That ghost was the "simple indivisible incorporeal substance", conscious only of its own ideas, and performing on them sundry ghostly acts, perception, volition, judgment, doubting, etc., which **Descartes** had foisted on philosophers as the human mind. Hume rejected the ghostly substance and its ghostly acts, but retained the "ideas", or "perceptions" as he preferred to call them, and attempted to reconstruct the world of common sense out of their spontaneous antics.

## V. MORAL PHILOSOPHY

Hume's contribution to Moral Philosophy is closely parallel to his contribution to the Theory of Knowledge. As he distinguished matters of fact from relations of ideas, so he now distinguishes ethical judgments from both of them. An ethical judgment states neither that something could not conceivably be otherwise, nor that something is as a matter of fact the case. And just as matters of fact cannot be inferred from relations of ideas, so ethical statements cannot be inferred from either. Just as the discovery of matters of fact depends on relations of necessary connexion, which seem to be objective, but are really dispositions of the mind, so ethical judgments depend on rightness and wrongness, goodness and badness, which seem to be objective qualities of persons and acts, but are really the approvals and disapprovals of the judger's mind. Just as our dispositions to expect depend on our experience of regular conjunctions, so our approvals and disapprovals depend on our past experience of pleasant and unpleasant consequences. Just as the task of the natural scientist is to regulate our expectations by the most general and well substantiated regularities, so the task of the moralist is to regulate our approvals and disapprovals by the most general and well substantiated tendencies of actions and character, to promote human happiness. Just as the task of the epistemologist is to describe the psychological mechanisms of belief, so the task of the moral philosopher is to describe the psychological mechanisms of approval and disapproval. And the psychological mechanisms which Hume describes are equally fantastic in either field, and equally irrelevant to his main contentions.

The main psychological principle which Hume seeks to apply in all his descriptions both of human behaviour and human approval and disapproval, is **hedonism**. Nothing but pleasure and pain influence voluntary action. The influence may be direct, as when I let go of a hot plate because it hurts my hand, or indirect, as when the fear of pain prevents me from touching a plate I believe to be hot. And this occurs because fear is a "disagreeable" sentiment. If heat were not painful, the belief that the plate is hot could not affect my actions. Reason by itself cannot influence conduct. It only does so "obliquely" either by discovering the means to gratify some "passion", or by discovering the existence of some object which arouses such a passion.

Hume is thus provided with two arguments against the widely held view that reason alone distinguishes moral good and evil. The first is that reason alone cannot influence conduct, but moral judgments sometimes do. This argument is based on his psychological theory. The second argument is that reason is the discovery of truth and falsehood, which belong only to statements about matters of fact and statements about relations of ideas. Since moral judgments are different from either of these, and cannot be deduced from them, reason cannot decide moral questions. This second argument is independent of Hume's psychological theories, and based on what is sometimes regarded as Hume's major contribution to Ethics: the contention that there is no logical argument from "is" to "ought", from description to evaluation.

The obligations of justice, i.e. keeping promises, respecting property, and allegiance to the state, present difficulties to Hume. For it is certain that the individual acts they require do not always increase the happiness of the agent, or even that of all concerned. Hume's answer is that these obligations rest on artificial conventions, without which society could not hold together, and which could not perform their function if each man supported them or not as it suited himself in the particular circumstances. Our sympathetic concern for the long-term happiness of our fellows creates a *moral* obligation to be just (which is not of much effect by itself), and our concern for our own and our friend's happiness leads us to set up a system of laws and penalties, which create a *natural* obligation to be just. And by "obligation" Hume means only a sort of motive.

This account enables Hume to argue forcibly against the **social contract** theory of political obligation, and to make a valuable suggestion about the nature of promises. Since contracts (i.e. exchanges of promises) and governments are both only useful artifices, and owe their obligatory power solely to their utility, it is pointless to try and base one upon the other, quite apart from the fact that the social contract is in fact a myth. Promising is neither uttering a verbal spell, nor performing a mental act by which a metaphysical entity called an "obligation" is created out of the void. It is simply operating the machinery of a convention, according to which, by general custom, if, after saying "I promise to do it", I do not do it, I am not trusted again. We have here the germs of the **speech-act** theory of language.

It will be seen that the impartiality of genuine moral approval is for Hume founded on "sympathy", which alone gives us a concern for the happiness of our fellows in general. Sympathy, he admits, is a pretty feeble motive, and moral principles control selfish passions mainly by means of the system of sanctions which self-interest leads us to set up. It may be asked then why virtue and vice seem to us so very important, independently of the rewards and punishments they sometimes receive.

Hume's answer is interesting but not convincing. If we approve and disapprove according to our personal interests and situation, our judgments will be variable and opposed to those of other people. Finding this *inconvenient* and looking for an invariable and common coin, as it were, for valuing human beings, we find none so suitable as sympathy, that mild preference we have for anybody's happiness, other things being equal. So we ask of any human characteristic or institution, is it in general likely to promote the long-run happiness of all whom it affects? The feelings of approval or disapproval which we experience through sympathy after asking this question are that which it is the proper office of ethical terms to express.

## VI. CONCLUSION

Hume can hardly be said to have succeeded in laying the foundations of an empirical science of human nature. His contentions rest not on discoveries of new facts, but on appeals to what we all already know. We have all learned how to distinguish causal connexions from coincidences, estimate likelihood, make and follow demonstrations, and make moral judgments. No one in common life looks for empirical exceptions to mathematical truths, or attempts wholly to anticipate by abstract reasoning the verdict of experience on questions of fact. It is perhaps not so clear that no one in common life approves what increases misery or disapproves what decreases it. But it can be said that many things have come to be recognized as certainly bad because of the misery they produce, and that no moral judgment has ever been justified in any other way except by appeal to some moral principle which itself either lacks justification or is controversial.

Hume's achievement is that he tries to describe clearly how we do certain things which we very well know how to do in familiar contexts, and so make it clear that in unfamiliar contexts we are sometimes not really doing these things, though we think we are. The metaphysician who pretends to reason concerning the origin of the universe or the immortality of the soul seems to be doing the same sort of thing as the person who reasons about the origin of Stonehenge or the evaporation of water. He is not really doing so. In fact he is doing things we have all learned *not* to do in the familiar contexts.

Since Hume, it has never been possible for anyone who understood him to do Metaphysics in the old way. Among the more important philosophers influenced by Hume were Jeremy **Bentham** and Immanuel **Kant**. Bentham said that scales fell from his eyes when he read Hume. Kant claimed that Hume woke him from his dogmatic slumber. Many of Kant's important tenets, especially his accounts of Space and Time, causality and substance, necessary truths, personal identity and practical reason are either explicitly or implicitly answers to problems raised by Hume.

(D.G.C.MACN.)

**Husserl,** Edmund (1859–1938), German philosopher, founder of the movement known as phenomenology. The main influence on Husserl's thought was the intentional psychology of **Brentano** under whom he studied in Vienna in 1884–86. Husserl taught at Halle, and held philosophical chairs at Göttingen and Freiburg. His principal works are: The *Philosophy of Arithmetic* (1891) much criticized by **Frege**; *Logical Investigations*, (1900–01), revised edition 1913–21); *Ideas for a Pure Phenomenology* (Book I, *General Introduction*, 1913; Books II and III posthumously published, 1952); *Phenomenology of Internal Time-consciousness* (1905–10, published 1928); *Formal and Transcendental Logic* (1929); *Cartesian Meditations* (1931); *Experience and Judgment* (1948); and *The Crisis of European Sciences* (1954).

Husserl's Phenomenology represents a vast extension and transformation of Brentano's "psychognosy", which was an attempt to work out a logical geography of mental concepts as a necessary preliminary to any empirical psychology. Husserl accepts Brentano's main thesis that states of mind are to be basically characterised in terms of "intentionality" or directedness-to-objects, all states of mind being *of* objects (whether real or unreal), and different states of mind being *of* their objects in varying manners. He also *starts* by building on Bretano's classification of mental states into Presentations, Judgments, and Affective-Desiderative attitudes. But he carries this psychognosy very much further, and develops it into such a ramifying tangle of fine distinctions, that it becomes an independent discipline rather than mere prolegomena to an empirical psychology. Husserl is, for example, deeply interested in the distinction between those conscious states in which something is merely "meant" and those in which it is concretely "present", the latter being said to "fulfil" the former; he is interested in the distinction, analogous to Frege's distinction between "sense" and "meaning", between the object as such and the object *as* it is meant – the victor of Jena is in a sense different from the vanquished of Waterloo; he is interested in the way in which successive thoughts or intuitions are "synthetized" in the developing consciousness of the "same" object, and in the way in which we pass from a problematic assertion to an assertion of probability; he is above all interested in the processes involved in the understanding and meaningful use of words.

Husserl also stresses, as Brentano does not, that the sort of investigation he is pursuing is conceptual or "eidetic" rather than empirical, that he is trying to see what factors are involved in, and what possibilities flow from, the mere *notions* of perceiving, believing, predication etc., rather than to find out what empirically obtains when we perceive, believe or predicate. A wholly imaginary instance may therefore be as decisive in a phenomenological investigation as one that is actual. Husserl further widens the scope of Brentano's psychognosy by making it include any and every *object* of a mental intention, not, however, in a naturalistic or realistic, but in a "bracketed" or phenomenological form. We can, that is, discuss the ideal objects of mathematics, sense-given natural objects or sociological groups, in so far as these latter are possible *cogitata* of mental references in which, to use Husserl's terminology, they are "constituted". As "constituted" in consciousness, the choir of heaven and the furniture of earth enter into the subject-matter of Phenomenology. The name "phenomenology" in fact derives its significance from this "bracketed" treatment of anything whatever. For its use connotes that we propose to study things as they *appear* in consciousness, and that, from the point of view of our study, we do not care whether what thus appears is ever *more* than an appearance. The things postulated by physics, theology or normative ethics remain phenomenologically interesting whether or not they are metaphysically real. Husserl's Phenomenology in its full development is in fact not unlike the philosophy of **Kant**, an affinity of which Husserl himself was fully conscious. Husserl, like Kant, wished to discover *a priori* principles governing mind, phenomenal nature, law, society, ethics, religion etc., which should never go beyond what *appears* to consciousness, and which should derive their warrant from the nature of such conscious appearances.

In the actual carrying out of his phenomenological venture there are, however, some singularities. Great use is made of the terms "intuition", "experience", "description" in contexts where the subject-matter is notional, and where such terms can only be misleading. The notion of "acts" is scrupulously explained, but their description reads like an account of ghostly performances. In the *Logical Investigations* there is even said to be a "categorical intuition" of the meanings of the logical connectives "and" and "or", and though this use, too, is innocuously defined, it leaves a legacy of misunderstanding. After 1907 Husserl also became addicted to a quasi-Cartesian approach; the phenomenological philosopher was represented as having to "put out of action" any sort of realistic conviction so that the "structures" of his own consciousness might become reflectively evident. Great use was made of the notion of an *Epoché* or transcendental suspension of belief: the abstraction necessary for a conceptual investigation became a mystical exercise for which the natural world dissolved, while phenomenological structures made their appearance. But Husserl, like other saints, fell a victim to his own ecstasy: he was unable to come out of this transcendental suspension. The harmless "bracketing" of commonsense realities became the metaphysical thesis that they can have none but an "intentional" existence in and for consciousness. Husserl does not see that we cannot suspend a belief if the belief suspended is meaningless. After 1907, therefore, Phenomenology passes over into a form of traditional German **idealism**.

The works of Husserl form a slowly declining series: as the fruitful analyses diminish, the metaphysical generalities increase. *The Logical Investigations*, with its fine studies of Meaning, Intentionality and Knowledge, is undoubtedly one of the greatest of philosophical masterpieces: in the later works there is much, but not so much, to admire. But the influence of Husserl's thought increased as its philosophical importance declined: hence the strange drop from Phenomenology to **Existentialism**.

(J.N.F.)

**Hutcheson,** Francis (1694–1747), born in the north of Ireland. He ran a private academy for a time in Dublin, and occupied the Chair of Moral Philosophy at Glasgow from 1729 to his death. His biggest work, A *System of Moral Philosophy*, was published posthumously by his son. Hutcheson opposed any "rationalist" and *a priori* account of value-judgment, such as that of **Clarke.** To Hutcheson, the discernment of value was not an activity of reason but of certain "internal senses" specially furnished by God for that purpose. The "moral sense", for instance, inclines us by "strong affections" to seek the greatest happiness of the greatest number. Hutcheson's doctrine looks back to **Locke,** with his distinction between the external and internal senses, and to Shaftesbury, whose somewhat untidy "moral sense" theory Hutcheson developed and systematized; and forward to **Hume** and the **Benthamites.** For it was through Hutcheson that Hume learned that moral judgments cannot be ultimately justified by reason alone – a view he was to extend far beyond ethics into his general philosophy. And here too is the first clear statement of the **utilitarian** "greatest happiness" principle. Seen in the light of both Hume and the utilitarian group, however, Hutcheson's philosophy – shored up by theology and proliferating in special *ad hoc* senses (sense of decency, of honour, of religion etc.) – shows up as a rather unwieldy and unstable structure.

(R.W.H.)

# I

**Iamblichus,** *see* Neoplatonism.

**Idealism.** "Idealism" in its philosophical sense is quite distinct from "idealism" as ordinarily used, when it generally refers to high moral aims. While the term has sometimes been employed by philosophers to cover all views according to which the basis of the Universe is ultimately spiritual, it has most commonly stood (in opposition to **realism**) for a theory according to which physical objects can have no existence apart from a mind which is conscious of them, thus not covering those who, while they believe in God, also ascribe a substantial existence to matter as quite conceivable independently of being experienced, although ultimately created by God.

Idealism in this narrower sense originated in the eighteenth century with **Berkeley.** He argued that the *esse* (existence) of physical objects was *percipi* (to be perceived) or that they were only "ideas" (hence the term "idealism"), mainly on the ground that we could not conceive as existing in abstraction from our sense-experience any of the qualities we ascribe to them. He also used the negative argument that we could not possibly know unexperienced physical objects. These two arguments in some form are common to most idealist thinkers. He then argued that ideas, being passive, cannot cause anything and in the absence of unconscious matter those which cannot be explained by human action must be due to the direct action of a non-human spirit, spirits being the only possible causal agents since they alone are "active", i.e. possess volition. The difficulty that physical things seem to exist when no one is perceiving them he met by saying that they exist in God's mind, thus providing a new argument for God.

Berkeley made practically no converts in his life-time, and the "idealist" school only began to gain ground with **Kant.** The latter however approached the subject in a very different way from Berkeley. He based his idealism on an argument, founded largely on his theory of knowledge, that everything spatial or temporal is only appearance. He contended that we can account for our *a priori* knowledge of things only by supposing that our mind has imposed on them a structure to which they must conform. The human mind could not impose a structure on reality but only on appearances, so for this very reason he held our knowledge to be limited to appearances. The latter only exist as objects of actual or possible experience and so must obey the conditions which our mind imposes, since otherwise they could not appear to us. This was the reason, he thought, why we are able to apply categories such as substance and cause to the physical world, but this very reason debars us from proceeding to metaphysics, as Berkeley did, and applying them beyond the realm of human experience. This, Kant insisted, does not cast any doubt on science; on the contrary it is the only way of saving science from the sceptic. Science tells us the truth, but only the truth about appearances (phenomena). If we claimed that its function was to tell us the truth about reality, we should have to admit that it was wholly illusory. Kant consequently called himself an "empirical realist" but a "transcendental idealist". By this he meant approximately what some twentieth-century thinkers have expressed by saying that physical-object propositions are true but have to be analysed in terms of our sense-data. He also argued that, if we hold that reality is in space and time, we are involved in certain self-contradictions ("antinomies"). We have in that case to hold either that the world in space and time is infinite or that it is finite, and either alternative he maintained leads to self-contradictory conclusions, so that the only solution is to say that reality is not in space or time at all. The physical world can still be said to be infinite in the potential sense that, however far we go, we can always find new phenomena. Kant did not, like Berkeley, use idealism as the basis of an argument for God but repudiated all theoretical arguments for theism and maintained an agnostic view as to the nature of reality, which he expressed by saying we can have no knowledge of "things-in-themselves". He did however think that there was an ethical argument which could establish the existence of God, not indeed with theoretical certainty or clarity, but sufficiently to justify belief. He was convinced of the objectivity of the moral law and argued that it commanded us to strive for ideals which could only be realised if we were immortal and if the world was ordered in the interests of the moral law, which we could only conceive by thinking of it as created and governed by an omnipotent and perfectly good being. His denial of the reality of time led to the paradoxical consequence that our own real self is timeless and therefore unknowable, a conclusion which he, however,

welcomed because it enabled him to solve the problem of freedom by saying that the real self is free, whereas our apparent self is completely determined by past appearances at least in the sense of being predictable from them, thus reconciling freedom with universal causality, which he thought necessary for science.

The chief idealists in the first half of the nineteenth century, **Fichte**, **Schelling** and **Hegel**, were all much influenced by Kant, but completely transformed his philosophy. The first element in Kant's philosophy to be rejected was the concept of unknowable things-in-themselves. It was argued that there could be no ground for asserting something quite unknowable and no meaning in doing so, and that Kant's attempts to exclude metaphysics involved inconsistencies since he himself only excluded it by making metaphysical assumptions of his own. Now, if we reject things-in-themselves, we have left only minds and objects of experience, so we have what Kant called dogmatic idealism again. The resultant philosophy which gradually developed ("absolute idealism" or "absolutism") held that reality can be known to be ultimately spiritual, but that spirit can only realise itself in relation to an objective material element and this is the reason for the existence of the latter. Object implies subject, but subject also implies object, though subject was viewed as ultimately prior. Reality as a whole was conceived not as dependent on a mind distinct from finite minds (God) but as itself a single all-embracing experience of which the finite minds are differentiations (the Absolute). Such a view stressed the unity and rationality of the cosmos and even described it as perfect despite the evil in its parts, which was conceived as arising from the fact that they were only parts.

It is reasonable to class Hegel as an idealist, as is usually done, but it is disputable in precisely what sense he was one. He undoubtedly thought that matter was the manifestation of spirit, but it is quite unclear what he supposed to be the status of unperceived physical objects (perhaps because he was not much interested in this problem). His philosophy centred on a "dialectic" by which he sought to show that, starting with the most abstract and empty of all concepts, mere being, we could pass by an *a priori* process of thought to the highest logical categories of the spiritual life. A leading characteristic of this mode of argument, which he also regarded as characteristic of reality itself, is that it proceeded in triads. An adequate concept was taken first, its inconsistencies led to its being replaced by the opposite extreme, but the latter displayed fundamentally the same defects, and the only cure was to combine the good points of the two in a third concept. This, though solving the previous problems and taking us to a stage nearer the truth, displayed inconsistencies in its turn so that a new thesis and antithesis arose, the antinomy between which was solved by a new synthesis, and so on till we reached the fundamental category of the "absolute idea" and proved the whole of reality to be the expression of spirit. Such a process of thought Hegel worked out both in logic and in the more concrete subjects of ethical and political thought. The dialectic was regarded not merely as an argument but as an account of the development of thought and civilization. Thus e.g. in politics men seek liberty at the expense of order, and order at the expense of liberty, but both when carried to the extreme turn into the same evil, the rule of the strongest regardless of others, and the story of political development is largely the story of the attempt to effect successive syntheses of the two which preserve more and more of what is of value in order and liberty. But unfortunately Hegel gave the impression that the final syntheses had already been achieved in the Prussian state of his day, so that his philosophy was used to bolster up stubborn conservatism, and still worse, the impression that the state is the representative of the Absolute on earth, and so can do no wrong. He was thus cited (probably unfairly) in favour of German imperialism. On the other hand the "Hegelian left" developed the almost equally one-sided doctrine of Marxism, which however repudiated idealism altogether and made the ultimate reality of matter and the dependence on it of the human mind a fundamental part of its creed. Though passages can be cited in which Hegel denies

that the universe is completely rational, his philosophy went very far in this direction. It may be doubted whether he believed in a personal God in any ordinary sense, but he called himself a Christian and attached to the Christian dogmas great importance as at least symbolic representations of the spiritual nature of reality. He however classed philosophy as superior to religion.

Idealism spread from Germany to Britain in the latter half of the nineteenth century and became dominant in Oxford and Scotland. Of the British school of idealists the following most deserve mention. T. H. **Green** (1836–1882), who exercised a great influence at Oxford, was specially concerned to bring idealism into connexion with Christianity and with liberal political ideas. He used a more subtle form of Berkeley's argument to show that physical objects cannot be conceived except in relation to mind and therefore should be thought as dependent on a divine mind, but he discarded Berkeley's empiricist tradition in theory of knowledge and insisted like Kant and Hegel on the place of thought in perception. His argument for God was based mainly on the view that relations imply mind and yet are independent of human minds.

F. H. **Bradley** (1846–1924), also of Oxford, in his leading work *Appearance and Reality* began with an attempt to show that all our ordinary concepts and especially the concept of relation are self-contradictory. This argument however led him not to scepticism but to the conclusion that we must suppose the existence of a perfect thought-transcending Absolute in which all these contradictions are reconciled. Everything is conceived as "appearance" because as taken by itself it is self-contradictory, since it cannot be rendered intelligible except in relation to the Whole, but it still really exists as an element in the Whole. Bradley developed the coherence theory of truth, according to which the definition and criterion of truth are both to be found in coherence in a system. Truth is for him a matter of degree, all our judgments being both partly false since they are all corrigible in the light of a wider system and partly true since they all embrace some elements in the real.

He did not mean to deny that in a limited system for ordinary purposes judgments could be taken as absolutely true or false. A coherence theory is expounded by B. **Blanshard** among twentieth-century Americans.

J. M. E. **McTaggart** (1866–1925), who taught at Cambridge, developed a form of idealism according to which there is no supreme divine mind or Absolute but reality consists of a number of spirits united in a supersensuous harmony, of which spirits every human being is one. He claimed by an elaborate argument, mainly *a priori* and not in any way dependent on the acceptance of religious authority or religious intuition, to have shown that matter, time and also almost all the unsatisfactory features of human experience are only appearance, that there is nothing in reality but spirits loving each other, and that we are immortal and will eventually all cease to experience things in time and come to realise our timeless nature, this involving the enjoyment of a bliss greater than anything we can now conceive. Especially in the twenties of the twentieth century, a great influence was exercised by the Italian idealists **Croce** (1866–1952) and Gentile (1875–1944). Croce has probably been the most influential philosophical writer of the present century on aesthetics.

It will be seen from the above that acceptance of the idealist case against independent matter still leaves room for a number of different views. It may be combined with theism, as by Berkeley, or it may take the form of absolutism, or of some kind of pluralism. It may even be maintained that physical objects are merely abstractions from human experience. Other idealists have taken the view that what we call inanimate matter is the appearance of very inferior minds, or at any rate psychic entities of some sort, if they are too inferior to be called minds (*panpsychism*). This view has been supported by the argument that the problem of the relation between the human body and mind can only be solved if we regard our body (or brain) as the appearance of our minds, which naturally led to the theory that everything else physical also is the appearance of something mental.

It would be hard to find many philosophers who would call themselves idealists today. There are indeed many who would reject the view that physical objects sould be regarded as entities existing independently of experience except in the hypothetical sense that under suitable conditions they would appear in experience; and some trends in modern science are widely regarded as supporting this conclusion. But it is not usual to call such thinkers idealists because in other respects they are usually so different from traditional members of the school. In particular they usually found their conclusion on an empiricist theory of knowledge and reject metaphysics. A term more commonly used of such things is "**phenomenalism**".

(A.C.E.)

**Ideas**. The term "idea" has a double history in philosophy in English. In neither case has its philosophical use been at all closely related to the current employment of the word in ordinary speech. In the first place, the word "idea" is a transliteration of the Greek word for "form", and hence occurs commonly in translations or discussions of **Plato**, and in the development of aspects of Platonism by **Kant**, **Hegel**, **Schopenhauer**, or **Husserl**. Secondly, the term "idea" was very extensively employed by **Locke** in the late seventeeth century, and it remained in current philsophical use for at least the ensuing hundred years. The expression "idée" had already been much employed by French writers, notably by **Descartes** and **Malebranche**, and Locke's use of "idea" no doubt derived from that source.

The word was in fact the cause of a very great deal of unclarity and confusion in the philosophy of the eighteenth century. An early critic of that philosophy, Thomas **Reid**, went so far as to suggest that all the major errors of Locke, **Berkeley** and **Hume** could be traced to this source, and that, but for unclarity at this key point, some of their tenets could scarcely have been stated. This contention, though somewhat extreme, was by no means baseless.

The root of the trouble was that the meaning of "idea", throughout that period, was either made undesirably wide, or – more frequently – left highly indeterminate. Locke, in introducing the expression, writes of it thus: "it being that term which, I think, serves best to stand for whatsoever is the object of the understanding when a man thinks, I have used it to express whatever is meant by *phantasm, notion, species,* or whatever it is which the mind can be employed about in thinking." This remark is conspicuously unclear. In actual fact Locke used the word "idea" in at least four ways. 1) He often uses it in the sense – itself not perspicuous – of the modern expression "sense-datum", to refer to the "immediate objects" of sense-experience. 2) He uses it also, occasionally, in the sense of an *image*, notably in his discussions of imagination and memory. 3) *Concepts* are often spoken of by Locke as ideas: for instance to have the "idea" of whiteness is to know what "white" means, to have the concept of that colour. Alternatively, one might say that, for Locke, the term "idea" sometimes designates the *meaning of a word*. 4) Less clearly, Locke sometimes seems to mean by "ideas" what one has in his mind when one *thinks* or *understands* (whatever that may be).

Now the greatest danger in such an excessively liberal use of a single term is that it makes it possible for the writer to discuss very different things in identical language, and hence constantly tempts him to forget how different they are. In the present case perhaps the most seriously harmful result was that, from Locke to Hume, no adequate distinctions were ever drawn between *perceiving, thinking, understanding, imagining,* and even *believing*. More accurately, there was a constant tendency to assimilate all the latter to *perceiving*, and thus to render malformed from the outset any attempted analysis of them. Hume, indeed, sought to improve the position to some extent by distinguishing ideas from "impressions" – the latter term being intended for separate reference to actual sense-data or sensations. Since, however, Hume now held ideas to be *like* impressions except for a lower degree of "force and vivacity", his subsequent analyses of belief, imagination, and thinking in general still retained the inappropriate underlying model of perception.

Berkeley's case is somewhat different, however. He accepted the term "idea" as so familiar in philosophical writing that he offers no account of its meaning whatever; he proceeds, with entirely unjustified confidence, as if it were already quite clear and well-understood. He employs the word from time to time in all of Locke's diverse senses, and is apt to fall into the resultant misconstructions particularly of thinking and understanding. But more important in his own case is the additional unclarity of one of these senses in particular, that, namely, listed as (1) above. Berkeley wished to combine the ontological thesis that there exist only "spirits" and "ideas", with the contention that this theory was really nothing more than an elucidation of common-sense beliefs. Though he wished to present a metaphysical doctrine, he wished also to maintain that it was *already* generally believed. He appears to succeed in this partly – as Reid contended – in virtue of his double, or at any rate fluid, use of the principle that we "perceive nothing but ideas". For in view of the indeterminate meaning of "idea", he is able at times to represent this principle as a truism – ideas just *are* "the things that we perceive"; but at other times he stresses that ideas are mental entities, that "they have not any existence without a mind"; and then combining these, he can appear to have shown that the things that we perceive exist only "in a mind". It would be unjust to the subtlety of Berkeley's argument to suggest that it rests wholly on so simple a manoeuvre. However, this concealed unclarity does probably account for Berkeley's strange conviction that his startling doctrines were *obviously* correct, and were scarcely in need of supporting argument; and it is, perhaps, in his writings above all that the employment of the term "idea" calls for critical scrutiny.

(G.J.W.)

**Ideology.** "Ideology" is an indispensable but highly controversial term in Marxist theory. Before **Marx** it referred to a supposed "science of ideas" devised in the 1790s by the French philosopher and political reformer Destutt de Tracy (1754–1836), and derived from **Locke**

and **Condillac**. Ideology was a branch of zoology; it analysed ideas into their sensory elements and dismissed any remainder (such as religion or metaphysics) as groundless. Its proponents believed that it would enable all citizens to decide matters of right and wrong for themselves. When Napoleon came to power in 1799, he derided the Ideologists for overestimating the reasonableness and malleability of human nature and the eliminability of religion, and the word "ideology" acquired a derogatory connotation which has clung to it ever since.

In an early work, Marx and **Engels** wittily denounced the Young Hegelians of the 1840s as the "German Ideologists", on the grounds that their understanding of society was based not on "material activity" but on "the ideological reflexes and echoes of this life-process" (see **dialectical materialism**). Beside Hegelianism, the chief examples of ideology were morality, religion and metaphysics; and "in all ideology human beings and their circumstances appear upside down."

The concept of ideology has thus acquired a double meaning. On the one hand it refers to "world-pictures" or bodies of ideas, as opposed to the real world which they (mis)represent. Thus in the "Preface" to the *Contribution to the Critique of Political Economy* (1859) Marx distinguished between his own topic – "the material transformation of the economic conditions of production" – and "the legal, political, religious, artistic or philosophical – in short, ideological – forms in which people become conscious of this conflict and fight it out." The Marxist doctrine that the course of history is determined by "material conditions" rather than "ideological forms" is known as "historical materialism."

But the concept of ideology also refers, on the other hand, to systems of ideas which are systematically deceptive, as opposed to scientific theories which reveal underlying truths. In this sense ideologies constantly confuse the natural with the social, the necessary with the contingent, the real with the apparent, and use-value with exchange-value; and the goal of Marxist theory is to decipher or "demystify"

the innumerable "fetishised" forms in which capitalist societies present themselves to their participants, or in other words to provide "critiques of ideology", allied with **hermeneutics**.

Much of the theoretical controversy within twentieth-century Marxist theory can be understood in terms of tensions between "historical materialists" and "critics of ideology". For the former, Marxism is a "natural science" of history, but can itself be treated as an ideology – the socialist ideology of the working class, for example. For the latter, Marxism is an open-ended art of interpretation, and is not itself ideological. In the formulations of Destutt de Tracy, and of Marx and Engels, the two meanings were of course not separated; despite the efforts of theorists like **Lenin**, **Lukács**, and **Althusser**, there must be some doubt as to whether they can ever now be reconciled.

[J.R.]

**Induction** is a technical term of **logic**; but unfortunately it is used in at least two ways. In one way it is used to stand for any procedure which is not **deduction** by which one attempts to justify the acceptance of some conclusion. Thus the procedures of mathematics and pure logic are deductive, but the arguments of the scientist and the detective are inductive. But the term is also used principally by **Popper** and those who agree with him, to stand for one particular view about how scientists and detectives do try to justify their conclusions, the view to be found in **Bacon** and J. S. **Mill** that the laws and theories of science are arrived at by a special sort of argument in which the premises are singular statements of observation and experiment; to this view is opposed the view that scientists arrive at their laws and theories by a process of testing hypotheses – but on the wider acceptation of the term this too would be a view as to the nature of induction. See also **Determinism**.

(J.O.U.)

**Intentionality.** In medieval philosophy, intentionality was a status attributed to objects of thought which are in the mind but which do not, or may not, actually exist (e.g. a unicorn, tomorrow's lucky bet). The concept was revived by **Brentano**, who used it to define the psychical as distinct from the physical world, and this usage was further developed by **Meinong, Husserl,** and **phenomenology** generally.

[J.R.]

# J

**James,** William (1842–1910), American psychologist born in New York. James' thought passed through three major stages: his work in psychology, his defence of **pragmatism**, and his "neutral monism". James was always more interested in the specific problems in which at any given time he was immersed, than in constructing a system which would demonstrate that all of his work would fit into a consistent pattern. But there is a very close affinity between his three periods. Each may be looked upon as a logical outgrowth of its predecessor; and all three can be read as the products of a single philosophical intent.

## I. PSYCHOLOGY

The key to James' work in psychology is his method, which is generally called "functionalism". At the outset of the *Principles of Psychology*, (1890) James stipulates that "the pursuance of future ends and the choice of means for their attainment are the mark and criterion of the presence of mentality in a phenomenon." Our conception of mentality must be rooted in careful and painstaking inspection of what mentality *does* – i.e. in the difference which its presence makes. Functionalism in psychology is a version of the general demand that anything whatsoever be understood as *being* no more and no less than precisely that which makes the differences in experience which its presence makes.

James was at the same time a thoroughgoing introspectionist. But paradoxically enough he was to set in motion a tendency which culminated in Behaviourism. By introspection James

reached his new classic conclusion that the essence of the mental life is experienced as a *"flow"* in which each succeeding moment grasps back upon and "owns" its predecessor; and then he came up with the startling conviction that "Whenever my introspective glance succeeds in turning around quickly enough to catch one of these manifestations of spontaneity in the act, all it can ever feel distinctly is some bodily process, for the most part taking place within the head."

Perhaps his most famous thesis so far as subsequent developments in psychology are concerned, is the "James–Lange" theory of the emotions. The thesis is that emotion is no more than the *feeling* of a bodily state. Crudely stated: I do not strike a man by whom I am insulted because I am angry; my anger is simply the feeling I experience as a result of being in the total bodily state part of which is striking the man.

## II. PRAGMATISM

James acknowledged C. S. **Peirce** as the source of his pragmatism. Peirce formulated his "pragmatic maxim" as one among several rules governing intelligent inquiry. For him it was a rule for achieving *clarity of meaning*. It demanded of any concept or hypothesis that its meaning be expressed by careful specification of the "sensible difference" its being true would make, but Peirce combined this demand with a strict correspondence view of truth.

In James the "pragmatic rule" assumes a far more over-arching status than the "pragmatic maxim" had for Peirce. James' view was that if a concept literally *means* what you do with it, then its *truth* must consist in a successful doing. Ideas, like minds, are to be treated in terms of their *function*. To judge that an idea is true is to claim that it successfully leads one through the labyrinth of experience. An idea is not a mystery but a tool.

According to James the errors of traditional **empiricism** were that too much attention had been paid to the origins of our ideas and not enough to their function as pointers to future experience; and that concentration on the discrete elements of experience had generated inattention to the equally real relatedness of those elements. For James the essence of pragmatism lay in its stress upon the *relatedness* of ideas as elements in experience to *future* experiences which fulfil their meaning. Thus pragmatism was the only genuinely radical empiricism.

James repeatedly defines the mental life as a continuous "substitution of concepts for percepts". But in the last analysis he always defines a concept as a *percept functioning in a certain way*. A concept for James is a percept which *functions* in human experience in a predictive manner. If James' psychology rests upon suspicion of any difference of kind between minds and bodies, so his theory of knowledge rests upon suspicion of any difference of kind between percepts and concepts.

In later life James defended a technical version of **realism** in philosophy under the label "Neutral Monism".

Latent in his psychology is a refusal to distinguish mental and material "stuff". If James as a realist was to commit himself to a "stuff" of the world which is independent of human investigation, he could not label it either "mental" or "material". He therefore took the bull by the horns and called the stuff of the world "neutral". Minds must be this stuff organized in one way; material objects the same stuff organized in a different way.

III. RELIGION

Amongst his more famous works two should be mentioned which have been ignored in the foregoing analysis. The first is his remarkable essay *The Will to Believe* (1897). Few philosophical essays are more clearly the product of personal experience. James here incorporates in his philosophy a decision which enabled him to surmount a period of acute melancholy and depression. His argument is threefold:

(1) There are "forced options" in intellectual life. By this he means that there are certain questions on which one *must* make up one's mind either for or against an urgent and important idea. There is no middle course. Thus, one must either believe that one is free or believe that one is not free; one must either believe that there is a God or believe that there is not

a God. In either case, according to James, the attempt to straddle the fence and *not* commit oneself, is pragmatically the equivalent of the negative option.

(2) In such cases, when decision transcends the evidence – that is to say, where in the nature of things evidence cannot settle the matter one way or the other – the only truly *empirical* approach is to recognize the need to transcend the evidence. To maintain a consistent empirical attitude one must look as it were for evidence at second remove; and this one does by examining the effects on the integrity and power of one's life which follow selection of one option rather than the other.

(3) But more than this, James makes the startling claim that in cases of this sort the very act of believing tends to make what is believed more true. Thus if I seriously believe that I am free I will in fact *act* as a free agent; whereas if I seriously believe that I am completely determined in all that I do I will *act* accordingly.

The other work which sould be mentioned is his monumental study *The Varieties of Religious Experience* (1902). The theme springs from the claim of *The Will to Believe* that where belief transcends evidence the only empirical approach is to examine the effects of belief upon the integration of men's lives. James claims that **religion** can be "justified" by its tendency to organize and energize men's lives. By "religious belief" James meant in general a more or less orthodox commitment to the divine or supernatural element in reality. He failed to anticipate that later and less orthodox pragmatists might claim that beliefs like communism and scientism can "integrate" one's life and actions more efficiently than the orthodox "over-beliefs" with which he was concerned. He did not foresee the expansion of the sense of the word "religion" to include *any* integrating belief; but his psychological approach to the justification of religious belief paved the way for that expansion.

(J.W.S)

**Jaspers,** Karl (1883–1969), next to **Heidegger,** the chief exponent of German **existentialism,**

although he repudiated both this label and the philosophy of Heidegger. He took his doctorate in medicine, published a *General Psychopathology* in 1913 and a *Psychology of Worldviews* in 1919, and then became a professor of philosophy at Heidelberg. In 1932 he published his chief work, *Philosophy*. Under the Hitler regime he was forbidden to lecture.

Jaspers represents a sustained protest against the "professors' philosophy" of the later nineteenth century. The two giants of the period after **Hegel** are, to his mind, **Kierkegaard** and **Nietzsche**. Kierkegaard's "forced Christianity" and Nietzsche's "forced anti-Christianity" are dismissed as immaterial: what matters is their concern with human existence and the unexampled fluidity and elusiveness of their thought: "Out of every position one may have adopted, out of every finitude, we are expelled: we are set *whirling*." It is only after reason has suffered "shipwreck" in its quest for certainty that true philosophizing can begin. Extreme situations (*Grenzsituationen*) confront us with the inadequacy of all philosophies and become, to cite Jaspers' characterization of his own *Nietzsche*, "an introduction to that shaking up of thought from which *Existenzphilosophie* must spring".

Jaspers' consistent disparagement of all content poses a problem about the contents of his own voluminous writings. They are very largely filled with highly subjective paraphrases of the alleged positions of other writers, followed again and again by an appeal to the reader (*appellieren* is one of Jaspers' key concepts) to be seriously concerned with his own existence instead of seeking refuge in finished positions.

(W.K.)

**Jevons,** William Stanley (1835–1882), was born in Liverpool and educated at University College, London. His early studies were in chemistry and after working for some years as a metallurgist in Australia, he went back to University College to study economics and philosophy. In 1863 he was appointed to teach logic and economics at Owens College, Manchester. He

returned to London in 1875 as professor in his old college. His chief works on logic were *Pure Logic* (1864), *Elementary Lessons in Logic* (1870), *Principles of Science* (1874) and *Studies and Exercises in Deductive Logic* (1880).

*Pure Logic* is a study of **Boole** which introduces some notational improvements and amends the meaning of the plus sign for the logical sum to the now generally accepted *inclusive* sense of "or", i.e. if "x" stands for the class of red things and "y" for the class of square things then "x+y" represents the class of those things which are red or square or both red and square. An appendix to the book contains some theoretical objections to Boole's system which are not, however, well founded. Jevons' later work on Boolean algebra included the construction of a logical calculating machine, the so-called "logical piano".

*Principles of Science* is a comprehensive work on the logic of induction. Written in conscious opposition to J. S. **Mill**'s account of induction as depending on a process of elimination, this book contains an elaborated account of inductive reasoning in which the hypotheses framed by the informed insight of the scientist are subsequently confirmed by evaluating the evidence in their favour in accordance with the calculus of probability. Jevons makes an important point against Mill by insisting on the essential uncertainty of all inductive conclusions. Though less attractively written than Mill's *System of Logic*, *Principles of Science* is a book that keeps much closer to the facts of scientific practice. Jevons' general view of induction has received a powerful and original formulation in the work of **Popper**.

(D.J.O'C.)

**John of Paris** or Jean Quidort (*c.* 1269–1306), Dominican friar and Paris Master. A brave thinker and an able political philosopher, he defended civil prerogatives against the Augustinian Giles of Rome, who taught that all dominion was subject to the spiritual power, and James of Viterbo, who taught that the Church was the paramount realm. His *Of Royal and Papal Power*, based on **Aristotle** and

Thomas **Aquinas**, defined and balanced two sets of divinely instituted rights, and anticipated the later doctrine of indirect control. He also defended Aquinas against the "Corrective" of the English Franciscan, William de la Mare. He denied that matter can exist without form, that matter exists within soul, and that a single organic substance needs a plurality of forms. He maintained the real distinction between essence and existence in finite things, but he seems to have made existence an entity apart from essence and not to have appreciated how far Aquinas had advanced from **Avicenna**.

(T.G.)

**Jurisprudence.** "Jurisprudence" is name of a loosely related group of studies concerned to investigate certain general questions about law which knowledge of particular legal systems does not suffice to answer. Among the general questions of Jurisprudence are: What is law? Can there be law without coercion? Is international law really law? How does law differ from and how is it related to morality and justice? How do Judges reason in deciding particular cases? How do social and economic conditions affect the law and how are they affected by it? Are there any fixed principles by which laws may be appraised as good or bad?

Jurisprudence may thus be distinguished from ordinary legal study as a discipline concerned to further the understanding and reasoned criticism of law as distinct from knowledge of its details. In pursuit of these general aims it has drawn heavily on other disciplines, especially philosophy. Distinctions are sometimes made between Jurisprudence, Philosophy of Law, and Legal Theory, but these mean little; it is more important to distinguish between different types of inquiry as follows.

1. ANALYTICAL INQUIRIES
The elucidation of the expression "law" and of terms embodying fundamental legal concepts (e.g. rights and duties, legal personality, ownership, sources of law) is now regarded especially in England as an independent and important study. The systematic analysis of

legal concepts was begun by **Bentham** in *The Fragment on Government* (1776), *The Principles of Morals and Legislation* (1789), and the *Limits of Jurisprudence Defined* (1782), and developed by his disciple John Austin in *The Province of Jurisprudence Determined* (1832) and in *Lectures on The Philosophy of Positive Law* (1863). Modern forms of analytical study of law have been developed in the "pure theory" of law of Hans Kelsen, described in *General Theory of Law and State* (1945) and by jurists influenced by linguistic philosophy. Analytical jurisprudence is usually associated with (though logically independent of) "legal positivism" i.e. the doctrine that there is no necessary but only a historical connexion between law and morality.

II. CRITICAL AND EVALUATIVE INQUIRIES
The doctrines of Natural Law developed by the scholastics (especially **Aquinas**) from Aristotelian metaphysics and Christian theology founded a lasting tradition in the criticism of law. Its distinguishing feature is the insistence (1) that there are fixed principles for the guidance of human conduct not made by man but discernible by reason; (2) that these principles constitute a *natural* law by which all man-made law is to be judged. Some theorists hold that failure to conform to natural law renders human law invalid; others look upon natural law not as a test of legal validity but only as a standard of criticism.

Criticism of law (on **utilitarian** grounds) was a major concern of Bentham and Austin in spite of their insistence on analytical studies and their objection to Natural Law doctrines. Most modern critical jurisprudence is based on a variety of social policies and is independent of natural law theory, though since World War Two its essentials have been reasserted in Germany and by neo-Thomists elsewhere.

Study of the judicial process especially in America stimulated two forms of jurisprudence, one constructive, the other sceptical. Both emphasized the fact that since all legal rules have only a central core of settled meaning, when Courts apply general rules to the many borderline cases, the reasoning involved is not (despite appearances) deductive but represents a choice between social values. One movement, led by Roscoe Pound (often termed "functional" jurisprudence) is concerned to determine the social interests which should guide Courts in the area left open by legal rules. The sceptical movement originating with O. W. Holmes (*The Path of the Law*, 1897) and J. C. Gray (*The Nature and Sources of Law*, 1902) stressed the diversity of non-legal influences on judicial decisions latent beneath the legal forms. Later "Realist" writers challenged the conventional conception of law as consisting of rules as distinct from more or less predictable operations of the Courts (see for example Jerome Frank's *Law and The Modern Mind*, 1930). These developments were anticipated by the advocacy of unfettered judicial discretion by Continental jurists of the "Free law" school (e.g. Ehrlich, *Freie Rechtsfindung*, 1903) and also by Scandinavian writers (especially Axel Hägeström 1868–1939).

III. SOCIOLOGICAL INQUIRIES

Various general theories concerning the interplay of law with economic and social forces fall under this head. The **Marxist** doctrine that law is determined by economic-conditions and destined to "wither away" has been developed by Russian writers, for example E. B. Pashukanis, in his *General theory of Law and Marxism* (1924). Official Soviet legal theory has suppressed the anarchical side of this doctrine. Non-Marxist theories such as E. Ehrlich's *Fundamental Principles of Sociology of Law* (1913) insist that the "formal" law to be found in statutes is a less important social influence than moral and other non-legal norms ("the living law"). Though general programmes for "sociological jurisprudence" have often been announced the best work consists of studies of the relation of special legal institutions to specific economic or social conditions, for example Berle's and Means' *The Modern Corporation and Private Property* (1932).

IV. HISTORICAL INQUIRIES

The work of Savigny, *The Vocation of Our Age for Legislation and Jurisprudence* (1814) and Sir Henry Maine's two works, *Ancient Law*

(1881) and *Early History of Institutions* (1875) are usually described as historical jurisprudence but no single form of inquiry is distinguishable under this name. Savigny thought that the naturally developing law of a society should be interfered with only in accordance with its natural genius which could best be grasped in the earliest of its legal forms. Maine wished to free the understanding of early law from modern preconceptions concerning the nature of law, and to exhibit characteristic stages of legal development followed by "progressive" societies.

(H.L.A.H.)

# K

**Kant,** Immanuel (1724–1804), the son of a saddler, born in Königsberg. He was educated at a grammar school of the city, and at its University, where he later taught first as a *Dozent* (lecturer) and afterwards, for many years, as professor. As a student he had, apart from philosophy, studied mathematics and physics; and, throughout life, he kept an interest in these subjects. What is known as the Kant-Laplace theory of the origin of the solar system is partly based on an early cosmological essay of his. Externally, he lived the quiet and uneventful life of an unmarried scholar, devoted to his work and his few friends. He had no particular taste for music and the fine arts but he was well acquainted with ancient and modern literature. His interest in the political events of his time was intense. He sympathized with both the American and the French revolutions. Kant is now widely acknowledged to have been one of the greatest of all philosophers.

Two main streams of European philosophy influenced his thought: **rationalism**, which reached him through his own teachers, in the form given to it by **Leibniz** and Wolff; and **empiricism**, the impact of which he felt most strongly when he came across some of **Hume**'s writings in a German translation. His own mature philosophy begins with the *Critique of Pure Reason* (1781), and is best known under the name of the Critical Philosophy. It is a synthesis – as distinct from a mere combination – of rationalism and empiricism, each of which, in his view, gave a one-sided and distorted account of the structure and content of human knowledge.

‾ Perhaps the best approach, though not the only one, to Kant's philosophical system is through his twofold classification of judgments. According to him every judgment is (i) either analytic or synthetic and (ii) either **a priori** or **a posteriori**. A judgment is analytic if its negation results in a logical absurdity. For example "A father is male", "A green thing is coloured" are analytic judgments, since their negations, namely "A father is *not* male", "A green thing is *not* coloured" are logically absurd. Their truth is clear from a mere analysis of the terms in which they are made. A judgment which is *not* analytic is synthetic. All judgments about empirical matters of fact are synthetic, in particular those stating empirical laws of nature, such as "Copper conducts electricity". These judgments, whether true or false, certainly can be denied without contradiction. A judgment is *a priori* if it is "independent of all experience and even of all impressions of the senses". Thus "Man has an immortal soul", which can be neither confirmed nor falsified by experience, is – if it is meaningful – *a priori*. Again all analytic judgments are *a priori*. Their truth, and indeed their logical necessity, can be made evident without resort to experiment or observation by a mere analysis of their terms.

If we combine these two classifications, and notice that all analytic judgments must also be *a priori*, we see that there are three classes of judgments, mutually exclusive and jointly exhaustive, namely: (i) analytic (and *a priori*) (ii) synthetic *a posteriori* and (iii) synthetic *a priori*. It is worth remarking here that Leibniz considers all judgments to be analytic. That is, even empirical judgments according to him could in theory have their terms analysed till their connection was seen to be logically necessary. According to Hume and his modern followers all judgments are either analytic (and so *a priori*) or synthetic *a posteriori*; none are synthetic *a priori*.

Kant is convinced to the contrary. He finds synthetic *a priori* judgments (i) in the mathematics and science of his day and (ii) in morality. An example would be the judgment "Every event has a cause". This can be denied without logical absurdity and yet, in its complete generality, is something neither confirmable nor falsifiable by sense-experience. (If no cause of an event is known, we can always go on looking for it. On the other hand even if we hold that all known events have causes, there may be others which have none. The dominant form of **quantum mechanics** at the present day does in fact successfully reject the principle of causality.)

The occurrence, then, of synthetic *a priori* judgments gives rise to two philosophical tasks, first to exhibit them clearly and, if possible, completely; and secondly to demonstrate not only that these judgments are made, both in the course of any theoretical inquiry and whenever moral duties are ascribed to a person, but further that one is justified in making them. Kant formulates this problem by asking "How are synthetic *a priori* judgments possible?" It is the central question of the Critical Philosophy. Its answer required a critique of all theoretical and moral knowledge as well as an examination of the claim of metaphysics to yield transcendent knowledge, i.e. knowledge of what transcends every possible experience.

## I. THE CRITIQUE OF PURE REASON

The task of the first critique is (i) to exhibit the synthetic *a priori* judgments which enter into pure mathematics and natural science, and show "how they are possible"; and (ii) to examine the claims of **metaphysics**. It is important to note that Kant was convinced that the mathematics of his day, Newtonian physics, and Aristotelian logic were complete to the extent that their analysis by the methods of the critical philosophy would yield all those fundamental synthetic *a priori* propositions from which any others could more or less easily be deduced by ordinary reasoning. Experts are divided on the question how far the development of non-Euclidean geometry, **relativity** and quantum theory and of the new mathematical logic forces one to admit that Kant cannot possibly have succeeded in producing the complete outline of *a priori* knowledge.

One of the fundamental assumptions of the Kantian philsophy is that perceiving and thinking are different. Following the psychology of his day, Kant attributes them to two distinct faculties of the mind, the one to sense and the other to understanding. Apart from analytical judgments – which merely elucidate the meaning of their terms – every judgment consists, or appears to consist, in applying a concept to some particular. Apprehension of particulars belongs to the faculty of sense; apprehension of concepts, and the rules according to which they are applied, belongs to the understanding. In order to grasp the function and the legitimacy of a synthetic *a priori* judgment it is necessary to inquire into its constituents – the type of concept and of particular which make it what it is.

Concepts are of three types. First, *a posteriori* concepts which are abstracted from sense-perception and applicable to it (thus "green" is abstracted from perceptual data and applied to them when we judge that something is green); second, *a priori* concepts which, though not abstracted from sense-perception, are nevertheless applicable to it; and thirdly, Ideas. These last are neither abstracted from sense-perception nor applicable to it. While Kant's account of *a posteriori* concepts contain nothing not familiar to traditional empiricism, his account of *a priori* concepts and of Ideas is all his own, and distinctive of the Critical Philosophy. We shall as we proceed see how essential this account is (i) to an understanding of the nature of those synthetic *a priori* propositions which are contained in mathematics, natural science, metaphysics, morality, aesthetic judgment and teleological explanation; (ii) to an understanding of their claim to be true; and (iii) to the decision whether and how far they are true in each of these cases.

(1) *Kant's philosophy of mathematics*. In discussing the mathematics of his time – arithmetic, classical analysis and Euclidean geometry – Kant is first of all trying to show that the propositions embodying their axioms and theorems are synthetic *a priori*. He is not concerned with analytic statements to the effect that the axioms of a mathematical theory logically imply its theorems. It is fairly generally agreed – since the discovery of non-Euclidean geometries and their successful use in physics – that the postulates of Euclidean geometry can be denied without logical absurdity, and that they are independent of sense-perception – which corresponds to what Kant meant by saying that they are synthetic and *a priori*. The synthetic *a priori* character of arithmetical propositions is disputed by many experts (see, however, section IV), although some arithmetical propositions concerning "the totality of all integers" have been denied without contradiction and are independent of sense in that they do not describe sense-perceptions of any kind. Kant holds that even such judgments as "$7 + 5 = 12$" are synthetic because the notion of "12" is not "contained" in the notion of adding 7 and 5.

Assuming now that the axioms and theorems of every system of pure mathematics are synthetic *a priori* judgments, Kant has to ask: How are they possible? Are there, perhaps, particular objects other than sense-perceptions which the concepts of arithmetic and geometry characterize? Kant's answer is that there are.

According to Kant space and time – as opposed to the sense-perceptions which are located in them – are (i) *a priori* and (ii) particulars rather than general notions. In one argument intended to show the *a priori* character of space and time he appeals to the possibility of varying in imagination all features of a perceptual object except its being in space and time. One of his arguments showing space and time as particulars and not general notions consists in emphasizing the point that "division" is a quite different process in the two cases. Space divides into sub-spaces and time into temporal intervals. Division of a general notion on the other hand is into its various species (as e.g. "animal" divided into "vertebrate" and "non-vertebrate").

Now if space and time are *a priori* particulars, then Kant can explain the legitimacy of the synthetic *a priori* judgments of arithmetic and geometry. Those of arithmetic describe the structure of time with its repetition of units; those of geometry describe the structure of space with its extended patterns. Mathematical synthetic *a priori* judgments are thus "possible" because they involve applying *a priori* concepts to *a priori* particulars – namely space and time. ⁻

Kant characterizes an explanation of the legitimacy of synthetic *a priori* judgments, such as the one just described, as "transcendental" and he calls his whole philosophy on this account not only "Critical" but also "Transcendental". Its concern is "not so much with objects as with the manner of our cognition of objects, in so far as it is possible *a priori*".

(2) *Kant's philosophy of science.* By an analysis of science and of common sense knowledge of fact Kant proceeds to show that in these fields too, just as in pure mathematics, synthetic *a priori* judgments are employed, which it is the task of the Critical or Transcendental Philosophy to exhibit, and to examine for their legitimacy. Here also, he urges, we must recognize our synthetic *a priori* possessions and prove our right to what we possess.

We all make judgments to the effect that this or that particular event *caused* something else to happen. Moreover, before the advent of quantum mechanics the general principle of causality – that every event has a cause – was generally accepted. The judgment expressing this principle is, according to Kant, a synthetic *a priori* one. Moreover, the concept "x causes y", which is involved in the general principle, and applied whenever we make a particular causal judgment, is an *a priori* concept. It is certainly not abstracted from any *perceived* necessary connexion, since all that we ever perceive is successions of occurrences. That we do not abstract the relation of causal necessity *from* perception had already been shown by Hume, whose views in this respect Kant substantially adopts. Yet we do apply this concept *to* perception. The name which Kant adopts for concepts which are not, as are the mathematical ones, characteristic of space and time, but which are applicable to perception, is *Categories*. The fact that they are constituents in synthetic *a priori* judgments makes it necessary to list them systematically.

There are certain clues by the help of which Kant believes that this can be done. First, we have the difference between subjective perceptual judgments and judgments which are objective and empirical. Compare, for example, the two judgments, "What now appears to me is green" and "This is a green object". The first judgment does not claim to be about a public thing independent of my perception. The second claims to be about a substance which exists independently of my perception. Yet both the subjective perceptual judgment and the objective, empirical one have the same perceptual content. Hence, Kant argues, in the subjective perceptual judgment the concept, or more precisely the Category, "substance" is not being applied. In the objective empirical judgment it is applied. This leads to the conclusion that if we compare objective empirical judgments with subjective perceptual ones which have the same perceptual content, and if we as it were subtract the latter from the former, what will remain is one or more Categories.

A second clue concerns not only the discovery of the Categories but also the criterion for judging whether we have discovered them all. This clue is the difference between the *matter* of objective, empirical judgments and their *form*. The matter of such a judgment is always expressed by its *a posteriori* concepts. The form can be expressed by the fact that the judgment has a certain structure. Thus the judgment "If the sun shines, the stone will get warmer" has the *if – then* form, or the structure of a hypothetical judgment. This, according to Kant, expresses the fact that in making the judgment we are applying the Category "x causes y". In considering on the one hand the difference between subjective perceptual and objective empirical judgments of the same perceptual content, and on the other hand the difference between the matter and the form of the objective empirical ones, Kant thinks we can see that the form or structure of objective empirical judgments embodies the Categories.

It follows that if we listed every form of judgment – all the varieties of logical structure – we would have a complete list of the Categories. Now Kant held that the traditional logic (slightly modified by himself) did contain a list of all the possible logical forms of judgment; and so it contained, implicitly, all the Categories. They are (i) The Categories of quantity: Unity, Plurality and Totality (ii) the Categories of quality: Reality, Negation and Limitation (iii) the Categories of relation: Substance-and-accident, Causality-and-dependence and Community or Interaction (iv) the Categories of modality: Possibility–Impossibility, Existence–Non-existence, and Necessity–Contingency.

Synthetic *a priori* judgments consist in applying the Categories to the data given to the senses in space and time, i.e. to the perceptual manifold. Since the Categories are *not* abstracted from the manifold so given, their application to it is not the mere declaration of what is found in perception. (How could we declare that we have found e.g. causal necessity in perception, when all we have perceived is regularity of sequence between events?) Kant's theory of the Categories applying to the manifold of perception is one of the central points of his philosophy. He himself compared it with the revolutionary idea of Copernicus who "made the observer turn round (the sun) and kept the stars still". Application of the Categories to the manifold of perception and indeed their bare applicability, is what constitutes the subjective manifold of otherwise disconnected appearances in space and time into an objective (or inter-subjective) reality, in which we discern physical objects as the source of systematically connected perception, as substances capable of causal relations and of interaction with other substances.

To be an object – as opposed to a mere subjective impression – is thus, for Kant, to be the bearer of Categories. The Categories are not abstracted from the manifold of perception but are, as it were, imposed by the subject on it. The reality of inter-subjective objects is due to the thinking subject – thinking being the connecting of the manifold by means of the Categories.

Kant distinguishes sharply between the *pure* Self which imposes the Categories and the empirical Self. All empirical self-awareness presupposes the application of the Categories. The empirical subject which apprehends its own states, and is thus aware of itself, is not the same subject which "imposes" the Categories. There is no self-awareness of the pure self.

Once we understand that the Categories, applied to the perceptual manifold, constitute objects we are on the way towards understanding those synthetic *a priori* judgments which are not mathematical. Kant conceives them as the principles according to which the Categories are applied to the manifold of perception. They express the conditions under which objective experience is possible. They are the presuppositions of our apprehending the objects of common-sense and science. The conditions for applying the Categories, expressed by non-mathematical synthetic *a priori* judgments, are according to Kant connected with the fact that objects and perceptions are all located in time. They are temporal conditions. (i) To the Categories of quantity there corresponds the principle "all perceptions are extensive magnitudes"; (ii) to the Categories of quality, there corresponds the principle "in all appearances the real which is an object of sensation has intensive magnitude, that is degree"; (iii) the principle corresponding to the Categories of relation, is that "objective experience is possible only by means of the presentation of a necessary connexion of perceptions." (This last principle is more concretely expressed in three synthetic *a priori* propositions which are presupposed in Newtonian physics: the principle of the conservation of substance; the principle of causality; and the principle of interaction.) (iv) To the Categories of modality there correspond three principles which are held to explain possibility, reality, and necessity as characterizing our judgments about the objective world.

Having found the synthetic *a priori* principles in their alleged completeness, Kant can enter upon the question of their justification. This takes place in the "Transcendental Deduction of the Categories". Its central point is that the application of the Categories to objects, in accordance with the principles, is legitimate because to be an object is nothing else than to be capable of being characterized by the Categories. That we employ Categories in our thinking about matters of fact and that their application constitutes objective reality is Kant's most important contribution to the theory of knowledge – whatever one may think about his claim to have discovered the presuppositions of *all* objective and scientific knowledge.

(3) *Kant's metaphysical views*. The analysis of mathematics and theoretical knowledge results in the thesis that all theoretical knowledge consists in "categorizing" perceptual material located in space and time. Knowledge is thus the joint product of perceiving and thinking. We can only think what cannot be perceived; we cannot know it. We cannot help thinking that there exists something apart from space, time and the Categories, a "thing in itself" an "intelligible" or "*noumenon*". Kant calls this doctrine "transcendental" idealism, as opposed to "transcendent" idealism which would claim knowledge of things in themselves. Any attempt to apply the Categories to things in themselves results in illusion and confusion.

Another source of such illusion is the improper use of the Ideas of Reason. Just as Kant derived the Categories from the possible forms of judgment, so he derives the Ideas from the possible forms of logical inference. In doing so he again accepts the traditional logic as, on the whole, complete. The guiding principle is this. We can always go on asking to have the premises of our inferences deduced from higher premises without limit. (We can always go on asking for the "conditions of the conditions, of the conditions. . .of the truth of any statement".) An Idea is formed when we assume that this *potentially* infinite series is *actually* given in its totality. Kant recognizes three types of deductive inference, each giving rise to a potentially infinite sequence of premises; and hence to three Ideas, namely (*a*) of the absolute unity of the thinking subject, (*b*) of the absolute unity of the sequence of the conditions of appearance, (*c*) of the absolute unity of the conditions of objects of thought in general. Each of these Ideas of Reason provides the spurious subject matter of a spurious metaphysical discipline; the first the subject matter of speculative psychology (containing alleged *a priori* knowledge about the soul); the second that

of speculative cosmology (containing alleged *a priori* knowledge of the world); the third that of speculative theology (containing alleged *a priori* knowledge of God).

According to Kant all metaphysical knowledge of matters of fact is expressed in or deducible from the synthetic *a priori* principles. If either (i) the Categories are taken as characterizing things in themselves; or if (ii) the Ideas are taken as characterizing something that is given in experience, metaphysics becomes spurious. The mistaken employment of the Categories and Ideas leads, so Kant tries to show, to obstinate fallacies. These can be recognized and resolved only when the nature and function of the Ideas and of the Categories is understood. Among these fallacies a special interest attaches to alleged proofs of the existence of God, in particular to the **ontological argument**. According to this we can deduce God's existence from the fact that we can conceive (think) the notion of a perfect being: A perfect being must exist since lack of existence would be imperfection. Kant's reply is that existence is not a predicate.

Other fallacies are so-called antinomies. Of these the most important for Kant's system as a whole is the antinomy between (i) the freedom of the will (where the will is considered as causing those actions of a morally responsible subject for which it is responsible) and (ii) the principle of natural causality which applies to all phenomena (and is among the conditions of objective reality). Here Kant distinguishes between the Idea of moral freedom, which has no application to phenomena, and the Category of causality which has such application. Our experience of moral obligation logically implies the Idea of moral freedom. It is a notion which we can and must think; but which we cannot know. We cannot think *and* perceptually apprehend it. The Idea of non-phenomenal freedom which we must assume if man is a moral being is quite compatible with the Category of causality, the application of which to phenomena is a condition of the knowledge of matters of fact. We return to this in Section II.

Whereas the application of the Categories to phenomena constitutes them as objects, the Ideas have only a "regulative" function.

They "direct the understanding to a certain goal. . .which serves the purpose of giving the greatest unity and the greatest breadth at the same time." The Ideas, we have seen, have their root on the one hand in the demand that we should search for the conditions of any true judgment; on the other hand in the assumption that the totality of these conditions, which form a potentially infinite sequence, is *actually* given. This assumption, unlike the demand, is the source of a pretended knowledge. But the demand does indeed confer greater unity on our judgment, since in following it we connect them systematically by deductive relations.

## II.  THE CRITIQUE OF PRACTICAL REASON

This part of the critical philosophy is concerned with the synthetic *a priori* principles which underlie our knowledge of what *ought* to be the case, in particular our knowledge of what we ought to do. It aims at exhibiting these principles and at demonstrating their legitimacy.

The moral law – by which we are enabled to decide whether an action is obligatory or not – is found by analysis of man's moral experience and of the language in which he formulates it. The morality or otherwise of an agent's action, Kant tries to show, is not a quality of his behaviour; nor is it a quality of any desire he has to bring about some state of affairs. These qualities do not imply that the person is doing his duty for the sake of duty. To know this we must know what Kant calls his maxim. An agent's maxim is the general rule which he would formulate in justifying his action.

Kant argues that a person's maxim is moral if it conforms to the moral law – provided that there is a moral law. The law which he derives from the analysis of moral experience is purely formal. It is the famous categorical imperative: the maxim of my action – and therefore the action performed in accordance with it – is moral if and only if I can will that it should become a universal law. By this formal test the maxims are divided into moral and non-moral, precisely as by purely formal tests syllogisms are divided into valid and invalid. The maxims are the material which is tested by the formal test. The most striking of

his alternative formulations of the categorical imperative is this: "Act in such a way that you treat humanity both in your own person and in the person of all others, never as a means only but always equally as an end."

By our experience of the conflict between duty and desire we are committed to the categorical imperative. Is this commitment, then, objective – not only in the sense of being true to our moral experience, but in the sense of being possible in a world which stands under the law of causality? Kant answers that the commitment is in the full sense objective. The Idea of freedom, which can be thought but not known, is not only demanded by our sense of duty. It is, as we have noted earlier, compatible with the rule of the principle of causality in the phenomenal world. Man *qua* phenomenal being is causally determined, but *qua* non-phenomenal or noumenal being he is free. He cannot know *what* his freedom is. He knows none the less *that* he is free. The consistency of moral freedom with the causal order of nature can be proved. But the nature of moral freedom must remain a mystery.

From the above account it is clear that according to Kant morality "needs neither the idea of another being above man, for man to recognize his duty, nor does it need another motive apart from the law that he should fulfil his duty." Unavoidably, however, morality gives rise to the assumption that virtue has some connexion with happiness, that the two are adequately correlated, and it thus suggests the Idea of a power which would secure this correlation. But the connexion between religion and morality is not logical. It is based on an act of faith which explains the otherwise mysterious consistency between moral freedom and causally determined nature. To have made room for this act of faith in the existence of God is, according to Kant, a greater achievement than to have provided fallacious proofs of it.

## III.  THE CRITIQUE OF JUDGMENT

In the first two *Critiques* Kant tried to discover and justify the principles which are presupposed in our *objective* judgments as to what is the case, and as to what ought to be the case.

In the Critique of Judgment he is concerned with discovering *subjective* principles which are at the root of (i) our search for system in our explanations of natural phenomena and (ii) our apprehension of beauty. The key notions into which this third Critique inquires are purpose and purposiveness (the latter in the sense of a harmony which we might apprehend without recognizing any *specific* purpose).

The notion of purpose is involved in *any* scientific explanation. Always, such explanation is based on the implicit assumption that the special empirical laws which we discover are something more than a heap of unrelated generalizations. We look for a certain systematic unity. This implies that they can be considered "*as if* an understanding (though not our own) had given them to our cognitive faculties, in order to make possible a *system* of experience in accordance with the laws of nature". This assumption, as is emphasized by the words *as if*, is not a statement of fact. It is a subjective, methodological principle.

Apart from the general assumption of a harmony between our understanding and the nature which we try to understand, Kant considers particular fields of inquiry, and the teleological explanations sometimes used in them. They have their use as preparing the way for causal explanations, or as filling temporary – perhaps even permanent – causal gaps. The notion of purposes in Nature is a methodologically useful and indispensable Idea; but as an Idea it has, unlike the Categories, no objective application.

Kant argues that teleological explanations foster the assumption that "the universe has its source in an intelligent being. . .existing outside the world." But not even the most complete teleology amounts to a proof of God's existence, since teleological principles are merely subjective expressions of "our cognitive faculties being what they are".

Kant, as we have seen, admits purposiveness without purpose. Indeed he defines beauty as "the form of purposiveness in so far as it is perceived *apart from the presentation of a purpose.*" The unity of aesthetic experience is due to an *indefinite* interplay of the faculties of perception and imagination on the one hand and

the understanding on the other. An aesthetic experience calls for the application of concepts by the understanding, but overflows every conceptual characterization.

Any aesthetic judgment, apart from ascribing purposiveness to what is judged beautiful, claims further that the beautiful object is necessarily connected with pleasurable feeling, that *qua* beautiful it is not an object of interest and that it pleases universally. This universality claimed for aesthetic judgments is quite different from the (objective) universality of synthetic *a priori* judgments. It has a merely subjective foundation in our cognitive faculties. In this respect aesthetic judgments are on an equal footing with teleological explanation.

Kant's *Critique of Judgment* was in no way meant to supersede the two other *Critiques*. Only by maintaining that he treated "purpose" and "purposiveness" as Categories constitutive of an objective reality could such an interpretation be supported. But he clearly treated these notions as Ideas.

## IV.  KANT'S INFLUENCE

As regards mathematics, Kant's view that it consists of synthetic *a priori* propositions describing the structure of space and time and constructions in them has been to a large extent adopted on the one hand by Hilbert and the formalist school and on the other by Brouwer and the Intuitionists. In addition Hilbert treats the actual infinite as a Kantian idea. As regards his philosophy of science, this has been kept alive by antiphenomenalists, and it has been substantially adopted by Einstein (see the *Einstein* volume in the *Library of Living Philosophers*, Chicago 1949). Kant's view of the function of Ideas influenced C. S. **Peirce** and other pragmatists such as Vaihinger. Kant's demonstrations of the antinomies which arise when Ideas are taken to characterize objective reality is one of the sources of the Hegelian doctrine that reality is self-contradictory and that the contradictions are resolved by a dialectical reconstruction of "the Idea".

This influence of Kant's anti-naturalistic views has been very strong among later ethical intuitionists; and his distinction between pure and practical reason is widely accepted by moral philosophers of most schools.

The Critical Philosophy, especially the Critique of Judgment, had considerable influence on the rise of German idealism particularly the philosophy of **Fichte** and his followers, who unlike Kant regarded the self as not only apprehending but somehow creating the world. See also **Categories**.

(S.K.)

**Kierkegaard,** Sören Aabye (1813–1855), Danish writer whose critique of contemporary Christianity contained a radical rejection of Hegelian philosophy, setting the stage (and providing the conceptual tools) for modern existentialism. He was born in Copenhagen, the youngest of seven children five of whom, along with their mother, died before he was twenty-one.

Kierkegaard's formative years were spent under the influence of his oppressively religious father. There ensued a period of extravagant socializing which, combined with a deepening personal despair, ended in an apparently rehabilitative decision to assume social responsibilities as cleric and husband. But shortly after completing his doctoral dissertation, *On the Concept of Irony* (1841), Kierkegaard gave up these plans and embarked on a writer's career which over the next ten years produced a constant flow of books and pamphlets including no fewer than twelve major philosophical essays.

Beginning with *Either-Or* (1843), the focus of the early works is on the task and rewards of adopting an ethical in preference to a consciously hedonistic or "aesthetic" way of life. From *Repetition* (1843) to *Stages on Life's Way* (1845) there emerges a need for a specifically religious orientation to support the openness required of an ethical mode of life. In *Fear and Trembling* (1843) the notion of actual conflict between ethical and divine duties is epitomized in the "teleological suspension of the ethical" of Abraham's decision to sacrifice his son in obedience to God's command. That these are all pseudonymous works is partly explainable by Kierkegaard's need to distance himself from their clearly autobiographical reference to the problematic status of the social outsider, but also by the fact – as Kierkegaard later says in reference to these particular works – that they were deliberately written from an "aesthetic" point of view to help people in the grip of that view to find their way back to an authentic religious understanding.

In *Philosophical Fragments* (1844) and *Concluding Unscientific Postscript* (1846) Kierkegaard's principal philosophical pseudonym attacks the Hegelian notion of an objective science of human spirit for obscuring the nature and place of Christian faith, as well as for eclipsing the subjective viewpoint from which alone the questions which prompt faith can meaningfully be raised. *The Sickness unto Death* (1849) offers a systematic psychopathology of progressively deliberate renunciations of a Christian ideal of human fulfilment. Kierkegaard also published in his own name a large number of "edifying" discourses dedicated to "that individual", as well as extensive works on specifically Christian themes, notably *Works of Love* (1847) and *Training in Christianity* (1850). When he died at the age of forty-two Kierkegaard had become a target of ridicule and public anger, the former through a feud he had himself provoked with a satirical weekly almost ten years earlier, the latter through a savage attack in the last two years of his life on the State Church, its dignitaries, and the naturalized form of Christianity he referred to as "Christendom".

Kierkegaard is widely admired for the profundity of his psychological insight, his moral fervour, and the subtle penetration of his thought. Among his many seminal ideas are a non-substantialist view of the self (or "spirit") as a "relation which relates itself to itself " the centrality of choice and commitment in the establishment of selfhood, and the communicative role of indirect communication. Kierkegaard rejects system-philosophy, but without denying that the kinds of questions it addresses have meaning once raised from the point of view of the "existing individual", who must still come to terms with them without recourse to rational philosophy or science. A number of modern thinkers, especially **Heidegger** and **Sartre**, owe much to Kierkegaard's writings. He

164

is also greatly admired as a literary stylist and innovator.

[A.H.]

**Knowledge,** *see* Epistemology, A *priori,* Empiricism, Rationalism.

**Kojève,** Alexandre (1900–1968), Hegelian Marxist born in Moscow, who studied in Germany under **Jaspers** and then taught in France. Between 1933 and 1939 he gave seminars on **Hegel**'s *Phenomenology of Spirit* in Paris. These were attended by, amongst others, Raymond Aron, Georges Bataille, Alexandre Koyré, **Lacan** and **Merleau-Ponty**, and they also influenced **Sartre** and **de Beauvoir**. Kojève held that "history can never refute Hegelianism; it can only choose between conflicting interpretations of it". His own interpretation focused on the discussion of "lordship and bondage" in the *Phenomenology* – the so-called "master-slave dialectic". On this basis Kojève constructed a Hegelian reading of **Marx**'s theory of history which bypassed **dialectical materialism** and connected with **existentialism**. He thereby initiated a Hegel renaissance in France, and is consequently often regarded as the "father" of French philosophy in the second half of the twentieth century. Raymond Queneau compiled an edition of the seminars which was published in 1947; the English translation (*Introduction to the Reading of Hegel,* 1968) is abbreviated.

[J.R.]

**Kripke,** Saul (1940– ). American philosopher born at Bayshore, New York State. His earliest published papers were in mathematical logic. In particular, his "Semantical Considerations on Modal Logic" (1963) showed how different modal logics could be semantically interpreted in terms of systems of possible worlds with different kinds of "accessibility" relationships between the worlds.

In *Naming and Necessity* (1973) Kripke developed his thinking about modal logic into a fundamental critique of description theories of reference and epistemological theories of necessity. He argued that identities involving proper names, like "Cicero-Tully", were *metaphysically* necessary, even though they could not be known to be true on the basis of the meanings of the names alone; and he accounted for this metaphysical necessity on the grounds that a proper name, like "Cicero", or "Tully", is a "rigid designator", which has the same referent in all possible worlds. Allied to the notion of rigid designation was the "causal theory of reference", according to which a proper name refers, not to the object that speakers recognize as its referent, but to the object that was the causal origin of the use of that name.

Other works by Kripke include "Outline of a Theory of Truth" (1975), which indicates how languages can contain their own truth predicates without running into the semantic paradoxes, and *Wittgenstein on Rules and Private Languages* (1982).

[D.P.]

**Kuhn,** Thomas S. (1922– ). American philosopher of science, born in Cincinnatti. He was trained as a physicist, but turned to history of science because he was amazed by the difference between the pretty picture of scientific rationality offered by philosophers (and eagerly accepted by scientists), and its actuality. In *The Structure of Scientific Revolutions* (1962) he argued that science is not a careful construction of theories on a basis of laboriously accumulated neutral fact, but a contingent social activity. "Normal science" is what scientists do "almost all their time", and consists in "puzzle-solving" within particular scientific communities. It assumes that scientists "know what the world is like"; but in reality it is based on "world views", and specifically "paradigms." Paradigms "provide models from which spring particular coherent traditions of scientific research", such as Ptolemaic astronomy, Newtonian dynamics, or wave optics. According to Kuhn, a choice of paradigm is presupposed by scientific rationality, not founded upon it; it belongs to "revolutionary" rather than normal science. Many critics have been alarmed by the apparent irrationalism or **relativism** of this approach. See also **history of philosophy, philosophy of science**.

[J.R.]

# L

**Lacan,** Jacques (1901–1981), the most controversial and influential French psychoanalyst of his generation; the papers collected in his *Ecrits* (1966) contributed greatly to the prestige enjoyed by **psychoanalysis** in France. The hallmarks of Lacan's work are a highly literary style, perhaps influenced by his early association with the surrealists, and a close but selective reading of Freud. Lacan concentrates his attention on Freud's earlier texts and makes a polemical attack on post-Freudian ego-psychology, which he sees as a quintessentially American deviation. This, together with a controversy over training methods and over the length of analytic sessions, led to conflict with the establishment and to Lacan's departure from the International Psychoanalytic Association. Lacan exploits the linguistics of **Saussure** and Jakobson, and the structural anthropology of Lévi-Strauss, to argue that the unconscious is structured like a language, but the emphasis placed on the role of language in the constitution of subjectivity also recalls **Heidegger's** dictum that language is the house of being. At the same time, Lacan draws upon **Hegelian** phenomenology, and particularly on the master-slave dialectic, for his theory of the ego and of inter-subjective relations. (See also **Kojève**.) Thus, intersubjectivity is always founded in a relationship of aggression and identification, whilst the ego is not the central agency of the personality but a false self with which the subject identifies in a dialectic of **alienation**.

[D.M.]

**Lakatos,** Imré (1922–1974), Hungarian philosopher of science who came to London in 1956, *see* Philosophy of Science, Relativism.

**Language,** *see* Chomsky, Saussure, Wittgenstein, Modernism, Analytic Philosophy, Structuralism.

**Law,** *see* Jurisprudence, Freedom of the Will, Induction, Logic.

**Leibniz,** Gottfried Wilhelm, (1646–1716) German philsopher, son of the Professor of Moral Philosophy at the University of Leipzig. At the age of fifteen he entered the University, graduating in 1663 with a thesis on the Principle of Individuation. This work contained many of the ideas of his later writings in embryo. From 1663 to 1666 he studied Jurisprudence at Jena and published a paper on legal education. This paper recommended him to the notice of the Archbishop of Mainz who thereupon took him into his service. He entered wholeheartedly into the Archbishop's plans for preserving peace within the Empire and between Germany and her neighbours. This led Leibniz to a search for a rational foundation for the Christian religion, acceptable to Protestants and Catholics alike, which would provide a sound basis for active religious toleration. Sent to Paris on a mission to Louis XIV, Leibniz stayed for four years, and made the acquaintance of **Malebranche**, Arnauld, Huygens, and Tschirnhausen. He also invented a calculating machine which was an improvement upon **Pascal's** machine in that it could extract roots, multiply and divide as well as add and subtract. In 1673, he visited London, met Boyle and Oldenburg and demonstrated his calculating machine to the Royal Society, which thereupon elected him to membership. In 1676, the Archbishop of Mainz died, and Leibniz became Librarian to the Duke of Brunswick at Hanover. On his way to Hanover, Leibniz spent a month at Amsterdam, where he met **Spinoza** and discussed with him those parts of his writings which he had been permitted to read. This was his last personal contact with fellow philosophers. From this time till his death he was at work on a history of the House of Brunswick. In his correspondence with Clarke, he attacked the absolute space and time of the Newtonian system, opposing to it his own system of monads and relative space and time which he set out in more detail in the *Discourse on Metaphysics* (1686) and the *Monadology* (1714). In his correspondence with Arnauld, he defended his view of individuality and human and divine freedom to which Arnauld had objected on reading a summary of the *Discourse*. In his later years, Leibniz was involved in a controversy with the friends of Newton as to the authorship of the Infinitesimal Calculus. In our day, he is largely valued for his original work on symbolic logic, but it was not until this century that it was known. His discoveries had to be made over again while his work lay buried in masses of manuscripts in the royal library at Hanover. Leibniz ended his life in a similar state of neglect. The Academy of Berlin, of which Leibniz was founder and first President, ignored his death as did the Royal Society of London.

Leibniz was a first-class mathematician and scientist, sharing with Newton the honour of having discovered the infinitesimal calculus and contributing the concept of kinetic energy to mechanics. He was also an excellent philosopher whose metaphysical system is peculiarly interesting in that it can also be interpreted as a system of logical doctrines. Leibniz established his basic positions with arguments drawn from science, logic and metaphysics and believed that his "new principle, pre-established harmony", was "proved" in all these disciplines, as well as in religious and moral theory.

Leibniz's account of substance as essentially active, arose out of his dissatisfaction with the extended substance of the "new philosophy" and his equal dissatisfaction with atoms and the void, and with the absolute space, time and matter of Newtonian mechanics. His objections to these concepts were both scientific and metaphysical. He showed that **Descartes'** formulation of the laws of motion was scientifically unsound, and that his view of motion as miraculously imparted to essentially inert matter was metaphysically unsatisfactory. He described "atoms of matter" as contrary to reason, since the "smallest particle of matter" is an absurdity. If it is extended, then it is

further divisible; if not it is not a particle of matter. Moreover, the laws of motion demand that the elements involved should be bearers of energy. No extended being can be active, nor can it be a true unity. The only possible element must be a "simple substance, without parts". This simple substance Leibniz called a monad.

Since the monad has no parts, it is indestructible except by annihilation and can come into existence only by creation. It can produce no effect on another monad, so there is no causal interaction. ("The monad has no windows.") Since it is non-extended it is neither in space nor in time, and it is not material. Furthermore, since the only essential characteristic of a monad is that it is active, all monads are of the same kind. However, there is no doubt that the observed world, which is the starting point for speculation about substance, *appears* to be spatiotemporal, and to have bodies moving about in it in causal relations with one another. It also appears that there are entities of different kinds, stones, plants, animals and men. These appearances are, in Leibniz's phrase, "well-founded", in that they can be systematically connected with real properties of the system of monads.

The proper description however, is of monads as varying in their degree of activity. There is an infinite series of monads ranging from the completely active to the almost inert. No created monad is completely inactive, and none is completely active. The proper activity of monads is perception, representation or "mirroring", to use Leibniz's metaphor. ("Perception" is applicable to stones and plants as well as to men and animals.) Every monad perceives all other monads with some degree of clarity, so that it has a multiplicity of aspects. Its perceptions are true in that they are in pre-established harmony with other monads. Pre-established harmony is "proved" by the joint fact of the impossibility of interaction and the actuality of perception. The less active monads present the well-founded appearance of materiality. High and low grade monads mutually mirror one another, and every "body" is a colony of monads of varying degrees of activity in pre-established harmony. A human being is such a colony and the relation between mind and body is no longer the Cartesian miracle but part of the natural order, one case of the universal mirroring. The history of each monad is the unfolding of its states in accordance with its own principle so that continued interaction is the appearance of the unfolding of the states of each monad in harmony with the unfolding of the states of every other monad. Leibniz used the figures of two synchronised clocks and of two choirs singing from the same score to explain how there could be the appearance of interaction without the reality. He described the unfolding of the states as "appetition", applicable equally to purposive human activity and to the moving of the iron towards the lodestone and the sunflower towards the sun.

Space is the well-founded appearance of the "order of possible co-existences" and time of the "order of possibilities which are inconsistent". Space and time as conceived by mathematicians are abstractions. The monads form an infinite series according to the principle of degree of activity, in which series each term differs infinitely little from the terms next to it. Similarly, successive states of a monad form a continuous series each according to its own principle. Leibniz described the "*plenum*" of the universe with its two ordered series of compossibles and incompatibles as the "actual infinite". His space and time are not only infinitely divisible, but infinitely divided, not into the mathematician's abstractions of atom, point and instant but into "real beings", the monads.

In describing the series of monads, Leibniz invokes his famous principle of the Identity of Indiscernibles. If two beings have exactly the same set of properties then they are "indiscernible", i.e. indistinguishable from one another. No two beings can have all the same properties but be in different places, because properties of a monad are a function of its place, so that to have the same properties, the two beings would have to be in the same place, i.e. be one and not two. Leibniz invokes the same principle in exhibiting absolute space and time

as absurdities. These absolutes have meaning only as the place of material bodies. To place a body here rather than there in absolute space, or earlier rather than later in time, would present no true alternatives. The two states of affairs in each case would be indiscernible, so that God in creating the world, could not make a rational choice. This objection is made in a letter to Clarke, who defended the Newtonian system. Clarke replied that no reason is needed for God's choice other than His will, but Leibniz maintained that the principle of Sufficient Reason was valid not only in relation to the various parts of the world, but also in relation to the acts of God. For every matter of fact, there must be a sufficient reason why it is so and not otherwise.

In the *Discourse on Metaphysics*, Leibniz presented arguments for the doctrine of monads drawn from the nature of propositions. The *Discourse* is an elaboration of a letter to Arnauld, presenting the outline of his logico-metaphysical system. In it, Leibniz assumed a close relationship between matters of fact and the propositions which stated them. He wrote that for philosophers, logical reasons would be convincing, but that they would not be suitable for ordinary men. The logical counterpart of the arguments for simple substances was that every proposition is of the subject-predicate form and that every true proposition has its predicate contained in its subject. Just as there is no interaction between monads, there are no relational propositions, and as a monad contains its states enfolded in it, so every true proposition contains its predicate in its subject. Leibniz's logical calculus presupposes that in its most satisfactory formulation, a true proposition would have as its subject a name showing the analytic constitution of the subject and a name for one or more of these constituents as its predicate. Any true proposition is expressible in the form ABC is A (or AB or B or AC or C or ABC). This view is closely connected with Leibniz's life-long search for a "universal characteristic", a language which could express truths established in any field, even in morals and aesthetics. False propositions in this language would appear as manifest absurdities, ABC is not A, or not B and so on. Disagreement would then disappear, for calculation has taken the place of inference.

The logical arguments aroused Arnauld's complete dissatisfaction on metaphysical, religious and moral grounds. If every true proposition is analytic, and the state of every monad contained in its concept, then human freedom is a myth and God constrained. Leibniz's reply was that every actual state of affairs has hypothetical but not absolute necessity. When God chose to create the actual Adam, everything that goes with him was created too, but God freely chose to create the actual Adam. Moreover, in creating the actual Adam, God had regard to all the free acts that would ever be performed by men, and adapted the whole state of affairs to them. Free and spontaneous activity is allowed for in the pre-established harmony of all monads and their states. All monads choose the best and their capacity to discern the best varies with the degree of clearness with which they mirror the world. God, with perfect knowledge and goodness, freely chose to create this, the best of all possible worlds.

This is one of the points at which Leibniz's system shows a fundamental inconsistency. Leibniz wanted both true contingency of matters of fact and yet such a complete system that the concept of every individual contained all that it was ever to become. He wanted to maintain a real distinction between mathematical and empirical propositions, the former true according to the principle of contradiction, and their opposites impossible, the latter true according to the principle of sufficient reason, but nevertheless, their opposites a manifest absurdity. Our reasons for our acts "incline without necessitating" yet Leibniz also maintained that the proposition "Julius Caesar did not cross the Rubicon", properly formulated by someone with complete knowledge of Julius Caesar, would appear as a self-contradiction. God, who alone possesses complete concepts of each individual, can "read off" any state of any monad from any other state of that or any other monad. The distinction that Leibniz certainly wished to maintain between the truths of logic and mathematics on the one hand and contingent truths on the other, was that the former are true of all possible worlds, the latter of this world only. The former depend on God's intellect but not on His will, but He wills that the latter shall be true in choosing to create this world. The true statements about this world form a system such that it is not possible that some of them should be true and the others false. Correspondingly, while it is abstractly possible that any part of the universe should be other than it is, no part can be other than it is and the other parts remain the same. A state of affairs must be not only possible, but also compossible with all other states of affairs. Leibniz provided a formal system by which possibilities as combinations of simples might be derived. He called this the "Combinatory Art", and it may be compared with a table of elements in chemistry. A formula for a possible combination of simples might lead us to the discovery of a hitherto unknown entity. Used with a well chosen system of "names", the combinatory art could provide an encyclopedia of all knowledge and a method of communication with people of all languages.

Leibniz's metaphysical system is completed by his proofs of the existence of God. The system of created monads is, in a sense, complete in itself, that is, it is necessarily as it is granted that any part of it exists. But no one part of it contains the reason for its own existence, so that the reason for its existence must lie in a being which does contain its own reason for existence, that is, in a necessary being, which we call God. This argument, the "cosmological argument", appears in the *Monadology* and there is nothing in it which is peculiar to Leibniz. The **rationalists**, generally, take the existence of God as the necessary creating and sustaining cause of the universe. Leibniz's formulation of the "ontological argument" is peculiar to him in two ways: he couples it with a new argument, from the existence of necessary truths, and he completes it by a proof that the concept "God" is a possible concept. Hitherto, according to Leibniz, philosophers have succeeded in proving only, that *if* God's existence is possible, then it is necessary. The argument from the existence of necessary truths presupposes that all truths are "made true by": facts of some sort. There is no difficulty with contingent truths – they are made true by empirical facts. What makes the truths of logic and mathematics true? What do we know when we are said to know them? Leibniz's answer is that we are knowing the truths as they are present to the mind of God. God's intellect is the "place" of the eternal truths. For contemporary philosophers, this is the solution of a pseudo-problem. Necessary truths are not true *of* anything; they are either analytic or self-contradictory and we do not need to look beyond our own concepts for their validation.

The ontological argument is preceded by a proof that the concept "perfect being" is possible. Leibniz first distinguished properties which were perfections from properties in the ordinary sense. A property is a perfection if it may be possessed in a superlative degree, and if its possession does not exclude other properties. Spatial and temporal properties are not perfections, since all superlatives involving them are self-contradictions, e.g. "greatest size", "last event", etc. Sensibly perceived properties are not perfections since their ascription to an object carries with it the denial of other properties; to ascribe "red" to an object implies that it is not blue, not green, etc. "Good", "wise", "knowledgeable" are all adjectives whose superlatives do not involve self-contradiction, so that they may be ascribed to the perfect being, who must possess all perfections *in* perfection. The concept "perfect being" is therefore a possible concept, and since existence is itself a perfection (assumed by Leibniz), "perfect being" is not only a possible concept, but actualized.

(R.L.S.)

**Lenin,** Ulyanov V. I. (1870–1924) born in Simbirsk, is best known as one of the great revolutionary political leaders and statesmen of the twentieth century. His claim ·to be taken seriously as a philosopher derives from three main sources: his book-length polemic against "Machism" amongst the Bolshevik philosophers; his posthumously published philosophical notebooks; and the supposed philosophical achievements implicit in his more substantive economic and political analysis and in his approach to political practice.

The ideas of the radical empiricist philosopher of science, Ernst **Mach**, became influential among Russian revolutionary intellectuals in the first decade of this century, and Lenin's *Materialism and Empirio-criticism* (1908) was devoted to a re-assertion of materialism as the philosophy of orthodox Marxists, against the "idealism" and "agnosticism" of Machism. In taking their cue from the recent revolution in physical science, the followers of Mach, according to Lenin, confused specific scientific *concepts* of matter with the philosophical *category*, which refers to the mind-independent reality which is the source and object of human perception and knowledge. Their rejection of this materialist category, he argued, could only strengthen idealism, fideism and reaction.

From the outbreak of World War I until 1916 Lenin was again preoccupied with philosophical issues. His *Philosophical Notebooks* contain extended quotation and commentary on works by **Hegel** and they suggest that Lenin was developing a new and more positive valuation of dialectics. Whilst his hostility to idealism was undiminished, his denunciation of "crude, simple, metaphysical materialism" became much sharper.

It is arguable that Lenin's reading of Hegel facilitated his subsequent dismissal of the orthodox view of rigidly demarcated "stages" in the historical process and so played some part in Lenin's change of strategic perspective in 1917. See also **Dialectical Materialism**.

[T.B.]

**Leucippus,** probably a native of Abdera, Greece, lived about the middle of the fifth century B.C. He was the first to formulate the **atomic** theory but he is a shadowy figure from whose work only one doubtfully authentic sentence survives. Our earliest authorities usually refer to Leucippus in conjunction with **Democritus**; it is quite impossible therefore to determine what was the original contribution of each. It is however reasonable to believe that Leucippus is in the tradition of the **pre-Socratic** Milesian philosopher-scientists, but his theory was designed to take notice of the criticisms of the **Eleatic** philosophers, with whom he was probably personally acquainted; in particular, the doctrine of the void was intended to answer the Eleatic difficulties about the notion of not-being, so that that which was not (the void) could be said to be (there was a void). The decisive importance of Leucippus in the history of thought is that he first proposed a completely mechanistic account of the world without reference to purpose or other teleological principles, and that he singled out as fundamental those properties of matter which can be the subject of quantitative science.

(J.O.U.)

**Levinas,** Emmanuel (1906– ), French philosopher born in Lithuania. He is indebted both to Jewish dialogical philosophy (Rosenzweig and to a lesser extent Buber) and to **phenomenology (Husserl,** of whom he was the foremost exponent in France in the 1930s, and **Heidegger**). *Existence and Existents* (1947) and *Time and the Other* (1948) presented original descriptions of the instant, time, death, the feminine and fecundity which forced him to the limits of phenomenology and, he claimed, beyond ontology. The confrontation with previous philosophy which these analyses represented was elaborated further when in *Totality and Infinity* (1961) they were integrated into an account of the possibility of ethics. The face-to-face relation with the Other, a relation with an exteriority irreducible to thematization, exposed the neutrality of previous philosophy. In *Otherwise than being or beyond essence* (1974) Levinas sought to restate this "beyond ontology" in a language which minimised its debts to the ontological tradition. This also led him to elaborate his account of language as an address to the Other – a "saying" – as well as a "said". Alongside his philosophical texts, there are a number of "confessional writings" on Jewish topics, mainly readings of the Talmud.

[R.L.B.]

**Lévi-Strauss,** Claude (1908– ), French anthropologist: *see* Structuralism.

**Lewis,** Clarence I. (1883–1964), American philosopher born at Stoneham, Massachusetts. He made fundamental contributions to mathematical **logic** and the theory of knowledge. His major achievement in logic was the calculus of "strict implication", one of the first successful symbolic systems of "modal" logic. It is called a modal logic because it employs the modal term "impossible" in defining "*p* implies *q*" as "It is impossible for both *p* and not-*q* to be true". Lewis developed his system as an alternative to **Russell**'s system of "material implication" because the latter yields such "paradoxical" theorems as "A false proposition implies every proposition", and does not capture the sense in which one proposition is commonly said to imply another. However, Lewis recognized that his and Russell's systems are but two out of a large number of distinct but self-consistent calculi which can be constructed, none of which is intrinsically superior to the others. He therefore held that the sole ground of choice between them is the pragmatic one of greater convenience in organizing our intellectual experience which may result from adopting one system rather than another.

Lewis generalized this claim in his pragmatic theory of the *a priori*. According to him, just as the map-maker must provide the principles of map-making in consonance with which he represents some territory on a map, so it is the mind which supplies the categories or principles in terms of which it interprets the sensuous content of direct experience. The categories and the relations of entailment between them are thus *a priori*, but place no limitation upon the content of the sensuously given. On the other hand, there are alternative systems of categories, just as there are alternative logics and alternative principles of map-making. But a choice between these alternatives can be made only on the pragmatic ground that some categorical schema may be more convenient than are others for organizing experience with a view to achieving the practical objectives of human beings.

However, so Lewis argued, every claim to knowledge of objective reality involves an interpretation of what is sensuously presented, and therefore makes a prediction concerning some future consequence of what is presented. To claim, for example, that the round rosy thing in my visual field is an apple, is to assert among many other items that if I were to bite into that thing I would experience a characteristic taste. But since such predictive judgments may be erroneous, Lewis concluded that all empirical knowledge is only probable. He then outlined a conception of probability akin to **Carnap**'s notion of logical probability. Lewis also applied the main principles emerging from his general account of knowledge to some outstanding issues in **ethics**, and claimed that judgments about moral values can be as objective as judgments about matters of fact.

(E.N.)

**Libertarianism**: the thesis which attempts to vindicate the **freedom of the will** and responsibility for action by denying the principle of **determinism** at least in the case of some spheres of human activity. It is not easy to state this thesis in a positive way. If it be said that human actions are uncaused it might seem that they are attributed to pure chance, in which case it would be absurd to attribute responsibility to the agent. If we are to be held responsible for actions it would seem that in some way they must arise out of our character; indeed it is often easy to predict the actions of people whom we know well on the basis of their character, and this is not naturally taken to diminish their responsibility. But if we say that action is determined by character we are not responsible for our inherited character or for the environment by which that character is modified. Thus the libertarian is faced with

172

a double problem; he has to justify rejection of the deterministic thesis and yet when he has rejected it he has no obvious alternative explanation of action which would preserve responsibility. It is in fact customary for libertarians to use such language as "a creative act of will" but it is not clear that such expressions can be used to do more than affirm choice without explaining it.

(J.O.U.)

**Locke,** John (1632–1704), born in Somerset, England, the son of a lawyer of no great distinction. He went to Westminster School and, in 1652, to Christ Church, Oxford. There he was trained in, but heartily disliked, the lifeless and obsolete philosophical orthodoxy of the day. In 1659 he was elected to a Senior Studentship in his college – an office supposed to be tenable for life, though Locke was actually dispossessed, on political grounds, in 1684.

In the early years after his election, Locke's main interests appear to have been scientific. Through his friendship with Sir Robert Boyle, who was in Oxford from 1654 to 1668, he was brought into close and practical contact with current work in physics and chemistry, and on his own account he had taken to the study of medicine. In fact he obtained, though with some difficulty, a medical degree from his University, and, in 1674, a faculty to practise medicine. His interest in philosophy, however, was eventually re-awakened by the study of **Descartes**; and Descartes' influence is clearly discernible, among many others, in the vocabulary and the pre-occupations, if not often in the conclusions, of Locke's own philosophical work.

His connection with Lord Ashley, afterwards Earl of Shaftesbury, began in 1666. They first met by chance in Oxford, but by the middle of the following year Locke had become one of Ashley's most esteemed friends and advisers, partly as his physician, but also generally on public affairs. In 1671 Locke composed two short drafts of what was to grow, over the next twenty years, into his *Essay concerning Human Understanding*; but for the present he was deeply engaged in the private and political affairs of his patron, who became Lord Chancellor in 1672. In 1680, after many vicissitudes in the scheming Shaftesbury's fortunes, and several journeys abroad for the sake of his own health, Locke was back in Oxford; but in 1683, after his patron's death in extreme political disfavour, Locke judged it prudent to retire to Holland, in the comparatively calm and liberal atmosphere of which he passed, to the great profit of his writings, the next five years. Henceforward, after the Whig revolution of 1688, he rapidly became a celebrated figure. His *Essay* and his *Two Treatises of Government* both appeared in 1690; and until 1700, when his health became precarious, he both wrote much on current issues of controversy and held various active political appointments. In that year he brought out a fourth edition of his *Essay*.

Locke's *Essay*, by far his most important work, is a vast, untidy composition, bearing all too clearly in its wanderings and repetitions the signs of having been written piecemeal over a period of many years. Its style is sober and, usually, clear; but Locke was not careful over points of detail, not always consistent with himself, and by no means rigorous in working out the full consequences of his position.

## I. THE WAY OF IDEAS

Locke's official concern is with **epistemology**, the theory of knowledge; his purpose is, as he puts it, "to inquire into the origin, certainty, and extent of human knowledge, together with the grounds and degrees of Belief, Opinion, and Assent". However, underlying this official "analytic", clarificatory programme, and greatly influencing its course, is the unsystematic and indeed almost unconscious statement of what can be regarded as a metaphysical doctrine. Locke believed that philosophers ought to take account of the impact of scientific discoveries upon their own beliefs, and on the ordinary opinions of "common sense". But, half unwittingly, he went much further than this. He evidently believed that the world is really what the physicist says it is. He even adapts

to this conviction a fragment of the medieval apparatus which he had reluctantly acquired in his student days: the "nominal essence" of a substance, he says, consists merely in those observable qualities which determine the ordinary application of its name; its *"real essence"*, on the other hand, consists in the physical structure of its "insensible parts". In this and in many other passages, Locke in effect erects the current physicists' atomic, or "corpuscular", theory of matter into the ultimate metaphysical truth. It was, incidentally, this aspect of Locke's position which was regarded by **Berkeley** as most odious, dangerous, and mistaken.

The general picture of the world which Locke thus took for granted may be summarised as follows: the physical universe really consists of indefinitely many material bodies, which are composed of corpuscles, or "insensible particles", which are themselves very small bodies. This whole system operates mechanically; Locke sometimes actually refers to ordinary objects as "machines", and he also says that impact, or "impulse", is "the only way which we can conceive bodies operate in". Now besides this system of mechanically interacting material bodies there exist also, Locke believes, *immaterial* substances, some at least of which are associated, in a manner not clearly understood, with particular material things, namely human bodies. These bodies have certain physical features known as sense-organs; and it is a fact, and in Locke's view a fact not further explicable, that when these sense-organs are stimulated – mechanically of course – the resultant motion "produces in us those different sensations which we have", or "produces in our minds. . .particular *ideas*". In addition to such "ideas of sensation", we acquire further "ideas of reflection" from "the perception of the operations of our minds within us, as it is employed about the ideas it has got". These **ideas** together, Locke holds, supply the whole of the material of consciousness, experience, perception, and thought; all are derived "from experience" (the vague but fundamental tenet of **empiricism**); and "we can have knowledge no farther than we have ideas".

**173**

Thus the mind, Locke says, "in all its thoughts and reasonings, hath no other immediate object but its own ideas, which it alone does or can contemplate". This conviction leads – though Locke does not follow it – to serious difficulties both as to perception and as to knowledge. As to perception, it is of course possible, on Locke's principles, to ask whether the "ideas" of which we are said to be aware in our minds do in fact faithfully represent to us the character of their causes, "external" material things. Locke's own answer to this question is that, in part, they do: our ideas of "primary qualities" – "solidity, extension, figure, motion or rest, and number" – do represent to us qualities that bodies do really possess. Ideas of "secondary" qualities, on the other hand – "as colours, sounds, tastes, etc." – are merely modes in which bodies happen to appear to organisms constituted as we are; there is "in truth nothing in the objects themselves, but powers to produce various sensations in us by their primary qualities, that is, by the bulk, figure, texture, and motion of their insensible parts". In making this distinction Locke gives striking expression to his conviction that the world *really is* nothing but a physical mechanism; it will be observed that the qualities he asserts to be really "in" bodies are precisely those relevant to their mechanical behaviour. However, he seems not to notice the difficulty that, if we can "contemplate" *only* our own ideas, it is at least not apparent how we could ever decide what relations hold between these and "external" bodies; how could we tell that our ideas were faithful representatives in *any* respect, if we can never contemplate that which they represent to us? It was indeed urged by Berkeley that, on Locke's view, we should have no solid ground even for the conviction that any "external" bodies exist; still less, then, is Locke in a position to assert so confidently that those bodies really do have certain qualities, but only appear to have others.

Locke's difficulties as to knowledge are somewhat similar. Defining knowledge as "the perception of the connexion and agreement, or disagreement and repugnancy, of any of our ideas", he is first obliged to add the inconsistent rider that our ideas must be perceived also to "agree with the reality of things", and then to evade the resulting question as to how, on his principles, this latter perception can occur. He sometimes appears to hold that knowledge, *strictly speaking*, can be *only* of the relations between ideas; but even if so, it is not clear how he could consistently admit that even so much as a well-grounded opinion could be achieved as to the relation between ideas and "the reality of things".

It will be observed that these major difficulties in Locke's position derive alike from his basic principle, that we can be actually – "immediately" – aware only of the contents of our own minds. It is in this way that ideas, in his system, become what has been described as an "iron curtain" between the observer and the world. And it is important to notice that this principle was not, as Locke seems to have supposed, forced on him by his adherence to scientific theory. For the scientific account of perception addresses itself to the question, how perception occurs – the orthodox answer being, in Locke's day, that it occurs by means of the mechanical operation of "insensible particles" upon the sense-organs. Now this is not an answer to the question, what it is that is really perceived. It may be that some occurrence "in the mind" is the last item in the causal transaction between the observer and his environment; but it does not follow that what occurs in his mind is all that he really observes.

## II. POLITICAL THEORY

Locke's political writings were for the most part avowedly directed towards supplying a theoretical justification for the political views of those who wished to overthrow the arbitrary government of the Stuarts, and to replace it by a monarchy of strictly limited powers. Of his *Two Treatises of Government*, the first is a successful refutation of a view that scarcely deserved such extended notice. Locke's target here is the absolutist theory, not, unfortunately, of the powerful **Hobbes**, but of the zealous Royalist Sir Robert Filmer. Filmer had argued that the authority of a king is identical with that of a father over his children, and is derived directly from God's grant of such authority to Adam. Locke gravely points out, first, that a father's authority over his children is not absolute, at least when they become adult; second, that the relation between a king and his subjects is not genuinely analogous with that between a father and his children; and third, that it would in any case be a matter of some difficulty to trace the direct descent of patriarchal authority from Adam to Charles II. It is in the second *Treatise* that Locke states his own case.

In the exposition of his political principles Locke adopted the pseudo-historical convention of the period. He describes, purporting to trace an actual process, societies as emerging from a pristine "state of nature", as a result of a "contract" made among individuals jointly to submit themselves, for the sake of certain advantages, to a ruler or rulers. Now Hobbes had argued that, in such a case, the designated ruler could only be absolute; if any members of society were to be effectively restrained, the ruler must have absolute power over all. Locke argues against this, first, that the ruler's rights are limited, as are those of everyone, by the "law of nature"; and second, that in any case his powers are assigned to him as a trust for the good of the members of society, and hence can properly be taken away again if that trust is broken. Though thus opposed to authoritarianism, Locke was of course in no sense a democrat. He had no uncritical faith in elected assemblies, still less in the populace at large; he did not envisage universal suffrage. He believed that monarchy was certainly the best political arrangement possible, provided that some assembly could hold the monarch to the terms of his trust, and itself be in some degree answerable to the people. Unlike Hobbes, he did not think it essential that any person or persons in society should be a centre of final sovereignty, and able in the last resort to settle all disputes. This, no doubt, was because, unlike Hobbes, he believed in the rational basis of the principles of conduct, and believed also that human beings were rational enough to be trusted, with certain safeguards, to follow those principles. This made it possible for him to rely

upon some measure of enlightened cooperation in political affairs.

It may perhaps be said, in summary, that Locke's real achievement was to bring together most of the threads of the "advanced" thinking of his time. In his philosophy he seemed to have escaped from the mazes of minute and insignificant subtlety into which the scholastic tradition had degenerated; to have taken account of the new stirrings of Cartesianism; and above all to have brought philosophy firmly into line with the latest and best in scientific theory. The general picture of the world, against the background of which Locke pursued his epistemological inquiries, was, as has been said, exactly that of the seventeenth– and eighteenth-century physicist; and there is little doubt that Locke's views owed much of their prestige to their declared alliance with the flourishing physical sciences. The fact that those views embodied serious misunderstandings was soon observed by philosophical critics, notably by Berkeley and **Leibniz**; they expressed so exactly, however, the spirit of the age, that they easily survived such criticism. Moreover, there is of course merit enough in Locke's many discussions of particular problems to ensure that he should still be read with close attention, as being at least in the historical mainstream of modern philosophy in the English language.

In his political theory also, unadventurous as it may seem, and artificially presented as it undoubtedly is, Locke was giving clear expression to the enlightened opinion of his day. It is true that his theory is presented as stating the conditions to be satisfied by any good society at any time; but in fact – not surprisingly – its real contribution was to the political thought of his own society and age. The seventeenth century in English politics was a period in which the character and role of kingship, or more generally the character and relations of ruler and subject, were topics of incessant uncertainty, conflict, and debate; that age was, even more than most, an age of transition. It can hardly be said that Locke contributed directly to the comparatively enduring settlement of 1688, but he did express the thought of those who worked for that settlement. In this also he was the embodiment of his age, and in his good sense, sobriety and devotion to reason, he remains a justly admired representative of it.

(G.J.W.)

**Logic**. Logic may be defined as the theory of the conditions of valid inference or, more shortly, as the theory of proof. Some remarks are necessary about this rough definition if it is not to be misleading. Inference is a process by which we pass from a belief in one or more statements (the *premises*) to a belief in a further statement (the *conclusion*) whose truth, if the inference is a good one, is either guaranteed or at least made probable by the truth of the premises. Inference is therefore a mental process and it might be thought that this means that logic is concerned with the processes of thought and so connected in some way with psychology. This is not so. The study of the *conditions* of valid inference does not involve studying any processes of thought. At least in the case of strict deductive proof with which we are chiefly concerned, it is the formal or structural properties of arguments in which we are interested. What this involves will be made clear below.

I.  THE SCOPE OF LOGIC
In its early stages, logic may be considered as a natural history of arguments. Just as the biologist studies the structure and working of plants and animals and tries to see how different species are related to each other, so the logician studies the structure and working of different types of argument and tries to relate them together systematically. But the logician is interested only in those features of arguments in virtue of which they are admitted to be *valid*. It is clear that we all rely on inference to provide much of our knowledge and that our inferences may be more or less reliable. At any rate, we all distinguish, at a common sense level, between good inferences and bad ones though we may not find it easy to say

what we mean by a satisfactory inference, still less to codify the rules which distinguish good inferences from bad. It is one of the tasks of logic to provide a systematic way of making these distinctions.

This is however only one of its tasks. In Greek and medieval times, logicians were interested mainly in the classification and working of arguments. And part of the interest of modern symbolic logicians has been to give a more detailed and complete account of the various kinds of valid arguments and their connexions. An equally important task of logic, at least since the work of **Frege**, has been the critical examination of mathematical concepts and methods. As mathematical proofs are a particularly striking and successful kind of proof, their study falls under the general heading of the theory of proof. But this aspect of logic, important as it is, is highly technical and difficult. No further reference will be made to it here where we shall be concerned only with elementary and practical aspects of logic. But it is necessary to remember that modern developments in logic (which now constitute the main body of the science) are almost entirely due to the work of mathematicians. This explains the highly formal character of its methods.

Two main types of inference have interested logicians, *deductive* and *inductive*. Well known examples of deductive inference are the geometry of Euclid or syllogisms such as:

(1) *If all mammals are warm blooded and all mammals suckle their young, then some warm blooded creatures suckle their young.*

That a deductive argument is valid is a guarantee that the conclusion cannot be false if the premises are true. The conclusion follows rigorously from the premises so that it is impossible, without self-contradiction, for anyone to affirm the premises together with the negation of the conclusion. It is part of the task of logic (and a matter of some difficulty) to give a complete and satisfactory account of the conditions under which a statement can be said to be inferable from, deducible from or entailed by others. Many logicians would say that the concepts of proof and valid inference are best restricted to cover only those cases that conform to the rules of deductive logic. However that may be, the process of inductive inference has received a good deal of attention from logicians. A brief account of some of its problems will be given in Section VI below. Sections II to V relate to deductive or formal logic.

## II. LOGICAL FORM

It has been a common practice of logicians since the time of **Aristotle**, who founded the science, to use symbolic devices for the expression and study of arguments. This is because logicians are not interested in particular arguments or the ordinary linguistic expressions into which they are cast or in the subject matter of arguments. They are interested rather in the *general rules* governing the validity of arguments and therefore in those features of arguments which are relevant to their validity. These features are structural ones, the form or skeleton of an argument which is often blurred or concealed by the way it is expressed in ordinary language. By the study of argument-structure, the enormous diversity of reasonings on all sorts of topics and in all sorts of languages can be systematically related together. That the validity of a deductive argument depends upon its structure (or *logical form*) and not upon its subject matter can be seen intuitively in the following examples. (2) and (3) below can be seen on inspection to be valid although they are concerned with different matters:

(2) *If no metals are soluble in water and some crystalline substances are metals, then some crystalline substances are not soluble in water.*

(3) *If no Christians are pantheists and some mystics are Christians, then some mystics are not pantheists.*

The logical form common to both can be represented thus:

(4) *If no A's are B's and some C's are A's, then some C's are not B's.*

Here the terms relating to the subject matter of these syllogisms have been replaced by *variables*, that is symbols that do not themselves name or refer to things or properties

but can, like pronouns, stand for (and may be replaced by) words or phrases referring to things or properties. They can be looked on as just a convenient way of marking blank spaces in the form of the argument, to be filled in at will with suitable terms. We could (rather less conveniently) write (4) as:

(5) *If no . . . are - - - and some • • • are . . . then some • • • are not - - -.*

The different ways of filling in the blanks are merely devices for labelling the positions of possible terms. Such labelling is obviously required if the logical form is to be preserved. The use of variables is familiar to most people in the use of *x*, *y* and so on in algebra.

Aristotle introduced the use of variables into logic in his treatment of the syllogism, partly, as it seems, to be able to formulate rules of logic that were universally true. Modern logic uses symbols other than variables, just as mathematics does, and some of these uses will be explained below. Meanwhile, it is worth noting that the use of symbols in formulating logical expressions has important advantages besides the exhibition of logical form and the statement of general rules. Their use brings a clarity and conciseness into logic without which little progress could be made. This can be appreciated if we consider how clumsy and inconvenient it would be to paraphrase in ordinary language even a simple algebraic expression like:

$$(x + y)^2 = (x^2 + 2xy + y^2).$$

The development of logic, like that of mathematics, depends on having available a concise and apt symbolism for its concepts and operations.

## III. PROPOSITIONAL CALCULUS

The basic branch of logic is the logic of propositions or, as it is often called, the propositional calculus. This was not the first part of logic to be developed. Aristotle paid little attention to it. And though Stoic logicians in ancient times and some of the medievals made contributions to this part of logic, its systematic development is the work of **Frege**, **Peirce** and modern logicians. The propositional calculus treats arguments whose basic constituents are propositions. The word "proposition" may be taken here to be synonymous with the phrase "indicative sentence". The defining property of a proposition for this purpose is that it must be either true or false and cannot be both. Thus questions or commands do not qualify as propositions. A typical example of a simple propositional argument is:

(6) *If smoking is not a cause of cancer, then statistical correlations are not a reliable sign of causal connexion. But statistical correlations are a reliable sign of causal connexion. Therefore, smoking is a cause of cancer.*

Its logical form may be shown by replacing the proposition "smoking is a cause of cancer" by "$p$" and "statistical correlations are a reliable sign of causal connexion" by "$q$" and rewriting as follows:

(7) *If, if not-p then not-q, and q, then p.*

(7) exhibits the logical form of (6) and is an *argument-form* which becomes a concrete argument if the variables "$p$" and "$q$" are replaced by particular propositions. And since this form is a valid one, whatever propositions we put for "$p$" and "$q$" will yield a valid argument.

In general, propositional arguments can all be conveniently symbolised by putting variables, $p$, $q$, $r$,. . .for the constituent propositions and finding further symbols for the words and phrases that bind the propositions together into their logical form. In (7), these words are "if. . .then. . .", "and" and "not". They are called in logic *propositional connectives* or *logical constants* and their symbolic equivalents in the commonly used notation of **Russell** and **Whitehead's** *Principia Mathematica* are:

not: $\sim$
and: .
if/then: $\supset$

A further commonly occurring constant is:

or: $\vee$

(here to be read in the *inclusive* sense of "or", that is, "$p \vee q$" means "either $p$ or $q$ and possibly both"). Thus (7) becomes under further translation:

(8)  $((\sim p \supset \sim q). q) \supset p$

178

Brackets are used here to show the *scope* of the logical constants. For example, (8) read without brackets would be ambiguous and could be understood in a number of different ways. Brackets or other similar devices are necessary to show the binding force of the constants.

All the argument forms of propositional logic can be expressed in symbolic form with the aid of this set of signs.

IV.  VALIDITY IN PROPOSITIONAL ARGUMENTS
Two problems arise once we have a method of formalizing propositional arguments:(i) How do we distinguish the valid argument forms from the invalid? (ii) How can we generate new valid formulas on the basis of those we already know to be valid?

(i) raises what is called the *decision problem*. At this level of logic, it can be solved easily enough. One simple decision procedure is the method of truth tables. By this method, we first list all the possible combinations of truth and falsity for the constituent propositions of the argument form in question. There will be $2^n$ of these where $n$ is the number of different propositions. For (8), there are $2^2$ or 4 such combinations; $p$ and $q$ both true, $p$ true and $q$ false, $p$ false and $q$ true, and $p$ and $q$ both false. We then find the truth value of the whole expression for each of these four cases. This is done by applying the definitions of the logical connectives in terms of truth-values. These definitions may be set out in a tabular form as follows:

| $p$ | $q$ | $\sim p$ | $\sim q$ | $p \cdot q$ | $p \vee q$ | $p \supset q$ |
|---|---|---|---|---|---|---|
| T | T | F | F | T | T | T |
| T | F | F | T | F | T | F |
| F | T | T | F | F | T | T |
| F | F | T | T | F | F | T |

Applying these rules to (8), we complete the truth-table in four stages, as follows:

*Stage 1.* We set out the truth-values of the negated and unnegated variables in columns according to the rules:

| (( ~p ⊃ | ~q) | . | q) | ⊃ | ·P |
|---|---|---|---|---|---|
| F | F | | T | | T |
| F | T | | F | | T |
| T | F | | T | | F |
| T | T | | F | | F |
| 1 | 2 | | 3 | | 4 |

*Stage 2.* We complete the column under the logical constant of narrowest scope according to the rules for "⊃" above:

| (( ~p | ⊃ | ~q) | . | q) | ⊃ | p |
|---|---|---|---|---|---|---|
| F | T | F | | T | | T |
| F | T | T | | F | | T |
| T | F | F | | T | | F |
| T | T | T | | F | | F |
| 1 | 5 | 2 | | 3 | | 4 |

*Stage 3.* We complete the column under the logical constant of next widest scope, i.e., we join columns 5 and 3 according to the rule for ".":

| (( ~p | ⊃ | ~q) | . | q) | ⊃ | p |
|---|---|---|---|---|---|---|
| F | T | F | T | T | | T |
| F | T | T | F | F | | T |
| T | F | F | F | T | | F |
| T | T | T | F | F | | F |
| 1 | 5 | 2 | 6 | 3 | | 4 |

*Stage 4.* Lastly, we complete the final column under the logical constant of widest scope joining columns 6 and 4 according to the rules for "⊃":

| (( ~p | ⊃ | ~q) | . | q) | ⊃ | p |
|---|---|---|---|---|---|---|
| F | T | F | T | T | T | T |
| F | T | T | F | F | T | T |
| T | F | F | F | T | T | F |
| T | T | T | F | F | T | F |
| 1 | 5 | 2 | 6 | 3 | 7 | 4 |

It will be seen that the argument form comes out true for all its truth-possibilities. This is the characteristic of a valid formula of the calculus of propositions, an invalid one reducing to F for at least one of its combinations of truth-values.

(ii) But a decision procedure merely tells us of any argument form taken at random whether or not it is valid. It provides no means of generating new valid formulas or of relating valid formulas

together into a system. A standard method for this is to construct an axiom system in which all the valid formulas of the calculus can be deduced from a small number of formulas (the *axioms*) taken as a starting point. (A very imperfect but well known example of an axiom system is the geometry of Euclid.) Deduction consists in operating on the axioms and on the formulas derived from them in accordance with the rules of the system. These rules must specify what symbols may be used and how they may be combined (Rules of Formation) and what manipulation of the axioms and derived formulas is permitted (Rules of Transformation). Axioms may be chosen in any convenient way provided that the set we select is consistent, that is to say, yields only valid formulas. It should also, if possible, be "complete" or be capable of yielding *all* the valid formulas of the system. Proofs must be found that these conditions of consistency and completeness are satisfied. For the calculus of propositions, this can be done without much difficulty.

## V. PREDICATE CALCULUS

The logic of propositions is only the first level of logic and most arguments cannot be expressed in its symbolism or tested by its methods. For example, even so elementary an argument as (2) above cannot be adequately formalized as an argument form of the propositional calculus. (Most syllogisms can be expressed in a calculus of properties which is an alternative interpretation of the calculus of propositions, presence or absence of a property being treated as analogous to truth or falsity of a proposition. But this cannot be developed into a general logic of predicates.) And a slightly more complex but still elementary example:

(9) *If A is larger than B and B is larger than C, A is larger than C,*

introduces still further complications.

An argument in the form of (2), that is (4), is clearly valid but it is not valid in virtue of its *propositional* form. For it is clear that:

(10) $(p.q) \supset r$

is not a valid form of the calculus of propositions. (2) is valid in virtue of the *internal structure* of its constituent propositions. More particularly, it is valid because of the way in which the words

179

"all", "some" and "not" and the descriptive phrases (or *predicates*) "metals", "soluble in water" and "crystalline substances" link the premises with each other and with the conclusion. To formalize such arguments we need, in addition to the symbolic apparatus of the logic of propositions, the following further signs:

(i) Variables $x$, $y$, $z$,. . .standing for *individuals*;

(ii) Signs for *predicates*, F, G, H,. . .These may stand for *monadic* predicates, like "blue", "square", *dyadic* predicates like "larger than", "loves" which need two individuals to complete their occurrence, *triadic* predicates like "between", "lends" and so on.

(iii) Quantifiers: (a) the universal quantifier, "$(x)$", read "for all $x$s";

(b) the existential quantifier, "$(Ex)$", read "There is an $x$ such that . . .".

With this additional apparatus, (2) can then be formalized:

(11) $((x)(Fx \supset \sim Gx)$ . $(Ex)$ $(Hx$ . $Fx)) \supset$ $(Ex)$ $(Hx$ . $\sim Gx)$

and (9) can be formalized:

(12) $(x)$ $(y)$ $(z)$ $(Fxy$ . $Fyz) \supset (Fxz)$

We are faced again in the *predicate calculus* with the same two problems that we met in the logic of propositions, the problems of finding a decision procedure and of constructing a satisfactory axiom system. There are axiom systems for the predicate calculus for which proofs of consistency and completeness can be given. But it has been proved (by Alonzo Church) that no general decision procedure is possible for this part of logic although decision methods can be devised for important fragments of it.

These are still comparatively elementary levels of logic and it is easy to find sentences which cannot be formalized by this apparatus. (For example: "There is only one god" or "2 + 2 = 4".) These must be taken care of by still further developments of logical technique which we can only mention here.

VI. INDUCTIVE ARGUMENTS

Reference was made in Section I to the study of inductive arguments. The basic importance of such arguments both in common sense reasoning and in natural science makes it necessary for logic to take account of them. Broadly speaking a proof by inductive methods is one which seeks to establish a general statement by considering a sample of the particular cases falling under it. This type of reasoning, in which inference proceeds "from the known to the unknown" is called *ampliative* or *problematic* induction. (It is much the most important of the various types of induction distinguished by logicians and the only one which will be considered here.) We may conclude, for example, that all green plants form starch in the presence of light on the basis of observations made on a limited number of specimens of a limited number of species. Since we go beyond our evidence in reaching the conclusion, the conclusion may turn out to be false. At any rate, it appears that such conclusions never follow rigorously from their premises. Whereas a deductive argument is either valid or invalid, the conclusion being either completely guaranteed by the premises or not at all, in an inductive argument the evidence will give more or less support for the conclusion but cannot guarantee it completely. Earlier logicians, in particular, J. S. **Mill**, thought that induction could be made to yield certain conclusions with the help of suitable ancillary premises to be provided by philosophical argument. But since the work of W. S. **Jevons** (1874) it has been generally accepted that inductive arguments cannot guarantee their conclusions.

The mere fact that we tend to make generalizations on the basis of our past experience does not of itself present a problem for logicians. All animals capable of learning show in their behaviour an expectation that future events will resemble past ones and that unobserved instances will resemble those which have been observed. The tendency to generalize is merely a fact of biology. It turns out however that some of our expectations about the future course of nature are justified by events and some are not. And it is clearly a matter of great importance to have procedures for distinguishing in advance expectations and generalizations that are well-founded from those that are not. The main task of inductive logic is therefore the study of the critical checks which are necessary in order to discipline our proneness to generalize.

Natural science provides us with a large body of well-established and closely knit generalizations of various kinds and so offers us a model of inductive reasoning. The influence of this model has been such that the phrase "inductive logic" has come to be synonymous with "the logic of science". And it is interesting to note that the earliest important study of inductive reasoning was made by Francis **Bacon** at a time when the experimental study of nature was beginning to play a significant role in the intellectual life of Europe. There is no doubt that the study of scientific methods and techniques is the surest guide to a correct view of inductive reasoning.

The example of natural science shows that to arrive at justified generalizations about nature is not the only aim of inductive reasoning. A major function of scientific reasoning is *explanation*. And an important part of inductive logic is the analysis of the notion of the explanation of natural phenomena. Indeed the existence of regularities or uniformities in nature has often been established in the course of seeking an explanation of some apparently exceptional observed event. It was in this way, for example, that attempts to explain Galvani's observation of a mysterious contraction in the muscle of a dead frog led to the formulation of laws about the behaviour of electric currents.

The logic of induction has had two main lines of development, the study of devices for *eliminating* irrelevancies and the study of methods for *confirming* hypotheses. The example of natural science shows that both elimination and confirmation are essential to scientific procedure. J. S. Mill's "methods of experimental inquiry", variously criticized and improved by later writers, consist essentially in a technique for eliminating irrelevant factors in phenomena under observation. They are embodied in a practical way in some of the various experimental techniques used in natural science. Indeed, this part of inductive logic may be said to consist in the logical analysis of experimental procedures. Recent developments in the study of experimental design link these matters closely with technical developments in mathematical statistics. So far, however, little work on these lines has been done by logicians. In the same way, study of the logic of confirmation which has in the past been associated with the theory of probability and its applications has now to take account of advances in statistical techniques. It has sometimes been said by logicians even in recent years that there are no precise rules for assessing inductive evidence. This was true only before the development of mathematical statistics which now provides very precise rules for just this purpose. The results of such assessments cannot indeed often be exact but the extent of their inexactness can usually be measured.

## VII. THE LIMITS OF LOGIC

Having considered both deductive and inductive methods of inference, we have made a very brief review of the elementary parts of logic. But the question naturally arises: Are all arguments either of the deductive or the inductive sort? If we use the word "argument" in its ordinary sense, the answer is clearly: No. Obviously, there are many fields of dispute such as literary criticism, theology, political theory, much of traditional philosophy and many parts of law where the issue cannot be decided by formalized deductive methods nor yet rendered more or less probable by inductive procedures. And it is clear that many of these arguments, though indecisive, look like rational procedures and are intended to be such, inconclusive as they are. It would seem therefore that logic ought to concern itself with them. Many contemporary philosophers would wish to support this view.

It would certainly be unwise to try to prescribe in advance what the science of logic can or cannot be expected to achieve. Conservative logicians at the end of the eighteenth century thought that logic was a completed science and would no doubt be astounded could they be shown its present state. But it must be emphasized that logic in its present state cannot take account of any argument which is not reducible to the standard forms of deductive logic or exhibited as a confirmable hypothesis. The example of inductive reasoning shows that not all legitimate types of reasoning need be demonstrative in character. But the types of reasoning in question here are those which not only fail to demonstrate but fail even to *support* their conclusions since they have no established and publicly agreed canons of propriety.

Such arguments are therefore "arguments" only in a vague and metaphorically extended sense of the word and cannot even qualify to be considered as evidence in favour of their purported conclusions. Whether future developments will extend the province of logic to include the "arguments" of the literary critic, the theologian or the metaphysician, no one can say. But it is clear in the light of the history of logic that the prospects for making such arguments respectable are not promising.

(D.J.O'C.)

**Logical Positivism.** "Logical Positivism" is a name given (by Blumberg and Feigl, 1931) to the philosophical movement emanating from the **Vienna Circle**. Often applied, in a vaguely opprobrious sense, to **analytic philosophy** in general, it is best confined to its original purpose, in which usage it is largely synonymous with so-called "logical", "scientific" or "consistent" empiricism.

The Vienna Circle originated in the early nineteen-twenties as an informal discussion group at the University of Vienna, presided over by Moritz **Schlick**. The more prominent members included Rudolf **Carnap**, Otto Neurath, Friedrich **Waismann**, Philipp Frank, Hans Hahn, Herbert Feigl, Victor Kraft, Felix Kaufmann and Kurt Gödel. Other associates, more or less remote in distance, time or opinion, were Hans Reichenbach, Carl Hempel, Karl Menger, Richard von **Mises**, Karl **Popper**, Joergen Joergensen, Charles W. **Morris** and A. J. **Ayer**. A fair number of the original circle were not philosophers by training, but mathematicians, physicists or social scientists, sharing a common interest in the philosophy of science and a common distaste for the academic metaphysics then prevailing in

Germany and Central Europe. Historically, their logic was that of **Frege** and **Russell**, while their "positivism" owed less to **Comte** than to the "neo-positivism" of **Mach** and Poincaré, Einstein's general **relativity**, and by way of these, to Karl Pearson, John Stuart **Mill**, the writers of the Enlightenment and the earlier British empiricists (most notably **Hume**). The strongest immediate influence, however, was that of **Wittgenstein**, who though not a member of the circle was acquainted with some of its members, and whose *Tractatus Logico-Philosophicus* (1921) supplied the background to many of its discussions, as also did Schlick's *Allgemeine Erkenntnislehre* (1918–25), and Carnap's *Logical Structure of the World* (1928).

After some years of comparatively private and unselfconscious existence, the group was formally constituted in 1929 as the Vienna Circle, the name – due to Neurath – being chosen for its agreeable associations with woods, waltzes and other local amenities. A manifesto-cum-bibliography (*Wissenschaftliche Weltauffassung: Der Wiener Kreis*) was issued under the auspices of a cognate body, the "Verein Ernst Mach"; a conference was held at Prague; and the journal *Annalen der Philosophie*, purchased in 1930, rechristened *Erkenntnis*, and edited by Carnap and Reichenbach, enabled the circle to establish and maintain contact with an increasing body of sympathizers in Britain, the United States and Northern Europe. Further conferences, in the name of the "unity of science", were held at Königsberg (1930), Prague (1934), Paris (1935 and 1937), Copenhagen (1936), Cambridge, England (1938) and Cambridge, Mass. (1939). Other enterprises included the publication of several series of books and monographs, the most ambitious of these being Neurath's uncompleted project for an "International Encyclopedia of Unified Science".

This enlargement of activities was accompanied by some loss of identity, and by the mid-nineteen-thirties logical positivism was already diffusing into the wider and vaguer movement of logical empiricism. The meetings of the Vienna Circle proper were abruptly terminated, in 1936, by the murder of Schlick; its dissolution soon completed by the pressure of events in Europe, whereby the majority of its members were driven into exile in Britain or the United States. The residual influence of the movement is probably strongest in the United States; elsewhere its explicit contentions have ceased to excite much controversy, though many of its ideals are still operative in present-day analytic philosophy.

The logical positivists preached a quasi-scientific agreement among philosophers, and at first were surprisingly close to practising it, at least among themselves. Some technical differences apart, it is therefore possible, if hazardous, to credit them with a collective point of view. Its main features are: a thoroughgoing empiricism, backed by the resources of modern logic and tempered only by a possibly exaggerated respect for the achievements and capabilities of modern science; an equally thoroughgoing rejection of metaphysics, on logical grounds, as not merely false or futile, but meaningless; a restriction of philosophy, therefore, to the task of eliminating its own problems, by clarifying the language employed in framing them; and the more constructive aim of analysing and unifying the terminology of the sciences, by reduction to a common denominator in the language of physics.

**Empiricism** is the doctrine that all knowledge is ultimately derived from experience. As stated by Hume, it involves the psychological claim that all ideas are direct or indirect copies of sense-impressions, from which the conclusion is drawn that knowledge is either of internal relations between ideas (as in mathematics), or else has reference, in the last resort, to the content of sense-impressions ("matter of fact and existence"); all else being committed to the flames as "sophistry and illusion". Following Wittgenstein, logical positivism began by adopting a more logically orientated version of the same view. Experience (it was held) can be resolved into its ultimate constituents, namely the immediate and incorrigible sensory observations of which the observer's world consists. The structure so presented is reflected in language; more precisely, it can be shown by logical analysis that the propositions in which knowledge is expressed are similarly reducible to elementary propositions, corresponding one-to-one with actual or possible items of sense-experience. The relation between complex and elementary propositions is "truth-functional", inasmuch as the truth of a complex proposition depends solely on the truth or falsity of its simple components. It is not a matter of adding anything more, but simply of a greater degree of logical complexity. Nothing is added, because the propositions of logic and mathematics are concerned only to regulate the formal relationships between symbols. In themselves, they say nothing about the world, and have no content; their function is to state equivalences and relations of derivation between other propositions, and although, if true at all, they are necessarily true, this is only because they are "tautological", true by definition, or, in an older terminology, "analytic". From this it follows directly, as Hume saw, that there can be no hope of a deductive metaphysics; for if logic is empty, the manipulation of empirical data cannot be expected to lead beyond experience. It remains to be shown that the propositions of metaphysics are literally without meaning.

Truth, on the above view, is either formal or factual, and consists, in the latter case, either in direct correspondence between elementary proposition and sensory datum, or else, at a more complex level, in an (implicit) correspondence of structure, plus the occurrence of appropriate sense-experiences. A proposition has meaning only if it can, in principle, be true or false. Hence the class of meaningful propositions is exhaustively divisible into those whose truth-or-falsity can be established on formal grounds (i.e., logic and mathematics), and those in which it is, or could be, factually confirmed by verification (or falsification) through sense-experience. The principle involved is known as the *verification principle*; it is crudely stated in the slogan that "the meaning of a proposition is the method of its verification". A more judicious, if less incisive, formulation would be that a proposition *has* meaning if sense-experience would be sufficient to decide its truth.

The "propositions" of metaphysics and theology are plainly not formal, since they claim to report on matters transcending ordinary experience. Yet metaphysicians have no dispute with ordinary facts, and from this it appears that no empirical evidence could serve to confirm or discredit their conclusions. Since their statements cannot be tested by experience, they are no more factual than formal, and must therefore be reckoned (in this somewhat technical sense) "nonsensical" or "meaningless". Strictly speaking, indeed, they are not propositions at all. The same applies to the "pseudo-propositions" of **epistemology** and **ethics**, so far, that is, as they refer to "things-in-themselves" or "subsistent values", and are not reducible, on the one hand, to factual statements about the psychology, etc., of perceptual or moral judgment, or, on the other, to logical analysis of the language in which these judgments are formulated. One result of such analysis has been the claim that ethical judgments do not state ethical facts, but express the emotions of the speaker, and perhaps incite others to share them. Metaphysical utterances may also be said to do this, and so to convey poetical emotion, or a possible "attitude to life". The objection to them is that they do so under a misleading appearance of imparting information about supersensible fact.

If all formal propositions belong to logic, and all factual propositions, in a broad sense, to the empirical sciences, it is not easy to find a haven for the propositions of philosophy, including, of course, the verification principle itself. Wittgenstein, faced with this difficulty, had been ready to denounce even his own arguments to this end as "nonsense", albeit of an important and elucidatory character. Unwilling to accept such a paradox, logical positivism was prepared to grant the legitimacy of analysis, which thus becomes the whole duty of philosophers. Philosophy is not a theory, but an activity – the logical clarification of the concepts, propositions and theories proper to empirical science. The verification principle was similarly interpreted as a definition, recipe or criterion of meaning, not as an assertion which could be either true or false.

The simple identification of meaning and method of verification has many curious and improbable consequences. The literature of logical positivism is much preoccupied with this problem, and attempts to deal with it have been largely responsible for later divergencies within the school. Briefly, the difficulties are that the principle appears to distort or deny the meaning of many propositions acceptable in science and everyday life; and that its conception of meaning is in any case private, incommunicable and variable from one observer to another.

Historical propositions, for example, are not directly verifiable in terms of events, and have to be interpreted as predictions about what *would* be found on a future inspection of records, etc. The content of such propositions is thus identified with the indirect evidence for their truth. Nor is there any means of distinguishing a future statement of observation from a present one, since their method of verification is the same. General propositions, such as natural laws, etc., are again in principle unverifiable, since no finite series of observations would be sufficient to guarantee them true. Similar difficulties attach to statements about material objects, whose verification in terms of immediate sensory observations would likewise require an infinite series of such experiences to complete it. Sooner than discard them as meaningless, it was declared that propositions of this type were not really propositions at all, but directions for making observations. Alternatively, they were hypotheses; capable of confirmation (or, as some said, falsification) by experience, and to that extent legitimate for the purpose of science. (Generalizations can, of course, be conclusively *falsified* by a single observation, and by that test would rank as genuine propositions; but the refutation of a particular claim that at least *one* X was Y, would then require an exhaustive enumeration, as before.)

In order to avoid these complications, some writers (notably Ayer) proposed to distinguish "strong" and "weak" forms of the verification principle. On the latter view, a proposition does not have to be conclusively verifiable, its meaningfulness being sufficiently warranted if there are sensory observations which would be "relevant" to its truth or falsity. The intention of this formula was to deny meaning to metaphysical propositions, while conceding it to empirical assertions of the kind mentioned above. As has since been recognized, however, it is altogether too lenient in this respect, since no metaphysician need scruple to declare that sense-observations are in some degree relevant to his speculations. Later formulations of the principle have sought to remedy this defect, only to run into other and more technical difficulties; with increasing complexity it has increasingly taken on the appearance of an *ad hoc* device for the exclusion of an already proscribed class of statements, rather than being in itself a reason for excluding them.

Further problems arise from the all-important role allotted to sense-experience in the process of verification. Since such experience is necessarily private to the observer, it would appear that propositions can only have meaning for him if they can be rendered in terms of what would, in principle, be accessible to his immediate experience. Carnap's *Logical Structure of the World* is an elaborate attempt to perform this reconstruction of scientific and empirical discourse from within the confines of an "egocentric" terminology. The **solipsism** involved is "methodological" only, since the aim is to effect a theoretical reduction of concepts and propositions merely, and not of facts. But the doubt remains as to how, on these assumptions, communication is possible, or how the data of the sciences are intersubjectively verifiable. Logical positivism was much divided on this question. The more orthodox opinion, expounded chiefly by Schlick, was that the "structure" of individual experience *could* be communicated and compared with that of others, though its "content" must remain ineffable, even to the observer himself. The more radical party, headed by Neurath and Carnap, would have none of this lapse into "metaphysics", and preferred to secure the objectivity of science even at the cost of abandoning its supposed sensory basis. Scientific hypotheses, they argued, are tested by referring them, not to private and unverifiable sensations in the observer, but to publicly observable facts. The mental life of the observer is of no interest to science, and allusions thereto are, indeed, strictly without meaning. The observer's reports, bodily states and general behaviour are another matter, however, since they can be publicly checked and recorded; and it is these, or rather the records thereof, that form the "protocols" or elementary data of scientific theory. This thesis, of "physicalism", has a close resemblance to behaviourism, but differs in that it does not explicitly deny the facts of mental life or reduce them to facts of bodily behaviour. Its contention, rather, is that statements in the language of introspective psychology are formally replaceable by statements in the language of physics; and that only in the latter format are they of any use to science. As such, the thesis is certainly questionable, but it is not refuted by the traditional arguments for dualism.

A more far-reaching claim of this sort, chiefly associated with Neurath, is that all the sciences depend ultimately on protocols couched in terms of physical objects and processes, and hence that all empirical statements can be expressed in the language of physics. Particular sciences may well have laws of their own – that is an empirical question; but the concepts employed can all be defined in physical terms, which thereby form a *lingua franca* of science. This was the theoretical foundation of Neurath's energetic campaigning for the "unity of science".

The physicalist retreat from empiricism was carried still further, for a time, by Carnap and Neurath, in proposing to dispense with the correspondence theory of **truth**. The parallel between language and fact is an essential, yet suspiciously metaphysical feature of Wittgenstein's theory of meaning, since, on his own showing, the extra-linguistic relationship involved is inexpressible within the resources of language. Schlick's pursuit of "incorrigible", immediately-verifiable protocols equally ends in the unutterable. Yet the problem is easily disposed of. Statements, it was insisted, are comparable only with other statements, not with external fact; and knowledge must accordingly be depicted as a system of mutually supporting statements, to which newcomers are admitted as true if found to be consistent with those already accepted. The belief in a set of "basic" propositions underlying knowledge thereby becomes otiose; the "protocols" required are simply a relevant selection of propositions drawn from the established system; and coherence becomes the test of truth. The difficulty, of course, is to know which system is the right one; for many are possible, and some, at least, must be false, since their internal consistency does not prevent them from being inconsistent one with another. Carnap's declaration of trust in the system underwritten by the protocols of accredited scientists was understandably viewed as an anti-climax, if not a confession of defeat – an impression soon confirmed by his abandonment of this theory and return to a qualified admission that sentences could be "confronted" with facts.

These changes of front are less radical than they seem, particularly when account is taken of Carnap's other views. Much of his energy as a logician has been devoted to "formalizing" the internal structure (or "syntax") of language, very much as Hilbert and his followers have formalized mathematics, by treating its propositions as meaningless marks on paper and discussing the rules for their combination (in a "metalanguage"). Carnap's "logical syntax" embraces the grammatical, or formation rules of language, whereby sentences are formed from its vocabulary, and the logical, or transformation rules, whereby sentences are formally derived from one another. Much importance is attached to a threefold classification of these sentences: syntactical sentences, which make reference to words or other sentences, are said to be in the "formal mode of speech"; empirical or object-sentences are those dealing with things and states of affairs; but there is also a third class, of "pseudo-object sentences", which *seem* to be about things (as when a table is said to *be* a thing), when in fact they really are, or can be translated into, statements about words (namely, that "table" is a thing-word). These are said to be in the "material mode of speech". The main point of these distinctions, in the present context, is to enable it to be argued that most, if not all, of the not hopelessly metaphysical propositions of philosophy, which appear to be alluding, e.g., to the existence or status of abstract entities, such as universals, are actually syntactical assertions about words, misleadingly cast in the material mode of speech. Philosophy is thereby identified with logical syntax, the higher-level discussion of language, and long-standing philosophical controversies, such as that between **idealism** and **materialism**, turn out, when translated into the formal mode, to be disputing a conventional choice between alternative "languages", rather than issues of transcendental importance.

Hence the ready and even nonchalant passage of logical positivism from the phraseology of a quasi-idealist sensationalism to that of a quasi-materialist physicalism; the decision between them being a matter of methodological convenience, not a substantial change of belief. Hence also the urge to eliminate the "semantic" element, of reference to external fact, from the notions of truth and meaning, and to bring the whole compass of language under one syntactical roof. The collapse of this position has since led Carnap to turn his attention to the semantic field itself, but his contributions to that subject scarcely belong to the literature of logical positivism.

If logical positivism has ceased to rank as a fashionable philosophy, the reason is largely that its approach to language now seems unnecessarily rigid and doctrinaire. Its assumptions have turned out too simple, its methods too elaborate, to deal successfully with the informality of "natural" languages, and restriction to the analysis of artificial model-languages has also restricted the interest of the results. Apart from some notable contributions in the relatively technical fields of **induction, probability** and the methodology of science, the main legacy of the school has been to concentrate attention on the problem of meaning, and to establish standards of logical rigour and clear, unrhetorical expression, that have since been generally emulated. The attack on metaphysics, if not wholly conclusive, may be said to have damped the ardour, chastened the style and improved the understanding of its remaining devotees. Nor is the influence of the controversy by any means exhausted; ethics and epistemology have both had something to learn from it; and its repercussions are still plainly audible in philosophical theology. See also **A Priori; Philosophy of Science.**

(P.L.H.)

**Lucretius.** Titus Lucretius Carus (98–55 B.C.), Roman poet. The only personal information we have about him is that he was driven insane by a love potion, wrote some books (which are presumably the six books of the philosophical poem *De Rerum Natura*) in sane intervals and committed suicide at the age of forty-four. There is no reason to doubt that this is true. The poem is a complete account of the Epicurean theory of the soul, sense-perception, astronomy, heredity, thunder, earthquakes, magnetism and indeed all that was most likely to seem to the credulous to be supernaturally caused and therefore a source of religious terror. There is not a systematic treatment of the Epicurean ethical theory, but the orthodox Epicurean view that pleasure is the sole good, that the most worthwhile form of pleasure is the freedom from fear and that the main reason for the study of nature is the practical one that it will help us to liberate ourselves from superstitious fears of the gods and life in the underworld is presupposed throughout. There is no reason to suppose that there is anything original in Lucretius; he himself makes no such claim; but his poem is an accurate and passionate statement of the Epicurean position. It is also one of the greatest masterpieces of Latin literature.

(J.O.U.)

**Lukács,** Georg (1885–1971), Hungarian Marxist born in Budapest, a student of Georg Simmel, whose friends included Ernst **Bloch,** Karl Mannheim, Max Weber and Bertolt Brecht. Lukács joined the Communist Party in December 1918, and was active thereafter, as conditions permitted, in Party and national affairs.

From his pre-Marxist *Theory of the Novel* (1916), which re-worked **Hegel's** critique of **Kant** in the context of the novel, to his last work, *The Ontology of Social Being* (1971), which includes chapters on Hegel and **Marx,** and treats labour as a model for social practice, Lukács' theoretical work focused on problems of dialectic. Throughout, dialectic is conceived of as a mode of historical and categorical thinking transcending the dualisms constitutive of modern philosophy: subject and object, freedom and necessity, theory and practice, history (time) and eternity. Dialectic, so conceived, is clearly of Hegelian inspiration.

Lukács' most important philosophical work is *History and Class Consciousness* (1923). In this work Lukács introduces the idea of **reification** as a cultural generalization of Marx's concept of commodity fetishism; this generalization entails the transformation of Marxism from a reified theory of the economy into a philosophy of praxis.

For Lukács the problems of modern philosophy are historical and social problems because the categories of philosophy are, in truth, historical and social categories. Hence the overcoming of categorial dualisms becomes possible in thought through their placement within the social totality, and in reality through the practical transformation of the categorial structures of modern society. Revolutionary praxis becomes, in Lukács, an ontological experiment.

*History and Class Consciousness* is the seminal work of "Western (Hegelian) Marxism" and is largely responsible for bringing the problems of Marxism into a philosophical purview.

Lukács spent the war years in Moscow. During this time he studied Marx's *Economic and Philosophical Manuscripts* of 1844. The impact of that reading is evident in *The Young Hegel: On the Relation between Dialectic and Economics* (1948).

Lukács' cultural conception of Marxism led him, throughout his long career, to write numerous works on literature and the philosophy of art. Prominent amongst these are: *The Historical Novel* (1938), *Goethe and his*

187

Age (1946), *The Meaning of Contemporary Realism* (1957), and *The Specificity of the Aesthetic* (1963).

[J.M.B.]

**Lyotard,** Jean-François (1924– ), *see* Postmodernism.

# M

**Mach,** Ernst (1838–1916), Austrian philosopher, Professor of Physics at Prague and then at Vienna.

Mach's lasting importance is as a philosopher and methodologist of science. His general philosophical position was extreme positivism; he held that **Kant**'s *Critique of Pure Reason* "banished into the realm of shadows the sham ideas of the old metaphysics", but that metaphysical notions were still prevalent in the philosophy of science and even within science itself. His main aim was therefore to give an account of the nature of science which would free it from all metaphysical and non-empirical elements and to reconstruct the basic science of mechanics in accordance with these philosophical requirements. "We know", he said, "only one source which directly reveals scientific facts – our senses"; therefore science must be reconstructed so as to be manifestly an account of sense-given facts. But the objects of our senses are colours, warmths, smells, sounds and the like, not bodies and still less atoms, absolute space, absolute time, absolute motion and other conceptions of Newtonian mechanics; therefore science must in the final analysis be an account of sensations. No other statements can have any scientific significance.

Experience, claimed Mach, provides us only with a manifold of constantly changing and unrelated sensations; we cannot claim to find objectively in the world any basis for our concepts of bodies in motion in space or of laws of nature. "According to our conception, natural laws are a product of our psychological need to feel at home with nature; all concepts transcending sensation are to be justified as helping us to understand, control and predict our

environment, and different conceptual systems may be used to this end in different cultures and at different times with equal propriety."

But Mach does not consider that there is nothing to choose between any two conceptual schemes. A conceptual system is better if it is simple, comprehensive and free from internal contradictions; such a system is more useful to us and more fruitful. But we must not be misled into saying that nature itself is simple, economical and the like; the difference between economical and cumbersome conceptual systems is one of utility, not truth. We must not however go to the other extreme and regard our choice of scientific laws as purely conventional; the system of concepts must be suited to the facts which it is used to describe and laws of nature are descriptions of the world, even if schematic, and so must be judged true and false by reference to experience. Critics have frequently noted the difficulty of reconciling Mach's empiricism with the more *a priori* elements in his view.

In accordance with the view of the nature of science described above, Mach claimed that it was misleading to talk of proof in science. If scientific laws are conceptual tools they cannot be inductively proved from the facts, and the deduction of laws from other laws is of no ultimate significance and may easily give a misleading appearance of rigour to science. The only justification that can be given or need be given for accepting a scientific law is, according to Mach, that it survives testing in use.

Mach was not satisfied with giving this general picture of the nature of science; he considered that contemporary science was to some extent vitiated by not conforming to this picture. In particular he held that science constantly hypostatized the elements in its conceptual system, ascribing to them counterparts in nature for which experience could give no warrant and which were therefore metaphysical. In *The Science of Mechanics* (1883) Mach therefore applied his general position to a criticism of the form given to mechanics by Newton and his successors and attempted to show how the scientific content of mechanics could be retained without appeal to absolute space and time, force and other non-empirical notions.

Mach's influence on the development of **empiricism** on the continent of Europe was very great; the **Vienna Circle** of logical positivists acknowledged him as their basic guide. His pure sensationalism was abandoned quite early in favour of "physicalism", but most of the leading ideas of logical positivism can be traced to him. On the other hand, **Lenin** attacked Mach as an enemy of materialism.

(J.O.U.)

**MacIntyre,** Alasdair (1929– ), Scots-Irish philosopher who has worked both in England and America. His abiding interests circle round the two poles of his first book, *Marxism and Christianity* (1954), which argued that **Marx** had "humanised certain central Christian beliefs" and that Christians ought to learn "from both the achievements and the failures of Marxism". Since then he has explored a wide range of topics in the history of philosophy (especially ethics) and the philosophy of social science, with an unusual sensitivity to their social, historical and political dimensions. But all his work is focused on a single object: the need for moral philosophy to ground itself in history so as to provide positive guidance amidst the dilemmas of **modernity.** A *Short History of Ethics* (1965) was an attack on the unhistorical approach of writers like **Hare** (author of the article on **Ethics** in this Encyclopedia). The strident polemic in *Marcuse* (1970) discovered élitism, intolerance and irrationalism in a thinker whose interpretation of Marxism is actually quite close to MacIntyre's own. *After Virtue* (1981) is a mournful analysis of the ways in which moral thought and practice have been wrecked by the liberal individualism of the Englightenment, and *Whose Justice? Which Rationality?* (1988) reinforces the argument by showing how "standards of rational justification themselves emerge from and are part of a history". See also **History of Philosophy.**

[J.R.]

**McTaggart,** John Ellis (1866–1925), Fellow of Trinity College, Cambridge. He was an admirer of **Hegel,** an idealist and a systematic metaphysician. In his great work the *Nature of Existence* (1921, 1927) he sets out, with the aid of two empirical premises to the effect that something exists, to show by rigorous a priori argument the general nature of the universe as a whole and of its constituent parts. The conclusion that the universe is a society of minds in close relation to each other is arrived at by a process of argument of great ingenuity and clarity; in the course of this argument occurs the celebrated proof of the unreality of time. In the second part McTaggart attempts to draw by less rigorous methods various conclusions from the results of the first part. The formal simplicity, rigour, lack of rhetoric and candour of this work, combined with unusual audacity of thought and ingenuity, make it of value even to those who are out of sympathy with idealistic metaphysics in general. Among his many uncommon views should be mentioned his belief in the immortality of the soul combined with atheism.

(J.O.U.)

**Maimonides** or Moses ben Maimon (1135–1204), a Spanish Jew, the most eminent of the medieval Jewish thinkers who attempted to find a synthesis of Greek, especially Aristotelian, philosophy and Jewish monotheistic religion. His writings greatly influenced not only his orthodox co-religionists but such unorthodox philosophers as **Spinoza** and such orthodox Christian philosophers as Thomas **Aquinas.** His most celebrated work is *The Guide of the Perplexed* in which he attempts to reconcile Aristotelian philosophy and the Greek sciences with the literal truth of the Old Testament; in this task he relies greatly on the Arab philosophers **Avicenna,** to whom he is much indebted for his doctrine of immortality, and **Averroes,** from whom he took the notion of the identity of essence and existence in God. Philosophy and revealed theology are treated by Maimonides as quite different in nature but as complementary. It is the task of philosophy to confirm rationally the truths of religion and to disprove doctrines which seem to contradict revelation.

(J.O.U.)

**Malebranche,** Nicolas (1638–1715), French philosopher. The heterodoxy of **Descartes** divided the philosophers of his time into bitterly opposed factions. Those who followed Descartes found their authority in **Augustine** and those who opposed him took **Aquinas** as their master. The most celebrated of the Augustinians was Nicolas Malebranche. Individual things he believed to be limitations of the one material substance and individual minds limitations of an immaterial substance, against which was contrasted the perfect freedom of God. Malebranche provided an **occasionalistic** solution of the problem of the causal interaction of the two substances, for he held that there was no capacity for action whatever in finite things, whether minds or bodies – a doctrine which he claimed to be the mark of a Christian philosophy. These considerations, coupled with the problem of how an immaterial mind-substance could perceive material bodies, led him to a kind of neo-Platonic metaphysics. We perceive nothing directly, but God implants in our minds the idea of a corporeal world. This world does in fact exist and corresponds to our ideas of it because the ideas of God which are the source of our perceptions are also the archetypes of the world of material things.

(R.HALL.)

**Marcel,** Gabriel (1889–1973), French philosopher and playwright. Marcel's philosophical work has been principally communicated to the world through his diaries, which have appeared in three parts: *Metaphysical Journal*, 1927, *Being and Having*, 1935, and *Presence and Immortality*, 1959. The Gifford Lectures on *The Mystery of Being* (1950) represent the nearest he has come to a sustained exposition of his views. While his use of the diary-form makes him an impossible writer to summarize, it gives to his philosophical work a suggestive and exploratory quality which is peculiarly valuable to those patient enough to read it.

Marcel is often characterized as a "Christian Existentialist", and as such contrasted with **Sartre**; but this is a serious misdescription. He wrote doctoral thesis on Coleridge's relation to Schelling, and was initially a student of the English-speaking idealists, **Bradley** and **Royce**, and of **Bergson**. With Royce he shared a profound sense of the depth of people's attachment to the community to which they belong. The reader will perhaps learn more from Marcel's diaries than from any other source, of the precise sense of **Collingwood**'s distinction between "proposition" and "presupposition". Marcel's diaries also reveal his preoccupation with the Cartesian problem of the relation of mind and matter. In his later years he gave serious attention to the implications of parapsychological phenomena, especially telepathy, interpreted as a mode of human communion.

Received into the Catholic Church in 1929, Marcel remained always aloof from the neo-Thomist enthusiasms of **Maritain**. For all its looseness of texture and diffuseness of exposition, Marcel's thought has a critical and analytical quality, evidenced, for example, in his discussion of the notion of an *argument* for the existence of God, in his laying bare of the precise content of the hope of immortality, in his contribution to the pervasive debate concerning the nature and possibility of metaphysics, and through his distinction between "problem" and "mystery". For all his stress on the dimension of subjectivity, he remains profoundly hostile to any sort of radical individualism, which he would judge false to the subtle actualities of the human situation.

(D.M.M.)

**Marcus Aurelius Antoninus** (121–180), Roman Emperor, and Stoic. In his latter years he wrote the *Meditations* as a personal spur and refreshment amid the burden of his lonely office. His Stoicism is rooted in **Epictetus** but he felt with a deeper religious fervour than other Stoics the natural communion of man in the organic unity of the universe. An all-beneficent providence has placed in men a divine control, reason; it is thus in their power to make themselves one with the rational purpose of the universe. This is man's active duty to himself as a citizen of God's State. But Marcus, as Emperor of Rome, saw equally important duties to his fellow men, his natural kin. Yet his love of humanity did not blind him to depravity; and, convinced of the transitory nature of temporal affairs, he found no incentive in his Stoic principles to fashion an ideal state, only a sense of urgency to do what he could in the post assigned to him by God. The philosopher-king remained a moral not a political ideal; Marcus is fundamentally concerned with his own moral character functioning in relation to others; his thoughts turn readily from Rome to the City of God.

(I.G.K.)

**Marcuse**, Herbert (1898–1979), German-American philosopher who developed his own version of "critical Marxism" in an attempt to update Marxian theory in response to changing historical conditions from the 1920s through the 1970s. Marcuse gained notoriety in the 1960s when he was perceived as both an influence on and defender of the so-called "New Left" in the United States and Europe. Marcuse's first published article appeared in Weimar Germany in 1928 and attempted a synthesis of **phenomenology, existentialism,** and Marxism of a kind, which was to be carried out again decades later by various "existential" and "phenomenological" Marxists. In 1933, he published the first major review of **Marx**'s *Economic and Philosophical Manuscripts* of 1844 and anticipated the tendency to revise interpretations of Marxism from the standpoint of the works of the early Marx. Marcuse's study of **Hegel**'s *Ontology and Theory of Historicity* (1932) contributed to the Hegel renaissance that was taking place in Europe.

In 1934, Marcuse fled from Nazism and emigrated to the United States where he lived for the rest of his life. His first major work in English, *Reason and Revolution* (1941), traced the genesis of the ideas of Hegel, Marx, and modern social theory. After service for the US government from 1941 to 1950, which Marcuse always claimed was motivated by a desire to struggle against fascism, he returned to intellectual work and published *Eros and Civilization* (1955), which attempted an audacious synthesis of Marx and Freud and sketched the outlines of a non-repressive society.

In 1958 Marcuse published *Soviet Marxism*, a critical study of the Soviet Union, and in 1964 *One-Dimensional Man*, a wide-ranging critique of both advanced capitalist and communist societies. This book theorized the decline of revolutionary potential in capitalist societies and the development of new forms of social control. The book was severely criticized by orthodox Marxists and theorists of various political and theoretical commitments. Despite its pessimism, it influenced many in the New Left as it articulated their growing dissatisfaction with both capitalist societies and Soviet communist societies. *One-Dimensional Man* was followed by a series of books and articles which articulated New Left politics and critiques of capitalist societies in "Repressive Tolerance" (1965), An *Essay on Liberation* (1969), and *Counterrevolution and Revolt* (1972).

Marcuse also dedicated much of his work to aesthetics and his final book, *The Aesthetic Dimension* (1979), briefly summarizes his defence of the emancipatory potential of aesthetic form in so-called "high culture." His work in philosophy and social theory generated fierce controversy and polemics, and most studies of his work are highly tendentious and frequently sectarian. Although much of the controversy involved his critiques of contemporary capitalist societies and defence of radical social change, in retrospect, Marcuse left behind a complex and many-sided body of work comparable to the legacies of Ernst **Bloch,** Georg **Lukács,** T. W. **Adorno,** and Walter **Benjamin.** See also **Alienation, Dialectical Materialism, Frankfurt School.**

[D.M.K.]

**Maritain,** Jacques (1882–1973), French Catholic philosopher. Originally a follower of **Bergson,** he later became one of the best-known modern exponents of **Thomism**; his *Introduction to Philosophy* (1920) is orthodox scholasticism in traditional scholastic terms. His best known philosophical work is *The Degrees of Knowledge* (1932), in which he distinguished natural scientific knowledge, metaphysical knowledge and mystical knowledge, which he regarded as all valid forms of knowledge, complementary to each other.

(J.O.U.)

**Marx,** Karl Heinrich (1818–1883), born at Trier in Rhenish Prussia. At the University of Berlin he came under the influence of the radical Young Hegelian movement. Because of these associations a University career was closed to him, so in 1842 he assumed the editorship of the *Rheinische Zeitung,* a new liberal paper at Cologne. The paper was suppressed in 1843, and Marx went to Paris where he made contact with German workers and French socialists and became a communist. Here he also met Friedrich **Engels** who became his life-long associate. Expelled from Paris at the end of 1844 he stayed in Brussels for three years and participated in the foundation of the Communist League. When the 1848 revolutions broke out he went back to Cologne to found the *Neue Rheinishche Zeitung.* After its suppression in 1849 Marx took refuge in London where he remained for the rest of his life, often in considerable poverty. In spite of all difficulties, he embarked on a massive research programme, using the facilities of the British Museum reading room. At the same time he was the moving spirit in the International Working Men's Association (1864–72), achieving more notoriety as a revolutionary than as a scholar in his lifetime.

Marx characterized his theoretical work as materialist, dialectical and scientific, and as expressing the standpoint of "the class that holds the future in its hands" – the proletariat. He was the founder of what Engels called "scientific socialism".

At the time of his death he was known mainly for *Capital* (Vol. 1, 1867) and the *Communist Manifesto* (1848). Also available were works of contemporary history such as *The Eighteenth Brumaire of Louis Bonaparte* (1852) and *The Civil War in France* (1871). The specifically philosophical elements of his work were known only through his critique of Proudhon, *The Poverty of Philosophy* (1847), and a two-page summary of historical materialism in the Preface to the *Contribution to a Critique of Political Economy* (1859).

It fell to Engels to articulate the philosophical views which, after later elaboration, became known in vulgarized form as **dialectical materialism.** But since then the gradual appearance of unpublished works and drafts by Marx has administered a series of shocks to this doctrine, and promoted a stream of reinterpretations of "what Marx really thought". Important manuscripts that became available were: *Theses on Feuerbach* (1845) – put out in edited form by Engels, 1888; *The German Ideology* (1845–46) – not available in full until the thirties; *Economic and Philosophical Manuscripts* of 1844 – published in 1932; and finally the *Grundrisse* (1857–58) – of which there was no accessible edition until 1953. These posthumous publications clarify Marx's relation to German philosophy, and especially the work of **Hegel** and **Feuerbach.**

The greatest shock was the publication of the *1844 Manuscripts*. Since then there has been considerable debate about the writings of the so-called "young Marx" and their continuity with the later, supposedly less philosophical, work. However, in the *1844 Manuscripts* Marx already saw productive activity as ontologically constitutive of human being, and the critique of **political economy** as the key task. In these manuscripts Marx argued that in the private property system labour is estranged from its object; that this state of estrangement is the result of the **alienation** of labour from itself; and that private property must be seen as the *product* of alienated labour. From this, Marx held, there flows an all-pervasive experience of alienation in modern social institutions and culture. The end of alienation requires "the positive supersession of private property", i.e. the reappropriation of the human essence presently estranged in it.

Marx acknowledged that his account of the way in which labour grasps its other (private property) as its estranged self, and negates this negation, has obvious parallels with Hegel's *Phenomenology of Spirit*; but he criticized Hegel for taking activity as essentially spiritual labour, and equating objectivity with estrangement.

Although the young Marx's theory of alienation is not simply a materialist inversion of Hegel's (as **Althusser** alleges) it is true that it treats the history of humanity as a development through self-estrangement to recovery of itself. Historical materialism, with its clear periodization of history in terms of successive modes of production, did not emerge till one or two years later. This theory is documented in the first part of the *German Ideology*, and the Preface to the 1859 *Critique*.

Marx distanced his materialism from that of Feuerbach through the key role he gave to practice, especially to productive activity. Because man is a natural being he has to interact with nature to secure his material existence. Labour converts the raw material provided by nature into goods for human use. This has to be done before anything else and hence fundamentally conditions everything else. Production, moreover, is always social production; and it is the guiding thread to history, Marx believed. History can be divided into distinct periods, in each of which a different mode of production prevails; but each system has its own laws of motion and considerable empirical work is required to discover them.

Marx begins by identifying the *relations* of production, which are seen as corresponding to stages in the development of the productive *forces*. ("The handmill gives you society with the feudal lord; the steam-mill, society with the industrial capitalist," as he wrote in 1847.) And in 1859, "The sum total of these relations of production constitutes the economic structure of society, the real foundation, on which rises a legal and political superstructure and to which correspond definite forms of social consciousness. The mode of production of material life conditions the social, political and intellectual life process in general. It is not the consciousness of men that determines their being, but, on the contrary, their social being that determines their consciousness." Social revolution arises out of class struggle rooted in changes in the economic foundation. Of course, the protagonists themselves are not typically aware of such changes. The French revolution, for example, was fought under the slogan "Liberty, Equality, Fraternity". But the development of a market economy and the rise of the bourgeois class was the real context of the event, and its outcome cleared the path for the capitalist mode of production.

It is unfortunate that Marx's architectural metaphor of foundation and superstructure suggests that social consciousness is merely epiphenomenal. In truth, Marx did not deny the reality of ideas, nor their effectivity in moving masses of people to act. He held only that reference to such ideas is not a "rock bottom" explanation.

Definite material and social preconditions must be fulfilled if revolution is to be on the historical agenda. Human liberation depends more on such premises than on any philosophy of freedom. Thus socialism is based on tendencies immanent in history, not on an ideal preached to people in abstraction from their present needs and interests. The historically created conditions for communist revolution include the development of productive forces adequate to sustain a society free from want, and also the emergence of a class that can solve its problems only by overthrowing the existing order.

Marx held that if history continually generates new structures of social being, and thus of individuality, then the socialist project cannot simply be dismissed as "against human nature". He had no quarrel with the visionary *aims* of Utopians like Fourier and Owen; he shared them (as the doctrine of "the withering away of the state" shows). But he differed from the Utopians in his conception of political practice. Where they looked with disdain on the existing class struggle, Marx held that the practical reality of communism lay in this very struggle, and that his science laid bare its motor of development and revolutionary potential. This was why Marx devoted most of his life to the study of the workings of capitalist society.

In *Capital* Marx acknowledged the influence of Hegel's *Logic*, but unfortunately he gave no details. One could mention such features as: the articulation of the whole as a hierarchy of determinations and its presentation at successively more concrete levels of mediation; the re-presentation of premises as results; the demonstration of capital's tendency to assimilate, and reproduce, its conditions of existence; the dialectic of essence and appearance; and the deployment of such categories as "contradiction" and "negation of the negation". It is also noteworthy that there are distinct parallels between Marx's criticism of the "mystified form" of Hegelian dialectic and his critique of the "fetishistic" forms of value – commodity, money, capital.

193

For Marx, philosophy is part of the "ideological superstructure". He sometimes spoke as if it had been superseded by his new science of history: "When reality is depicted, philosophy as an independent branch of knowledge loses its medium of existence" (1846). But more significant is his famous verdict: "The philosophers have only *interpreted* the world, in various ways; the point is to *change* it" (1845). Thus philosophy is to lose its independence not so much in its subjection to positive science, but through changing its conditions of existence, overcoming in reality the dualities of subject and object, real and ideal, duty and inclination, that bedevil it. Scientific socialism conceives itself as the theoretical expression of a revolutionary process which will put an end to philosophy in so far as it abolishes the alienating material relations which require such compensatory speculation. Marx's project of displacing philosophy from its throne in favour of a unified science of man, nature and history thus itself speculatively prefigures such a non-alienated society. But philosophy has effective social reality still. And, as long as the revolutionary project of transforming society in its totality lacks immediate historical actuality, Marxism is condemned to remain engaged *with* philosophy as such. See also **Ideology**.

[C.J.A.]

**Materialism.** Philosophical materialism is the view that all that exists is material or is wholly dependent upon matter for its existence. This view comprises (*a*) the general metaphysical thesis that there is only one fundamental kind of reality and that this is material, and (*b*) the more specific thesis that human beings and other living creatures are not dual beings composed of a material body and an immaterial soul, but are fundamentally bodily in nature.

The best known form of materialism is the speculative **atomism** of **Democritus** and **Epicurus**. This view arises as an attempt to give an account of change in terms of the ultimate elements of the world. According to this theory, the ultimate elements are indivisible and indestructible particles moving about in empty space.

The things, animals and people of the natural world are formed by the coalescence of these particles. On this view, thought is a form of sensation and sensation is explained in physical terms. When the body decays or is destroyed, sensation is no longer possible and the soul itself disintegrates into it ultimate atoms. Thus the distinction between soul and body is not a distinction between the immaterial and the material, but between different sorts of material wholes. Materialistic atomism was revived in the seventeenth century and became the creed of such eighteenth-century atheists as the Baron d'Holbach, who defines feeling in physical terms as a way of being moved and of receiving impulses through the body.

With the growth of the physical sciences speculative atomism was adopted as an explanatory principle of physics and chemistry and thus gave rise to scientific materialism. This outlook gained support from the evidences of geology and the theory of organic evolution, from which is appeared that life and mind had developed from inanimate matter. Advances in physiology reinforced this view, since it was claimed that the existence and scope of mental life depended upon the size and configuration of the brain. The German physiologist Karl Vogt (1817–1895) became notorious for his statement that thought was related to the brain much as bile is related to the liver and urine to the kidneys. (In fact Vogt's utterance was an echo of some phrases from Cabanis' *Relations of the Physical and the Moral in Man* (1802) where it is suggested that the brain may be regarded as digesting impressions or secreting thoughts.) But neither Vogt nor his better known contemporary Ludwig Büchner (1824–1899) provided any clear account of the nature of mind. Thus, although Büchner recognised that thought is not something that could be "secreted", he has little positive to say about it except that it is "caused" by physical processes.

In the twentieth century there have been two main forms of materialism, **dialectical materialism** and physicalism. Dialectical materialists describe Vogt and Büchner as "vulgar materialists", but their own view, while it is clear as regards the dependence of mind upon matter, is vague as regards the nature of mind itself.

Physicalism was formulated by some members of the **Logical Positivist** movement. It rests upon the view that whatever can be meaningfully said must state what is verifiable. The Physicalists argue, however, that there can be no genuine verification of a statement purporting to state the private experiences of one individual. One may say that one feels a pain, but no one else can test this. What others can do is hear utterances or see movements. Nothing can be verified publicly by more than one observer except physical occurrences. From this the Physicalists concluded that the only meaningful statements about minds must refer to bodily behaviour of some sort. It was therefore their view that psychology was, in a broad sense, a part of physics. Whereas some psychologists had advocated Behaviourism as a policy of only admitting those data that could be observed by more than one observer, the Physicalists advocated it on the ground that any other policy would have no meaning.

It is important to notice that materialists do not deny the existence of mind or consciousness, for to do so would itself be an exercise of the very thing it purported to deny. What they deny is that mind or consciousness are characteristics of immaterial souls. The strength of the case of materialism is a result of the obscurities in the notion of a wholly incorporeal existence. This is held to be non-spatial and hence incapable of movement. But then its mode of operation on and with material bodies seems inexplicable. On the other hand to describe sensation in terms of physical movements or chemical changes is obviously to omit what is most characteristic of it. The most acceptable form of materialism appears to be the view that mind is not a thing, whether material or immaterial, but the powers, capacities and functioning of certain sorts of bodies. Yet the critic of materialism is on strong ground in insisting on the gulf between experience on the one hand and physical processes on the other.

(H.B.A.)

**Material mode** of speech, as distinct from "formal mode", concerns objects as opposed to words. See **Logical Positivism**.

**Mathematics** has always been a subject of great interest to philosophers not only in its own right but also as of crucial importance for the problem of the nature and extent of the knowledge that the human mind can gain through pure reasoning and without recourse to observation or experiment. No doubt we come to grasp such truths as that $2 + 2 = 4$ only in the course of experience, but this is not an experimental truth as it is an experimental truth that if two drops of water are put with two drops of water one small puddle results. If mathematical knowledge is occasioned by experience it is not based on experience; we do not need to send expeditions overseas to see if $2 + 2 = 4$ holds there also. Thus mathematical knowledge seems to be a case of pure rational knowledge, gained by thinking alone and independent of empirical verification; it is what is technically called **a priori** knowledge. Consequently mathematics appears to be a refutation of the empiricist thesis that all knowledge is based on sense-experience, a counter-example so indisputable that among empiricists only J. S. **Mill** has been so bold as to try to deny it by claiming that mathematical truths are really but well-established empirical generalizations.

But mathematics is a challenge to philosophy in yet another way, for it is a hard problem to discover what mathematics is about; what is the number two, and what is it to add two to two? Two is surely not a physical thing and adding is not putting with as two eggs can be put with two eggs? The problem arises also with regard to geometry, for if the theorem that the internal angles of a triangle are equal to two right angles be understood to refer to triangles drawn on paper it is almost certainly false; what then are the triangles, rectangles, lines and points of which the geometer speaks?

When we consider these difficulties it is not surprising that **Plato**, the first great philosopher of mathematics, regarded mathematics as the supreme example of knowledge of a supra-sensible world of intelligible entities accessible to the reason alone and that **Russell**, at the beginning of his career, accepted an essentially similar position. Yet such a view is not one which can appeal to a robust common-sense; the empiricist must find an alternative to it. The most famous attempt prior to the end of the nineteenth century is that of **Kant**, for whom the problem of mathematics was central.

Then **Frege** in Germany and, independently, Russell in England developed the Logistic theory. Briefly, their view was that mathematical, terms – number, addition and the like – could be defined in purely logical terms and that mathematical theorems could be deduced from purely logical axioms; mathematics was therefore an extension of **logic.** This theory will now be briefly sketched.

In the late nineteenth century the Italian mathematician Peano had succeeded in showing that the arithmetic of finite cardinal numbers could be derived from five primitive propositions or axioms and three undefined terms – *zero, number* and *successor of*. Now it is clear that mathematics cannot be regarded as continuous with logic unless all the terms of mathematics can be defined in terms of logic; this meant that Russell and Frege, basing their work on that of Peano, had to define *zero, number* and *successor of* in logical terms. This task they claimed to have successfully performed, Frege in *The Foundations of Arithmetic* (1884), a masterpiece of philosophical writing that is neither very long nor very difficult, and Russell in *The Principles of Mathematics* (1903). The key terms Russell used in his definition are *class, belonging to a class* and *similarity*; thus he defined number in general as "the class of classes similar to a given class". Definitions of the basic terms of mathematics were given so that any mathematical proposition could be rewritten so that every reference to numbers was replaced by reference to classes, membership of classes and relations between classes.

But if mathematics is to be identified with logic we must not merely be able to reduce the vocabulary of mathematics to that of logic; we must also be able to deduce the five axioms of Peano, or whatever else we take as a set of axioms for mathematics, from purely logical axioms. This gigantic task was undertaken by Frege in *The Basic Laws of Arithmatic* and by **Whitehead** and Russell in *Principia Mathematica*. Many philosophers would claim that Whitehead and Russell essentially succeeded in this project, and regard the logistical theory of mathematics

as established. The whole of mathematics, it is claimed, has been shown to be but an elaboration of a set of trivial logical axioms.

Opponents of the logistic thesis urge that not all the axioms required are so trivial; we may shortly consider the *axiom of infinity*. Russell's definition of number is such that to speak of the number three is to speak of the class composed of all classes having three members and to speak of the number nine is to speak of the class of classes with nine members and so on; but if there were only eight objects in the universe then the class of classes with nine members would be empty – it would be a null class – and similarly for all numbers greater than eight; so that all numbers greater than eight would be equal to each other and equal also to zero, which is absurd. To avoid ever getting to a stage in the sequence of finite integers when they would all become equal to zero Russell and Whitehead introduced the axiom of infinity which in effect says that there are an infinite number of objects in the universe; but this is not obviously true and if true is not obviously a logical truth. Whether such difficulties can be surmounted without abandoning the logistic thesis is still an open question.

Of alternative theories, the best known is formalism; as stated by its best known exponent, Hilbert, this is the view that mathematics is to be regarded as an abstract calculus of which the terms, numbers, are given no interpretation beyond being things which satisfy the axioms; the essential characteristic of mathematics is self-consistency, which is a purely formal property. Critics of this view claim that mathematical terms must be given more than this purely formal meaning if mathematics is to be applied – as it obviously can be; even within mathematics we need to say such things as that four has two square roots, and here "two" must be given more than a formal meaning.

There is no agreed answer to the central problems of the nature of mathematics; but in spite of disagreement it becomes more and more probable that an account of mathematics can be given which, while admitting its *a priori* character, will not require us to accept a Platonic view involving some rational insight into a world of eternal essences which are the subject of mathematical investigation.

(J.O.U.)

**Medieval Philosophy.** The Middle Ages are significant in the history of thought as the period in which living religious traditions came into full contact with Greek philosophy. This experience was common to Muslims, Jews and Christians, and in each case the chief philosophical factor was the text of **Aristotle**, accompanied by a vague current of **neoplatonism** which affected the interpretation of Aristotle and occasionally showed itself independently. All three religions were faced with a choice between the primacy of theology, the primacy of philosophy, and the possibility of a harmonious synthesis of both. The efforts at synthesis provided the most interesting thinking of the period.

The Muslims came into contact with Greek philosophy as they extended their conquests over Asia Minor towards the gates of Constantinople. **Avicenna** succeeded to his own satisfaction in harmonizing the Koran with a neo-platonic doctrine of the emanation of all things from God, worked out in Aristotelian terms. **Averroes** was regarded throughout the Middle Ages as the Commentator of Aristotle *par excellence*, but his adherence to the theory of the eternity of matter and his denial of personal immortality were incompatible with orthodox Islam. After his death a theological reaction, already preluded by the notable mystical thinking of Al Gazali (1058–1111), put an end to the creative period of Arabic philosophy.

Jewish thinkers living in Muslim countries, especially Spain, underwent similar philosophical influences. Avencebrol (Solomon ibn Gabirol, 1021–1058), the author of *The Source of Life*, was thoroughly neoplatonic in spirit. **Maimonides** wrote *The Guide of the Perplexed*, which is the most remarkable development of Aristotelian philosophy in harmony with Jewish monotheism and had considerable influence on **Aquinas.** A theological reaction also stifled medieval Jewish philosophical speculation.

The earliest period of Christian philosophy in the Middle Ages, from the end of the eighth to the end of the eleventh century, saw a gradual but by no means uninterrupted recovery from the barbarism of the Dark Ages. Philosophy had no independent existence, but philosophical notions persisted through the study of the Fathers, especially **Augustine**, and through the reading of **Boethius.** The more elementary parts of Aristotelian logic were taught under the name of dialectic among the seven liberal arts, and the remarks of Porphyry in his *Isagoge* directed attention to the question of the relation of universal concepts to fact. The neo-platonic system of **Erigena** in the ninth century was an isolated product.

The twelfth century was the period of the recovery of the text of Aristotle, but already the need of more material for study was evident in the new speculative urge of **Anselm**, the originator of the **ontological argument.** The brilliant speculative mind of **Abelard** was partly stultified by the lack of material for reflection and criticism. In the course of this century however, and in the earlier part of the next, the writings of Aristotle were made available in Latin translation and came to be understood. It should be borne in mind that for the Middle Ages Aristotle was the leading source of what we should now call science as well as what we should now distinguish as philosophy. The rise of universities, as at Paris and Oxford, was also a stimulus to systematic study.

The thirteenth century was the most important in medieval philosophy because it was the period of the critical assimilation of Aristotle. The more conservative theologians, who are sometimes described as Augustinian because their leading authority was Augustine, made use of the new Aristotelian knowledge and method while keeping them in strict subordination to the tradition of Christian theology. Such was **Bonaventura. Albert the Great** gave himself wholeheartedly to the new learning, and his disciple **Aquinas** provided the classical medieval synthesis of Aristotelian philosophy and Christian theology. His pacific manner sometimes obscures the fact that he was ready to suggest modifications on either side whenever he thought them desirable. The nearest comparable synthesis is that of **Scotus** in the next generation.

Meanwhile the more radical Aristotelians, sometimes called Averroists arrived at philosophical conclusions which they could not square with theology. **Siger** of Brabant seems to have honestly expounded his difficulties, but others come under theological suspicion of substituting philosophical conclusions for doctrines of faith.

While Aquinas remains important as having tried to erect a metaphysical philosophy on an empirical basis, that basis needed further analysis. In the fourteenth century the criticism of **William of Ockham** brought philosophy to a more completely empirical starting point. This might have been an invitation to a more critical metaphysic, but there was no great mind to take up the challenge. Medieval philosophy tended to decline into that sterile logic-chopping which a later age was to consider characteristic of scholasticism. The neo platonic system of Nicholas of Cusa (1401–1464) was again an individual achievement.

The revival of scholastic philosophy after the Renaissance, associated above all with the name of Francisco Suarez (1548–1617), falls outside the Middle Ages, but it failed to last because it did not come to terms with the rise of modern science. For the more recent revival see **neo-Thomism**. The spirit of medieval philosophy is sometimes summed up in the phrase which speaks of philosophy as the handmaid of theology, but this was coined by a conservative theologian, Peter Damian (1007–1072), who was anxious to curb the pretensions of rational speculation. It is better summarized by Anselm when he speaks of faith seeking understanding. The great medieval philosophers, while presupposing the truth of Christianity, sought with candour and persistence for whatever new light could be thrown on their view of the world by what they could recover of Greek philosophy.

(D.J.B.H.)

**Meinong,** Alexius, (1853–1920), Austrian philosopher, who developed **Brentano**'s intentional psychology, and whose **realism** greatly influenced **Russell, Moore** and other British and American Realists. Meinong spent most of his life as a professor at the University of Graz. His principal works are: *Hume Studies* (1877, 1882); *Psychological-ethical Investigations towards Value-theory* (1894); *On Assumptions* (1902); *On Possibility and Probability* (1915); *On Emotional Presentation* (1917); *Ground-work of the General Theory of Value* (1923).

Meinong's Psychology is rooted in that of Brentano: he assumes that directedness-to-objects is the distinguishing property of the mental. The analysis of mental states is, however, complicated by distinguishing two "elements" in them: (a) an "act-element" which represents the *manner* in which a state of mind is directed to its object, and (b) a "content-element" which is defined as that which gives a state of mind its direction to one object rather than another. The difference between thinking of dragons and believing in dragons is a difference in "act", whereas the difference between believing in dragons and believing in ghosts is a difference in content. By the "content-element" Meinong does not mean any mental image or representation, much less the object itself: the use of the term only expresses the fact that its being *of* a certain object is intrinsic to, and not adventitious to, a state of mind. Meinong builds on Brentano's threefold classification of states of mind into Presentations, Judgments and Affective-Desiderative attitudes. But he divides Presentations into those involving Passive Perception and those involving *Active Production*, for example, ideas of relations. He also places beside Judgments certain judgment-like attitudes which lack *conviction*, that is, *Assumptions (Annahmen)* and shows how important these are in art, play, pretence, fantasy, hypothesis etc. And he separates the affective and desiderative attitudes which Brentano confounded.

The main interest of Meinong's doctrine does not, however, lie in his Psychology but in his Object-theory. According to Meinong, if we ask ourselves exactly what our various mental states bring to mind, we shall see that different types of mental state correspond to typically different objects. Thus our various "productive presentations" introduce us to various "objects of higher order" which are founded on the objects of passive perception. For example, a particular grouping or pattern is "objective" and yet is not something that we passively see. Such founded objects are said to Meinong to *subsist (bestehen)* or have subsistence *(Bestand)*, and not to *exist*, a use of terms taken over by Moore and Russell. Meinong further held that *what* we judge and *what* we assume is a peculiar complex object called an "objective", which involves other objects as its material, and which cannot be said to exist, but which may or may not be *a fact (tatsächlich)*. "Objectives" are the Russell-Moore "propositions". They are expressed by a complete sentence or that-clause, for example "that Caesar conquered Gaul", but their status *as* objectives does not depend on their being expressed or thought.

The most famous (or notorious) of Meinong's doctrines is concerned with objects which do not exist or with objectives which are not facts. According to Meinong such objects or objectives are *genuine* objects or objectives, with a make-up which is independent of thought or expression. Their very non-existence or not-being-the-case entails this objective status, for the non-existence of a golden mountain is quite *different* from the non-existence of a round square, and the not-being-the-case of the former differs from the not-being-the-case of the latter. But Meinong does *not* hold, as Russell for a time did, that non-existent objects *subsist*, or have any sort of being *(Sein)*. He only maintains that they have a describable *nature* or *Sosein*, which is unaffected by the circumstance of their existence or non-existence. We may say, for example, that a round square is round and square, but not that there is a round square. For Meinong, therefore, "Something is F" is *not* equipollent to "There is an F", as it is for Russell. Meinong holds further that objects which cannot be said to exist play an extremely important role in knowledge. Objects *incompletely determined*, and which violate the law of excluded middle, are none the less the means through which the mind refers to objects which exist and are completely determinate. In his theory of knowledge Meinong makes use of Brentano's concept of self-evidence *(Evidenz)*, but he adds to absolute self-evidence the important notion of a surmise-evidence *(Vermutungsevidenz)*, with

which he justifies sense-perception, memory and induction.

In his theory of Value, Meinong holds that feelings may fuse either with the act or content element of our presentations or judgments, yielding *four* types of feeling: (*a*) presentation-act-feelings in which we *sensually* like or dislike something, without caring about its reality or its character; (*b*) presentation-content-feelings (aesthetic feelings), in which we do not care about the reality of something but do care about its character; (*c*) judgment-act-feelings, in which we do care about the reality of something but not about its character (scientific feelings), and (*d*) judgment-content-feelings, or *valuations* proper, in which we care about both the reality and character of something. In Meinong's earlier work no absolute or impersonal values are admitted: so-called absolute values are merely values for an impartial spectator. But in his later work he argues that feelings and desires may be the mental index or "content" corresponding to peculiar objective determinations. Feelings introduce our mind to "dignitatives", for example, beauty, goodness, while desires introduce them to "desideratives", that is to various objective "oughts" – that a picture *ought* to be rehung for instance. The objects thus introduced *sometimes* really subsist and there can be considerable surmise-evidence that they do so.

(J.N.F.)

**Merleau-Ponty,** Maurice (1907–1961), French phenomenologist. Co-founder and leading proponent of French existentialism, and co-editor with **Sartre** and **de Beauvoir** of the influential journal, *Les Temps Modernes*, Merleau-Ponty also taught for many years at the Collège de France in Paris. The publication of his monumental *Phenomenology of Perception* in 1945 established his reputation as one of the foremost academic philosophers of post-war France. The principal originality of this work was to apply **Husserl's** phenomenology of intentional consciousness to the *corporeal* dimensions of human existence: hence his description of human existence in terms of a "body-subject" which is always "situated" in a concrete lived experience. The fact that we are bodies, pre-reflectively immersed in the "flesh of the world" is in no way incompatible with our status as free and creative subjects intentionally related to history. Merleau-Ponty rejects the positivistic view of the body as a mere object amongst objects. It is to be understood rather as an expressive subject which reveals itself through our everyday perceptions, gestures and symbols.

Merleau-Ponty criticized his existentialist colleague, Sartre, for his excessive emphasis on the autonomy of human consciousness, arguing that all subjectivity is intersubjectivity – that the freedom of consciousness is inextricably bound by with pre-conscious structures of collective meaning. On this point, he came close to Lévi-Strauss and **structuralism.**

This analysis of the body-subject as both a producer and product of historical meaning gave rise to a philosophy of ambiguity, which expresses itself in the following basic phenomena:

(1) Physically, the human hand can both touch and be touched.

(2) Linguistically, we create new meanings on the basis of a language already acquired.

(3) Politically, we are both agents who transform society and recipients of the "sedimentations" of our social institutions and traditions. (This political ambivalence was evident in Merleau-Ponty's controversial exchanges with Sartre on the nature of revolutionary Marxism – which they both supported in different ways – in *Les Temps Modernes* and in his collection of political essays, *Adventures of the Dialectic,* 1955.)

(4) Ontologically, human existence is expressed in the intertwining of the visible and invisible dimensions of being. This last phenomenon was a central preoccupation of Merleau-Ponty's two final works, *Eye and Mind* and the unfinished *The Visible and the Invisible*, both published posthumously in 1964. It also recapitulates his life-long interest in the "indirect languages" of art and literature as evidenced in earlier works such as *Sense and Non-Sense* (1948) and *Signs* (1960).

Merleau-Ponty's preference for an aesthetic reading of existence – in terms of style and signification – over a scientific one in terms of objects and statistics, epitomizes his conviction that truth is an ongoing project rather than a fixed possession, a task of living experience rather than a *fait accompli*. See also **Philosophy of Mind**.

[R.K.]

**Metaphilosophy** is theory about the nature of philosophy.

**Metaphor. Aristotle** spoke of ability to use metaphor as a "sign of genius". His own definition, in the *Poetics*, is a useful starting point: "the application to one thing of a name belonging to another thing". Although it blurs the finer rhetorical discriminations of metonymy, synecdoche, and catachresis, this definition nevertheless highlights the central philosophical question about metaphor, namely: how is it possible to apply terms "figuratively", beyond their normal range of application, without lapsing into nonsense? What theory of meaning, or communication, or thought, is required to explain this possibility? A second, related, philosophical concern is with the truth-bearing potential of metaphor. Do metaphors afford a special kind of cognition?

Philosophical attitudes have been mixed. **Hobbes** and **Locke** dismissed figurative usage as a superfluous distraction in intellectual discourse, a sign of sloppiness or deceit. Other philosophers have argued that metaphor is pervasive and inescapable; **Nietzsche** and **Derrida** draw the sceptical conclusion that the pervasiveness of metaphor undermines any search for fixed, timeless truths. A third attitude, hinted at by Shelley but refined by recent analytical philosophers, associates metaphor with unique truth-bearing, even truth-creating, possibilities.

In contemporary philosophy of language the debate is initially focused on meaning. Two general approaches are discernible here, loosely labelled "semantic" and "pragmatic". Semantic theories locate metaphorical meaning in *langue*, the language system. Metaphoricalness is seen as a complex semantic property of phrases or sentences. If metaphor has cognitive potential then, according to this view, it resides in the embodiment of a novel thought or proposition within this special semantic content. Pragmatic theories, in contrast, locate metaphorical meaning in *parole*, as a property of specific, contextualized utterances. What cognitive potential there might be is thought to lie not in the linguistic representation of a thought but in the evocation of a particular response, imaginative or intellectual.

The simplest, most traditional, semantic theory identifies the semantic content of a metaphor with the literal meaning of a corresponding simile. Thus "Time is a tyrant" is taken to mean the same as "Time is like a tyrant". However plausible for certain examples, this account is now widely regarded as inadequate. In a complex metaphor, like **Wittgenstein**'s famous aphorism "a cloud of philosophy condensed into a drop of grammar", it is not always possible to construct an exactly equivalent simile. In any case, the standard criticism remains that something integral to metaphor is lost in literal translations of this kind.

A further objection to reducing metaphors to similes is that a metaphor and a corresponding simile might have different truth-conditions. John Searle illustrates this with the example "John is a gorilla", which would normally be taken to imply, metaphorically, that John is fierce, nasty, prone to violence, and so forth. However, gorillas, as we now know, are shy and sensitive creatures, so quite different implications are carried by the literal comparison "John is like a gorilla".

Responding to the weaknesses of the simile account, other semantic theories have tried to capture the features that make metaphor distinctive. Max **Black**, in a landmark paper of 1955, argued that the terms in a metaphor *interact* by invoking and "filtering" systems of associations. This interaction, elsewhere described as "interanimation" (I. A. Richards) or "tension" (Monroe Beardsley), generates a novel semantic content, going beyond the literal meanings of the metaphor's constituent elements. An important aspect of Black's theory is the appeal to language-users' empirical *beliefs*, over and above the *meanings* of words, in the creation of metaphorical meaning.

The introduction of non-semantic factors, in the form of beliefs, might seem to weaken the claim that metaphor is a purely semantic phenomenon. Some theorists, notably L. J. Cohen, have argued for a more uncompromising semantic position, whereby metaphorical meanings are deemed to be already present in literal meanings and reachable by a process of selection and elimination. Such austere semantic accounts, however, face the problem of explaining the spontaneity and novelty of certain metaphors.

Interaction theories like Black's confront other difficulties of detail. First, there is the problem of how semantic interaction could discriminate relevant from irrelevant "associations". What semantic rule selects the connotation of fierceness for the interaction of "John" and "gorilla", but not the connotation of, say, living in Africa or being popular in zoos? Second, it is hard to see how the relevant associations in some metaphors, for example "Time is a tyrant", could be transferred in any non-metaphorical sense from one constituent to another. Few, if any, properties of tyrants could be attributed literally to time. But then the semantic content yielded by the interaction is just a further series of metaphors.

A problem for all semantic theories lies in the initial identification of a phrase or sentence as metaphorical. Although some metaphors, again like "Time is a tyrant", contain semantic clues to their metaphorical nature, in the form of anomalies, mixed categories or patent falsehoods, other metaphors, like "The rats went down with the ship", display no semantic irregularities and rely entirely on the context of utterance to prompt a metaphorical reading.

Pragmatic theorists use the relativity to context and the dynamics of metaphorical interpretation as their starting point. Their paradigm is this: a speaker issues a metaphorical utterance on a particular occasion and intends thereby to invoke a certain kind of response in the hearer. Different accounts have been offered of such metaphorical communication. One view, widely held, and expounded in detail by Searle, is that metaphor is an instance of "speaker's meaning" rather than "sentence meaning", that is, a speaker says one thing (S is P) and means something else (S is R). Recognizing that the speaker cannot mean (literally) what he says, given the context of utterance, the hearer then invokes principles of (metaphorical) interpretation to recover the meaning intended. This account allows that there might be different features of the context, not only semantic anomalies in the sentence, which prompt the search for a metaphorical reading. One major criticism of this view is that it demands too determinate a meaning for metaphorical utterances, failing to acknowledge their "openendedness". Another is that it gives undue authority to a speaker's intentions.

A different pragmatic approach is to postulate a distinctive speech act associated with metaphor. One suggestion is that a metaphorical utterance is an "invitation" or "instruction" to a hearer to think of one thing in terms of another. Here the speaker might have no special authority over how the instruction might be carried out. Speech act accounts, however, face the complication that metaphors themselves can occur in different speech acts and in *oratio obliqua*. Does the metaphorical speech act override, or get subsumed by, the wider speech act?

A far more radical theory, introduced by Donald **Davidson** in a seminal paper of 1978, proposes that there is no such thing as metaphorical meaning, either semantic or pragmatic. "Metaphors mean what the words, in their most literal interpretation, mean and nothing more" (Davidson). The power and interest of metaphorical utterance, according to this theory, lies in its ability to jolt us into new ways of thinking. A metaphor does not convey a propositional content, other than that of its literal sense, so there is no question of "metaphorical truth".

This "no-meaning" view of metaphor emphasizes the causal and psychological features of language use. But psychological responses can be unpredictable and arise under a variety of conditions. To retain any distinctive concept of metaphor the no-meaning view needs to offer some constraints on the relevant responses and also on the modes of utterance that are their causes. It also needs to account for the prominent role of metaphor in cognitive discourse, including science and philosophy, where rational

argument, rather than causal efficacy, is paramount. Finally, whereas this view presupposes a secure concept of literal meaning, in fact the boundaries between literal and metaphorical language or even between "dead" and "live" metaphors remain blurred. That encourages the thought that metaphors are more pervasive and more intractable than neat theories of meaning are prepared, or able, to acknowledge.

[P.L.]

**Metaphysics.** Metaphysics is that part of philosophy which has the greatest pretensions and is exposed to the greatest suspicions. Having the avowed aim of arriving at profound truths about everything, it is sometimes held to result only in obscure nonsense about nothing. This equivocal status is not the least of those features of metaphysics which require explanation.

I. DESCRIPTIONS OF METAPHYSICS
It will be well, first, to set out a number of descriptions of the subject given by some who are themselves metaphysicians or critics of metaphysics or both. From these descriptions we may gather a list of characteristics each of which we may expect to find in some examples of metaphysics and some of which we may find in all. The task will then be to explain how these characteristics are related; to decide, if possible, which of them are central; and perhaps to distinguish different kinds of metaphysics.

The name of the subject is the name given by scholars to a treatise of **Aristotle**. Aristotle described the subject of his treatise in a number of different ways which he regarded as equivalent. He called it the study of the first principles of things. He said it was the science of existence in general, or of "being as such", contrasting it in this respect with the various special sciences which each studied only one part or aspect of being. He described it also as the study of "substance", a term which occupies a central position in the work of most of the great metaphysicians who came after him. Substance he declared to be what primarily existed, and was prior to all other things in respect not only of existence, but of explanation and of knowledge as well; that is to say, the explanation of anything else involved the idea of substance; knowledge of anything else involved knowledge of substance; and the existence of everything else depended on the existence of substance. Metaphysics, then, is regarded by Aristotle as a single, comprehensive study of what is fundamental to all existence, all knowledge and all explanation. It will at once be evident that different identifications of substance, i.e. of what has this fundamental character, will yield different systems of metaphysics.

If we set beside Aristotle's account of his subject the words of the English metaphysician **Bradley**, we notice a different element in the definition. Bradley says: "We may agree, perhaps, to understand by metaphysics an attempt to know reality as against mere appearance, or the study of first principles or ultimate truths, or again the effort to comprehend the universe, not simply piecemeal or by fragments, but somehow as a whole". The mention of first principles, the contrast with "piecemeal" studies, are Aristotelian. But the emphasis on knowledge of reality *as against mere appearance* is an additional element.

There is a more striking shift of emphasis when we turn to the great critical metaphysicians, **Hume** and **Kant**. Kant emphasized above all the non-empirical character both of the subject-matter and of the method of traditional metaphysics. Its method was **a priori**, the employment of pure reason alone; its subject matter was transcendent. Neither its results nor its methods could be checked by experience. For it argued to conclusions about things which transcended experience, in accordance with principles which experience did not establish. The resulting controversies were endless; and "the battlefield of these endless controversies is called metaphysics". Kant concluded that we should turn the light of reason on reason itself, that we should undertake the critical examination of pure reason in order to determine what it is, and is not, capable of. The first, and perhaps the only, task of metaphysics is to determine its own limits. Kant here echoes, in a more specific form, the suggestion of Hume that we should "inquire seriously into the nature

of human understanding and show, from an exact analysis of its powers and capacity, that it is by no means fitted for such remote and abstruse subjects". This inquiry Hume describes as "cultivating true metaphysics with some care in order to destroy the false and adulterate".

There is a certain modern account of metaphysics which does not seem at all obviously related to what has gone before. **Wisdom** describes a metaphysical proposition as, characteristically, a sort of illuminating falsehood, a pointed paradox which uses language in a novel way in order to make us aware of differences and similarities which are concealed by our ordinary ways of talking. And **Wittgenstein** compares a metaphysical suggestion to the invention of a new kind of song. The thought common to both is, perhaps, that it is characteristic of the metaphysician to propose for use, or to offer for contemplation, a shift in our ideas, a revision of our concepts, a new way of looking at the world.

## II. CHARACTERISTICS OF METAPHYSICS

The composite picture which these descriptions yield is not a very clear one. (1) Metaphysics is a comprehensive study of what is fundamental in the order of knowledge, explanation and existence; (2) it is the study of reality as opposed to mere appearance; (3) its subject is, or has been, what transcends experience; (4) it is, or ought to be, a study of the intellectual equipment and limitations of human beings; (5) its method is, or has been, *a priori* rather than empirical; (6) it proposes a revision of the set of ideas in terms of which we think about the world, a change in our conceptual scheme, a new way of talking.

This list of characteristics is heterogeneous, and may seem scarcely coherent. Before we relate the list to actual examples of metaphysics, perhaps we can trace some general connections between some of its items. For instance, while it might be possible to interpret a metaphysical system as (6), a proposal for conceptual revision, an invitation to look at the world in a new way, the system will not generally be presented by the metaphysician as such a proposal, but rather as (2), a picture of things as they really are instead of as they delusively seem, a description of reality as opposed to appearance. Again, starting with a concern with (1), what is fundamental to existence, the metaphysician may reach the same antithesis, (2); for he may express his sense of the importance of what he regards as fundamental by saying that it alone really exists and all else is appearance. If this revised picture of reality is a radical enough revision, the distinction between appearance and reality may have to be drawn between what falls within and what lies outside experience, (3); and evidently, if the concern is with what transcends experience, the method must be non-empirical (5). It is obviously less easy to connect (4), the recommendations of Hume and Kant, with many of these characteristics; but at least there is an easy connection between the examination of the intellectual equipment of human beings and part of (1), viz. the determination of what is fundamental in the order of knowledge and explanation.

III. THE HISTORY OF METAPHYSICS

Now to compare this list of characteristics with actual systems of metaphysics. It is certainly true that most of the great metaphysicians have proposed radically revised pictures of the world, bold, comprehensive and often startling; and that most of them have accorded a central place in the picture to some few key concepts, or to some specially favoured type of entities given the title of "substance". It is also true that the choice of key concepts and entities, and the resultant picture of the world, have varied greatly from one metaphysician to another. Sometimes even "substance" has been dethroned, e.g. in favour of "process"; and among candidates for the role of substance the choice has been wide. Besides God, the divine substance, who has a place in most systems, **Descartes** recognized two types of substance, matter and minds; **Berkeley** one only, minds or spirits; **Leibniz** a class of entities (monads) each of which, though non-spatial and non-temporal, was somehow a model of the entire universe. **Spinoza** recognized only one comprehensive substance, God or Nature, infinite and eternal, of which mind and matter were merely two aspects. Kant regarded substance as belonging to the world of our

ordinary experience, yet set Reality itself, as totally unknowable, outside that world. Hume, though inclined to deride the whole notion of substance, thought that if anything deserved the title, as being capable of independent existence and fundamental in the order of knowledge, it was particular sense-impressions and the imagination's copies of these. It is inevitable that we should inquire into the reasons for this diversity; and it is impossible not to decide that it reflects in part historical changes in the general intellectual situation as human thought advances or develops in different particular spheres, and in part individual variations in the interests, attitudes and preferences of different metaphysicians. These interests and preferences, those advances and developments, are dramatised into cosmic *tableaux*, expressed in the form of highly abstract myth, uncontrolled, as Hume and Kant remarked, by a critical examination of the kind of reasoning employed. The point may be illustrated from the case of Descartes. His main interest was in the development of science, and he had very clear ideas about the proper direction for this development. Mathematics, and in particular geometry, seemed to him to provide the model for scientific procedure. He thought that the fundamental method in science was the deductive method of geometry, which he conceived of as rigorous reasoning from self-evident axioms; and he thought that the subject-matter of all the physical sciences must be fundamentally the same as the subject-matter of geometry, and hence that, from the point of view of science in general, the only important characteristics of things in the physical world were the spatial characteristics which geometry studies. It is not the holding of these beliefs which makes Descartes a metaphysician. It is rather the dramatic expression they receive in his doctrines about the essential nature of knowledge and existence. He offers a picture of a world in which the only realities, apart from God, are purely material substance with none but spatial characteristics, and pure thinking substances whose being essentially consists in the ability to grasp self-evident axioms and their deductive consequences. Knowledge is nothing but the results of exercising this ability.

Whatever else ordinarily passes for reality or knowledge is downgraded, given an inferior status. Such a drastic revision of our ordinary scheme of things naturally creates problems, and calls for further explanations and adjustments. Thus Descartes teaches, on the one hand, that it is only through confidence in God's veracity that we can have reason to believe in the existence of material things; and on the other that it is only through our wilfulness that we ever believe what is false.

Again and again in the history of the subject such a preoccupation with some advance, achieved or hoped for, in a particular branch of thought, has found expression in some similarly bold new vision of the nature of the world. Not only mathematics and the physical sciences, but history, biology and formal logic as well, have all inspired metaphysics. Developments in the study of history underlay the Hegelian system; and the late metaphysics of Logical Atomism can be seen, in part, as the expression of a profound satisfaction with advances in formal logic at the end of the nineteenth and the beginning of the twentieth centuries. Nor is it only a concern with theoretical disciplines that supplies the drive to. metaphysical revision. Religions and moralities too may seek and find metaphysical support. Elements of diverse kinds may be fused in a single system, such as that of Spinoza, which expresses an attitude at once thoroughly scientific and profoundly moral.

## IV. CRITICAL METAPHYSICS

The critical metaphysicians, Hume and Kant, demand separate and special attention. Kant pointed out that the metaphysician necessarily employed concepts which have an application in our ordinary experience or at least are derived from concepts so employed; but that the metaphysician's own use of these concepts characteristically ignored or went beyond the empirical conditions of their employment. Any such extension of the use of these concepts, so far from extending our knowledge beyond the limits of experience, was quite illegitimate, and the results were empty or senseless. Kant maintained that the positive task of metaphysics was to

show how the most general and fundamental concepts we employed were interrelated to form an organizing framework of ideas and principles, a framework which supplied the necessary conditions of the kinds of knowledge and experience which we in fact possessed. The negative task was to show both how inevitable was the metaphysical temptation to use these general concepts in ways which disregarded the empirical conditions of their employment, and how inevitably empty were the results of succumbing to this temptation. At this point we find in Kant a residue of that very kind of metaphysics which he declared to be impossible. For the framework of ideas which it was the positive task of metaphysics to elucidate was thought of by Kant as the framework of things only as they appeared to beings with our cognitive constitution, not of things as they were in themselves. What was ultimately real was in principle unknowable; and this unknowable reality acquired a more positive role when Kant was concerned to secure metaphysical foundations for morality: it appeared as the authoritative source of morality's commands. Hume, Kant's predecessor in time, shared with Kant the conviction that significant discourse was limited by the conditions of actual experience, and that much traditional metaphysics trespassed beyond those limits. But Hume inherited from **Locke** and Berkeley a curiously limited conception of what experience actually supplied us with. The real elements of experience, he held, were separate and fleeting impressions of sense and feeling. Our ordinary picture of a world of continuously existing and interacting material things and persons could not be rationally justified on this basis; but it could be explained, as the product of the associative mechanism of the imagination set in motion by the ultimate elements of feeling and sense.

It will be obvious that both Hume and Kant, while criticizing in principle the revisionary schemes of other metaphysicians, were to some extent metaphysically revisionary themselves. Kant's doctrine that only what is unknowable is ultimately real, and Hume's doctrine that it is imagination which makes us believe in the existence of material bodies, are alike in doing violence to the concepts of imagination, reality and knowledge which we actually employ. Nevertheless, in virtue both of the positive and of the critical aspects of their work, these two great philosophers exercised an influence on metaphysics which may well appear decisive. This is particularly true of Kant. Both philosophers concerned themselves with the general structure of our thought about the world. Both wrote, much of the time, in an idiom more suggestive of empirical psychology than of an investigation into concepts and the conditions of their use. But behind the psychological idiom of Kant we can find the outline of a far more coherent account of the general structure of our conceptual scheme than we can find either in Hume or in those later empiricists who wrote in the spirit of Hume while discarding much of his psychology. The criticisms made by both Hume and Kant of the metaphysical employment of concepts without regard to the conditions of their empirical use still stand. But on the critical as on the positive side Kant's contribution is ultimately more effective than Hume's. For though these criticisms were later expressed most vociferously and in their most extreme form by the school of Logical Positivists who were heirs of Hume rather than of Kant, the effectiveness of this expression suffered from the weaknesses and limitations of the associated empiricist metaphysics.

## V. REPUDIATIONS OF METAPHYSICS

Over much of the philosophical world in this century the doctrine of the impossibility of metaphysics became almost an orthodoxy, and the adjective "metaphysical" a pejorative word. Some of the reasons for this devaluation should now be clear. The conceptual distortions and final incoherence of systems, the abstract myths parading as Reality, the grandiose claims and the conflicting results – these seemed to many the essence of the metaphysical enterprise and sufficient reason for condemning it; and the extravagances of metaphysics were by some of them contrasted with the sobrieties of a method of philosophical analysis which aims to make clear the actual functioning of our concepts in use. But though the repudiation of

metaphysics was natural, it does not follow that it was justified. Metaphysical excess might be no more essential to metaphysics than tyranny to government. To show that the repudiation was not justified calls for some reordering of the facts which we already have before us.

When Aristotle described the subject of his treatise, he distinguished it sharply from the special or departmental disciplines. But the distinction was not drawn in a wholly clear way. It was implied that the "science of being as such" was more general and comprehensive than the special sciences. Clearly this most general science was not to be merely a *compendium* of the others; yet when the special sciences are put on one side, what subject for study is left? It is difficult to avoid the impression that the projected science of being, if such a study exists at all, must have some curiously elusive yet very fundamental subject-matter of its own, somehow lying behind those aspects of reality which are studied in departmental disciplines. Behind these aspects of reality is Reality itself, "being as such", the subject-matter of metaphysics. Already the tendency of metaphysics towards the transcendent becomes intelligible. In default of a further clarification of the nature of the enterprise, it will inevitably appear as the gropings of pure reason in a mysterious realm to which ordinary access is impossible. Another consequence may appear equally inevitable. For in order to describe this realm, the only materials that we have, or can make, available must be taken, or fashioned, from the conceptual equipment which we use for the less rarefied purposes of daily discourse or departmental studies. If we are to put such concepts to work to describe the transcendental realm, we must cut them off from the conditions of their ordinary employment and deprive them of their ordinary force; yet they must *seem* to retain something of their ordinary force, or we shall not even seem to be saying anything significant. So transcendental metaphysics proceeds by way of conceptual distortion to a termination in uncashable **metaphor**.

This is a kind of caricature of the rake's progress of metaphysics. Its purpose is to enable us to see more clearly the significance of the Kantian revolution. When Kant denied that knowledge of reality was possible, he was in effect denying that metaphysics had, or could have, any such peculiar subject-matter of its own. But he did not thereby deprive the metaphysician of employment. The positive task of the metaphysician was not to think about a special world, but to think about the structure of our thinking about the ordinary world; not to acquire knowledge of objects beyond our experience, but to clarify the nature and conditions of knowledge of objects within our experience. So metaphysics is indeed a more general and comprehensive study than any special science; for it aims to make clear the fundamental general structure of all our ordinary and scientific thinking. Its method is indeed non-empirical; for it inquires into the conceptual structure which is presupposed by all our empirical inquiries.

This conception of metaphysics may appear to differ from the Aristotelian conception. There is no mention of "being as such", of what is prior in the order of existence. But this difference is apparent only. If we investigate the fundamental categories of human thought, the connexions between them, and the dependencies of one on another, we are thereby committed to inquiring into the relations between the various types of entity, or being, which we admit into our conceptual scheme. The idea of ontological priority is not discarded, but simply given a clearer meaning. It is the idea of a transcendent reality as a possible subject of inquiry which is abandoned. The Aristotelian conception is not rejected, but rescued from perversion.

It might be said that the aims of metaphysics, so understood, are no different from those of philosophical **analysis** in general, which also proposes to investigate the actual functioning of our concepts; or that, at most, the difference will simply be one of scope and generality. But this is an important difference, which entails another: a difference in method. When the analytic philosopher proposes to investigate some particular concept – say that of memory, or cause, or truth – he finds the surest method of procedure to lie in a careful examination of the actual use of the verbs, adjectives and nouns by means of which we introduce this concept into our discourse. Such an examination has great power to reveal the complexities of the concept, the multifariousness of the phenomena which it covers, and, up to a point, its connexions with other concepts. The results arrived at in this way may be perfectly adequate for the purposes of a regional analysis, which legitimately takes much for granted; and they provide an indispensable corrective to the conceptual distortions to which metaphysics is prone. But this method of illuminating the workings of a particular part of our conceptual apparatus is apt to assume, rather than to reveal, the fundamental structure of the apparatus as a whole; and it is precisely this general structure which the metaphysician wishes to understand. The connexions and dependencies which the metaphysician has to make explicit lie below the surface of the linguistic phenomena. They do not lie so far below the surface that they cannot be detected and recognized. But their detection and recognition require a wider-ranging vision than is compatible with attention to the surface phenomena alone.

We have seen that many traditional metaphysicians have not been content to describe the actual structure of our thought about the world in its most general and fundamental aspects. Rather they have wished to substitute a revised structure, which somehow symbolized their own intellectual preoccupations and attitudes. It is almost as if, in order to record their sense of the importance of a certain change of direction in thought, they had to exaggerate the extent and implications of the change; as if our *whole* view of the world had to be at least temporarily altered, in order to accommodate a new vision of one of its aspects. Perhaps indeed there was a certain historical necessity about this; and it is not surprising that to some historically-minded critics this side of metaphysics has seemed to be the only side. We have seen reason to think that this is a mistake. The most fundamental concepts and categories of human thinking are not those which undergo drastic changes with advances in the sciences or alterations in social living; and the investigation of this central core of thought provides metaphysics with a constant subject-matter. But it would be a mistake on the opposite side to suppose that the central tasks of metaphysics can be performed once for all, and the subject regarded as closed. For even though its central subject-matter does not significantly change, the idiom, the needs, and the emphases of metaphysical elucidation vary from age to age and even from one philosopher to another. Old truths have to be restated in a new idiom; different parts of the picture call, from time to time, for more or less emphatic illumination. Metaphysical elucidation can reach no final and complete form. But that does not mean it is impossible. Some projections of the picture involve less distortion than others; and even those projections which involve the grossest distortions of the picture as a whole may nevertheless represent a part of it with a peculiar clarity.

(P.F.S.)

**Mill,** James (1773–1836). Born in Aberdeenshire, Scotland, Mill studied for the ministry at Edinburgh University but religious doubts led him to give up this career and at twenty-nine he went to London. In 1808 Mill met **Bentham**, converted him to Radicalism and became his chief lieutenant. In 1819 he entered the East India Company and lived to become its chief administrator. A remarkable account of his character and opinions is given in the *Autobiography* of his eldest son, John Stuart **Mill**.

In his *Analysis of the Phenomena of the Human Mind* (1829) Mill tries to show that all knowledge is reducible to feelings (sensations, ideas, pleasures, pains) occurring in certain orders – some successive, some simultaneous. Feelings tend to become associated in regular patterns if they occur *together*. To explain a notion is always to analyse it into ideas that have become associated. The doctrine is reductionist, atomistic, and did not succeed in the author's intention which was to make the human mind as plain as the road from Charing Cross to St Paul's.

The doctrine of association encouraged Mill to think that almost anything could be accomplished by education; and that men (who necessarily seek only their own happiness) could be so constituted by education as to find their own happiness in devotion to the common good (*Encyclopedia Britannica*, 1820, "Education"). The test of right actions lies in their consequences; it is a universalistic test – the right is that which promotes general happiness, not the happiness of the agent. Moral praise and blame, reward and punishment constitute a social device for the artificial encouragement of actions useful to society and discouragement of those that are harmful to society.

Mill rejects all notions of "natural rights" and makes an attempt (perhaps the first ever made) to defend representative institutions on purely utilitarian lines (*Encyclopedia Britannica*, 1820: "Government"). People need government in order to defend their lives and interests from other people: but any government is made up of people – who will have a private interest in plundering and enslaving their subjects. A power is therefore needed to act as a check upon the "sinister interests" of government; and the only effective way of setting up such a power is by choosing representatives. But how can we ensure an identity of interest between community and representatives? By frequent elections. Mill advocates not a representative government but a representative anti-government. Who is to choose the representatives? Mill excludes women and children and younger men on the ground that they have a *natural* identity of interest with their husbands and fathers. Mill contemplates other exclusions and finally advocates votes for the middle class since they are the real leaders of society and have been throughout the whole history of the world. Mill had unbounded confidence in representative institutions accompanied by complete freedom of discussion.

Certain critics are inclined to rank James Mill above John Stuart Mill. However it can hardly be denied that James Mill is doctrinaire in all that he attempted. This weakness shows most in his treatment of government. The argument proceeds from assumptions without historical backing: only one reason is given for each step taken – one is supposed to be decisive and one is therefore enough. Macaulay's attack (*Edinburgh Review*, 1829) fastens upon this deductive method.

(K.B.)

**Mill,** John Stuart (1806–1873), born in London. J. S. Mill was educated at home by his father James **Mill.** At eighteen he entered the East India Company, where his father was also employed, and remained with the Company until its extinction in 1858, by which time he had become its chief London administrator. At the age of twenty, Mill suffered a "mental crisis" followed by a long period of depression and disillusion, during which he found consolation in Wordsworth's poetry. On his recovery he reacted for a time against the intellectual and moral opinions of his father and his circle, and came under the influence of Coleridge, Carlyle and John Sterling. In 1831 he met Harriet Taylor and the two formed a passionate attachment which gradually came to be tolerated by her husband but not by most of their friends. It seems that on the whole Mrs Taylor's influence helped to free Mill from his Coleridgean inclinations.

Mill's first original work consisted of essays on economic questions (written 1830–34, published 1844). At about the same time he began work on the philosophy of logic and devoted to it the "spare time" of his most fruitful years. *A System of Logic, Ratiocinative and Inductive* was published in 1843 and made Mill famous. *Political Economy* appeared only two years later. In 1851 John Taylor died, and thereafter the two friends married and began work together on a number of essays and on the *Autobiography.* They both worked in the shadow of death, and were attempting to complete a bare outline of their views – "a sort of mental pemmican, which thinkers, when there are any after us, may nourish themselves with, and then dilute for other people". The partnership came to an end in 1858, when Harriet died at Avignon. *On Liberty* (a "joint work") was published in the following year. Mill now retired, living partly at Blackheath and partly at Avignon and carried out many of the projects he had discussed with his wife. He became a well-known public figure, a champion of women's rights, of the working-classes and of electoral reform. In 1865 he was elected M.P. for Westminster and was then able to propose votes for women as an amendment to Disraeli's Franchise Bill.

He died at Avignon at the age of sixty-seven, the outstanding English radical of his day and a main link between liberal thought in England and the rest of the world.

### I. ETHICS

At the age of fifteen, Mill gave his enthusiastic assent to the ethical system of **Bentham**: admiring, even at that age, Bentham's total rejection of intuitive modes of reasoning in morals. Bentham introduced scientific methods into the discussion of moral questions. This position Mill never consciously abandoned: and in his logical inquiries, and in his later reflexions on Justice and Liberty, he attempted to show that the ultimate test must be an experimental and **utilitarian** one. Mill also agreed with Bentham in holding that all our conduct is determined, and that all our deliberate acts are motivated by the belief that a certain line of conduct will lead to our own greatest good. Our decisions rest upon our characters and beliefs, as well as on our situations. Mill held that we can to a degree correct our beliefs and improve our characters – if we *want* to do so. The desire to have or to know may be efficacious: and so also may the desire *to be.* This (Mill says) embodies what is really inspiriting and ennobling in the (incorrect) doctrine of **free will.** Mill at least makes clear that moral discussion has point: it may help people to decide what sort of person they would like to be.

The fundamental principles of Mill's ethics are (1) That pleasure alone is good or desirable in itself; (2) That actions are right in proportion as they tend to promote the happiness of all concerned, wrong as they tend to promote unhappiness; and happiness means pleasure and the absence of pain.

(1) "Happiness is desirable, and the only thing desirable, as an end; all other things being desirable as means to that end." Mill demurs about giving a proof of this thesis but tries to connect pleasure or happiness with being the object of a desire; and being good in itself. We can see that each man desires his own happiness; that, of course, does not imply that happiness is desirable or good. But Mill was neither the first nor the last to hold that there must be

some intimate connexion between being good and being desired. Perhaps his view is that we learn to call things *good* and *bad, desirable* or *undesirable*, through our experience of desiring and getting or not getting what we desire. Some of the things we have desired turn out to be worth while; others not. Is happiness one of the things men desire – and one which turns out to be *good?* Mill says that to desire a thing is to think of it as pleasant – to hold that it brings or would bring pleasure. This evidently widens the meaning of "pleasure": the word becomes a technical term for whatever anyone desires for its own sake; and certainly not all these things can be called "desirable" or "good". In fact Mill is not at all prepared to treat all objects of desire alike: he makes many distinctions and conveys his own definite preferences. Some desires are primitive: others the result of experience, training, self-discipline and special associations. A hungry man (whatever his character) desires food; a miser desires to have money and a spendthrift to spend it. The pleasures of the miser, the spendthrift and the virtuous man are educated pleasures. Mill points to the qualitative differences between *kinds* of pleasure, which are readily recognizable, while quantitative differences (Bentham's "circumstances") are often difficult or impossible to assess. Mill may have supposed that qualitative differences are ultimately reducible to quantitative ones: but he is at no pains to say so. In effect he says that we ought in all our decisions to give preference to the "higher" pleasures, which include the social and generous pleasures and those of cultivated feelings and intellect.

(2) "Actions are right in proportion as they tend to promote happiness". The happiness to be considered is not that of the agent, but that of all concerned in the action. Mill is not often critizised for holding this universalist view; but for having pretended to prove that the general happiness must be something which "the aggregate of all persons" in fact regard as desirable or good. There are two points to be distinguished: (*a*) What is the nature of a right action? (*b*) Who will be moved to do it? On the first question, Mill may be taken either as offering an analysis of the accepted definition

of "right action" or as putting forward a point of view. In the main he seems to be doing the second – and seems to recognize clearly that other views are meaningful though mistaken. On the second question Mill argues that men have natural social impulses which lead them to consider the good of all concerned in an action: these may be strengthened by training and experience.

Some actions will in fact bring happiness in the long run, others will not. In effect Mill argues that we ought to choose the action which (at the time of decision) *looks most likely* to produce most happiness: it is the only possible practical version of Utilitarianism. But even this seems to ask more than is reasonable: how can one always stop to calculate? Mill answers very definitely that one should usually be guided by those *general rules* which have been formulated as a result of the long experience of men in society: "the beliefs that have come down are the rules of morality for the multitude, and for the philosopher, until he has succeeded in finding better". The philosopher is entitled to test traditional rules; to ask whether the general observance of a rule makes for greater happiness than the general observance of any alternative rule would do, or than leaving the matter outside the scope of rules. And in applying such a test, preference must be given to the "higher" kinds of pleasure. The place assigned to rules is a marked departure from the view of Bentham: Mill actually defines morality as "the rules and precepts for human conduct". Only where there is a clash of duties (where one and the same action is required by one rule and forbidden by another) should one choose simply by reference to the probable consequence of the action individually considered. Mill seems to commit himself to the view that in all other cases the right act is the one which is in accordance with a valid rule. A rule is valid only because it passes the utilitarian test: and it is difficult to believe that Mill meant us to follow such a rule where it is *known* that on this occasion it will bring more harm than good. (Perhaps this is meant to be covered by his remarks on conflicting duties.) The rules of justice – which forbid us to harm, trespass upon, or interfere with the liberty of, another – are to be observed, no matter what advantage might *seem* to come from setting them aside: for a strict and reliable adherence to these rules is itself of the greatest utility to everyone.

However, Mill is prepared to restrict the sphere of duty. Duty is something which a man may be compelled to do: and should not be widened beyond necessity. There are many good, noble and generous deeds which a man is rightly praised for doing, but which should not be required of him by any rule. The sphere of virtue includes that of duty but extends beyond it. Mill also denies that we have any duty to ourselves: if a man fails to take proper care of his own interests this is not itself a case of wrong-doing.

Mill's somewhat negative view of duty leaves to the individual a wide choice to do or become what he wishes. In *On Liberty*, he argues that this freedom is being endangered by the interfering powers of public opinion. Society has a right to make laws for that part of a man's conduct which may damage the interests of others; in this sphere the question whether a particular rule is justified is a proper question. "But there is no room for entertaining any such question where a person's conduct affects the interests of no person besides himself, or need not affect them unless they like". In the private sphere, the question whether to regulate or not is an improper question. The argument begins to look like a rehabilitation of Natural Rights. Mill argues, for example, that censorship *could not be* expedient in any civilized society. Utilitarian language hardly suffices to convey the moral importance which Mill attaches to proper pride, love of liberty, and sense of dignity. "It is the privilege and proper condition of a human being, arrived at the maturity of his faculties, to use and interpret experience in his own way." It may now seem odd that Mill should have worked to bring about a government based on the working classes and committed to Socialism. But he believed the workers could be educated in time and hoped for constitutional safeguards of the rights of minorities; the State was to pay for education but not to undertake it, and a social ownership did not for him imply ownership by an omnicompetent State.

## II. POLITICS

Mill's thinking on politics began when he read Macaulay's attack on the essay on Government by James Mill. Macaulay denied the possibility of making deductions from principles: the only study of politics must be the direct study of history. Mill came to disagree both with his father and with Macaulay. In Book VI of the *Logic*, he distinguishes two quite different types of sociological inquiry. The first is both specialized and hypothetical: e.g., What would be the effect of repealing the corn laws in the present condition of society and civilization in England? We suppose that "the state of society generally" remains constant, and use the deductive method as employed in physics. The causal factors to be changed must be analysed and their laws known (e.g. the psychological laws governing trade): the answer holds good only in the present state of society. But societies pass through different general states and we must suppose that the total causes of any such state are to be sought in its immediate predecessor. Mill believed (with **Comte**) that economic, social, and cultural conditions mutually affect each other, the state of knowledge being the most important factor. History does, when judiciously examined, afford empirical laws of society: e.g. an age of Faith leads to an age of Reason; and an age of Reason to a scientific or "positive" age. We could not have predicted such changes but we can do something to understand the law which governs them. This *general* science of society does not begin with a hypothesis and go on to verify it. It begins with generalizations from history and tries to show how a given type of transition can be explained by reference to laws discovered in the special sciences (geology, botany, economics, psychology, genetics). This "inverse deductive method" was taken from Comte – whose "friendship" with Mill shows some analogies with **Rousseau**'s for **Hume**. Mill's modest-seeming account of a general science of society has been totally rejected by K. R. **Popper**, who argues that the whole notion of a "law" of the successive total states of society is a misuse of the concept of law.

211

## III. LOGIC

In his philosophy of politics Mill fights on two fronts: against *a priori* and intuitive philosophy and against simple empiricism. The same situation is seen in his logic. Mill insists that his logic is "a logic of experience" but goes on to show that science must be systematic, analytic and (at some vital points) deductive. In the *System of Logic*, Mill attempts to show (1) that "necessary propositions" are merely verbal; (2) that the traditional immediate inferences are "merely apparent" and not real inferences; (3) that the syllogism, considered as an argument from the premises to the conclusions, is also "merely apparent" inference; (4) that the syllogism is important on account of the assertion of the major or universal premise; (5) that the assertion of a universal proposition on the basis of particular evidence is a genuine inference; hence pure deduction is not, but induction is, genuine inference; (6) that the principles of mathematics are inductive and rest upon observation; (7) that in some cases we can properly claim to know universal propositions based on induction.

Mill has not much interest in formal logic for its own sake; his main theme is *generalization* and the grounds on which it rests; and the methods appropriate to the sciences. It should be admitted at once that Mill's account of mathematical knowledge has satisfied nobody. Mill never properly distinguished between pure and applied mathematics, and confused the errors of counting and measurement with those of calculation. It was left to others to show that Mill's own highly original account of deductive reasoning as a system of tautologies, can be extended to cover mathematical reasoning also.

The logical doctrine rests on an account of meaning which introduces the notion that not all words are simply names for things. Mill uses "names" for all terms in a proposition: John, George, Mary are "singular names" and so is "the King who succeeded William I" – a many-worded name. Predicates are "general names" (e.g. man, old, white) which are "capable of being truly affirmed, in the same sense, of an indefinite number of things". But Mill picks out proper

names from all other terms; they are arbitrary in the sense that they merely denote a person or place: they are not bestowed in virtue of any property supposed to belong to it. Mill says they merely "denote"; but descriptive words and phrases say something which may be true or false. "The King who succeeded William I" denotes Rufus for anyone who understands what the phrase *means*, and sees its truth. This other sense of meaning, Mill calls "connotation". "Man" connotes certain properties: and Mill says "it denotes whatever individuals have those properties" e.g. John, George, Mary. Thus general names both connote and denote. Here Mill is mistaken: a definite description may denote an individual (Rufus) but a predicate term does not denote: I can state that J. S. Mill was not a great scientist without referring to any great scientist – which one would it be? General terms are not names: and Mill at all events makes clear that they have a meaning which does not involve naming at all. He also says that such words as "and", "of", "in", "truly", while they contribute to the formation of names, "have no title whatsoever to be considered as names".. Naming, then, is not the only kind of meaning: a truth not fully assimilated by philosophers for several generations.

A proposition which merely asserts part of what its subject-term *means* (connotes) is "merely verbal" or tautological. The immediate inferences of traditional logic are also tautological, depending for their truth (although Mill does not state this very clearly) on the *meaning* of the logical words employed. (If all men are mortal then some men are mortal: the transition depends on the meaning of "all", "some". "If... then... ".) But what of the syllogism? It is notorious that the conclusion of a syllogism must be "contained in" the premises – otherwise it is invalid. All the same I can know that all men are mortal without knowing that the Duke of Wellington is so: I might never have heard of the Duke of Wellington. Mill sees that the "novelty" of the conclusion of a syllogism arises from the fact that we can know a universal proposition without knowing all its particular instances: when I discover a new instance I make a new *application* of the universal proposition and so reach a new conclusion. But Mill is more concerned with the question, How can we know factual universal propositions? We come to know them by inference from a set of instances. This inference is inductive. The whole importance of syllogistic argument in science depends on our having universal premises. And this comes from induction: it is the only "genuine" inference.

## IV.  INDUCTION

In *Logic* Book III, Mill examines the nature of induction. It depends on the "assumption" that the course of nature if uniform, that what happens once in certain circumstances, will always happen again if like circumstances occur. And we know by an examination of nature "that the assumption is warranted". The simplest induction proceeds on the basis of simple enumeration of like instances: "The swans we have seen are all white – therefore all swans are white". It is by this very method that we learn that nature is uniform. Mill distinguishes between uniformities of co-existence and uniformities of sequence. The former include the "togetherness" of the properties of natural kinds, and of spatial and numerical properties. These can be known only by observation (including counting and measurement): in many cases the evidence for them is superabundant. Uniformities of sequence may be characterized loosely as *causal*: one sort of event leading always to a certain sequel. We learn then in the first place by simple enumeration: but Mill holds that in *causal* inductions something more like a deductive proof is possible by the help of his celebrated "Methods of (Causal) Induction".

By "cause" Mill means a sufficient cause – or rather that factor which added to the ordinary course of events in the universe, is sufficient to produce a given effect. We know (according to Mill) a most important truth about such causes: that every event has one. This we learn by simple observation, but having learned it we can use it to discover and prove particular causal laws. For the sufficient cause of X must lie in its immediate antecedent events and circumstances. This limits the search for the cause of X: we find it preceded by the circumstances A, B, C etc., and one or other of these, or some

combination of them, must have caused X. The Methods (Agreement, Difference, Agreement and Difference, Concomitant Variation) may do two things: (1) enable us to eliminate the circumstances that are not always found preceding X; (2) provide us with more and more cases where a certain other factor is found in X's antecedent environment. Of course the second part is enumeration; what Mill emphasises is that an elimination is itself a kind of proof. If we can find an instance of A not followed by X, then A cannot itself be the sufficient cause of X. And this, he holds, must strengthen the case for the remaining candidates, B, C etc. Mill writes of his Methods as constituting "a scientific test": but this claims too much. For, first, the picking out (from X's antecedents) of likely factors must depend on a knowledge of the field got without the help of these Methods: and second, this "knowledge" is itself subject to revision. (What we thought could not possibly be relevant may turn out to be the vital factor.) Methods of elimination cannot lead to a *decisive* verdict in favour of the candidates that remain, unless the set of possible candidates is decisively limited, which strictly speaking it cannot be in such inquiries. That repeated experiment does, at least by elimination, increase the *probability* of remaining factors, is hard to doubt: but a decisive test is of course quite another matter.

The Methods are common to all *causal* inquiries at the basic experimental level: at a higher level different sciences employ methods or strategies or experiment. In Book VI of the *Logic* Mill distinguishes four methods: The Geometrical Method, applicable where different laws do not modify each other's action (Mill's example suggests that this method hardly belongs to observational and experimental science at all); The Chemical Method, of direct experiment, which has to be applied where the causes combine in a way that has defied analysis; The Physical Method, which can be used when the laws of different causal factors are already fairly well known. It is then possible to suggest that a certain change was the result of a certain combination of forces, and continued experiment will provide a test. Finally Mill recognized the Historical Method, which is applicable where phenomena are complicated and beyond the scope of experiment, as in the social sciences.

Mill refers to his own views as "the experience philosophy". The point of this description comes out in his constant appeal to facts (which can be known by experience) and – at a metaphysical level – in his **phenomenalistic** account of our knowledge of things and of minds. Mill's approach is near to Hume's: he adopts an account of bodies in terms of our perceptions of them. He distinguishes clearly (as **Berkeley** did not) between two kinds of order in experience: (1) the uniform causal order which connects together bodies or physical changes of certain kinds; (2) the order which connects different ideas or impressions in our minds and leads us to form the notion that they are all perceptions of the same individual thing. The second kind of order (as Hume saw) is not a uniformity in the succession of our ideas: the *uniformities* we look for are between bodies and not between sensations. Mill attempts an analysis of this order and goes on to define a body as a "permanent possibility of sensation": i.e. to talk of a table is to talk of an order of this type in actual or possible sensations. No attempt is made to found this possibility upon an actual external substance, nor upon God. But Mill recognizes that there are "other successions of feeling besides those of which I am conscious". How are we to describe the order of experiences which constitutes an individual mind? Mill here comes upon "a final inexplicability" – the fact that a mind which is a series of feelings should be aware of itself as past and future.

In his essays on natural theology Mill defends the possibility of a mind existing without a body, hence the possibility of immortality. He also examines, in a scientific spirit, the question whether the world as we know it is largely the work of a divine intelligence; and if so, whether that divine intelligence has communicated with man by a miraculous revelation. The argument from design carries some weight: it suggests that there is a God who desires the good of his creatures (i.e. those of his creatures known to us) but that he has many other tasks in hand. At this point Mill switches the question from the region of belief to the region of simple hope. Without actual belief, a man may contemplate the notion of divine perfection, meditate upon the gospels, hope for immortality. This has a practical value. These reflections are found in Mill's letters and connect with his early serious Wordsworthian concern for the cultivation of the best that is to be found in human feeling and imagination. But his *Essays on Religion*, which appeared after his death, surprised his more downright agnostic and atheistic friends. See also **Philosophy of Science.**

(K.B.)

**Miracles,** *see* Theism.

**Mises,** Richard von (1883–1953), a prominent associate of the **logical positivists** of the **Vienna Circle** until he sought refuge from Hitlerism in the USA. He wrote a general account of positivism in 1939, but it is as a theorist of probability that he is best known. His main work in the field of probability was *Probability Statistics and Truth* (1928). Von Mises aimed to set up a scientific definition of probability to replace our vague notions in everyday thought. He defined probability as the limiting value of the frequency of an event within a collective; a collective is an indefinitely large reference class whose members occur in a random order, that is, a class in predicting the character of whose members no gambling system will be of avail. Thus to say that the probability of heads is one half is to say that the limiting value of the fraction given by dividing the number of heads by the number of tosses is one half. The series of tosses constitutes the collective. Von Mises was able to show that the axioms of mathematical probability followed tautologically from this definition, which has however been attacked, especially for its use of the notion of limiting frequency outside pure mathematics; others have objected to von Mises allowing no meaning to probability statements which were not of the form "The probability of event *e* within the collective *K* is P".

(J.O.U.)

**Modernism.** According to a widely accepted but not unquestionable theory, the last few years of the nineteenth century witnessed an international upheaval in the arts which was to continue for at least thirty years. It was called modernism and it overthrew "traditional" forms which, it is argued, had unthinkingly presupposed an incontrovertible "real world" which art was expected to "express" or "represent". Thus modernist writers replaced narrative and dialogue with "stream of consciousness", modernist composers moved to "atonalism", and modernist painters discovered "abstraction"; in general the medium, or "language", was treated as an object in its own right, rather than a stand-in for an ulterior reality. **Phenomenology** and **logical positivism, relativity** and **quantum mechanics** are sometimes seen as further manifestations of modernism. In original intention, modernism appears as a rejection of the domineering epistemological optimism of **modernity**; but in a wider perspective it can be seen as a continuation of it by sophisticatedly self-conscious means: see **post-modernism**.

[J.R.]

**Modernity.** The idea of modernity – which is common to sociology, economics and historiography, both in their professional and in their popular or "folk" forms – is an attempt to grasp the peculiarity of the present by contrasting it with a preceding age. Various criteria of modernity have been proposed: science, commerce, capitalism, police, print, surveillance, cheap travel, atheism, bureaucratic rationality, urbanism, consumerism, or democracy, and above all, **alienation**. But the underlying contrast is always epistemological: the modern world is enlightened, scientific, and disappointed, whereas its predecessor was superstitious, gullible and magical. Hence philosophical debates about the scope and limits of reason or science touch the crux of the concept of modernity.

Within philosophy, "modernity" has been used to designate various moments of abundant epistemological optimism. In the fourteenth century, **nomialism** was the *via moderna* in contrast with the discredited *via antiqua* of realism; in the

eighteenth, **Descartes** was hailed as the "father of modern philosophy" thanks to his confidence in mathematics and natural science.

**Rousseau** initiated a reaction in which reason was seen as an ailment rather than an adornment of humanity; and **Hegel** consolidated this argument by invoking a superior form of knowledge – dialectical or speculative reason – which was supposed to transcend the rationalistic one-sidedness of the eighteenth-century "enlightenment". Thus it became a commonplace to blame "the Enlightenment" for the calamities of modernity, and particularly for the excesses of the French Revolution. The same theme was carried forward by **Marx's** theory of **ideology**; and in **Nietzsche** (followed by **Heidegger** and **Derrida**) it was inflated into a blanket condemnation of the whole of Western philosophy since **Socrates**.

The old ambitions of modernity have occasionally been reactivated in twentieth-century philosophy, notably by **logical positivism** and **dialectical materialism**; but the barrage of criticism has been sustained by philosophers like **Horkheimer** and **Adorno** (see their *Dialectic of Enlightenment*, 1944), **Marcuse, Habermas,** and **MacIntyre**. The philosophers of **post-modernism**, however, have attempted to trump these criticisms of modernity by accusing them of a secret complicity with what they criticize, in that they cling to the "enlightenment" idea of a final truth toward which, in spite of everything, we may at least hope to draw nearer. See also **History of Philosophy**.

[J.R.]

**Monads,** *see* Leibniz.

**Monism.** Monism is any doctrine that there is only one substance, or one "world", or that reality is in some sense *one*, that is, unchanging or indivisible or undifferentiated. For instance, the alternative claims that "everything is mental" or "everything is material" are crudely expressed forms of monism, each opposed to the common sense **dualism** of mind and matter. The term was invented by Christian Wolff (1679–1754), who used it only of these two theories, which have the best right to the labels **"idealism"** and **"materialism"** respectively. It later came to be used also of the theory of absolute identity held by **Schelling** and **Hegel,** namely, that mind and matter are not reducible one to the other, but both to one common substance of which they are phenomenal modifications. (Compare the later "neutral monism" of William **James** and, at one time, **Russell.**) Subsequently the term was more widely applied, to any theory attempting to explain phenomena by, or reduce them to, a single principle; and opposed not merely to dualism but often also to pluralism, of which an example is Russell's Logical Atomism, which he also called "absolute pluralism". As a result of these extended uses, the term is systematically ambiguous. (1) *Substantial* monism is the view that the apparent plurality of substances is due to different states or appearances of a single substance, which was God-or-Nature to **Spinoza,** for example, and the Absolute to **Bradley.** (2) *Attributive* monism, on the other hand, is the view that whatever the number of substances, they are of a single ultimate kind, that is, there is only one realm of being. One could also distinguish from these absolute views (3) *partial* monism, namely that within a given realm of being (however many there may be) there is only one substance. These varieties of monism need not all stand or fall together; and have, for reasons requiring lengthy argument, been held selectively: for example, Spinoza held (1) and hence trivially (3), but rejected (2) in favour of an infinity of ultimate kinds, whereas **Descartes** rejected (1) and (2), but accepted (3) within the material realm, and **Leibniz** rejected (1) and (3), but accepted (2), all monads being souls; thus each of these thinkers accepted monism in at least one sense but not in others. The appropriate sense of "monism" always needs to be made clear from the context. But in each of its forms it is the supreme expression of metaphysical tidiness. See also **Philosophy of Mind.**

(R.HALL)

**Montesquieu,** Baron de (1689–1755), French political theorist, *see* Encyclopedists.

**Moore,** George Edward (1873–1958). English philosopher, lecturer and, subsequently, Professor in the University of Cambridge. His direct personal influence on British philosophers of his time was immense.

The three main topics dealt with in Moore's writings are philosophical method, ethics, and perception. He wrote little about his method because his energies were given to practising it, but probably it is as a contribution to the right method of doing philosophy that his work will be of lasting importance.

This method clearly appears in an article in 1900 on *Necessity*, is proclaimed in his programmatic essay of 1925, *A Defence of Common Sense*, and is reaffirmed in his autobiographical remarks of 1942 in *The Philosophy of G. E. Moore*. What interests him about the things we say in ordinary life is neither their meaning nor their truth, since he believes them to have a well-known meaning and to be in many cases certainly true, but something about them which he calls an analysis of their meaning. With philosophical views, on the other hand, he is anxious to discover what they could mean and whether they are true, because they are often attempted analyses whose results deny the commonly accepted meaning and truth of what they analyse.

In these investigations Moore makes two appeals, which have often been confused by critics, namely an appeal to the truth of what we hold in common sense and an appeal to the propriety of what we say in ordinary language.

His attitude to common sense, like that of Thomas **Reid** in the eighteenth century, is that many of its beliefs are such that, though, like the laws of **logic,** they are neither *provable* nor *disprovable*, there are far better reasons for accepting them than for accepting any of the philosophical doctrines which contradict them. Unlike any philosophical belief, we all do hold and cannot help holding them, and various kinds of inconsistency issue from our attempts to deny them.

Since the expressions, like "good", "know", "see", "real", whose meaning Moore analyses are in common everyday use, he has felt justified in assuming that we all understand them very well, and, therefore, justified in using them to interpret some of the strange things that philosophers say and in accusing any philosopher who goes against them of "an abuse of language".

In common with many philosophers since **Plato**, Moore holds that the meaning of an expression is a kind of entity, often called a concept, notion, or proposition, which the expression stands for, conveys, represents, or names, and which is called up before the mind of anyone who understands the expression. Hence his contrast between knowing the meaning of an expression and knowing the analysis of the meaning, which one might express as that between knowing how to use an expression and being able to say how it is used, is put by Moore himself as a contrast between having the concept expressed by a given expression before the mind and being able to say or do something in regard to that concept. As to what exactly an analyst has to do in regard to the concept before his mind, Moore seems to have had three separate views, often held in the same work. In general the analyst has to *inspect* the concept and try to describe it; in particular he has *either* to say how it can be *divided* into a set of constituent concepts and how these constituents are interrelated *or* to say how the concept is to be *distinguished*, by way of similarity and difference, from other concepts which are brought before the mind by the given expression and by other related expressions. The division method, with its dependence on the concept theory of meaning, has a very ancient history and predominates in the work of Russell and the early Wittgenstein, while the distinction method, in a form uncommitted to the concept theory, is favoured by Wittgenstein's later work and by later analysts.

Again, Moore often thought that in order to give an analysis of a concept one must find a concept or set of concepts identical with the concept to be analysed and, therefore, also find an expression synonymous with the expression used to express the concept to be analysed.

Taking "what is good?" as the central question of ethics, Moore distinguished the sense in which the question demands an inquiry into the analysis of the notion of *good* from the senses in which it seeks to know either what things are good or what kinds of things are good. Although in *Principia Ethica* (1903), he attempts a brief answer to the question "What kinds of things are good?", according to which there is an "immense variety" of such kinds of things, including "the pleasures of human intercourse and the enjoyment of beautiful objects", most of his work here and elsewhere is devoted to an analysis of the notion of *good*. In accordance with his method of inspection, he advises the analyst of *good* to "attentively consider what is actually before his mind" in the hope that "if he will try this experiment with each suggested definition (i.e. analysis) in succession, he may become expert enough to recognize that in every case he has before his mind a unique object". Under the influence of the method of division, he has said that a definition "states what are the parts which invariably compose a certain whole; and in this sense the notion 'good' has no definition because it is simple and has no parts". This simple concept for which he thought the expression "good" stood he called a "non-natural" quality, and any attempt to identify it with another concept he called a commission of the "naturalistic fallacy". When, however, he used the "distinction" method of analysis, he counted it as an analysis of *good* if he could "distinguish this from other" concepts. In his later writings he has inclined to hold that the word "good" is not after all the "name of a characteristic" but that its use *may* be to express an attitude or approval. The notion of *right* is made dependent on the notion of *good* in that, agreeing with the **utilitarians**, Moore analyses it as the cause of things which are good in themselves.

In discussing the notion of perception, Moore assumes that there is no doubt about the meaning of such expressions as "I see a book" and "This, which I see, is a book" and usually no doubt about the truth of what they say. He then argues that whenever we see an opaque material object, such as a book, we *ipso facto* see, in a second sense, a particular part of it, such as the surface turned towards us, and also see, in a third sense, what he calls a sense-datum, such as a particular patch of colour. His task then is to distinguish and relate the three concepts expressed by the one word "see" and the three concepts expressed by their respective grammatical objects, namely "material object", "part of the surface of a material object" and "sense-datum". To the

217

question how these various concepts are related to each other, he has provided many answers but never one which satisfied either himself or other philosophers. The reason for this failure is mainly due, it seems, to two assumptions, namely, that the word "sense-datum" is the name of a peculiar kind of *entity*, which is present in every perceptual experience, and that when I say "This, which I see, is a book", I must be trying to *identify* the *sense-datum with* something.

(A.R.W.)

**More,** Henry (1614–1687), English philosopher and poet, *see* Cambridge Platonists.

**Morris,** Charles (1901– ), American philosopher. His main contributions were to the philosophy of language. He sought to fuse the behaviouristic pragmatism of his teacher, George H. Mead, with the logical empiricism of the **Vienna Circle,** and to develop systematically the fertile but sketchily worked out ideas of Charles **Peirce** on signs within this conceptual framework. However, Morris went far beyond Peirce in taking into account non-linguistic as well as linguistic signs. His division of semiotics (or the general theory of signs) into three major branches, has been widely adopted. The first is syntactics, which studies the relations signs have to one another in virtue of their purely formal or structural properties. The second is semantics, which analyses the relations of signs to what they designate. The third is pragmatics, which examines responses to uses of signs.

(E.N.)

# N

**Nagel,** Ernest (1901– ), born in Czechoslovakia, emigrated to the USA in 1911. He is best known for his work in the philosophy of science. His *The Structure of Science* (1961), is generally acknowledged to be a modern classic in this field. In **metaphysics** Nagel counts himself as a **naturalist,** holding that the world must be understood in terms of efficient causation and as

involving no ultimate ingredients beyond matter. Nagel is the author of articles on **Carnap, Cohen, Lewis, Morris,** and **Popper** in this Encyclopedia.

(J.O.U.)

**Naturalism.** Like most of the words ending in "ism" and used to name a type of philosophical position, "naturalism" has only a vague and imprecise sense, or set of senses. More widely, a naturalist considers that the totality of things which we call "nature" and which are studied in the natural sciences is the totality of all things whatever, and denies the need of any explanations of the natural in terms of the super-natural; such a philosopher will normally hold that any reference to a deity, or to a realm of values, or to mind as something more than a natural phenomenon is illegitimate. With such nineteenth-century thinkers as T. H. Huxley, naturalism connoted especially a belief that life and thought could be completely explained, in principle, as arising by evolution from matter. In **ethics** naturalism is the view that statements about the rightness, wrongness, goodness and badness of things are statements about the natural world and not about special values beyond the ken of science; thus a naturalist might maintain that to say that something is good is to say that it is likely to satisfy desire, which is a scientifically testable statement. But in *Principia Ethica* G. E. **Moore** widened the notion of naturalism for his special purposes so that everyone was guilty of the "naturalistic fallacy" who attempted to define ethical concepts in terms of concepts which were not specifically ethical; thus even those who defined "good" as meaning "willed by God", a view clearly utterly opposed to naturalism as ordinarily understood, were said by Moore to have committed the naturalistic fallacy. Unfortunately this usage of Moore's has become so widely known that the term "naturalism" has probably now lost whatever utility it ever had. See also **Analytic Philosophy.**

(J.O.U.)

**Natural Law,** *see* Jurisprudence, Grotius, Hobbes, and Political Philosophy.

**Negative Theology,** see Neoplatonism.

**Neoplatonism.** The term "neoplatonism" designates the last creative effort of pagan antiquity (*c.* 250 to 550 A.D.) to produce a comprehensive philosophic system which could satisfy all the spiritual aspirations of man by presenting an inclusive, logically coherent image of the universe and of man's place in it and by explaining how man can achieve salvation, i.e. be restored to his original condition. It should be stressed that "Neoplatonism" is a modern term. Those to whom we apply it claimed to be simply Platonists. Whether this claim was legitimate or whether Neoplatonism radically differs from original Platonism is controversial. In any case Neoplatonism succeeded in synthesizing most earlier philosophic thought (particularly that of **Aristotle,** the **Stoics,** and the **Pythagoreans,** only **Epicureanism** was excluded) with Platonism. But it also assimilated many religious beliefs, myths, rites, and cults of Greek and of Oriental polytheism, including alchemy, magic practices (often based on affinities between planets and metals etc.) and in its universe could find a place for all the traditional deities and semi-deities of popular religions.

Neoplatonism teaches belief in a deity (or a supreme principle) which is the source out of which everything flows without ever becoming separated from it, so that it is also immanent in everything. This "flow" is not a temporal process; it is, so to speak, timeless history. What starts it is not an intentional, creative act; it is rather a timeless, involuntary, permanent effulgence or emanation. But this emanation does not consume its source, which on the contrary remains forever undiminished and full. Some scholars describe the relation between the supreme principle and all its emanations as "dynamic pantheism".

As the supreme principle is above being, no predicates can really be applied to it. The best we can do is speak of it as "One", to express that it is undifferentiated and simple and therefore without quality. If we think of it as the source of all being, we can also refer to it as "goodness" in the sense that it is the ultimate "Why" of everything.

The timeless process of effulgence is best described as a gradual "dispersion" of the original unity, by which it passes into ever-increasing multiplicity. It begins with the realm of the supra-sensible reality (first: mind, or thought thinking itself, or spirit; next: the soul); then comes sensible reality (in time and space). One more step and the dispersion becomes annihilation (as light, emanating from its source, gradually fills progressively larger parts of space, becoming progressively dimmer, until it fades into complete darkness). This annihilation is seen by Neoplatonism as the result of matter. In some way, this matter, although sheer nothingness, is at the time the "Why" of nothingness. The supreme principle as the source of all being was "goodness"; and matter was "evil", or "not-goodness".

The successive steps or, as they are often called, hypostases are the results of some kind of necessity. From this point of view, the universe is flawless. Everything is as it ought to be. But Neoplatonism is keenly aware of human imperfection which stems from the soul's remoteness from the deity. Thus effulgence, though necessary, engenders a longing to "revert" and so to undo the "progress" which may now be interpreted as some kind of flaw or fall. Man shares this longing with all other beings. The way to its satisfaction is taught in **ethics.** Thus, whereas in its theoretical aspects Neoplatonism is monistic, its practical aspects are dualistic.

The concept of a deity which is inaccessible to reflective thought demands as its correlate a kind of knowledge transcending rational, reflective thinking. To acquire this higher kind of knowledge man must suppress all determinateness of thought, and call himself back from his "dispersion". Having finally become one, he is able in rare moments to face the One, a condition described by some Neoplatonists as rapt contemplation of the One, by others as absorption into unity with the One. It is the condition of ecstasy, the main purpose of moral life. The virtues of steadfastness, self-control, fairness, and prudence serve this purpose. Depending on how far man has progressed on his return

219

journey, they appear on the different levels of his spiritual life in appropriate forms, for example, as civic, purificatory or exemplary virtues. In the moment of ecstasy all the intellectual and moral aspirations of man are satisfied.

One of the most striking aspects of Neoplatonism (and one which makes it totally unacceptable to an empiricist) is its derivation of all sensible reality from a supra-sensible one (the latter being more real than the former), this derivation representing a type of causation radically different from causality in space and time. The Neoplatonist would think of modern scientific explanations as shallow; the scientist, on the other hand, is likely to consider Neoplatonism utterly fantastic.

It is customary to see in **Plotinus** the founder of Neoplatonism (though Platonism from the time of **Cicero** on – so-called Middle Platonism – can be seen as the fertile soil out of which Neoplatonism developed). It is also customary to consider the year 529, in which the Emperor Justinian ordered the school of Plato (the Academy) in Athens closed, to be the end of pagan philosophy in general and of Neoplatonism in particular. In these three hundred years different neoplatonic schools developed. We particularly distinguish the school of Plotinus, the school of Pergamum, and the school of Alexandria.

Two outstanding representatives of the early phase of the school of Plotinus are Porphyry (234–c. 305) and Iamblichus (died c. 330). The former edited the writings of Plotinus, and attacked Christianity in *Against the Christians* with great acumen and erudition. Some of his arguments, particularly in matters of chronology and the authorship of parts of the Scriptures, have not yet been superseded. His *On the Cave of the Nymphs* is a good example of the allegorizing interpretation of poetry (in this case Homer), practised by many Neoplatonists. His aphoristic *Starting Points* are an excellent introduction to the main Neoplatonic doctrines. His consolatory *Letter to Marcella*, his wife, is very readable. Particularly influential was his *Introduction to Aristotle's Categories*, a commentary on five fundamental concepts (genus, species, difference, property, and accident, later called the predicables). A passage in which he poses (but does not answer)

the question whether **universals** have an existence independent of both minds and particular things gave impetus to the medieval controversy between **nominalism, realism** and **conceptualism**. He, much more than Plotinus, stresses will as the factor responsible for the "fall" of the soul.

In a series of treatises (*Exhortation to Philosophy*, *Life of Pythagoras*, *General Mathematics* etc.) Iamblichus expounded what he considered to be Pythagorean doctrines. His *Egyptian Mysteries* is a philosophico-allegorical interpretation of Egypt's rites and religious doctrines. Perhaps he himself instituted something like neoplatonic mysteries, a blend of Greek and Oriental mystery religions. He is inclined to subdivide the entities of the supra-sensible realm (for example, he has two Ones, two Minds)' and later Neoplatonists carried such subdivisions and distinctions further and further.

The school of Pergamum, founded by a disciple of Iamblichus, Aidesios, was particularly interested in the practice of magic. Its best known representative is the Emperor Julian the Apostate (born 332 A.D.). In his attempts to stem the growth of Christianity he tried to revive polytheism with the help of Neoplatonism. Neo-platonism was to provide polytheism with allegorico-philosophical interpretations, thus making it attractive again to the educated, while permitting the uneducated to practise it according to tradition.

The main representatives of the later phase of the school of Plotinus were Proclus (410–485 A.D.) and Damascius. The former, sometimes called Neoplatonism's schoolman, gave a particularly comprehensive and systematic presentation of Neoplatonism in two works, *Elements of Theology* and *The Theology of Plato*. In his writings some tensions inherent in Neoplatonism come to light. Though he derives everything from the One alone and is second to none in characterizing it by absolute simplicity (and therefore ineffability), he at the same time derives all reality from two principles (ultimately Pythagorean and Platonic), viz. the Limit and the Unlimited, these being in some way present also in the One. In addition to the One he assumes the existence of Ones, immediately following the One and identifies them with gods. And he explicitly derives matter from the One. Of great importance for him is the "triadic" principle according to which everything remains, in one aspect, in that from which it emanated, in another is turned away from it, and in a third turns back to it. A number of his hymns are remarkable documents of Neoplatonic religiosity.

An author not yet identified, but pretending (and for centuries believed) to be Dionysius the Areopagite, St Paul's disciple, and therefore enjoying great authority, compiled a series of writings, for example *Divine Names* and *Mystical Theology*, which combine Proclus with Christianity. They are particularly well known as representing "negative theology".

Damascius was the head of the Academy at the time of its closing. In a way, he presents the consummation of a tendency latent in all Neoplatonism in that he declares *all* rational knowledge to be merely parabolic so that no aspect of reality is accessible to it.

The school of Alexandria occupies a special position. Its Neoplatonism is comparatively simple (in some respects closer to Middle Platonism than to Plotinus) and a number of its members accepted Christianity, whereas the school of Athens to the very last remained one of the strongholds of polytheism. Hypatia (murdered by Christian fanatics) and her pupil, Bishop Synesius are among its representatives.

Despite the anti-Christian attitude of many Neoplatonists (inherited by men like Marcrobius or Symmachus) Neoplatonism had always had great attraction for philosophers within the orbit of Christianity and, after the Arabs discovered and assimilated Greek philosophy also within the orbit of Islam and Judaism. On the one hand this is natural, considering Neoplatonism's sympathy for religion in general, the loftiness of its concept of the divine, its assumption that the supra-sensible is more real than the sensible, and its asceticism. On the other hand, there is something paradoxical about it. Christianity is a strictly historical religion (as are Judaism and Islam). Incarnation, central for Christianity and considered to have absolute and unique importance, is an event in time with all the contingency of an historical event. Neither it nor the moment at which it occurred can be logically deduced. But Neoplatonism, true to its Hellenic heritage, always remained a rational system, in the sense that it presented the universe as a kind of giant syllogism, with one event following from another in the same timeless manner in which conclusions follow from premises. What happens in time is contingent and can therefore have no essential, ultimate significance for the universe at large or for man. But in spite of this fundamental difference, Christian thinkers time and again tried to express Christian doctrines in terms of Neoplatonism. Even in our times we find such attempts. Perhaps some of them are simply the result of the willingness to become entirely reconciled to the contingent, historical character of Christianity. See also **Augustine, Cambridge Platonists, Cudworth, Erigena.**

(P.M.)

**Neo-Thomism.** The scholastic philosophy which had its origin in the Middle Ages gradually faded out in the course of the seventeenth and eighteenth centuries on account of its failure to maintain contact with the development of the experimental sciences and the new approach to the theory of knowledge. Since the later scholastics had failed, it was assumed that their medieval predecessors were equally unworthy of attention. But the incapacity of modern philosophy to evolve a realistic metaphysic eventually aroused the suspicion that it might be useful to re-examine the thinkers of the creative period of medieval philosophy, especially **Aquinas.**

The pioneer of this Thomistic revival was an obscure seminary lecturer at Piacenza, Vincenzo Buzzetti (1777–1824). Among his students were the brothers Domenico Sordi (1790–1880) and Serafino Sordi (1793–1865). Both became Jesuits and tried, at first with little success, to influence the fellow-members of their order in the direction of Aquinas. In the end, however, they won over a few thinkers of some prominence in Italy, Luigi Taparelli d'Azeglio (1793–1862), Matteo Liberatore (1810–1892) and Giovanni Maria Cornoldi (1822–1892), together with the German Joseph Kleutgen

(1811–1883). These, along with Gaetano Sanseverino (1811–1865) at Naples and the Dominican Tommaso Zigliara (1833–1893), made the movement known. Another supporter was Giusepppe Pecci (1807–1890), whose brother Giocchino became Pope under the name of Leo XIII and lent his official support to the revival of Thomism and its application to modern intellectual needs.

What was required to make the revival effective was both an intensive study of the history of medieval thought and a practical demonstration that it was still relevant to contemporary philosophical problems. Here the leadership of the movement passed to France, Belgium and Germany. In Italy and Spain Neo-Thomism has tended to remain in isolation as a clerical preserve. But the Institut Supérieur de Philosophie at Louvain, founded in 1889 under Désiré Mercier (1851–1926), has been the most powerful centre of a progressive Thomism. Thanks to scholars like Martin Grabmann in Germany and **Gilson** in France the history of medieval philosophy has gradually been revealed. **Maritain** is the Neo-Thomist whose name is most familiar to the general public.

Neo-Thomists claim that the central tradition of Greek thought was continued and developed legitimately in a theistic direction by the medieval Aristotelians. They hold that this tradition has not been made out of date by modern philosophy. They have, therefore, to produce a theory of knowledge which will satisfy the questions and difficulties which have arisen from **Descartes** onwards and to show that this theory of knowledge justifies the main outline of Aristotelian and Thomistic metaphysics. They have to show also that this philosophical view of the world harmonizes with the approach of the modern scientist. They must be as ready to shed what time has really destroyed of the medieval outlook as to assimilate the positive contributions of later philosophy. And they have to talk a language which their contemporaries can understand. Among books which make a notable effort to fulfil these requirements are Gilson's *Being and Some Philosophers* and *The Unity of Philosophical Experience*. That Neo-Thomism has not yet attained the results for which its

originators hoped is evident, but it can be judged fairly only as a movement which is in progress and is capable of further development. Of late it has begun to come into fruitful contact with the **phenomenologists,** the followers of **Husserl,** and with the recent evolution of formal logic.

(D.J.B.H.)

**Neurath**, Otto (1882–1945), Austrian philosopher, Marxist sociologist, and logical empiricist who also pioneered a system of visual design known as "Isotype", *see* Carnap, Logical Positivism.

**Nietzsche,** Friedrich (1844–1900), born at Röcken, Prussia, profoundly influenced continental European philosophy and literature, especially in Germany and France. In the English-speaking world, especially among philosophers, he has won relatively few admirers. Amateur psychologists have often tried to "explain" his ideas, but Sigmund Freud, according to Ernest Jones' biography, "several times said of Nietzsche that he had a more penetrating knowledge of himself than any other man who ever lived or was ever likely to live". Freud also remarked that Nietzsche's "premonitions and insights often agree in the most amazing manner with the laborious results of psychoanalysis".

Nietzsche was the son of a Protestant minister and the grandson of two. He studied classical philology and was appointed to a professorship at Basel, Switzerland, before he had completed a doctoral dissertation. The degree, a prerequisite for such a position, was conferred hurriedly, and Nietzsche went to Basel in 1869 and became a Swiss subject.

In the Franco-Prussian War of 1870–71 he served briefly as a medical orderly on the Prussian side and returned to Basel with shattered health. He formed a friendship with Richard Wagner, but the composer, born like Nietzsche's father in 1813, appreciated Nietzsche mainly as a brilliant apostle and errand boy. Whenever Nietzsche showed an independent mind, Wagner showed no interest. A break was thus inevitable, and it came about when Wagner made his peace with the young German Empire, which Nietzsche loathed, and settled in Bayreuth where his anti-Semitism became as influential as his music. Nietzsche had no sympathy for the idealization of "the pure fool" in Wagner's *Parsifal*, which he considered an insincere obeisance to Christianity, and Wagner, a Francophobe, was so displeased by Nietzsche's enlightened, anti-romantic *Human, All-too-Human*, also published in 1878, with a dedication to Voltaire, that he refused to read it.

The following year, Nietzsche retired from his professorship for reasons of health, and during the next ten years he devoted himself entirely to writing. He lived very modestly and in utter solitude in Switzerland and Italy, and every book represented a hard-won triumph over half-blind eyes, intense migraine headaches, and manifold physical agonies. His writings were ignored until Georg Brandes (né Cohen) began to lecture on them in Copenhagen in 1888. During the following decade Nietzsche attained world-wide fame, without knowing it. For he suffered a mental and physical breakdown in January 1889, and remained insane until his death.

His first book, *The Birth of Tragedy* (1872) was ill-received by German scholars; but by 1912 F. M. Cornford, the great British classicist, hailed it as "a work of profound imaginative insight which left the scholarship of a generation toiling in the rear" – an estimate shared more or less by most German classicists today. The book broke with the "sweetness and light" conception of Greek culture and called attention to the "Dionysian" element and the tragic outlook.

He published four more, equally unacademic essays, collected as "Untimely Meditations" (the title alludes to **Descartes**), before he changed his style to write books of aphorisms, studded with psychological observations: *Human, All-too-Human* (1878, with two sequels, 1879 and 1880), *Dawn* (1881), and *The Gay Science* (1882; second edition with substantial additions, 1887). Nietzsche thought that his aphorisms, though lacking the gravity of the German academic style, were closer to the true scientific spirit and to the experimental method in particular. After

attempting all kinds of psychological explanations of diverse phenomena, he was struck, for example, by the apparent importance of the striving for power and of fear, and in *Dawn* tried to see how far he could explain all kinds of behaviour in terms of these two concepts.

Eventually he came to the conclusion that Greek culture had been based on an unsentimentally competitive spirit and that "the will to power" is the most basic human drive. What man – and, according to Nietzsche's next book, *Thus Spoke Zarathustra*, every living being – wants above everything else is a higher, more powerful state of being in which the manifold frustrations of his present state are overcome. It is only when man fails in his endeavour to perfect himself, to recreate himself, to become a creator rather than a mere creature, that, *faute de mieux*, he often settles for the hunt after crude, physical power over others. Of many of his critics Nietzsche might well have said, substituting "powers" for "pleasures" in one of J. S. **Mill**'s remarks that *they*, and not he, represented "human nature in a degrading light, since the accusation supposes human beings to be capable of no powers except those of which swine are capable".

Nietzsche's conception of "the will to power" cannot be understood apart from "sublimation" – a word which he was the first to use in its modern sense. His anti-Christian polemics, which became more and more central in his later works, depend in part on his claim that Christianity "demands not the control but the extirpation of the passions". Christianity, he says, failed to realize that the sex impulse, for example, is "capable of great refinement" and it "made something unclean out of sexuality".

Still, Christianity itself is an expression of the will to power – but the will to power of the weak and frustrated whose resentment gave rise, he argues, to a pervasive antagonism against all physical intellectual excellence, a predisposition in favour of everything low, a levelling tendency, a hatred of sex, and the depreciation of body and intellect in favour of the soul and of this whole world in favour of another, fictitious world. In one of his last works, *The Antichrist*, in which his style has become shrill, and no attempt is made to offer judicious qualifications, he cites

I Corinthians I to illustrate his claims: "God has chosen the weak things of the world to ruin what is strong, and base things of the world... and what is nothing, to bring to naught what is something". Here he finds an outlook "born of resentment and impotent vengefulness". And he also cites Chapter 6, "the saints shall judge the world" and "we shall judge angels". Here he finds a will to power that has run amock.

His critics feel that it is Nietzsche who has run amock; but they have generally misunderstood him because they overlooked the fact that he did not find in Christianity what they have found in it. Few indeed are aware of the fact that Nietzsche says, also in The Antichrist: "When the exceptional human being treats the mediocre more tenderly than himself and his peers, this is not mere politeness of the heart – it is simply his duty". Christianity he associated with resentment and the hope for boundless power in another world from which, according to some of the greatest Christians, the blessed will behold the torments of those who got the best of things in this world.

Nietzsche was not only a moralist but also a moral philosopher. His view of traditional ethics might be summed up in the words which F. H. Bradley used to characterize metaphysics: "the finding of bad reasons for what we believe on instinct". But Nietzsche did not believe that moral idiosyncrasies were literally instinctive. On the contrary, he was struck by the great variety of moral views in different times and places; and he derided the philosophers' "conceit that they have long known what is good and evil for man".

His views on this subject are best cited from Beyond Good and Evil (1886), especially from sections 186 and 260: "With a stiff seriousness that inspires laughter, all our philosophers... wanted to supply a rational foundation for morals; and every philosopher so far has believed that he had provided such a foundation. Morality itself, however, was accepted as 'given'." "Because our moral philosophers" were parochial and myopic, "poorly informed, and not even very curious about different peoples, ages, and the past, they never laid eyes on the real problems of morality; for these emerge only when we compare many moralities".

Nietzsche poses two questions: how does our prevalent morality compare with other moralities? and what can be said about morality in general?

In answer to the first question we must try to construct as a first step "a typology of morals"; and Nietzsche finds "two basic types": "There is master morality and slave morality". Our prevalent morality, for which different moral philosophers have sought different "rational foundations" is one of the many mixed types and profoundly inconsistent. For it originated historically out of two different traditions.

Nietzsche does not believe that every man is by nature either a master or a slave. What he claims is rather that moral codes have originated "either among a ruling group whose consciousness of their difference from the ruled group was accompanied by delight – or among the ruled group, the slaves". The first type of morality is rooted in self-affirmation. The noble type calls itself "good" and those who are not noble "bad" – and Nietzsche adds: "The opposition of "good" and "evil" has a different origin". He does not glorify brutality. "The noble man, too, helps the unfortunate, but not, or almost not, out of pity, but more prompted by an urge which is begotten by the excess of power".

In Aristotle's words, Nietzsche's "masters" feel that "it is vulgar to lord it over humble people." Indeed, Nietzsche's "masters" closely resemble Aristotle's portrait of "the great-souled man". This parallel is not accidental: Aristotle's ethics greatly influenced Nietzsche and helped to convince him that modern bourgeois morality is not morality par excellence; also that Christianity represented the "revaluation of all the values of antiquity".

The first of the three essays that comprise Nietzsche's next book, Toward a Genealogy of Morals (1887), bears the title: "Good and Evil versus Good and Bad". It deals at length with slave morality which contrasts good and evil. According to Nietzsche, it is rooted "in the resentment of those who are denied the real reaction, that of the deed, and who compensate with an imaginary revenge". Not self-affirmation but resentment is primary here: evil is the slave's primary concept "from which he then derives, as

an afterimage and counterinstance, a 'good one'
– himself ".

The strong and noble man is above resentment. "Here alone it is also possible... that
there be real 'love of one's enemies'. How much
respect has a noble person for his enemies!
And such respect is already a bridge to love".
"Beyond good and evil" does not mean beyond
good and bad. What it does mean is stated
repeatedly in Zarathustra: "you are too pure for
the filth of the words: revenge, punishment,
reward, retribution", "that man be delivered from
revenge, that is for me the bridge to the highest hope".

In one of his last works, Twilight of the Idols,
Nietzsche leaves no doubt that, although he far
prefers master morality to slave morality, he
does not by any means accept master morality. On the contrary, he calls attention to its
inhuman aspects; and in the final analysis he
finds both types of morality "entirely worthy of
each other".

This brings us to the second question
Nietzsche pressed: what can be said about morality in general? Nietzsche makes two points in
reply. First, "every morality is, as opposed to
laisser aller, a bit of tyranny against 'nature'; also
against 'reason'; but this in itself is no objection". Some discipline and constraint, although
arbitrary in a sense, is the prerequisite of all
achievements "for whose sake life on earth is
worthwhile; for example, virtue, art, music,
dance, reason, spirituality". Point two: a morality
is a prescription for living with one's passions.
Nietzsche tries to show this in the cases of **stoicism,**
**Spinoza,** Aristotle, and Goethe, and claims that
moralities are "baroque and unreasonable in form
– because they are addressed to 'all' and generalize where generalizations are impermissible". It
would be folly for St Francis to try to live like
Goethe, or vice versa.

Nietzsche finds the greatest power in those
who can sublimate and control their passions,
employing them creatively. The libertine, who
lacks self-control, has less power; and the ascetic, who cannot master his passions short of
extirpating them, strikes Nietzsche as weaker
than such men as Socrates of Goethe.

Although religion and ethics constituted
Nietzsche's primary interests, he also ventured

into epistemology and metaphysics. In epistemology he made many interesting suggestions without ever working out any theory. His importance
for metaphysics is twofold. First, he offered a
psychological analysis of belief in *another* world
and argued that *this* world is the only one.
And he criticised, especially in Twilight of the
Idols, metaphysical conceptions of mind, consciousness, ego and will. He even derided "the
will" as a phantom which "does not explain
anything". Secondly, he offered a metaphysic
of his own when he suggested earlier, especially
in Zarathustra, that "the will to power" is the
ultimate reality. His psychological explanations
can probably be reconciled with his critique
of metaphysical conceptions, but his reification
and cosmic projection of the will to power
seems clearly inconsistent with his own central
intentions. It appears as a misguided attempt to
outdo **Schopenhauer,** whom the young Neitzsche
had admired. Nietzsche's doctrine of the eternal
recurrence of the same events at gigantic intervals, finally, has struck practically all his readers
as merely bizarre. But this was not intended as
a metaphysical theory: Nietzsche was under the
demonstrably mistaken impression that modern science, if it refrains from inconsistently
postulating a Creator, entails such a view. And
he thought that for almost all men nothing could
be more depressing than this prospect, while the
overman (Übermensch), the human being who
has overcome himself and given his life meaning
by becoming a creator, might actually say, unlike
Goethe's Faust: abide, moment – and if you
cannot abide, at least return.

Nietzsche's influence on the existentialists and
psychoanalysts, on N. **Hartmann,** Scheler,
Spengler, Rilke, Buber, Thomas Mann,
Malraux, and Gide has been very pronounced.
The literature about him is vast, and includes
poems and novels. Richard Strauss wrote a tone
poem, Thus Spoke Zarathustra.

(W.K.)

**Nominalism:** the theory that the objects of
thought are simply words and that there is
no more to the meaning of a general term

225

than the set of things to which it applies. At its most modest nominalism holds that there is no independently accessible thing, **universal** or concept, which constitutes the meaning of a word. The only way to find out the meaning of a word is to see what things it is applied to. To say that the meaning *is* this class of things, the word's extension, is to go further and seems to entail that we never really know the meaning of any general word since many words with the same extension differ in meaning (e.g. *man* and *featherless biped*). A more traditional version of nominalism contends that there is nothing more in common to the things a general term applies to than the fact that it applies to them. But to say this, it is argued, makes classification arbitrary and cannot explain why it is that people have made the classifications they have or how it is that they all make the same classifications. In practice, therefore, most nominalists follow Hobbes in holding that the things a general term applies to are related by resemblance. But this similarity theory, it is often claimed, is only a disguised form of **realism**, since resemblance is itself a universal. Nominalism was one of the possibilities envisaged in **Porphyry**'s celebrated comment on the *Categories* of **Aristotle** which posed the problem of universals for medieval philosophy. Roscellinus believed that only individual sensible things were real and took the doctrine of the Trinity to be an assertion of the existence of three gods and, on similar grounds, Berengar of Tours rejected transubstantiation. Many contemporary analytic philosophers follow Hobbes in upholding the similarity theory but **Russell** remained faithful to realism.

(A.Q.)

**Nozick,** Robert (1938– ), American philosopher born in New York, author of *Anarchy, State and Utopia* (1974). This is a work of **political philosophy** which argues (against **Rawls** in particular) for an "entitlement theory" of justice based on the primacy of individual rights. Acknowledging that this "libertarian" conclusion is "apparently callous toward the needs and suffering of others," Nozick nevertheless holds that anything more than a "minimal state" is

morally wrong. "The state," he says, "may not use its coercive apparatus for the purpose of getting some citizens to aid others, or in order to prohibit activities to people for their *own* good or protection." This minimal state – "the only morally justifiable one" – is also, Nozick claims, "the one that best realizes the utopian aspirations of untold dreamers and visionaries." Nozick is the author of several other works, notably *Philosophical Explanations* (1981).

[J.R.]

**Number,** *see* Frege, Russell, Mathematics.

# O

**Occasionalism.** For **Descartes** a human being was the point of union of material substance and immaterial substance. Descartes' followers were unable to accept his own curious doctrine of the mechanism by which one of these disparate substances could act upon the other. It was to provide a solution to the problems raised by the undoubted action of one substance on another that the theory of Occasionalism was developed. In each substance, mind and body, the chains of cause and effect were supposed to be complete and independent, since it was clear that modifications of an immaterial substance could be neither the causes nor the effects of modifications of material substance. The correlation between the run of events in the one substance and the run of events in the other was explained by the intervention of God. Geulincx (1624–1669) gave the doctrine its characteristic form. Since doing something involves how to do it, material bodies, knowing nothing, cannot act; their apparent action upon each other is the act of God. Since God is the sole cause, apparent psycho-physical causation need present no problem since the occurrence of an event in the one substance, mind, provides the Occasion for a Divine Act in the other substance, body.

(R.HAR.)

**Ockham,** *see* William of Ockham.

**Ontological Argument**: the argument that, since God is conceivable as a necessary existent, God exists. See **Anselm, Descartes, Leibniz, Kant, Theism.**

**Ontology** is theory as to what exists.

# P

**Pantheism** is the doctrine that everything is divine, that God and Nature are identical. Pantheism is more often discovered as an instrument of poetic expression than as a conclusion of philosophical argument. The great exception here is **Spinoza**. Spinoza's initial definition of substance inexorably leads on to the conclusion that there can only be one substance, truly so-called, and that it must be infinite. For there could be nothing other than itself to limit it and so constitute it finite. Spinoza's definition of God, which follows the traditional definitions, makes God the possessor of infinite attributes. But the only being of infinite attributes is the one substance, which is Nature. Hence God and Nature must be identical. The history of Spinoza's reputation illustrates the knife-edge along which the pantheist walks. From the stand-point of the theist, a pantheist appears one who reduces God to Nature, and is thus essentially an atheist. From the standpoint of the Sceptic, the pantheist takes an unwarrantedly religious view of Nature, and appears as a covert theist. All metaphysical doctrines, such as **idealism**, which assert that the Universe is a Unity tend towards pantheism. For the Universe is then something more than any of its finite parts; and there can be no deity distinct from it. It may be surmised that the collapse of such metaphysical doctrines deprives intellectual pantheism of its only support.

(A.MACI.)

**Parmenides,** Greek philosopher of Elea in Southern Italy, born about 515 B.C. He wrote a philosophical poem consisting of a prologue and two parts, of which considerable fragments have survived. The prologue describes Parmenides' meeting with a goddess who reveals the truth outlined in the first part of the poem; of the two possible paths of inquiry, It is and It is not, only the first is tenable – "for you could not know what *is not* (for this is impossible), nor could you give expression to it". Thus Parmenides recognized the existential "is not" as an artificial concept, but was misled by his inability to distinguish the existential and predicative "is" into denying that negative predication was possible. This seemed to entail that there could be no differentiation in the real world (since if A can be distinguished from B then A *is not* B, which was, by Parmenides' logic, impossible). Thus reality, "that which is", must be single, homogeneous, indivisible, everlasting, and motionless. Being itself was spatially finite, "like the mass of a well-rounded sphere". Some of Parmenides' arguments against not-being were perhaps directed particularly against **Pythagorean** dualism. But he himself, in the fragmentary second part of his poem, which professedly gave "the opinions of mortals" and was "deceitful", outlined a cosmology in which the world was composed of two opposed substances or "forms", fire and night. What was evidently quite an elaborate account included explanations of thought and knowledge (produced by the excess of one opposite, the hot or the cold, in the limbs), and astronomy, which had points in common with **Anaximander**. The purpose of this "Way of Seeming" is obscure. Perhaps Parmenides felt that his true conception of Being was too austere for practical life and ordinary people, and wished to show that the apparent world could be accounted for on the basis of a single pair of apparent sensible opposites, without introducing so-called reality-principles like the Limit and Unlimited of the Pythagoreans.

(G.S.K.)

**Pascal,** Blaise, (1623–1662), French mathematician, scientist and theologian, and one of the earliest great French prose writers. His earlier years were devoted to mathematics and the physical sciences; his experiments with the barometer are famous, the ascent of the Puy de Dôme by his brother at his direction being a decisive confirmation of the new theory of air pressure. In 1654 Pascal underwent a profound experience of religious conversion; he became a strong adherent of the Jansenists and much of his energy was henceforth devoted to theological and religious propaganda and controversy. He continued however to work occasionally at mathematics, doing work on the theory of the cycloid preparatory to the theory of the calculus, and laying the basis of the mathematical theory of **probability**. Pascal's posthumously published *Pensées* constitute the part of his work most interesting to a philosopher; most notably he argues for the reasonableness of faith on the ground that there are no rational grounds either for belief or disbelief and so belief is not less reasonable than disbelief; but this being so it is wiser to gamble on the truth of religion since this policy involves success if religion is true and no significant loss if it is false. The section on geometry also has some wise and clear remarks on definition and the nature of deductive systems.

(J.O.U.)

**Peirce,** Charles Sanders, (1839–1914), born at Cambridge, Massachusetts, son of America's leading mathematician Benjamin Peirce. Much of his early formation was scientific; he came to philosophy through reading Schiller and was later enthralled by **Kant**. He associated with most of the leading American thinkers of his day – among them **James**, Wright and Holmes. But he obtained little academic recognition and was never appointed to a permanent university post. He spent most of the latter part of his life almost as a recluse and died in comparative poverty in 1914. He published a number of articles but no book on philosophy. Much of his best work remained unpublished until it was edited in the *Collected Papers of C. S. Peirce* (8 volumes: 1931–58).

I. EPISTEMOLOGY

The central problem in modern **epistemology** has been to reconcile the subjective nature of thought with our claim to know things distinct from thought. This had not been a problem for **Aristotle**, who considered that the mind simply discovered an order in reality. But Kant inverted Aristotle's position and claimed that the order in our knowledge came from the mind. Peirce accepted the modern problem and offered his own solution.

Peirce began by holding that we are conscious that we experience the real directly. The real consists of the things that exist whether we think about them or not. Moreover, if we are to avoid unpleasant surprises, we must endeavour to adapt our conduct to these things. So far he agrees with Aristotle. But it is clear that we deal with things according to the ideas we have of them. Our ideas however are selective constructions, based on partial experience coloured by our history, circumstances and purpose. The selective nature of knowledge led Peirce to agree with Kant that the mind constructs to some extent the order in knowledge. He next set about showing that if we examine what an idea or concept is we should be able to reconcile what is true in Aristotle and Kant.

In reply to the question: What is a concept?: Peirce formulated in 1878 his famous **pragmatic** maxim: "Consider what effects, which might conceivably have practical bearings, we conceive the object of our conception to have. Then, our conception of these effects is the whole of our conception of the object." He illustrates the maxim by saying that our idea of "wine" means nothing "but what has certain effects, direct or indirect, upon our senses". So too, if we call a thing "hard", we mean that "it will not be scratched by many other substances". He summed up: "Our idea of anything is our idea of its sensible effects." Peirce offers his maxim as an instrument for distinguishing true knowledge from false. True knowledge – a correct idea of an object – enables us to predict what will happen when we come to deal with that object. In fact for Peirce all our ideas are analogous to scientific hypotheses.

Peirce's 1878 formulation of the maxim contained in germ his later views. But it was formulated for explaining our ideas of material things. It gave the impression of leaving no place for a *regulative* idea such as moral goodness. Furthermore, William James and the popular pragmatists took the maxim in a phenomenalist sense.

Peirce in later years insisted that pragmatism (or "pragmaticism" as he called his teaching, to distinguish it from that of James and others) teaches that an idea has meaning through any possible practical conduct that it can lead to or regulate. An idea does not necessarily have to lead to immediate sensory verification. It is enough if it gives meaning to our conduct. For example, the notion of truth as an ideal-limit, though it has no direct sensory content, inspires us to keep on adding to our knowledge. Peirce completed his theory by saying that each idea gives rise to a possibility of regular conduct in regard to what the idea expresses. Hence each idea is finally interpreted in a "habit". These habits, interpretants of our ideas, are "guides to action". Our ideas find living and consistent expression in our habitual modes of conduct.

But since the knowledge of an object or situation that an inquirer possesses is always inadequate, it is not enough that any single individual should apply the maxim. The community of research gathers more knowledge than any single individual and works to overcome mistakes in individual verification. Knowledge is pooled and correction is a cooperative affair. But since the community may be wrong, every inquirer has to envisage his research within the indefinitely continuing, constantly growing company of inquirers. Hence the community seeks truth as an ideal-limit. Searchers after truth make their way all the time towards a state of perfect knowledge; but they will never arrive at this state.

The need for honesty in scrutinizing one's data, for integrity in cooperating with others and for a genuine love of truth led Peirce to believe that truth is not only to be seen intellectually, but has to be won morally. The work of forming concepts, drawing consequences, and verifying them must be carried out in a self-disciplined and cooperative way within the community of seekers and against the background of the social ideal-limit of truth.

## II. CATEGORIES

Like Aristotle, Peirce wanted to classify the main aspects of reality through a doctrine of **categories**. Aristotle's categories however had

been objectivist. Peirce believed that categories should express aspects of the world in terms of our direct perceptive experience. He formulated three such categories: Firstness, Secondness, and Thirdness.

Firstness is the spontaneous aspect of things: it is exemplified especially in the free surge of the mind in the formation of hypotheses; it indicates life, growth and variety in the universe. In any single instance of Firstness, such as an act of immediate consciousness before it is reflected on, there is undifferentiated unity. But otherness and the struggle resulting from it are also an inescapable fact of experience. Hence comes the next category.

Secondness points to the element of duality in experience. Through this category Peirce emphasises existence, "that mode of being which lies in opposition to another.... A thing without oppositions *ipso facto* does not exist." In this sense existence is not a predicate but something that is experienced in willing and perceiving as we come up against the "brute" aspect of the world and the sheer individuality of each thing over and against every other thing. But spontaneity and opposition do not exhaust our experience of reality; there is continuity or regularity.

Peirce calls Thirdness "law". He means that we can reflect on an idea like "wine" or "hard" and see that it applies to many things; this shows that there is regularity in the real, and this is the foundation of law. He speaks of "law" or "general principles" as "active" in things: the uniformities we discover in the real order have meaning for us only in so far as we ourselves can act regularly in their regard. So we can conceive the laws of the universe as analogous to our own habits of action.

## III. GOD, SELF AND IMMORTALITY

(1) Peirce accepted as a philosophical hypothesis the idea of a personal and omnipotent God. He then outlined several different ways of arguing the reality of such a Being. (*a*) The living variety of the universe and the spontaneity that finds its highest expression in human personality enables us to *perceive* (he uses the term in a wide sense) an infinite

Spontaneity or Firstness at the source of limited instances of Firstness. (*b*) It is clear that an order of dynamic finality exists in the world. The manner in which the human mind is adapted to interpreting and predicting the course of nature through the hypotheses of science brings out such purposiveness most clearly. The only full explanation of this adaptation of parts of the world to one another and of the mind and the world is that an absolute Mind has presided over the creation and development of things. Peirce adds that the evolutionary hypothesis supports this for there has not been time enough to allow for haphazard and unguided development from chaos to the present order. (*c*) When we reflect on the hypothesis of God as the creative source of the universe, we are gradually impelled to accept this as the only possible explanation of existence. An instinctive belief in God fits every movement of our nature. Our inclination to pray and our awe before the totality of things go to confirm the truth of the hypothesis.

Peirce concluded that God is unlimited in knowledge and power. Nothing is opposed to his Being (no Secondness in him) and he is above all conceptual order (no Thirdness). But we are forced to conceive him to some extent in the image of a man. Such anthropomorphism is not false: rather it is figurative. It is justified in its intention provided that we do not seek to make our representation of God too precise.

(2) Peirce rejected the Cartesian self. Indeed he stressed the connexions that each *ego* has with others and the universe so much that some passages suggest that he rejected a unitary self. He also insisted that we have to interpret our own thoughts. They are as much signs to us as are the words of other people and the things of the universe. But if he rejected the Cartesian self, he had no time either for the view current among the other pragmatists that reduced human personality to a "bundle of habits". He argued that "unity must be given as a centre for habits". Firstness presupposes some minimum unity; Secondness is based on the self as distinct from everything else; and Thirdness of its nature points to unified continuity in human thought.

(3) Peirce never made up his mind about immortality. Early in his career he admitted

that in its favour was the failure of **materialism** to explain much of the universe. But against it was the dependence of the working of the mind on the body. As the years went on he laid more and more stress on the spiritual aspects of the universe as evidence for personal immortality. But he stopped short of saying that such evidence was conclusive.

Peirce exercised little real influence during his life. William James popularised a form of pragmatism derived largely from a misunderstanding of Peirce's pragmatic principle and his insistence on moral effort in the search for truth. **Royce**'s theory of the social infinite owes a lot to Peirce's teaching on the community of inquirers but Peirce dismissed Royce's logic. **Dewey** took over some of the empirical emphases in Peirce's methodology. But by and large Peirce's general philosophy made no impact until the publication of the *Collected Papers*.

(J.O'C.)

**Peter of Spain,** also known as Petrus Hispanus, lived in the thirteenth century. He is now generally identified with Petrus Juliani who was born *c.* 1210–1220 at Lisbon, studied at Paris, and was elected to the Papacy as John XXI in 1276, dying in 1277 owing to the collapse of a study which he had had built.

His *Summulae Logicales* remained a fundamental logical text till the seventeenth century. Of the twelve tractates in the *Summulae*, 1–5 and 7 correspond in their own admirably concise and formal way to the books of **Aristotle**'s *Organon*, with the exception of the *Posterior Analytics*, those on the *Predicables* and *Predicaments* (2 and 3) being, however, placed after that corresponding to the *Peri Hermeneias*. This order had already been adopted by William of Shyreswood, a master under whom Peter may have studied in Paris, in his *Introductiones in Logicam*. The remaining tractates, 6 and 8–12, forming the *logica moderna*, are concerned with the "properties of terms", supposition, amplification etc. being interrupted by the last tractate of the *logica antiqua*, on fallacies.

A notable innovation in the *Summulae*, destined for enormous influence, is the method of describing the syllogism. The major premise is by definition that which is first stated, and the major extreme is by definition that extreme which appears in the major premise. Here Peter was extending to the first figure the definitions which Shyreswood, following **Boethius**, had adopted only for the second and third. Exclusion of all reference to the conclusion is fully explained by his definition of a syllogism as consisting not of three but of two propositions (the premises). This metalogical apparatus is of course quite distinct from the much later decree that the major premise, defined as that containing the major extreme, itself defined as the predicate of the conclusion, must stand first. But there is some reason to think that in the sixteenth and seventeenth centuries the Petrine method was mistakenly taken as asserting this, and that it was failure to distinguish the two sets of definitions which occasioned the rise and spread of this curious tenet.

Peter also wrote a *Syncategoremata*, in which is to be found the principle that "when an entire copulative (conjunctive) proposition is negated, no determinate part of it is negated, but each of its parts under disjunction." This is one of the two equivalences relating negation, conjunction and disjunction formerly ascribed to De Morgan, now often named after **William of Ockham**.

(I.T.)

**Phenomenalism**: the doctrine that human knowledge is confined to the appearances (phenomena) presented to the senses or, less restrictively, that appearances are the ultimate foundation of all our knowledge. It takes two main forms: first a general theory of knowledge and secondly, a theory of perception.

(1) As a general theory of knowledge phenomenalism is the view that we can know nothing that is not given to us in sense-experience and it denies, with more or less thoroughness, the validity of inferences made from things that fall within our sense-experience to things lying outside it. One version, sometimes called agnosticism, asserts that, although we cannot infer the character of what lies outside our sense-experience, we can at least infer that there is something outside it. **Kant**'s Thing-in-itself, **Hamilton**'s Unconditioned and **Spencer**'s Unknowable are outcomes of this line of thought. Some philosophers, understandably reluctant to suppose that we can know that there is something that lies beyond the bounds of possible knowledge, maintain that nothing at all exists beyond the appearances presented to our senses. This view, sometimes called sensationalism, is roughly exemplified by the doctrines of **Hume**, J. S. **Mill** and **Russell**, although both Hume and Mill were dissatisfied with their attempts to explain the observing mind that is the subject of sense-experience in terms of the appearances presented to it. To describe phenomenalism, as is often done, as the view that we do not know things as they really are but only as they appear to us, is misleading. By implying that there are things over and above the appearances presented to us, it begs the question in favour of agnosticism.

(2) In its usual modern form, as a theory of perception, phenomenalism was first clearly expounded by J. S. Mill in 1865 and his compact formula – that a material thing is a permanent possibility of sensation – is as good as any. Much the same point is conveyed by Russell's remark that the thing is the class of its appearances. More recent phenomenalists have preferred to state their doctrine in a linguistic, instead of an ontological, idiom. Material-object statements, they say, are reducible to or translatable into statements about sense-data. The whole content of our beliefs about material things can be expressed in terms of what is immediately given in sense-experience. The usual argument for this conclusion starts from the straightforward consideration that everything we know by perception must be either inferred or uninferred. Now unless some of it is uninferred we are landed with an infinite regress. This inescapably uninferred perceptual knowledge, it is widely agreed, is knowledge of appearances, that is of sense-data. So much is common ground to many theories of perception. The characteristic phenomenalist contention at this point is that there can be no valid inference from appearances which purports to conclude to the existence of

transcendental things, to things, in other words, that do not appear to us and so of which we have no direct knowledge. What reason could we have for believing that there now exists something unobserved that stands in a certain relation, that of being its cause for example, to what we are now observing? Only that we have in the past actually observed such things regularly standing in that relation to sense-data like our present ones. It is, of course, logically impossible that we should have such evidence for things transcending sense-experience since these are unobservable by definition.

Phenomenalists are not, however, solipsists. They do not believe that there is nothing we can know to exist apart from our own sense-experiences. But, while not rejecting all inference from sense-data, they will only countenance inference to things that could in principle be experienced. The permitted variety of inference is simple extrapolation to what are variously called possible sensations (Mill), sensibilia (Russell) and hypothetical sense-data. Our actual experience displays enough regularity for us to establish laws of correlation between experiences of different kinds. When some part of one of these regular patterns is presented to us we can reasonably understand that the rest of the pattern is available if we modify the conditions of observation appropriately (for example, by stretching out our hands or opening our eyes). Our experience, though fragmentary, is orderly enough to enable us to construct from it a material world that is, in Hume's phrase, "continuous and distinct". There is some disagreement about the way in which this conclusion should be expressed. Russell speaks of "sensibilia", actual entities just like sense-data except that no observer is aware of them. Others, feeling that there is still a faint whiff of the transcendent, even of the self-contradictory, about this, prefer to say that what we infer is the truth of hypothetical propositions.

There are three main lines of objection to this theory. First, it is argued that the phenomenalist translation could never, even in principle, be carried out, either because we lack the verbal means to effect it or because

the appearances associated with a given material object are infinitely numerous and complex. Secondly, it is said that the translation is spurious since the antecedent clauses of the hypothetical statements making up the translation must themselves mention material objects, for example the bodies and especially the sense-organs of observers and the physical conditions of observation. Thirdly, a lot of discomfort has been felt, even by philosophers well-disposed to phenomenalism such as H. H. **Price**, about the fact that unobserved material things, which are only clusters of possibilities according to the theory, exert a causal influence. How can the collection of possible sense-data, which is all the water at the bottom of a well consists of, manage to emit an actual noise when an unobserved, and so equally hypothetical, stone strikes it? A more fundamental line of objection starts further back by attacking the presumption shared by phenomenalists with many other theorists of knowledge, that the only immediate objects of perception are sense-data.

Phenomenalism has close affinities with the theory of perception put forward by **Berkeley**, who at one point, indeed, explicitly propounds phenomenalism but fails to follow it up. What we infer, in his view, is not possible experiences of our own but actual, and pretty transcendent-looking, experiences of God's. Mill could be said to have derived his phenomenalism from Hume's account of perception by making one crucial change: what Hume regarded as an imaginative fiction Mill saw as a legitimate intellectual construction. Russell with his theory of sensibilia, was never a complete phenomenalist and Price was led by the argument about the causal efficacy of clusters of mere possibilities to augment his families of sense-data with ghostly relics of Lockean substance called Physical Occupants. The most thorough and unwavering phenomenalist of recent times is **Ayer**.

Phenomenalist theories of mind (which see the mind as simply a related cluster of actual experiences) have been advanced with more or less conviction and enthusiasm by Hume, Mill, Russell and Ayer. **Mach** and Pearson expounded a phenomenalist philosophy of science which gives an attractively hard-headed account of the theoretical entities of natural science (electrons, viruses etc.). In **Carnap's** *Logical Structure of the World* a completely generalised phenomenalism is worked out in impressive formal detail in which our entire conceptual apparatus is decomposed into its ultimate phenomenal constituents.

(A.Q.)

**Phenomenology.** In its broadest meaning, "phenomenology" signifies a descriptive philosophy of experience. The name of **Husserl** is most closely associated with this term in twentieth-century thought. C. S. **Peirce** defined the descriptive discipline of "phaneroscopy" or "phenomenology", but no relationship between him and Husserl has been established. Husserl's version of phenomenology is unrelated historically to **Hegel's** "phenomenology of spirit". Although there can be no doubt about Husserl's gradual tendency, in later years, to evolve a "philosophy of spirit", he was hostile to speculative philosophy in his formative period. The indebtedness of Husserl's phenomenology is nevertheless many-sided. The influence of **Brentano, James**, the British empiricists, **Descartes, Leibniz** and **Kant** is to be noted particularly.

The Husserlian version of phenomenology was developed slowly and painstakingly. Husserl hoped to extend the scope of the *a priori* to the entire field of experience, so as to construct a science of "pure" phenomenology. Phenomenology was first defined as "descriptive psychology". Husserl managed to clarify that definition by elaborating a "transcendental" phenomenology. From the beginning, phenomenology was committed to the ideal of the greatest possible freedom from presuppositions. Accordingly, speculative constructions were ruled out, and there could be no talk of a "transcendent" realm, beyond possible experience. Husserl's slogan "Back to the things themselves!" expresses this principle very well.

The term "transcendental" implies pure reflection. Kant indicated its general nature when he explained "transcendental" as meaning attending to the experiencing of an object, rather than to the object itself. The aim of phenomenology is to make this reflection as "radical" as possible, proceeding to the sources of certainty or "evidence" in immediate experience, and "questioning" everything for its evidence. Toward that end, a procedure of "reduction" is instituted, requiring the suspension of all beliefs, and of all scientific knowledge as well. Descartes' method of doubt serves as a convenient means of introducing the method of phenomenology. One could be mistaken in judgments about the world, or anything "transcending" experience, but "immanent" experiences concerning the world, or concerning any alleged or imagined objects, could not be doubted.

The aim of phenomenology is, then, to delimit the entire, endless realm of experiences, in all their types – perception, phantasy, etc. All beliefs in truths of any kind are suspended, and we are left with the experiences themselves, and with the objectivities meant by them. The two aspects – the meaning and the meant – are called the *noetic* and *noematic* sides of experience. This "correlative" or "intentional" mode of viewing experience is essential to the procedure of phenomenology. With all beliefs placed in abeyance as a matter of method, one can speak of "pure subjectivity", or of "pure experience". It is a "radical" procedure because all natural and traditional assumptions have been suspended. It would be a misunderstanding, however, to infer that the world has been "discarded" or denied. The "thesis" of existence is simply "put out of play",,and the "world" is the correlate of my meaningful experience, not regarded as independently real. It is a "bracketed" world.

The "reduction" to the stream of inner experiences must begin with the individual thinker. Because one must begin with one's own experiences, "transcendental egology" is the first stage. The "exhibiting" of other minds must be provided for if solipsism is to be avoided. In the language of phenomenology, that is made possible by "empathy", "appresentation", and "apperception by analogy", based upon the resemblance of other bodies to one's own. The phenomenologist then speaks of "transcendental intersubjectivity", and of the "constitution" of the objective world.

The term "constitution" is unfortunately used in more than one sense in phenomenology.

It really names the *constructive* programme of descriptive analysis, which is called for once "purification" by "reduction" is completed. The "constitution" of the world within the frame of pure consciousness does not mean that it is made out of consciousness. But when all things are viewed as objects for experience, it is appropriate to speak of the synthetic and "idealising" processes by which complex structures and meanings are "constituted" out of the stream of experiences. The meaningful (noetic) experiences and the meant (noematic) objects are both included in the scope of phenomenology.

The value of phenomenology from a critical point of view is evident. The programme of reflecting upon all knowledge and experience, with the ideal of the "self-givenness" in experience of what is meant, may well have an emancipating effect.

The "transcendental" or purely reflective "reduction" to one's stream of experiences is united with the "eidetic reduction". "Eidetic" means "essential", and under the eidetic reduction one's interest is restricted to the descriptive analysis of essential structures and relations in all types of experience, such as perception, remembrance, etc., and in all the "intentional" or meant objects of experience.

The procedures of phenomenology are supposed to have the advantage of avoiding the doubts and errors of ordinary natural experience. The investigator of the "immanent" realm of experience allegedly has the advantage of not being "at the mercy of the facts". He may indeed make mistakes in his descriptions. But he is incomparably more secure than the natural investigator. At least, that is the argument. It is unfortunate that the attempt to justify the pure "inner" realm of inquiry against severe opposition has led phenomenologists to underestimate natural experience and its methods.

Historically, phenomenology was a means of outflanking **naturalism.** In this respect it was in harmony with the dominant academic philosophers of the time, who were concerned with circumscribing the methods of the sciences, and with defending the traditional preserve of a spiritual philosophy of values. Although phenomenology is a highly distinctive philosophy in its methods and descriptive results, it has little new to offer in its basic arguments for **idealism.** If mind or spirit were removed, Husserl argues, there would be no nature; for spirit is what gives meaning to being.

The chief justification of phenomenology lies in the value of its descriptive findings. Its studies of time-consciousness, its "origin-analyses" of the basic concepts of **logic,** and its analyses of perception and other modes of experience have greatly extended the range of our descriptive vision. It is on "seeing" that the greatest emphasis is placed. "Seeing" cannot be based upon anything more fundamental. The field of description encompasses the whole network of psychical relations, and particular attention is devoted to the process of "idealisation", without which scientific experience and thinking would not be possible.

The subjective method of phenomenology should not be presumed to displace the objective empirical methods of the sciences. Like many other innovators, Husserl did not know when to stop, in his relentless drive toward a universal philosophy. At times, he revealed awareness of the limits of his achievements, as when he mused that he would never set foot on the "promised land". The pure eidetic science of transcendental phenomenology, which would enable philosophy to provide scientists with thoroughly clarified concepts and basic principles, remained an ideal for him, just as it had been an unfulfilled promise for the great rationalists.

The charge has been made that phenomenology has no access to the "problem of being". As a "pure" subjectivistic procedure, it excludes all judgments of existence. From its point of view, all the special sciences are "dogmatic", because they make assumptions concerning being, and their concepts and principles have not been rendered "evident" in immediate experience. How, then, can a phenomenologist speak of "being"? The answer can only be given by emphasizing the specialized service which phenomenology can render. It is not equipped to deliver a universal philosophy, which requires active cooperation with the sciences. It can, however, make important contributions within the limits of its area of activity, as determined by its carefully defined conditions for inquiry. The "clarification" of the basic concepts and principles of the sciences in terms of immediate experience, is in itself an indispensable discipline. The descriptive analysis of experience from the radically reflective point of view undertakes to make clear the contributions of the knower to experience. That has already been carried to a point hitherto scarcely approached in the history of philosophy.

The impact of phenomenological findings on psychology has been impeded by sharp critical exchanges, caused by misunderstanding on the part of some psychologists, and righteous indignation on the part of Husserl. The critique of the "natural science of psychology" was intended by Husserl to show the need for a "rational psychology", which would do for naturalistic psychology what geometry has done for physical science. Husserl portrayed phenomenology as the "mother-ground" for all the basic concepts and principles of the sciences. The "First Philosophy" which he envisaged was to be truly the "foundation" for all knowledge which could hope to be scientific.

The influence of phenomenology has been extensive, and to some extent it has borne fruit of a type quite uncongenial to Husserl. He regarded the so-called "realistic" phenomenologists as dogmatic metaphysicians. The broader phenomenological movement includes a prominent religious wing, with some evidence of mysticism. The "intuition of essences" of phenomenology has not only been misused to include the nonrational, but has also at times deteriorated to the level of banal descriptions of familiar objects of experience. Attempts have been made, with varying degrees of success, to develop phenomenological approaches to social science history, art, mathematics, psychology, **psychoanalysis,** and Marxism (see **Frankfurt School**), as well as logic and the philosophy of values. Husserl denounced the "existentialist" movement, despite its debts to phenomenology.

It is possible to formulate a strictly methodological version of phenomenology, with no ulterior commitments to idealism or any other dogma. The phenomenological procedure is then regarded as one method of inquiry alongside all the "objective" methods – inductive, causal, and explanatory. Although its findings may well be valuable for all other disciplines, it could have no subject-matter without the factual "mother-ground", which is primarily represented by the natural and cultural sciences. A strict phenomenology, freed from all pretence to metaphysics, and from excessive claims to "absoluteness", would, however, be as defensible in its way as symbolic logic has always been in its own.

(M.F.)

**Philosophy of Mind.** The philosophy of mind is a certain area of problems commonly recognized by English-speaking philosophers. But it is not an accident that this expression is hard to translate into other languages. This is only partly due to the fact that the English word "mind" has no exact equivalent in the other main European languages. It is also a reflection of the fact that the classification in which this label figures is itself based on certain profound philosophical assumptions, often unexpressed.

The crucial assumption can perhaps be tersely described as the view that a whole host of rather different things belong together, and can usefully be treated as members of one class. The items which are gathered together under "mind", or under the associated adjective "mental", include such disparate things as tickles and pains, feelings of nausea and discomfort, emotional experiences like love or anger, perceptions of the world around us, and thoughts of the most abstract and exalted character. The idea of treating all these together is perhaps first clearly propounded by **Descartes,** and contrasts strikingly with the preceding dominant view, descended from **Aristotle,** which offered a highly differentiated picture of our experiences and capacities and located sensations and thoughts, for example, in distinct parts or faculties.

What all the items on the long, diverse list of the "mental" have in common for Descartes, is that they are all essentially present to first-person experience. That is, there cannot be such a thing as a thought, or a perception, or a tickle, without a thinker who can experience it as his; whereas this is manifestly not true of a rock or a tree or

235

a house. Descartes' crucial move was to deem all such things as consisting exclusively in what they present to experience, and hence to see them as distinct from "outer" realities, even though causally related to these. This way of sorting things into "inner" and "outer" is what gives rise to the philosophical category of the "mental", and what licences the grouping together of all sorts of problems under the heading "philosophy of mind".

Descartes' inner/outer sorting was motivated by a number of things, of which two are perhaps crucial: the essential place in his method of a kind of self-scrutiny which circumscribes inner experience the better to focus on it; and his uncompromisingly mechanistic notion of body, which forces one to the complementary category of the mental as what is excluded from the physical and cannot be perceived in outer reality. The continuing force of both these leading ideas in modern philosophy, particularly in the Anglo-Saxon world, is what ensures the currency of the term "philosophy of mind". By the same token, the dominance in French and German philosophy of views which are highly critical both of these notions of method and of mechanistic reduction helps explain the relative untranslatability of the expression.

It is also understandable in the light of this background that the major problem of the philosophy of mind is the "mind-body problem" itself. This is the term for a congeries of difficulties which beset any attempt to relate into a coherent whole "mind" and "body" once distinguished by the inner/outer sorting. Descartes' own approach was a metaphysical **dualism:** mind and body are in fact different substances, causally related in virtue of being brought together in a substantial union by God. But this solution has very little support three centuries later. There are some neurophysiologists who espouse it, like Sir John Eccles; but generally it has seemed incredible for a number of reasons. One is the difficulty of conceiving causal relations between mind and body once separated in this way. This is what led **Malebranche** and **Berkeley** to even more extravagant views, respectively **occasionalism** and a denial of matter altogether. But beyond that, dualism has seemed to many incompatible

with the obvious dependence of mental function on the physical substrate. And in addition, one important stream of European philosophy has rebelled against Descartes' downgrading, as irremediably obscure and confused, of our experience of ourselves as embodied and social agents. **Heidegger** and **Merleau-Ponty** are among the most influential philosophers in our century to have articulated this reaction.

The obvious recourse for those who hold to mechanism is a kind of materialist **monism:** mind is just a reflection of underlying material process. Thoughts reflect the firing of neurones in the brain, emotions our endocrinological state, and so on. A number of theories of this kind have been propounded. Recently the most fashionable have taken up computer technology as a source of models, and propose to see mental functions as the inner reflection of highly complex programmes of computation.

But monism presents its own problems. Quite apart from the possible objections to reductive mechanistic explanations of our thought, action, language and social life, there is the difficulty of placing the inner "reflections" themselves in a monistic world-view. The analogous situation is well-understood, where a solar system in which the earth "really" spins on its axis and orbits the sun "looks" to us as though the sun were circling an immobile earth. The appearances here are external to the phenomena explained (the solar system) and can be disregarded when explaining them. But when we come to consider "inner" experience as the reflection of neural process, it cannot be so easily sidelined. In this case, it is part of our brief to account for there being such a thing as an inner reflection at all. Why is it that ordinary computers made of transistors don't have such an inner life and we do? Or perhaps they do after all? Or at least their more sophisticated descendants will? The discussion goes off into bizarre science fantasy at this point, which is a sign of deep malaise.

The difficulty is that here the "appearances" themselves are part of the explicandum, and it is hard to conceive how they can find a place in a monistic materialist world. Either they are left unexplained; or various heroic attempts are made to subsume them under physical reality, though they fall short of explaining why the problem should ever have arisen in the first place.

It would appear that there is a better hope of making coherent sense of ourselves if we start from a perspective which makes embodied agency central, as Merleau-Ponty does, for instance. But that entails abandoning the inner/outer sorting altogether, and hence the portmanteau categories of "mind" and "mental". These approaches take us outside the classification in which the "philosophy of mind" figures as a term.

The actual situation in English-speaking philosophy is a mixed one. The traditional Cartesian sorting is still sufficiently acknowledged, so that the classification "philosophy of mind" is a recognized one, and lots of people worry over the "mind-body problem". But at the same time, Cartesian assumptions are often challenged in some of the particular fields which are included in the broad category. These include the philosophy of action, analyses of feeling and emotion, issues about the **freedom of the will**, and questions about the self and personal identity. The philosophy of mind also overlaps with **epistemology**, because any theory of knowledge must make some assumptions about philosophical psychology in the very choice of its key terms. Thus the classical Cartesian and empiricist epistemologies relied on the notion of an "idea", or "impression", or "sense-datum", as the immediate object of consciousness.

Now Cartesian, dualist assumptions are strongly challenged in the field of philosophy of action, partly under the influence of the later **Wittgenstein**. Most contemporary philosophers reject a construal of action as an external movement caused by an inner act of will, and search for an account which does not artificially separate mind and body. Some attempts in this field also draw on European developments, like the notion of **intentionality,** as defined in the work of **Brentano** and **Husserl**. At the same time, the philosophical psychology of classical epistemology is widely considered outdated if not absurd. Very few thinkers defend **sense-data**, and many have become sensitive to the role of language, which in turn has led them to recast

the problem entirely. Since language is a social institution, the question arises whether we can offer a coherent view of the origin and bases of knowledge confined to the individual mind, as classical epistemology tries to do.

But alongside this, other questions, such as the issues about freedom and determinism, continue to be treated very much on the old assumptions. The conception of determinism, in relation to which freedom and responsibility seem to be problematical, is itself largely inspired by a mechanistic view of the human subject. And the most widely-discussed issue in this field is that about "compatibilism", i.e. whether there is, after all, any conflict between a deterministic account of human action and the kind of freedom that seems to be inseparable from moral responsibility. The thesis that there is no such conflict goes back to the period of origin of the inner/outer sorting, with Hobbes and Hume.

The self and personal identity are also often discussed in traditional terms, as though the main issue were that of the unity of an object through time. The idea that the self may have another kind of unity has barely begun to impinge on this debate.

The whole field of the philosophy of mind offers a strange and contradictory prospect, in that it is held together by certain fundamental ideas which are nevertheless frequently challenged in the discussion of some of the particular issues which fall within it.

[C.T.]

**Philosophy of Science.** The questions that arise in the philosophy of science fall roughly into three divisions: (A) those about science in general, (B) those bearing on groups of sciences, or relations between them, and (C) conceptual problems in individual sciences.

*A. Science in general.* (1) **Epistemology**, and, in particular, questions about reasonable grounds for knowledge: Is scientific method the only rational route to knowledge and understanding? Is it rational at all, and if so, why? Are there best methodologies? What might support a theory that cannot be directly checked by observations? The problem of induction: to what extent can we assume that the future will resemble the past, or that past generalizations will hold up in the future? Probability: can one measure the degree to which a hypothesis is supported by or made credible by evidence? The relations between experiment and theory: is scientific knowledge founded upon observation independent of theory, or are all observations "theory-laden"?

(2) **Metaphysics**, and, in particular, questions about reality: Is a scientific theory a representation of the world? Is a theory a set of statements trying to describe, in literal terms, how things are? Or is a theory only an instrument for organizing experience and experimental results, an instrument that is used to make better predictions and reveal interrelations between phenomena? What are causes: constant regularities in experience, or necessary connexions in nature? What is an explanation? Many theories postulate entities that cannot be observed – for example, electrons, the superego, the money supply. Do these literally exist, or are they merely intellectual constructs? Sometimes these questions are expressed semantically: Do the very words such as "electron" refer to or denote something, or is their role in language quite different from words such as "coal" or "window"?

(3) **Ethics**: What are the responsibilities of a scientist in choosing fields of research, and in communicating or using discoveries that may be harmful? What are the parallel responsibilities of society, and of public or private patrons of science? Issues range from debates about weapons research through the use of scarce resources (including mental resources) to questions about whether it is immoral even to investigate certain areas, e.g. correlations between race and physical and intellectual abilities, or brainwashing, or the discovery of ever more potent modes of destruction.

B. *Groups of sciences.* Many of these questions bear on the "unity of science". Should the human or social sciences use a methodology which is fundamentally different from that of the natural sciences? Or is there a single scientific method, appropriate to all fields

of inquiry? There are related questions about nature itself. Are all phenomena ultimately the consequence of the same basic laws of nature? On one simplistic picture, sociology is reducible to psychology, which is reducible to biology and biochemistry, and those in turn to chemistry, which reduces to physics, with an ultimate goal of a "Grand Unified Theory" in physics. There are logical issues here (what is meant by "reduction?"), factual ones (has unification been proceeding apace, or are we witnessing increasing diversification?), and methodological ones (does the drive towards unifying theories always tend to produce greater or deeper knowledge?).

C. *Individual sciences.* The list of these questions is as long as any list of sciences. How to understand space and time after **relativity** theory? How to understand causality and determinism after **quantum mechanics?** What, in evolutionary biology, is a species? What is the relation between artificial intelligence and human thought? Some writers hold that the only function for philosophy of science is participation in conceptual debates within the special sciences.

I. ORIGINS OF THE PHILOSOPHY OF SCIENCE

**Aristotle, Descartes** and **Leibniz** made contributions of the first rank to both of what we now call science and philosophy, and Francis **Bacon** is widely regarded as the first philosopher of the scientific revolution of the seventeenth century. A distinct family of inquiries to be called "philosophy of science" arises, however, only in the nineteenth century. It was then that distinct sciences such as what we now call biology or physics emerged and were "professionalised". Philosophy of science grew up around this development. Many of the issues mentioned in (V) did of course arise earlier. **Empiricist** and **rationalist** traditions in the seventeenth century divide on questions of methodology. There were important **realist**/anti-realist controversies about, for example, the "reality" of gravitational force, or whether it is literally true that the earth rotates about the sun. And **Hume** is commonly considered the originator of a well-defined problem about induction, and author of the definitive "constant conjunction" analysis of causality. Nevertheless philosophy of science as a fairly autonomous branch of philosophy is a creature of the nineteenth century. Important figures in the first generation are Auguste **Comte**, William **Whewell** and J. S. **Mill**. The first two represent opposed attitudes to the sciences that persist to this day.

Comte invented the label **positivism** for his philosophy. Positivism includes the following ideas: the only significant propositions of science are those that can be verified or falsified in experience; there is no power of necessity in nature: causality is no more than the regularities and uniformities that we observe: theoretical entities are intellectual constructs, invented to enable us to organize phenomena and to make successful predictions. Many positivists have said outright that they were opposed to metaphysics. Hume is often cited as a forerunner.

Whewell's *Philosophy of the Inductive Sciences* (1840) was in contrast strongly influenced by **Kant**. It was committed to the existence and possible discovery of fundamental but unobserv--able entities, and to explanations that reveal the necessary causes of events. The progress of science was, in Whewell's opinion, a matter of comprehending the reality that underlies phenomena.

Many discussions among today's philosophers of science can be seen as continuations of the disagreement between Comte and Whewell. Notice, however, that science has changed since the nineteenth century. As Alexander Bain (an admirer of J. S. Mill) said near its end, atoms, electrons and the like were just "representative fictions". There was nothing one could conceive of doing to or with such postulated entities. If one believed in them it was only because of the role that they played in organizing one's understanding of experimental results. This is no longer the case. Nuclear fission and genetic engineering are dramatic examples of our now commonplace ability to manipulate and use what, even at the outset of our century, could still be regarded as "representative fictions". Note that not only was there no nuclear fission then, but even the nucleus of the atom was first proposed only in 1911 – a consequence of

Rutherford's experimental, rather than theoretical, work. A similar tale can be told for genes.

## II. LOGICAL POSITIVISM

The most influential twentieth-century school of philosophers of science originated with groups in Vienna and Berlin, meeting in the 1920s. Impressed by positivist doctrines, and by the results of symbolic logic, many gladly called themselves **logical positivists**, later preferring the term "logical empiricist". Major figures were Moritz **Schlick**, Hans Reichenbach (1891–1953), Rudolf **Carnap** and Karl **Popper**. All were deeply moved by the triumphs of relativity and quantum mechanics, and wished to produce criteria that would distinguish science like that from what they regarded as pseudoscience, e.g. Marxist history or Freudian **psychoanalysis**. Most emphasized that scientific propositions should be verifiable, but Popper, who always distanced himself from the others, and rejected the "positivist" label, insisted that verification and confirmation were not decisive; instead scientific assertions should be testable and open to refutation. He strongly urged that all scientific pronouncements are fallible. Carnap spent many years attempting a theory of probability, to be called inductive logic, which would explain how generalizations are supported by positive instances. In contrast Popper, like Hume, argued that all such induction is invalid. Instead we learn from experience by a process of conjecture, testing, and refutation.

All living members of this group emigrated in the 1930s. They became influential in the English-speaking world. Although recently there has been a revival of interest in their work in Germany, opposition there is more marked, as shown for example by a debate between **Adorno** and **Habermas** on the one hand, and Popper on the other, published as *The Positivist Dispute in German Sociology* (the discussions took place in Germany in 1961, and were published in translation in 1976). The main issue was the question of whether there are distinct methodologies and types of knowledge for the natural and for human sciences.

## III. THE HISTORICAL DIMENSION

Criticism of a different sort arose in America. Popper and the positivists were committed to a strong contrast between what Reichenbach called the context of justification and the context of discovery. There might be an economic, historical, sociological or psychological explanation of why a particular discovery (or error) was made, but such "external" circumstances had nothing to do with the correctness, grounds of belief or acceptance of the discovery. A number of writers, of whom T. S. **Kuhn** is by far the most widely influential, fundamentally challenged this confident rationalist picture of science. His *The Structure of Scientific Revolutions* (1962) describes scientific development dialectically, in terms of periods of "normal" science being followed by "crisis", then "revolution" and then new normal science. Kuhn is not speaking of science as a whole, or even one of the sciences such as chemistry, but rather of small fragments of a field in which there may be only a hundred or fewer significant workers. Normal science conducted by these research workers is a matter of solving puzzles or problems according to an established pattern, or "paradigm". Crisis arises when central problems become intractable, when there is no way, for example, to explain anomalous results inconsistent with a theory. New concepts are evolved which displace old ones, so that there may be no way of systematically comparing the successes and failures of abandoned theories and their successors. Thus the very notion of "the facts" is called in question, and doubt is cast on the most fundamental of positivist tenets, that theory-neutral observations suffice to decide between competing theories. It is suggested instead that all observations are tinctured by theory.

Kuhn's work forced a rather radical reassessment of the ideas in anglophone philosophy of science that had been inculcated by its German and Austrian teachers. Some wanted to preserve their rationalist ideology. For example, one of the more iconoclastic and polemical retorts to Kuhn was that of Imré Lakatos (1922–1974), a Hungarian refugee who settled in London. His *Methodology of Scientific Research Programmes* (1970, 1978) is a revision of Popper's philosophy, aiming at criteria of rationality couched in terms of the track record of an entire programme of investigation. It is notable, however, that for all his criticism of Kuhn's work, on one point he is in complete agreement. Where the logical empiricists had thought of the logic of scientific method as being essentially timeless, Lakatos' philosophy of science is entirely historicized.

This historical dimension is now represented in most philosophers of science discussing the general issues described in (A) above. It is not strictly new, but rather a return. Whewell's *Philosophy of the Inductive Sciences* was preceded by a three volume *History of the Inductive Sciences*, and Comte's monumental *Course on Positive Philosophy* is first of all an overview of the history of science. In consequence of this return to an historical vision of scientific activity, some Anglo-American philosophers have found that their concerns had been partially addressed already by French historian/philosophers of science such as Gaston **Bachelard** and Georges **Canguilhem**.

A more critical attitude towards science itself has also blossomed. It is epitomized by Paul Feyerabend's question in *Against Method* (1975), "What's so great about science?" Many of Kuhn's core ideas had been put forward simultaneously and independently by Feyerabend, who went on to argue, most specifically against Lakatos, that there is no peculiarly "scientific" method. Adherence to any canons of procedure led to stultification. Feyerabend has on occasion urged that the present scientific establishment is as effective in closing minds as was the religious orthodoxy challenged at the time of Galileo. He has described himself as an "anarchist" about science.

A related critique is advanced by a younger generation of workers; it has been called the "strong programme in the sociology of science". We are accustomed to providing sociological explanations for the acceptance of patently false theories, e.g. the preference for Lysenko's over Western genetics during the Stalinist period in the USSR. Most philosophers have supposed that no comparable explanation is needed for the discovery of truths. A chief tenet of the strong programme is that the truth of a proposition, the compelling character of the evidence, or the rationality of a method, never explains the acceptance of a discovery. Exactly the same kind of explanation is needed as for Lysenkoism.

Moreover the notion of a "discovery" is held to be disingenuous. It suggests an analogy to discovering a continent or an island, which we think of as being there in the ocean whether people get to it or not. One should think not of discovering scientific facts, but of constructing them in the course of an ongoing process of social interaction among research workers. Thus the strong programme and its variants tend to be anti-rationalist in epistemology, and anti-realist in metaphysics.

## IV. PLURALISM

Most philosophers of science hold such views to be extreme and wrong-headed. The strong programme does, however, indicate a substantial shift in philosophical interests in the sciences since the days of the logical positivists. These days were perhaps too much dominated by a certain image of science furnished by the twin successes of relativity theory and quantum mechanics. Since then, people have become more aware of the enormous diversity of scientific activities. Where the logical empiricists and Popper alike wrote extensively about theory and said virtually nothing about experiment, there has recently been a good deal of work on experimental science in its own right. Sometimes this has been combined with the attitudes of the strong programme, with philosophically minded participant-observers describing what goes on in a laboratory in the course of making a "discovery".

These tendencies towards pluralism on the part of philosophers have also affected the tenor of discussions about the relationship between the natural and social sciences. Anti-positivist philosophers once argued that the social sciences had to have their own methodology, which was autonomous and independent of the methods of the natural sciences. But as scientific methodology has increasingly come to seem very piecemeal and fragmented, this debate has appeared less pressing than it was.

It must be emphasized that this summary has concerned only the most general of the philosophical issues mentioned in (A1) and (A2) above. These are undoubtedly the ones that have attracted the attention of philosophers with little interest in science for its own sake, and also of the reading public at large. But if one turns to books, journals, or conference proceedings in the philosophy of science, one finds that by far the larger part address the more specific sorts of issue sketched in (C).

[I.H.]

**Plato** (c. 427—347 B.C.), was born in Athens and lived there for most of his eighty years. Though at first marked out for politics, both by his lineage and by his interests, he devoted himself almost wholly to study, theory and teaching. One cause of this was the disgust he came to feel at the low level of politics in his time; he found that bad faith and injustice and cynical selfishness were widespread, and that ingenuous good faith could not stand against them. The only hope for politics, it seemed to him, was to found a school and create therein a new kind of political character.

The main cause of his renouncing political practice was probably **Socrates**. He fell deeply under the spell of Socrates' magnetic and searching thought, and was profoundly shocked when, at the age of about 27, he saw Socrates condemned to death on the absurd charge of corrupting the young and not believing in the city's gods. He has left us unhistorical but magnificent pictures of Socrates' defence, imprisonment, and execution, in his *Apology, Crito,* and *Phaedo.*

After this disaster, most of Socrates' friends left Athens for a time. Plato visited the Greek cities of Sicily and southern Italy, and made political and scholarly friends there. By about 385, at the latest, he was back in Athens, and was founding, near the grove of the hero Academus, what has come to be called the "Academy", which may loosely be called the first university. He gathered about him a number of pupils and fellow students, who united themselves in a "museum", or society dedicating itself to the patrons of letters and music, the Muses. The members might stay there for twenty years or even for life, taking part in common studies, religious exercises, and meals. The ultimate practical purpose of the society was the restoration of decent government to the Greek cities. Some of the members left after a time and went into

241

*Plato*

practical politics. Some, including Plato himself, wrote political advice to their friends elsewhere. But the studies were far from wholly practical. Plato held the restoration of decent government to require a complete foundation of theoretical knowledge; and he sought to lay such a foundation, as deep and as firm as possible. The studies which he encouraged hence came to appear to the man in the street as obscure, fine-drawn, and impractical; and there is a story that, when he advertised a lecture on "The Good", people came hoping to learn how to be happy, but heard only what seemed to them to be higher mathematics. Mathematics certainly became, after philosophy, the study most pursued by the society.

Plato devoted himself to his school for most of the remaining forty years of his long life. He had, however, two very important relations with the outside world; his interventions in the politics of Syracuse and his published writings.

During his travels Plato had made a friend of Dion at the court of Syracuse. In 367 Dion urged Plato to come to Syracuse and instruct the new ruler, Dionysius II, who being young and well-intentioned might be made into the new kind of statesman desired by Plato. Plato went; but he had little hope of realizing his ideal in Dionysius, and had probably lost by this time most of his original eagerness for political practice. The matter turned out very badly. This was not because the royal pupil had no relish for Plato or philosophy. On the contrary, he became very attached to his teacher and to the subject. But Plato had not been at Syracuse six months before Dionysius expelled Dion on the ground that he was plotting against him. Loyalty compelled Plato to support Dion and demand his recall, while jealousy and suspicion drove Dionysius to try to separate Plato from Dion. Dionysius never let Dion return, and for some time he did not let Plato leave.

Six years later, in 361, Dionysius sent for Plato again, and ensured Plato's compliance by making it a condition of the restoration of Dion. Once he had Plato, however, he did not recall Dion but on the contrary confiscated Dion's property in Syracuse. Plato had to use the influence of a neighbouring ruler in order to be allowed to return to Athens.

Jealousy begins with false beliefs, but by acting on them makes them true. Dion now became the irreconcilable enemy of Dionysius. He invaded Syracuse and drove Dionysius from it in 357, ruled it himself for four years, and was then assassinated. The assassin had apparently had relations with Plato and was considered a member of the Academy. This was a terrible blow to Plato.

Plato's publications are all preserved, and make five large modern volumes. They constitute not merely the greatest philosophical work there is, but also one of the greatest pieces of literature in the world. If anyone asks what philosophy is, the best answer is: "read Plato". For it was Plato who brought the word "philosophy" into use; and it was he who mainly invented and first practised the sort of study for which "philosophy" is the name. To say that there is little philosophy in a major work by Plato is self-contradictory; or it expresses an arbitrary change in the meaning of the word. The so-called **pre-Socratic** philosophers, and even Socrates, were not philosophers in the full sense of the word, though they were certainly Plato's inspirers.

I. THE EARLY DIALOGUES

Plato's works can for the most part be confidently assigned to one of three periods, the early, the middle, and the late. The early works constitute an extremely striking presentation of the figure of Socrates.

All but one of these works are dialogues; and this is part of Plato's conception of philosophy as well as part of his literary originality. Philosophy is essentially a kind of *logos*; and Plato's notion of *logos* may be analysed in modern terms as "the reasonable use of words in thinking". The reasonable use of words involves submitting them to criticism by others and testing their implications; and this involves dialogue. The typical early Platonic dialogue draws out the implications of a statement, in order to test it for consistency with itself and other statements. The question whether to adopt a statement must not be answered until we have discovered its implications and connexions. Since more implications may become visible to us in the future, it is usually better to adopt a view provisionally and until someone persuades us otherwise with a better argument.

242

## II. THE MIDDLE DIALOGUES

In his middle dialogues Plato shows some dissatisfaction with the hypothetical and negative procedure of his Socrates in the early dialogues, and some hope of finding an unhypothetical starting-point on which to base intuitive certainty and good politics. He thinks that such a starting-point can be found, if at all, only in the region suggested by the following statements.

Through all the multiplicity and variety of just and unjust acts, persons, and situations in this world, there evidently is in some way only *one* Justice and *one* Injustice. And so with every other collection of things to which we apply the same name, as "beautiful" or "couch". Various and divergent as beautiful things are, there is only *one* Beauty. We can distinguish from each and all of the many beautiful things the *one* Beauty itself, what Beauty itself *is*, which must be there because otherwise there would be no sense in calling anything beautiful.

The one Beauty itself is not merely distinct from each and all of the beautiful things. It is also separate from them. For it must be completely beautiful, purely beautiful, unchangingly beautiful; and no beautiful thing is such. This comes out very clearly when we consider the one Equality itself; for probably no two sticks in this world ever are exactly equal; and if they were our measurements would never be able to tell us that they were. Thus we arrive at an astounding and thrilling conclusion: there is a second world, other than our world of visible things, consisting of the Ones Themselves, each of which is perfectly, purely, and eternally what it is, visible only to the mind itself, or rather not visible but intelligible, grasped only by the pure intellect using bare words.

Can this be right? Let us go back and approach by a slightly different way. Socrates has made us familiar with the enterprise of asking what a thing *is*. He has asked what courage *is*, what virtue *is*, what knowledge *is*. And he has rejected all such answers as: "Well, look at Laches if you want to know what courage is; he is a courageous man". Socrates has replied that he wants, not this or that courageous man or act, but courage itself. And surely he was right. The question "What is courage?" expresses a possible enterprise which

is not that of collecting examples. The Socratic search for "Definitions" was in fact the search for one or other of these elusive but necessary Ones in Themselves. They must be there, to make sense of our world and our speech; but their forms are to be discerned only by the eye of the mind. There is an intelligible world of "Forms" or "Ideas".

To Plato the word "idea" meant first visible form and then form in general. Thus it meant something objective. It never carried the subjective meaning it has today. In any case it is hardly more than a label to him, a label for "that one thing itself which (something) in itself is, complete, pure, and eternal"; and this phrase in turn is Plato's distillation from Socrates' search for definitions and from the fact of common names.

These Forms, then, so unexpectedly but so simply discovered, are the required starting-point, both for good practice and for good theory and indeed for a kind of religion (for Plato called them divine). To believe in them and to pursue them is to be a philosopher; that is the deeper definition of what philosophy or the pursuit of wisdom *is*. To be ignorant of them, or to disbelieve in them when they are pointed out (which unfortunately is the usual human state), is to be essentially not a philosopher. Knowledge of them is the first possible kind of knowledge. Indeed it is strictly speaking the only kind of knowledge; for strictly speaking only the unchangeable can be known, and only the Forms are unchangeable. If you say that the moon is full, and then the moon wanes, you cannot strictly speaking have known that the moon was full. Only what completely is can be completely known. There is a difference of kind between knowledge which has the Forms for its object, and opinion, which has for its object this transitory and confused world.

The Forms are, however, the explanation of the visible world, so far as it has one. This cosmos is the mixed result of Mind and Necessity, and hence our account of it cannot be better than a likely story. But certainly whatever reality there is in visible things comes to them from the Forms after which they are called. A visible couch shares in, or perhaps imitates, couch itself, and derives its half-reality therefrom. We may also suppose that, beside the Forms and the visibles, there is a Third Thing, a receptacle of

Plato

all becoming, which like gold takes any shape, and is to the Forms as mother is to father, a sort of room or seat of becoming, to be grasped imperceptibly by a kind of bastard reasoning.

## III. POLITICS AND PHILOSOPHY

All opinion is defective; but it is not all equally defective. On the contrary, those who know the Forms will have far better opinions about this world than those who do not. And that is the key fact for good politics, since it implies that kings should be philosophers. The only good government is by those who know, and this means those who know the Forms. The ideal city would be a philosophocracy.

Whether such a city could ever come into existence is very doubtful; but how it would maintain itself if it did come into existence is clear. The ruling philosophers would take care to see that their rule was absolute and not limited by unchangeable laws or by popular votes, that they handed it over only to other equally adept and right-minded philosophers, and that the supply of suitable successors was assured by appropriate education of the best persons. Education would be in fact by far the most important part of practice. Those chosen to receive it would be primarily the children of the rulers; but impartial selection would reject some of these as inferior, and add some superior children from the common people. The same kind of impartial search for the best, overriding all useless customs however dear, would give us women as well as men rulers, would make these women exercise naked as well as the men, and would abolish family life among the rulers in favour of a conventional system of common parents and common children, which, together with communion of property, would fuse the whole ruling class into a united and selfless whole whose ascendency would never be in doubt.

The primary education of these rulers would not be very different from what Plato had himself received. It would, however, be publicly organized and intense; and the physical or gymnastic part would be more military in character. The two greatest differences would be, first, the ever present risk of failure in the next examination and consequent relegation to the masses, and,

second, the complete absence from their music and poetry of all corrupting or degrading suggestions, such as frenzied music and Homer's assertion that the gods could not restrain their laughter on a certain occasion. For whatever is read in literature in early years goes deep into the soul, especially any suggestion of self-abandonment.

Those who passed all tests up to the age of twenty would be sure of some sort of place in the ruling class for life; but whether this was ever to be higher than that of a private in the army would depend on their success in the studies and exercises and examinations in the following fifteen years. Here Plato is strange indeed; for what he proposes as a suitable training for the higher ranks of the army and for administrators and rulers, is advanced **mathematics** followed by abstract study of the Forms and finally of the Form of the Good. Nothing is said about history or politics or economics. His reason is that those who are to keep a city as good as possible must above all know what pure and absolute Goodness Itself is, to which end they must previously know about the other pure and absolute Forms Themselves, to which end in turn they must first know mathematics. Mathematics provides a bridge from the sensible to the intelligible world. For in mathematics we draw sensible squares and triangles, and yet are interested in intelligible triangles and squares. We use the visible as a suggestion of the intelligible, and thus are gradually brought to the desire and power to study the intelligible itself, by mere words without accompanying visible images, as the adept philosopher does.

Only those who can and will persevere the whole way up this path will be governors of our ideal city. They will by then be at least fifty years old. One curious consequence of this education will be that the rulers will dislike ruling. They will have a passion for the Forms and wish to be left alone with them. But this is no disadvantage. On the contrary, the love of power makes bad rulers; and our reluctant rulers will nevertheless rule willingly enough, because they are just and they recognize the justice of recompensing their city for the supreme education it has given them. Besides, they will have plenty of leisure to devote to abstract philosophizing.

This ideal city of Callipolis, the first surviving Utopia and by far the most interesting one, is constructed in Plato's splendid dialogue *Republic*, which is one of the ten best books there are. It is a work of his maturity, and the high point of his powers. Later in life he published two more dialogues on politics, and they show a change of interest. Here he still affirms that knowledge is the only right basis for government, that it may and should dispense with laws, and that communal living is best. But he seems to think now that knowledge and communal living are hardly ever practical possibilities, and therefore we had better spend our efforts in finding what is best to do in their absence. He has no doubt that in their absence we should have recourse to the reign of law. Law, while much inferior to the man who knows the Good, is much the best ruler for us ignorant and ill-tempered persons; and should be sacred among us. So when in his old age he plans another ideal city, which he calls Magnesia, his account consists mainly in a mass of legal details, and the dialogue describing Magnesia is named *Laws*.

IV. THE LATER DIALOGUES

Philosophy in the narrow sense is the analysis of conceptions; and this is mainly the invention of Plato's later dialogues. However, Plato himself continued to think of his theoretical philosophy as a study of the world rather than of man, as metaphysics rather than as logic and epistemology. And his results were often not of great value; there are weary wastes of logical and metaphysical oddities, tiresome enough in Plato himself, intolerable when expounded by devoted interpreters. Yet it is never to be forgotten that these late dialogues, or rather that activity in the Academy of which these dialogues are an expression, formed the best analytical thinker there has yet been, **Aristotle**.

The best of the late dialogues are the first two, *Parmenides* and *Theaetetus*. The conflict of opposed views natural to a good dialogue is at its greatest in the *Parmenides*, which consists of two parts. The first appears to destroy Plato's own theory of Forms with well-founded and unanswerable arguments. The second appears to be a formidably long and boring kind of metaphysical nonsense; it is described by the main speaker as "a laborious game", and ends with the following words: "Let this be said, then; and also that, as it seems, whether one is or not, both itself and the others, both to themselves and to each other, all in every way both are and are not and appear and do not appear. – Very true." Whatever this be, a joke, or ultimate truth, or something between, it is a remarkable achievement and has a queer value of its own. The discussion of the Ideas in the first part does in fact amount to a pretty clear revelation of the reasons that make the theory impossible, and is therefore a fine example of candid self-criticism. It is very strange that the *Parmenides* thus contains both an extreme example of frankness and an extreme example of mystification.

The *Theaetetus* is Plato's most successful work in purely analytical philosophy. The conceptions analysed are perception, knowledge, subjectivity, truth, change, error, *logos*, simplicity, and (by implication) definition. Plato introduces there the classical comparisons of the mind to a wax tablet and to a dovecote, and the classical comparison of Socrates' conversation to midwifery. The conclusions of the dialogue are mostly negative and valueless by themselves: "Knowledge is not perception: it is not true opinion; it is not even true opinion with *logos*. Error is not thinking one thing instead of another, or misrelating what I see to what I know, or misusing the knowledge that I have; it is hard to see how it can occur at all." Nevertheless, anyone who studies and absorbs this dialogue will be greatly enlightened.

After the *Theaetetus* and the *Parmenides*, the *Sophist* is the greatest of Plato's late works. In outline it is a series of attempts to define the sophist by successive divisions of a genus, as when we define the angler by dividing the genus craft, to which he belongs, into acquisitive and constructive craft, and place the angler in acquisitive craft. We can then subdivide acquisitive craft into acquisition by consent and acquisition by subjugation, and again place the angler in the half to which he belongs. If we continue long enough, we should come to a class that is co-extensive with the angler and constitutes a definition of him. This process of definition by division is prominent in the late dialogues. Plato appears to have hoped that it would supply a sure way of constructing definitions, as opposed to merely destroying definitions as Socrates' technique had done. Aristotle, however, showed that there is nothing sure about procedure; every step in it is merely an unsupported assertion. And its prominence in the late dialogues is a large cause of their relative unfruitfulness.

The *Sophist* fortunately contains, besides six long divisions, a long passage of much more value. Here Plato resumes from the *Theaetetus* the puzzles in the notions of not-being, error, and falsehood. He then discovers as many puzzles in the notion of being. He finds difficulties both in the notion of being as many and in the notion of it as one only. He finds that in the battle of giants between materialists and idealists neither side can defend itself. If we say that the real is what we can grasp with our hands, we deny the obvious facts of justice and wisdom and soul. On the other side, if we say that only the Ideas are real, we deny that the real can live or move or think.

Plato believes that he now has a solution of these difficulties. It consists in analysing the way in which we apply many names to the same thing (whereas the theory of Ideas was reached by considering that we apply one name to many things). From the fact that we may call the same man both white and squat and short and brave he develops the doctrine that some pairs of things communicate with each other and others do not, and that some things communicate with everything but most do not. Among the things that communicate with everything are Same and Other; for everything is the same as itself and other than every other thing. But to be other than another thing is *not to be* that other thing. Thus otherness is a kind of not-being; and this kind of not-being is omnipresent, since everything is other than every other thing. Now this is a perfectly respectable kind of not-being, unlike the not-being that has puzzled us; for there is nothing queer about being other than something else. This kind of not-being is not opposite to being but merely other than being. Not-being therefore firmly exists and has its own nature, although **Parmenides** forbade us to say so.

Not merely does not-being exist; it is also shared in by thought and statement, which

therefore admit of being false. That appears as follows. A simple statement consists of a name followed by a verb, as "man learns"; and cannot consist of anything less complicated. It necessarily has a subject and is either true or false. It is false if what it says about its subject is *other* than what is true about its subject. As it really can say, about a really existing subject, something really other and not so as if it were so, it really can be false. False statement is possible. But then false thought is possible; for thought is the same as silent internal statement.

Once in his old age Plato returned to the ethical topics of Socrates and made Socrates his main speaker again. This was in the *Philebus*, an ugly and disappointing but acute and still useful dialogue. It begins with a last statement of his method of division, the most puzzling and least rewarding of them all. It then devotes itself to what appears to be a solution of the problem left open in the *Republic*, namely, what is the Good? The Good must be perfect, adequate, and desired by all who know it. The main contenders for the place are pleasure and knowledge. No one would choose either alone if he could have both; but which is the better? Socrates develops a strange classification of things into the definite, the indefinite, the mixture of these two, and the cause of their mixture; and decides that pleasure falls into the indefinite class but mind falls into that of cause. He then goes into a long and close analysis of pleasure. It is caused by the restoration of living substance. But there are also mental pleasures of expectation. Pleasures are often accompanied by false opinions, and can themselves be false. There is a neutral state of neither pain nor pleasure; and pleasure itself is not the mere absence of pain. The greatest pleasures and pains occur in bad states of the body or soul. States of pleasure mixed with pain can occur in several ways. But there are also true and absolute pleasures. Pleasure cannot be the Good, because it is a genesis, and therefore exists for the sake of something other than itself. In the course of this long psychological analysis of pleasure, Plato has some useful remarks on perception, memory, desire, imagination, envy, comedy and laughter.

He then gives a much shorter analysis of knowledge. He observes that some arts are more exact and mathematical than others. He distinguishes between popular and philosophical arithmetic. Dialectic is the most accurate of all the arts, though perhaps not the most useful. Finally the dialogue returns to the Good. This cannot be either knowledge or pleasure alone, for neither of them is perfect. It must be a mixture of the best of each of them, including all the sciences, and those pleasures that are pure and necessary. In this mixture the most valuable part is beauty and symmetry and truth, and that is the cause of its goodness. Each of these three is more akin to knowledge than to pleasure. Knowledge therefore stands nearer than pleasure to the Good. And we may finally announce the following order of value: measure, beauty, mind, science, pure pleasure.

Another dialogue of Plato's old age, the *Timaeus*, is devoted to the physical world, and offers an elaborate cosmogony, cosmology, physics, chemistry, and human physiology, pathology, and medicine, while at the same time declaring in the manner of the middle dialogues that there can be no science of such matters. For a long time the western world read only this dialogue of Plato's, thus obtaining a very inaccurate impression of him. At all times, however, most of Plato's readers have tended to take his second-best and leave two thirds of his best. They have tended to take his authoritarian politics and his mystical religion of the Ideas with its inclination to unreason. But of his best they have taken only his literary beauty. They have ignored his great lead in the analysis of conceptions, that is, his invention of philosophy in the narrow sense; and they have ignored his magnificent ideal of reasonable thinking and acting. This ideal is presented to us in the person of Socrates; but it is presented only by the writings of Plato. See also **Political Philosophy**.

(R.R.)

**Plotinus** (205–270 A.D.), the originator of the philosophy known in modern times as **neoplatonism**. We know nothing of his background, though the not very reliable fourth-century writer, Eunapius, says that he came from Upper Egypt. His education and cultural background were completely Greek. In 232 he came to Alexandria to study philosophy. He could find no teacher to satisfy him until he was introduced to Ammonius Saccas, with whom he remained for eleven years. Ammonius was a self-taught, non-writing philosopher and we know next to nothing of his teaching, but his influence on Plotinus and his other pupils (who probably included the Christian Origen) was very considerable. In 243 Plotinus started for the East with the Emperor Gordian's expedition, in the hope of learning something about Persian and Indian philosophy. But Gordian was murdered in Mesopotamia in 244 and Plotinus escaped with some difficulty to Antioch, and went from there to Rome. There is no evidence that at this or any other period in his life he acquired any knowledge of Indian thought.

Plotinus spent the rest of his life in Rome teaching philosophy, and after ten years began to write the treatises which were collected by his disciple and editor, Porphyry, into the edition which we know as the *Enneads* (composed of six sets of nine treatises each). Porphyry also wrote his master's life which is our main source of information about Plotinus. It gives a vivid and detailed picture of the man and his method of work at Rome. His method of teaching was informal, based on the reading of **Plato** and **Aristotle** and their commentators, and including a great deal of free and vigorous discussion of difficulties raised by members of his audience; traces of these discussions are to be found in the published treatises.

The philosophy of Plotinus, though professing to be an exposition of the real thought of Plato and owing a great deal to close and critical study of Aristotle and of the Platonists, Pythagoreans and Aristotelians of the century or so before his own time, is in many ways thoroughly original. The primary purpose of his teaching was to lead people – those few who were capable of it – back to the source from which they and all things came, the One or Good, which in giving them being gave also the impulse to return. This required perfect moral purity and the utmost intellectual effort. Those who think that mysticism has nothing to do with virtue or intelligence are not recommended to read the *Enneads*.

It is, then, to show the way back to the ultimate goal, the Good, that Plotinus expounds his view of the nature and structure of reality. The One or Good himself (Plotinus always tends to use the masculine pronoun in speaking of his First Principle) the source or first principle of being is beyond all determination or limitation and so beyond description or definition. Language can only point the way towards him without reaching him. Even the names of One or Good are not adequate descriptions of him. But though he is beyond the reach of language he is by no means mere negation or abstraction. It is because he is more, not less, than any conception we can form of him that he is beyond thought and language. He is present to all according to their capacity to receive him.

From the One or Good reality proceeds in a series of stages of steadily increasing multiplicity, limitation and separation. Its generation from the One is both free, in the sense of being perfectly spontaneous and unconstrained, and necessary, in the sense that it is not conceivable that it should not happen. The Good cannot but be self-diffusive or self-communicative. This is the significance of the metaphor of emanation or radiation (as of light from the sun) which Plotinus often uses, with full consciousness that it is a metaphor. The whole process of production or generation is timeless, and all the stages of reality are eternal. Even the last and lowest, the physical universe, is eternal as a whole, though in the sublunary world its individual parts are continually perishing and being replaced by others. But in the timeless process of generation, at each stage, two elements can be distinguished in thought, one in which the product proceeds from the producer as an unformed potentiality, the other in which it returns upon its source in contemplation and so is formed and actualised by it and gains in its turn (except at the last and lowest stage) the power to produce. This double rhythm of outgoing and return runs through the whole of Plotinus' universe.

The One is beyond being, and the source of being. In the Platonic language of Plotinus "being" cannot be used by itself except to denote the sum or totality of beings, and there is no such thing as indeterminate or unlimited being. True

being for Plotinus is the first level of reality which proceeds from the One, the Divine Intellect which is also the totality of Platonic Forms or Ideas. In this Divine Intellect thought and its content are one, and the Ideas are themselves living intelligences, so that it can be regarded as either a unity-in-diversity of Forms or a unity-in-diversity of minds, each of which thinks and so is the whole. In terms of our consciousness Intellect is the level of intuitive thought which is identical with its object and does not see it as in some sense external to it. The Forms of Intellect are, as in Plato, the archetypes of the quasi-realities of the world of the senses. They are finite in number, though infinite in productive power. Plotinus, in those of his writings where he considers the question most carefully, makes an important departure from Plato in admitting individual as well as universal Forms, a Form of Socrates as well as a Form of Man, an admission which he reconciles with the traditional doctrine that the Forms are finite in number by adopting the **Stoic** idea of cyclic world periods, repeating themselves endlessly in every detail.

From Intellect proceeds Soul, the active principle which forms and orders the visible universe. Its characteristic intellectual activity is discursive thought. Time is the life of the soul in this discursive motion. But Soul in Plotinus has a very wide range. At its highest it is fully illuminated and formed by Intellect and raised to its level: and it has a lower phase (which Plotinus often calls Nature) which is the immanent animating principle of the material universe and all animal and plant life within it (and indeed of the life which Plotinus recognizes in things which we should regard as inorganic). From Nature come the forms of bodies, the lowest and weakest of realities, incapable of further production. All levels of soul from the lowest to the highest are permanently present in us and we have to choose whether we will remain on the level of the lower soul, immersed in the concerns of body, or whether we wake to the consciousness of the higher realities present in us.

For Plotinus the material universe is a living organic whole, bound together by that universal sympathy in which his contemporaries, philosophers and magicians alike, believed. Plotinus himself believed in the reality of magic, but since it could not affect the higher life of the soul, it was of no importance to him. Matter itself, though it proceeds like all else from the Good, is the principle of evil because it is the absolute limit, the utter negation and deficiency of being that marks the end of the descent from the Good through the successive levels of reality. But the material universe for Plotinus, though affected (at least in the regions below the moon; celestial matter is not evil for Plotinus) by the evil of its materiality, is good and beautiful as a living structure of forms and the best possible work of soul, and Plotinus' attitude to it is by no means merely negative or pessimistic, as was that of the Gnostics whom he detested and vigorously attacked.

The direct and indirect influence of Plotinus on the Christian theologians of the fourth and following centuries was considerable, as was his influence later on the philosophy of Islam. The indirect influence on Christian thought continued throughout the Middle Ages in the West; and the publication of Ficino's Latin translation of the *Enneads* in 1492, and of the *editio princeps* of the Greek text in 1580 made Plotinian Neoplatonism an important influence on the thought of the Renaissance. The philosophical changes of the seventeenth century led to a decrease in the influence of Plotinus; the last group of philosophers who were deeply influenced by his thought were the **Cambridge Platonists**.

(A.H.A.)

**Political Economy** is a school of social theory created in the eighteenth century by James Stuart and Adam **Smith**. It describes how the mechanisms of a modern commercial society ought to ensure that the uncoordinated activities of individuals pursuing their private interests will automatically maximize the wealth of a nation, without any need for political intervention. Ruskin and other romantic anti-capitalists denounced political economy as "a lie"; but **Marx** respected it enough to devote his theoretical energies to providing a "critique" of it.

[J.R.]

**Political Philosophy.** The term "political philosophy" can be used loosely to cover almost any abstract thought about law, politics, and society, particularly if it addresses normative questions about the way in which political power should be used or the way citizens should behave. Thus, democratic theory, jurisprudence, political morality, **applied ethics**, social theory, and **political economy** have all been thought of as parts of political philosophy. A political philosopher might study subjects as diverse as punishment, representation, feminism, private property, judicial review, economic inequality, civil disobedience, rational choice, and the morality of abortion. In these and similar areas, people who think of themselves primarily as philosophers have become immersed in recent times in the study of what we may call "public affairs", and they have contributed to a large body of literature in which the issues and controversies of public life are debated and discussed.

Behind this concern with public issues, however, there is a deeper and more abstract agenda which defines political philosophy as a branch of philosophy proper. That agenda consists in the traditional questions that have dominated the subject since **Plato**'s time. What is the state? What is society? What is the human individual? How are they related to one another? Is a society greater than the sum of its individual parts? Is the state just a social construction or a construction of individuals, or does it have an irreducible reality of its own? Unless these questions are addressed, the study of "public affairs" is bound to remain superficial. Apart from anything else, we need to be able to answer these questions before we can say with any confidence what makes an issue "public" or "political", what it is for something to be an issue or a concern for a whole society as opposed to an issue or concern for some of the individuals who make it up.

Philosophical questions about the relation between society and the individual spring from a deep paradox in our thinking. On the one hand, it is beyond question that each of us is the product of a particular society: I do not make myself; I owe everything I have, including my sense of self, to the community and culture in which I live. On the other hand, as soon as I start thinking or reflecting on society and the way it has constituted me, I appear to be doing so *as an individual,* and my own thoughts, preferences and purposes seem more real to me than the community in which they were fashioned. Society may have made me, but what it has made is something that can regard society as separate from itself.

The two sides of this paradox mark a fundamental division in political thought. If we take society as our point of reference and regard the individual as derivative, then our values and ideals will be defined in terms of forms of communal life. We will not, of course, be unconcerned with individual men and women, but we will value their aspirations and fulfilments strictly as part of an overall communal ideal. However, if we take the individual as our fundamental point of reference, then community will appear valuable only as a means to the goals and ideals that individuals have adopted as their own. We may still think it desirable that one person's behaviour should be constrained by respect for others. But it will be respect for the interests of the other *individuals,* rather than a respect for social life as such.

Individualists differ about the nature and importance of individuality. For **Hobbes,** the individual is a voracious consumer of utilities, driven inevitably into deadly competition with his fellows. For others, in the tradition of Immanuel **Kant,** man is better conceived as a moral being, autonomously pursuing goodness as he happens to conceive it. Such a being still has needs which must be fulfilled and ideals which may be better pursued depending on the resources at his disposal. But he aims to *make* something of his life, not simply engage in accumulation and consumption for their own sake. It is arguable that principles of individual *liberty* and *rights* are much easier to defend from this second perspective than from the first, for there seems nothing intrinsically important about the unimpeded motion of a utility-seeker. Still, philosophers in the individualist tradition have been wary of tying the value of freedom too closely to the idea of striving after goodness. That may lead to the illiberal conclusion – sometimes described as "positive liberty" – that freedom to do wrong is

not worth having or not worth fighting for. And it would move them uncomfortably close to the communitarian version of that idea – that true freedom involves submerging oneself in the life of a well-ordered society.

It is perhaps easier to maintain that man is essentially a *social* animal than that he is a *political* animal, for law, politics, and the state seem to be artificial constructions in a way that basic human sociability is not. When we talk about *politics,* we seem to be talking about the way people come together deliberately to express their sense of how society should be run and to articulate their differences; and we are talking about the relatively formal practices and institutions of debate and conflict that make this expression possible. Because it has this formal and artificial character, both individualists and communitarians may view the realm of politics as something derivative, to be judged in terms of more fundamental values and ideas that are not themselves political.

One way of approaching the matter is to think of the social and political structure of a society as something which people design, as an architect designs a building, and hence as answerable to the "specifications" that such a designer might have in mind. The earliest example of this type of thinking is found in Books II and III of Plato's *Republic,* where justice is thought of as the idea of order and harmony that would guide the founding of a new colony or the institution of a new society.

In Plato's approach, both the social designer and the specifications he is guided by are thought of as external to the society he is constructing. That approach can be contrasted with the more individualistic view of politics as artifice expressed in the theory of the **social contract,** propounded by thinkers like Hobbes and **Locke.** Here political society is taken to be designed by the very people who are to live in it, and the specifications for the design are not derived from any transcendent ideal but are simply their individual needs and purposes. The state is thought of as the product of an agreement among men to remedy certain problems that arise for them when large numbers of individuals, each with his own interests and concerns, try to make lives for themselves in circumstances of moderate scarcity. On this account, government and law do not come naturally to us, but we agree to set them up so that each of us can realize gains from cooperation and mutual forbearance that would otherwise be unobtainable. This agreement then provides an artificial basis for political authority: it legitimizes institutions like legislatures and courts, it obligates each contracting party to respect the decisions of those institutions, and it places limits on what can be done with state power.

There are, however, a couple of well-known difficulties with the social contract view. First, though everyone gains from cooperation, an individual may do even better for himself if he defects from a cooperative arrangement while others do not. The contractarian, like every other political philosopher, has to find some response to the question posed by Plato in the *Republic*: "What advantage is there in being just?" Secondly, even if it can be shown to be rational to keep one's agreements, it is implausible to claim that any of us has ever *actually* agreed to abide by the principles of the state. In fact, most of us were never given the opportunity; the social contract seems to be an elaborate fantasy. And if it is just a fantasy, it is hard to see how it can provide any actual basis for political obligation.

These worries have led people to try and express the individualist approach in other ways. If we take individual values as the basis of political evaluation, surely we can simply ask how well a given set of institutions serves those values now. We don't have to assume that it was set up for that purpose; the question is whether we should alter it or abolish it. Of course, that is not a straightforward question, for a given set of institutions may serve some individuals better than others. **Utilitarianism** is the theory that we should maximize the existence of whatever we take to be valuable: if individual satisfaction is valuable, we should seek to promote a set of social arrangements that satisfy as many individual preferences as possible. Other theories take *equality* as their basic value, or stress that certain interests – in liberty or basic well-being – should have priority as matters of right over ordinary utility.

For much of this century, it seemed that this more direct approach to social and political evaluation was preferred to the social contract approach. The publication in 1971 of John **Rawls'** book, *A Theory of Justice*, however, heralded a revival of interest in contractarianism. Rawls argued that one could use the image of the social contract as a theoretical or intellectual device for expressing the force of certain individualist values, particularly non-utilitarian ones. As much as any critic of the contract idea, he conceded that society was not actually a voluntary arrangement. Nevertheless, he thought that by asking, "What basis for institution-building *would* people have agreed to, if (contrary to fact) they had come together to settle terms for cooperation instead of having institutions thrust upon them?", we could come up with answers that were, in some sense, impartial *between* individuals, while retaining the image of the consent of each and every individual as our fundamental point of orientation. Rawls' answer to this question – his principles of liberty and economic equality – have not been universally accepted, but his book has had an enormous influence in setting the modern agenda for political philosophy in the English-speaking world. It has initiated an intense discussion of the basis of social justice, liberty, equality, rights, and – most recently – community, which has dominated the subject ever since.

Among those who regard the state as an artificial construction, not all view it in individualist terms. **Marx** for example maintained that though man is naturally social there is nothing natural about political life. Rather, politics is the institutional expression of class struggle, the state serving to maintain the conditions for the economic dominance of one class and the orderly exploitation of others. Many Marxists maintain that, with the overcoming of class struggle, the need for a specially organized apparatus of power, superimposed on the forms of society, will gradually "wither away".

Other philosophers have taken an even more jaundiced view of the state than this. In the anarchist tradition, the institutions of state and law have always been thought disruptive of social and moral life. Either the state is seen as a coercive

251

order superimposed on what would otherwise be a well-functioning social organism. Or it is seen as an order which, in the force it uses and in the obsessive sense of obligation it evokes, precludes and interferes with the exercise of autonomous moral judgment by the individual. Either way, it is seen as a structure of force, representing an attempt by some faction in society or some gang of individuals to gain the upper hand over others.

So far we have discussed those approaches which seek to explain the state in terms of something else – as the embodiment of some ideal, as an instrument for the fulfilment of individual interests, as a crystallization of class conflict, or as an excrescence of power. On the other side are those philosophies which accord the state and politics reality and moral significance in their own right, and which use this as their point of reference for thinking about justice and political obligation.

In modern times, the most striking theory of this kind has been that of **Hegel** and of the English idealists who followed him like T. H. **Green**. According to Hegel, the institutions of the state embody the reality of human consciousness. In the life of an individual, consciousness is something incomplete, but in the life of the state it attains what Hegel calls "final unity" and "universality": "Since the state is mind objectified, it is only as one of its members that the individual himself has objectivity, genuine individuality, and an ethical life." From this perspective, patriotism, legality, and the performance of social duty take on aspects quite different from what they have in an instrumental, individualist tradition.

Between the individualism of the social contract and the collectivism of Hegel are theories like those of **Aristotle** and Jean-Jacques **Rousseau** which see in political life a possibility of transforming man from an animal dominated by its natural desires into a genuinely moral being. Rousseau, like the anarchists, was profoundly sceptical about existing political forms. But he held open the prospect that active participation in the democratic life of a small-scale polity might still "enlarge" and "ennoble" the human spirit.

Aristotle's theory was expressed slightly differently. "Man is by nature a political animal," he said, "It is his nature to live in a state." He argued that man was naturally fitted for political life by his ability to engage in discourse about the good, to reach conclusions in ethics that would be impossible for individuals to reach on their own, and to live in a society with others on the basis of a shared and articulate view of right and wrong, just and unjust.

This Aristotelian view of society as essentially a *moral* community has always been worrying to liberal individualists, who stress the diversity of moral conceptions and argue for political structures which are, as far as possible, *neutral* between rival accounts of what makes life worth living. Liberalism is in part the product of an attempt to disengage the state from the enforcement of virtue (not to mention religious belief). It should be clear, nevertheless, that liberal arguments, however well-founded, are not themselves "neutral" between different views of political morality. We have seen that political philosophy is still largely a debate about the basis on which judgments and evaluations are to be made in the political realm. Respect for the moral autonomy of the individual is one possible basis, but it has to be one that can defend itself against the rival claims of Aristotelian, communitarian, and collectivist approaches to politics.

[J.J.W.]

**Popper**, Sir Karl R. (1902– ), born and educated in Vienna, taught in New Zealand and later in London. His major contributions have been to the **philosophy of science**. Although he never subscribed to the early **phenomenalist** tendencies of the **Vienna Circle** or to the instrumentalist interpretation of scientific theory professed by some adherents of logical empiricism, the general orientation of his thought is similar to that associated with this philosophical movement.

In his first book, *The Logic of Scientific Discovery* (1935), Popper defined scientific statements as ones which deny that something logically conceivable is actually realized. Accordingly, for a statement to be counted as scientific it was not sufficient that there should be confirmatory observational evidence for it; it was essential that such a statement should be capable of being disproved by some conceivable spatio-temporally located event exemplifying a possibility which the statement excludes. It is this feature of its statements that Popper thinks demarcates science from non-science. He therefore proposes an amended version of the relative frequency notion of **probability**, in order to make such probability statements refutable and so scientific; but he also outlines a conception of logical probability which, unlike the frequency notion, he believes to be relevant for the task of assessing evidence for a hypothesis. (See **Carnap.**) In addition, the book contains a vigorous critique of **Bacon**'s view of scientific procedure (which he calls "inductionism"), and argues that it is the use of the hypothetico-deductive method which is distinctive of modern science. These themes are developed further in the essays comprising *Conjectures and Refutations* (1963).

Popper is perhaps better known as the author of *The Open Society and Its Enemies* (1945). Although it contains many reflections on the logic of science, the book is primarily a thoroughgoing criticism of social philosophies (in particular, those of **Plato, Hegel** and **Marx**) which minimize the efficacy of individual human effort and subscribe to a belief in laws of inevitable historical development. In opposition to such philosophies, Popper advocates piecemeal social engineering as the sound scientific approach to social problems. Popper pursued this argument further in *The Poverty of Historicism* (1957). See also **Philosophy of Science, Relativism.**

(E.N.)

**Porphyry,** *see* Neoplatonism, Plotinus.

**Positivism.** "Positivism" is the name given (*a*) to the doctrine and movement founded in the nineteenth century by the French philosopher Auguste **Comte** (1798–1857), and (*b*) to the general philosophical view of which Comte's Positivism is only one instance. Positivism in the broader sense (referred to in this article with a small p) is the view that since all genuine knowledge is based on sense experience and can only be advanced by means of observation and experiment, metaphysical or speculative attempts to gain knowledge by reason unchecked by experience should be abandoned in favour of the special sciences. All positivists hold that the task of philosophy is to understand the methods by which the sciences are advanced but not to seek for any independent knowledge of the world. They often argue that as soon as means have been found for advancing knowledge of a subject, it ceases to belong to philosophy and becomes a separate science, or a part of one.

Francis **Bacon**, who considered himself the "trumpeter" of the new sciences which were becoming detached from philosophy in the sixteenth and seventeenth centuries, may be regarded as the source both of positivism and of the name that was given to it in the nineteenth century. In his *On Principles and Origins* (1623–24) he refers to an ancient legend according to which Cupid was the oldest of the gods and existed at the beginning of things alone with Chaos. Cupid, according to this myth, had no parents, and Chaos no beginning. Bacon interprets the absence of parents to mean the absence of any cause, and surmised that by "Chaos" was meant the ultimate matter from which all material things are formed. This ultimate matter, he writes "is a thing positive and inexplicable and must be taken absolutely as it is found, and not to be judged by any previous conception". It is improper, he says, "to require or imagine a cause when we come to the ultimate force and positive law of nature. . . . For nothing has corrupted philosophy so much as this seeking after the parents of Cupid; that is, that philosophers have not taken the principles of things as they are found in nature, and accepted them as a positive doctrine resting on the faith of experiences; but they have rather deduced them from the laws of disputation, the petty conclusions of logic and mathematics, common notions, and such wanderings of the mind beyond the limits of nature."

Bacon here gives expression to a number of important items of the positivist doctrine. He rejects the idea of "deducing" the ultimate facts of nature. He believes that philosophers should not attempt to wander beyond "the limits of nature". He thinks that there are ultimate facts that should be approached without any "previous conception". He warns against a too enthusiastic search for causes. He says that there are ultimate facts that should be accepted "on the faith of experience". When he applies the adjective "positive" to these "inexplicable" facts and to the doctrines based on them, he is not using the word in the sense in which it is opposed to "negative", but in the sense in which positive religion (consisting of revealed doctrines, accepted by faith, and not proveable by reason) is opposed to natural religion (the doctrines of which are established by rational proof), or in which positive law (laid down by specific authorities for particular populations) is opposed to natural law (held to be rationally apprehended and independent of the will of legislators). Probably as a result of Bacon's usage – Bacon was much admired by the eighteenth-century empiricist philosophers both in England and in France – the adjective "positive" came to be applied to the methods of the natural sciences in respect of their reliance on observation and use of experiment. Saint-Simon, whom Comte later served as secretary, in his *Essay on the Sciences of Man* (1813) applies the word "positive" to the sciences which are based on "facts which have been observed and analysed". The sciences which are not so based Saint-Simon calls "conjectural". Comte himself uses the word in this sense in an article entitled *Plan of the Scientific Works necessary for the Reorganisation of Society* which was published under Saint-Simon's auspices in 1822. He later brought it to full prominence in the title of his major work, *Course on the Positive Philosophy* (1830–42). Comte here explains that he used the word "positive" to emphasize his view that the function of theories is to co-ordinate observed facts rather than to explain in terms of causes. It is Comte's "Positive Philosophy" which later came to be called "Positivism", a name which Comte welcomed but did not himself invent.

Comte's Positivism can best be understood in terms of his famous Law of the Three Stages according to which the human mind advances from a theological stage through a metaphysical

stage to the final positive stage. At the theological stage the attempt is made to penetrate to the inner nature of things and to explain their behaviour in terms of supernatural beings. At the metaphysical stage, which is really only a sophisticated modification of the earlier one, explanations are given in terms of abstractions, essences or forces, which, on Comte's view, are nothing but depersonalized deities. As examples of this mode of thought Comte cites the physical doctrine of the ether, the chemical doctrine of affinities, and the biological doctrine of vital spirits. At the final, positive stage the attempt to penetrate to the inner nature of things and to discover the origin and destination of the universe is abandoned. Instead, the positive thinker tries to establish, by means of reasonings based on observations, the invariable co-existences and sequences of phenomena. It was Comte's view that all the sciences pass through these stages, as for example, astronomy in its development from sun-worship and astrology, and chemistry in its development from alchemy. Like Bacon, Comte emphasized the enhanced power over nature that the advance of science brings with it.

Comte's Positivism, however, was much more than a philosophy of science and an account of intellectual development. Comte held that the time must come when human society itself is studied by the positive methods. He called this positive science "sociology" and sought to lay its foundations in the *Course on Positive Philosophy* and later writings. It was his view that to each of the three stages of intellectual development, the theological, metaphysical and positive, there corresponded forms of society and social outlook. There is the theological social outlook in which there is respect for tradition and authority upheld by priestly learning. Metaphysical criticisms of the traditional doctrines bring with them an era of social criticism when such unverifiable doctrines prevail as belief in natural rights and the sovereignty of the people. In Europe this was the era of the Reformation and the French Revolution. With the advance of positive social science the negative and sterile disputation of the revolutionary era would be replaced by a stable society where agreement is established on the basis of incontrovertible social knowledge.

A new form of authority would then reside in a new spiritual power consisting of men of science whose knowledge would enable humanity to achieve a peaceful unity of thought and action. In his later years Comte elaborated this part of his doctrine into a Religion of Humanity, of which some account is given above (pp. 63–4). Some of the most eminent of his early supporters such as Littré in France and George Eliot and J. S. **Mill** in England refused to follow him in this. Nevertheless, Positivist Societies were established in various parts of the world on the model of that which Comte himself had founded in 1848. In these Humanity was the object of ceremonial worship, and sociology was taken as the warrant for sociolatry. The movement was particularly strong in Latin America, but flourished for many years in England, mainly in London and Liverpool. Leaders of the movement here were Richard Congreve, who resigned his fellowship at Oxford in order to devote himself to its promotion, and Frederick Harrison. *The Positivist Review*, later called *Humanity*, was published from 1893 until 1925. An attempt was made to revive Positivism in England, just after the Second World War.

Both the theoretical side e of Comte's Positivism and positivism in the more general sense are natural growths in the age of scientific advance. Bacon may be regarded not only as the first positivist, but also as the forerunner of Comte's ceremonial Positivism, since in *The New Atlantis* he writes in some detail of a cult of great men. Positivism has formed a part of the empiricist tradition in philosophy. Thus **Hume** argued that all genuine human knowledge is concerned either with matters of fact or with logic and mathematics – called by Hume "relations of ideas". The latter kind of knowledge is certain. It has that character of not being otherwise thinkable which philosophers call "necessity". But no mathematical or logical reasoning, can, on its own, tell us anything about the nature of the world. Its conclusions are, in that regard, as Bacon said, "petty". Knowledge of matters of fact, on the other hand, is knowledge about what is in the world. To that extent it is not "petty". But such knowledge can never have the certainty and necessity of logic and mathematics. We can

always conceive of the facts of the world as different from what they actually are, and there is no means of proving that the world must have been as it is. But this is just what metaphysical philosophers have tried to prove. They have claimed to provide knowledge of the world which has all the necessity of mathematics. But this is confusion. On the one hand there is knowledge of matters of fact – of how things are and which things accompany which others. And on the other hand there is logic and mathematics which are not about the world at all. All the books which fall into neither of these categories can contain nothing but "sophistry and illusion".

This view was very widely held in the nineteenth century, especially by men of science. It was not, hoowever, strongly represented in the universities, where various forms of Idealist metaphysics prevailed. But in the twenties of the twentieth century Hume's positivist arguments were revived and strengthened. It was now argued that a form of words that expressed neither a verifiable matter of fact nor a truth of logic or mathematics was meaningless. The field of what is meaningful contains only what is in principle verifiable or what is a mere matter of logic. This criterion excludes most of the things said in books on metaphysics which are therefore not false but without sense. This view is known as **logical positivism**.

Positivism gets much of its strength from the contrast between the continuous and agreed progress which has been achieved in the natural sciences since the time of Galileo, and the situation of deadlock and disagreement that has at all times obtained in metaphysical philosophy. This seems to suggest that in the special sciences a fruitful method has been employed, whereas metaphysical philosophers have got lost in an intellectual impasse. Comte and the earlier positivists argued that metaphysical problems are beyond the power of man to solve. The Logical Positivists of our own day have argued that when verifiability is taken as a criterion of meaning, the problems of metaphysics are seen to be mere pseudo-problems which remain unsolved not because they are difficult but because they have no sense. The weakness of all types of positivism is the assumption that there are facts, each distinct from every other, which observation and experiment can reveal and correlate. When they attempt to explain what these facts are, positivists give as widely different answers as the metaphysicians. Bacon's "simple natures", Hume's "impressions", and the "atomic facts" of twentieth-century positivists raise theoretical problems which are as elusive as those of self-confessed metaphysicians.

(H.B.A.)

**Post-modernism.** The word "post-modern" gained currency in architectural criticism in the 1950s and 1960s, where it designated a movement away from the shiny machine-like austerity of the "International Style": soon it was extended to apply to reactions against **modernism** in other branches of art as well.

In the 1970s the term was adopted within philosophy as a rough synonym for deconstruction (see **Derrida**) and post-structuralism (see **structuralism**). Philosophical post-modernism has two aspects: it is a reaction against both modernism and **modernity**. According to its most prominent advocate, Jean-François Lyotard, the essence of post-modernism is a carefree scepticism about every possible attempt to make sense of history. It anarchically rejects all the "meta-narratives" of progress – whether Marxist or liberal – by reference to which modernity and modernism have identified themselves (see *The Post-modern Condition*, 1979).

However, the fact that modernism is itself acutely critical of modernity threatens the coherence of the whole project of philosophical post-modernism. Moreover, the post-modernist desire to escape the superstitions of a preceding epoch is not so much a break with traditional modernity, as a repetition of its oldest refrain. Post-modernism has encountered formidable criticism in **Habermas'** *Philosophical Discourse of Modernity* (1985).

[J.R.]

**Post-structuralism,** *see* Structuralism.

**Pragmatism.** The word "pragmatism" was very little used in the English language, and not at all in philosophical contexts, until it was introduced by the American philosopher C. S. **Peirce** in 1878 as the name of a logical maxim for determining the meaning of words which he had formulated. In his own words, Peirce offered the rule: "Consider what effects, which might conceivably have practical bearings, we conceive the object of our conception to have. Then our conception of these effects is the whole of our conception of the object"; alternatively Peirce said that pragmatism was "the theory that a conception, that is, the rational purport of a word or other expression, lies exclusively in its conceivable bearing upon the conduct of life; so that, since obviously nothing that might not result from experiment can have any direct bearing upon conduct, if one can define accurately all the conceivable experimental phenomena which the affirmation or denial of a concept could imply, one will have therein a complete definition of the concept, and there is absolutely nothing more in it". Thus if we wish to determine the meaning of the word "hard" we should consider the experimental phenomena which would be implied by saying of something that it was hard, such as that it would scratch most things and few would scratch it – which is therefore part of the meaning of "hard". Undoubtedly this doctrine has, and was intended by Peirce to have, important consequences, such as that "almost every proposition of ontological metaphysics is either meaningless gibberish… or else downright absurd". But it is important to realize that Peirce took "pragmatism" as a name for a special maxim for getting clear about the meanings of words and not for a complete philosophical position; being a confirmed coiner of technical terms he would have been quite as willing to subscribe to "synechism" and "fallibilism" as to "pragmatism". Above all, Peirce certainly did not regard his pragmatic maxim as being in any way a theory of truth but of meaning; to him it seemed evident that truth consisted in correspondence between statement and fact.

But very early the word "pragmatism" was borrowed by other philosophers who gave it new and vaguer meanings; so much was this so that Peirce wrote that "to serve the precise purpose of expressing the original definition, he begs to announce the birth of the word 'pragmaticism', which is ugly enough to be safe from kidnappers". The earliest philosophers thus to borrow and distort the concept of pragmatism were William **James**, F. C. S. **Schiller** and John **Dewey**; what they have in common with each other is first and foremost a theory about truth which has since been regarded as the essence of pragmatism. In his *Pragmatism* James said that "ideas become true just so far as they help us to get into satisfactory relations with other parts of our experience" and that "the true is the name of whatever proves itself to be good in the way of belief". If we wish to find the connexion of this view with that of Peirce it perhaps comes out in the following quotation: "Pragmatism... asks its usual question. Grant an idea or belief to be true", it says, "what concrete difference will its being true make in one's actual life? How will the truth be realized? What experiences will be different from those which would obtain if the belief were false? What, in short, is the truth's cash-value in experiential terms?". The superficial similarity here to the words of Peirce is obvious but the position utterly different; the doctrine that the meaning of an hypothesis can be determined by considering its experimental consequences is conflated with the doctrine that the true is the good in the way of belief to yield the conclusion that the true is what has good experimental consequences.

The notion of pragmatism has become particularly connected with this doctrine about truth, partly owing to the controversies between James, Dewey and Schiller on the one side and **Russell** on the other. The gravamen of Russell's attack is that the pragmatists have confused the meaning of "true" with the criteria that we may use for deciding whether a belief is true and have thereby surrendered to an irrationalist position; two of his most important articles are "Pragmatism" and "James' Conception of Truth" which are printed in *Philosophical Essays*. Largely as a result of Russell's attacks Dewey simply abandoned the use of the word "true" and claimed that it could be adequately replaced by a notion of "warranted assertibility".

Lying behind this view about truth is the conviction of James and Schiller that everything must be understood in the light of human purpose, including thought; thoughts are but tools by which human beings try to achieve ends and they must be judged by their efficiency in subserving these ends; thus beliefs are tools for dealing with experience and must be judged as such. From this "pragmatism" has come to be a name for any position which lays emphasis on results as a test of satisfactoriness. The sense which Peirce, its inventor, gave to the word "pragmatism" is now obsolete except in historical discussion of Peirce.

(J.O.U.)

**Predestination,** *see* Freedom of the Will, Determinism.

**Prescriptivism**: the doctrine, derived from **Kant** and revived by **Hare**, that ethical judgments are essentially commands or imperatives, rather than representations of facts. See **Ethics**.

**Pre-Socratics.** The term "Pre-Socratics" refers to a dozen or so of the earliest Greek thinkers, down to the time of **Socrates**, who attempted to define the constitution of the world and the nature of reality. They range from **Thales**, active in the early sixth century B.C., to **Democritus** in the latter part of the fifth. The earliest Pre-Socratics came from Ionia, the Greek colonization area in the centre of the west coast of Asia minor. City-states like Miletus were materially prosperous in the first half of the sixth century B.C. and in close contact through trade with the foreign cultures of Egypt and Lydia (and so with Babylonia) as well as with the Greek colonies of the Black Sea and the west. In addition, Ionia was itself heir to an old literary culture going back beyond Homer. These conditions encouraged the surge of speculative thought in Miletus, Ephesus, Colophon and Samos. The interest in philosophy soon spread overseas: **Pythagoras** migrated from Samos to one of the Greek colonies of Southern Italy, while **Xenophanes** wandered all over the Greek world. **Parmenides** and **Zeno** were natives of Elea in south-west Italy: **Empedocles** belonged

257

to Acragas in Sicily. Thus most of the Pre-Socratics belonged either in the east or the west of the Greek world, and Athens became involved only when **Anaxagoras** moved there from Ionia in the seventies of the fifth century B.C.

In spite of their differences from each other the Pre-Socratics form a logical, not merely a chronological, category. Socrates turned Greek speculative thought in a totally new direction by rejecting physics and concentrating on ethical questions. Except for the **sophists,** in whose tradition Socrates in this respect belonged, earlier *philosophoi* or "lovers of wisdom" had subordinated human problems to the assessment of external physical reality. Thus those whom we term Pre-Socratics were called by **Aristotle** "investigators of nature", *physiologoi*: for they studied the *physis*, the nature or constitution, of things as a whole. Many of them had more specialized physical interests too; indeed some of the earlier ones, like the Milesians Thales and **Anaximander**, were men of many-sided intelligence who won fame with their contemporaries not for their theoretical accounts of reality, which in some cases may have been of only incidental importance even to their authors, but for their ability to solve practical problems like the measurement of the distance of a ship at sea, the transport of an army over a river, or the accurate delimitation of the seasons. All the Pre-Socratics tried to describe the nature of the heavenly bodies; some, Thales and Pythagoras most conspicuously, had special mathematical interests apart from astronomy; Empedocles, Anaxagoras and Diogenes of Apollonia were concerned with medicine and embryology; and most of them seem to have attacked notorious natural problems like the causes of earthquakes, of rainbows, of magnetism, or of the flooding of the Nile. It is important not to overlook this strong practical interest, combined as it surprisingly was with a quite unempirical dogmatism when it came to dealing with larger problems of the nature of the world. What gave these men the right to be considered as philosophers, unlike the other astronomers, geographers and doctors who were active especially in the latter half of the period, was their common assumption that the world possessed some kind of integral unity

and determinability which could be understood and explained in rational terms.

The first part of this assumption can be seen in earlier quasi-mythological cosmogonies and theogonies; but it was the treatment of these problems in straightforward descriptive terms and the rejection of personification that gave Thales and his successors, for later Greeks as for us, the title of "philosopher".

Although they abandoned much of the mythological language, the Pre-Socratics continued to be affected at certain points by pre-philosophical assumptions. Thales, in declaring that all things came from water, was probably giving rationalistic expression to a partly mythopoeic Egyptian idea, paralleled also in Babylonia, that the world had arisen from Nun the goddess of primeval waters; though this was itself a reflexion of the annual re-appearance of the earth as the Nile recedes. A more important debt to myth appears in the central presupposition that the world is coherent and intelligible, is somehow a unity in spite of the diversity of its appearance. This presupposition formulated itself in the anthropomorphic *genetical* tendencies of traditional mythology. Thus in the Hesiodic *Theogony*, a poem put together perhaps in the early seventh century B.C., the family of gods is traced back to the very beginning of the world, when Gaia, mother earth, together with the different parts of the underworld, appears as the first distinct cosmological entity out of an originative gulf called *Chaos* (which means, not confusion, but simply "gap"). At the same time Eros or sexual love, the anthropomorphic motive for further differentiation, comes on the scene. Gaia gives birth to the male sky-god, Ouranos, also to mountains and the inner seas; then sky-god and earth-goddess mate together to produce the encircling river that connects them, Okeanos. Further generation takes place from these same parents; according to other accounts rain is the seed of sky which fertilizes earth so as to produce plants and crops. This quasi-mythological cosmogony is complicated by confusions produced by the synthesis in the *Theogony* of several different versions. A cruder and more completely mythopoeic story which occurs later in the poem, according to which

Ouranos lies continuously with Gaia and refuses to allow her to bring forth offspring until he is mutilated by Kronos, probably represents a more primitive version by which the original *chaos* or gap was that produced by the initial separation of earth and sky. At all events the mythological idea that different components of the world are connected with deities who have a traceable ancestry, as human beings have, led on to the view that the world as a whole can be derived from a single ancestor or pair of ancestors – for example earth, or earth and sky. This assumption deeply affected the earlier Pre-Socratics, who for the Gaia or *Chaos* of Hesiod substituted a single originative material like the water of Thales or the air or mist of **Anaximenes**. Even where cosmogony was rejected – as for example by **Heraclitus**, who declared that the world-order was made by neither gods nor men, but had existed always – the assumption of an essential unity and determinability in the world was retained. This important general presupposition, the reasons for which were not discussed by the Greeks themselves, was presumably also due in part to the observation of natural regularities, of the sun, the seasons and so on, which encouraged the comfortable belief that the world worked in accordance with laws not completely unlike those which ordered human societies. The narrower view of the main natural constituents as divine people with a single remote ancestor was a more specialized manifestation of this anthropomorphic approach.

The survival of anthropomorphism can also be seen in the devices used by some Pre-Socratics to account for the ultimate source of physical change. The Eros or sexual love of Hesiod found its counterpart in the idea of legal retribution in Anaximander, of war or strife in Heraclitus, or of love and strife in Empedocles. Indeed, less primitive thinkers have had to fall back on metaphor here; for example Aristotle used Eros to explain how the Prime Mover can move without being moved. Two other points at which the Pre-Socratics were influenced by inherited pre-philosophical assumptions were in their conceptions of divinity and of the soul. To a large extent they had abandoned the traditional Olympian pantheon. Yet they all retained the idea that what was all-powerful and indestructible was divine; thus the Milesians seem to have applied this description to their primary kinds of matter. As for soul, its constitution was largely ignored by the earliest Pre-Socratics; but for the Pythagoreans, Heraclitus and Empedocles it served as a physical link between man and the outside world. These thinkers were reinterpreting the popular idea that the soul is related to *aither*, the material of the pure upper air and of the stars. At the same time confusion was caused in Pre-Socratic psychology by failure to distinguish perception and intelligence or mind; here the effects are evident of the influential but inconsistent treatment of soul in Homer, where *psyche* meant sometimes life-stuff, sometimes consciousness-stuff, and sometimes intelligence.

## I. SOURCES

Before summarizing the main development of Pre-Socratic thought it must be emphasized that our knowledge of these thinkers is very incomplete. We do not possess anything like the intact works of any Pre-Socratic. What we have is in the form of short isolated fragments, varying in length from one word to a few sentences, which have survived through being quoted by later authors of antiquity. Of the Milesians there is almost nothing – a phrase or a sentence of each; of Pythagoras nothing; of Heraclitus just over a hundred genuine sayings, mostly very short (the longest consists of fifty-five words). There remain about one hundred and fifty hexameter lines of Parmenides, about three hundred and forty of Empedocles; this, little as it is, may have formed something over a third of the original works, which were probably quite brief. Of Anaxagoras we possess about a score of fragments amounting to approximately a thousand words in all; these form probably not less than an eighth and not more than a half of his original book. Of Democritus, known to have been an extremely prolific writer, only between two and three hundred fragments survive, nearly all of an ethical character and largely irrelevant to his more unusual physical theories. Extracts from original works are, of course, only one source of information about the ideas of a dead thinker, and we rely heavily for our knowledge of the Pre-Socratics upon summaries and commentaries made by historians of thought in ancient times. Thus **Plato** himself made brief incidental judgments, many of them of a humorous or ironical kind, upon some of his predecessors – Heraclitus, Parmenides and Anaxagoras in particular. Plato seems to have taken Pythagoreanism seriously, but used most of the other Pre-Socratics as symbols for various kinds of wrong-headedness. Aristotle, on the other hand, believed in the systematic assessment of his predecessors. The Pre-Socratic physicists were of special interest because, in spite of grave misunderstandings of causation, they seemed to him to have been making what he called "lisping" but not valueless attempts to express the truths which he revealed. There has been dispute between twentieth-century critics about the value of Aristotle's detailed opinions on his early predecessors. It has certainly been demonstrated that he was capable on many occasions of seriously distorting their views. At the same time Aristotle's information and judgments are always valuable and often indubitably correct; and they can only be safely rejected in those cases where we possess reliable contrary evidence, which for the most part can be provided only by relevant original fragments, and where in addition his motives for distortion can be detected.

The correct assessment of Aristotle's judgments is particularly important because virtually all subsequent ancient accounts of the Pre-Socratics were strongly influenced by him. The chief source of information for later writers was *The Opinions of the Physicists*, a history compiled by Aristotle's colleague **Theophrastus** as part of the great Peripatetic encyclopedia of knowledge. But Theophrastus himself, although on many points he seems to have checked original sources, was also heavily influenced by Aristotle's opinions, which are sometimes reproduced in words borrowed from Aristotle's *Physics* and *Metaphysics*. In many cases he seems to have been unable to ascertain disputed points, no doubt partly because not all the Pre-Socratics were still readily available in their own words. Indeed, although the Greeks themselves assumed that each Pre-Socratic (though not Pythagoras) wrote at least one book, to which they usually assigned the stock title "On Nature", it is doubtful whether

some of the earlier ones produced writings that achieved wide currency even in their own time. They perhaps relied more on oral propagation, and the extracts from Heraclitus, notably, are primarily framed as oral apophthegms. Even when Pre-Socratic books were available their often metaphorical and poetical language did not always meet with sympathetic interpretation from the scientist Theophrastus. Thus his history, even if it had survived entire, would itself require much interpretation and modification, and even then would often not take us back beyond Aristotle; but except for a section on sensation it too exists only in fragments. Fortunately an unknown Stoic in the second century B.C. made a summary of it; this was recopied and expanded by one Aetius three or four hundred years later, and his work has been reconstructed from extracts in two slightly later extant writers. One more source must be mentioned: the Neoplatonist Simplicius is of great importance because, although he lived a thousand years after the Pre-Socratics, he found it desirable for the purposes of his commentaries on two treatises of Aristotle to set out the views of some of Aristotle's predecessors in their own words; for by his time many of the Pre-Socratic writings, and even the later summaries of them, had become extremely rare. To him, then, we owe in particular a great proportion of what we possess of the original words of Parmenides, Empedocles, Anaxagoras, and Diogenes of Apollonia.

Of the chronology and biography of the Pre-Socratics we are also imperfectly informed. For a crucial hundred years between the rise of the Sophistic movement and the foundation of the Lyceum they did not greatly interest most Greeks. Aristotle was interested in their ideas, not in their personal lives; so it was left to the mendacious Alexandrian biographers from the third to the first century B.C. to produce such dubious stories as that Heraclitus buried himself in dung or that Empedocles cast himself into Mount Etna. A few plainer facts have survived, which depend upon more reputable sources. Most of the chronological information, too, goes back to a more respectable but still largely speculative side of Alexandrian learning. Sotion classified the Pre-Socratics into eastern and western schools and, following Theophrastus, related them to each other as master and pupil. Then the chronographer Apollodorus left a standard account, in verse, of the dates and opinions of philosophers and others; he assumed that each thinker's period of greatest activity came at the age of forty, which he made to coincide with the nearest of a series of epochs or dated historical events. Further, a pupil was regularly made forty years younger than his putative master. Fortunately we know a few objective dates by which to check Apollodorus: for example the eclipse predicted by Thales must have been that of 585 B.C., and Melissus, the follower of Parmenides, was Samian admiral against Athens in 441 B.C. In general the Apollodoran dating, though overschematic, seems to be roughly reliable.

The ancient distinction between East-Greek and West-Greek schools is useful up to a point. The westerns were less materialistic in their search for unity, indeed the Eleatics rejected the sense-world altogether. In Pythagoras and Empedocles there was a mystical or religious trend that would not have been tolerated in the more matter-of-fact, if no less dogmatic, atmosphere of eastern, Ionian thought. But there are many exceptions: Pythagoras was an Ionian by upbringing, though he moved to southern Italy; the Ionian Heraclitus discovered unity in structure rather than material; Melissus, though a follower of Parmenides, was an Ionian from Samos. Apart from the Sicilian Empedocles, the post-Eleatic pluralists came mostly from the eastern end of the Greek world (for example, Anaxagoras, and the Atomists Leucippus and Democritus) and tended to revert to traditional Ionian explanations of detailed cosmological phenomena.

## II. THE MILESIANS

Thales and his two successors, Anaximander and Anaximenes, are sometimes grouped together as "the Milesians". They considered that the unity which they assumed to exist in the world was to be found in the material of which the world was made or from which it had originated. Thales thought this material to be water. Aristotle, unfortunately vague here, wrote as follows: "Thales. . . says that it [namely the element and first principle of existing things] is

water – and therefore declared that the earth is *on* water – perhaps taking his supposition from seeing the nurture of all things to be moist". Now Thales may have been affected by this and similar observations, but his primary stimulus for the choice of water was probably the Near-eastern story that the world arose from a great surrounding flood. He was undoubtedly interested in Egypt and also had opportunities, through Sardis, for contact with the Babylonian records on which his most famous exploit, the prediction of an eclipse during a particular year, must have depended. Unfortunately it is hard to tell how far Thales carried the theories that he founded on Near-eastern empiricism. Was the unity of the world simply based, in the old genetical manner, on a distant origin from a single parent, namely water? Or is the world still somehow made of water? Aristotle naturally assumes the latter, since it fits his own idea of a persistent material substrate. Probably Thales did not distinguish very clearly between the alternatives; if things came from water, they must still be watery in a way – after all they are still supported and surrounded by an indefinite watery mass. Nor, probably, did he specify precisely how the world assumes its present diversity. According to Aristotle he declared that all things are full of gods, and that magnetic stone must possess soul because it can move iron. If, then, apparently inanimate things like stone possess soul and therefore life, then the world as a whole might seem to be penetrated with soul or life, which because of its immense power and scope must be divine and so could cause the development of the present plurality.

Anaximander was somewhat younger than Thales, whom he must have known. He seems to have felt that if the originative stuff were identical with a present world-component like Thales' water, then the other components, for example fire, which is in many ways opposed to water, could not have asserted their identity. Anaximander accepted the idea of the single originative material, divine and all-encircling, but called it "the Indefinite" – implying that it was both boundless in extent and not identical with any nameable constituent of our world. Cosmogony took place when a nucleus that produced fire and dark mist separated off from the Indefinite.

261

The mist solidified at its centre into earth, and was surrounded by a ball of flame which burst to form the heavenly bodies. These were wheels of flame encased in mist, each shining out through a single aperture. The earth, a broad flat-topped cylinder, stays in its place because it is equidistant from from everything else – a brilliant advance on the idea of Thales or Anaximenes that the earth floats on water or air. Within the world things are divided into mutually opposed substances like heat and cold, winter and summer, day and night, the interactions of which are both motivated and regulated by a sociological metaphor: first they encroach on each other and then they "pay penalty and retribution for their injustice according to the assessment of Time". (The anthropomorphism here may lie partly in the language; but the use of traditional poetical language and the absence of an abstract vocabulary was a constant brake on philosophical development at this period.) The cosmological regularity was derived from the divine Indefinite substance itself, which thus transmitted its unity to the developed world.

In the next generation Anaximenes reverted to the concept of a specific cosmogonical substance: air/mist (*aer* in Greek) or breath. The objection probably felt by Anaximander was overcome by the important idea that the originative stuff can take on other forms, and so turn into the other materials of our world, by condensation and rarefaction – variation of its amount in any one place. This explanation of physical change, which was wrongly thought to be confirmed by the observation that the temperature of exhaled breath varies with the compression of the mouth, succeeded in making material monism logically feasible for the first time. The consequent cosmogony and cosmology were not too implausible; for mist, as Thales may have observed of water, seems to permeate many changes in Nature – rarefied, it turns into fire (for lightning bursts out of cloud), condensed, it becomes earth by way of water, which seems to turn into earth, for example when the sea recedes. But Anaximenes' choice of basic substance was not entirely scientific; for the cosmic material, also called "breath", was likened by him to the human soul, often associated with breath,

and so had a vital kinetic, directive power in the world. Thus the motive of change was still largely anthropomorphic.

## III. PYTHAGOREANISM

In Anaximenes' maturity, around 535 B.C., Pythagoras migrated from Samos to Italy and established an exclusive semi-religious, semi-philosophical society. He wrote nothing himself, and assessment of him is particularly precarious. He taught that the soul migrates from one body and species to another; consequently all living things are akin, and abstinence from meat, as well as other taboos, had to be observed. In common with those known as Orphics he believed that the soul must be kept pure. An important means of purification was music. Here the mystical and scientific trends link up; for Pythagoras discovered by the experiment of stopping a single string that the musical scale is numerical – that the major harmonic intervals can be expressed in ratios of whole numbers. If music, which is related to soul, is numerical, then the whole world must somehow be numerical too; Pythagoras' followers, developing this typically over-bold induction, seem to have assigned concrete bulk (still assumed to be the mark of existence) to the points which, as units, both made up numbers and delimited lines, planes, and volumes; so that physical objects, composed as they were of determinable geometrical shapes, could be resolved into sums of concrete unit-points. Further, the world could be analysed into ten pairs of opposites, of which the archetype was limit and the unlimited. These were the elements of number, too: odd numbers are limited, even numbers unlimited. The world came into being when the unit as limit drew in the unlimited and subjected it to various determinations. Most of these ideas were probably later than Pythagoras; but the master himself had ascribed special importance to the decade, and there is no reason to remove from him the famous theorem associated with his name. It may have been a follower, though, who drew the full damaging implication from the consequent irrationality of the diagonal: that some natural lengths, all of which should be composed of unit-points, could not be expressed in terms of whole numbers at all.

Pythagoras' longer-lived coeval Xenophanes, likewise an emigrant from Ionia, devoted much of his poetry to attacking the traditional Homeric description of the gods – both their immortality and the very basis of their anthropomorphism: for each species should on this view envisage gods in their own shape, which seemed absurd. Xenophanes put in their place a single, motionless god who "shakes all things by the thought of his mind". This idea of a divine, intellectual source of change may have affected Empedocles and Anaxagoras; his destructive rationalism was probably more generally influential. Apart from attacking anthropomorphism he appears to have parodied the exaggeration and dogmatism of Ionian physical theories by such suggestions as that the sun continues each day in a straight line. Although not primarily interested in physics, and a professed sceptic over the acquisition of certain knowledge, Xenophanes is not without scientific importance, since he used the testimony of marine fossils found inland to show that the earth must once have been mud – a rare use at this period of rational inference from a well-testified and correctly assessed observation.

Further modifications of the Milesian approach were made by Heraclitus, active in Ephesus probably around 510–480 B.C. Philosophically as well as socially an extreme individualist, he undermined the general conception by abandoning cosmogony and stating that the unity of things was to be found in their essential structure or arrangement rather than their material. This common structure or *Logos*, which was not superficially apparent, was chiefly embodied in a single kinetic material, fire. It was responsible both for the regularity of natural changes and for the essential connexion of opposites – Heraclitus adopted this traditional analysis of differentiation – through balanced interaction. The regularity underlying change was for Heraclitus the significant thing, but like the Greek poets he also emphasized the ubiquity of change (and was consequently subjected to exaggerated interpretation, *see* **Cratylus**), which he termed strife or war; for without reaction between opposites and world-masses the *Logos* and the unified cosmos would cease to exist. Philosophy was not a game: knowledge of physics was

ethically essential, for man is part of his environment; his soul, which in its unadulterated state is a kind of fire, is connected through sensation and breathing with the fieery *Logos*-constituents of the outside world. This enabled understanding to be distinguished from mere perception.

## IV. THE ELEATICS

Development of these fruitful ideas was interrupted by a philosophical explosion on the other side of the Greek world. Parmenides wrote a poem claiming that we can only meaningfully say of anything that "it is". The predicate "is not" is literally nonsense: not-being is impossible, inexpressible, and inconceivable. Since not-being was equated at this time with empty space, there could be no movement; but Parmenides rejected change on metaphysical rather than physical grounds, since any change involved its subject in *not-being* what it was before. This confusion between the existential and the predicative "is" was not cleared up until Plato. From the single premise "it is" Parmenides proceeded to the conclusion that reality or "being" is homogeneous, motionless, solid, and indivisible. "Since there is a furthest limit, it [Being] is bounded from every side, like the mass of a well-rounded sphere"; he was still obliged to use materialistic language, and would no doubt, if pressed, have said that his reality was concrete. From now on, however, there was a gradual development of more abstract language which could attribute to the new and odd kinds of philosophical reality a status different from that of phenomena. Parmenides, ignoring Heraclitus here, seems to have started from the old problem of how an initial unity can turn into a plural world. His emphasis on "limit" suggests that he was deliberately rejecting the "unlimited" component of Pythagorean **dualism.** His follower **Zeno** of Elea, too, is thought by many to have directed his paradoxes (which show that space is continuous, not composed of discrete points) against the Pythagorean view of matter. A curious and professedly "deceitful" appendix, in which Parmenides outlines a cosmology based not on one but on two substances probably reflects, as well as some reaction against Pythagoreanism, his doubts over rejecting the world of manifest experience. Certainly it gives a hint that pluralism is a possible escape from his dilemma.

To meet this dilemma Empedocles posited no less than four "roots" or permanent kinds of matter: fire, water, earth (Heraclitus' world-masses), together with air, the concrete exist-ence of which Empedocles had now confirmed by special observations. To these were added two kinetic agents, Love and Strife – motives of attraction and repulsion which, anthropomorphic as they obviously are, were described concretely as "equal in length and breadth" to the four roots. The different substances in Nature, apart from unmixed earth, water, and so on, were compounds of roots welded together by the admixture of Love. Empedocles felt obliged to propose a uniform stage of existence – not a true cosmogonical origin, which might imply illegitimate "becoming", but a recurrent period in a cycle – in which all things are mixed by Love in a homogeneous mass equivalent to Parmenides' "sphere" of Being. Only Strife, by coming somewhat obscurely to "the lowest depths of the vortex", is excluded. Then, by the gradual intrusion of Strife, the roots begin to separate into different combinations, until eventually Love is excluded in turn and Strife has separated the roots into isolated masses. A world could only be formed in one of the two intermediate stages between the total domina-tion of Love or Strife: our world belongs to the stage when Strife is increasing. Each inter-mediate cosmological stage produces different stages of animal evolution, causing monsters and bisexual creatures as well as the more efficient species of our present world. Sensation can be valid, since it is caused by material effluences from objects entering pores in the sense-organs: earth is perceived by earthy components in the body, fire by fire, as in vision, and so on. Empedocles also wrote a more mystical poem called "Purifications", according to which the soul, originally divine, is polluted by Strife and cast into the world of opposites; after successive incarnations it may purify itself and regain the realms of Love.

Anaxagoras, like Empedocles active around the middle of the fifth century B.C., similarly maintained that physical change, being merely the aggregation and dispersion of different kinds of permanently-existing matter, did not imply that "what is" must turn into the vicious "what is not". But for him these kinds of matter were not four or six, but as many as there were dif-ferent natural substances. Originally these were all mixed together in a sort of Parmenidean One; then the motive substance, now described as Mind, and as "subtlest of all objects and purest", started a rotation and so, by separation and re-aggregation, a cosmogony. Objects in the world are compounded of lumps or particles called "seeds". There is "a portion of everything in everything" – a portion, probably, of every natural substance (except Mind, which only exists in some things) in every seed. Each seed possesses the apparent character of the portion that predominates. Thus the original unity is preserved in the developed world, and yet evi-dent alterations can be explained in the ratio of the portions between different seeds. Anaxagoras argued against both the Pythagoreans and the Eleatic Zeno that matter is infinitely divisible, but evidently did not notice the incompatibility of this principle with "a portion of everything in everything". At all events his theory, though complicated and in places self-refuting, preserved appearances without contradicting the Eleatic premise; it further avoided the difficulties of Empedocles' cyclical scheme, and the objection that the formation of natural substances out of Empedoclean "roots" *did* seem to involve coming-to-be of a kind.

## V. THE SOPHISTS

It was at about this time that the Sophists, pro-fessional teachers of wisdom, made themselves felt. They believed that the current physical systems and the Eleatic rejection of the phe-nomenal world were either over-complicated or absurd or both, and were in any case irrelevant to practical life and quite unconfirmed by evidence. **Protagoras** and **Gorgias**, the most important of them, taught that knowledge of the constitution of the world lay outside human reach, that man should assess things on the basis of his own individual experience. Yet there now appeared a much simpler physical explanation of the world and its changes: **Atomism**, a system originated perhaps around 440–430 B.C. by **Leucippus**, of whom we know very little, and elaborated by Democritus. (It was also, of course, later adopted by **Epicurus** and expounded by **Lucretius**.) The Atomists began by denying the Eleatic implication that empty space, the void, cannot exist. There *is* not-being, in this sense. In addition there is homogeneous, solid matter, which is not continuous (as was Parmenides' Being) but is contained in an infinite number of indivisible, and also invisible, atoms. Reality consists, then, in atoms and the void. The atoms are constantly in motion, because of their collisions with and rebounds from each other; no metaphorical cause of motion was needed. They differ only in position and shape; sometimes atoms of different shapes get caught up with each other to form complexes. A world arises when collisions and rebounds in an isolated group of atoms happen to start a vortex, which causes heavy complexes of atoms to go to the centre, light ones to the circumference. Man himself is a complex of atoms and his soul is made of mobile spherical ones. Leucippus adapted the Empedoclean theory of sensation: objects emit effluences, "membranes" of atoms which, sometimes distorted in passage, make physical contact with the atoms of the sense-organ and then of the soul. It follows that there are no real qualities: appearances are secondary (but not therefore negligible; Democritus had a developed ethic, aimed at moral well-being), and in reality there are only atoms and void. Thus Atomism simultaneously fulfilled the conditions of Eleatic logic and the aims of Milesian material monism. Entirely an *a priori* construction, it has almost nothing in common with contemporary atomic theory, though this itself has grown out of **Gassendi**'s direct revival of Democritean atomism.

Various other theories of an eclectic nature were propounded from the mid-fifth-century B.C. onwards; by Hippon, for example, and Archelaus. Cratylus exaggerated Heracliteanism by holding that everything is in flux all the time, while Diogenes of Apollonia produced an unusually coherent old-style monistic system in which air is basic substance, with warm air as divine and intelligent, directing all things for the best. This was the kind of teleology that Socrates wanted; but Socrates rejected physics and concentrated on ethics and the soul – soul or mind being the obvious teleological agent in his still anthropomorphic view. In many ways the Socratic reaction, aided by the Sophists and by current anthropological, medical and social ideas, brought physical speculation to a depressingly sudden halt; but by his interest in definitions Socrates initiated a deeper study of logic, without which philosophy could make no further real progress.

The Pre-Socratics, who for the most part made little appeal to their lay contemporaries, plainly had great influence on their philosophical successors; negatively, in the main, on Plato, but positively on Aristotle in his revival of physics. Atomism, furthermore, survived for centuries through Epicurus, while Stoicism was deeply indebted to Heraclitus. Great historical importance in the development of thought the Pre-Socratics certainly had; but it may legitimately be asked whether their fragmentary science and philosophy have any value other than as a necessary primitive stage on the way to serious speculation. The inevitable deficiencies of these lively thinkers are striking but instructive: their love of inference unconfirmed, for the most part, by observation, let alone experiment; their retention of mythical and metaphorical explanations of change; their inadequate linguistic resources, which delayed or distorted the formation of abstract concepts; their reluctance to examine what was implied by knowledge, and their rudimentary logic. Yet they also had great virtues; and apart from the admirable quality of the rapid and systematic intellectual progress from Thales to Democritus, or the comprehensiveness of systems like that of Heraclitus, the Pre-Socratics illustrate in a particularly clear form certain problems of materialistic philosophy and the limitations of some of their classical solutions: problems, for example, of presupposed unity and observed plurality; of unseen or structural types of unity; of the physical source of change; of the evaluation of sense-perception, and the interrelation of ethics and physics. It is perhaps in this respect that Pre-Socratic thought may be said to have philosophical as well as historical value.

(G.S.K.)

265

**Price,** Henry Habberley (1899–1984), English philosopher, who worked at Oxford and wrote mainly on perception and the philosophy of mind, and also on psychical research.

In his first book, *Perception* (1932), he rejected previous theories about the relation between **sense-data** and material objects, especially the theory that the latter *cause* the former and so are known solely by their effects. In his own view, the sense-data not only belong directly to the physical object, but are related intimately among themselves, forming a "family", that is a set of series each converging on a standard member; these standard members compose the Standard Solid, which has the shape ordinarily called "the real shape of the thing". For Price a "thing" is a family of sense-data *together with* the coincident physical object, but he can say so little about the object that he runs close to **phenomenalism**.

His later *Thinking and Experience* (1953) rejects theories which make thinking consist entirely of the use of symbols or of images or of concepts treated as subsistent objects, and contends that recognition is basic, concepts being "recognitional capacities".

(R.HALL)

**Price,** Richard (1723–1791), English theologian, a Minister at Newington Green, London and a D.D. of Glasgow. His *Review of the Principal Questions in Morals* (1758), is the earliest clear and cogently developed **deontological** theory – that is, an account of morality which makes "right" and "obligation" the fundamental concepts. Price see these as indefinable, *a priori* and objective, and thus is at loggerheads with the school of **Hutcheson** and **Hume**. He attacks not simply the detail of their arguments in support of an ethic of "sentiment", but the basis of their **empiricism** itself. Universal notions and concepts such as substance, duration, infinity, cannot, he thinks, be explained from a radical empiricist standpoint. No more can the basic notions of morals.

Price followed **Butler** in his rejection of psychological **hedonism,** but did not fully share Butler's confidence that duty and interest for the most part coincide in this life. He argued that a hereafter must be postulated in order to make sense of our moral experience; but he saw that an *infinitely* long after-life cannot be demonstrated in this way.

Particularly valuable throughout Price's moral philosophy are his serious acknowledgement of the facts of moral conflict and his tough-minded refusal to accept over-simplifying "supreme principles", such as those of the egoists and utilitarians of his day.

(R.W.H.)

**Prichard,** Harold Arthur (1871–1947), English philosopher, probably the outstanding member of the realist movement at Oxford of which Cook **Wilson** was the officially acknowledged leader. His only largescale publication on theory of knowledge was *Kant's Theory of Knowledge* (1909), a polemical work in which he opposes his realism to **Kant.** In later years he rather modified these views, holding that we perceived only coloured patches and not bodies, of which we could have only inferential knowledge. In moral philosophy his paper "Does Moral Philosophy Rest on a Mistake?" (1912) was influential in the revival of intuitionist ethics; Prichard claimed that we could know simply by attending to the matter that certain acts were duties and that any attempt to produce a general theory of why such acts were duties was a mistake. In ethics, however, as in epistemology, he grew sceptical in later years; in *Duty and Ignorance of Fact* (1932) he admitted a considerable element of subjectivism into our assessment of our duties.

(J.O.U.)

**Probability.** Probability has given rise to several conflicting philosophical theories. If we concentrate on such statements as "The probability of heads when a penny is tossed is ½ the *Frequency Theory* of probability may well seem most plausible. According to the frequency theory the above statement means, roughly, that in the long run the frequency with which a tossed coin will fall heads upwards will be one in two. Special attractions of this theory are that, in a well-known version of it, it follows from the definition of probability that the axioms of the mathematical theory must be applicable and that it manifestly ties up probability very closely with statistical data. On the other hand it is very difficult indeed to give a satisfactory version of this theory when, as is necessary, more accurate expressions are substituted for "in the long run" to indicate what frequency is relevant. The frequency theory was first stated in detail by **Venn** in his Logic of Chance; other well known exponents are von **Mises** and Reichenbach.

If we turn our attention to such statements as "Probably there is life on Mars" the frequency theory becomes specially unplausible; when dealing with the probability of theories, hypotheses and special events it is hard to see how we could be referring to any sequence of events or any frequency within such a series, though some philosophers have attempted to sustain such a view. When dealing with such examples it is much more plausible to regard the word "probable" as indicating that the statement "There is life on Mars" should be accepted with some reserve; that it is made in a condition of *evidential satisfactoriness* midway between those that we might indicate by such expressions as "We know that there is life on Mars" and "There is no ground for supposing life on Mars."

**Carnap, Braithwaite, Russell** and many other philosophers agree that notion of probability is used in both the frequency way and in the evidence-assessing way and that we must understand it according to context. When a numerical statement is in principle possible in the form "The probability of an X being Y is p", some explanation of a frequency type is given; but where a statement is of the form "Probably it is the case that so and so", where no numerical valuation seems plausible, the word "probably" is taken to be indicative of caution.

It should be added that the classical definition of probability, found in the great French mathematical writers on probability, was that the probability of an event was the ratio of favourable to total possibilities; for the purposes of philosophy this is quite inadequate, since it seems that the "possibilities" referred to are hardly distinguishable from probabilities and it is hard to see how to add up favourable possibilities without falling into severe logical difficulties.

(J.O.U.)

**Proclus,** *see* Neoplatonism.

**Protagoras** of Abdera, the Greek Sophist, flourished *c.* 450–440 B.C. He was famous as a teacher of *arete*, practical excellence or political and rhetorical skill; he worked in different cities and took fees for his teaching. He was credited with several books, on logic, cultural origins, and human behaviour. Protagoras attacked the dogmatism of contemporary religion and philosophy. Of the gods he said: "I am unable to know about the gods either that they exist or that they do not, and what form they have; for there are many things that prevent knowledge – both the obscurity of the subject and the shortness of human life." Contradictory statements could be made on any subject, and each could be true according to circumstances; there was no single absolute truth to be discovered by man, since a man's own nature was intimately involved in any judgment. This is probably the reference of Protagoras' famous dictum "Man is the measure of all things, of the existence of the things that are and the non-existence of the things that are not." This seems to be directed particularly against the extremism of **Eleatic** ontology, which was subjected to critical examination by Protagoras' contemporary, Gorgias, also. See also **Pre-Socratics**.

(G.S.K.)

**Psychoanalysis,** or "depth psychology", was invented in Vienna in the 1890s by Sigmund Freud (1856–1939), who described it as "a procedure for the medical treatment of the nervously ill". But it is a very unusual kind of medicine: it consists in frequent and regular private consultations between a patient and an analyst, sometimes lasting for many years; and as Freud said, "nothing takes place between them except that they talk to each other."

The patient's side of the conversation comprises reminiscences, self-descriptions, reports of dreams, and verbal free associations. The analyst's contributions are carefully-considered "interpretations" of what the patient has said. The aim of psychoanalysis is to discover experiences which haunt the patient's memory, but which are so painful that they have been "repressed" into "the Unconscious". It is these repressed memories, according to Freud, rather than physiological abnormalities, which cause most nervous illness; they are also the nucleus of non-neurotic personalities. Freud's enormous experience as an analyst persuaded him that the crucial memories in everyone's life refer to early childhood, and that they are all essentially concerned with the child's experience of itself as either a boy or a girl and its sexual feelings about its mother-figure, its father-figure, and itself (the "Oedipus Complex").

Freud made two basic claims about psychoanalysis: that it affords unrivalled insight into individual personalities; and that skilful "interventions" by analysts can cure nervous disorders, and so replace "misery" with "common unhappiness". Logically these claims are independent, of course: psychoanalytic treatment might be successful even if the interpretations on which it was based were untrue; and profound insight into neuroses need not necessarily help to cure them.

Freud conceived of psychoanalysis as part of the inexorable progress of dispassionate scientific materialism, the third and final blow to humanity's inflated view of its uniqueness and importance. Copernicanism, Freud said, had demonstrated that the earth is not the centre of the universe; Darwinism, that *homo sapiens* is not the lord of the animal kingdom; and now psychoanalysis proved that the conscious self "is not master in its own house". Philosophy, according to Freud, was incorrigibly prejudiced in favour of consciousness, and hence inseparable from pre-scientific superstition.

In fact, however, many philosophers have welcomed psychoanalysis. Freud's apparent faith in the healing powers of self-knowledge could be assimilated to the traditional Socratic imperative: "Know thyself "; and followers of **Wittgenstein** could see the philosopher and the analyst as engaged in essentially the same enterprise – offering painstaking and intricate therapy so as to relieve people of conceptual and psychic disorders, respectively. Their main reservation about psychoanalysis concerned Freud's tendency (as they saw it) to treat concepts like "repression"

as literal descriptions of quasi-hydraulic processes inside a pseudo-material machine called "the mind", rather than as **metaphors**.

Some philosophers have been totally hostile to psychoanalysis. Ironically, these critics align themselves with the very same current of scientific materialism as Freud. To the **logical positivists**, for example, or to **Popper**, psychoanalysis is a perfect example of a psuedo-science: the analyst's "findings" are protected from open scientific scrutiny by the confidentiality of the psychoanalytic session; and the idea of the inexhaustible interpretability of the Unconscious prevents analysts from venturing specific predictions which could be definitively tested.

The third and most prolific philosophical response to psychoanalysis regards it as a significant event within philosophy itself. According to **Gadamer**, for example, Freud taught philosophy to "get behind the surface of what is meant" and to "go behind the subjectivity of the act of meaning"; for him, as for **Habermas** and **Ricoeur,** Freud was a key innovator in the development of philosophy as **hermeneutics**. To socialist philosophers like **Marcuse**, psychoanalytic ideas of repression and the Unconscious are in part descriptions of the misery and **alienation** peculiar to modern capitalistic bureaucracies. Moreover, as **Althusser** noted, the idea that people's consciousness is systematically at odds with their real situation corresponds closely to the Marxist theory of **ideology**. **Sartre**, though critical of Freud's "materialism", thought of his own phenomenology as "existential psychoanalysis". According to Sartre, Freud's leading achievement (especially in the later writings, where the conceptions of "consciousness" and "the Unconscious" were overlaid by the more developmental ideas of "Ego", "Id", and "Superego") was that, like **Hegel**, he devised a way of thinking of the mind, and particularly the "I" or the "Ego", as constructed in a historical, social world, rather than as the expression of some pre-established interiority. For many feminists, Freud's achievement was to uncover one of the repressed themes of philosophical thought, namely **gender**.

The philosophical adoption of psychoanalysis has been taken still further by **Lacan**, and by neo-Nietzscheans like **Deleuze** and neo-Heideggerians like **Derrida**: for them, Freud has unmasked the self-deceptions not just of consciousness and the Ego, but also of the very ideas of "Reason" and "the Real", which they take to be the unquestioned presuppositions of the entirety of Western philosophy. Like **Foucault**, they criticize Freud for failing to pursue his ideas to their true conclusion, namely that the whole idea of pursuing the truth is dangerous and deluded. Freud, of course, would hardly recognize these philosophical views as developments of his own work; but, given his doctrine of the Unconscious, he could not consistently claim the authority to disown them. See also **Philosophy of Mind**.

[J.R.]

**Pyrrho** of Elis, *see* Scepticism, Sceptics.

**Pythagoras** of Samos, Greek philosopher, flourished *c.* 530 B.C. He left Samos to escape the tyranny of Polycrates and settled in Croton in South Italy, where for a time he had great political influence. He established there a community of disciples, partly religious and partly scientific. The master himself wrote nothing and since his followers attributed their own developments to him out of piety it is especially hard to assess his ideas. Some lines of Xenophanes prove that Pythagoras believed in the transmigration of the soul – even between different species, since all living things were akin. He was also renowned for his scientific and mathematical knowledge, and there is no reason to disconnect from him the theorem that bears his name. He also probably made the important discovery that the musical scale has a numerical basis, that is, that its main harmonic intervals can be expressed in ratios of the first four integers. These integers together formed the Decad, to which sacred significance was attached in the community; but whether Pythagoras himself maintained like his successors that not only music, but the whole world, was somehow numerical and was made up out of "limit" and "the unlimited", is uncertain. See also **Pythagoreans** and **Pre-Socratics**.

(G.S.K.)

**Pythagoreans.** The community founded by **Pythagoras** in Croton in Southern Italy split into a mathematical and a religious group. The latter lived according to taboos based on Pythagoras' idea of the kinship of living things and the necessity for purification of body and soul. The "mathematicians", while probably not rejecting these ideas, associated them with developments of Pythagoras' discovery that the musical scale is numerical. Since music was held to have special power over soul, which permeated the cosmos, the whole world must be somehow made out of number. The elements of number, and thus of the world, were the even, representing the unlimited, and the odd, representing limit. A table of ten pairs of basic opposites within the world was drawn up, in which odd, male, straight, good, at rest, etc., came under "limit", their contraries under "unlimited". Unfortunately there is little evidence here apart from Aristotle's rather vague account, which did not distinguish early from later Pythagoreanism. Most of these ideas were probably formed by the time of **Parmenides**, who seems to attack Pythagorean dualism. By this time, too (though one piece of ancient evidence may suggest that the development was later), the units which formed number were probably conceived as possessing spatial magnitude; so that lines, surfaces and solids could be expressed as sums of units, and objects were literally made out of number. The Pythagorean cosmogony may have developed a little later: an initial unit "drew in" the unlimited, in the form of the void, and somehow divided into other units separated by the unlimited. These unit-point-atoms then grew into lines, planes and solids. At the centre of the universe lies fire; the stars, of which the earth is one, each produce a sound according to the speed of their revolution, and these make up a "harmony of the spheres" inaudible by men. See also **Pre-Socratics** and **Zeno**.

(G.S.K.)

# Q

**Qualities,** Primary and Secondary, *see* Atomism, Descartes, Locke.

**Quantum Mechanics.** Planck, Einstein and Bohr originally developed Quantum Theory in the early 1900s, to explain the interactions between atoms and radiation. "Energy" was found to be packaged in finite "quanta", so that the energy in a light "wave" behaved like a stream of "particles". In the 1920s de Broglie extended this "duality" by showing that material "particles" could behave like waves and a radically new mechanics was created by Schrödinger, Heisenberg, Dirac and von Neumann. As a formal calculus for predicting experimental results it is astonishingly successful, but its interpretation is racked with controversy.

Quantum Mechanics is philosophically interesting because of its implications for **determinism** and **realism** – indeed some argue that it also has implications for **logic**. A remarkable body of "meta-theory" has developed on the question of whether its revolutionary features could be reversed by future science.

Quantum Mechanics represents a system by a complex mathematical function which ascribes ranges of *potential* properties to the component entities in a coordinated fashion. Which properties are realized when a measurement is performed is a matter of probability. Furthermore, certain properties are "paired" so that, according to Heisenberg's Uncertainty Principle, closer definition of one implies more "uncertainty" in the other. Since this appears to make precise prediction impossible in principle, quantum mechanics is often taken to have refuted determinism.

Bohr's Complementary Interpretation sets its face against theoretical realism by treating the micro-system and the measuring apparatus as an indivisible whole. Thus properties whose measurement requires mutually exclusive experimental arrangements cannot be simultaneously real. In Quantum Mechanics the **holistic** coordination of a system remains even when its components are apparently separate, so a measurement on one "entity" fixes the state of another. Alternatives to quantum mechanics, such as Bohm's, which treat properties as real, can model this only if they permit instantaneous action-at-a-distance.

But can it be measurement which makes properties actual? If Bohr's way of looking at the situation is applied to an enlarged system which incorporates the observer, then his argument

seems to imply that the new system will be undefined – until observed by someone else! And so on *ad infinitum*. To cut this regress Wigner argues that *consciousness* makes measurement definite, thus committing physics to **idealism**. Conversely Everett and Wheeler's Many-Worlds Interpretation rescues realism, but only at the cost of claiming that interactions continually split the world into more and more parallel universes. The theory's technical triumphs only deepen our metaphysical perplexity.

[J.H.P.]

**Quine,** Willard V. O. (1908– ), American logician and philosopher, born in Ohio. He was a pupil of **Whitehead** at Harvard, where he was to spend the rest of his life. In the early 1930s he was converted to **logical positivism** and went to Warsaw to study with **Carnap**, whom he regarded as his "greatest teacher". Carnap migrated to America in 1936 and Quine recalls how he, **Goodman** and other young American philosophers "moved with Carnap as henchmen through the metaphysicians' camp".

Quine never broke with Carnap's orientation toward the natural sciences and his belief that the heart of philosophy is mathematical logic. But his numerous writings, all cast in a bright laconic style resembling those of Chandler and Runyon, have apparently left Carnap's vision of scientific philosophy in ruins, since in Quine's system natural science is presented as a (superior) form of metaphysics, not as a radical alternative to it.

Carnap and other logical positivists had divided knowledge into two components: empirical propositions, which were supposed to correspond one-by-one to sensory experiences; and logical propositions, which were no more than explications of structural properties of signs. Quine came to believe, however, that this view of knowledge depends upon an indefensible "myth of meaning": it proceeds "as if there were a gallery of ideas, and each idea were tagged with the expression that means it". So, according to Quine, the stark anti-metaphysical programme of logical positivism was secretly in league with an extravagant metaphysic; and the "linguistic theory of logical truths", so dear to Carnap and other logical positivists, had "less to it than meets the eye".

Quine's "adverse treatment", as he put it, of the idea of meaning, led him to discard two cardinal doctrines of logical positivism. The first was the "belief in some fundamental cleavage between truths which are **analytic**, or grounded in meanings independent of matters of fact, and truths which are **synthetic** or grounded in fact." The second was the "reductionist" doctrine that "each meaningful statement is equivalent to some logical construct upon terms which refer to immediate experience."

The effect of abandoning these "two dogmas of empiricism" was, so Quine intended, "a blurring of the supposed boundary between speculative metaphysics and natural science", and "a shift towards pragmatism". Observations, experiments, and common sense formed, together with logic and the sciences, parts of a seamless "web of knowledge". The laws of logic were statements which we are particularly unwilling to revise, but they are not in any way necessary; they shade off into empirical statements which we would freely alter, even though no experience could definitely require us to do so. **Locke** and **Hume** had espoused "term-by-term empiricism"; **Frege** had attended to "statements" rather than "terms"; but, for Quine, "the unit of empirical significance is the whole of science." Quine drew the conclusion that "our statements about the external world face the tribunal of experience not individually but as a corporate body" – a doctrine which he credited to **Duhem**, and which has come to be known as the "Duhem-Quine thesis".

These arguments are all contained in "Two Dogmas of Empiricism" (1951), which was anthologized in *From a Logical Point of View* (1953). This also contains "On What There Is" (1948) which argues that every theory involves an ontology. Of course, many of the objects apparently named in a theory may not actually be required by it: their apparent names can be eliminated by **Russell**'s theory of descriptions. Then, and according to Quine's doctrine of "ontological relativity", "to be is to be the value

of a variable". On pragmatic grounds (for he acknowledges no others), Quine implores scientists to reduce their ontological commitments to a minimum, so as to escape, if they can, from "Plato's beard" – a "tangled doctrine" which, with its luxuriant population of shadowy entities, "has proved tough, frequently dulling the edge of Ockham's razor".

For Quine, the objects of the physical sciences and of ordinary common sense are "cultural posits", just like Homer's Gods: "in point of epistemological footing the physical objects and the gods differ only in degree and not in kind." Or, as he argued in *Methods of Logic* (1952), "statements, apart from an occasional collectors' item for epistemologists, are connected only deviously with experience", so that "there is many a slip twixt objective cup and subjective lip."

Quine gave a systematic portrayal of his position in *Word and Object* (1960), which proposed an austere "canonical notation", purged of singular terms, as the likeliest framework for scientific progress. In this notation it was manifestly absurd to yearn for a solid foundation for empirical knowledge – "a fancifully fanciless medium of unvarnished news". Quine's scepticism about the very idea of meaning was dramatized as "the indeterminacy of translation". This went far beyond "the platitude that uniqueness of translation is absurd", to the astonishing thesis that there could be different ways of translating one language into another, which would offer incompatible translations of the same sentences but which would still fit all the observed facts. This thesis does not assert, of course, that there are shades of meaning which no translation can capture; on the contrary, it implies that the very idea of uncaptured shades of meaning is pointless. Critics have wondered, nevertheless, whether the indeterminacy thesis, and the idea of rival translations, can have any sense at all within Quine's system. Quine's other books include *The Ways of Paradox* (1966); *Philosophy of Logic* (1970); *Ontological Relativity* (1969); and *Quiddities: an intermittently Philosophical Dictionary* (1987). See also **Philosophy of Science, Relativism**.

[J.R.]

# R

**Rationalism**. In the usage of philosophers, rationalism is the characteristic of a philosophical theory which claims that by pure reasoning, without appeal to any empirical premises, we can arrive at substantial knowledge about the nature of the world. There is also a well-known use of the word in which it refers to the view that faith in the supernatural is inadmissible and that religious claims must be tested by rational criteria, but, in the absence of clear evidence to the contrary, the former sense of the word should be presumed in modern philosophical literature. It is in that sense that **Descartes**, **Leibniz** and **Spinoza** are quoted as classical examples of rationalism.

Rationalism is opposed to **empiricism**, the doctrine that experience is a necessary basis to all our knowledge; but neither of these terms has a precise meaning. Thus we might expect that a pure empiricist would claim that all knowledge requires empirical premises, and J. S. **Mill** did at times make this claim; for him even mathematical truths are empirical generalizations. But most empiricists have admitted that mathematical truths are *a priori*; they are still considered to be empiricists if they claim that mathematical truths are analytic, formal truths which give no information about the nature of the world. Thus there is a tendency to consider that a rationalist is one who claims to have synthetic *a priori* knowledge, who claims to know, wholly or in part, what the world is like by pure reason. But Leibniz is usually considered to be the most extreme of the rationalists because he claimed that in principle all truths could be known by pure reasoning, experience being but an inferior substitute for reason; yet Leibniz held that all truths of reason were guaranteed by the principle of contradiction and therefore, in modern terminology, analytic. However, Leibniz's claim that the contradictory of every true proposition is self-contradictory, is very paradoxical, and we may say that the rationalist is one who claims knowledge which is not based on sense-experience and which cannot be regarded without paradox as being purely formal. But this is still not precise; **Kant** claimed synthetic *a priori* knowledge, but claimed that he was not a rationalist because it was not dogmatic knowledge about things themselves but only about phenomena; he thought that it was one of the main virtues of his critical system that it avoided being either rationalist or empiricist.

(J.O.U.)

**Rawls**, John (1921– ), American political philosopher, born in Baltimore, who transformed Anglo-American **political philosophy** by means of a series of articles published in the 1950s and 1960s culminating in A *Theory of Justice* (1971). In opposition to **utilitarianism**, with its exclusive concern with aggregate happiness, Rawls argues that the fundamental political value is individual rights, or "justice as fairness".

Rawls proceeds by reviving and generalizing the hypothesis of the **social contract** as found in **Locke**, **Rousseau**, and **Kant**. The best political principles, he argues, are those which rational citizens would agree upon if they were to choose the "basic structure of society" whilst a "veil of ignorance" prevented them from knowing their own eventual position within it. According to Rawls they would recognize a general presumption in favour of equality, and hold that "all social values – liberty and opportunity, income and wealth, and the bases of self-respect – are to be distributed equally unless an unequal distribution of any, or all, of these values is to everyone's advantage."

On this basis, Rawls attempts to justify two principles of justice. The first and over-riding one states that "each person is to have an equal right to the most extensive basic liberty compatible with a similar liberty for others". The second specifies conditions under which inequalities may nevertheless be justified: "Social and economic inequalities are to be arranged so that they are both (a) to the greatest benefit of the least advantaged and (b) attached to offices and positions open to all under conditions of fair equality of opportunity."

Debate about Rawls' system has focused on part (a) of the second principle, which is known as "the difference principle". It implies that inequalities cannot be justified unless they are to the advantage even of the least privileged. Left-wing critics have feared that this opens the way for attempts to justify unacceptable inequalities. Right-wing critics (such as **Nozick**) have argued that, provided that the better-off gain their advantages rightfully they are under no obligation to bother about the disadvantaged. Either way it seems that "self-respect", which Rawls regards as "perhaps the most important primary good", may not be safe in Rawls' system.

[J.R.]

**Realism.** Realism is sometimes said to be the view that some things exist essentially independently of any mind. For example, realism about **universals** holds that they exist independently of any mind; nominalism denies this. Mathematical realism claims that numbers exist independently of mind, which discovers rather than creates them. Realism about the external world asserts that physical objects exist essentially independently of the mind of any perceiver. **Phenomenalists** (often called "subjective idealists") deny realism about external physical objects; John Stuart **Mill**, for instance, held that physical objects are nothing more than sets of actual and possible sensory data, which themselves have existence only as the contents of a mind. Realists about social phenomena deny that social wholes can be accounted for entirely in terms of the psychological states of individuals, (cf. **holism**).

Some realists word their claims in terms of essential independence from human activity, since acting, in its proper sense, presupposes that the actor has intentions and purposes, and hence a mind. Contemporary thinkers normally restrict "mind" to human minds; but traditionally, anti-realists such as **Berkeley** and **Hegel** allowed objects to be essentially independent of all human minds, but dependent on infinite mind, or the Deity.

It is important, in characterizing realism, to insert the qualification, "essentially". It would not refute a realist about the external world if every bit of reality had depended in some causal or contingent way upon mind, and one can be a realist about objects (for instance, to use **Marx**'s example, a cultivated cherry tree), which would

not have existed without human activity. If such dependence is inessential to the thing, in the sense that the object logically could have existed independently of mind or activity, it poses no problem for a realist.

However, this characterization of realism has the unfortunate consequence of rendering realism about the mind impossible by definition, since obviously no mind can exist essentially independently of itself. One could avoid this difficulty by defining realism as the view that a thing could exist independently, not of mind in general, but more specifically of any beliefs or thoughts we might have about it. We are realists about mental contents like pain if we hold that one can be in pain even if one does not believe it. We are realists about morality if we think that actions can be right, or things can be good, whether or not anyone believes that they are. In this sense, realism is connected with the epistemological idea that what is real can always serve as an objective "other", against which we can test our beliefs. The important point for realism, recharacterized in this way, is that it is always possible either that our beliefs are wrong, or that we are wrong about which beliefs we have. Error and mistake are always possible. In epistemology, the correspondence theory of **truth** is naturally associated with the metaphysical doctrine of realism.

Scientific realism can be characterized using this second definition. It is the view that scientific theories about unobservable entities should be construed at face value, as attempts to describe an independent even if unobservable reality. Instrumentalists (like **Peirce**) and phenomenalists (like **Mach**) argue for an anti-realist view, that scientific theories do not refer to an independent reality, but are either heuristic tools for the prediction of empirical data, or shorthand summaries, equivalent to the set of empirical statements which follow from them. Of course, scientific realists need not deny a factual or causal dependence of any part of reality upon theory, as, for example, in the case of self-fulfilling predictions which bring about the facts that make them true. But for the scientific realist, any factual ties between reality and scientific theory are always logically or conceptually inessential.

Sometimes anti-realism is described more weakly as the view that our knowledge of reality is theory-dependent, or necessarily depends on language. It then might seem an easy step to conclude that reality itself is language-, or theory-, dependent. This characterization is a mistake. A clear distinction must be drawn between the mind-dependence of language or theory and the alleged mind-dependence of the world itself. A scientific realist can accept that all descriptions of the world are theory-dependent (**Popper** is a clear example of this). Suppose we must use some theory T, in order to describe reality. All of our descriptions of the world will be T-dependent, and T is certainly something which we have created. However, it does not follow from this that without theory T the world could not have been the way it is. All that follows is that without the theory, we would not be able to describe the world in that way.

The great problem that faces realism is that, since it places a gap between mind on the one hand and reality on the other, it has to say that real objects transcend the contents of our experience. Realists believe that material objects and theoretical entities are more than the experiential content of our minds; that social phenomena are more than the individuals who participate in them; and that universals are irreducible to the particulars of which those universals are true. But if real objects transcend experience, how is knowledge of reality possible? See also **Religion**.

[D.-H.R.]

**Reid,** Thomas (1710–1796), the originator of the Scottish philosophy of common-sense. He was himself a Scot, educated at Aberdeen and a professor first at Aberdeen and then at Glasgow, where he succeeded Adam **Smith**. Reid, like **Kant**, was prompted to his original philosophical position by reading the works of **Hume**. To Reid it seemed that the immediate objects of the human mind in thought and in perception are peculiar mental entities called **ideas**. This starting-point, Reid considered, was common to other modern philosophers – **Descartes**, **Locke**, and **Berkeley**, for example – but only Hume had

recognized that if we have access only to discrete and unconnected ideas we cannot have connected knowledge transcending ideas. But Hume's conclusions, so extreme in scepticism, were untenable. Therefore his basic premises, the theory of ideas, must be abandoned. In his *Inquiry into the Human Mind* (1764) Reid therefore attacked the theory of ideas as neither intuitively evident nor a hypothesis successfully helping to explain what it was introduced to explain.

In the *Essays on the Intellectual Powers of Man* (1785), Reid set out a realist, but by no means rationalistic or speculative, account of perception, memory and conception to take the place of the way of ideas. Common sense is, he says, "that degree of judgment which is common to men with whom we can converse and transact business". But, Reid held, "all knowledge and all science must be built upon principles that are self-evident, and of such principles every man who has common sense is a competent judge when he conceives them distinctly." First principles may be necessary, as in mathematics, or contingent. Reid gives a list of principles of common sense in the contingent sphere which are very similar to the list which G. E. **Moore** gave in his "Defence of Common Sense"; they include (1) "the existence of everything of which I am conscious", (2) "that the thoughts of which I am conscious are the thoughts of a being which I call myself, my mind, my person", (3) "that those things did really happen which I distinctly remember", (4) "our own personal identity and continued existence", (5) "that those things do really exist which we distinctly perceive by our senses, and are what we perceive them to be". Anyone who doubts these principles will be incapable of rational intercourse and those philosophers, such as Hume, who profess to doubt them do not do so sincerely and consistently. Reid's critical work is at all times clear and acute, though his own positive views do not emerge so clearly from his writings as do the inconsistencies and unplausibilities of Locke and Berkeley.

(J.O.U.)

**Reification**: the mistake of treating an abstraction or relation, or convention, or artificial construct, as if it were a natural *thing* (Latin, *res*). See **Alienation**.

**Relativism**. Relativism can be characterized as the view (which **Plato** reports **Protagoras** as expressing) that "man is the measure of all things". Plato's discussion of the saying shows that it was construed as asserting that any person's views are as good as any one else's. Relativism, then, is a doctrine about differences between individuals (individualistic relativism) or between societies (social relativism). It may focus on differences in factual beliefs (scientific relativism); in morals (ethical relativism); in concepts (conceptual relativism); or in logic. Relativism asserts that in some sense what is true in one situation may not be true in another; that what is right or good in one situation may not be right or good in another; that the concepts used in one situation might be unintelligible in another; or that what is rational in one situation may not be rational in another.

Relativism does not simply assert that different things are believed or said or done in different times and places. Such differences may be only derivative and therefore compatible with there being some fundamental higher-order principles or rules or concepts, valid always and everywhere, which explain, in combination with different local facts about the circumstances in which the two things occur, such variations.

For example, there might be a single rule of scientific support which licenses inquirers with different information to believe incompatible theories. Or there might be a single ethical principle which entitles or requires persons in different circumstances to perform different actions. The mere fact that some languages use several concepts where other languages use only one (e.g. English and Eskimo concepts of snow) does not show that there are no fundamental concepts common to all languages. Nor does the fact that a sentence such as "It is raining", can be true in one situation but not in another prove that truth is relative. Relativism should be defined as the assertion that some of these differences are (or at least may be) fundamental rather than derivative.

The idea that what is true in one situation might not be true in another may seem more plausible than it is. This may arise from two confusions: the belief that "true in one situation but not in another" means nothing more than "believed to be true in one situation but not in another", and the failure to fully specify a statement. The truth of "It is raining" appears to be "relative" because the sentence is incomplete; but the truth of "it is raining at place p at time t" does not even appear to be relative.

Is there some scientific methodology, valid universally, for judging when one scientific theory or set of empirical beliefs is better than another? **Popper** and **Lakatos** believe that there is; **Kuhn** and **Feyerabend** deny it. Popper, for example, requires that the theory withstand attempts to falsify it. Kuhn, on the other hand, basing himself on an examination of episodes in the history of science, argues that scientific change from one theory to another is essentially non-rational. On his view, such changes between scientific paradigms can be explained but never justified in terms of methodological considerations.

Some writers have held that different societies or individuals could employ fundamentally different logics (either deductive or inductive). Nelson **Goodman**'s famous "new riddle of induction" poses the possibility of an inductive logic fundamentally different from our own. There is also a great deal of controversy concerning the possibility of non-standard deductive logics; certainly, the possibility of a logic which rejected the law of excluded middle, and thereby modified the classical conception of **truth**, seems coherent. On the other hand, the attempt to describe a society whose logic differed from the classical logic by rejecting the law of non-contradiction does seem deeply incoherent.

Conceptual and ethical relativism are more plausible. It is unlikely that we will find genuine empirical evidence of societies that differ fundamentally from us in concepts or in morality, but we can pose the question in thought experiments: Is it logically possible for two societies to differ in the most fundamental concepts they employ? **Quine**, with his doctrine of the indeterminacy of translation, thinks it is: that there could be a society which used concepts of object stages or undetached object parts, for instance, rather than our concept of an object as enduring through space and time. If one society used a fundamental concept that another society had neither as a fundamental nor as a derived concept, the languages of the two societies would be, to that extent, mutually unintelligible.

Could what was fundamentally right or good in one society differ from what was fundamentally right or good in another? The answer to this depends on whether one regards values as being as much a part of the universe as facts are. If they are, then there is no more reason for good or right to differ fundamentally between societies than there is for truth to differ. But if, as for example **Hare** and **Sartre** say, values are something we create, then there is a logical possibility, even if not a real one, that different societies or individuals could create fundamentally different moralities.

[D.-H.R.]

**Relativity.** The theory of Relativity is primarily due to Albert Einstein (1879–1955). Its philosophical interest lies in the overthrow of what had been regarded as *necessary* truths about space and time. The theory derives its name from the so called Principle of Relativity, according to which the same laws of physics obtain whatever frame of reference is adopted.

Special Relativity Theory (1905) removed a deep conflict between classical mechanics and electromagnetic theory, by making the astonishing "Light Postulate" – that the velocity of light is *invariant*, i.e. the same in every frame of reference. Einstein explains this postulate by showing that any measurement of velocity requires the synchronization of spatially separated clocks. His method is based (with benign circularity) on the Light Postulate, which implies that distances and time-intervals are relative to frame of reference. Thus "relativity" undermines the idea that there is a unique, universal "flow" of time.

Special Relativity Theory was devised in opposition to "Aether Theories" which attempted to interpret phenomena in terms of picturable mechanisms. Einstein's idea of "invariance" generated more elegant and more fruitful strategies for theory construction. Contrary to popular

belief, the theory does not abolish "absolute" (i.e. invariant) quantities but creates new, "four-dimensional", ones (Minkowski 1908).

In General Relativity Theory (1916) Einstein attempted to show that the structure of space is determined by matter, thus eliminating "Absolute Space" from physics. By taking the paths of light rays in a vacuum to define "straightest lines", Einstein was able to treat "gravitation" as the curvature of space-time, and show that the world has a non-Euclidean geometry. The theory explained known anomalies and predicts novel effects (most dramatically the Expansion of the Universe).

Relativity's success in displacing Newtonian theory shows how hazardous it is to claim a *priori* status for concepts in physics, and how easy it is to mistake a long-lived theory for the final truth. Nevertheless some argue that the general outline of Relativity Theory can be deduced *a priori*. At any rate is seems certain that future developments will not reverse the changes wrought by Relativity.

[J.H.P.]

**Religion.** The human race seems small and weak compared with the vastness of nature, and each of us occupies the stage of history but briefly. Are our lives really significant? If so how? In all cultures over recorded human history religions have offered answers to such questions through ideas rooted in experiences which seem to transcend the mundane routines of ordinary life. Typically a religion traces the value of human life to a "transcendent realm" *beyond* nature and human society. Rituals, prayer, and meditation are justified by sacred stories about transactions between the two realms.

Philosophers who interpret the religious idea of a transcendent realm in a **realist** fashion face a dilemma: either this realm has effects on the world of everyday experience or it does not. If it does not, then it is difficult to see how it can have any relevance for human life. But if it does, then it seems that the progress of science threatens its "transcendent" status. Since the scientific revolution of the seventeenth century, one tendency, running from **Descartes** to **Whitehead**, has endeavoured to construct metaphysical systems which encompass both sides of this dilemma. But another tendency, from **Berkeley** to **Duhem**, has counter-attacked with anti-realist interpretations of science, intended to leave room for realist accounts of Religion.

Following **Kant**, most philosophers have accepted that *knowledge* of a transcendent reality is unattainable, and religious thinkers, such as Karl Barth (1886–1968), have welcomed this conclusion, believing that it leaves room for "faith". Indeed Barth embraced the logical positivists' conclusion that the tenets of faith are literally meaningless, arguing that this underscores our utter dependence on Divine Grace. Religious language provides a means for talking about experiences of "numinous" awe, or "mystical" ecstasy or tranquility. It is clear that religious symbolism can express or evoke such experiences, and that those who have them feel that they are of immense significance – it matters a great deal to them that their "nirvana" is attained through a moral and meditative discipline and not by injecting a chemical which disrupts their normal brain function. However it is hard to see how the occurrence of such experiences can provide a basis for religious conviction. **Nietzsche** and the **existentialists** took the collapse of theistic realism to signal the need for a fundamental reappraisal of human values, and many followers of **Wittgenstein** have come to the conclusion that statements like "God is love" can only be understood as expressions of belief in the importance of human love. Such analyses accord with Matthew Arnold's comment that religion is "morality touched by emotion".

Anthropological studies have vastly extended our understanding of different forms of religious life. These studies have shown how religious doctrines can fulfil such social functions as legitimizing the distribution of power by reference to a "transcendent" source of authority supposedly beyond renegotiation. This complements philosophical scepticism about realist accounts of Religion.

Some thinkers (such as **Hegel**) have argued that the philosophical quest and the religious quest have the same goal, and indeed that the questions with which religions are concerned can

be answered only by philosophy. Much philosophical analysis is destructive of the metaphysical pretensions of traditional religious doctrine and of the idea that religious commitment can yield knowledge which cannot be attained by other means. At the very least the philosophical enterprise calls for detachment from one's preconceptions and a refusal to adopt beliefs which cannot be rationally justified. That such a commitment can be as total as any religious commitment is symbolized in the story of how **Socrates** met his death. Although philosophy no longer seems able to offer metaphysical consolations of the sort which sustained him, the quest for significance remains at its roots.

[J.H.P.]

**Ricoeur,** Paul (1913– ), French phenomenologist born in Valence. He has been hailed as one of the few modern thinkers to surmount the division between European and Anglo-American philosophy. Ricoeur is principally renowned for his original development of the **hermeneutic** method in philosophy, which consists in interpreting the meaning contained within pre-rational signs or symbols. Ricoeur's famous phrase "the symbol gives rise to thought" expresses the basic premise of hermeneutics: that the symbols of myth, religion, art and ideology all carry messages which may be uncovered by philosophical interpretation. Hermeneutics is defined accordingly as a method for deciphering indirect meaning, a reflective practice of unmasking hidden meanings beneath apparent ones. While this method had originally been used by theologians to investigate the inner meanings of sacred texts, it was radically redeployed by modern thinkers like **Dilthey**, **Heidegger**, **Gadamer** and Ricoeur to embrace man's general being in the world as an agent of language.

While a prisoner of war in Germany during the Second World War, Ricoeur became acquainted with the writings of German phenomenologists and existentialists. After the war, he launched his philosophical career with major works on **Jaspers** and **Marcel** and an extensive commentary on and translation of **Husserl's** *Ideas* (1950).

In contrast to **Sartre** and **Merleau-Ponty**, who developed French phenomenology in a polemical existentialist direction, Ricoeur turned it into a hermeneutic project. Concerned throughout his career with the ultimate ontological question – the meaning of Being – Ricoeur refuses what he sees as the "short cuts" of Hegel and Heidegger. He proclaims the inevitability of a "truncated ontology" which instead of presuming direct access to truth, accepts the obligation of always approaching it sideways – through the mediation of symbols, images, stories and ideologies. This indirect questioning of meaning, necessitated by the finite nature of human understanding, is what Ricoeur calls the "hermeneutic detour". It has led him through such inquiries as *The Symbolism of Evil* (1960), which analysed the symbols of myth and religion, and *Freud and Philosophy* (1965), concerned with the interpretation of dreams and unconscious desires, to an impressive variety of studies of the signifying activity of language, ideology and fiction – *The Conflict of Interpretations* (1969), *The Rule of Metaphor* (1975), *Hermeneutics and the Human Sciences* (1981), and *Time and Narrative* (1984–85).

Unlike the existentialists, who held that the human subject is the ultimate origin of all meaning, Ricoeur insisted that meaning is always mediated through cultural, linguistic and social signs. But unlike the **structuralists**, Ricoeur never abandoned the basic phenomenological notions of world, self and history.

An astute synthesiser of rival theories, Ricoeur has sought to chart a course beyond both the traditional ontology of absolute truth and the *avant-garde* ideology of the absolute text. Relentlessly faithful to an open-ended "conflict of interpretations", Ricoeur would seem to place his own philosophical bet on the possible existence of some transcendent meaning – although on his own principles such a meaning could never be known directly.

[R.K.]

**Rorty,** Richard (1931– ), American philosopher born in New York, whose central interest is in **metaphilosophy**. Starting from the work of **Quine** and others he has developed a comprehensive criticism of **analytic philosophy**. In the editorial introduction to his anthology, *The Linguistic Turn* (1967), Rorty argued that "the entire philosophical tradition" had been put "on the defensive" in the twentieth century. "What makes most philosophers in the English-speaking world linguistic philosophers," he wrote, "is the same thing that makes most philosophers in continental Europe phenomenologists – namely, a sense of despair resulting from the inability of traditional philosophers to make clear what could count as evidence for or against the truth of their views." This raised the question whether modern culture was moving into a "post-philosophical" phase, in which "philosophers will have worked themselves out of a job", and also posed problems for "talking about the history of philosophy". The way forward, Rorty suggested, might lie in overthrowing the "spectatorial account of knowledge" which had dominated philosophy "since Plato and Aristotle". Rorty detected "the beginning of a thoroughgoing rethinking" in the works of **Dewey, Hampshire, Sartre, Heidegger** and **Wittgenstein**.

Rorty executed this programme in *Philosophy and the Mirror of Nature* (1980), which argued that "traditional philosophy" in general is a desperate "attempt to escape from history". Ever since Descartes' "invention of the mind", philosophers had hoped to provide timeless "foundations" for knowledge, morality, language, or society; but they had never been able to establish that they were doing anything more than "eternalize" contingent prejudices. To replace the pretensions of "systematic philosophy", Rorty recommended the "edifying philosophy" which he claimed to find in Wittgenstein, Heidegger and Dewey – philosophers who had aimed "to help their readers, or society as a whole, break free from outworn vocabularies and attitudes, rather than to provide 'grounding' for the intuitions and customs of the present". Philosophy as Rorty conceives it is "a voice in a conversation", rather than "a subject" or "a field of professional inquiry". He has elaborated this conception in *Consequences of Pragmatism* (1982) and in later work on the theme of contingency. See also **History of Philosophy**.

[J.R.]

278

**Ross,** Sir W. David (1877–1971), Scots philosopher who taught at Oxford. He has two reputations. First, he was an Aristotelian scholar of the first rank; his editions of Aristotle's *Metaphysics*, *Physics* and *Analytics* with elaborate commentary and textual apparatus, are among the most important work on Aristotle in the twentieth century. Secondly, he was responsible for an influential re-statement of intuitionist **ethics**: the doctrine that we apprehend our various duties directly and do not derive them from any ulterior principle such as that of utility. Ross' statement of the position is a model of precision, clarity and moderation.

(J.O.U.)

**Rights,** *see* Ethics, Political Philosophy, Locke, Nozick, Rawls.

**Rousseau,** Jean-Jacques (1712–1778), French writer. Rousseau spent his life wandering from country to country, from faith to faith, from job to job, often in bad health and always the victim of his over-sensitive and emotional temperament.

His early essays portray the natural man as a creature of good instincts and simple tastes who has been corrupted and deprived of happiness by civilization, and particularly by urban life, class distinctions, and governmental tyranny. His novel *La Nouvelle Héloïse* (1761) glorified sentiment and emotion against the contemporary claims of reason and self-restraint. Its popularity and influence were immediate and immense. His next tale *Emile* (1762), the greatest of all writings on education, had an even wider and more lasting effect. It held that education should not curb or discipline the natural tendencies of the child but encourage them to grow and blossom. Teaching should come not from books and verbal instruction, but by example and direct experience of people and things. The family, not the school, is its proper field; and love and sympathy, not rules and punishments, the tools for the task. Religion should not be an affair of creeds and dogmas, of texts and formalities, but the infusion of the heart with feelings of awe and worship, feelings revelatory of a God who is beyond our reason. In his posthumously published *Confessions* Rousseau claimed to be giving the world the first completely uninhibited picture, in all its colours bright and dark alike, of a human soul.

Rousseau's work was of great historical importance as the first attack of the romantic movement against the eighteenth-century stronghold of classical rationalism. But the works noted above are not in the narrow sense philosophical, and his claims as a philosopher must rest on his theories of government. These are found chiefly in the *Discourse on the Origins of Inequality* (1755) and the *Social Contract* (1762). Rousseau was not a systematic nor even a coherent and orderly thinker. His writing is passionate and rhetorical; he saw society as Carlyle saw history – by flashes of lightning.

In the *Social Contract* Rousseau urges that government is justified only if sovereignty remains with the people. Every law must be passed by the direct votes of all the citizens. Representative democracy is rejected. He saw that this system gives absolute power to the majority and he makes various unconvincing attempts to explain why minorities must acquiesce. He rejects any limitation on the majority and any notion of individual rights. He realized that such a system would work only in very small states (and he was much influenced here by the examples of the Greek city-state and the Swiss canton). To remedy the weakness of such states he looked to federation but he never worked out this solution.

The application of laws to particular cases was assigned to a body which Rousseau called "the Government" whose constitution would vary according to the size of the state and other local conditions. All associations within the state should be eliminated so that the individual should feel no rival loyalties to his citizenship. The book remains the classic defence of democracy.

Rousseau, however, was well aware of the objections to direct democracy. It is incapable of continuous legislative activity, and he appears to have met this by the belief that laws could be few and general and that much of what we should call legislation could be left to "the Government". The people may also be ill-informed, short-sighted, and irrational. The remedy here is a "Legislator" a semi-divine individual who should draft legislation and persuade the assembly to enact it.

In the course of formulating these problems he was led to his key conception of the "General Will" and the "Will of All". The former is the will of a body of men directed to their own common interests, the latter a mere aggregate of private individual selfish wills. This conception had two separate aspects each of which had a more subtle and long-term influence than the obvious revolutionary implications of the theory of direct popular sovereignty.

First there is the suggestion that a state is a person with a will of its own distinct from the individual wills of its citizens and entitled to override them. This foreshadows much difficult and debated work on corporate personality and group psychology and it can be argued that it leads to a mystic nationalism with unlimited claims on individual loyalty.

Second there is the suggestion that the General Will is infallible. We cannot call any law an expression of it unless that law is genuinely in the public interest. Thus the General Will becomes an ideal conception to which actual laws may only approximate. Direct democracy is justified by the argument that if the people themselves make the laws under which they live they lose no freedom. But obedience to the General Will is justified by the argument that it is directed to the common good which is my good (or at least the good at which I am morally obliged to aim). Law is not an external command with the sanction of force, but the voice of my own moral or higher or true self. So political obligation can be (like the service of God) "perfect freedom".

But now it was not obvious why democracy was needed. As **Spinoza** has said: "Provided the laws are good, it does not matter who makes them". This tendency foreshadowed the theories of **Kant** and **Hegel** which identified duty with freedom, the State with the moral ideal, and laws with right and justice. This led to the glorification of the State as the supreme expression of morality.

Rousseau never clearly distinguished nor successfully reconciled these different strands. His work is therefore important as a source of ideas rather than as a system of arguments. See also **Political Philosophy.**

(J.D.M.)

**Royce,** Josiah (1855–1916), born in California, American spokesman for **idealism**. His philosophy had two main elements, the first of which may be called the principle of self-applicability. This requires that every philosophy should be able to account consistently for the very fact of its being expressed. By means of this weapon Royce sought to discredit virtually all alternatives to his own version of idealism – especially evolutionism and **pragmatism**; he believed that his idealism alone satisfied this principle.

The second principle is that of idealism itself. Royce insisted that everything has both a "that" and a "what", and that no philosophy is satisfactory which is forced to assert "that" when unable to specify "what". Now, the "what" of anything is simply its "meaning"; and it therefore follows for Royce that the core of a sound philosophy is a clear account of meaning. There are, he maintains, two types of meaning: external and internal. The external meaning of a thing consists in its relations to all other things; its internal meaning, or what it itself is, consists in its peculiar "embodiment of purpose". Royce then argues that "embodiment of purpose" is the mark of "mentality", and that, therefore, the internal essence of anything is mental. This is his version of idealism.

But if everything (including the false and the fictitious) embodies purpose, what is the criterion of truth or reality? Royce's answer is that the test of reality is conformity with the "ideal community" of purposes of humanity as a whole, past, present and future. Thus Royce's "Absolute", his "ultimate Real", is the ideal community of all human purposes. Aware that absolutism in Germany had led to anti-individualism, Royce devoted much labour to a defence of American democratic individualism, based on proofs of the reality of Time, Evil and Freedom. Royce's efforts to interpret Christianity in terms of natural science also had considerable influence upon theology.

(J.W.S.)

**Russell,** Bertrand Arthur William, third Earl Russell, (1872–1970), English philosopher. His father, Viscount Amberley, was the eldest son of Lord John Russell, the Liberal statesman, who became the first Earl Russell, and his mother was a daughter of the second Lord Stanley of Alderley. He was their second son and third child. His godfather was John Stuart **Mill.** Both his parents died before he was four years old and he was brought up by his grandmother, Lady Russell. After being privately educated, he won a mathematical scholarship to Trinity College, Cambridge, in 1890. In 1893 he turned from mathematics to philosophy, obtaining first class honours in 1894. Two years later, he published a work on German Social Democracy, the first of his many books. He was a Fellow of Trinity College, Cambridge, from 1895 to 1901 and a Lecturer in Philosophy from 1910 to 1916. During this period he was mainly occupied with mathematical logic, but he retained his interest in politics and in 1907 unsuccessfully fought a by-election at Wimbledon as candidate of the National Union of Women's Suffrage Societies. He was a militant pacifist in the First World War and was dismissed by Trinity College in 1916 after he had been prosecuted and fined for writing a leaflet about the case of a conscientious objector. In 1918 he was again prosecuted for writing an article in which he was held to have libelled the British Government and the American Army and he was sent to prison for six months. While in prison, he wrote his *Introduction to Mathematical Philosophy* (1919) and began work on the *Analysis of Mind* (1921).

In the years following the war Russell paid visits to Russia and China. He was disillusioned by the results of the Russian revolution, of which he had at first approved, but very favourably impressed by the old civilization of China. Though reinstated by Trinity in 1919, he resigned before taking up his duties there. He stood unsuccessfully as a Labour Candidate for Chelsea in the General Elections of 1922

and 1923 and in 1924 went on the first of many lecture tours to the United States. In 1927, in collaboration with his second wife, he founded a progressive school at Beacon Hill near Petersfield and there put into practice his theories on education. In the following decade he engaged extensively in political and social journalism. He continued to uphold pacifism but renounced it on the outbreak of the Second World War, the greater part of which he spent in the United States. After holding professorships at the Universities of Chicago and California, he was in 1940 as the result of social and religious prejudice judicially pronounced unworthy to be a professor at the College of the City of New York. He was then employed to lecture at the Barnes Foundation in Philadelphia, from which he was ejected in 1943, in circumstances which led him to bring a successful legal action for wrongful dismissal. In 1944 he returned to England having been re-elected to a fellowship at Trinity. After the war he continued to write, lecture and broadcast on a variety of subjects, his numerous books including two volumes of short stories. For a time he was in favour of the atomic bomb as a deterrent to the Russians, but he was later a protagonist in the Campaign for Nuclear Disarmament. Russell succeeded his elder brother in the earldom in 1931 and in 1949 was awarded the Order of Merit.

I. LOGIC AND MATHEMATICS

We have seen that Russell started his career as a mathematician and he stated that he was induced to take an interest in philosophy by his desire to find some reason for believing in the truth of mathematics. Under the influence of the works of F. H. **Bradley** he became a convert to **Hegelian** Idealism, but was soon re-converted by G. E. **Moore** to an extreme form of **realism**. Among other things, he was impressed by the argument that the fundamental idealist doctrine, that what is known is conditioned by the knowing of it, denies to the properties of mathematics any objective validity. Further, it seemed to him clear that mathematical propositions are irreducibly relational, and this led him to reject both the idealist thesis that relational judgments are vicious abstractions and the view, ascribed

Russell

to **Aristotle** and **Leibniz**, that all propositions are of the subject-predicate form. In his early book on Leibniz, Russell argued that it was Leibniz's acceptance of this view that provided the key to his metaphysics. On the other hand, while admiring John Stuart Mill, Russell was not satisfied with his theory that the propositions of pure mathematics are empirical generalizations, for this did not seem to him to afford a sufficient guarantee of their truth.

His own solution was to reduce mathematics to **logic**. This involved, first, the analysis of the fundamental terms of mathematics into purely logical concepts, and secondly the elaboration of a system of logic which was adequate to furnish the premises from which the propositions of mathematics could be deduced. The first part of the undertaking was carried out in the *Principles of Mathematics* (1903) and the second in *Principia Mathematica* (1910–13). His definition of number, in which he had been anticipated by the German mathematician **Frege**, made use of the concept of a one-one relation; that is, a relation such that if x is so related to y, no other term is so related to y and x has the relation to no other term. Two classes are said to be similar if their members can be correlated by a one-one relation. Then the number of a class is defined as the class of all those classes that are similar to it, and a cardinal number is defined as anything which is the number of some class. At that time Russell believed in the existence of classes. Later, he came to think that they were logical fictions, and thereby put the status of numbers again in question. But this was a difficulty which he did not resolve.

*Principia Mathematica* occupies an architectonic position in the development of symbolic logic. The breach with Aristotelian logic consisted not so much in the use of a special notation as in the greater generality of Russell and **Whitehead**'s system, and above all in their attempt to make it rigorously formal. How far they succeeded in this, or in their programme of deriving mathematics from logic, is a technical question about which there is still dispute. Other systems of logic have since been developed which lay claim to a greater rigour, but to a large extent they are constructed on the basis of Russell and Whitehead's work.

Perhaps Russell's most original contribution to this field was his introduction of the theory of types. This arose out of his discovery of a contradiction which made Frege say, when the news was communicated to him, that the whole foundation of mathematics had been undermined. It can be fairly easily set out. Most classes appear not to be members of themselves: for example it is not true that the class of men is itself a man. But some classes do appear to be members of themselves. For instance, the class of all the things that can be counted would itself appear capable of being counted. Now consider the class of all classes which are not members of themselves. Is it or is it not a member of itself? If it is, it is not, and if it is not, it is. Similar contradictions can be found in other fields. A notorious example is the paradox of Epimenides the Cretan who said that all Cretans were liars. Another starts from the point that some words are predicable of themselves and others not. Thus the word "short" is short but the word "long" is not long. Let us call those that are so predicable "autological" and those that are not "heterological". Then is the word "heterological" predicable of itself? If it is, it is not, and if it is not, it is.

Russell's solution of the paradoxes was to arrange objects into a hierarchy of types, so that what can be true or false of objects of one type cannot significantly be said about those of another. In particular, if a given class is the extension of a given predicate, it is nonsensical to apply that predicate to that class. Thus it is not false but nonsensical to say that the class of men is human: the question whether the word "heterological" is itself autological or heterological is a meaningless question. Even when a predicate does appear to characterize objects of different types, it does not have the same meaning in each case. Thus a predicate like "being countable" becomes, as Russell put it, systematically ambiguous.

The theory of types, of which only the outline has been given here, has a certain *ad hoc* air about it. Not all forms of self-reference are logically vicious: and we seem to have no adequate rules for picking out the cases in which it is to be prohibited. But the theory has had a strong historical influence. By calling attention to the fact that a sentence might be grammatically well-formed and yet succeed in saying nothing, it prepared the way for the **logical positivists'** rejection of metaphysics, their declaration that the statements typically made by metaphysicians were not even false but literally meaningless.

## II. THEORY OF KNOWLEDGE

Russell always tried to integrate his logic with his theory of knowledge, and he accordingly identified his statements of lowest type, the statements that formed the basis of his semantic hierarchy, with those that were epistemologically primitive. In *The Problems of Philosophy* (1912) he drew a distinction between what he called knowledge by description and knowledge by acquaintance and he took as his basic propositions, as those which supply the foundation for all our empirical knowledge, propositions which refer only to things with which one is directly acquainted. The meaning which he here gave to "acquaintance" was such that if one was acquainted with an object it followed that the object really existed and really had the properties that it was apprehended as having. The existence and properties of things that were known only by description he regarded on the other hand as being problematic.

At that time Russell held that the things with which one could be acquainted were one's own private sense-data, images, thoughts and feelings (both present and past since he allowed memory to be a form of direct knowledge), one's own self and **universals**. Subsequently he dropped one's self from the list, for he came to hold that selves did not exist as separate entities, that is as distinct from the experiences which were attributed to them, but he continued to hold that we are acquainted both with our own sense-data and with universals. Contemporary criticisms of the notion of sense-data did not disturb him but there is reason to think that he would have liked to dispense with universals. The recognition of such abstract entities runs counter to the "robust feeling for reality" which he always claimed for his philosophizing. He did not, however, see how it is possible to dispense with them. He allowed, it

may be wrongly, that one can successfully take the nominalist step of reducing them all to the single relation of resemblance, that one can, for example, substitute for the quality "whiteness" the relation of resemblance in being white: but he did not think that much is to be gained by this as resemblance, in his view, is itself a universal.

When he wrote *The Problems of Philosophy* Russell believed that physical objects were known only by description. They were postulated as the causes of sense-data. But following his principle "Wherever possible substitute constructions out of known entities for inferences to unknown entities", a principle which he called the supreme maxim in scientific philosophy, he abandoned this view in favour of the theory that physical objects are logical constructions out of actual and possible sense-data. This amounts to claiming that statements about physical objects can be faithfully translated into statements about sense-data. This theory was developed by Russell in *Our Knowledge of the External World* (1914) and in two of the essays reprinted in *Mysticism and Logic* (1918). Roughly speaking, his view was that at any given moment each observer perceives a private three-dimensional world with its own private space, or spaces, since he distinguishes the space of sight from the space of touch. He called such private worlds "perspectives". In addition to these perceived perspectives, there exists also an infinite number of unperceived perspectives, namely all those that would be perceived if an observer were in the appropriate state and position. These contain not sense-data but what Russell called "sensibilia", entities which are generically similar to sense-data but are not actually sensed. He did not fully work out this theory, which encounters obvious difficulties even if one is willing to assume that sensibilia and unperceived perspectives literally exist.

In later years, Russell reverted to a causal theory of perception. He came to think that it alone can do justice to the evidence which is furnished by science. A curious feature of his causal theory was that he located sense-data in the percipient's brain. He did not mean by this that when we think that we are perceiving the world around us we are, in any literal sense, really observing only our own brains. His argument was rather that an event's position in space-time is determined by its causal relations and that "the causal and temporal connections of percepts with events in afferent and efferent nerves gives percepts a position in the brain of the observer". It might be thought that if percepts are to be admitted as entities one would do better to maintain that they are not the sort of things that can be located in physical space at all.

Russell's reductionism was carried to its furthest point in *The Analysis of Mind* (1921), where he adopted a theory which is akin to the neutral monism of William **James**. He there held that both mind and matter are logical constructions out of elements, primarily sense-data, which are themselves neither mental nor physical. They are distinguished by the fact that certain elements, such as images and feelings, enter only into the constitution of minds, and by the operation of different causal laws. Thus the same sense-data when correlated according to the laws of physics constitute physical objects and when correlated according to the laws of psychology help to constitute minds. In their mental aspect they engage, among other things, in what Russell called *mnemic causation*, a kind of action at a distance by which experiences produce subsequent memory images. Though Russell gave up the reductionist view of the nature of physical objects, he retained it with respect to minds, in the sense that he rejected the notion of consciousness or the self as a substantial entity. On the other hand, while he dallied with behaviourism, he never denied the existence of states of consciousness which are not definable in physical terms.

III. NAMES AND DESCRIPTIONS

Russell's predilection for William of **Ockham**'s razor was not merely due to a love of intellectual economy for its own sake, though this may have played its part. His main reason for using it was epistemological; his belief that the more entities you allow yourself to postulate, the greater the risk of your being wrong. There are also semantic considerations which are displayed in his famous theory of definite descriptions, a theory which he himself regarded as one of his most important contributions to philosophy. This theory was sketched in the paper "On Denoting" (1905),

more rigorously formulated in the first volume of *Principia Mathematica*, and further explained in the *Introduction to Mathematical Philisophy*. The philosophical problem which gave rise to it was that of showing how it was possible to speak meaningfully of non-existent objects, such as the present King of France, or even of objects which could not possibly exist such as the round square, as in the statement "The round square is a contradiction". His solution was to show that expressions of the form "the so and so", at least in this usage, never function as names. It does not follow from the fact that they are meaningful that there is any object which they mean. His method of showing this was to give a rule for translating the sentence in which the definite descriptive phrase occurs, in such a way that the phrase no longer looks as if it were a name. Thus, to take his own best known example, the statement "The author of Waverley was Scott" becomes in his translation a conjunction of the three statements "At least one person wrote Waverley"; "At most one person wrote Waverley"; and "It is not the case that anyone both wrote Waverley and was not identical with Scott". To put it symbolically, as Russell would have preferred, he held that to say that the thing which has $\phi$ has $\psi$, when $\phi$ is the property concealed in the definite description and $\psi$ the property attributed to what it describes, is to say that there is an $x$, such that $x$ has $\phi$, and, for all $y$, if $y$ has $\phi$ $y$ is identical with $x$, and $x$ has $\psi$. Thus, any description of the subject goes into the predicate, and what Russell called a "bare particular" is left to be the value of the variable $x$.

This theory, which has been called "a paradigm of philosophy", later came in for criticism on the ground that it makes definite descriptive statements false when they fail in their reference, whereas it would be more in accordance with ordinary usage to say in that case that they were neither true or false. A more serious objection, which does not directly impugn the truth of the theory but does diminish its importance, is that Russell throughout assumed a defective view of meaning, in that he identified the meaning of substantives with their denotation. The main reason why definite descriptions, and even ordinary proper names, like "Homer" and "Napoleon", are turned by him into predicates is that they do not guarantee the success of their reference. It is always logically possible that they should denote nothing. But if the statements in which they occur are to be meaningful Russell thought that their analysis must terminate in statements containing substantival words whose denotation was guaranteed. The ultimate values of his existential variables are denoted by what he called logically proper names.

This is the basis of the doctrine of Logical Atomism which Russell, under the influence of his pupil **Wittgenstein**, put forward in the years following the First World War. The view is that, in the last analysis, the world consists of atomic facts and these facts are characterized by their directly, as it were photographically, corresponding to elementary propositions. The elementary propositions are those which are expressed by conjoining a lowest level predicate with one or more logically proper names. And once more tying up his logic with his theory of knowledge, Russell tended to assume that these logically proper names stood for sense-data: for it is plausible to argue that only demonstrative expressions which stand for sense-data are bound to succeed in their reference. It may be thought, however, that the whole enterprise was misconceived, since there seems no good reason to suppose that for a referential statement to be meaningful it is necessary that its reference should be logically guaranteed.

In the *Inquiry into Meaning and Truth* (1940), Russell gave this theory a new aspect by identifying particulars with qualities. His motive was to eliminate what he regarded as the metaphysical notion of substance. He therefore followed **Berkeley** in treating the things of common-sense as collections of qualities, united by what he called the relation of compresence. This view is retained in Russell's last important philosophical work, *Human Knowledge: Its Scope and Limits* (1948), which is otherwise of interest chiefly for his attempt to deal with the problem of induction. He took the view that inductive reasoning stands in need of justification and he elaborated a set of principles which he thought would be sufficient for the purpose. He did not,

however, claim that any of these principles can be known to be true.

From the purely philosophical point of view, Russell's work in the field of ethics and of social and political philosophy was not of comparable interest with his work on logic and the theory of knowledge. He had been persuaded that ethical statements have no objective validity, a conclusion which he confessed to disliking on emotional grounds; and was therefore inclined to hold that the main questions in ethics are psychological and social; the question of what people desire and how they may attain it. In the sphere of education and of politics he was above all an advocate of liberty. Though he was more keenly aware of the irrational features in human conduct, his political position was in many ways strongly reminiscent of that of John Stuart Mill.

It has been shown that Russell often changed his philosophical views, but his approach to philosophy was highly consistent. His aim was always to find reasons for accepted beliefs, whether in the field of mathematics, natural science, or common sense. He was a consistent Sceptic, not in the sense that he denied our claims to knowledge, but that he questioned them. He adhered also to a single method: the method of starting with propositions which are the least susceptible to doubt, and trying to reconstruct the edifice of knowledge on this basis, with as few assumptions as possible. The result of this was that his justifications usually took the form of analyses: even so he was not interested in analysis for its own sake, but only as a method of proof. In this way, as in the power and elegance of his literary style, he remained in the high tradition of British Empiricism, the tradition of Hobbes, Locke, Berkeley, Hume and Mill. He was its outstanding representative in the twentieth century.

(A.J.A.)

**Ryle,** Gilbert (1900–1976), born in Brighton; Professor at Oxford and probably the most widely influential British philosopher of his generation.

He was at one time much influenced by the earlier writings of **Husserl**, but already in the early nineteen-thirties he was adumbrating one of the characteristic doctrines of modern linguistic analysis when he suggested that the task of philosophy was "the detection of the sources in linguistic idioms of recurrent misconceptions and absurd theories". In *Dilemmas* (1954) he suggested that philosophical problems arise from apparent conflicts between general truths none of which we could sincerely abandon; the task of philosophy was therefore to resolve these apparent conflicts by an elucidation of the concepts which were used in stating these truths; philosophy was then essentially the dissolution of dilemmas arising from our imperfect understanding of our own conceptual apparatus. This position is akin to, but not identical with, that of the later **Wittgenstein**.

Ryle's best known work, *The Concept of Mind* (1949) exemplifies this theory of the nature of philosophy. Ryle considers that problems about the nature of mind and the relation of the mind to the body arise from a misunderstanding of the concept of mind and of concepts of such mental "states" and "activities" as willing, thinking or imagining. We are inclined to construe the mind as an extra object situated in the body and controlling it by a set of unwitnessable activities; this is what he calls the dogma of the ghost (the mind) in the machine (the body). Ryle regards this picture as totally misleading and in a series of brilliant studies he attempts to disabuse us of it by showing that mental concepts refer not to ghostly acts but to dispositions to behave in certain ways in appropriate circumstances, to the style of actual witnessable performances and similar unproblematic matters. He protests vigorously that he is not putting forward a doctrine of behaviourism, not denying in any way the reality of the mental life, but only attempting to clarify the nature of the mental. But the work has often been attacked as behaviouristic and it has been suggested that Ryle at this stage had not wholly freed himself of the "reductive" tendencies of **Russell**.

In his treatment of mind and elsewhere Ryle has made much use of the notion of a "category mistake"; we make a category mistake when we misunderstand what kind of concept we are using or considering, as if we were to think that the University of Oxford were something that we could visit in addition to the Colleges. To think of the mind as a hidden substance is such a category mistake.

Apart from his studies in the nature of philosophy and the concept of mind Ryle's main work has been on the nature of meaning and the philosophy of logic; he has also contributed to Platonic scholarship. Ryle is also the author of articles on **categories**, **epistemology**, and **solipsism** in this Encyclopedia.

(J.O.U.)

# S

**Saint-Simon,** Claude-Henri de Rouvroy, Comte de (1760–1825), French socialist and philosopher of history, *see* Comte, Positivism.

**Santayana,** George (1863–1952), American philosopher born in Spain. As a **Sceptic**, he denied that the existence of anything can ever be proved, and insisted that all beliefs as to existence are based upon "animal faith". As a Platonic **realist**, however, he insisted that we have indubitable knowledge of **universals** or "essences". The proposed bridge between these two sides of his thought is the claim that essences (which both are and are not real) do not *exist*.

The above paragraph has used the word "real" in **Plato**'s sense, but Santayana does not generally so use it. "To be real" for him means to exist in space and time; and he insists that all reality in this sense is material. In his metaphysical scheme the "Realm of Matter" is the basic real. Essences, according to this way of talking, are ideal only. Thus, in an unorthodox way, Santayana seeks to combine **realism** and **idealism**.

Another strange union in his philosophy is between hard-boiled naturalism and aesthetic romanticism. He could combine the harshest naturalistic description of what exists in space and time (the stone of sculpture, the canvas of painting, the sound waves of music) with the most sensitive appreciation of the ideal content of the work of art. His metaphysical distinction between the "reality" of matter and the "ideality" of essence assists him in this. He was himself a poet of considerable talent; and the literary quality of his prose is generally very high.

In **religion** Santayana repeatedly proclaimed his **naturalism** and materialism, insisting that the essence of religion is myth and poetry. Emotionally, however, he was unquestionably Roman Catholic. He never concealed his utter disdain for Protestantism, and his later works show that his Catholicism was more than skin deep. The last years of his life were spent in a Catholic retreat in Rome.

(J.W.S.)

**Sartre,** Jean-Paul (1905–1980), born in France. His name is almost synonymous with **existentialism** throughout the world. A highly original and talented thinker, who expressed himself with equal facility in philosophical and literary works, Sartre was the epitome of the "committed" intellectual. Instead of opting for the life of a professional philosopher in an academic institution, he communicated his ideas to a wider audience by adopting a popular style in several of his theoretical works and by composing a series of plays and novels which earned him international acclaim as a writer. He was offered the Nobel Prize for literature in 1964, but refused it.

Having taught for a brief spell at a Lycée in Le Havre, Sartre travelled to Germany in 1933 to study **phenomenology** at first hand. **Husserl** and **Heidegger** – the principal exponents of German phenomenology – were the main influences, though **Hegel, Kierkegaard** and **Kant** also figured strongly in his existentialist writings. What most fascinated him about the phenomenological movement was its determination to describe human consciousness as it exploded into the world, intentionally relating to the everyday things around it and dynamically projecting new meanings for its future. (See **Intentionality.**) Human existence was revealed accordingly as first and foremost a being-in-the-world (*être-au-monde*). And this meant in turn that even the most ordinary objects of our environment could be treated as matters of immediate philosophical concern. Sartre has described the enthusiasm with which he and other

French thinkers like **Merleau-Ponty** and Simone **de Beauvoir** greeted the phenomenological invitation to "philosophise about everything – even the essence of a gas street lamp". Nothing appeared more important to these French existentialists than the "promotion of street lamps to the dignity of philosophical objects". Philosophy had abandoned its academic haven and was now to be found in the streets.

All of Sartre's works share a commitment to a philosophy of freedom. His famous claim that existence precedes essence exemplifies this. There is no such thing as a given "human nature", determining how we act and behave. On the contrary, it is our everyday acts and choices that make up our identity. Man first of all exists, Sartre argues, and defines himself afterwards.

Sartre did not deny that we are always "situated" in a concrete world. His claim was that it is precisely our way of responding to such situations which constitutes our freedom. We can choose either to abandon ourselves to the prevailing state of affairs, passively conforming to the *status quo* and reducing ourselves to the status of a mere object among objects. Or we can choose to transcend what is given by projecting ourselves authentically towards a new horizon of possibility. Either way, we are always choosing what we are, and never able not to choose. We are what we make of ourselves, as Sartre proclaims in his polemical essay *Existentialism and Humanism* (1947).

It follows from this that "man is condemned to be free". Even such factors as the unconscious or social class could not, for Sartre, deprive man of his ultimate responsibility and freedom. While we do not of course decide what class, sex, language or world we are born with, we do decide what is to be made of them. In other words, we are at all times free to create and recreate the meaning of our world in terms of a project of possibilities reaching into the future.

Not surprisingly, Sartre's first two philosophical works, published in the thirties, were devoted to an analysis and assessment of imagination (see *Imagination*, 1936 and *The Psychology of Imagination* 1940). His basic argument in these works is that consciousness negates the world as it is and invents a possible one in its stead. Here we find the seeds of Sartre's decisive ontological conviction that human being is free and for-itself because it has this capacity for negation – the power not to be what it is and to be what it is not.

This conviction was developed in Sartre's subsequent writings – and most notably his monumental work *Being and Nothingness* (1943). Here Sartre explored the central existential dilemma – how can human consciousness relate positively to other people and things in the world if its very freedom as a being-for-itself is defined *against* what is other than itself? Existence is described accordingly as an absurd conflict between freedoms, each one trying to "nihilate" the other in order to preserve its own sovereign autonomy.

But how is moral action or political commitment possible? This question was relentlessly pursued in Sartre's novels (*Nausea* and the *Roads to Freedom* trilogy) and plays (*No Exit*, *The Condemned of Altona*, *The Flies*, *The Respectful Prostitute* and *The Devil and the Good Lord*). It also figured centrally in most of his post-war philosophical works and accounts for his growing interest in Marxism – an interest which began as early as *What is Literature?* (1947) where Sartre first raised the controversial notion of "committed writing". The attempt to reconcile the existentialist claim for individual freedom and the Marxist claim for collective revolution became most explicit in *The Critique of Dialectical Reason*, the first volume of which was published in 1960 (Volume Two appeared posthumously in 1985.) Indeed the debate between existentialism and Marxism dominated much of French intellectual life in the post-war period and featured centrally in the columns of *Les Temps Modernes*, the left-wing journal founded and co-edited by Sartre, Merleau-Ponty and de Beauvoir.

In his later writings, Sartre seems to have rediscovered his early fascination with the powers of imagination. He devoted several full-length works to the study of the existential crisis of creativity experienced by writers such as Genet, Mallarmé and Flaubert (the last of which extended to three massive volumes published in 1971–72). He even wrote an autobiographical

account of his own imaginative journey through childhood (*Words*, 1964). But Sartre's return to the theme of imagination was not a retreat from the political fray. Up to his death in 1980, Sartre retained his combative stance, frequently crossing swords with structuralists, psychoanalysts, doctrinaire Marxists, and of course the right-wing French bourgeoisie whom he took great delight in denouncing as "salauds". Perhaps the most abiding feature of Sartre's work was his unswerving attachment to the freedom of a critical intellect that always refused the compromise of certainty.

[R.K.]

**Saussure,** Ferdinand de (1857–1913), Swiss philologist who founded modern structural linguistics with his *Course in General Linguistics* (1916). The book was created after his death, out of various sets of students' notes, by two of his disciples. To this apocryphal but seminal text we owe above all a theory of the sign, conceived as the union of a signifier, a form, and a signified, an idea. The relationship between these is not natural, but arbitrary; nor is it autonomous: it depends on the network of relationships within language as a whole – a sign has a "value" before it has signification. Thus, language is conceived as a system: the *Course* distinguishes *langue*, the code common to all the speakers of a language, from *parole*, the individual speech-act which externalizes the system. Finally, the object of linguistics is defined as synchronic rather than diachronic: the linguist studies the system in a particular state, without reference to its evolution in time. There is another, darker side to Saussure: the never-published notebooks in which he develops the theory that Latin poets concealed anagrams in their texts. This dubious theory nevertheless anticipates contemporary conceptions of the free play of the signifier.

[J.-J.L.]

**Scepticism.** Scepticism is a doctrine which holds the possibilities of knowledge to be limited. In one form it contends that there are things which cannot, in principle, be known at all; in another that knowledge of some things can only be attained with difficulty and given certain precautions. In this second form it supports a methodological policy of reserve and circumspection in the formation of beliefs. Its opposite is dogmatism. Different species of scepticism are distinguished in two principal ways: by reference either to the methods of inquiry whose reliability is questioned or to the kind of objects whose knowability is doubted. Doubt of methods may be general, on the ground that there is no infallible way of getting knowledge and that all methods have failed at some time or other. But more usually scepticism of methods is partial and depreciates the trustworthiness of one recognized source of knowledge in the interests of another. Reason and sense-experience have been set against one another and again jointly defended against the pretensions of authority, revelation and intuition. On the other hand, defenders of faith like **Pascal**, have expressed a radical scepticism about the ability of reason to arrive at religious truth. Thus **Averroism**, which distinguishes the natural truth accessible to reason from the supernatural truth that is beyond its reach, is ambiguous. It may be a sincere belief that the unaided human intelligence cannot acquire religious knowledge, but it may also be ironical and imply that since reason is unable to acquire such knowledge it cannot be acquired at all.

It is more usual for particular and limited varieties of scepticism to be defined by means of the objects held to be unknowable. Sceptical arguments have been used to deny that we can get knowledge of any matters of empirical fact, of the external world of material objects, of the minds of others, of the past, of the future, of nature as a whole, of values and of any objects of religious or metaphysical speculation which lie beyond sense-experience. Scepticism about objects has three levels or degrees. The Sceptic may admit that the objects in question exist but deny that we can ever know any more than this about them. **Kant**'s position on things-in-themselves is sceptical in this sense as is that of the inductive Sceptic about laws of nature. Secondly, he may assert that the objects in question do not in fact exist: the standpoint of the ordinary religious Sceptic about God, of

the ethical Sceptic about an order of values and of many philosophers about a substantive and immortal soul. Finally, he may assert that the objects in question could not possibly exist and therefore that knowledge of the sort he is doubting is logically ruled out. **Berkeley**'s attitude to material substance and **Hume**'s to real or intrinsic connexions between events are instances of this type.

General or total scepticism has always been rare, most Sceptics being the partisans of one method or one type of object. There are good reasons for taking general scepticism to be a kind of dialectical extravagance. To start with there is an obvious air of paradox about it. It seems self-refuting to say that nothing at all can be known, for to assert it is to claim at least one piece of knowledge, the truth of the sceptical principle itself. This was clear to Pyrrho, the first sceptical philosopher who concluded that the principle could only be held tentatively, a rather enfeebling manoeuvre. According to **Russell**'s theory of types general scepticism, since it refers to itself, is not capable of significant formulation. In general, it can be argued, if one is to have any reasonable ground for scepticism there must be something of which one is not sceptical. The usual reason for sceptical doubt is the experience or possibility of failure in claims to knowledge. Failure reveals itself through inconsistency and to recognize this we must be aware that contradictory statements have been made and that the law of contradiction is true. Furthermore past experience of failure in a given type of thinking is only relevant to one's future confidence in it if the rationality of inductive argument is assumed. A man could conceivably exhibit complete scepticism by refusing to claim any knowledge at all. What he could not do is offer a rational defence for his procedure.

Scepticism as a philosophy began with Pyrrho (c. 300 B.C.) in the same way as it has from time to time recurred, as the expression of discontent with the intellectual chaos produced by the conflict of dogmatic systems. For Pyrrho philosophy was a practical art whose aim was detachment and peace of mind (*ataraxia*). This goal could not be attained unless the inevitably frustrating search for truth were abandoned. Most of the conceivable arguments for scepticism are to be found in the thought of the Greek Sceptics as reported by Sextus Empiricus. Aenesidemus put forward ten "tropes" which set out in detail the reasons for doubting the reliability of perception. Agrippa's five "tropes" are more compact and more far-reaching. As well as the relative or subjective nature of perception, he lists the infinite regress of proof propounded by Carneades, the conflict of opinions between men, the inevitably hypothetical character of all ultimate premises and the logical circularity of the syllogism, later emphasised by J. S. Mill. Some Sceptics, Arcesilaus for example, concluded that since certainty was not to be had men must make do with probability and Carneades suggested that coherence of beliefs was a measure of reliability, that the more systematic one's body of beliefs the more reason there was for confidence in it. Since the period of the Greek Sceptics (of the fourth to second centuries B.C.) scepticism has reappeared from time to time in the history of thought. Abelard's Sic et Non, (Yes and No) a collection of contradictory opinions by the Fathers on points of doctrine, introduced a sceptical technique that was used by Kant in setting out the antinomies with which he sought to prove the impossibility of constructive metaphysics. The anti-Aristotelian and anti-Scholastic logicians of the Renaissance prepared the way for the more thorough-going Sceptics of the sixteenth century whose most distinguished representative was Montaigne. Hume is the most penetrating and comprehensive of modern Sceptics. He argued that our belief in bodies, minds and causes rested not on reason or the senses but on the workings of the imagination which was naturally constituted so as to make a coherent structure out of the disorderly flux of sense-impressions that was all we really knew. Hume's intentions are ambiguous and insecure enough for it to have been plausibly argued that he was not really a Sceptic at all but rather a defender of "natural belief" against irrelevantly rigorous criteria of knowledge.

This interpretation is in sympathy with a doctrine deriving from G. E. Moore, and ultimately from Reid, which argues that common-sense beliefs are more deserving of our confidence than the arguments of sceptical philosophers and that philosophical scepticism is insincere, or, at best, "methodological", a technique for bringing to light principles and criteria of knowledge ordinarily taken for granted. To the followers of Wittgenstein philosophical scepticism is a symptom of conceptual confusion and disorder, an indication that language is being misunderstood and put to an improper use. It is argued that we can only learn what "knowledge" and "certainty" mean by hearing them used in connection with material objects, past events, other people's feelings and so on, and that it is senseless to inquire whether these paradigm cases are genuine instances of knowledge and certainty.

Wisdom and Ayer have suggested that problems in the theory of knowledge have a characteristic pattern and commonly arise in a sceptical form. In each case there is an apparent conflict between (1) our evidence, what is given or known directly (sense-impressions, present events, other people's words and deeds, particular occurrences), (2) what we claim to know (material things, past events, other people's feelings, laws of nature) and (3) the fact that what we claim to know goes logically beyond the evidence for it. Sceptical theories say that we must abandon the claims to knowledge (2). But there are less catastrophic ways out of the difficulty. Causal and analogical theories resolve the inconsistency by appealing to principles that validate inference from the evidence to logically distinct conclusions. Reductive theories like phenomenalism deny (3); intuitionist theories like naïve realism deny that we are confined to the evidence specified in (1). To many philosophers scepticism is of no serious importance as a philosophical theory. Its point is to make us aware of what is involved in our claims to knowledge and perhaps, by doing so, to render them more secure.

(A.Q.)

**Sceptics.** "Sceptics" is a name given to certain groups of philosophers in the Hellenistic-Roman period who, doubting the capacity of senses and reason to furnish knowledge of the nature of things, advocated suspension of judgment. There are three phases: (1) Pyrrhonism (late fourth and third century B.C.), inaugurated by Pyrrho, expounded by his pupil Timon; (2) the Middle and New Academy (third to first century B.C.), represented by Arcesilaus, Carneades, Clitomachus and Philo of Larissa; (3) the new Pyrrhonism of Aenesidemus and Agrippa (from the first century B.C.).

The common ground of the Sceptics was an epistemological attack on all philosophies which were dogmatic, that is which claimed to have discovered truth. There seems no way, said the Sceptics, of penetrating beyond "appearances" to a knowledge of external objects. Sense perception gives contradictory reports and there is no criterion in sensation itself to distinguish true from false impressions. Nor is there any criterion of correct judgment, and an attempt to find one must lead to an infinite regress. Thus we must withhold our judgment.

(1) To Pyrrho of Elis (c. 360–c. 270 B.C.) the ethical end of imperturbability was the mainspring of philosophy. This was a typical goal of his troubled age; the novelty of Pyrrho lay in the method by which he sought to attain it. With no means of arriving at knowledge, no single thing could be said to be in itself any more this than that; no argument could be judged more certain than its opposite. The external stimulus of belief, desire, emotion was thus severed, which produced indifference, on which followed tranquility; and one is left with no guide for action other than custom.

(2) Pyrrhonism faded out before the dialectical scepticism of the Middle and New academy, a logical attack directed principally against the **Stoic** theory of knowledge, which held that special sense-perceptions caused by real objects irresistibly demanded the assent of the wise man. Arcesilaus of Pitane (315 – 241–0 B.C.) argued that there is no discernible difference between true and false perceptions, and that the latter may be as irresistible as the former. In teaching he adopted the basic sceptical practice of arguing impartially on both sides of any question. His scepticism may have had roots in **Socrates** as well as Pyrrho.

Carneades of Cyrene (214–213 – 129–8 B.C.), the most formidable of the Sceptics, systematized the attack on dogmatism. With a wealth of brilliant argument against the possibility that true and false sense-impressions are distinguishable in themselves, and against the capacity of any rational process to do more than test formal validity, he swept the **epistemology** of the Stoa from the field. He severely damaged their anthropocentric theology and their theories of divination, providence and fatalism. In a systematic review of all ethical ends he demonstrated logical difficulties in the Stoic moral goal, and on a famous embassy to Rome in 166–5, he argued the relativity of moral terms. In practical life he proposed a theory of probability as a guide for action; there were three grades of probability: the probable; the probable and undisputed; the probable, undisputed and tested; the latter being the highest state of belief that is reached when a whole system of connected ideas is formed agreeing logically with each other. Carneades left no writings, but was fully reported by his voluminous successor, Clitomachus of Carthage. Philo of Larissa was still maintaining scepticism in the first century B.C. but his successor, Antiochus of Ascalon, turned the Academy to an eclecticism in which Stoic views were incorporated.

(3) It was outside the Academy that the sceptical movement flowed strongly for the next two or three centuries. The new sect professed to look beyond the Academy to the more complete scepticism of Pyrrhonism. Academic Sceptics had no right to deny the possibility of knowledge; assent should be witheld even from this. On the other hand there seemed no basis even for opinion; a man could but take things as he found them and live by custom, convention, tradition. But the new Pyrrhonists gladly accepted the Academic tradition of dialectical argument, and combining with this the **empiricism** of the Empiric Medical School, drew up a complete systematisation of sceptical arguments. Aenesidemus of Cnossus, probably an earlier contemporary of Cicero, dealt with the relative nature of sense-perception in his Ten Tropes (or Modes) of Witholding Assent. Every perception was relative to the percipient, object and concomitant external and internal circumstances, so that the

object itself was inapprehensible. Later Agrippa in his Five Modes of Attack used relativity like Aenesidemus and found four types of fallacies in dogmatic arguments: discrepancy of theories, infinite regress, hypothetical assumption, and circular reasoning. We finally hear of two ultimate Modes: nothing is apprehended intuitively, as is shown by the disagreements of philosophers; nor can anything be apprehended through something else, or one is involved in circular reasoning or infinite regress. The sceptical attack on causation is likewise classified by Aenesidemus in Eight Modes, directed against the inadmissibility of a dogmatic jump to the non-apparent, unconfirmed by any evidence from appearances. There is no certain connexion between reality and phenomena; a reason is arbitrarily chosen to suit the theory of the moment. There is also an interesting argument on the relativity of cause and effect: if cause is productive of effect it must exist before it (which will lead to an infinite regress); but since cause is relative to effect it cannot be prior in existence (and their relativity makes any argument concerning them circular). The whole edifice of scepticism may be explored in the works of Sextus Empiricus (late second century A.D.) which are all the more valuable for their lack of originality.

Scepticism was of immense importance in an age dominated by the dogmatic philosophies of stoicism and epicureanism; indeed a persistent movement of doubt and inquiry which insists on keeping open for examination any assertion seems fundamental for all philosophy. In addition, stoic examinations of sense-perception, causality and probability are of great interest in much recent philosophy.

(I.G.K.)

**Schelling**, Friedrich W. J. (1775–1854), the *Wunderkind* of German **idealism** and "the Proteus of philosophy" to his contemporaries, must be recognized as a magnificent failure. However, the failure is that of **metaphysics** and moral philosophy themselves. The fact that failures are often more instructive than successes may explain why after long being buried under a flourishing **Hegel**

renaissance Schelling has now returned to haunt contemporary philosophy. Recent research has concentrated less on his last, highly religious works, *Philosophy of Mythology* and *Philosophy of Revelation* (1821–43), than on the major works of his early and middle periods, e.g. *Ideas for a Philosophy of Nature* (1797), *On the World-Soul: A Hypothesis of Advanced Physics toward an Explanation of the Universal Organism* (1798), *System of Transcendental Idealism* (1800), and *On the Essence of Human Freedom* (1809), along with a series of sketches, *The Ages of the World* (1810–14). As the titles indicate, the two principal themes in Schelling's philosophy are **nature** and **freedom**. Yet why "failure"? And why "magnificent"?

The problems of nature and freedom in modern philosophy arise from the notorious Cartesian split between extended substance and thinking substance. Schelling regards all philosophy after **Descartes** as sterile and even mutilated, inasmuch as its "subjective idealism" has cut it off from nature. He traces the Cartesian split back to the Manichaean-Augustinian tradition in theology. As long as **dualism** vitiates philosophy, with its oppositions of mind/matter, subject/object, good/evil, etc., the genuine problems remain insoluble. Schelling tries to confront those problems head-on by developing an "objective" or "real" idealism and a philosophy of absolute "identity". Yet as he tries to absorb the negative sides of each duality back into the positive sides – matter back into spirit, evil back into the good, etc. – in order to account for their ultimate unity, the entire Judaeo-Christian tradition of **ontology** and **ethics** is made to tremble. Whereas Hegelian dialectic often seems to be a machine that bulldozes its path of Progress, Schelling's meditation never forgets the damage done: however nostalgic for "eternal joy", it stresses the "source of sadness" in moral philosophy, "the veil of melancholy draped over all nature, the profound and indestructible melancholy of all life".

Major influences on him were **Plato** and **neoplatonism**, Bruno, Jakob Böhme, **Kant**, **Fichte**, Hegel and Hölderlin. Schelling, in turn, should be studied by philosophers interested in **Schopenhauer, Nietzsche, Heidegger, Whitehead, Merleau-Ponty**, contemporary philosophy of biology, ecology or **animal** rights, and also by anyone interested in the fate of Kantian "moral freedom".

[D.F.K.]

**Schiller,** Ferdinand Canning Scott (1864–1937), British philosopher who worked in Oxford and, in later life, in Southern California. He was a personal friend of William **James**, with whose pragmatic philosophy he was in close sympathy, though he claimed to have arrived at the basic principles of **pragmatism** independently. Unlike James he was a polemical writer; he was convinced that the fashions in philosophy prevalent at his time in Oxford were obscurantist and quite without worth. As a result most of his writings are attacks, particularly on F. H. **Bradley** and those whom he called the "formal logicians", often couched in an *ad hominem* form which at a later date is somewhat tedious. But he had a powerful and original mind and his now little-read works contain much that is worth reading.

Schiller's basic thesis was that all human activities are moulded by human purposes and are only intelligible by reference to them. This, he held, was true of thinking as well as action; the conceptual frameworks we employ, the modes of reasoning that we adopt and the beliefs we hold can have their only justification in their utility for human aims. To call a statement true is to evaluate it favourably, just as to call an action good is to evaluate it favourably.

Much of Schiller's effort was devoted to the application of his "humanist" thesis to this logic. In his *Formal Logic* (1912) and his *Logic for Use – An Introduction to the Voluntarist Theory of Knowledge* (1929) Schiller maintained that the (then) prevalent view of reasoning as exhibited in logic books was wholly mistaken; his principal charges were that formal logic operated with illegitimate abstractions in speaking of propositions since meaning and truth were dependent on the time, place and circumstances of communication, and secondly that validity as a criterion of success in reasoning was useless since no concrete argument could be formally valid and unquestionably good arguments in all fields made no attempt even to approximate to such an ideal. In place of formal logic he offered an account of reasoning

which in its stress on verification, hypothesis and approximation anticipated later accounts of scientific thought.

(J.O.U.)

**Schiller,** Johann Christoph Friedrich von (1759–1805), German poet, philosopher and aesthetician whose *Letters on the Aesthetic Education of Man* (1795) developed **Kant's** theory of art to the conclusion that "Beauty" and "Play" jointly constitute the ethical ideal.

**Schlick,** Friedrich Albert Moritz (1882–1936), educated in Berlin, originally as a physicist, in 1922 he took over **Mach's** chair of the Philosophy of the Inductive Sciences in Vienna, where he later founded the **Vienna Circle** (see also **logical positivism**). Schlick was assassinated in Vienna by a demented student. The impending break-up of the Vienna Circle was hastened by his death.

Despite his scientific training, Schlick's early writings are largely on moral and aesthetic questions, and display a poetic sensibility not conspicuous in his later work. He subsequently gained notice as an expositor of **relativity**-theory (1917), and as the author of a treatise on **epistemology** (1918) in which many of his more characteristic doctrines occur in preliminary form. Here, in opposition to **Kant**, it is argued, from an **empiricist** standpoint, that the propositions of **logic** and **mathematics** are not synthetic **a priori** but true by definition, **analytic**, and hence empty of content. Scientific theories, on the other hand, are a posteriori systems of concepts, whose truth depends on correspondence, inasmuch as the consequences drawn from them must be capable of verification by observed facts. Nor are these facts sensations merely, as they were for Mach; anything answering to a scientific concept may legitimately be taken as real. More typical than this temporary acceptance of realism are Schlick's views on the mind-body problem, which he regards as spurious, in that the supposed dualism involved is merely a duality in our ways of describing the phenomena.

Schlick's later opinions reflect the influence of **Wittgenstein** and **Carnap**, and consist, in effect,

293

of an extension of his views to all the traditional problems of philosophy. Such problems arise "only from an inadequate description of the world by means of a faulty language", and the task of philosophy is not to solve them, but merely to clarify the question in dispute. It will then appear that the answer is either ascertainable, in principle, by scientific methods, or else void from the start, since the question itself is so framed that there could be no evidence relevant to is decision. The metaphysical assertions of **idealism, materialism, realism**, etc. are all meaningless in that no possible combination of sense-experiences could either verify their claims or prove them false.

In basing verification (and meaning) on immediate sense-experience, Schlick, like other empiricists, was seeking an incorrigible foundation for knowledge. But the attempt leads to many paradoxes, and even imperils the foundations of communication, since meaning defined in terms of private experience is plainly inaccessible to anyone else. Schlick's explanation, that the "structure" of experience is communicable, but its "content" beyond description, did not give general satisfaction, and the problem of formulating the "basic" or incorrigible propositions required by this theory was a source of much subsequent dissension in the Vienna Circle.

(P.L.H.)

**Scholasticism,** *see* Medieval Philosophy.

**Schopenhauer,** Arthur (1788–1860). German metaphysician, best known for his main work, *The World as Will and Idea* (1818) and for his acid essays. After his father's death he devoted himself entirely to philosophy, being able to live comfortably on his inheritance. His ridiculously vehement essay *On Women*, which has probably been read more widely than anything else he wrote, airs a deeply personal resentment.

His diatribe "On University Philosophy" also has a personal background. He applied to become a lecturer at the University of Berlin, was found acceptable by a committee on which **Hegel** sat, and then decided to offer his lectures at the

same hours as Hegel. But he failed to win away students from Hegel, and so his university career ended in failure. After that, he outdid himself in vituperating Hegel, **Schelling**, and **Fichte**, calling them windbags and charlatans, although his own philosophy owed a great deal to Fichte's conception of the will, and he heard Fichte as a student.

The two philosophers he admired most were **Kant** and **Plato**, and he considered himself the rightful heir of Kant, while regarding Fichte, Schelling, and Hegel as usurpers. Like Fichte, he found Kant's doctrine of the unknowable thing-in-itself unacceptable, and thought that he had discovered what the ultimate reality is: will. This will has no purpose or aim and is not reasonable or rational; it is blind striving. At this point, Schopenhauer may have been influenced by the First Part of Goethe's *Faust*. He personally knew and greatly admired Goethe, and, like Hegel, sided with Goethe's Doctrine of Colours against Newton.

The details of Schopenhauer's **metaphysics** and **ethics** have had little influence. His historical importance is conveniently summed up in terms of three points. First, he was the first major European philosopher to make a point of atheism. **Hobbes** and **Hume** went out of their way to dissociate themselves from atheism, while von Holbach is remembered, if indeed he is remembered, mainly because he was an atheist. Schopenhauer's fame was based on other grounds.

Secondly, he was the first major European philosopher who called attention to, and was profoundly influenced by, the Upanishads and Buddhism. He insisted on the universality of suffering and probably described it in greater detail than any philosopher before him. He is therefore frequently referred to as a pessimist. And he claimed that man can find salvation only by overcoming the blind cosmic will. Outright suicide will not do because it is an assertion of will. (Since Schopenhauer did not accept the Indian doctrine of the transmigration of souls, this point remains unclear.) There are mainly three aids to salvation: philosophic knowledge, contemplation of works of art, and sympathy for others, based on the recognition that we are only phenomenally distinct from others while in reality we are one. This ethic of sympathy contrasts very sharply with the ethic by which Schopenhauer himself lived: few philosophers have been more lacking in sympathy for others.

Finally, Schopenhauer's voluntarism inaugurated an increased emphasis on the will and on the irrational in modern philosophy. Although **Kierkegaard and Nietzsche**, Vaihinger and **James, Bergson** and Freud clearly did not agree with him, their ideas suggest that Schopenhauer marks an important point of departure in the history of thought. His conception of the intellect as an instrument of the will is especially noteworthy in this connexion.

Initially, *The World as Will and Idea* attracted no attention at all, even after Schopenhauer added a second volume (1844) by way of elaborating his metaphysic. Of two essays on ethics which he submitted for two prize contests in Scandinavia, one won a prize, the other did not; so he published them together, specifying on the title page "crowned by . . ." and "*not* crowned by . . ." – confident that he would thus immortalize in infamy the academy that had passed him by. Late in life, he witnessed and relished his growing fame. It may be that the widespread disillusionment after the unsuccessful revolutions of 1848 helped to make his pessimism popular. Certainly, his clearly written essays, published as *Parerga and Paralipomena* (1851) helped to find him an audience.

Among his declared and devoted admirers were Richard Wagner, whose *Tristan and Isolde* tries to realize in music Schopenhauer's blind will; the young Nietzsche, who later outgrew his earlier infatuation with Schopenhauer; and Thomas Mann.

(W.K.)

**Scotus,** John Duns (c. 1266–1308), born in Scotland. Scotus joined the Franciscan order in 1281 and later studied and taught both at Oxford and at Paris.

His main works are the two commentaries on the Sentences of Peter Lombard named after the place of their delivery *Opus Oxoniense* and *Reportata Parisiensia*. Understanding of the true character of his thought was for a long time hampered by the false attribution of the later *Theoremata* and *Grammatica Speculativa* to him.

Scotus combines acceptance of the typically Aristotelian theory of knowledge directed to the nature of physical objects and achieved by the abstractive power of the intellect with the more typically Franciscan view of the soul as a substance in its own right, hence with powers of intellection not confined to sensible reality. The subtle mingling of these two divergent tendencies earned him his title of *Doctor Subtilis*.

Scotus argues that the proper object of philosophical speculation is reality or being, without any of the determinations which restrict it to one mode (for example, infinite being or God) rather than to another (for example, sensible being). But the human mind is hampered by having to draw its knowledge from the sensible. So **metaphysics** is an abstract science of essences bearing upon a univocal field of being which is differentiated in terms of formal distinctions. These fall short of actual differences but are not merely the product of the mind's activity. Actual distinctness or the physical existence with which we are acquainted is finally accounted for by a form of "thisness" or *haecceitas*.

There can be no doubt that Scotus himself was a profound and able thinker but later, in the hands of less able followers, his *Formalism* degenerated into endless verbosity which contributed greatly to the collapse of scholastic thinking.

(J.G.D.)

**Semiology,** *see* Structuralism.

**Seneca,** Lucius Annaeus (c. 5 B.C.–65 A.D.), of Cordoba, Spain, a Roman **Stoic**. He switchbacked from a dangerous philosophical and rhetorical eminence under Caligula, to banishment under Claudius; soared as millionaire tutor and confidant of Nero, to sink into prudent retirement and death by enforced suicide. In the main a follower of **Chrysippus**, he was also influenced strongly by Panaetius and Posidonius, but his works have a Latin flavour both in thought and presentation; Cato was his hero, Roman rhetoric his medium. He most notably changed the doctrine of the Stoics by grafting the Roman concept of will on to their intellectualism, and altered its direction by applying their individualistic philosophy to the government of the Roman Empire. His shortcomings as philosopher and politician are due to contradictory tendencies towards worldly ambitions on the one hand and stoic **idealism** on the other; the resulting discrepancy of actions and professions may be mitigated by his honest belief that he was compelled politically to justify means by ends, and that his philosophical teaching was the result of examination of his own moral struggles. But the weakness of his character formed his stoicism, rather than his philosophy his character; thus the question of the capacity of the Stoa as an educative force in politics remained unanswered.

(I.G.K.)

**Sense-data.** The term "sense-data" (singular: sense-datum) is a comparatively new word for an idea that is almost as old as philosophy, namely the immediate object of sense-perception. In the past, philosophers have spoken of sensible species, ideas, impressions, representations, sensations and the given. "Sense-datum" has been preferred to these on the grounds of its comparative neutrality. As a technical term it presupposes as little as possible about the nature and the origins of perception's immediate objects. It is as hard to find a neutral definition for sense-datum as it is to find a neutral term for the idea it expresses. From the time of **Heraclitus, Protagoras** and **Democritus** many philosophers have been persuaded that independent, external, material things are not the direct or immediate objects of perception. In any perceptual situation we can always doubt that what we perceive is a real material thing. It might be a hallucination or we might be dreaming. But there is something we cannot doubt, for whatever, if anything, may be going on outside us, we may be sure that our senses are affected in a certain way and this indubitable residue is our current sense-datum. Though we may be in doubt as to how things are, we cannot be in doubt as to how things appear to us to be now. So to say how things appear to us

now, with no implication that this is how they really are or how they would appear to anyone else, is to describe our current sense-data. Most of our ordinary perceptual beliefs involve a good deal of inference. In taking what I now see to be a chair, I ascribe to it a back, a texture and a weight, but none of these are at the moment present to my senses. The inferred elements of our perceptual beliefs are the dubitable ones. The sense-datum is what remains when they are suppressed.

It is clear that sense-data are private. My sense-data may resemble yours but this likeness can only be established by a complex and precarious inference and is always a contingent matter. The fact of hallucination shows that it is possible for a man to have a sense-datum to which nobody else's sense-data correspond at all. The privacy of sense-data follows from their being defined in terms of what appears to *me*. There is no very clear or uniform convention about the extent or complexity of sense-data. Are we to call all dreams, hallucinations, memories and images sense-data even when we are not in the least tempted to suppose that we are perceiving some real material thing? Is my current sense-datum the whole of what I am sensibly aware of at this instant or is it what I am aware of by means of any one sense, my current visual field for example; or is it any one discriminable part of a current sense-field? Philosophical usage tends to favour the last of these. A more substantial problem arises about the duration of sense-data. Can I be aware of the same sense-datum twice or do sense-data endure only for one specious present? Some philosophers have held that sense-data can have properties which they do not appear to have. Against them **Ayer** has argued that sense-data are by definition precisely and entirely what they appear to be.

There are two main arguments to prove that sense-data are necessarily distinct from material objects. First, the argument from illusion. My sense-datum, what I immediately perceive, may be just the same in a case where I am really perceiving a friend as it is in a case where I am undergoing the hallucination of seeing him. Since what I immediately perceive is precisely the same in both cases and cannot be a material object in one of them it cannot be a material object in either. Secondly, the causal or time-lag argument. The perception of very remote events, such as the explosion of stars, brings out dramatically that perception is always of something that is temporally earlier, even if only minutely, than the event of perceiving it. But, it is argued, we can only perceive what is present, since to say that something is present is simply to say that it is contemporary with my current perception.

If sense-data are distinct from material objects, the fundamental and traditional problem of perception presents itself: what is the relation of sense-data to material objects, and how can we have any knowledge about material objects if all we immediately perceive is sense-data? Some philosophers, **Hume** for instance, have been sceptical of the validity of any inference from sense-data to material things. More commonly it has been held either, with **Locke**, that we can reasonably infer material objects as the causes of our sense-data, or, with **Berkeley** and **phenomenalism**, that material objects are entirely composed of sense-data, actual or possible or both. In opposition to the sense-datum theory two main tendencies can be discerned in contemporary philosophy. One view, that of **Ryle**, is that there are no such things. Another, less radical, view is that though there are sense-data they are not the only things that we immediately perceive: they are the causes rather than the grounds of our perceptual beliefs and for the most part their existence and character is a matter of inference.

(A.Q.)

**Sextus Empiricus,** *see* Sceptics.

**Sidgwick,** Henry (1828–1900), English philosopher and Professor at Cambridge. He wrote on economics as well as on philosophy and was a founder member of the Society for Psychical Research and its first President.

The work for which Sidgwick is remembered is *The Method of Ethics*, published in 1874 but modified and expanded in subsequent editions. He there adopted a hedonistic **utilitarian** position,

but with a far clearer recognition of the many-sidedness of moral problems. Having denied that moral terms can be defined in non-moral terms Sidgwick goes on to contend that morality is founded on **a priori** moral intuition that "we ought to aim at pleasure". Any other basic moral knowledge is concerned with the way pleasure should be distributed; thus we know that similar cases ought to be treated similarly and that "the good of any one individual is of no more importance, from the point of view of the universe, than the like good of any other". From these basic positions Sidgwick deduces the principle of benevolence: "each one is morally bound to regard the good of any other individual as much as his own". Sidgwick acknowledges that in practice people are swayed morally by rules of conduct and not by general principles of universalistic hedonism; he himself is willing to accept these rules of conduct on the ground that they are a means to the utilitarian end. This position is however complicated by the fact that Sidgwick finds himself compelled to acknowledge as self-evident the principle that "it is irrational for me to sacrifice my happiness to any other end" the principle of rational ethical egoism. Sidgwick is well aware of the apparent incompatibility of this principle with the universalistic hedonism which is his other main contention; he regards this incompatibility as the basic problem of ethics, but simply finds himself unable honestly to deny either the principle of egoism or the principle of benevolence. His solution of the dilemma is to suggest that the universe is so arranged that egoism and universal benevolence never come into conflict and that we can follow the principle of benevolence with the assurance that we shall not thereby violate the rational principle of egoism. Thus Sidgwick, in his anxiety to do justice to all the facets of morality, attempts to harmonize a number of positions which are usually regarded as essentially opposed; he is utilitarian and **deontologist**, egoist and universalist.

(J.O.U.)

**Siger** of Brabant (1235/40 – 1281/84), French philosopher, with Boethius of Dacia and Bernier of Nivelles, a leader of the so-called Latin **Averroists**, who claimed to be pure philosophers, of the school of **Aristotle**, and in no way theologians. They accepted the distinction of truths of reason and truths of faith which had been made by Averroes and proceeded to work out ruthlessly their philosophy, which was an Aristotelianism coloured by the interpretation of Averroes and **Avicenna**. Some of their doctrines, such as that of the eternity of the world, the unity of intellect in all human beings and the determination of human affairs by astral influences, went straight against the Christian dogmas of creation, the individual soul and divine providence; these doctrines and others which they held were condemned in 1270 and again in 1277, but their authors maintained that these philosophical tenets did not conflict with their faith in the truth of revelation.

(J.O.U.)

**Smith,** Adam (1723–1790), was one of the greatest of that line of eighteenth-century Scottish philosophers who shifted the study of human nature from its traditional concerns with theology and the pursuit of happiness in the life hereafter, to one which was based on philosophy, history and the pursuit of happiness in the world of common life. In doing so he helped to challenge the claims of the theologians to provide an adequate guide to the problems of living in the increasingly complex world of commerce.

Like his close friend David **Hume**, Smith was interested in the principles of social interaction and the processes by which we acquire the metaphysical, moral, political and religious skills which are necessary to ordinary living – matters which he discussed in his first book, *The Theory of Moral Sentiments* (1759). But he was also interested in the role of labour and property in shaping social behaviour and social institutions and in transforming society from its barbarous to its civilized state – matters which he discussed in his greatest work, *The Wealth of Nations* (1776). All of this required him to develop an elaborate and fine-meshed account of the way in which any

society disposes of its land, labour and capital resources and develops the political, cultural and religious institutions it needs in order to maintain its stability. In so doing, he developed the first, fully-fledged "materialist" model of society and its history on which all subsequent models have been based. See also **Political Economy**.

[N.P.]

**Social Contract.** Social contract theories attempt to explain the duty of obedience to the laws and civil authority by reference to a contract or compact or promise to obey made for the sake of the benefits gained from the civil society thereby instituted. There are many different versions of the contract theory; a version, not accepted by **Plato**, is given in *Republic* Book II; famous modern versions are those of **Hobbes** in the *Leviathan*, **Locke** in the *Second Treatise of Civil Government* and **Rousseau** in the *Social Contract*. These versions differ from each other as regards both the parties to the contract and its terms; they also differ in the degree to which the historicity of the contract is affirmed, since some authors content themselves with a tacit or implied contract. The theory was destructively criticized by **Hume** in his Essay "Of the original contract" and by **Hegel** in his *Philosophy of Right*. See also **Political Philosophy, Rawls**.

(J.O.U.)

**Socrates** (469–399 B.C.), Greek philosopher of Athens. He left no writings of his own, and probably never made any. Our information about him comes from four sources: Aristophanes, Xenophon and **Plato**, whose lives overlapped his, and **Aristotle**, who was probably born some thirteen years after the year in which, according to Plato, Socrates was tried and put to death for "corrupting the young men and not believing in the gods of the city".

(1) The only statement common to all four of these writers is that there was a philosopher called Socrates. Beyond that, the picture of Socrates in Aristophanes' farce *The Clouds*

should be entirely disbelieved, because it contains nothing agreeing with the other three and nothing individual or unusual, but on the contrary appears to be just the popular idea of a sophist dubbed "Socrates" and given a mask with the pronounced features of the real Socrates.

(2) Xenophon left us the *Memories of Socrates*, a work of some 180 pages, consisting mainly of amusing little dialogues between Socrates and various other persons, at some of which Xenophon says he was present; an *Apology of Socrates*, a short report of the trial, which, however, Xenophon does not claim to have attended; the *Oeconomicus*, in which Socrates discusses household management; and a *Symposium*, depicting a party at which Socrates is present. Though in some of his works Xenophon is a serious historian, it is quite clear that his Socratic writings are fictions got up to look like truth by the storyteller's device of saying "I was there". They should be believed only so far as they agree with Plato or Aristotle.

(3) In the *Metaphysics* Aristotle gives us the most likely account we have of Socrates' thought: "Socrates 'occupied' himself with the excellences of character, and in connexion with them became the first to raise the problem of universal definition . . . . It was natural that Socrates should be seeking the essence, for he was seeking to syllogize, and 'what a thing is' is the starting-point of syllogisms . . . . Two things may be fairly ascribed to Socrates, inductive arguments and universal definition, both of which are concerned with the starting-point of science; but Socrates did not make the universal or the definitions exist apart." All of these points except the last, which will be considered near the end of this article, are well supported by Plato and not contradicted by Xenophon, and had therefore better be accepted.

(4) Plato's portrait of Socrates is by far the most copious and impressive. Socrates is the main speaker in all Plato's early and middle dialogues. His conversation there concerns the nature of virtue and of particular virtues, and tends to the view that virtue is knowledge and vice is ignorance. He takes a particular virtue and tries to find its essence by giving a general definition of it. He produces syllogistic arguments,

that is, arguments where two premises when put together necessitate a new proposition, the conclusion. And often he recommends one of the premises by an inductive argument from similar cases. In these respects Plato agrees excellently with Aristotle.

But Aristotle does not prepare us for the strange fact that the Platonic Socrates uses his inductions and syllogisms not for but against proposed definitions of the virtues. His conversation takes the form of putting questions to a single respondent. The first question, being a request for a definition, does not admit the answers yes and no and is a matter of doubt. The subsequent questions, however, demand the answer yes or no. Having obtained a number of apparently disconnected answers in this way, Socrates "syllogizes" them, as Aristotle says, and shows that they refute his respondent's answer to the first question. He then asks the respondent to find another answer to the first question, and treats that in the same way. The effect is to show that the answerer is contradicting himself, and does not know what he thought he knew. Socrates does not, however, claim to understand the matter himself. On the contrary, he denies all knowledge of it. He even denies that he intended to convict his answerer of ignorance. "I was never a teacher of anybody." He says that his questions might, for all he knew beforehand, have led to the establishment instead of the refutation of the answer given. This latter denial is, however, impossible to believe. Hence his victims tend to call him "sly", as pretending that he knows less than they do when actually he knows more. The Greek for slyness is "irony"; and this is the origin of the conception of irony as the conveyance of a statement by words which literally convey the contradictory.

There is something repellent about this pattern of talk; and Plato represents it as incurring condemnation from some people. He represents the extraordinary personality of Socrates as including some other questionable traits, but there is no doubt that he succeeds in making us feel that Socrates' character was wonderful and uniquely valuable. In his *Symposium* he shows us Socrates first as the deep thinker who has got stuck in contemplation outside the host's door, then as the pretended lover easily obtaining the seats next the most attractive young men, then as a benign cross-examiner of his host, then as the philosophical sublimator of earthly love into a **religion** of Beauty, and then as the subject of a daring encomium by Alcibiades. Alcibiades calls him an ugly statue of Silenus that opens to show hidden beauties within. He confesses to having persistently tempted Socrates and thus experienced his unbreakable self-control. He praises Socrates' formidable calmness and endurance on campaign, and affirms his wonderful unlikeness to every other human being alive or dead. All this is to be believed.

Like Xenophon, Plato offers us an *Apology of Socrates*, professing to be the three speeches made by Socrates at his trial. They are certainly not transcripts. They bear at the best only a remote resemblance to what was actually said. Some think that Socrates made no defence at all. But probably the indictment really was that "Socrates corrupts the young men, and does not believe in the city's gods and believes in new divinities." Probably if thirty more jurors had voted the other way he really would have been acquitted. Probably Socrates really did propose as a penalty that he should be fed at public expense, and really did change this to a fine at the request of Plato and other friends in court. And, if we believe that he was intransigent in his choice of a "penalty" after conviction, we should believe that Plato's work is probably true to life in the magnificently proud and unbending tone it makes Socrates take with the court.

It is very probably true that Socrates had, as Plato makes him say he had, firmly opposed at one time the injustice of tyrants and at another time the injustice of the people, both at great risk to himself. It is also very probably true that Socrates did sometimes declare himself to enjoy a mysterious "divine sign", a sort of inner voice which frequently forbade him to do something he was thinking of doing, and whose advice he believed to be always good. It is doubtful, however, whether Socrates really thought that he had been "ordered by the god, both by oracles and by dreams and by every means by which a divine destiny was ever imposed on a man", to convict men of their ignorance by refuting their opinions in cross-examination.

It was easy to escape from the prison at Athens; and probably many of those who voted for his death assumed that Socrates would do so. Plato has an exquisite little dialogue, *Crito*, in which he shows Socrates' old friend Crito pleading with him to escape, and Socrates refusing. The reason he gives is that, by his choice in pursuing his life in the city of Athens, he has in deed, though not in word, promised to obey the laws of Athens, and he will keep his promise.

Finally, in the magnificent *Phaedo* Plato depicts the last conversation and death of Socrates, while letting us know that he himself was not there. We may believe Plato when he tells us that Socrates' wife and children visited him on his last day but were not present at his death; that his friends wept loudly when he drank the poison and were rebuked for it by the unmoved Socrates; that his last words were "Crito, we owe a cock to Asclepius; pay it and do not neglect it"; that Crito answered "That shall be done; think if there is anything else"; and that no answer came to this. The last pages of the *Phaedo* are of extraordinary beauty and grandeur.

We had better not believe, however, that Socrates really defended the doctrines which Plato represents him as defending on his last day. In the *Phaedo* Plato shows Socrates convinced that there is a life after death; he is more likely to be historical on this point in the *Apology*, where he makes Socrates treat it as an open question. In the *Phaedo* Plato makes Socrates say that in his youth he had a period of interest in physical questions; he may have had, but the *Phaedo*-passage is probably only a dramatic way of setting certain points of view in opposition to each other. In the *Phaedo* Plato makes Socrates expound and assume the theory of Ideas, thus coming into conflict with Aristotle's statement that "Socrates did not make the universals or the definitions exist apart." It is very probable that Aristotle is right, as the tradition holds, in saying that the theory of Ideas was the invention of Plato. It was a natural step forward from Socratic definition, but not one that ever occurred to Socrates himself. Plato introduced it into his *Phaedo* as a way of dedicating to Socrates the fruits of Socrates' teaching, not as a record of that teaching itself.

The greatest value of Plato's Socrates is his superb championship of the ideal of reason, and his high and clear conception of what reason demands. He impresses us, more than any other figure in literature, with the supreme importance of thinking as well as possible and making our actions conform to our thoughts. To this end he preaches knowledge of one's own starting-points, hypothetical entertainment of opinions, exploration of their consequences and connexions, willingness to follow argument wherever it leads, public confession of one's thoughts, invitation to others to criticize, readiness to reconsider, and at the same time firm action in accordance with one's present beliefs. Plato's *Apology* has in fact made Socrates the chief martyr of reason as the gospels have made Jesus the chief martyr of faith.

(R.R.)

**Solipsism.** Sometimes we idly fancy that the whole world is merely our dream. Solipsism is a theory, rather like this fancy, but based on argument. If asked why I believe in the existence of stars, trees and people, I have to reply "My sight, hearing, touch, in short, my perceptions tell me so. Certainly my perceptions are sorted and supplemented by memory, inference and conjecture, but without perceptions such thinking has nothing to work on. Now perceiving is having sensations. But you cannot have, for example, my visual or tactual sensations, any more than you can have my toothaches. So you cannot perceive anything that I perceive. The world that my senses acquaint me with is private to me. Even the *you* that I see and hear could no more exist without my existing than my toothaches could. I hanker to believe that independently existing, unperceived things tally with the perceivced contents of my private world, but I ought to believe that I alone (*solus ipse*) exist in my own right, all else depending on me as my toothaches do." No important philosophers accept this repellent conclusion. But many, accepting the argument for it, have to postualte non-perceptual reasons for believing in independently existing things and people. We should, instead, reject the step in the argument "perceiving is having sensations".

(G.R.)

**Sophists.** In ancient Greece traditional education had consisted of music (poetry, drama and in general the subjects presided over by the nine muses) and gymnastic. In the more sophisticated social conditions of the fifth century B.C. the need for a further education became apparent. The sophists were men who offered this higher education; they were itinerant professors who wandered from city to city giving courses of lectures, mainly on rhetoric and the art of getting on, in return for fees from their audiences. Thus originally the term sophist was not in any way a term of opprobium – it meant something like "professor" – and the sophist was not specially concerned with philosophy; certainly it is quite mistaken to think of the sophists as forming some philosophical school. Some of the sophists, such as **Protagoras**, were indeed very brilliant and influential philosophers, but others confined themselves almost entirely to rhetoric. The establishment of such permanent centres of higher education as the schools of **Plato, Aristotle** and Isocrates (all of whom were sophists to the general public) led to the disappearance of the sophists in the middle of the fourth century B.C.

The opprobrium which now attaches to the word "sophist" is due to the skilful propaganda against the sophist, their rivals, by Plato and Aristotle. The basic charge was that the sophists pretended to teach knowledge whereas they taught an art of getting on which neglected the highest values. Among the sophists the best known names are Protagoras, Gorgias, Prodicus, Hippias, Antiphon, Thrasymachus, Lycaphron and Isocrates.

(J.O.U.)

**Speech Acts,** *see* Austin.

**Spencer**, Herbert, (1820–1903), English philosopher who achieved an enormous popular reputation in the later nineteenth century by projecting a "System of Synthetic Philosophy" which would unify the biological and social sciences by means of a generalized philosophical notion of evolution.

In *First Principles* (1862) Spencer maintained that we could have knowledge only of phenomena, but that we could nevertheless infer to an Unknowable, an Incomprehensible Power which is the source of phenomena, the most important of which is the Law of Evolution which he obscurely phrased as follows: "an integration of matter and concomitant dissipation of motion, during which the matter passes from an indefinite incoherent homogeneity to a definite coherent heterogeneity". He also defined progress as a change from homogeneity; thus he identified evolution and progress and could claim that "progress is not an accident, not a thing within human control, but a beneficient necessity". This general conception of evolution is based on the work of German biologists and antedates the publication of Darwin's work.

Life was defined by Spencer as a continuous adjustment of the internal to the external environment; to live is to be the sort of thing which continually adapts its own nature to be able to deal better with its environment. This is the fundamental viewpoint of the *Principles of Biology* (1864–67) and *Principles of Psychology* (1870–72). He claimed in the *Principles of Ethics* (1879–93) that the principles of **ethics** "have a natural basis", for moral conclusions follow the general law of evolution. Man is capable of indefinite change by adaptation to circumstances, in particular to the change from wild to settled, civilized life; in this adaptation man represses old selfish traits and develops new ones by virtue of a principle of sympathy. Moral principles are rules which aid the harmonious, readjusted life of civilization. A hedonistic element can be legitimately recognized since "pleasure promotes function" and the law of evolution ensures that those actions we find pleasant will be such as tend to have survival value. Spencer's attempt to draw ethical conclusions from evolutionary principles still has imitators today.

(J.O.U.)

**Speusippus,** an Athenian, born towards the end of the fifth century B.C., died 339. He was

302

Plato's nephew and a member of the Academy, and he was head of the Academy from Plato's death in 347 until his own death. Only fragments of his many works survive and we cannot get a comprehensive view of his philosophy. Four main points may be mentioned.

(1) Speusippus maintained – against Eudoxus – that pleasure is not good but that pleasure and pain are opposite evils. Plato's *Philebus* is partly concerned with this controversy in the Academy.

(2) He wrote a number of works of "Classifications". He seems to have held that no one thing can be satisfactorily defined unless all other things are also; to understand a concept is to know how it is related by similarities and differences to all others.

(3) Speusippus held that the account in Plato's *Timaeus* of the making of the world was simply an expository device (like mathematicians' talk of "constructing" figures or proofs).

(4) From Aristotle's *Metaphysics* it is clear that Speusippus abandoned Plato's theory of Ideas and also recognized more kinds of entity than Plato, assigning different principles to each kind.

(J.L.A.)

**Spinoza,** Benedict de, (1632–1677) born in Amsterdam of Jewish parents. Spinoza was brought up to speak Spanish, Portuguese and Hebrew, but he had a less sure command of Dutch. He attended a Jewish High School in Amsterdam where one of his teachers was Rabbi Manasseh ben Israel, who negotiated with Cromwell the re-entry of the Jews into England. At the age of eighteen, Spinoza went to a Dutch teacher, Van den Ende, to learn Latin and the "new science", studying the works of Copernicus, Galileo, Kepler, Harvey, Huygens and **Descartes.**

Spinoza wished to lead a quiet life, attending the Synagogue and pursuing his studies. He was becoming critical of orthodox interpretations of the Bible, but he had no wish to disturb the beliefs of others. When eventually his orthodoxy was called in question, the leaders of the Synagogue offered him a pension if he would leave Van den Ende and conform. Spinoza refused and was excommunicated, thereupon moving to a suburb of Amsterdam. In conformity with

Jewish custom which required all men to learn a trade, he had mastered the art of grinding and polishing lenses, and he now proceeded to earn his living by his art. His *Short Treatise on God, Man and his Wellbeing* was composed at this period. In 1661, he moved to a lodging in a small house at Rhijnsburg, where he wrote his *Tractatus de Intellectus Emendatione*. This house is now the Spinoza Museum. At this period Spinoza became acquainted with Henry Oldenburg, one of the Secretaries of the Royal Society. Their correspondence lasted for fifteen years and throws light on some of the more difficult points in Spinoza's philosophy. In 1663, Spinoza moved to Voorburg, near the Hague. By now his fame was considerable: a society had been formed to study his writings and Spinoza published his *Renati des Cartes Principia Philosophiae*, with an appendix *Cogitata Metaphysica* (1663). A Dutch translation immediately appeared. His room in Voorburg became a meeting place for the intellectual leaders of the day, among them Huygens and Jan de Witt. In the *Tractatus Theologico-Politicus* (1670) Spinoza tried to show that the Bible gave no ground for violence and intolerance. The work was published and immediately condemned by the theologians. In 1673, Spinoza was offered the Chair of Philosophy at the University of Heidelberg, but declined; he wished to pursue his investigations "in accordance with his own mind".

Spinoza now moved into Amsterdam, and completing the *Ethics*, designed to publish it. Information was laid against him to the authorities and Spinoza withdrew the book. He worked on a Hebrew grammar and a translation of the Old Testament into Dutch, with the object of enabling his fellow citizens to become acquainted with the Bible which they so misinterpreted. These plans were brought to a sudden end by his death, at the age of forty-five. The *Ethics* was published immediately afterwards.

In the *Tractatus de Intellectus Emendatione* Spinoza declared the object of his work to be the discovery of "the life of blessedness for man". It entailed a search for that "by whose discovery and acquistion I might be put in possession of a joy continuous and supreme to all eternity". Spinoza called this "the intellectual love of God", and it consists in a clear understanding of human nature, the universe, and the rejoicing which is essential to human beings. Knowledge for Spinoza is to be pursued by freeing the understanding from the vague and confused ideas of sense-perception and imagination, and from inappropriate attachment to objects. It is for these reasons that Spinoza's main work, a largely metaphysical treatise, is called the *Ethics*. In it we are shown finding our freedom and blessedness in the realization that we are part of a system which is determined throughout. We rejoice in this state, and in Spinoza's sense of the word, this is to love God.

When the intellect is working well it is in possession of true ideas and of certainty. ("He who has a true idea knows at the same time that he has a true idea.") True ideas are expressed in definitions which may then be deductively developed, the connexion between each proposition and the next being self-evident. We thus reach a system of true propositions. Those who proceed in this way enjoy knowledge of the second grade, *ratio*; knowledge of the highest or third grade, *scientia intuitiva*, belongs to God alone. The lowest grade, *imaginatio*, is knowledge by sense perception and imagination, by vague signs and hearsay. These are not erroneous in themselves, but they lead to error unless they are placed in their right context, as states of the body, not parts of a system of ideas. Error is a privation of knowledge, a confusion of ideas not seen as confusion. Vague signs are ones like "man" and "horse", which stand confusedly for any number of particulars, in contrast to "Peter", which stands unequivocally for one body-mind in a determinate place in the spatio-temporal system. "Man" has no place in a system of ideas, but "Peter" may be understood as a body-mind in a system of interacting bodies or body-minds.

The *Ethics* consists of a system of definitions, axioms and theorems. The definitions in Part I are not derivable from any more fundamental concepts. Taken together, they form a basis for rational theology and the sciences. Substance is defined as "that which is in itself and is conceived through itself ", attribute as "that which the intellect perceives of substance as if constituting its essence". Definition VI equates "God" with "substance consisting of infinite attributes". Taken with axioms III and IV, these definitions yield the concept of God as One, infinite, necessarily existing, containing all being and the sole cause of every existing thing. Axiom III is the axiom of causality and axiom IV gives Spinoza's special meaning of "cause". "The knowledge of an effect depends upon and involves the knowledge of the cause". That is to say, the causal relation for Spinoza is the relation of ground and consequent. Substance, since it is conceived through itself, is its own ground, i.e. it is self-caused and so necessarily existing. There could not be two such beings, for if there were, then either one would have to be understood in terms of the other, or both would have to be understood in terms of a third thing which would then itself be substance. Everything except substance is "in something else, through which also it is conceived", so that there is nothing outside substance.

Substance is also manifested in infinite attributes, each infinitely modified into "modes" which are "conceived through" substance under one or other of its attributes. Of the infinite number of attributes, we know only two, extension and thought. They are perceived *as if* constituting the essence of substance. Philosophers have mistakenly supposed that thought and extension were substances, so creating the problem of connecting things "which have nothing in common with one another, and so cannot be conceived through one another". Extension and thought are two attributes of the one substance, not interacting, but each infinitely diversified into modes which occur together. The most interesting case of this "occurring together" is in human beings, where mental events are paralleled by physical events. The mind is "the idea of the body".

The system of extension is *facies totius universi* (the aspect of the entire universe). It is studied at different levels in the sciences of geometry, mechanics and biology. In geometry, the concepts of point, line and plane are appropriate; in mechanics, smallest bodies, motion and rest. In biology, the concept of *conatus* is fundamental: it is "the endeavour with which each body perseveres in its own existence". In human bodies, it is sometimes accompanied by awareness, when

it is called desire. These sciences are founded in the metaphysical concept of substance under the attribute of extension. There has been no comparable development of the concept under the attribute of thought, but this is what Spinoza hoped to provide: "I shall consider human actions as if I were considering lines, planes or bodies". Just as a human body is to be described in terms of "smallest bodies" acting on one another, their motions determined by earlier motions, so a human mind is to be described in terms of action, passion and adequate ideas, and mental events in terms of earlier events. The essence of an individual is its *conatus*, and the cohesion of physical parts is patterned by the mind's awareness of its own unity and of its union with the body.

The differences between simple bodies are expressible in terms of degrees of motion-rest: between complex bodies in terms of their own motion-rest and that of their parts. The differences among minds are expressible in terms of the degrees of clearness and adequacy of their ideas. People whose ideas are clear are said to be free and active in the sense that the causes of their actions lie, as far as is compatible with their finitude, within their own nature. The causes of action of a finite being cannot lie completely in its own nature; the body is a part of a system of interacting bodies. Free persons have an adequate idea of their own state as such an effect; and even though it may be painful, the appropriate emotion is joy, in that the pain is known to be occurring in its proper place. If the pain has arisen as the result of the action of other human beings, the free person will neither blame nor hate them. Love is "joy accompanied by the idea of an object", and "hatred is sorrow accompanied by the idea of an object". The free person, who sees all human beings as parts of a determined system, can only rejoice in this knowledge, and so cannot hate anyone.

The important concept in explaining human actions, as in explaining any other event, is cause, not purpose. Spinoza's favourite example of error is our belief in free will. People are aware of their "actions" but ignorant of their causes; they therefore say that they freely choose to act in this way, but this only shows a confusion in which the causes of our "actions" are for the most part hidden. "Action" is in inverted commas because, in Spinoza's terminology, the doings of those whose ideas are confused and inadequate are "passions". The explanations of the passions are to be sought in our circumstances, not our nature. There are three primary emotions, desire which is *conatus*, joy which is the passage of the organism to a higher state of perfection, and sorrow which is the passage to a lower state. All other emotions are compounded of these three, together with the ideas of objects appropriately or inappropriately conjoined. To pass to a higher or lower state of perfection is not to become better or worse in the moral sense, but to become more or less active. People with inadequate ideas are passive in that what they do depends on what happens to them, not on what they are.

Spinoza's moral theory is relativistic and naturalistic. ("We call that good which we certainly know to be useful to us.") In itself, nothing is either good or bad, and persons with adequate ideas will attach the term suitably to that which increases their power of action, whilst those who are passive will apply it to that which they mistakenly see as ministering to their purposes. They attach emotion to objects instead of seeing it in its right place in the causally connected phases of their mental life. Praise and blame are equally inapplicable to human action, though they may be used as causes in affecting the actions of those for whose conduct we feel responsibility. Nothing can be more useful to the free than the society of other free people, so that Spinoza's "good man" will be good in the normal sense. He will naturally try to bring it about that others are free and wise, understanding that hatred and resentment are as inappropriate towards human beings as towards rocks and stones. He knows that the only object worth pursuing, knowledge, is better attained in companionship than alone, but he also knows that every other being has its own *conatus*, and no matter how mistaken he may be in his idea of how best to "persevere in his own being", he has an equal right with the wise so to persevere. The wise will be tolerant of others, interfering with the harmless beliefs of nobody, whether in politics or **religion**. They will choose the religion which promotes a good

life, and the social system which gives security to its citizens and strengthens their "natural right to exist and work without injury to themselves or others". Since there are people of all grades of perfection, some must be led by authority. For this reason, it is of immense importance that theologians and civic leaders should understand the conditions of the good life.

If resentment of other people is inappropriate, it is a thousand times more inappropriate towards God. God is above good and evil, and though He is equally the cause of perfect and imperfect beings, His power is equally manifest in both. A physical or mental cripple is such because of its place in the system: God has not tried to produce perfection and failed. ("To Him material was not wanting for the creation of everything, from the highest down to the very lowest grade of perfection: or to speak more properly, because the laws of His nature were so ample that they sufficed for the production of everything which can be conceived by an infinite intellect.") Such a God can be loved and worshipped by the wise, but they will not expect Him to love them in return, or to allot rewards and punishments. One who loves God does not look to a future life: this life may be one of blessedness; and in thinking adequately, we think God's thoughts, and share in God's rejoicing self-knowledge, that is to say in "the love with which God loves Himself"; and to this extent, we may be eternal.

(R.L.S.)

**Stevenson,** Charles Leslie (1908– ), American philosopher, best known for *Ethics and Language* (1944). In this book Stevenson gives an elaborate statement of the emotivist theory of the significance of ethical terms, which had been hinted at by **Hume** and summarily stated by the **logical positivists**, but never previously been so carefully treated. Stevenson's principal contention is that to say that something is good is to state that one approves of it and to seek to evoke the same attitude in one's hearers. He also maintains that in moral discourse we can attempt to persuade others to agree with us, but that the concept of valid argument is not applicable to such discourse. The book in undoubtedly the classical statement of the emotivist position.

(J.O.U.)

**Stoicism**: one of the dominant philosophies of the Hellenistic-Roman period. It was founded by **Zeno** of Citium at the end of the fourth century B.C., receiving its name from the Painted Stoa (colonnade) where he taught in Athens. To him are attributed all the fundamental doctrines. In the following century **Chrysippus** formulated the definitive system in an extensive series of works. But Stoics did not shrink from change within the framework, and in the second and first centuries B.C., Panaetius and Posidonius made some changes of emphasis and detail. In the Roman Empire it was modified still further by **Seneca, Epictetus** and **Marcus Aurelius**, but it always remained in essence the unified comprehensive system of Zeno and Chrysippus. It faded out after the end of the third century A.D.

The Stoics divided their philosophy into **logic** (dialectic and rhetoric), **ethics**, and physics (which included theology); these were intertwined and interdependent, but not of equal importance. Their interest in logic was mainly confined to perfecting their own arguments in defence of their system; it was the wall protecting the garden, the shell safeguarding the egg. Physics, on the other hand, was in a sense at once the starting point and culmination of their ethics; Chrysippus said there could be no other starting point for justice than physics and their definition of happiness (the end of man) was "to live in harmony with nature"; in other words, like most Greeks, they based their philosophy on a conception of nature. Yet their interest in nature was confined to its relation to and importance for human action; Stoicism was primarily an ethic for which physics provided the foundation.

Their ethics was formulated in response to the needs of the time. At the close of the fourth century, the break up of the Greek city state produced not only physical, economic and political insecurity but also a moral vacuum. The response of the philosophical schools reflects this: the Academy allowed ethics to slip into the background and turned **Sceptic**; the **Peripatetics** engaged in scientific research, and in ethics were content to acknowledge as many human goods as possible; the **Epicureans** offered **hedonism**.

Zeno's reaction was to devise a philosophy of security for individuals without divorcing them from the circumstances in which they found themselves. His starting point was the same as that of the **Cynics**, the belief that insecurity and unhappiness were the result of pursuing what was not wholly under the control of the individual. Health may deteriorate, a fortune be lost, reputation vanish through external causes; so no physical or external "goods" can be end goods. The only thing completely in our power is the correct moral attitude of mind, which is virtue. Further, this attitude is based on knowledge (courage was the *knowledge* of what was and was not to be feared); for the Stoic, happiness was derived from knowing what was the right thing to do at any given moment, and knowing that the actual attainment of the object was irrelevant to happiness, which depended solely on the moral functioning of the rational element in man. It was argued that the wise man wants only what he can achieve; thus he could always achieve what he wants.

So far the Cynic ingredients. But to understand the Stoic flavour one must turn to the Stoic conception of the universe. All reality was material, mind as well as matter; for, they argued, only matter can move or be moved. But there was an important distinction between active force and passive matter; the active force was *logos*, divine reason, the governor of the universe. Indissolubly permeated throughout passive matter which it qualified, it fashioned the universe into one rational purposeful living whole of which man was an integral part. It was this *logos*, identified with creative fire (or warm air) among the elements, which was the substance of the human soul. Just as reason in the universe is all-important as the ruling active force, so is reason in us and happiness must depend on it alone; and since human reason is the same as the universal reason, our knowledge of ourselves and our duties cannot be complete until it comprises the universe and our place in it. For by understanding the working of reason in the universe we can identify with its purpose. We thus have the power to accommodate our own nature to universal Nature, or in the Stoic phrase, to live in harmony with nature.

Physics afforded the justification for the supremacy of moral intelligence, not an account of its field of exercise; for that the Stoics turned to psychology. They observed certain natural impulses and aversions which point to certain ends; the attainment or avoidance of these appear natural for a human being and involve appropriate actions. For example, the principle of all life, the securing of one's own existence, led to physical and external satisfaction, health, comfort, adequate wealth, etc. The instinct to perpetuate the race was the basis of family life and then in general of society, friendship, (and the responsibilities and duties involved). The impulse of the intellect fostered reflection, curiosity, fine arts. As we have been shaped by nature along these lines, the pursuit of all these and avoidance of their opposites are according to our nature and therefore appropriate. But as they are based on the conception of human nature alone, and not on human nature as part of the universe, their importance is subordinate to that of the rational. They form a class of intermediate objects with relative value, but morally indifferent in having no absolute (i.e. moral) value. Their relative value, fixed from an intelligent survey of human psychology, makes possible the formation of general rules for their attainment or avoidance which is the subject of "appropriate" duties. (The Stoics supplied their own terminology.) But the attainment of "intermediates" cannot be good, nor "appropriate" duties perfect acts because sometimes the general rule is wrong; such actions may be done by good people or bad, or for a wrong or insufficient reason; owing to external circumstances it is not completely in our power to fulfil all or any of them. Nevertheless the "intermediates" are involved in virtue because they are also the material (though not the end) of perfect duties; they are the field in which virtue functions; but virtue alone is good, the attainment of the "intermediates", whatever their worth, never so. The "intermediates" are according to human nature, but only the right exercise of moral choice among

them can bring us into harmony with universal nature. So Stoicism retained the self-sufficiency of the Cynics, but like the Peripatetics refused to divorce morals from human nature.

It is just this distinctive relationship between virtue and "intermediates" which formed the core of Stoicism and roused most criticism and misunderstanding; this was fostered by certain shifts of emphasis in different Stoics, and not least by their love of paradox. They were fond of stressing the absolute importance of moral intelligence by insisting that there were no half measures. If a man perfected it, all his acts were right, if not, none were; he was either perfectly good and wise, or fool and knave; all mistakes or vices were equal. Although all Stoics accepted this position, some emphasized it more than others, notably Ariston (a pupil of Zeno), whose unorthodox attitude of complete indifference to the "intermediates" largely eliminated the practical side of Stoicism. Chrysippus showed once and for all that the paradox "all sins are equal" meant that all moral mistakes were equally mistakes in comparison with perfect virtue, but regarded solely by themselves one could be worse than another. The objects of our natural impulses and the "appropriate" duties involved were not in every case valueless; some had a *prima facie* "worth" and were to be "preferred", others "unworth" and to be "relegated"; others were completely indifferent. The relative value of all this lies only within its class (i.e. the class of "appropriate" duties); health is to be preferred as a general rule without outside considerations, as pain is to be avoided; but circumstances may arise where it is right to reject the preferred or vice versa; for neither health nor pain is good or evil in itself. "Appropriate" duties receive absolute value in each case only from the decision of moral intelligence; nevertheless this decision is concerned with them; one is to incline this way or that. The position is most clearly marked in the educative methods of the Stoa; for while he who was not a wise man was a fool, yet fools could progress towards virtue, (and indeed the Stoics made a serious attempt to trace the growth of moral notions in the human mind). Fools were led along the path by the rules of "appropriate" duties, which acquainted them with the material of ethics. But Stoicism concentrated on concrete acts, and in each case the rules required interpretation. So although fools made progress, they remained fools, being fallible and vulnerable, until they understood that the infallible directing principle of morality came from within, the divine control of reason. They must know in each instance what they should choose and why; for this they must comprehend the logos. Each individual alone can be the captain of his own soul. Yet it was apparent that most if not all men were still in the progressive stage; consequently Panaetius (c. 185–110 B.C.) and Posidonius (c. 135–50 B.C.) in particular, when faced with a Roman audience demanding a more practical approach than Greek theory, concentrated on the department of "appropriate" duties, with its emphasis on man as a human being and in relation to others in society, on the study of human nature and human psychology. Thus Panaetius derived from the virtues a series of moral and political rules for action. This could not mean that he had abandoned the higher study of man in the universe and the logos philosophy; but it led in the last century B.C. to the criticism that the Stoa was saying nothing different from Peripatetic ethics; which is true if confined to this intermediate stage, but nonsense when it is remembered that this stage could not produce happiness, which was completely in man's power to achieve.

It was this essential framework of the end and scope of morality which gave unity and shape to the diverse ramifications of Stoicism. In *ethics*, since the condition for right action was the soundness of moral reason, the greatest danger came from the passions, as irrational movements of the mind. Stoics classified the passions under the *genera* pleasure, pain, desire and fear, and regarded them as springing from impulses externally roused and overriding correct judgment. Chrysippus, whose intellectualism brought him to regard all mental forms as modes of reason, went so far as to call them evil reason arising from mistaken judgments; but this embarrassing psychology was criticized by Posidonius, who once more posited an irrational faculty in the mind to explain the moral predicament. But for the Stoics passion involved an assent which

could only be given if reason was weak. Therefore the passions had to be eradicated. The Stoics in their moral teaching attempted to effect a prophylactic cure for this mental sickness. But they never banished emotion; the sage felt correct emotions derived from his sound state; but emotion from other sources was never permitted to cloud his reason. In politics the Stoics were in a curious position; they had a duty to enter politics since they had duties to their fellow human beings. But despite the influence of Panaetius, Stoicism remained fundamentally an ethic for the individual. In the last resort duty to the community had to give way to duty to oneself; and Stoics tended to think of a community based on the individual, or of a community of the wise in divine nature. So their politics tended to remain general rather than particular, or to withdraw to a higher plane, as in the cases of Seneca and Marcus Aurelius. Since the end for a person lay solely in virtue, or the soundness of moral reason, should extraordinary circumstances arise whereby this was threatened, the wise were at liberty to commit suicide. Life and death were alike indifferent compared with the end; the door was always open; one would merely be following the summons of the divine purpose in the universe. There were periods in Stoicism when suicide became almost an obsession, although Stoics had no belief in an after-life.

In *physics*, the Stoics, despite their interest in nature, did not engage in scientific research. Even to Posidonius, who had the most scientific mind of all Stoics, physical phenomena had interest purely as displaying the rational purposive nature of the universe. This the Stoics regarded not with scientific curiosity, but with a religious awe. They argued: the universe is completely material without void; everything is a mode of the original single being, combining passive unqualified matter and force; the latter is reason and god. By a theory of mixture whereby a drop of wine would be diffused over a whole ocean, the subsequent complete blend producing a new whole, so divine reason is diffused throughout the universe making of it an organic whole. There is nothing without a tincture of the divine (thus they are both monotheistic and pantheistic); there is nothing which is not subject to the rational law. This position involved firstly a rigid fatalism: all events are part of an unbroken chain of cause and effect; chance is a name given by human ignorance; possibility means that a future event is not excluded by a known law of nature; (compare **Spinoza**, who distinguishes between "contingent" and "possible", but both words merely reflect human ignorance). Secondly, since god is good, providence rules all for the good of the whole. There were gradations here; the logos varied in purity and "tension" in different forms (e.g. man, animal, plant); the parts contributed to the good of whole, the lower forms to the good of higher; e.g. animals which do not possess active reason are created for the use of humans who do. While the position of moral reason is thus buttressed, critics of the Stoa lost no time in pointing out two consequent difficulties for their ethics. In the first place, the problem of evil became acute. While Stoics maintained that most things regarded as evil are morally indifferent, only vice being evil, yet they did recognize its existence, and the variety and contradictory nature of their answers show that they did not quite know how to meet the problem. There are three main lines of argument: *a*) God could not create evil for its own sake; it is the result of the material in which he has to work, or a secondary result of his provisions for the world. *b*) Evil is not the fault of God, but of man's misuse of his bounty, for they have been granted control of their own virtue or vice. *c*) Evil is necessary (i) for there to be good, since opposites only acquire meaning from each other (compare Plato, *Theaetetus*); (ii) as a punishment or an example or to test us; (iii) by some arrangement beyond human comprehension, for the good of the whole. Secondly, Fatalism was involved in Stoic physics, **freedom of will** in their ethics. Chrysippus' defence consisted of a distinction between the initial external cause which immediately preceded the action, and was part of the infinite chain of cause and effect, and the all-important internal cause furnished by the nature of the thing. A stone when moved falls downward by its own nature. The external stimulus to human action binds man to the fatalistic chain, but from his own nature

he has the power of decision for his own virtue and vice. Yet even so he can do no more than run willingly between the shafts along the road appointed by fate; otherwise he will be dragged willy-nilly in the same direction. A man's nature is subject to Nature's direction, but it is in his power to work hand in glove with Nature itself. His own happiness alone is in his control, not his part in the functioning of the universe. Their physical theories attracted Stoics to divination and astrology. They were supremely conscious of themselves as members of a divine organism through which extended a sympathy affecting all. There is a deep religious feeling especially marked in Cleanthes (pupil of Zeno), Posidonius, Epictetus, and Marcus Aurelius. Like the microcosm, the living universe was thought to have an eternal cycle of change. There will come a period of "conflagration", when everything is converted to the divine fire, becomes soul only, and evil disappears. Then the fire in turn becomes a wet mass from which the seeds of reason initiate an identical cycle.

Since virtue depended on knowledge, one of the principal tasks of Stoic *logic* was to provide a theory of knowledge. Since all reality was material, knowledge depended on sense-perception, tested by reason. Material images of objects were reproduced directly on the mind. Some images, called "comprehensible" or cognitive, corresponded so exactly to the real object as to demand unconditional assent from reason when in a sound condition; "comprehension" (the term meant "grasping", as one grasps an object in the hand) or cognition followed this assent, and became knowledge as an unshakeable certainty in the sage. The extreme weaknesses of this rather mechanical process were rightly attacked by the Sceptics, who pointed out that there is no distinguishable mark between true and false perceptions, that the latter may be as irresistible as the former and that there is no criterion of judgment. This remained the weakest link in Stoicism. In their desire to perfect their arguments, the Stoics made considerable contributions to the study of the syllogism; being empiricists and interested primarily in concrete moral acts they devoted themselves to the hypothetical and disjunctive syllogism, which they classified as **Aristotle** had classified the categorical. Since speech, they believed, was thought in sound, and words arose from the nature of things, they engaged in etymology, and, to far greater effect, in the study of grammar, the development of which owed much to Stoicism. The sage, perfect in all spheres, was also the perfect orator, concentrating on truth and preciseness, and eschewing emotional devices.

Most of the components of Stoicism are not original, but in the attempt to unify much previous philosophical thinking, including apparently incompatible theories, into a comprehensive system, something new was produced. It is true that the two impulses towards comprehensiveness and towards internal unity and consistency produced a magnificent crop of paradoxes. While the Stoics emphasized them in the Socratic tradition for teaching purposes, they remained inherent in the system. Not least paradoxical was their emphasis on the power of all people to achieve their happiness in an all-beneficent universe, combined with the admission that the world was full of human depravity. In the history of the School, the sage tended to become more and more of an ideal, but he always remained a practical ideal; we were not born perfect, but it was in our power to become so. In fact in the later Stoa, during the Empire, most emphasis was laid on practical ethics. This combination of practicality and noble ideals made the Stoa perhaps the most popular and dominant School of philosophy for some five or six hundred years; it survived both the devastating attack of the New Academy, and the acquisitive eclecticism of later Academics and Peripatetics. Although its natural basis and intellectual framework was Greek, and completely alien to Christianity, there were many points of contact between the two in ethics; Seneca was later represented as a secret Christian in correspondence with St Paul; and Epictetus appeared in the Christian curriculum. The influence of Stoicism on later philosophy is not easy to trace, but there are some remarkable similarities to the Stoa in the philosophy of Spinoza.

(I.G.K.)

**Strawson,** Peter Frederick (1919– ), English philosopher and Professor in the University of Oxford. In his *Introduction to Logical Theory* (1952) he examined the general nature of formal **logic**, demonstrating that the gulf between formal and informal discourse is wider than orthodox accounts suggest. He has criticized the semantic and correspondence theories of **truth** and put forward the view that the phrase "is true" has no assertive or descriptive function but is used to perform the act of confirming or endorsing a statement. In "On Referring" (1950) he criticized **Russell's** theory of descriptions. His most important work is *Individuals: An Essay in Descriptive Metaphysics* (1959); in this he studies the ways in which we actually distinguish individual things of all kinds, and concludes that the space-time location of bodies is fundamental to all our ways of locating all kinds of things, including ourselves. This study he calls descriptive **metaphysics** in contrast with speculative metaphysics which, in Strawson's opinion, is largely concerned to set up new conceptual systems. Later works include *The Bounds of Sense, an essay on Kant's Critique of Pure Reason* (1966), and *Freedom and Resentment, and other Essays* (1974). Strawson is also the author of the article on Metaphysics in this Encyclopedia.

(J.O.U.)

**Structuralism**: one of the dominant philosophies of Continental Europe in the post-war period. The method of structural linguistics was first developed by the Swiss theorist, Ferdinand de **Saussure**, early in the century. But it was not until the sixties that a structuralist movement took shape and began to occupy a commanding role in European thought, vying with **Existentialism, Phenomenology** and humanist Marxism for the centre stage. The proliferation of a number of controversial works by French thinkers like Roland Barthes, Louis **Althusser**, Michel **Foucault**, Jacques **Lacan** and Claude Lévi-Strauss, put structuralism on the intellectual map. These thinkers developed Saussure's rather abstract model of linguistic structures into a fully-fledged "semiology" – that is, a science of signs which goes beneath the surface events of language (*parole*) to investigate a variety of concealed signifying systems (*langue*).

Although few of these thinkers adopted the label "structuralist", the term did have some general basis in its reference to a number of diverse applications of Saussure's method. Most structuralists also shared a predilection for the psychoanalytic model of the unconscious and the Marxist model of determining social structures. For the French structuralists, Saussure, **Freud** and **Marx** represented a new intellectual trinity which radically challenged the prevailing existentialist gospel of the autonomous human subject. In contrast with existentialism, structuralism was deeply anti-**humanist**. In response to Sartre's maxim that each man is what he makes of himself, the structuralists declared that man is what he is made by structures beyond his conscious will or individual control. It is not man who speaks language, they argued, but language which speaks man.

While Saussure was the first to adumbrate a science of structural linguistics, or semiology, it soon became evident that such a project could be extended to embrace a considerable range of "trans-linguistic" signifying systems. These could include mass media communications, anthropology, literature, social science or information theory. As Roland Barthes argued, semiology can account for any system of signs, regardless of content or limit – "images, gestures, musical sounds, objects, and the complex association of these, which form the content of ritual, convention or public entertainment: these constitute, if not *language*, at least systems of signification" (*Elements of Semiology*, 1964). Barthes' own most spectacular contribution to the structuralist debate was probably his analysis of the signs of popular media culture in *Mythologies* (1957). This was followed by Foucault's interrogation of the underlying assumptions guiding Western notions of reason and madness, sexuality, sickness and crime; Lacan's exploration of the unconscious structures of desire in speech and language; and Lévi-Strauss' painstaking disclosure of a hidden "wild thought" (*pensée sauvage*) which operates as a timeless mythological logic beneath the veneers of cultural and historical

progress. Rigorously analysing the systems of binary opposition governing the patterning of mythic narratives and rites, Lévi-Strauss concluded that "myths are machines for the suppression of time". They attempt to resolve the fundamental contradictions of human existence – e.g. the conflict between the one and the many, eternity and transience, permanence and change – by translating the disorder of our empirical experience into the order of systematic structures. What cannot be solved at the everyday level of fact can be resolved at the structural level of fiction.

The polemical public disputes which raged between structuralists and humanists in the fifties and sixties were by no means confined to Paris. Structuralism exerted an enormous influence on intellectual life throughout Europe and the English-speaking world, particularly in the fields of literature, linguistics, humanities, history, politics, social science and media studies. In the seventies, structuralism began to be challenged and in many cases superseded by a movement called post-structuralism. The basic structuralist claim to uncover hidden unconscious structures behind surface meanings was now being questioned by **Derrida** and the deconstructionists. The post-structuralists rejected the binary oppositions between surface and depth, event and structure, inner and outer, conscious and unconscious as revived forms of metaphysical dualism. They renounced the structuralist quest for a science of signs, celebrating instead the irreducible excesses of language as a multiple play of meaning.

[R.K.]

**Subjectivism.** Like most terms ending in "ism", the term "subjectivism" is used very vaguely and loosely in philosophy; roughly a view is said to be subjectivist if it maintains that the truth of some class of statements depends on the mental state or reactions of the person making the statement. Thus in **ethics** and **aesthetics** a subjectivist will hold that to say that something is good or beautiful is to say something about one's reaction to something, perhaps that it gives one a special feeling of pleasure, and not to say anything about the "objective" characteristics of the thing; it is necessary to distinguish such a subjectivist view from the expressive theory (found for example in **Ayer's** *Language Truth and Logic*) which holds that when we say something is good we do not make a statement about our reactions to the thing but rather are thereby reacting to the thing in words in a way analogous logically to cheering or throwing one's hat in the air. The view that what is perceived exists only when and because it is perceived, expressed by **Berkeley** in the words *"esse est percipi"*, is also termed subjectivism or subjective **idealism**; such subjectivists believe, usually on the basis of the fact of perceptual illusion and the physical and physiological theories of science, that colours, sounds, smells, etc. exist only "in the mind" and not in the natural world.

(J.O.U.)

**Substance,** *see* Aristotle, Descartes, Spinoza, Leibniz, Locke, Dualism, Monism, Universals.

**Syllogism,** *see* Logic, Peter of Spain.

**Synthetic,** the opposite of **analytic**. For "synthetic *a priori*", see *A priori*.

# T

**Tarski,** Alfred (1902– ), Polish-American logician, *see* Truth.

**Taylor,** Alfred Edward (1869–1945), British philosopher. He began his philosophical career as an idealist and a follower of **Bradley**. But in *The Faith of a Moralist* (1930) he argued that our moral knowledge necessarily presupposes the existence of a God who controls the universe with a moral purpose, and the immortality of the human soul. But Taylor is better known as a Platonic scholar than as an original philosopher.

(J.O.U.)

**Teleological Argument,** *see* Theism, Deism.

**Thales** of Miletus, a Greek seaport in Asia Minor, predicted an eclipse which occurred in 585–4 B.C. He was a *sophos* or sage of many interests: among other things he organized the diversion of a river, and urged federation on the Ionians. His mathematical and astronomical discoveries, later somewhat exaggerated, included methods of mensuration, for example of the height of pyramids, and the compilation of a star-catalogue for nautical use. He probably visited Egypt, and for his estimation of the eclipse must also have had access to Babylonian celestial records. How prominent and how precisely formulated was his more theoretical cosmology we do not know. He certainly believed that the flat earth floated on water, from which it had originated. Here he was probably adapting a common motif of Near-Eastern, and especially Egyptian, mythology. He may also have thought, as **Aristotle** asserts, that the world and its parts were still essentially watery. He seems to have said that "all things are full of gods", meaning that they are permeated by soul. Even the magnet-stone, apparently inanimate, causes motion and is therefore alive. By abandoning personification and attempting to explain the whole world rationally Thales earned his traditional title of the originator of Greek philosophy. See also **Pre-Socratics**.

(G.S.K.)

**Theism.** Theism is the belief that there is a God and that God is omnipotent, omniscient and benevolent, distinct from the universe which he has created and in which he intervenes. To be a theist is not in itself to hold a philosophical theory, but it is to be committed on philosophical issues, both of truth and of meaning. At the same time, a belief shared by **Aquinas, Descartes** and **Berkeley** obviously has a certain chameleon-like quality.

The grounds on which the existence of the God of theism has been asserted are very various. There is first the Cartesian view that "God exists" is a necessary truth: "recurring to the examination of the idea of a Perfect Being,

I found that the existence of the Being was comprised in the idea in the same way that the equality of its three angles to two right angles is comprised in the idea of a triangle . . . and that consequently it is at least as certain that God, who is this Perfect Being, is, or exists, as any demonstration of geometry can be". Descartes' mistake, which Aquinas had identified four centuries earlier, in thinking that any assertion of existence could be a necessary truth is not committed by those who have accepted either the cosmological or teleological arguments.

Both these arguments attempt to derive the conclusion that God exists, from premises about the world. The cosmological argument takes as its premise the assertion that something exists, the teleological the assertion that the universe manifests traces of intelligent design. The cosmological argument then proceeds by way of the assertion that the existence of anything at all can only be explained by supposing that there exists an uncaused First Cause. The teleological argument passes from the assertion of design in nature to the assertion of a supernatural designer. Both arguments have been, perhaps over-frequently, pulverized by the charge that they attempt a causal inference from the universe to its maker; and **Hume** has shown that it only makes sense to speak of causal relations as holding between observable states of affairs, and, whatever God is, he is certainly not an observable state of affairs.

The Cartesian, or ontological, argument, the cosmological and the teleological arguments became a standard triad in eighteenth-century apologetics. The habit of reading the arguments of medieval theism as earlier versions of these is however a questionable one. Clearly the chief difficulty in advancing a proof of the existence of God lies in the elementary logical point that in a valid proof nothing can appear in the conclusion which was not already contained in the premises. A valid proof of God's existence could therefore be nothing other than the making explicit of a belief which was implicit in the premises. Those who are prepared to deny not only those premises which state, but also those which imply, divine existence must necessarily be left untouched by the theistic arguments. The concept of theistic proof as proceeding by unquestionable inferences from undeniable premises is ruled out not by any special difficulty in theism but by the prerequisites of proof in general. Aquinas, at least, was well aware of the central issues here. All that you can do, on a matter of first principles such as theistic belief is to show that your opponent's position fails.

The failure of the eighteenth-century triad, however, led not to a re-examination of the notion of proof but to an appeal to inner religious experience. This appeal became characteristic of Protestant philosophy of religion and led to the quest for an experience at once plainly identifiable as *the* religious experience by those who enjoyed it and as plainly witnessing to the existence of God. Schleiermacher's "feelings of absolute dependence" and Otto's "numinous" are the most notorious candidates in this field. This whole movement had fruitful consequences for the phenomenological study of religious experience. But as an attempt to provide grounds for theistic belief it fails, for it becomes either another version of the familiar and invalid causal inference, passing in this case from an alleged introspectible state of affairs to an unobserved author of this state of affairs, or a simple irrationalist affirmation that because I feel that it is so, it is so.

The latter alternative must be distinguished from another Protestant position, which rests belief neither on argument nor on experience. For some Protestants the whole ground for belief is faith in a divine revelation; the belief that there is a God is from the standpoint of rational argument simply groundless. This is not to say that theistic belief lacks grounds which it might possess, but that theistic belief necessarily lacks grounds. Such a belief is not however invulnerable to rational argument even on its own assumptions. For, if God has revealed himself, it must be at some time and place to some specific person and the allegation that there was such a person is a purely historical affirmation which can be challenged on historical grounds. So the revealed belief of Islamic theism depends upon historical assertions about Mahomet and that of Christian theism depends on assertions about Jesus.

How in any case can the assertion that this or that event is revelatory of the divine be warranted? A necessary condition presumably is that the event in question should either be a miraculous occurrence or be accompanied by such occurrences. In this way the problem of miracles arises for the theist, and since the assertion that God intervenes miraculously is essential to theism, as contrasted with **deism**, an *a priori* proof of the impossibility of miracles would be a disproof of theism. That Hume provides such a proof has often been asserted. Hume accepts the theological definition of a miracle as a breach of a law of nature, and he argues that when we speak of a law of nature we mean that a certain course of events has been uniformly experienced to occur. Now where such a sequence of events has been uniformly experienced by the whole of mankind it is to the highest degree improbable that such a sequence should be interrupted. And when someone testifies that such a sequence has been interrupted, as the apostles testified that Jesus walked on the water, it is always more probable that the testimony is erroneous than that the hitherto observed regularity of nature should have been contravened. But this is an argument against accepting reports of the miraculous rather than against believing in the possibility of miracles; and it ignores one essential feature of claims about the miraculous.

What distinguishes a miraculous event is not just its apparent inexplicability; but also the fact that it appears as an answer to a human command or need. The concept which demands scrutiny is not that of a "miraculous event" but rather that of "doing a miracle".

This relationship between divine intervention and human life is characteristic of the religious content of theism and it is therefore not surprising that it should affect the conceptual problems which theism raises. It emerges notably in the difficulty posed for theistic belief by physical and moral evil. If God is all-powerful, then he must be able to prevent evil. If God is all-good, then he must wish to prevent evil. But evil occurs. So that God cannot be both all-powerful and all-good. And to assert that he is both these things and to allow that evils occur is to admit

that theism involves the starkest contradiction. The Theistic answer to this charge is usually that God's willing some good end such as human freedom and the possibility of human moral achievement made it logically necessary that God should create a world with possible or actual evils in it. Among the difficulties which this answer encounters is the fact that so much animal suffering, for example, must have taken place before man ever appeared and must therefore be considered irrelevant to any divine purpose for human freedom. Theists however are normally disposed to admit that the facts of evil constitute at least a *prima facie* objection to theism. That they admit this perhaps assists them in meeting another type of problem.

Critics of the theistic proofs argue that there are no good reasons for believing that God exists; exponents of the problem of evil are apt to claim that there are good reasons for believing that God does not exist; neither scepticism cuts as deep as that which claims that it is equally meaningless to assert or to deny the existence of God. This may be asserted on the general positivist ground that the meaning of a statement is the method of its verification, and that there is no method of verifying theistic statements. But the same charge can also be made in a way that brings out the nature of theistic belief more strikingly. For to make an assertion is always to allow that one may be wrong, that there is some conceivable state of affairs incompatible with one's assertion which, if it occurs, shows that one's assertion is false. If one does not rule out anything by making what appears to be an assertion, then one simply has not succeeded in asserting anything. But the theist does not seem to allow that anything conceivable could falsify his assertion that there is a good and all-powerful God. Whatever disasters happen, he claims that their occurrence is not incompatible with the care of an all-loving, all-powerful God. This seems to evacuate words like "loving" and "powerful" of all meaning. To this the theist will reply that his assertions would be falsified by the occurrence of pointless and irredeemable evil, but that no actual evils can be shown to be pointless and irredeemable, especially in the light of the possibilities of an after-life. Thus the theistic claim comes into logical connexion with the claim that human beings are not mortal, a connexion which is already made in most of the great religions on theological grounds.

There is no one problem or group of problems which can be labelled "the theistic question". Proof, introspection, laws of nature, free-will, falsifiability – almost all the topics of philosophy – arise in a theistic context. The conceptual problems of the theistic philosopher are thus for the most part the ordinary conceptual problems of philosophy, raised from a particular point of view. See also **Religion**.

(A.MACI.)

**Theophrastus** (*c.* 370–*c.* 286 B.C.), born in Lesbos, a Greek island in the Aegean, was **Aristotle**'s most famous pupil. He succeeded as head of the Lyceum when Aristotle left Athens in 323. Most of his many writings are lost and it is hard to get a true picture of his contributions to philosophy. He remained fundamentally an Aristotelian, but he criticized Aristotle on particular points and made useful additions to Aristotle's work, for example in logic. In some respects he paved the way for the teachings of **stoicism** and **epicureanism**. Three of his works may be mentioned. (1) The *De Plantis* (which we have) laid the foundations of scientific botany and introduced important botanical concepts. (2) The *Metaphysics* (also extant) raised problems about Aristotle's metaphysical doctrines, especially the doctrine of a Prime Mover. (3) Theophrastus compiled a large work containing the views of previous Greek philosophers on nature, God etc. This became the source for numerous later historians of Greek philosophy. (See **Pre-Socratics**.) It is not too much to say that until comparatively recent times historians of pre-Socratic philosophy were dominated by the influence of Theophrastus. This was unfortunate because Theophrastus saw all earlier philosophers as mere precursors of Aristotle and forced their ideas into an Aristotelian framework.

(J.L.A.)

**Thomism**, *see* Aquinas, Neo-Thomism.

**Thomas of Sutton**. One of the Oxford Dominicans who rallied to the support of Thomas **Aquinas** after the Kilwardby and during the Peckham offensives from Canterbury. His early writings, which began from about 1286, centre on the soul as single substantial form of the body. His later writings, to about 1315, find him facing a new attack, from the developed Aristotelianism of **Scotus**. He became a resolute defender of the distinction between essence and existence in finite beings.

(T.G.)

**Toulmin,** Stephen Edelston (1922– ), English philosopher, based in the United States. His *Place of Reason in Ethics* (1950) was the earliest book on **ethics** from the viewpoint of linguistic analysis. In *Philosophy of Science: An Introduction* (1953) Toulmin gives an account of scientific theorizing as being more like the making of maps to enable one to find one's way about than the process of generalization which is described in the classical theories of induction. His *The Uses of Argument* (1958) is an attempt to redescribe the nature and function of arguments in terms more revealing than those traditionally used in logic textbooks. He has also written widely on the history of science, and produced a systematic treatise on *Human Understanding* (1972).

(J.O.U.)

**Transcendental Arguments**. Transcendental Arguments move from the premise that a certain kind of knowledge is possible (say, arithmetic), to the conclusion that a priori "conditions of its possibility" must be fulfilled. The view that such arguments are crucial to philosophy is due to **Kant**'s proposal for a "transcendental" philosophy, "concerned not so much with objects as with the mode of our knowledge of objects". **Husserl**'s project of **phenomenology** can be seen as an extended Transcendental Argument, as can **Wittgenstein**'s argument against the possibility of a private language. Indeed the term can be applied to any argument purporting to establish a proposition by showing that if it were false, it would not even be possible to discuss it: for example **Aristotle's** argument that the law of contradiction must be assumed even by those who would argue against it.

[J.R.]

**Truth**. Philosophers have been concerned principally with two questions about truth; the first problem is concerned with the meaning of the word "true", the second with the criterion or criteria by which we can decide on the truth or falsity of statements. Most commonly philosophers have failed to distinguish these two questions and have offered as an answer to one of the questions what might be regarded as a possible answer to the other. But it is easy to see that there is such a distinction if we consider the views of a philosopher who does see and make the distinction; thus F. C. S. **Schiller** maintained that in meaning "true" was an evaluative term, meaning something like "good to believe", but as a **pragmatist** he maintained that the criterion of truth was utility.

The two most famous theories of truth, the correspondence theory and the coherence theory, have usually been represented as theories about the meaning of "true"; so interpreted the correspondence theory asserts that "true" means "corresponds to the facts" and the coherence theory asserts that "true" means "coheres with the body of accepted statements". The most obvious criticism of the coherence theory is that while it has considerable plausibility as a statement of one criterion of truth it hardly gives the meaning of "true"; we do treat the coherence of a statement with what we already believe as one reason, though not a sufficient reason, for accepting it as true, but if coherence is a test of truth it cannot be the same thing as truth. Criticism of the correspondence theory is more difficult and complex; from one point of view it seems that to say that truth is correspondence with fact is a mere platitude, but we get into difficulties when we try to give clear meaning to "correspondence" and "fact". No doubt it is true that there are no centaurs, and we

may say that the statement that there are no centaurs corresponds with the facts; but it is hard to see what sort of status the "fact" of there being no centaurs has and what sort of relation, called "correspondence", it can enter into with a statement. Thus the correspondence theory is liable to resolve itself into a mere metaphor.

A difficulty much noticed in recent years is that the phrase "it is true that" seems to add nothing to the meaning of sentences in which it occurs; it is hard to see what extra value is added if, instead of saying "the cat is on the mat", we say "it is true that the cat is on the mat". The real use of the word "true" appears to be in such expressions as "that is true", where it enables us to confirm a statement without repeating it. These points have led some philosophers, notably **Strawson**, to hold that the word "true" is rather a signal of assent, or concession, or admission, functioning more like the word "yes", than like a word signifying a quality or relation. Schiller's view, mentioned above, that "true" is a term of evaluation is closely related to this view.

Incautious pragmatists have sometimes spoken as though they identified the meaning of "true" with "useful to believe", though cautious pragmatists like Schiller avoided this trap. In putting forward utility as a criterion of truth, the pragmatists were not wishing to say that if it would be pleasant if something were true, we should count it as true; they rather wished to emphasize that systems of human beliefs and the concepts employed in them are interpretations of the world designed to help us cope with it. If we thus think of statements as interpretations, we cannot divorce the question of their satisfactoriness from the question whether they do the job that they are intended to do.

Finally, a very celebrated paper by Tarski, "The Concept of Truth in Formalized Languages" should be mentioned. In this paper Tarski defines "truth" in a way that gives it a function in a calculus analogous to the function of "true" in ordinary language. It is quite certain that this definition cannot be applied directly to our ordinary notion of truth; whether it has any relevance to the philosophical problem of truth is a highly technical and disputable question. Such views as Tarski's are called semantical theories of truth. See also **Davidson**.

(J.O.U.)

# U

**Universals.** In the first instance, Universals are abstract objects such as qualities, relations and numbers, things which cannot be straightforwardly located in space and time. They are contrasted with particulars and are sometimes defined as the objects of thought, while particulars are the objects of perception or sensation. Particulars are sometimes identified with concrete objects in space and time, sometimes with that element of a concrete object which individuates it, that is, distinguishes it from everything else however similar in character. It is perhaps preferable to retain the term "particular" for the latter idea and to call concrete objects "individuals", as being made up of both a particular and universals. On this view a particular would be an uncharacterized spatio-temporal position, the bare possibility of an object. Some such idea is one of the roots of the traditional concept of substance.

Two main sorts of universals can be distinguished: predicative universals, the properties and relations that are the meaning of general terms or predicates, and formal universals, the abstract entities of **mathematics**. The difference is that while predicative universals can and usually do have instances, formal universals are rather ideal limits to which actual things more or less closely approximate. The existence of predicative universals (redness, justice, betweenness etc.) is argued for as a necessary condition of the predicative use of general terms. We cannot think or speak without general terms: every statement contains one such term as "red" or "earlier than", and we are never aware of anything except as having some property or standing in a relation. In other words, individual things fall into kinds, and the world exhibits recurrences and similarities. Clearly there are general terms and they have meanings. But does it follow that there actually exist things which

are the meanings of general terms? Could one not say that there is one set of things, namely concrete objects, to which singular terms are related in one way (each standing for one concrete thing) and general terms related in another (each applying to many)? The difficulty with this view (a form of **nominalism**) is that we can use general terms correctly without having been told in advance all the things to which they apply. There are, that is to say, sets of things in which a few members of the set are representative of the rest. Positive theories of universals are attempts to explain this peculiar and important fact. A predicative universal is what the members of a natural set of this kind have in common.

The existence of formal universals is argued for on two related grounds: abstract reference and necessary truth. Some true statements ("2 × 2 = 4" and "tuberculosis is decreasing") refer not to concrete things but to entities that are neither in space nor time. But what a true statement refers to must exist. Again, there are some truths which we know for certain simply by the use of reason and without any observation of the spatio-temporal world (such as "axb = bxa" and "Red is a colour"). Universals, then, may be thought of as the subject-matter of necessary or **a priori** knowledge; to use one's reason is to examine and elicit their invariable qualities and relations. The argument from predication is more emphasized at the present time than the argument from abstract reference and necessary knowledge. For it is widely held that all abstract reference is apparent rather than real and that the principle of reference does not apply to necessary truths. Contingent propositions with abstract subjects must refer to existing things if true. But what they refer to, and so presuppose the existence of, is ordinary concrete things. "Tuberculosis is decreasing" really refers to tuberculosis sufferers, not to the disease itself. It is an idiomatic, and potentially misleading way of saying "fewer people suffer from tuberculosis nowadays". Necessary propositions refer to nothing, for they depend for their truth, not on the existence of anything, but on the meaning of the words to express them. "Mary's husband is married to Mary" is a necessary truth whether Mary is married or single.

The most famous account of our ability to apply predicative general terms to things we have not come across before is **realism**, or, less confusingly, conceptual realism. On this view we can apply one general term to many things because we are aware of the common property they possess. This common property cannot be in space and time since, if it were, it would exhibit the logically insufferable characteristic of being in many different places at one and the same time. Furthermore there would be many such properties in many places at the same time. This theory suggests that universals are directly accessible to the mind in a way that is not easy to accept. It also has a formal defect common to all theories of universals in seeming to generate an infinite regress. I can tell that this particular thing is hard because I am aware of the abstract universal Hardness and of the fact that the universal inheres in the thing. But to discern this fact of inherence I must be aware of the abstract universal Inherence and so on. This defect of platonism, first formulated in **Plato's** *Parmenides*, led **Aristotle** to say that universals were not abstract and "separated" from the things they inhered in but were to be found in the common world of space and time along with particular objects. What this presumably means is that Hardness is a vast fragmentary object, cropping up here and there all over the place. If so it would be little suited to its theoretical task, for people who know the meaning of the word *hard* perfectly well are acquainted with only a minute portion of this total object. They could only find out what the rest of it was composed of if they already knew the meaning of the word. Furthermore universals with no instances such as *Ghost* and *Female Pope* would be one and the same universal and the two terms would have one and the same meaning, which they plainly do not.

The two traditional alternatives to realism are **conceptualism**, which asserts that we apply general terms to new things through the use of some mental standard, a concept or image, and nominalism, the view that the things to which a general term applies have no more in common than the fact that men apply that general term to them. In practice neither of these theories is often held in its full rigour. Without some basis in the nature of the things in question, the general correspondence between different people's concepts and linguistic practices would be an unintelligible miracle. Thus conceptualists like **Abelard** and **Locke** say that concepts are based on the similarities of things; and nominalists like **Hobbes** and many contemporary philosophers explain the application of general terms by the similarity of the things they apply to either to one another or to some standard thing or group of things. Realists argue that since similarity is itself a universal these modifications are no more than realism in disguise.

Apart from absolutely pure nominalism all theories of universals are exposed to the regress argument. But this does not mean that what they say is false. It is rather that what is really a repetition in other words of the puzzling fact of the reapplicability of general terms has been misinterpreted as an explanation of it. To say that we can recognize hard things as hard because they all have the common property of being hard or fall under the concept of hardness is uninformative. To be aware of the common property or to possess the concept is simply to know how to use the general term, above all in the recognition and classification of things.

(A.Q.)

**Urmson,** James O. (1915– ), English philosopher, a compiler of posthumous editions of works by **Austin**, a sympathetic but critical historian of **analytic philosophy** (see *Philosophical Analysis*, 1956; *The Emotive Theory of Ethics*, 1968), the original editor of this Encyclopedia, and author of many articles in it and also of *Berkeley* (1982). Although many of his writings focus on theories about the nature of philosophy, he holds that "on the whole the best philosophy is little affected by theory; the philosopher sees what needs doing and does it".

[J.R.]

**Utilitarianism,** is a theory of ethics combining two basic theses. (1) The *rightness* of an action is to be judged by the contribution it makes to the increase of human happiness or .the decrease of human misery. The moral validity of a law or rule, or the value of an institution, depends on the same considerations. Nothing else matters: not conformity to revelation, authority, tradition, nor even "moral sense" or conscience or contract or history. An action may pass any of these tests, flatter the conscience of the doer, and yet bring misery and ruin. The only thing that matters is its contribution to happiness. (2) Pleasure is the only thing *good in itself* and pain the only thing evil in itself. Happiness includes pleasure and freedom from pain: perhaps such a balance of pleasures as itself produces further pleasure. For example, **Bentham**'s formulation in *Principles of Morals and Legislation* (1789) is: "By the principle of utility is meant that principle which approves or disapproves of every action whatsoever, according to the tendency which it appears to have to augment or diminish the happiness of the party whose interest is in question . . . if that party be the community in general, then the happiness of the community". If the tendency of an action to increase the happiness of the community is greater than any tendency it has to diminish it, then it is "conformable to the principle of utility". One may then say that it is a right action or at least that it is not wrong.

Utilitarianism has its origins in Greek thought: in modern times it is derived from certain views of **Hobbes** and **Locke**, and was formulated by **Hutcheson** in 1726. A version of the theory was elaborated by **Hume** as a purely descriptive account of the way in which men make moral judgments; directly moralistic versions were given by Joseph Priestley and William Paley; and practical applications in **jurisprudence** were worked out by Helvétius in France and Beccaria in Italy. Jeremy Bentham drew upon all these predecessors, setting out a clear and solid theory and making the widest possible use of it in his attacks upon the constitutional, economic, legal and social problems of his day. James **Mill**'s version is simpler and more egotistical. J. S. **Mill**'s *Utilitarianism* (1863) is much more complicated, and re-introduces many factors which Bentham had painstakingly eliminated. Henry **Sidgwick** and (with a difference) Herbert **Spencer** are in the same tradition. G. E. **Moore** (*Principia Ethica*, 1903) made a fundamental modification. He accepted the view that the rightness of an action depends on the good or bad consequences that follow it, but held that many sorts of things apart from pleasures and pains are good or bad in themselves. Rejecting the original utilitarian view that what matters is human happiness or pleasure, Moore argued that what matters is what is *good*, and that what kinds of things are good is to be learned by intuition.

"Pleasure and pleasure alone is good in itself." We may imagine the pleasure of someone tasting food, or settling to rest, or zestfully attacking a victim. We may think of these pleasures as if they were a kind of sensation and suppose that it is for the sake of this sensation that we eat, or rest, or do violence, and that it is for the sake of remoter pleasures or avoiding greater pains in the future that we work or save or suffer pains. Then it is the pleasure that an object brings that makes us call it "good", and the pain that makes us call it "bad". In effect Bentham regards "good" and "bad" as expressive terms which we apply to things that bring pleasure or pain. And he is content to say that one pleasure is *better* than another only if it is *a greater pleasure*. This ethical view is often associated with psychological **hedonism**. On that view all the objects which we aim at "for their own sakes" or "as ends not simply means", must be "pleasures". But the ethical doctrine is weakened by this association. Mill appeals to this metaphysical doctrine in order to establish the view that the person who aims at knowledge or virtue *for its own sake*, is still pursuing "pleasure". There are (he says) many objectives which were once pursued only as means to some pleasant end, but which (by association and habit) have come to be pursued without reference to the original end. Saving money is one of Mill's examples; abiding by the rules of virtue at all costs, is another. But this means that "pleasure" includes things that are desired only by a confusion of thought and things that are pursued by mere habit and without desire: nor is there any clear distinction between things desired as means and things desired for their own sake.

Mill goes on to introduce a distinction between "lower" and "higher" pleasures. The higher pleasures are not known to be "greater" by Bentham's criteria: but nevertheless they are to be preferred. On this view it is a trivial point that only pleasure can be desired for its own sake: what really matters is that *some* of the objects of desire are higher pleasures. Mill's position is a half-way house on the road to the ideal or agathistic theory of G. E. Moore. "Pleasure and pleasure alone is good in itself" has some value as a war-cry: but so hospitable a doctrine is bound to include the *oddest* pleasures and ends up by counting as "pleasure" whatever is the object of desire. The moral justification of this can hardly be that all these pleasures are good: it is rather that it is right or proper for *persons* to choose for themselves. This doctrine (wholly congenial to Bentham as to Mill) lacks the characteristic "scientific" features which the calculation of pains and pleasure was supposed to introduce.

"Actions are right in proportion as they tend to produce happiness, wrong as they tend to produce the reverse of happiness." G. E. Moore, in his account of utilitarianism, maintained that an action is right if its consequences would in fact be better than those of any other action which could be performed instead. Since we can never *know* what the consequences of an action will be (but can only judge what they are likely to be), it follows that when one debates whether to do action A or action B, one can never *know* which action is right. The earlier utilitarians sometimes suggested this: but their real view seems to have been that "right" and "wrong" are to be attributed by reference to probable consequences. We think of the right act as what a man ought to do, and this has to be judged by reference to probable consequences as they appear at the time of decision. So we may conclude that on this point Moore was mistaken.

Moore also held that in deciding whether or not a given action would be right, it is the consequences (he should have said probable consequences) *of that action singly considered*, which are to be taken into account. (So also Bentham.) Such a view seems to offend against common-sense. We are accustomed to think of actions as falling into certain kinds: some of

these kinds are never to be performed; others whenever opportunity arises; and then there are other kinds where we must choose by considering consequences. For example, in making choices for one's own life one has often to decide simply by reference to probable consequences. But one ought not even to consider cheating or lying as possible actions because all actions of those sorts are always wrong. On this point the Utilitarians will say (1) No doubt cheating and lying and killing have got a bad name because they almost always have very bad consequences. A moral rule against an action of a certain *kind*, may be regarded as a rule of thumb which shows us that such actions are to be avoided on almost all occasions; (2) Social Life is possible only if certain conventions are almost always followed, for example telling the truth. On a given occasion an immediate consequence of a lie may be good: but in almost all cases there is a further consequence to be considered. Any breach of the convention is likely to weaken it, chiefly by lowering public confidence in it. And although this consequence may touch the parties immediately concerned very lightly, it is not to be taken lightly, because it is an injury to "the general happiness". For this reason it is indeed *generally* wrong to lie even where the more obvious consequences are good. But if there should be a case where the consequences of telling a lie are not so bad as the consequences of not doing so then the utilitarian would hold that in this case lying is right.

In this connexion, it has been argued that the utilitarianism put forward in Mill's essays is not the same as that of Bentham, Sidgwick and Moore. Mill's utilitarianism (it is said) is *restricted* in a most important way. For Mill recognizes that the test of the rightness or wrongness of individual actions is not normally the test of their consequences: the test lies in the application of a moral rule – or (as Mill calls it) a secondary principle. Thus an act of theft is wrong because there is a rule against stealing: and morality consists of "rules and precepts for human conduct". But these rules may themselves be tested and found to be valid or invalid. The test is a utilitarian one: a rule is valid if the consequences of its being generally observed are better than the consequences of its not being generally observed. According to this interpretation, Mill would hold it proper to follow the moral rule unless (1) one were prepared to question the validity of the rule in general on utilitarian grounds; or (2) there was a conflict of rules. In the latter case Mill clearly says that the proper procedure is to appeal directly to "first principles" – i.e. to test the consequences of doing or not doing the action in question.

Certainly Mill attaches great importance to following moral rules even at great cost to oneself. But can a utilitarian hold that there is a virtue in following a rule *for its own sake?* The situation is complicated in the case of what Hume called the "artificial virtues" (justice, keeping promises, telling the truth etc.). As he showed, these virtues are possible only where certain rules of conduct are generally followed. One cannot keep a promise or break a promise without the institution of promising; and one cannot defraud a residuary legatee in a society which has no law or custom of testation. In the case of the artificial virtues, then, one *could not* display them if one were guided simply by the first principle of doing the action which promises the best consequences. The institutions which give rise to honesty in property, or good faith in promises presuppose that *most people* are bound by the rules of property or good faith. This shows that the artificial virtues are particularly liable to be undermined by *irregular* conduct, since *our chief reason* for observing them is the expectation that everyone else will do the same. (This is not so in the case of kindness, generosity, saving life etc. – Hume's "natural virtues".) The argument cannot of course go so far as to show that such rules ought never to be broken. The question is: does it succeed in explaining, on utilitarian principles, why the rules about justice and promise-keeping are so important, and why it is always such a serious matter to break them? It is argued by anti-utilitarians that we know that certain rules are binding: and know which of the rules are the most binding: and that we know this without having the information that would be necessary to infer it on utilitarian grounds.

(K.B.)

# V

**Venn,** John (1834–1923), English logician, who taught philosophy at Cambridge. He wrote three influential books on **logic**. *The Logic of Chance* (1866) gives the first statement of the "frequency" theory of **probability**. His work is largely original though he worked from suggestions put forward by the mathematician, R. L. Ellis. Venn's account of probability has been extensively developed and criticized in the present century.

*Symbolic Logic* (1881), though containing little original work of importance is a thorough and readable survey of previous work in symbolic logic. It contains an extraordinarily full bibliography drawing attention among other important books to **Frege's** *Begriffsschrift*, then very recently published. *Principles of Empirical or Inductive Logic* (1889), is a less important book relying largely though not uncritically on the work of J. S. **Mill**. Curiously, Venn's own ideas on probability are little used there.

(D.J.O'C.)

**Verification Principle:** the thesis, central to **logical positivism**, that the meaning of a propostion is the method of discovering whether it is true.

**Vienna Circle.** The Vienna Circle was the group of logical **positivists** or, as they are sometimes called, logical **empiricists** who belonged to the University of Vienna in the nineteen-twenties and thirties. In 1895 a Chair of Philosophy of the Inductive Sciences had been founded in Vienna for Ernst **Mach**. Moritz **Schlick** was elected to this chair in 1922 and very soon an informal circle of colleagues and senior pupils formed about him; they were united by a common interest in the sciences and mathematics, a general acceptance of the positivistic outlook of Mach and a rocognition of the importance of the developing science of mathematical logic. Among the more important of these are Friedrich Waismann, Rudolf **Carnap**, Otto Neurath, E. Zilsel, Herbert Feigl, B. von Juhos, Felix Kaufmann, Victor

Kraft, Hans Hahn and Kurt Göedel. Though **Wittgenstein** was living in Austria at this time and was a personal friend of some of the members of this group he was never a member of it; but his *Tractatus Logico-philosophicus* greatly influenced it. In 1929 the Circle was given a more formal status and a pamphlet was issued setting out its basic tenets and aims. In 1930 the magazine *Erkenntnis* was founded as the organ of the group. Immense interest in the work of the Circle was aroused in the early 1930s both in Europe and in America; the group itself, however, was soon to be dispersed, because of the assassination of Schlick in 1936, the hostility of the Nazis after the *Anschluss* and finally the War in 1939. Many members of the group subsequently led distinguished philosophical careers in other countries and the circle has had its greatest influence outside the German-speaking countries in which it originated.

(J.O.U.)

**Vitoria**, Francis de, born between 1483 and 1486 in Old Castile, Spain. A Dominican Master of Paris, Valladolid, and Salamanca, he brought to the teaching of scholastic philosophy in his *Relectiones*, or published lectures, a new dignity and warmth. The founder of the great School of Spanish Thomists, he took a leading part in the university movement for promoting justice for the natives of Spanish America which earned the grateful admiration of Dr Johnson. He criticized the prevailing **nominalism** in philosophy, but above all is famous as the Father of International Law. He developed the jurisprudence of Thomas **Aquinas**, extending the *Jus Gentium* (law of nations) of the Roman legal texts into an organic instrument of concord for the whole *Respublica Humana* (community of mankind) which allows for pacts between States but also appeals to a higher sovereignty.

(T.G.)

**Voltaire**, François-Marie Arouet de (1694-1778), French dramatist and philosophical writer, *see* Encyclopedists. .

# W

**Ward,** James (1843–1925), English philosopher who taught at Cambridge after resigning from the Congregational ministry, for which he had been educated in Birmingham, besides studying philosophy at Berlin and Göttingen. His interests were wide, ranging from biology to his elaborate **metaphysics**. His *Naturalism and Agnosticism* (1899) is mainly critical of **Spencer** and "physics treated as metaphysics", preferring history as a model of reality. *The Realm of Ends* (1911) develops under the influence of **Leibniz** and Lotze a pluralistic system of minds, (matter being composed of interacting mindlike monads), which is intended to "leave room for" a unifying **theism**.

But it is his work as a philosophical psychologist which gives him historical importance. His *Encyclopaedia Britannica* article "Psychology" in 1886 brought about the downfall in Britain of the associationist psychology, which had attempted to reduce mental life to a system of experiences, or "presentations", mechanically interrelated by laws like those which relate bodies in physics. Most notably, Ward maintained that there must always be a *subject* to which these presentations occur. This psychological subject, or "Pure Ego", is not only aware of presentations, but feels pleased and pained in consequence, and has the power of variously distributing attention to the presentations, which form a continuum at any one moment (a "field of consciousness") and from one moment to another. The bulk of the article was eventually incorporated in his book *Psychological Principles* (1918). Ward's views in this field continue the intermixture of philosophy with the empirical science of psychology, on account of which **Bradley** accused Ward of confusion.

(R. HALL)

**Weil,** Simone (1909–1943), born in Paris, is best known for the Christian and mystical doctrine of her later works. She established her reputation in France as a radical and iconoclastic teacher of philosophy and revolutionary trade-union activist. She was schooled in the "activist" Cartesianism developed by Jules Lagneau and her own teacher, Alain, and her philosophy is marked throughout by a belief in the importance of the individual quest for knowledge and self-enlightenment. Its particular character, however, derives from its synthesis of Marxist, pre-Socratic, Platonist, pacifist and religious arguments.

One of her major concerns, made more acute by her own experience as a factory worker, was the servitude and humiliation of the industrial worker. Her positive philosophy of human dignity and humility was developed through her conception of "decreation", which means a systematic release of the self from the "personal", modelled on God's abdication of interference in the universe.

Weil's most important work of social philosophy, *The Need for Roots*, 1949, was written in an occupied and defeated France. It is an extended indictment of a politics which substitutes the pursuit of power and national glory for the realization of the more fundamental spiritual needs of the collectivity.

Other principal writings translated into English include: *Gravity and Grace* (1947), *Waiting on God* (1950), and *The Notebooks of Simone Weil* (1953, 1956). Several anthologies are also available.

[K.S.]

**Whewell,** William (1794–1866), British philosopher who taught at Cambridge.

Whewell pioneered the study of scientific method, stressing the importance of induction; but in line with Kantian philosophy he regarded the "mysterious step" from the observation of particular facts to the discovery of general principles as dependent on **ideas** formed by the understanding. That is to say, for the production of a scientific theory the mere collection of facts is inadequate; what is necessary is "a true *colligation* of facts by means of an exact and appropriate conception. Here and elsewhere he is in effect describing the *hypothetico-deductive* method: for example, "success seems to consist in framing several tentative hypotheses and selecting the right one". This emphasis on the value of hypothesis in science is his permanent

contribution. It led directly to controversy with J. S. **Mill** because Whewell maintained that the formation of an explanatory hypothesis *was* the induction, and since the facts explained could then be deduced from the hypothesis, **induction** and **deduction** were not different kinds of reasoning as Mill thought, but each the other in reverse: "deduction justified by calculation what induction has happily guessed". The dispute was unreal, for Whewell was interested in, and undoubtedly right about, the method of discovery in science, whereas Mill was mainly concerned with the logic of induction as a method of proof, or "process of analysis", proceeding from particular premises and usually terminating in a general conclusion.

Whewell's views on induction and scientific method appeared in his *Philosophy of the Inductive Sciences* (1840). They rested on the immense store of information in his earlier *History of the Inductive Sciences* (1837), without which Mill, by his own confession, would have been unable to write the parts of his *Logic* dealing with induction and attacking the later book. Whewell also wrote on mathematical and moral philosophy, in both as an intuitionist, and in both Mill selected him for attack, accusing him of making all philosophy a support for "any opinions which happened to be established". Whewell was indeed the champion of the established order in every field.

Whewell was probably the most learned man of the early Victorian age, when he was famous; as a philosopher of science he deserves more attention than Mill. See also **Philosophy of Science.**

(R. HALL)

**Whitehead,** Alfred North (1861–1947), English philosopher, born in East Kent, where his father was a vicar. His boyhood gave him a strong sense of the continuity of the life of a society over the generations, and of **religion** as intimately bound up with its way of life. He went to Cambridge in 1880, and was subsequently elected to a fellowship in **mathematics**. Here he began the collaboration with **Russell** on the logical foundations of mathematics which led to the three volumes of *Principia Mathematica*. This interest was first shown in the *Treatise on Universal Algebra* (1903), and in *Mathematical Concepts of the Material World* (1905). Whitehead held the chair of Applied Mathematics at Imperial College, London from 1910 until 1924, when he was invited to Harvard University as Professor of Philosophy, remaining in Cambridge, Massachusetts, until his death.

Whitehead's philosophy was an attempt to combine (a) a logico-mathematical interest in abstract relational systems, (b) "cosmology" (in the broad sense of an interpretation of the world suggested by general notions underlying physical science); and (c) a moral, religious and aesthetic interest in human relationships within societies. (Whitehead's interest in religion was not, however, merely sociological; he saw it also as concerned with man's relation to God as the permanent ground of the world process.) In his early logical work he pursued the suggestion, originating from **Frege**, that mathematics is derivable from certain formal logical relationships. These make possible the development of deductive systems which supply, as it were, blank cheques of possible forms of relations, some of which may be filled in by "values" in empirical applications. In his interest in the general ideas underlying the physical science of his time, he was impressed chiefly by the field theories in physics, and the notion of energy as he learnt it from J. J. Thompson, by whom it was presented as a vector magnitude, a measurable flux passing from one natural event to another. This notion, he thought, implied that the physical ultimates should be thought of as lines of force with a direction, not as particles of matter occupying points of space at instants of time. This led him, as early as the 1905 paper on *Mathematical Concepts of the Material World*, to an attack on the classical Newtonian concepts. The notion of lines of force overlapping one another in "fields" was seen as analogous to the logico-topological device of "Extensive Abstraction" a method he had devised by which geometrical elements such as points and lines are defined not as real or ideal entities, but relationally in terms of ways in which volumes of different kinds, such as circles rectangles or ellipses, may systematically extend over or overlap one another. The logical and epistemological notions connected with this way

of regarding the physical world were developed in the three books of Whitehead's "middle" period, *The Principles of Natural Knowledge* (1919), *The Concept of Nature* (1920), and *The Principle of Relativity* (1922). Here he was concerned on the one hand with framing deductive systems of precise concepts, and on the other hand with the interpretation of these in the data of experience. "Experience", he believed, comes to us in the first instance in the form of vaguely interconnected *continua* of feelings, and not in the form of clear-cut sense-data. Thus he considered that his basic logical notions of the relations of "Whole and Part", systematic overlapping, and "Extensive Connexion" were more congenial than atomistic notions in the analysis of our basic experience; we should start, he believed, not from clear cut items, but from the sense of *something going on*, with a spatio-temporal spread. Whitehead at times claimed that his logical schemes could be reached by a process of idealizing and abstracting from the crude data of experience. This seems to underestimate the extent to which a notion such as the Method of Extensive Abstraction is a topological device for defining points and straight lines, and very unlike anything than can be derived from sense experience. But in seeing the need to devise logical and topological notions to deal with structures within an indeterminate continuum, he was fastening on a genuine problem, even if his own formulation of it was not sufficiently clearly developed to hold the attention and interest of his contemporaries or immediate post-contemporaries, most of whom have continued to work with logical notions related to the atomistic form of analysis.

In the books of his middle period Whitehead tried to give a general account of the "relatedness of nature" in terms of a logical scheme based on the notion of "Extensive Connexion". In the books of his last period – *Science and the Modern World* (1926), *Process and Reality* (1929) and *Adventures of Ideas* (1933) – he turned to the construction of a comprehensive metaphysical system, based on these notions but centring in a speculative account of what it is to be an "actual entity" in process of development within nature. Here he presents a perspectival view of structures within the continuum of natural events, each unified from its own centre, this centre being looked on as the locus of an active subject of experience, forming itself from its interrelations with the whole of its environment; in Whitehead's own terminology, it is a "concrescence of prehension". The nearest analogy among traditional metaphysical views would be **Leibniz**'s monads; Whitehead's "actual entities" are, however, not "windowless", but in active interaction with each other throughout nature. Whitehead looked on this as a generalized notion of organic interconnexion; indeed he described his later work as a "philosophy of organism". Its treatment in his later books is complicated by the use of terminology drawn not only from biology but from introspective psychology (for example the notion of "feelings" is used in a highly general sense). It is also complicated by his attempt to combine logical, mathematical, physical, biological, psychological, and indeed aesthetic and religious notions within the same scheme, looking on these as all in various ways descriptive of elements in real processes within nature, and also (he hoped) all finally to be seen as particular exemplifications of certain very general "metaphysical" principles. He acknowledged that the attempt to reach these completely general principles was unlikely finally to be successful, although he hoped metaphysical schemes might be produced which should approximate to them. His belief in the importance of aiming at a comprehensive system led him to try and produce such a scheme by generalizing principles derived from varied sources. These, however, may belong to different levels of abstraction or to different logical types, so that as Whitehead presents them they do not readily cohere in a single system. In the earlier work he had been concerned with logical devices by which orderly schemes of exact concepts could be connected with sensory experience, which is vague and fragmentary and also (he believed) qualitative, emotionally toned and teleologically directed. In this later work there is a gigantic attempt to bridge this gap by representing the scheme of general notions itself as derived by "descriptive generalization" from the kind of structure he believed we find in our actual experience. In this way he hoped to overcome the "bifurcation" between human beings and nature, and also the gap between general theory and actual experience. But in so doing he may have underestimated the artificial nature of general theories, and his phenomenology of actual experience may at times be overinfluenced by his theoretical schemes.

Whitehead's work is many-sided, and has the faults as well as the virtues of a vast attempt to construct a comprehensive system which will "get everything in". Except for the great influence of the work on Symbolic Logic with Russell in *Principia Mathematica*, it has remained on the whole a self-contained form of thought with little direct effect on contemporary philosophy. But some features of his view of organic interconnexion, thought of in terms of overlapping fields of relationships, have been drawn on in sociological theory. And certain of his books, notably *Science and the Modern World* and *Adventures of Ideas* and *The Aims of Education* (1929), are likely to be read not only for the theoretical notions which they only partially present, but for their wealth of humane, and sometimes witty and penetrating, observations on the history of ideas and on man's life in society.

(D.M.E.)

**William of Ockham** (?–1347), English scholastic philosopher, a Friar Minor. He began to lecture at Oxford as a Bachelor about 1318 and since he never proceeded Master became known to his followers as *Venerabilis Inceptor*. In 1324 he was summoned to Avignon at the instigation of the Chancellor of his University, to reply to criticisms of his teaching before a Papal commission. After four years there he threw in his fortunes with the Emperor Lewis of Bavaria a few weeks after the latter had declared Pope John XXII deposed. Thenceforward till his death his pen was at the service of the Empire. He died at Munich while negotiations for his reconciliation with the Holy See were still in progress.

The dissolvent influence of Ockham and the "terminist" school which he founded on previous ways of medieval thought was immense and lasting; many of his writings were political in purpose, but his logic (in a wide sense), developed at Oxford, was always basic and operative.

In **epistemology** Ockham propounded an intuitive knowledge of material singulars which he held to act directly, naturally and infallibly on the mind to produce a total impression of themselves. Theories of abstraction or of illumination are thus discarded. Direct and immediate, this intuition yet issues in concepts which are signs and representatives of their source, representatives with plenary powers so that their marshalling and analysis is a faithful presentation of their original. Here the by now traditional grammatical and logical treatises on modes of signification and the properties of terms, metaphysically neutral in the hands of earlier writers, acquire a definitely conceptualist tinge; Ockham himself cannot be said to have neglected the intuitive approach to singular reality, but his followers widely surrendered themselves to the technicalities of this conceptual reflection, so that logic and nominalism have been and still are often identified as by definition.

Ockham's *formal* logic displays some idea of material implication and a preference for propositional logic, which he understood to be more basic than the syllogistic. (At the same time we have to reckon with texts which show that his ideal of demonstration was explicitly syllogistic.)

In ontology the singular object of intuition was, for Ockham, often composite indeed, but always irreducibly singular. No common or universal nature is to be discovered in it, no distinction of essence and existence, no principles of change on the Aristotelian pattern, above all no relations. Matter and form he admitted, but conceived of as no less absolute and singular than the singulars composed of them. "I say then . . . that no natural reason can be found to prove that there is anything imaginable which is not absolute, and hence that no one thing depends on another or postulates another, and conversely that the fact that some things coexist does not prevent each being absolute."

"Plurality is never to be posited without need" is one form of the principle known as "Ockham's razor", because he applied it frequently and thoroughly. Change is a mere re-shuffling of the singulars, and their origin in creation is a simple positing by God which remains wholly exterior to them. Unlike **Aquinas**, Ockham denies that the causality of the first cause permeates their being and operations without exception.

This atomistic theory of knowledge and being is faithfully reflected in the moral order. The obligatory law of right reason is in the last analysis imposed by an inexplicable divine command in no way rooted in the nature of God or the world. With regard to it every human will has the fullest autonomy, as indeed has God himself. For Ockham the will is not essentially a power of choosing between goods, with which as goods it has a natural affinity, but a power of self-determination in face of isolated beings in respect of which it has been given some arbitrary rights and duties, such as it can further establish for itself.

(I.T.)

**Wilson,** John Cook (1849–1915), British philosopher, Professor of Logic at Oxford. He published little in his lifetime; his one book *Statement and Inference* (1926) is a compilation from the lecture-notes of his pupils made after his death. But his personal influence in Oxford was immense; though brought up in the idealistic tradition of the late nineteenth century he was regarded as the leader of the Oxford realists, of whom **Prichard** and **Ross** are other notable examples, in their opposition to the hitherto supreme idealistic movement represented by F. H. **Bradley**. In particular he insisted that knowledge was a simple indefinable apprehension of the real in opposition to the idealistic contention that the given was inevitably affected by thought. He was also a notable Aristotelian scholar and was deeply interested in the philosophy of **mathematics**, regarding which he bitterly opposed the logistical theory of **Russell**.

(J.O.U.)

**Wisdom,** (Arthur) John Terence Dibben (1904– ), British philosopher, formerly Professor of Philosophy at Cambridge. Though his work touches on an enormous variety of topics, it is remarkably consistent in method, following up the making of almost any philosophical assertion by saying just the opposite and seeing what comes to light. Even of one of his main theses, that philosophical statements are verbal recommendations, he is quite prepared to say the contradictory since, in this way *both* likenesses *and* differences between philosophers' statements and those of others will be brought out; and thus philosophy shows up the logic of different kinds of statement. He is heavily indebted to **Wittgenstein**, not least in rejecting traditional **metaphysics** regarded as dealing with strange entities but still finding it valuable because it expresses dissatisfaction with our ordinary linguistic usage where this contains conflicting conventions or none at all. It is these conflicts which are illuminating, says Wisdom, and he compares them to the obsessional doubts of the neurotic, which also have a point; indeed, philosophy has a therapeutic value in ridding us of perplexity, and is in some ways comparable to **psychoanalysis**.

(R.HALL)

**Wittgenstein,** Ludwig Josef Johann (1889–1951), by birth an Austrian of Jewish descent. He studied engineering at Berlin and then, from 1908, at Manchester where he became especially interested in aeroplane engines and propellers. The mathematical aspects of this work led Wittgenstein to develop an interest in pure **mathematics** and the philosophy of mathematics and he thus became aware of the work of **Russell** and **Frege** on mathematical logic. Consequently he moved to Cambridge where he spent the greater part of 1912–13 working with Russell, first as a pupil but soon as a partner. Wittgenstein served in the Austrian army in the First World War, being captured in Italy at the end. By this time he had completed his *Tractatus Logico-Philosophicus* which was published in Germany in 1921 and in London in 1922. At this time Wittgenstein believed that this work was a definitive solution to the problems of philosophy; he had also undergone a deep mystical experience while on the Eastern front during the war, apparently as a result of reading Tolstoy. On his release after the war he

consequently gave away the considerable fortune which he had inherited and went to work as an elementary schoolmaster in Austria; at this time also he began to lead the very simple life which he never abandoned. However, during the nineteen-twenties he began to re-establish contact with philosophy; under the auspices of J. M. Keynes he revisited Cambridge in 1925 and about the same time he established personal contact with **Schlick** and Waismann, two of the leaders of the positivist movement in Vienna. In 1929 he returned permanently to Cambridge; he became a British subject at the time of the *Anschluss*. During the next three or four years he was gradually led, largely through self-criticism, to a new position in philosophy, so influential on Anglo-Saxon thought in the fifties and sixties, which was first stated in the *Blue and Brown Books*, which are notes of lectures dictated to pupils in 1933–35 and published posthumously in 1958. He became Professor of Philosophy at Cambridge in succession to G. E. **Moore** in 1939; but on the outbreak of war he went to work as a porter in a hospital. In 1947 he resigned his chair in order to devote himself entirely to research; but his health soon deteriorated and he died of cancer in 1951.

He was an unusual man; even as a professor he invariably wore an open-neck shirt; his room in Trinity College, Cambridge, was furnished by little more than a few deck-chairs; he never dined at the High Table; his candour was so extreme that it could easily be regarded as rudeness; to the philosophical world in general he often gave the impression of being the high priest of a secret cult rather than a fellow-worker.

Wittgenstein's work as a philosopher divides clearly into two periods. The definitive account of his earlier views is contained in the *Tractatus Logico-Philosophicus*, written in 1914–18; he himself published no account of his later views, but we have an earlier version of them in the *Blue and Brown Books* and a later version in the *Philosophical Investigations* (published 1953) which contain his thoughts, constantly revised, from the mid-thirties until his death. *Remarks on the Foundations of Mathematics* (1956), contains his most mature views on the philosophy of mathematics. Many other posthumous publications have followed.

The *Tractatus Logico-Philosophicus* is without doubt a modern classic of philosophy; but it is a very difficult work, written in aphoristic style. It presents a position in many ways similar to Russell's logical atomism; but it has been perhaps too frequently interpreted-in Russellian terms, for Wittgenstein differed from Russell on important points and adopted a much more extreme and consistent **empiricism**. Wittgenstein first states a metaphysic according to which the world consists entirely of simple facts, none of which is in any way dependent on any other, these facts being the ultimate subject-matter of empirical science. Wittgenstein, unlike Russell, gives no examples of what he regarded as simple or elementary facts; there must be such in the last analysis but he is not prepared to claim that he has identified any. However he would presumably have regarded John's shooting at Johann as being more nearly a simple fact than Britain's being at war with Germany, and would have regarded most of what are usually called facts as being in truth mere assemblages of elementary facts. Language, he held in the *Tractatus*, has as its purpose the stating of facts, which it does by picturing the facts. By saying that language pictures facts Wittgenstein especially wanted to claim that language must have a structural similarity to what it describes; an informative statement will be a picture of some possible state of affairs in the same way as a sketch-map can picture a battle or the arrangement of the furniture in a room. This is true even though ordinary idiomatic language is so full of special conventions and *ad hoc* rules as to be hardly recognizable as a picture – just as a map of Australia might have such a queer projection that we would not recognize it intuitively as such. But a perfect language is imaginable and in principle constructable in which, for example, the spatial relationship of objects will be pictured quite clearly by the spatial relationship of their names. The only fully significant use of language is thus to picture facts; beyond this there is a derivative but legitimate use of language for stating tautologies, of which a simple example would be "It is raining or it

is not raining", but which Wittgenstein held to include the whole of logic and mathematics, which are vacuously true and tell us nothing. Beyond the fully-meaningful picture of fact and the legitimate but empty tautology there is no legitimate use of language, and any attempt to use it otherwise will be nonsensical: in particular all ethical or metaphysical utterances will be but pseudo-propositions, nonsensical violations of the proper use of language, since they are neither empirical nor tautologies (here we have a clear glimpse of what the **logical positivists** were later to call the verification principle as a criterion of significance). By a famous paradox, but as consistency requires, Wittgenstein denounces his own metaphysics and theory of language in the *Tractatus* as meaningless nonsense; for to say, for example, that language pictures facts is to try to give a picture of the pictorial relation which holds between statement and fact, which is absurd; this pictorial relation shows itself and what shows itself cannot be said. Wittgenstein regarded his metaphysics as useful or important nonsense which helped one to recognize it itself and all other nonsense as such. Our tendency to talk nonsense, particularly in philosophy, is caused by the complicated, untidy character of ordinary language, and Wittgenstein devotes a great deal of attention to the technical problem of constructing an ideal language which will never tempt anyone to talk nonsense. Finally, once one has understood the *Tractatus* there will be no temptation to concern oneself any more with philosophy, which is neither empirical like science nor tautological like mathematics; one will, like Wittgenstein in 1918, abandon philosophy, which, as traditionally understood, is rooted in confusion.

Wittgenstein's later philosophy was given its most simple, general and intelligible, though not its most mature and complete, statement in the *Blue Book* of 1933. It is largely directed, though not explicitly, to showing why the whole way of thinking adopted in the *Tractatus* is mistaken, though it tends also to destroy all traditional approaches to philosophy. The basis of the new approach is a new view of language; the old view in the *Tractatus* that there is in principle the one perfect scientific language with the sole task of describing the world is abandoned and language is seen as an indefinite set of social activities, each serving a different kind of purpose. Each of these distinct ways of using language is called by Wittgenstein a language game. No doubt there is a use of language for describing the world, and there may be one way of doing so which may reasonably be called "picturing" as in the *Tractatus*; but there is a host of other uses of language – giving orders, asking, thanking, cursing, greeting, praying. Wittgenstein gives a considerable list of such different language games in paragraph 23 of *Philosophical Investigations* and ends with the remark: "It is interesting to compare the multiplicity of tools in language and of the ways they are used, the multiplicity of kinds of word and sentence with what logicians have said about the structure of language (including the author of the *Tractatus Logico-Philosophicus*)".

Though, in Wittgenstein's opinion, we learn to play all these language games correctly, by training in childhood rather than by theoretical instruction, we are liable to become over-impressed with one or two of the possible ways of using language, giving ourselves an over-simplified account even of these (as his own account of the language of science had been over-simplified). Thus we think of a word as being always the name of something, to be learnt by ostensive definition or pointing ("That is a cat"), and of sentences as typified by "The cat is on the mat" or "Tom is fat" – accounts of the way the world goes. It thus comes about that when we reflect on uses of language which are in fact quite different, and of which we are masters when we employ language unreflectingly in its proper context, we try to force them all into one pattern. We may for example reflect on the language game of wishing or hoping and try to force it into the pattern by taking is as "a description of my present mental state"; we may then introspectively attempt to isolate the special mental event of hoping or wishing. Wittgenstein sees here the main root of philosophical perplexity and metaphysical paradox; philosophical puzzlement arises when we utterly misunderstand the functioning of some of our conceptual tools. We may talk as though our problem is of precisely defining a hope or wish,

as though we knew well enough roughly for ordinary purposes but in philosophy needed greater accuracy; whereas, Wittgenstein held, what we need philosophically is to see that we are utterly misconstruing the concept of hoping if we take "hoping" as the name of some psychic process. Therefore to have a philosophical problem is like not being able to find your way about a town through not understanding its plan, like being a fly in a bottle, buzzing against the side instead of flying out of the top; it is a bewitchment of the intelligence. What is needed in such a predicament is not a revelation of the hidden, a subtle theory or explanation, a fine-spun analysis, for these do not cure radical misunderstanding. The concepts which perplex us are ones over which, out of our studies, we have complete mastery (in railway travel the notion of time does not perplex us). What we need, therefore, are simple reminders of the purposes for which we make use of these concepts, judiciously assembled so that we cease to be blind to what "already lies open to the view". A well-arranged selection of such reminders, to produce which requires philosophical gifts and is no automatic procedure, will make us see how we employ the concepts in question, the general nature of the language game; having seen this we shall cease to be victims of philosophical puzzlement.

We have just observed that Wittgenstein found one source of philosophical puzzlement in our tendency to try to interpret all uses of language in terms of one over-simplified model, the attempt to assimilate the different. Another important source of philosophical perplexity he found in the search for the feature common to all things called by the same name. Thus we may try to find, and even invent, some feature common to all games, in virtue of which they are called games. But Wittgenstein held that there need be no such feature; if we call tennis a game it is easy to find similarities between it and bridge and between bridge and patience, and this is enough to explain the common name "game" without our looking for some feature common to both football and patience and possessed by all games and only games. In such a situation as this Wittgenstein spoke of a family resemblance. Thus we may tend to look for some psychic occurrence common to all cases of hoping or intending not only because we think that the verbs "hope" and "intend" must name some process but because we think that there must be a common feature to all cases of each; Wittgenstein will then suggest to us that there may be only a family resemblance between them.

The bulk of Wittgenstein's later work consists of the application of this method of philosophy to a wide variety of problems and tracing their interconnexion. He will take a set of concepts, from mathematics or from ordinary conversation, set out the paradoxical things which we are inclined to say about them under the influence of philosophical puzzlement, and then attempt to banish the puzzlement by reminding us of the normal use of these concepts, by inventing new language games which will be both revealingly similar and revealingly different, always by description of actual and possible uses of language in various contexts.

Given this view of philosophy as being a fall into conceptual puzzlement from which one is rescued, or rescues oneself, by reminders of the use of these concepts in their natural context, Wittgenstein could find no place for any philosophical theories, doctrines or opinions. He conceived his task to be to remind us of what lay on the surface, not to express any opinions or offer deep explanations. In his own words (*Investigations*, 126 and 129): "Philosophy simply puts everything before us, and neither explains nor deduces anything . . .. Since everything lies open to view there is nothing to explain . . .. The aspects of things that are most important for us are hidden because of their simplicity and familiarity." This makes the actual content of Wittgenstein's later work quite impossible to summarize; there is no doctrine and the method of description of conceptual matters that he employs has no theoretical rules of procedure: one must simply describe things in such a way as to end the intellectual bewitchment of the perplexed.

The influence of Wittgenstein on modern philosophy, particularly in the English-speaking countries, has been very great. His *Tractatus Logico-Philosophicus* was also of great importance for the growth of logical positivism in Continental countries, particularly in Austria; many of the modern logical empiricists who have been little affected by his later work are thus under a debt to his earlier views. The direct influence of the *Tractatus* on Anglo-Saxon philosophy was considerably lessened in earlier years by a tendency to think of it as being simply a rather extreme and paradoxical version of Russell's philosophy; it was also positively misinterpreted in the light of Russell's logical atomism and because of a translation which, as well as being inaccurate, made use of Russell's technical vocabulary (e.g. "atomic fact").

Very few modern analytic philosophers would accept Wittgenstein's views that the whole object of philosophy is to banish puzzlement. Moreover we can find other philosophers moving independently in the same direction as Wittgenstein at the same time; for all his great originality Wittgenstein was of his time. But few would dispute that among analytic philosophers – between whom there is but a family resemblance – Wittgenstein stands out as a great and original philosophical genius. See also **Philosophy of Mind**.

(J.O.U.)

# X

**Xenophanes,** Greek poet and thinker who lived at Colophon, 570–c. 475 B.C. Leaving Ionia when young, he travelled round the Greek world, particularly Sicily and the west, reciting his poems, which ranged from banqueting-songs to speculations on physics. He attacked the immoral gods of Homer and indeed the whole concept of anthropomorphism, stating that there was one single deity "in no way like men in body or in thought", but "shaking all things by the thought of his mind". Xenophanes was treated as the first **eleatic** by later Greek historians because of the superficial resemblance of his one god (which according to **Aristotle**'s conjecture was coextensive with the world) to **Parmenides'** Being. Some of Xenophanes' physical ideas were also interesting: the heavenly bodies were ignited clouds; things were originally all mud, because fossils of sea-creatures are found inland; the sea will dry up, and then the process will be reversed. Other rather fantastic physical suggestions were perhaps intentional parodies of the excesses of Milesian dogmatism. Xenophanes certainly stated salutorily that positive philosophical certainty lay out of men's reach – "seeming is wrought over all things". See also **Pre-Socratics**.

(G.S.K.)

# Z

**Zeno** of Citium, Cyprus, (*c.* 333–262 B.C.), Greek philosopher, founder of **Stoicism**, which was so named from the Painted Stoa (colonnade) where Zeno taught. He came to Athens in 312–11, attended the lectures of Polemo, head of the Academy, studied dialectic under Stilpo and Diodorus of the Megaric School, but was most strongly influenced by Crates the **Cynic**. The immense literary output and authority of **Chrysippus**, the third head of the School, has made it difficult to penetrate to Zeno. But the fundamental doctrines and the outline of the system are certainly due to him. His philosophy proceeded from the Cynic base of the self-sufficiency of virtue, but he incorporated much from other sources, such as **Socrates** (probably through the works of **Antisthenes**) and the Peripatetic development of **ethics**.

(I.G.K.)

**Zeno** of Elea, Greek philosopher and follower of **Parmenides**, flourished in Greece *c.* 450 B.C. He wrote a book defending Parmenides' single motionless Being by showing that plurality and motion entailed logically contradictory consequences. Fragment 3 gives a typical argument against plurality. "(a) If there are many, there must be just as many as there are and neither more nor less. But if they are as many as they are, they must be limited. (b) If there are many, existing things are infinite; for there are always other things between the things that are, and again others between those. And thus the things that are are infinite." Against motion there were four related arguments: the stadium, Achilles and the tortoise, the flying arrow, and the moving rows. In the first, for example, Zeno argued that it is impossible to cross the stadium; for you must first reach half-way across, and before that quarter-way across, and so *ad infinitum*. Thus the distance is infinite. These arguments against motion assumed that space could be divided into portions which could be correlated with portions of time. The **Pythagoreans** believed that things were composed of discontinuous units, and many scholars think that Zeno was attacking their kind of plurality in particular. His arguments seemed, nevertheless, to be valid against other pluralistic systems in general.

Many of them were fallacious, since Zeno ignored the fact that the sum of an infinite geometrical progression is finite if the common ratio is less than 1. See also **Eleatics** and **Pre-Socratics**.

(G.S.K.)